COMMERCIAL BANK MANAGEMENT

COMMERCIAL BANK MANAGEMENT

Benton E. Gup
The University of Alabama

Donald R. Fraser
Texas A & M University

James W. Kolari
Texas A & M University

WILEY

JOHN WILEY & SONS
New York   Chichester   Brisbane   Toronto   Singapore

Library of Congress Cataloging in Publication Data:

Gup, Benton E.
    Commercial bank management / Benton E. Gup, Donald R. Fraser,
James W. Kolari.
        p.   cm.
    Includes index.
    ISBN 0-471-84676-7
    1. Banks and banking—Management.   I. Fraser, Donald R.
II. Kolari, James W.   III. Title.
HG1615.G875 1989
332.1'2'068—dc19 88-28272

Printed in the United States of America

10 9 8 7 6 5 4 3 2 1

To Jean, Lincoln, Andy,
and Jeremy
B. E. G.

To Lyn and Eleanor
D. R. F.

To Karie
J. W. K.

ABOUT THE AUTHORS

Benton E. Gup holds the Chair of Banking at The University of Alabama. He is the author of *Bank Mergers: Current Issues and Perspectives; Cases in Bank Management; Financial Intermediaries; Management of Financial Institutions;* and other books. His articles have appeared in *The Journal of Finance, The Journal of Financial and Quantitative Analysis, Financial Management,* and elsewhere. Dr. Gup is a nationally known lecturer in executive development programs and seminars, and has served as a consultant to government and industry.

    Donald R. Fraser is the Alumni Professor of Finance at Texas A & M University. His books include *Banking Deregulation and the New Competition in Financial Services, Financial Institutions, Financial Institutions and Markets in A Changing World, The Financial Market Place, The Future of Small Banks in a Deregulated Environment,* and others. His articles have appeared in *The Journal of Finance, The Journal of Financial and Quantitative Analysis, Journal of Bank Research, Journal of Banking and Finance,* and elsewhere. He is Associate Editor of the *Journal of Financial Research* and the *Journal of Retail Banking.*

    James W. Kolari is an Associate Professor of Finance at Texas A & M University. His books include *The Future of Small Banks in A Deregulated Environment, Bank Costs Structure and Performance,* and others. His articles have appeared in *The Journal of Finance, Journal of Banking and Finance, Journal of Financial Research, Issues in Bank Regulation, Journal of Marketing,* and elsewhere. He is on the Editorial Board of the *Journal of Economics and Business.* Dr. Kolari has served as a consultant to various government agencies and private organizations, including the American Bankers Association and the Independent Bankers Association.

PREFACE

There is a saying, "the more things change, the more they stay the same." That saying is applicable here because major changes are occurring in the financial structure of the United States; but the fundamental business of commercial banking is the same—acquiring funds and making investment and lending decisions. The changes in our financial structure are the result of a dynamic economy, increased competition, the growth of technology, and financial innovations. Because of these factors, traditional differences between various types of financial institutions have become obscured to such an extent that it is difficult to distinguish commercial banks from other types of financial institutions and from businesses offering financial services. There is little practical difference between a commercial bank and a savings and loan association or a savings bank. And firms such as Sears, Merrill Lynch, and General Electric Credit provide some of the same services as those offered by banks and vice versa. It follows that the banking practices presented here apply to other providers of financial services too. Stated otherwise, if you can manage a bank, you can manage other types of financial institutions that provide similar services.

This book is about commercial banking in the new environment. The new environment is competitive, innovative, dynamic, and international in scope. It includes a never-ending stream of financial innovations—interest rate swaps, securitization, and financial futures contracts to name a few—that are altering the way banking is done. These innovations have fostered new techniques for managing bank assets and liabilities. Today, it is not uncommon for a Japanese-owned bank located in the United States to lend funds to firms located in Brazil and then to sell the interest received from those loans to a bank located in Germany. In addition, a bank may pool its home mortgage loans or car loans and sell the packaged loans to other investors. Or a bank may buy or sell financial futures contracts to hedge interest rate risks or to create synthetic Certificates of Deposits. These and other processes of managing banks and financial institutions are covered in this book.

Our text was written for those who want to learn about managing banks and financial institutions from a practical point of view. It is divided into six parts. Part One gives an overview of the banking system and bank investments. Parts Two and Three cover bank assets, liabilities, and equity. Heavy emphasis is placed on lending activities. Part Four is about asset/liability management. Part Five focuses on international banking. Part Six concerns off balance sheet products and services.

Writing a book about banking is especially difficult because of the dynamic nature of the subject. New laws, regulations, and innovations date some material before the ink is dry on the page. Keeping this in mind, we present the key concepts and the intuition behind them. Thus, it makes little difference whether primary capital is 4 percent or 6 percent, if you understand what the concept is and how it is used.

We thank the following individuals for their helpful comments and suggestions in the preparation of this book: Donald Mullineaux, University of Kentucky; Donald Tuttle, Indiana University; Donald G. Simonson, University of Oklahoma; Robert Eisenbeis, University of North Carolina; and Charles Haley, University of Washington. Their contributions have enhanced the quality of our offering. Additional thanks to Robert N. Stone and T. H. Mattheiss, The University of Alabama.

Benton E. Gup
Donald R. Fraser
James W. Kolari

Contents

PART ONE   INTRODUCTION *1*

   CHAPTER ONE
   OVERVIEW OF THE BANKING SYSTEM *3*

   CHAPTER TWO
   FUNDAMENTALS OF BANK INVESTMENTS *25*

PART TWO   ASSETS *47*

   CHAPTER THREE
   EVALUATING BANK PERFORMANCE *49*

   CHAPTER FOUR
   LIQUIDITY MANAGEMENT *87*

   CHAPTER FIVE
   INVESTMENT MANAGEMENT *109*

   CHAPTER SIX
   PRINCIPLES OF COMMERCIAL LENDING *135*

   CHAPTER SEVEN
   THE PROCESS OF COMMERCIAL LENDING *167*

   CHAPTER EIGHT
   THE PROCESS OF COMMERCIAL LENDING, CONTINUED *197*

   CHAPTER NINE
   REAL ESTATE LENDING *215*

   CHAPTER TEN
   CONSUMER LENDING *241*

PART THREE   LIABILITIES AND EQUITIES 263

CHAPTER ELEVEN
MANAGING BANK LIABILITIES 265

CHAPTER TWELVE
BANK CAPITAL MANAGEMENT 299

PART FOUR   ASSET/LIABILITY MANAGEMENT 325

CHAPTER THIRTEEN
AN OVERVIEW OF ASSET/LIABILITY MANAGEMENT:

CHAPTER FOURTEEN
TECHNIQUES OF ASSET/LIABILITY MANAGEMENT:
Dollar Gap and Duration Gap 327

CHAPTER FIFTEEN
TECHNIQUES OF ASSET/LIABILITY MANAGEMENT:
Futures, Options, and Swaps 365

PART FIVE   INTERNATIONAL BANKING 389

CHAPTER SIXTEEN
INTERNATIONAL BANKING 391

CHAPTER SEVENTEEN
INTERNATIONAL FINANCE AND LENDING 411

PART SIX   OFF-BALANCE SHEET PRODUCTS AND SERVICES 443

CHAPTER EIGHTEEN
OFF-BALANCE SHEET ACTIVITIES 445

CHAPTER NINETEEN
THE PAYMENTS SYSTEMS *465*

CHAPTER TWENTY
BANK MANAGEMENT ISSUES *483*

INDEX *505*

DETAILED CONTENTS

PART ONE   INTRODUCTION *1*

CHAPTER ONE
OVERVIEW OF THE BANKING SYSTEM *3*
What Is a Bank? *4*   What Do Banks Do? *5*   Motivation for Bank
Activities *8*   Why Are Banks Regulated and What Have Been the
Consequences of Regulation? *13*   Summary *21*   Important Concepts *22*
References *23*   Questions *23*

CHAPTER TWO
FUNDAMENTALS OF BANK INVESTMENTS *25*
Measures of the Rate of Return on a Loan or Security *26*   Risk and
the Market for Financial Instruments *30*   Determinants of Value *31*
Components of Risk *36*   Risk Management: a Synthesis *42*
Summary *42*   Important Concepts *43*   References *43*
Questions *44*   Problems *45*

PART TWO   ASSETS *47*

CHAPTER THREE
EVALUATING BANK PERFORMANCE *49*
A Framework for Evaluating Bank Performance *50*   Analyzing Bank
Performance with Financial Ratios *56*   Trends in Bank Performance *69*
Regulatory Monitoring of Bank Financial Condition *74*   EWS *74*
CAMEL *76*   Summary *77*   Important Concepts *78*
References *78*   Questions *79*   Problems *79*   Appendix *82*

CHAPTER FOUR
LIQUIDITY MANAGEMENT *87*

Estimating Liquidity Needs *88*   Asset Liquidity *91*   Liability
Liquidity *98*   Funds Management of Liquidity *99*   Summary *104*
Important Concepts *105*   References *106*   Questions *106*
Problems *107*

CHAPTER FIVE
INVESTMENT MANAGEMENT *109*

Developing Investment Policies and Goals *110*   Types of Investment
Securities *111*   Evaluating Investment Risk *115*   Investment
Strategies *127*   Summary *131*   Important Concepts *131*
References *132*   Questions *132*   Problems *133*

CHAPTER SIX
PRINCIPLES OF COMMERCIAL LENDING *135*

Traditional Lending by Commercial Banks *136*   Current Lending Role of
Commercial Banks *136*   Types of Commercial and Industrial Loans *138*
Collateral *143*   The Dollar Size of Commercial Loans *150*
Federal Limits on the Size of Bank Loans *150*   The Lending Decision *151*
Written Loan Policy *156*   Summary *159*   Important Concepts *159*
References *160*   Questions *160*   Appendix *161*

CHAPTER SEVEN
THE PROCESS OF COMMERCIAL LENDING *167*

Asking for a Commercial Loan *167*   Evaluating a Loan Request *173*
Structuring Commercial Loan Agreements *183*   Loan Pricing *186*
Summary *192*   Important Concepts *192*   References *193*
Questions *193*   Problems *194*   Appendix *194*

CHAPTER EIGHT
THE PROCESS OF COMMERCIAL LENDING, CONTINUED *197*

Loan Review *198*   Problem Loans *199*   Loan Losses *202*   Private
Financial Guarantees *205*   Loan Sales and Participations *210*
Summary *212*   Important Concepts *212*   References *213*
Questions *213*

CHAPTER NINE
REAL ESTATE LENDING *215*

Selected Characteristics of Residential Real Estate *216*   Residential
Mortgage Loans *219*   Adjustable Rate Mortgages (ARMs) *224*
Federal Laws in Residential Real Estate Lending *228*

Commercial Mortgage Loans *234*   Mortgage Banking Companies *236*
Real Estate Investment Trusts *237*   Summary *237*
Important Concepts *238*   References *239*   Questions *239*

CHAPTER TEN
CONSUMER LENDING *241*

Consumer Loans at Commercial Banks *242*   Finance and Interest
Charges *248*   Consumer Credit Regulation *254*   The Credit
Decision *258*   Summary *260*   Important Concepts *260*
References *261*   Questions *261*   Problems *262*

**PART
THREE   LIABILITIES AND EQUITY 263**

CHAPTER ELEVEN
MANAGING BANK LIABILITIES *265*

Structure of Bank Liabilities *265*   Managing Bank Liabilities *280*
Summary *294*   Important Concepts *295*   References *296*
Questions *297*   Problems *297*

CHAPTER TWELVE
BANK CAPITAL MANAGEMENT *299*

Definition of Bank Capital *300*   Role of Bank Capital *302*   Capital
Adequacy *303*   Trends in Bank Capital *319*   Summary *321*
Important Concepts *321*   References *322*   Questions *322*
Problems *323*

PART FOUR ASSET/LIABILITY MANAGEMENT 325

CHAPTER THIRTEEN
AN OVERVIEW OF ASSET/LIABILITY MANAGEMENT *327*

The Focus of Asset/Liability Management *329*   Asset/Liability
Management in Historical Perspective *330*   The Influence of Rate,
Volume, and Mix *333*   Measuring Interest-Rate Sensitivity *334*
Asset/Liability Management, Interest-Rate Risk, and Credit Risk *341*
Summary *341*   Important Concepts *342*   References *342*
Questions *343*   Problems *343*

CHAPTER FOURTEEN
TECHNIQUES OF ASSET/LIABILITY MANAGEMENT:
Dollar Gap and Duration Gap *345*

Instruments Used in Asset/Liability Management *346*   Appropriate
Degree of Interest-Rate Risk *346*   Dollar Gap Management *347*
Duration Gap Analysis *352*   Managing Assets and Liabilities
over the Business/Interest Rate Cycle *357*   Interest-Rate Risk
Management and the Yield Curve *359*   Simulation and Asset/Liability
Management *360*   Interest-Rate Risk and Liquidity Risk *360*
Summary *361*   References *362*   Questions *363*

CHAPTER FIFTEEN
TECHNIQUES OF ASSET/LIABILITY MANAGEMENT:
Futures, Options, and Swaps *365*

Using Financial Futures Markets to Manage Interest-Rate Risk *366*
Using the Futures Options Markets to Manage Interest-Rate Risk *375*
Interest Rate Swaps *379*   Summary *384*   Important Concepts *384*
References *385*   Questions *385*   Problems *386*

PART FIVE   INTERNATIONAL BANKING *389*

CHAPTER SIXTEEN
INTERNATIONAL BANKING *391*

Distinguishing Features Between Domestic and International Banking *392*
How U.S. Banks Engage in International Banking *394*
Foreign Banks in the United States *397*   Regulating International
Banking *399*   Insurance for International Loans *401*   The Debt
Crisis *403*   Summary *407*   Important Concepts *407*   References *408*
Questions *408*

CHAPTER SEVENTEEN
INTERNATIONAL FINANCE AND LENDING *411*

Foreign Exchange Markets *411*   Credit Risk *427*   International
Lending *429*   Letters of Credit *431*   Collections *435*
Summary *437*   Important Concepts *437*   References *438*
Questions *438*   Problems *439*

PART SIX   OFF-BALANCE SHEET PRODUCTS AND SERVICES *443*

CHAPTER EIGHTEEN
OFF-BALANCE SHEET ACTIVITIES *445*

Risks Inherent in Financial Instruments *447*   Trade Finance *447*
Financial Guarantees *448*   Investments *454*   Services for Fees *460*
Summary *461*   Important Concepts *461*   References *462*
Questions *462*   Problems *463*

CHAPTER NINETEEN
THE PAYMENTS SYSTEM *465*

Benefits of the Payments System *466*   Check Clearing *469*   The
Elusive Dream of a Cashless Society *471*   Automated Clearinghouses *472*
Wire Transfers *474*   Automated Teller Machines *475*
Point of Sale *476*   Bank Credit Cards *478*   Summary *481*
Important Concepts *481*   References *482*   Questions *482*

CHAPTER TWENTY
BANK MANAGEMENT ISSUES *483*

The Evolution of Funds Management *484*   Organizational Structure *492*
Product and Service Strategies *496*   Restructuring the Financial
System *499*   Summary *501*   Important Concepts *501*
References *502*   Questions *502*

INDEX *505*

INTRODUCTION

OVERVIEW OF THE BANKING SYSTEM

Commercial banks have for many centuries played a vital role in the financial system. That vital role continues today, although, as with other financial institutions, the functions of commercial banks have changed as the needs of the economy have changed. The present chapter provides an overview of the role of commercial banks through concentrating on six topics.

1. What is a bank?
2. What do banks do?
3. Why do they perform those services?
4. How do banks compare with other financial service organizations?

3

5. How and why are banks regulated and what are the consequences of such regulation?

6. What changes have been occurring in the functions and regulation of commercial banks and in the competitive environment within which banks operate?

The discussion of these topics focuses on the manager of the banks; that is, the focus is from inside the banking institution looking outward at the environment within which banks operate. In examining each of these questions, the basic aim is to acquaint the existing or potential manager of the bank with the information and/or techniques necessary to succeed in managing the organization.

WHAT IS A BANK?

It might seem that the answer to this question is quite simple. In fact, however, the answer is rather complicated. A bank offers transactions accounts (such as demand deposits) to its customers. It also offers various types of savings accounts and certificates of deposits and makes a variety of loans. It might be argued then that a bank is an organization that offers these services.

Two problems immediately come to mind with such a definition. First, other organizations in addition to commercial banks provide these services. Obviously, savings and loan associations, savings banks, and credit unions provide deposit and loan services that are virtually identical with those of commercial banks. But money market funds and investment brokers such as Merrill Lynch also provide similar services. Second, banks do many things that are not included in the functions of offering deposit and loan services. They provide trust services, they arrange mergers and acquisitions, and they guarantee payment for one party to another through letters of credit and other devices.

Perhaps the best definition of a bank is the following: "A bank is an organization that has been given banking powers either by the state or the federal government." Although this definition might seem to be somewhat circular (a bank is as a bank does) and somewhat trivial, the definition provides useful insight into the nature of the institution by recognizing the dynamic and ever changing nature of banking.

Imagine the entire range of financial services that exists in a modern economy. The number would certainly be in the hundreds, perhaps in the thousands. At a given time, government will allow banks to provide some of those services. At that time, commercial banks may be defined in terms of those services. Over time, however, new financial services will be created and attitudes may change about the desirability of allowing banks to offer existing financial services. As a result, the range of financial services permissible for commercial banks may be altered—either expanded or reduced. In the last 20 years, the range of permissible services has been expanded considerably, both because of deregulation and the actions of bank managers in innovating new financial services not expressly prohibited by legislation or regulation. Hence, a bank today is different than a bank 20 years ago (in terms of the services offered), which is again different than a bank 20 years earlier. Yet all are commercial banks.

Defining a commercial bank in terms of permissible activities also provides insight into the perpetual dispute over the limits of bank powers. Not surprisingly, managers of commercial banks attempt to get laws and regulations changed in order to obtain expanded powers to provide additional financial services. Managers of the firms that provide those financial services not now permitted to banks work as hard to prevent bank competition in those areas. Much of the debate over bank regulation centers on the controversy between bankers and other financial service firms over the limits of bank powers.

WHAT DO BANKS DO?

Because banks perform a large number of different functions, it may be preferable to discuss the general activities of banks rather than attempt to describe in minute detail the activities of banking organizations. Most of the functions performed by commercial banks may be subsumed under three broad areas:

1. Payments
2. Intermediation
3. Other financial services

Payments

Banks are at the very core of the payments system. Most of the money supply of the United States is held in the form of bank money (i.e., transactions accounts at commercial banks). Because an efficient payments system is vital to a stable and growing economy, the role of banks in the payments system takes on an important social dimension. At one time, commercial banks had a monopoly of transactions accounts, but in recent years, savings and loans, mutual savings banks, and credit unions (known collectively along with commercial banks as depository institutions) have obtained the authority to offer transactions accounts. Also, other types of financial service organizations, such as mutual funds, have developed financial products against which checks may be written.

Intermediation

Commercial banks intermediate between those who have money (i.e., savers or depositors) and those who need money (i.e., borrowers). To the saver or depositor, commercial banks offer various types of deposits that meet the needs of those customers better than alternative uses of funds. Commercial banks are able to provide deposit instruments with low denomination, low risk, and high liquidity, characteristics that meet the needs of most savers better than stocks and bonds, which often have high denominations, high risk, and lesser liquidity. Commercial banks in their intermediation function are able to package large amounts of small deposits and lend those funds to borrowers. Although at one time commercial bank loans were concentrated in short-term commercial lending (hence the term **commercial** bank), most banks now make any type of loan legally permissible that meets internal credit-quality standards.

Some banks, however, do concentrate in drawing funds from business and in lending to business (those banks are known as wholesale banks), whereas other banks draw their funds from consumers and concentrate their lending to consumers (those banks are known as retail or consumer banks). In either case, however, the banks are performing an intermediation function.

Financial intermediation between savers and investors is crucial to the efficient operation of the economy. Economic growth fundamentally depends upon a large volume of saving and the effective allocation of that saving to productive uses. Efficient financial markets contribute to such an allocation. By offering depositors financial instruments that have desirable risk/return characteristics, commercial banks are able to encourage a greater volume of saving and, by effectively screening credit requests, they are able to channel funds into socially productive uses. Although the social role of commercial banks in financial intermediation is somewhat different than in the payments function, it is no less important.

Other Financial Services

In addition to their traditional role of providing a means of payment through offering transactions accounts and financial intermediation between depositors and borrowers, commercial banks provide a variety of other financial services. It is among these existing and potential activities that the controversy exists about the proper scope of commercial banking activities. The most important of these are:

Fiduciary Services

Commercial banks have operated separate "trust" banks for many years in which they manage the funds of others. In contrast to deposit accounts, however, in which banks accept the legal responsibility to repay the principal (either on demand or at maturity), with trust accounts, the bank merely agrees to manage funds, for a fee, under the guidance of a trust agreement. Because the bank does not "own" the assets held in trust, they do not show up on the bank's balance sheet. In its fiduciary role, the bank manages employee pension and profit-sharing programs and handles a variety of securities-related activities for corporate businesses.

Securities Related Services

Commercial banks provide a number of brokerage and investment banking related services. However, the nature of these services is severely restricted by the Glass–Steagall Act of 1933 (which was enacted because of the erroneous belief that the wave of bank failures in the early 1930s was caused by the mixture in one organization of commercial and investment banking). Commercial banks may offer discount brokerage services (and many do) but not general-purpose brokerage services. Commercial banks may underwrite U.S. Treasury securities and general obligation municipal securities but not (as of mid 1988) revenue municipal securities or corporate stocks and bonds. Commercial banks also are engaged in facilitating mergers and acquisitions and in trading currencies and U.S. government securities. A great deal of controversy exists about the desirability of allowing commercial banks to further expand their activities in the investment banking area.

Off-Balance Sheet Risk Taking

One new area of rapid growth has been in the off-balance sheet risk taking whereby banks (especially large banks) generate fee income by assuming certain contingent liabilities. For example, a bank may guarantee the payment of another party. These guarantees are contingent claims (the bank must pay only if the party defaults) and do not appear on the bank's balance sheet. The standby letter of credit is perhaps the best known of those contingent claims and involves the agreement by a bank to pay an agreed-upon amount upon presentation of evidence of default or nonperformance of the party whose obligation is guaranteed. Standby letters of credit exceed $200 billion.

Insurance and Real Estate-Related Activities

Commercial banks currently are able to offer only a limited set of insurance and real estate related activities, principally those that involve brokerage rather than underwriting or ownership. However, considerable pressure exists to expand the range of bank activities to encompass these functions.

The activities of the commercial bank in offering payments services, financial intermediation, and financial services ultimately show up in the balance sheet of the bank. Table 1.1 shows the principal balance sheet items. On the asset side, the largest use of funds is to make loans, of all types and maturities, reflecting the intermediation role of the bank. Funds for loans, securities, and cash assets are drawn from transactions accounts (reflecting the payments functions of the banking system), savings and time deposits (reflecting the intermediation function), as well as nondeposit borrowings and (to a minor extent) equity capital.

TABLE 1.1
ASSETS AND LIABILITIES OF COMMERCIAL BANKING
INSTITUTIONS (billions of dollars), August 1987

Assets		
Investment Securities		501.7
U.S. government securities	312.7	
Other	189.0	
Trading Account Assets		20.0
Total Loans		1,820.5
Interbank loans	162.5	
Loans excluding interbank	1,658.0	
Commercial and industrial	551.6	
Real estate	552.7	
Individual	317.2	
All other	236.6	
Total Cash Assets		209.3
Other Assets		190.7
Total Assets		2,942.2
Total Liabilities and Capital		
Deposits		1,926.4
Transaction deposits	572.6	
Savings deposits	535.2	
Time deposits	818.6	
Borrowings		435.1
Other Liabilities		209.2
Residual (assets less liabilities)		171.4
Total Liabilities/Capital		$2,742.2

Source. Federal Reserve Bulletin, November 1987, p. A18.

MOTIVATION FOR BANK ACTIVITIES

Commercial banks are private, profit-seeking business enterprises. They provide payments services, financial intermediation, and other financial services in anticipation of earning profits from those activities. Along with other profit-seeking businesses, their principal goal is to maximize the market value of the equity of the common stockholders. Thus, decisions on lending, investing, borrowing, pricing, adding new services, dropping old services, and other such decisions ultimately depend on the impact on shareholder wealth. Because shareholder wealth is determined by three factors—the amount of cash flows that accrue to bank shareholders, the timing of the cash flows, and the risk involved in those cash flows—management decisions involve evaluating the impact of various strategies on the return (the amount and timing of the cash flows) and the risk of those cash flows (see Figure 1-1).

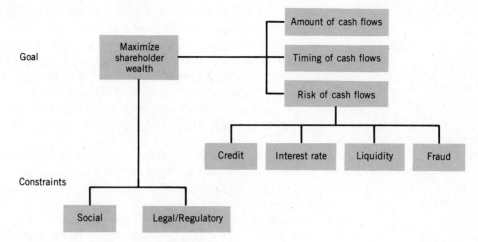

FIGURE 1.1   Bank goals and constraints.

Risk Management

In essence, bank management is **risk** management. Banks accept risk in order to earn profits. They must balance the various alternative strategies in terms of their risk and return characteristics with the goal of maximizing shareholder wealth. In doing so, banks must recognize that there are different types of risk and that the impact of a particular investment strategy on shareholders depends upon the impact on the **total risk** of the organization. That total risk is composed of four components.

Credit Risk. The risk that the bank will not get its money back (or that payment will be delayed) from a loan or investment.

Interest Rate Risk. The risk that the market value of the asset will fall with increases in interest rates. For a commercial bank that promises to pay a fixed amount to depositors, any decline in the value of assets due to interest rate increases could have serious implications for the solvency of the organization.

Liquidity Risk. The risk of being unable to turn an asset into cash (or being unable to borrow funds when needed) quickly with minimal loss. Given the large amount of bank deposits that must be paid on demand or within a very short period, liquidity risk is of crucial importance in banking.

Fraud Risk. The risk that officers or employees will steal from the bank through falsifying records, self-dealing, or other devices. A large number of bank failures, especially at small banks, have resulted from fraud.

A Federal Deposit Insurance Corporation study of bank failures in the 1971–1982 period revealed that credit risk associated with defaults in the loan portfolio was the primary factor in 66 percent of large bank failures.[1] Interest rate risk was the primary cause of failure in 14 percent of the cases; liquidity and fraud each accounted for 10 percent of the failures. Obviously, a single failure may be associated with a combination of factors, and the relative importance of different factors may vary for banks of different sizes. However, the dominant reason for failure for all size groups of banks was credit risk.

The fact that the principal risk that has caused problems for bank management is credit or default risk is important in the education of bank managers. Although banks fail for many reasons, the principal one is that they make bad loans. Recent problems with energy loans, agricultural loans, and loans to less-developed countries certainly illustrate this point. The crucial importance of credit risk in the loan portfolio has contributed to the extensive treatment of loans and the loan portfolio in this book.

Constraints

Bank management must carefully balance risk and return in seeking to maximize shareholder wealth. However, such decisions are constrained by a number of factors. Of course, all businesses face constraints in their decision making, but the constraints under which banks operate are particularly important. These constraints may be classified into two separate though overlapping areas: social constraints and legal/regulatory constraints.

Social Constraints. These stem from the historical position of the commercial bank at the core of the financial system. As such, banks often become the lender of next to last resort in times of financial crisis (the Federal Reserve is, of course, the lender of last resort) in providing credit to distressed institutions and in providing deposit and credit services to their customers. Because the financial performance of a bank is intimately linked with the economic health of the community it serves, banks often perform numerous social functions (and are expected to do so) despite, in many cases, being unable to determine the contributions of such activities to shareholder wealth.

Legal/Regulatory Constraints. Perhaps more significant is the enormous variety of legal and regulatory constraints on the portfolio management (i.e., its risk/return position) of a commercial bank. These are discussed in considerable

---

[1] Federal Deposit Insurance Corporation, *Deposit Insurance in a Changing Environment,* Washington, DC, 1983, pp. 11–17.

detail in other parts of the book. It may be sufficient at this point to mention the following constraints on bank operations:

Constraints on balance sheet composition, including the prohibition on holding equity securities, minimum capital requirements, reserve requirements, and limitations on real estate investments.

Constraints on pricing, including (until the mid-1980s) maximum limits on the interest rates that may be paid on deposit accounts and (with usury laws) limits on the amounts that may be charged on loans.

Constraints on geographic expansion, including the inability in some states to operate in more than one geographical location (i.e., unit banking states) and significant limitations on multi-office banking through the holding company device.

Constraints on entry, including significant hurdles on chartering a new bank and, to a lesser extent, opening a new branch of an existing bank.

Constraints on customer relationships, including a large number of consumer protection laws.

Most constraints on bank behavior are designed either to reduce the risk of failure or to affect the price and allocation of bank credit. The risk reduction constraints stem primarily from the banking collapse of the 1930s. The legislation of the 1930s fundamentally changed the operations of commercial banking organizations. In contrast, many of the constraints designed to restrict the relationship of banks with their customers stem from the consumerism movement of the 1960s and 1970s. These motives are discussed more fully in the next section.

Sizes and Market Shares of Banks and Other Service Firms

Table 1.2 provides information on the total assets (as of 1986) of the principal financial service firms of the United States and their market share (their total assets expressed as a fraction of the total assets of all financial service firms). In terms of the prior categorization, payments services are offered primarily by commercial banks, savings and loans, mutual savings banks, and credit unions (collectively known as depository institutions), although mutual funds and securities brokers and dealers also offer some form of transactions services. Intermediation services are offered principally by the depository institution, the finance companies, and real estate investment trusts, in the sense that they are involved both in borrowing and lending. The remaining financial institutions may be classified as providing insurance, funds management, or broker/dealer financial services.

TABLE 1.2
FINANCIAL ASSETS AND MARKET SHARES OF DIFFERENT
FINANCIAL SERVICE FIRMS
June 30, 1986 (billions of dollars)

	Dollars	*Percent*
Commercial banks	2033.2	28.6
Savings and loans	1121.0	15.8
Savings banks	226.2	3.2
Credit unions	156.9	2.2
Life insurance companies	833.1	11.7
Private pension funds	831.5	11.7
State and local government employee retirement funds	486.3	6.8
Other insurance companies	317.8	4.5
Finance companies	380.0	5.4
Real estate investment trusts	6.4	0.1
Mutual funds	414.5	5.8
Money market funds	222.0	3.1
Securities brokers and dealers	67.4	1.1
	$7096.3	100.0

Source. Federal Reserve Flow-of-Funds Accounts.

The principal financial service firms held total assets in 1986 that exceeded $7 trillion. Commercial banks held almost 30 percent of the total assets of all financial service organizations, with slightly over $2 trillion in total assets. Depository institutions together held over $3 trillion, or almost one-half of the total for all financial service organizations. Savings and loans were the second largest individual financial service organization, with private pension funds and life insurance companies close behind.

The market shares of the different financial service organizations are undergoing significant change. Commercial banks continue to lose market share, savings and loans have also lost market share, and life insurance companies have experienced an erosion of their asset base. In contrast, pension funds (both private and state and local government) have increased the percentage of assets under their control. Mutual funds experienced explosive growth in the early and mid-1980s, reflecting falling interest rates and rising stock prices.

Financial service organizations differ considerably in terms of the level and stability of their profitability. As shown in Table 1.3, commercial banks seem to be among the least profitable of the major financial service organizations in the period from 1975 to 1984. They were particularly less profitable than securities-related firms (especially investment banking organizations). On a year-by-year basis, however, the profitability of commercial banks has generally been more stable than the earnings of other major financial service firms.

TABLE 1.3
PROFITABILITY IN FINANCIAL SERVICES[a]
(Average After-Tax Return on Equity)

Industry	1980–1984	1975–1984
Commercial banking	12.2%	12.3%
17 multinational BHCs	13.0[b]	13.1[b,c]
Finance companies[d]	12.6	11.4
Mortgage companies[d]	13.1	13.7[e]
Securities	18.7	16.4
Investment banks	26.0	21.5
Other securities	15.8	14.5
Life Insurance	13.4	13.7
Stockholder-owned	15.2	15.6
Mutual	10.5	10.6
Property and casualty insurance	7.4	10.9[f]
Stockholder-owned	7.7	11.2[f]
Mutual	7.4	9.8[f]
Insurance brokerage		
Large firms	18.3	22.5[f]
Small firms	9.2	12.5[f]

[a] Returns for commercial banks, securities firms, life insurers, and property and casualty insurers are based on average equity. Because of limited availability of data, returns for finance companies, mortgage companies, and insurance brokers are based on year-end equity. By way of comparison, nonfinancial firms (represented by those included in Standard & Poor's 400 stock index) reported average returns of 13.7 percent over 1980–84 and 14.0 percent over 1975–84.

[b] Excludes Crocker and Continental Illinois in 1984.

[c] 1976–1984.

[d] Excluding subsidiaries of bank holding companies.

[e] 1978–1984.

[f] 1976–1984, one complete underwriting cycle.

Source. Trends in Commercial Bank Profitability, Federal Reserve Bank of New York, 1987.

WHY ARE BANKS REGULATED AND WHAT HAVE BEEN THE CONSEQUENCES OF REGULATION?

The Nature of Regulation

The three principal reasons for the regulation of commercial banks are:

1. prevention of banking market failure
2. prevention of concentration and monopoly
3. achievement of desired social goals

Banking Market Failure

Because most money is bank money and the general agreement that changes in the amount of money outstanding affect the levels of employment, production, and income, it follows that banking market failure cannot be tolerated. The collapse of the banking system and the fall in the amount of money (i.e., transactions deposits at banks) would have potentially grave consequences for the economy. As a result, public policy must prevent such a development.

The concern is with the failure of the banking system, not the failure of an individual bank. However, the immediate availability of many bank liabilities in the form of transactions accounts and many time deposits makes the prospect of bank runs, panics, and contagion a distinct possibility. The failure of an individual bank could easily lead to the withdrawal of funds from another bank, which could cause that bank to fail, which could then have a domino effect on the banking system.

The possibility of banking market failure has led to two kinds of regulation. First, constraints on the ability of banks to take risks have been created (as discussed earlier). The purpose of these constraints is to reduce credit, interest rate, liquidity, and other types of bank risk and thereby, presumably, to reduce the number of bank failures. As the number of bank failures is reduced, the probability of bank runs is also reduced. This policy, coupled with a relatively stable economic environment since World War II, has contributed to a sharp decline in the number of bank failures (although the number of failures did rise sharply in 1985, 1986, and 1987). In fact, the decline in failures is remarkable; more than 4,000 banks failed in 1933, whereas fewer than 800 banks failed in the entire 50-year period from 1934 through 1983.

The second type of public policy action designed to deal with the apparently inherent tendency of the banking system to be subject to runs and panic was the establishment of deposit insurance in 1933. The fundamental purpose of deposit insurance was to break the link between the failure of an individual bank and the banking system. By assuring depositors that their funds were safe even if their bank failed, deposit insurance has removed the incentive for runs (at least for insured depositors).

The deposit insurance system has been remarkably successful in accomplishing its basic purpose. There have been no bank panics since the FDIC was established. As discussed in a later section, however, deposit insurance has had some unintentional and undesired effects on bank risk taking.

Concentration

The second principal motivating factor for bank regulation has been to prevent the growth of exceedingly large banking institutions that would dominate the financial system and perhaps the entire economy. Concentration of economic power is also considered undesirable, because it might lead to concentration of political power. The principal types of regulations that seek to achieve a deconcentrated banking system are limits on the geographical extent of bank operations through restrictions on branching and holding company acquisitions and the enforcement of the antitrust laws to limit mergers in the banking industry.

A number of states have prohibited branching entirely. In these "unit" banking states, an individual bank has been limited to operations at one geographical location. Some states have limited branching to certain specified portions of the state, such as a particular metropolitan area, whereas other states do allow banks to branch statewide; interstate branching is prohibited. Similar restrictions exist for holding company affiliations, although interstate acquisitions by a bank holding company are allowed if specifically authorized by state law. In any case, these geographical constraints have made the growth of giant banks more difficult in the United States.

Antitrust law in the United States also has restrained the growth of large banking organizations. Combinations among banks that would tend to create a monopoly are prohibited. Moreover, under the Bank Merger Act, the regulatory authorities are instructed to disallow a bank merger or holding company acquisition if it would have a serious, negative impact on competition.

Consumer Protection

The decades of the 1960s and 1970s brought a wave of federal (and some state) legislation designed to protect consumers and insure that they were treated fairly. Some of the major types of consumer protection legislation include the following:

The Truth-in-Lending Act of 1968 required full disclosure of credit costs and terms on consumer loans. The act also provided for regulation of the content of credit advertising.

The Fair Credit Billing Act of 1974 regulated credit card distribution, terms, and cardholder liability.

The Fair Credit Reporting Act of 1970 provided for regulation of credit reports furnished to creditors, employers, and insurers.

The Community Reinvestment Act of 1972 forbade discrimination by home lenders on the basis of age or location of buildings and requires regulators to consider the degree to which an institution is satisfying community credit needs when evaluating requests from that institution to branch or merge.

Consequences of Regulation

Although there are a number of significant effects of bank regulations, two in particular stand out: the effect on the structure of American banking and the effects on risk in banking.

Banking Structure

Constraints on the geographical expansion of banks have produced a fragmented banking structure that stands in remarkable contrast to the concentrated banking structure of most nations. The United States has an enormous number of commercial banks (over 14,000) whereas most advanced nations have a very small number (usually under 100). Reflecting the large number of banks, the "typical" commercial bank is relatively small, yet a few large banks hold a large percentage of the assets of the banking system, reflecting their wholesale and international orientation.

Table 1.4 illustrates this peculiar American banking structure. Forty percent of all U.S. banks have assets of less than $25 million, but those 5820 banks hold only 4 percent of the total assets of all banks. At the other extreme, the largest 1.8 percent of all banks hold over 50 percent of all the assets of the banking system.

Most of the smaller banks are unit banks, that is, they do not have branches. As late as 1986, roughly 7,000 U.S. banks (about one-half of the total) operated without branches. However, the number of U.S. banks that do not have branches has been shrinking dramatically, whereas the number of banks with branches has been growing. Many of the unit banks (and also a number of the branch banks) are connected through common ownership by a holding company. By 1986, more than 6,000 bank holding companies were registered with the Federal Reserve. These holding companies controlled roughly 90 percent of the assets of all banking organizations.

Risk

Bank regulation inevitably affects the risk of bank failure, sometimes in intended ways but at times in unexpected ways. As discussed earlier, many of the restrictions placed on bank activities in the 1930s were intended to reduce bank risk through forcing banks to hold low-risk assets and, through Regulation Q,

TABLE 1.4

ASSET SIZE DISTRIBUTION OF DOMESTIC INSURED COMMERCIAL BANKS IN THE UNITED STATES December 31, 1983

Size Range of Total Assets Held	Number of Commercial Banks	Percent of All Banks	Total Assets	Percent of All Assets
Less than $25 million	5,820	40.2	82.1	4.0
$25–49.9 million	3,747	25.9	134.1	6.6
$50–99.9 million	2,623	18.1	181.0	8.9
$100–499.9 million	1,836	12.7	347.6	17.1
$500–999.9 million	191	1.3	132.5	6.5
$1 billion or more	256	1.8	1,150.0	56.7
	14,473	100.0	$2,027.3	

Source. Federal Deposit Insurance Corporation, Statistics on Banking.

placing a ceiling on the bank's cost of funds. However, other regulations may actually increase risk. In particular, restricting banks to limited geographical areas makes it difficult, if not impossible, for them to obtain a diversified loan portfolio. Forcing banks to concentrate their lending within a limited geographical area leads to a portfolio concentrated in one industry (or in very few industries) with the result that the bank experiences severe loan quality problems when the industry is distressed. The experience of commercial banks in the farm and energy states in the late 1980s provides ample evidence of this risk. Bank risk is also increased to the extent that the cost of adhering to extensive regulations (such as consumer credit regulations) is greater for banks than for their competitors.

The Changing Bank Environment: Regulatory and Competitive

Changes

The environment within which bank managers make decisions has changed dramatically in recent years. The major changes in the regulatory and competitive environment include the following:

1. *Financial Reform.* The process that is known loosely as deregulation has profoundly affected the operations of commercial banks. Collectively, the actions of the regulators and of Congress through the Depository Institutions Deregulation and Monetary Control Act of 1980 and the Garn-St Germain Depository Institutions Act of 1982 have given banks (and other depository institutions) much greater operating flexibility. Perhaps the most significant aspect of financial reform is the elimination of deposit rate ceilings. However, banks have also obtained powers to offer a larger number of financial services. Moreover, with most states now allowing some form of interstate banking (through holding company affiliates), the geographical barriers to bank operations have been substantially reduced.

2. *Greater Competition.* The market within which banks operate has become intensely more competitive. This greater competition comes from two sources. First, the deregulation embodied in DIDMCA in 1980 and Garn-St Germain in 1982, as well as regulatory initiatives for financial reform, have markedly increased the competition for banks from nonbank depository institutions. For example, prior to 1980 commercial banks had a virtual monopoly of transactions accounts. After 1980, all depository institutions could offer transactions accounts and do so on an equal basis with commercial banks. In fact, most of the financial reform in the early 1980s involved allowing other depository institutions (especially savings and loans) to offer financial services traditionally reserved for or dominated by commercial banks.

The second and perhaps more significant source of competition for commercial banks has been the expansion of services by financial and nonfinancial conglomerates. Financial conglomerates include such firms as American Express and Merrill Lynch, which have transformed themselves from narrowly based providers of financial services to broad-based financial service providers, as well as firms such as Sears and Ford, which mix retailing or manufacturing with various types of financial services. The diversity of product offerings of these financial conglomerates appears in Table 1.5, which shows that insurance companies, retailers, and security dealers offered only a few of the same products as commercial banks in 1960; their organizations essentially operated in segmented markets. By 1984, not only did these financial conglomerates offer the same financial services as banks, but they also had many that banks were prohibited from offering. In terms of the earlier discussion of the three types of activities that banks engage in—offering transactions accounts, financial intermediation, and other financial services—the financial conglomerates (as well as savings and loans) offer each one of these products and also have fewer regulatory constraints on offering a diversity of financial services.

3. *More Unstable Interest Rates and Economic Conditions.* Not only has the environment within which commercial banks operate become more competitive, it has become less stable. This instability is reflected in the volatility of interest rates, with the prime rate, for example, exceeding 20 percent in the early 1980s, declining to less than 8 percent in 1986, and then beginning to increase again in 1987. Such volatility of interest rates makes it difficult for commercial banks to make a reasonable profit from their financial intermediation function of taking (and paying for) deposits and making loans. Earning a satisfactory and stable margin between the cost of funds and the earnings on loans (and other uses of funds) is exceedingly difficult in a period of unstable interest rates.

TABLE 1.5

FINANCIAL SERVICES OFFERED BY DEPOSITORY AND CONGLOMERATE INSTITUTIONS 1960 and 1984

Financial Services	Commercial Banks		Savings and Loans		Insurance Companies		Retailers		Security Dealers	
	1960	1984	1960	1984	1960	1984	1960	1984	1960	1984
Transactions	X	X		X		X		X		X
Saving/Time deposits	X	X	X	X		X		X		X
Installment loans	X	X		X		X		X		X
Business loans	X	X		X		X		X		X
Mortgage loans	X	X	X	X		X		X		X
Credit cards		X		X		X	X	X		X
Insurance				X	X	X		X		X
Stocks, bonds										
Brokerage		X		X		X		X	X	X
Underwriting									X	X
Mutual funds				X		X		X		X
Real estate				X		X		X		X

Source. D. Koch, "The Emerging Financial Services Industry: Challenge and Innovations," *Economic Review,* Federal Reserve Bank of Atlanta, April 1984, p. 26.

Related to unstable interest rates has been the instability in the underlying economy. The most severe economic contraction since the Great Depression occurred in the early 1980s. Although economic growth began again after that recession, the pace of expansion was quite uneven; whole sectors, states, and regions were not part of that expansion. In particular, the agricultural and energy sectors, and the states that depend upon those industries, fell into depression in the mid-1980s despite prosperity in other parts of the nation. At the same time, growth of many less developed nations (especially in Latin America) came to a halt, and in some cases the economies suffered severe economic decline. The net effect of all of these factors was to raise, in some cases sharply, loan losses at commercial banks, leading to a sharp increase in the number of bank failures.

4. *Declining Market Shares for Commercial Banks.* The market share of commercial banks in the financial intermediation function has declined in the past decade. This decline reflects two factors. First, the growth of competition from nonbank depository institutions such as savings and loans has contributed to a decrease in bank market share. Second, and perhaps more important, an increasingly larger share of credit flow (especially business credit) is being provided directly by the capital markets, bypassing the traditional flow of funds indirectly through such financial intermediaries as commercial banks. This direct finance by which borrowers directly access the capital market is referred to as *securitization* and promises to significantly affect the role of commercial banks. In fact, commercial banks have participated in the securitization process by packaging their loans into securities and selling these securities directly into the capital markets.

5. *Globalization of the Financial System.* The operations of commercial banks have been affected greatly by the increasing links between the U.S. financial system and the financial systems of other countries. There are many examples of such links. Financial instruments are now traded around-the-clock, around the world; U.S. stocks and bonds trade in London and in other foreign financial markets. Increasing links have been forged between markets whereby a financial contract may be bought in one market and simultaneously sold in another market (e.g., Chicago and Singapore). Equally important, the operations of many commercial banks have become global. Many large U.S. commercial banks operate throughout the world. In such operations these banks face not only the traditional types of bank risk such as interest rate and credit risk, but also must deal with foreign exchange risk caused by fluctuations in the value of the currencies in which they operate, as well as potential government interference with their operations, including expropriation or nationalization of their assets.

Domestically, U.S. banks face substantial and growing competition from foreign banks. By late 1985, there were almost 400 foreign banking organizations operating in the United States, with assets of almost $500 billion. The impact of foreign bank penetration of the U.S. market has been most noticeable in the market for business loans. In some states, especially California and New

York, however, foreign banks have purchased U.S. banks in order to enter the retail or consumer markets.

6. *Proliferation of Financial Instruments.* One of the most significant developments in the financial system has been the incredible proliferation of financial instruments. Partially, this proliferation reflects the attempt by financial market participants to shift risk. Futures, options, and options on futures were (partially at least) intended to allow market participants to shift interest rate risk. The development of adjustable rate loans reflects the same motivation. In other cases, such as various types of off-balance sheet financing, commercial banks have created or participated in financial instruments where they explicitly accept risk in order to increase their returns.

Consequences

Two consequences of this changing financial environment are of particular concern to bank managers: **risk and complexity.** Bank managers operate in an environment of greater risk and more difficulty in earning a profit, and they face a much more complicated financial world. In addition and, more important, the

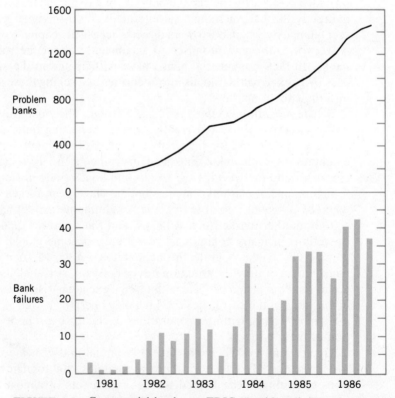

FIGURE 1.2 Commercial banks on FDIC "problem list" and commercial bank failures. *Source.* Federal Deposit Insurance Corporation, *Banking and Economic Review,* January/February 1987, p. 1.

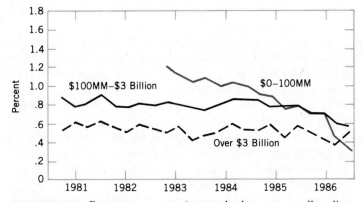

FIGURE 1.3   Returns on assets (quarterly data, seasonally adjusted). *Source.* Federal Deposit Insurance Corporation, *Banking and Economic Review,* January/February 1987, p. 3.

traditional risks are greater, and thus bank failures are greater (see Figure 1.2) and bank profitability has eroded (see Figure 1.3). In facing these risks, bank managers confront an extraordinarily complicated environment. Their operations are complicated by the number of competitors and the wide variety of alternative techniques available to deal with their risk management.

At one time, commercial bank managers operated in a relatively stable economic environment and with regulatory protection from their potential competitors designed to assure bank profitability and minimize the number of bank failures, but those days are gone. Commercial banks face intense competition from a variety of different sources and operate in an unstable, often hostile economic environment. Bank managers can produce satisfactory returns for their shareholders if they have the tools to deal with these risks, to properly evaluate the degree of risk in each one of their operations, and to make appropriate risk/return decisions. The principal purpose of this book is to provide bank managers with these tools.

SUMMARY

A bank is an organization that engages in the business of banking. The scope of the business changes over time and in recent years has broadened considerably. In essence, banks perform three functions: (1) provide the means of payment through administering the checking account system; (2) intermediate between depositors and borrowers by offering savings and time deposits to depositors and providing all types of loans to borrowers; and (3) providing a variety of financial services, encompassing fiduciary services, investment banking, and off-balance sheet risk taking. The controversy over the proper scope of banking activities centers on the issue of how far to allow banks to enter into these financial services activities.

Commercial banks are private, profit-seeking enterprises, balancing risk and return in their portfolio management with the goal of maximizing shareholder wealth. Shareholder wealth depends upon three factors: (1) the volume of cash flows resulting from portfolio decisions, (2) the timing of those cash flows, and (3) the risk or volatility of the cash flows. Risk itself may be viewed as composed of four types: (1) credit or default risk, (2) interest rate risk, (3) liquidity risk, and (4) fraud risk. The maximization of shareholder wealth is constrained by certain social responsibilities of banks as well as extensive legal and regulatory restrictions, including balance sheet, pricing, geographical, entry, and customer protection constraints.

Commercial banks are regulated for at least three reasons: (1) to prevent banking market failure, (2) to prevent concentration and monopoly, and (3) to achieve certain social goals such as allocating credit to socially meritorious uses. The desire to prevent banking market failure has produced significant limits on the ability of individual banks to take risk, with the goal of reducing the number of bank failures. In addition, the FDIC was established to prevent panics through the contagion of the failure of an individual bank to the failure of the banking system. The desire to prevent concentration has led to limits on branching and holding company expansion, as well as to the application of the antitrust laws to bank mergers. The use of regulation to achieve social goals has given rise to a large number of consumer protection laws, including the Truth-in-Lending Act and the Community Reinvestment Act.

The extensive regulation of commercial banks has produced a number of consequences, some of those intended and others unintentional. Constraints on the geographical expansion of banks has resulted in a fragmented banking system with a large number of small banks. Bank regulation has also reduced the number of failures dramatically. Also, the establishment of deposit insurance in 1933 has eliminated bank runs, although recent deregulation combined with the existing deposit insurance system has encouraged banks to take excessive risk.

The environment within which bank managers operate has changed dramatically. The principal regulatory and competitive changes are: (1) financial reform, (2) greater competition, (3) more unstable interest rates and economic conditions, (4) declining market shares for commercial banks, (5) globalization of the financial system, and (6) proliferation of financial instruments. The net result of these changes is to increase sharply the risk involved in bank management and the complexity of bank decision making.

IMPORTANT CONCEPTS

definition of a bank	credit risk
bank functions	interest rate risk
bank risk management	liquidity risk

social constraints   consumer protection
legal/regulatory constraints   banking structure
banking market failure   financial reform
concentration

REFERENCES

Aspinwall, Richard, and Robert Eisenbeis, (eds.). *The Banking Handbook.* New York: Wiley, 1985

Cooper, Kerry, and Donald Fraser. *Banking Deregulation and the New Competition in Financial Services,* Cambridge, Mass. Ballinger, 1986.

Crane, Dwight, Richard Kimball, and William Gregor. *The Effects of Banking Deregulation.* Washington, D.C., Association of Reserve City Bankers, 1983.

DiClimente, John. "What Is a Bank?" Federal Reserve Bank of Chicago, *Economic Perspectives,* January/February 1983, pp. 20–31.

Hempel, George, and Jess Yawitz. *Financial Management of Financial Institutions.* Englewood Cliffs, N.J.: Prentice-Hall, 1977.

Mason, John. *Financial Management of Commercial Banks,* Boston: Warren, Gorham and Lamont, 1979.

QUESTIONS

1.1. Why is it insufficient now to define a bank as an institution that provides both demand deposits and commercial loans?

1.2. List three broad functions of commercial banks. What other financial institutions compete with banks in providing payments services to the public?

1.3. What does efficient allocation of savings to investment mean?

1.4. What securities activities are (and are not) allowed by commercial banks under the Glass–Steagall Act of 1933.

1.5. What are standby letters of credit? Would the interest rate on corporate bonds backed by such letters be related to the credit risk of the firm or the bank?

1.6. What is the principal goal of a commercial bank? How does profitability of a bank and the risks it faces affect this goal?

1.7. It is sometimes argued that bank managers are fundamentally involved in risk management. In what sense are they risk managers? Is their risk management similar to or different from that of managers of manufacturers and other nonfinancial firms?

1.8. Which risk historically accounts for most bank failures?

1.9. With what constraints must banks cope in achieving their goal(s)?

1.10. Discuss market share trends over time among commercial banks, savings and loans, life insurance companies, pension funds, and mutual funds.

1.11. Give three key reasons for regulating commercial banks. Is the failure of an individual bank important?

1.12. What are the social benefits of deposit insurance? Are there any problems with allowing banks to purchase federal deposit insurance?

1.13. What is concentration in the banking industry? Is it good or bad?

1.14. What did the following consumer acts do?
    The Truth-in-Lending Act of 1968
    The Fair Credit Billing Act of 1974
    The Fair Credit Reporting Act of 1970
    The Community Reinvestment Act of 1972

1.15. How does the U.S. banking system differ from most foreign nations? Are the differences becoming more or less pronounced?

1.16. How did DIDMCA of 1980 increase competition for commercial banks?

1.17. What is securitization? What type of bank risk is reduced by securitization?

1.18. Many changes in the financial environment have occurred in the 1980s. How have these changes affected bank managers?

1.19. It is sometimes argued that risk in banking has increased. What evidence would support this argument?

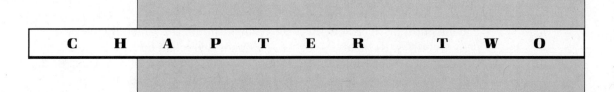

CHAPTER TWO

FUNDAMENTALS OF BANK INVESTMENTS

A substantial amount of bank managers' financial management decisions involves evaluating and pricing risk. By their very nature, commercial banks must accept risk. A bank that takes too little risk will be unable to earn a sufficiently high return to compensate depositors and, at the same time, attract and retain equity capital. On the other hand, a bank that takes excessive risk may encounter such losses that its profitability and solvency may be threatened. Effective bank management must structure its financial management decisions to accept neither too much nor too little risk, a task that is often very difficult to implement.

This chapter is designed to provide potential bank financial managers with the skills necessary to evaluate and price risk and to balance risk and return in

25

making portfolio decisions. Because bank portfolios are generally restricted to debt securities, the analysis focuses on bonds and loan contracts. The chapter begins with a discussion of measurement of rates of return. It distinguishes the risk evaluation process in price-taking and price-making markets. This is followed by a discussion of the basic determinants of value and the factors that cause value to change. The chapter concludes with a discussion of the components of risk and factors that may cause risk to change. Understanding risk and its influence on value is fundamental for effective bank portfolio management.

MEASURES OF THE RATE OF RETURN ON A LOAN OR SECURITY

A number of measures of rates of return exist for loans, securities, and other fixed income instruments. Knowledge of these alternative measures is vital to bank management in making loan and investment decisions. The most commonly used measures of rates of return are discussed in the following sections.

Coupon Rate

The coupon rate is the contractual rate that the security issuer (i.e., borrower) agrees to pay at the time the security is issued. The total amount of interest that the security issuer has agreed to pay to the lender is obtained by taking the coupon rate and multiplying it by the par or stated value of the instrument, as shown in equation (2.1).

$$\text{Coupon rate} \times \text{Par} = \text{Dollar interest} \tag{2.1}$$

For example, if the coupon rate was 12 percent and the par value of the debt instrument was \$1,000, the borrower would agree to pay \$120 per year in interest. If paid semiannually, the payment would be \$60 per period, if quarterly, \$40 per period, and if monthly \$10 per period.

The coupon rate is a meaningful measure of the rate of return on a debt security only if the price of the security is at or near par. Except at the initial creation of the security, however, its market value will seldom equal par.

Current Yield

The current yield takes the interest paid on a debt security and divides it by price, as in equation (2.2). The current yield is preferable to the

$$\text{Current yield} = \frac{\text{Annual interest}}{\text{Market value of security}} \tag{2.2}$$

coupon rate as a measure of return to the investor in that it reflects any differences between market value and par value. It is still deficient, however, because it ignores the price at which the investor can redeem the security at maturity. For example, assume a 12-percent coupon security selling at a price of $800 per $1,000 of face value. The current yield would be 15 percent, but this would ignore the fact that the investor purchased the security at $800 and can redeem it at $1,000 at maturity. Because the current yield ignores this gain or loss at maturity, it will understate the "true" yield when the security is bought at a price below par and overstate it when the security is bought at a price above par.

Yield to Maturity

The yield to maturity (also known as the internal rate of return) is probably the most widely used measure of return on a security. It is preferable to the coupon rate and the current yield in that it recognizes the amounts and timing of all cash flows from a security and adjusts for the time value of money. The yield to maturity is the rate of discount that equates the present value of all cash flows with the purchase price on a security. It may be expressed as in equation (2.3).

$$P = \frac{I_1}{(1 + y)^1} + \frac{I_2}{(1 + y)^2} + \frac{I_3}{(1 + y)^3} + \ldots \frac{I_n}{(1 + y)^n} \qquad (2.3)$$

where I is the income from the security (interest on a bond or loan plus principal payments), n is the number of payments, and y is the yield to maturity.

Holding Period Yield

The holding period yield is essentially the same as the yield to maturity except with the assumption that the security is sold prior to maturity. This concept is expressed mathematically in equation (2.4).

$$P = \frac{I_1}{(1 + h)^1} + \frac{I_2}{(1 + h)^2} + \frac{I_3}{(1 + h)^3} + \frac{P_s}{(1 + h)^n} \qquad (2.4)$$

where I is the annual income from the security as in equation (2.3), P_s is the selling price of the security prior to its maturity, and h is the holding period yield.

The holding period yield and the yield to maturity are, of course, equal if the security is held until maturity. If the security is sold prior to maturity, however, the holding period yield may be above or below the yield to maturity.

Bank Discount Basis Yield

Many money market securities carry no coupons (they are zero coupon issues), are sold at a discount, and are quoted using a bank discount basis yield method. The bank discount basis yield is calculated by subtracting the price of the security from par in order to obtain the discount (D), dividing the discount by par (P), and annualizing the discount on the basis of a 360-day year. For example, assume a 147-day treasury bill selling at a price of $97.55 per $100 face value. The bank discount basis yield on this security may be obtained through the use of equation (2.5).

$$\text{Bank discount basis yield} = \frac{D}{PR} \times \frac{360}{DM} \times 100 \qquad (2.5)$$

where D = dollar value of discount, PR = par value, and DM = days until maturity.

$$BDBY = \frac{2.45}{100} \times \frac{360}{147} = 6 \text{ percent}$$

Although widely used, the bank discount basis yield obviously understates the "true" yield on the security, because it divides the discount by par rather than price and because it annualizes the discount on the basis of a 360-day rather than a 365-day year. The bond equivalent yield is used to determine the true yield on a discount money market instrument such as a treasury bill. The bond equivalent yield may be calculated with the use of equation (2.6).

$$BEY = \frac{D}{\text{Price}} \times \frac{365}{DM} \times 100 \qquad (2.6)$$

In the preceding example, the 6-percent Bank Discount Basis Yield is, in reality, a 6.24-percent Bond Equivalent Yield, calculated as in equation (2.6).

$$BEY = \frac{2.45}{97.55} \times \frac{365}{147} \times 100 = 6.24 \text{ percent}$$

Simple and Compound Interest

These measures of return are commonly used on loan and deposit contracts. Simple interest is the interest charged or paid for exactly 1 year and paid at the end of the year. The coupon rate on a single payment security maturing in exactly 1 year is simple interest. In contrast, with compound interest, interest is earned on interest. For example, the coupon rate on a security that matured in exactly 1 year but that paid semiannually or quarterly interest would be less than the compound interest rate on that security. Assuming a 12-percent security, and a par value of $1,000, with a single payment at maturity, the simple interest paid (and received) would be $120. With monthly payments, which allow for compounding (i.e., interest paid on interest), the total interest paid is $127 (this may be verified from any compound interest rate table) so that the compound interest rate is 12.7 percent. For a given simple interest rate, the more frequent the compounding, the higher the compound interest rate.

Equation (2.7) illustrates the relationship between simple and compound interest.

$$(1 + r) = (1 + i/m)^m \qquad (2.7)$$

where r is the compound interest rate, i is the simple interest rate, and m is the number of times per year that the interest is compounded. Equation (2.7) can be simplified as in equation (2.8).

$$r = (1 + i/m)^m - 1 \qquad (2.8)$$

For example, with quarterly compounding (as with a savings account), a simple interest rate of 8 percent would compound to a rate of 8.24 percent. With monthly compounding, a simple interest rate of 8 percent would compound to more than 8.24 percent.

Add-on Interest, Discount Interest, and the Annual Percentage Rate

Bank lending rates are frequently stated according to the "add on" or discount method. With the add-on method, the total amount of interest is added to the loan and the sum of the interest and principal is divided by the total number of payments in order to obtain the dollar amount of each payment. For example, again assume a 12-percent coupon or stated rate and a $1,000 par value, the total interest paid on the security is $120. If the security was to be paid off in equal monthly installments, the amount of each payment would be $1,120/12 or $100. Note that if the security pays only once (at maturity), the add-on interest and the simple interest are the same. If the security pays more than once, however, then the effective interest rate is higher than the simple interest rate.

With a discount loan the interest is deducted from the amount advanced on the loan. In the 12-percent coupon rate, $1,000 par value illustration, the interest of $120 is deducted at the time of the loan. The lender advances only $880 to the borrower, but the borrower must repay $1,000 at maturity. The effective interest rate for a 1-year single payment discount note may then be calculated as the ratio of interest paid to the net funds advanced multiplied by 100 or 120/880 × 1000 = 13.6 percent. Most discount loans are single payment and thus do not call for intermediate payments.

Neither the add-on nor discount methods provides an accurate measure of the yield (or cost) on a loan. For this reason, the Consumer Credit Protection Act was passed in 1968 by the U.S. Congress, requiring lenders to inform borrowers of the "true" rate paid. This rate is known as the Annual Percentage Rate (APR). A frequently used approximation to the APR is given in equation (2.9). (The true APR is the internal rate of return.)

$$APR = \frac{\begin{array}{c} 2 \times \text{number of payment periods in a year} \\ \times \text{ annual interest cost in dollars} \end{array}}{\begin{array}{c} \text{Total number of loan payments} + 1 \\ \times \text{ Principal of the loan} \end{array}} \times 100 \qquad (2.9)$$

In the 12-percent *single* payment example, the APR can be obtained from equation (2.10).

$$APR = \frac{2 \times 1 \times 120}{2 \times 1,000} = \frac{240}{2,000} = 12.00 \text{ percent} \qquad (2.10)$$

If the loan were to be repaid in monthly installments, the APR would be given by equation (2.11).

$$APR = \frac{2 \times 12 \times 120}{13 \times 1,000} = \frac{2,880}{13,000} = 22.15 \text{ percent} \qquad (2.11)$$

RISK AND THE MARKET FOR FINANCIAL INSTRUMENTS

Bank management must properly evaluate and price risk if the bank is to make effective portfolio management decisions. However, the precise steps taken by bank management in implementing its risk management strategy depend upon whether the bank is a price maker or a price taker in its financial markets' operations. A price maker is one that determines the price (or interest rate) on a financial instrument. In contrast, a price taker is one that accepts the price (or interest rate) on a financial instrument.

The bank is a price maker in many of its loan markets, which means the bank may vary the interest rate charged on loans without driving off all its loan customers. Naturally, in setting the price the bank must recognize the law of the downward sloping demand curve; that is, the higher the interest rate on the loans the smaller the quantity of loans that the bank will be able to make. Also, the bank must recognize that loans to large, well-established companies are much more price sensitive than loans to smaller firms and consumers. The bank is a price taker if it has no control over the price (or interest rate) on the financial instrument. The bank is a price taker in most securities markets; in these markets, the market price and interest return are established by the interplay of market supply and demand. The bank may buy as much as it wishes at the market price but cannot buy at a lower price.

The risk evaluation process for bank management is quite different in the two types of markets. In the price-maker market, the bank evaluates the risk of the financial instrument (most commonly a loan applicant) and determines the appropriate price or interest rate to compensate for the risk. The lender controls the compensation received for risk bearing and can adjust that compensation as risk changes. Of course, the applicant can always reject the terms of the loan offer or attempt to modify them through negotiation. Setting the terms of a financial contract in a price-maker market frequently involves negotiation between the lender and the borrower.

In a price-taker market, the price (and hence the interest return) is given to the bank. The bank may (and should) determine the degree of risk in the financial instrument and then decide whether the asset was appropriately priced. The sole decision of the bank, however, would be whether to buy or not buy (or sell if the bank held the asset) the financial instrument. The bank would not be involved in setting the price nor would there be negotiations concerning the price and other terms of the financial instrument. Pricing is not an issue in price-taker markets.

DETERMINANTS OF VALUE

General Concept

What determines value? What factors determine the price of a financial instrument (or the interest rate set on that instrument) in the price-maker or price-taker market? Although many variables enter into the determination of value, three in particular are relevant (they were discussed briefly in Chapter 1):

The amount of cash flow

The timing of cash flow

The riskiness of cash flow

The value of an asset is determined fundamentally by the cash benefits (interest) and/or principal payments that the seller *expects* to receive from the asset. In terms of the present value concept, the value of an asset is the present value of all its expected cash flows discounted at the appropriate discount rate that reflects the risk of those cash flows. This approach may be expressed algebraically as in equation (2.12).

$$V_0 = \frac{CF_1}{(1 + r)^1} + \frac{CF_2}{(1 + r)^2} + \frac{CF_3}{(1 + r)^3} + \cdots \frac{CF_n}{(1 + r)^n} \qquad (2.12)$$

where V_0 = present value (or price) of the asset at time zero, CF = expected cash flow that accrues to the owner of the asset during the owner's holding period, r = required rate of return or discount rate, and n = amount of time the asset is held or is expected to be held.

In this approach three factors will cause an increase in the value of the asset:

1. An increase in the amount of cash flow to be received from the asset.
2. Earlier receipt of the expected cash flow.

3. A decrease in the required rate of return.

Conversely, three factors will cause a decrease in the value of the asset:

1. A decrease in the amount of cash flow to be received from the asset.
2. Later receipt of the expected cash flow.
3. An increase in the required rate of return.

An example of the determinants of value and how value would change may assist in understanding the concept. Assume that the cash benefits from holding an asset for 5 years are $200 per year. Further assume that the holder expected to be able to sell the asset for $1,000 at the end of the fifth year (if the asset were a bond, for example, this might be its principal or maturity value), and that the required rate of return is 12 percent. Then the value of the asset, using equation (2.12), is

$$V_0 = \frac{200}{(1.12)^1} + \frac{200}{(1.12)^2} + \frac{200}{(1.12)^3} + \frac{200}{(1.12)^4} + \frac{200}{(1.12)^5} + \frac{1000}{(1.12)^5} = \$1,287 \quad (2.13)$$

The value of the asset can be determined easily with the use of present value tables, as shown in Table 2.1. The present value of a financial instrument that offered $200 per year for 5 years with the expectation of receiving $1,000 at the end of the fifth year is $1,287. If the required rate of return on this financial instrument were 12 percent, then the current equilibrium market value would be $1,287.

Equation (2.12) and Table 2.1 can be used to show the effects of changes in the determining variables on the value of a financial asset. For example, suppose that the cash flow from an asset increased from $200 to $400. Then the present value of the cash flows would be given in equation (2.14).

TABLE 2.1
PRESENT VALUE OF CASH BENEFITS

Time	Cash Benefits	Present Value Interest Factor	Present Value
1	200	.893	179
2	200	.797	159
3	200	.712	142
4	200	.636	127
5	200	.567	113
5	1,000	.567	567
			1,287

$$V_0 = \frac{400}{(1.12)^1} + \frac{400}{(1.12)^2} + \frac{400}{(1.12)^3} + \frac{400}{(1.12)^4} + \frac{400}{(1.12)^5} + \frac{1000}{(1.12)^5} =$$

$$= 358 + 318 + 284 + 254 + 226 + 567 = \$2,007 \qquad (2.14)$$

As another example, suppose that the cash flow to be received in the original example of $200 per year plus $1,000 at maturity (a total of $2,000) was accelerated to $1,000 in year one and $500 each in years two and three. The present value of these cash flows is given in equation (2.15).

$$V = \frac{1000}{(1.12)^1} + \frac{500}{(1.12)^2} + \frac{500}{(1.12)^3} = 893 + 388 + 356 = \$1,637 \qquad (2.15)$$

In this example, the value of the asset would increase from $1,287 to $1,637 simply because the cash benefits were received earlier.

As the third example, assume that the required rate of return fell from 12 percent to 10 percent. In that case, the new value of the asset could be calculated from equation (2.16).

$$V_0 = \frac{200}{(1.10)^1} + \frac{200}{(1.10)^2} + \frac{200}{(1.10)^3} + \frac{200}{(1.10)^4} + \frac{200}{(1.10)^5} + \frac{1000}{(1.10)^5}$$

$$= (200)(.909) + (200)(.820) + (200)(.751) + (200)(.683) + (200)(.621) \qquad (2.16)$$

$$+ (1000)(.621) = 182 + 164 + 150 + 136 + 124 + 621 = 1377$$

The value of the asset was increased from $1,287 to $1,377 because of the decline in the discount rate.

Applications to Bonds and Other Fixed Income Instruments

Because commercial banks are principally engaged in acquiring bonds, mortgages, and various types of loan contracts, all of which are generally referred to as fixed income instruments, application of the general concepts of valuation focuses on these types of assets. In the case of a bond, the cash flows are the regular interest payments plus the return of principal at maturity. In the case of a mortgage, the cash flows are the regularly scheduled interest and principal payments (assuming the mortgage is amortized), plus any prepayments, including early payoff. In the case of a loan contract, the cash flows are the regularly scheduled interest and principal payments if the loan is amortized or the interest and principal payments at maturity if the loan is a single payment (at maturity) loan. For purposes of simplicity our examples are for bonds, although the basic principles of valuation are generally applicable to other fixed income instruments.

The following **principles of valuation** are useful guideposts for bank managers in making these loan and investment decisions:

1. Par, Discount, and Premium Assets.

(a) If the interest payment on the asset is equal to the required rate of return, the asset will sell at par.

(b) If the interest payment on the asset is less than the required rate of return, the asset will sell below par. It will be a "discount" instrument.

(c) If the interest payment on the asset is greater than the required rate of return, the asset will sell at above par. It will be a premium instrument.

2. Prices and Required Rates of Return. An increase in the required rate of return (commonly referred to as the yield to maturity for a bond) produces a decline in the market value of the asset. Conversely, a decrease in the required rate of return produces an increase in the market value of the asset. In short, **asset prices and required rates of return are inversely related**.

These two principles of valuation have great relevance for bank managers in the selection of assets and liabilities in their portfolios. Two examples, one dealing with the bond portfolio and the other with the loan portfolio, illustrate this point.

Assume that bank management is considering the purchase of a bond. Most bonds trade in well-defined markets so that the bank is a price taker rather than a price maker in this market. If the bank finds the bond attractive at the market established price, it must be concerned about what would happen to the price of the bond if interest rates (i.e., the required rate of return) were to rise. If interest rates did increase, the bank would suffer a loss through the depreciation of the market value of the bond. Even if the bank does not plan to sell the bond, it would incur a loss in the sense that the cash flow on the bond would be less than that available on other bonds after interest rates increased.

In the case of a loan contract, the principle is the same although the process is somewhat more complicated. Banks are price makers in most loan markets. Bank management must appraise the risk dimensions of the loan and set an interest rate that adequately compensates for that risk. If, for example, the bank and the borrower negotiate a contract interest rate on the loan that is less than the rate that the market requires for that type of loan, then the bank could sell the loan (and loans increasingly are sold in the secondary market) only at a discount. Even if the bank were to retain the loan on its own books, it would not be earning a sufficient return to compensate for assuming the risk of that loan.

3. The longer the "life" of an asset, the greater the fluctuation in price for a given change in the required rate of return. Valuation principle 2 (given previously) states that asset prices move inversely to interest rates but does not specify the exact amount of the price change for a given change in interest rates. If the price change were the same for assets of different lengths of lives, this issue would not be significant. But because the price changes vary substantially with the life of the asset, management of the life of the portfolio is crucial to the bank.

The maturity of an asset is conventionally used to measure its life. Maturity only measures the last date on which a cash payment is made, however, and ignores all intervening cash flows. Two assets could have the same maturities but be quite different in terms of their "lives" and the sensitivity of their market values to interest rate movements. Take a zero coupon (single payment at maturity) 30-year bond, for example, and compare it with a 30-year amortizing mortgage. Their maturities are the same, but because their cash flows are quite different, their market value sensitivities to interest rate changes are very different. In fact, accurate predictions of the sensitivity of asset price changes to interest rate changes cannot be made based upon the maturity of the asset. Such accurate predictions can be made based upon duration.

Duration is a useful concept in measuring the effects of changes in interest rates (i.e., required rates of return) on the present value (or prices) of cash flows from an asset. Duration may be defined as the period of time that elapses before a stream of cash flow generates one-half of its present value. It may be measured by weighting the present value of each future cash flow by the number of periods until the receipt of the cash flow and then dividing by the present value (or price of the asset) as in equation (2.17).

$$D = \frac{\sum_{t=1}^{N} tpv(CF_t)}{\sum_{t=1} pv(CF_t)} \qquad (2.17)$$

where D is duration, t is the length of time until the date on which the cash flow is to be received (measured in days, weeks, months, or years), and $pv(CF_t)$ is the present value of each cash flow to be received. The cash flows are discounted at whatever is the appropriate market rate.

Duration is a particularly important measure of the average life of a security because it recognizes *all* cash flows from an asset, not just the final cash flows at maturity. For a zero coupon instrument (with no intermediate cash flows), the duration of the asset and its maturity are the same. For financial instruments with intermediate cash flows, as with most bonds and mortgages, duration is less than maturity. By using the concept of duration, it is possible to relate accurately the changes in prices of financial assets to changes in interest rates.

An example of the calculation of the duration for two bonds may help to illustrate the concept. Assume that one bond is a zero coupon instrument with a 5-year maturity (a zero coupon instrument has no intermediate cash flows). Assume that the second bond is a 10-percent coupon bond (with the interest paid once a year at the end of the year) with a 5-year maturity. Assume further that the required rate of return is 10 percent for both bonds. Then by equation

(2.17), the duration of the first bond is 5 years ((5 × 1000)/1000) and the duration of the second bond is 1.7 years (1 × 91 + 2 × 83 + 3 × 75 + 4 × 68 + 5 × 62 + 620)/1000.

The change in the price of the asset resulting from interest rate changes can be estimated with the use of equation (2.18).

$$\frac{\Delta p}{p} = -D\frac{\Delta i}{(1 + i)} \approx - D\Delta i \tag{2.18}$$

where p = price of the asset, i = yield of the asset or required rate of return, and Δ = change from previous value.

By equation (2.18), the percentage change in the price of the asset is equal to its duration (with a negative sign) multiplied by the change in the interest rate, divided by one plus the interest rate. Hence, for a given change in interest rates, the decline in price for a 10-year duration bond will be double that of a 5-year duration bond (although the decline in price may not be twice as great for a 10-year maturity bond as that of a 5-year maturity bond).

Knowledge of the concept of duration leads logically to a fourth principle of valuation.

4. For assets of a given maturity, the greater the intermediate cash flows (due to higher coupon rates or amortization of principal), the more stable will be their prices for a given change in interest rates. That is, price volatility will be less for an asset of a given maturity if more of its cash flow is received early in the life of the asset. This reduced risk for high intermediate cash flow occurs because these assets have shorter durations; that is, for an asset of a given maturity, the ratio of its duration to its maturity is smaller if a greater fraction of its cash flows occurs early in its life.

COMPONENTS OF RISK

Commercial banks deal primarily in assets that are commonly referred to as fixed income instruments. Although the determinants of value for these assets are the same as for all other assets—the amount of cash flow, the timing of the cash flow, and the risk of the cash flow—changes in the market value of the assets stem principally from changes in the required rate of return due to risk changes. Hence, in evaluating the desirability of portfolio adjustments, bank management must understand the determinants of the risk of individual assets and the factors that would cause risk to shift.

The required rate of return may be thought of as being composed of the following elements as shown in equation (2.19).

$$\text{Required rate of return} = f \begin{bmatrix} \text{Real rate, inflation premium, default risk,} \\ \text{duration, taxes, marketability,} \\ \text{other factors} \end{bmatrix} \tag{2.19}$$

Equation (2.19) indicates that the required rate of return on an asset is determined by two basic factors: economy-wide factors and firm or asset specific factors. The underlying real rate of interest and the premium for inflation are common factors for all securities. They establish a floor for the interest rate for any security. This basic economy-wide interest rate must then be adjusted for the specific firm or asset characteristics associated with a particular asset. These include the probability of a default on the required cash payments (referred to as default or credit risk), the life of the asset, proxied by its duration, the way in which the asset is taxed, the marketabiliity of the asset, and a variety of other (generally less significant) factors.

Economy-wide Factors

The underlying base rate for all assets is the nominal riskless rate of interest. This interest rate (or required rate of return) can be viewed as the sum of the real rate of interest plus a premium for expected inflation. Following the work of Irving Fisher, the nominal riskless rate of interest can be specified as in equation (2.20).

$$i = r + p \qquad\qquad (2.20)$$

where i = nominal riskless rate of interest, r = the real rate of interest, and p = premium for anticipated inflation.

Fisher argued that the nominal interest rate could be thought of as being composed of two parts—a constant real rate and a premium for anticipated or expected inflation. Assuming a constant real rate produces the conclusion of a 1 for 1 relationship between chances in expected inflation and the nominal interest rate. Although there are disagreements about the stability of the real rate, nevertheless, the *Fisher effect* (the name given to Fisher's hypothesized relationship) provides insight into the fundamental driving force behind changes in the overall level of interest rates. Bank managers, in structuring their portfolio of assets and liabilities, should recognize the fundamental importance of expected inflation in affecting the level of interest rates and should structure their assets and liabilities accordingly.

Specific Factors

Although changes in the general level of interest rates obviously are important in the management of a bank's portfolio, banks buy and sell individual assets. Prices on their individual assets respond not only to economy-wide factors but also to factors specific to the firm issuing the security or to the individual asset. These include:

Default Risk

This refers to the probability that the borrower will be unable or unwilling to make the agreed-upon payments on a debt contract in a timely fashion. Default occurs whenever the borrower does not make a required payment or whenever the required payment is late. In either case, the lender has suffered a loss. If the payment is never made, the lender is unable to invest the funds and earn interest during the period of the delay. As a result, the realized rate would be less than the rate agreed upon in the loan contract.

Banks do, of course, accept default risk in their entire portfolio (with the exception of the holdings of U.S. government securities). Default risk exists in their holdings of corporate and municipal bonds and even in their money market investments, such as lending in the federal funds market. However, most default risk in a bank's portfolio is concentrated in its loan portfolio. Because most recent bank failures have been associated with loan defaults, managing default risk and obtaining adequate compensation for accepting default risk are crucial to the successful operation of the bank.

Financial markets provide useful information to bank managers on pricing default risk. Bond markets establish default risk premiums on securities, and thereby create a risk structure of interest rates. This risk structure may be envisioned by relating a risk premium (the difference between the yield on a risky security and the yield on a risk-free security) to some measure of default risk (e.g., a bond rating).

Figure 2.1 shows the risk structure of interest rates for corporate bonds. Default risk is proxied by the bond ratings and the risk premium is measured as the difference between the yield to maturity on corporate bonds of a given rating group and the yield to maturity of U.S. Treasury securities (presumably default risk-free) of similar maturity. The risk premium increases as the credit quality of the corporate bonds diminishes, reflecting the need to compensate investors for accepting additional default risk. This risk premium line represents the market price of risk at a given time.

Knowledge of the market price of risk is extremely important for bank managers because it provides a reference point for evaluating risk for assets

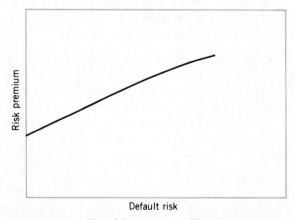

FIGURE 2.1   The risk structure of interest rates.

without markets or with very limited markets. Such knowledge is especially important in managing the bank's loan portfolio. In establishing an acceptable interest rate for a loan, the bank begins with some measure of its cost of funds (or some other base) and adds to that number an amount to compensate it for unusual handling costs and for accepting a credit or default risk. But how much should it add for accepting default risk? If it can determine the financial condition of the borrower and relate that financial condition to the financial condition of companies with different bond ratings, it can obtain some estimate of the appropriate risk premium. For example, suppose a prospective borrower has a financial profile equivalent to a Baa-rated security. Suppose further that Baa-rated securities carry a default risk premium equal to 325 basis points, as shown in Figure 2.1. Any premium less than this amount (assuming the data used in the analysis were correct) would be too small to justify accepting the risk. Of equal importance, if market conditions or competitive factors made it impossible for the bank to obtain this premium from the borrower, the bank should (absent other overriding factors) not make the loan and use the funds for some other purpose. Many banks have experienced severe earnings problems because of their policy of underpricing risk in their lending decisions.

Duration

The life of the asset, proxied by its maturity or better by its duration is another factor that affects the risk. The relationship between the yield to maturity on a group of assets identical in all respects except their durations and the duration of the assets is referred to as the yield curve. In most circumstances, the yield curve is upward sloping; that is, the longer the duration of the asset, the greater the required return or yield. Figure 2.2a shows a "normal" or upward-sloping yield curve. Given that assets of longer durations have a greater price volatility, it is not surprising to observe that these assets normally have a higher required rate of return. In some periods, however, the yield curve becomes inverted (i.e., downward sloping) as shown in Figure 2.2b. Downward-sloping yield curves usually appear in periods of high interest rates and reflect portfolio adjustments by financial market participants in anticipation of falling interest rates in the future.

Taxes

Obviously, the way in which the returns from the asset are taxed is very relevant to bank managers in structuring their portfolio decisions. Bank managers, as with other investors, are interested in after-tax return, that is, the cash flows from an asset less the tax payment that must be made to governmental entities. Cash flows that banks receive from corporate and consumer borrowers generally are fully taxed. However, certain tax benefits from the cash flows come from holdings of U.S. government securities and some issues of state and local governments (referred to as municipals). Interest income on U.S. government securities is exempt from income taxation by state and local govern-

Normal yield curve

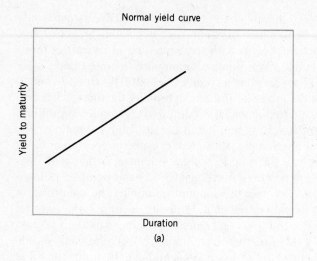

(a)

Inverted yield curve

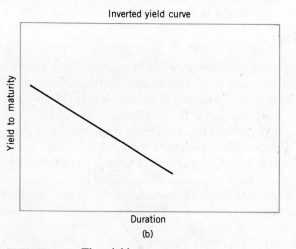

(b)

FIGURE 2.2   The yield curve.

ments. More significantly, interest income on certain issues of state and local governments are exempt from federal income tax (unless the bank purchased the securities with borrowed funds). In structuring its portfolio, the bank can easily apply its relevant tax rate to the earnings from taxable assets in order to determine whether they are preferable, on an after-tax basis, to the assets that are tax-free or whose interest earnings are subject to a reduced rate of tax.

The yields on taxable and tax-exempt securities may be compared with the use of equation (2.21).

$$\begin{array}{c}\text{Tax}\\ \text{equivalent}\\ \text{yield}\end{array} = \frac{\text{Tax-exempt yield}}{(1-t)} \qquad (2.21)$$

where t = appropriate tax rate.

For example, a 5-percent tax-exempt yield is equivalent to a 5.88-percent yield on a taxable security for an investor in the 5-percent marginal tax bracket. For an investor in a 25-percent tax bracket, however, a 5-percent tax-exempt yield is equivalent to a 6.66-percent yield.

Marketability

The ability to dispose of an asset in the secondary market at a reasonably stable price is also a relevant feature of an asset to a bank (or other investor). Many assets traditionally held by banks have been highly illiquid, with little or no secondary market. The lack of marketability has been especially pronounced for the loan portfolio. With securitization, however, more and more assets are traded in the secondary market. This makes marketability an even more important characteristic in bank investing decisions.

Other Factors

Any other factors that might affect the risk of an asset obviously must be considered in the bank's investment decisions. Those assets in which the borrower has the right to prepay with little or no penalty (such as mortgages) must be considered separately in an analysis of assets that are not redeemable. For bonds, the ability of the issuer to retire an issue prior to maturity voluntarily through a call feature or through planning with a sinking fund is certainly relevant.

Diversification and Risk Management

The risk embodied in a bank's portfolio of loans and investments depends not only on the risk of the individual assets in the portfolio but also on the degree of asset diversification. More specifically, the risk of the portfolio depends upon the risk of the individual assets and the correlations among those assets. Presumably, the greater the degree of diversification, the smaller the degree of portfolio risk for a given level of risk in the individual assets. Of course, some types of portfolio diversification policies will reduce risk more than others. For example, making a number of loans to firms in the same industry will reduce risk less than making the same number of loans to firms in different industries. Similarly, buying municipal bonds from different government units within a small geographical area will generally reduce risk less than buying those bonds from different governmental units in different geographical areas.

A number of bank management policy implications flow from the recognition of the importance of diversification. Although many are discussed throughout the book, two are particularly important and warrant discussion at this point.

First, recognition of the importance of diversification in portfolio risk management suggests that bank management should attempt to spread the loan portfolio over a relatively large geographical area and over many different types of loans. For banks that are part of extensive branch or holding company systems, such a diversification is relatively simple. For smaller, community banks, or for very small unit banks, however, achieving adequate diversification is more difficult. These banks should consider purchasing loans in the secondary market or participation in loan pools as ways to reduce credit risk through diversification.

The benefits of diversification may exist not only in credit risk management but also in interest rate risk control. Because interest rates for different maturity assets seldom rise or fall precisely together (i.e., the yield curve seldom shifts up or down by exactly the same amount for all maturity securities), bank management may be able to reduce risk in the investment portfolio by a careful selection of different maturities in the investment portfolio. A computer simulation could then be done to determine the effects of alternative changes in the yield curve on the income and portfolio value of different investment portfolios.

RISK MANAGEMENT: A SYNTHESIS

Commercial bank managers attempt to maximize the value of the owners' equity, subject to regulatory and other constraints. Such share maximization comes from maximizing the value of the assets. Those values will increase or decrease with their cash flows and with the discount rate required to determine their present values. Increases in the required rate will lower the value of the bank, absent increases in expected cash flows from the asset. Those increases in the required rate may be due to industry-wide or firm/asset-specific factors. Bank management must anticipate (to the extent reasonably possible) such changes in the required rate of return.

SUMMARY

Bank management must be able to measure and appraise accurately the return and risk dimensions of their portfolio choices. A number of measures of return exist on financial instruments that commercial banks normally deal in. These include: coupon rate, current yield, yield to maturity, holding period yield, bank discount basis yield, simple interest, compound interest, add-on interest, discount interest, and the annual percentage rate. In some markets, especially the securities market, the bank is a price taker, reacting to the market determined price and deciding whether the yield on the asset justifies its risk. In other markets, especially the loan markets, the bank is a price maker, setting the yield to compensate itself for risk.

The value or price of a financial asset (investment security or loan) is determined by the amount, timing, and risk of cash flows from the assets. In present value terms, the value or price of an asset is the present value of the cash flows discounted at some required rate of return reflecting the risk of the asset. Increases in the required rate of return lower the value of the asset, and the longer the "life" of an asset the greater will be the change in price for a given change in interest rates. Duration, the most precise measure of the life of an asset, is the period of time before a stream of cash flow generates one-half of its present value.

The required rate of return on an asset fundamentally reflects its risk. More specifically, the required rate of return is composed of some real rate of interest (i.e., the pure cost of money) plus various premiums for risk. These premiums include inflation risk, default risk, duration, taxes, marketability, and any other factors that would affect the required rate of return.

IMPORTANT CONCEPTS

coupon yield	tax effects
current yield	marketability
yield to maturity	discount interest
holding period yield	annual percentage rate
bank discount basis yield	price maker
simple interest	price taker
compound interest	determinants of value
add on interest	duration
default risk	Fisher effect

REFERENCES

Bierwag, Gerry, George Kaufman, and Alden Toevs. "Duration: Its Development and Use in Bond Portfolio Management," *Financial Analysts Journal*, July–August 1983, pp. 15–35.

Cramer, Robert and Jones Siefert. "Measuring the Impact of Maturity on Expected Return and Risk," *Journal of Bank Research,* Autumn 1976, pp. 229–235.

Fama, Eugene. "Short Term Interest Rates as Predictors of Inflation," *American Economic Review,* June 1975, pp. 269–282.

Fisher, Lawrence. "Determinants of Risk Premiums on Corporate Bonds," *Journal of Political Economy,* June 1959, pp. 217–237.

Homer, Sidney and Martin Leibowitz. *Inside the Yield Book,* Englewood Cliffs, N.J.: Prentice-Hall, 1972.

Jaffee, Dwight, "Cyclical Variations in the Risk Structure of Interest Rates," *Journal of Monetary Economics,* July 1975, pp. 309–325.

Taylor, Herbert. "Interest Rates: How Much Does Expected Inflation Matter?" Federal Reserve Bank of Philadelphia *Business Review,* July–August 1982, pp. 3–12.

Yawitz, Jess et al. "The Use of Average Maturity as a Risk Proxy in Investment Portfolios," *Journal of Finance,* May 1975, pp. 325–332.

QUESTIONS

2.1. Compare and contrast the coupon rate, current yield, and yield to maturity as measures of the return on a fixed income instrument.

2.2. How does the yield to maturity compare with the holding period yield? Under what conditions would the yield to maturity and the holding period yield be the same? Different?

2.3. What is the bank discount basis yield? Why is it different from and lower than the "true" yield?

2.4. Show an equation relating the simple interest rate to the compound interest rate. As the number of compounding periods increases, how does this relationship change?

2.5. How does add on interest compare with discount interest? How do both compare with the Annual Percentage Rate?

2.6. What is the difference between a price taker and a price maker for financial instruments? Of what relevance is this difference for bank management?

2.7. Explain the relationship between the interest payment and the required rate of return for par, discount, and premium assets.

2.8. If the required rate of return on an asset increases but the interest payment stays constant, in what form are earnings increased to the purchaser of the asset?

2.9. What is duration? Why is it preferable to maturity as a measure of the "life" of a financial asset?

2.10. Distinguish between economy-wide and specific factors as determinants of the required rate of return on a financial instrument.

2.11. What is the Fisher Effect? How does it influence the required rate of return?

2.12. What is the default risk premium? Is it a greater fraction of the required returns for a low rated or high rated issue?

2.13. What would be the effect of an increase in the tax rate on the tax equivalent yield on a municipal security? How would the tax rate change affect the desirability of holding municipals as compared to U.S. government bonds?

2.14. What is the yield curve? What yield curve shape is most common? When might the yield curve be inverted?

2.15. What is diversification? How can a bank use it to control different kinds of risk?

PROBLEMS

2.1. What is the current yield for a $1,000 par bond paying a 6-percent coupon and selling at a price of 90? What is the yield to maturity on the bond (assume a 10-year maturity)? Suppose that you bought the bond at 90 and sold it one year later at 95, what would be your holding-period yield?

2.2. In problem 2.1, what would be the price of the bond if the required rate fell to 6 percent? If it fell to 5 percent?

2.3. Calculate the bank discount basis yield for a 91-day treasury bill selling for $98 per $100 face value. What is the bond equivalent yield? Why is it necessary to calculate this yield?

2.4. If the simple interest rate is 6 percent on a savings account, and interest is compounded annually, what is the annualized compound rate of interest earned?

2.5. What is the duration of a zero coupon, five-year bond? What is the duration of a 10-percent coupon, five-year bond, with a 12 percent required rate of return?

2.6. If a bond has a duration of 5 years, and interest rates are expected to increase by 2 percent, calculate the new price of a par bond valued at $1,000 after such a rate increase.

2.7. Which 2-year certificate of deposit has the greater yield?
(a) 7 percent interest rate compounded daily.
(b) $7\frac{1}{4}$ percent interest rate compounded annually.

2.8. Suppose that you want to borrow $50,000 for 6 months and the bank deducts interest in advance at the rate of 10 percent. How much would you have to borrow? What is the effective rate? What is the Annual Percentage Rate?

2.9. Given a financial instrument with expected cash flows at year-end for four years of $100, $100, $100, and $1,100. If the required rate of return was 14 percent, solve for the value of the instrument. How would a lower required rate of return affect this value?

PART TWO

ASSETS

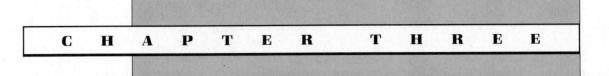

EVALUATING BANK PERFORMANCE

Deregulation of interest rates, rising competition from bank as well as nonbank competitors, continuing development of innovative ways to provide financial services, and interstate banking are all contributing to a heightened awareness in evaluating bank performance. Banks can no longer earn legally mandated yield spreads between the average interest rates earned on sources and uses of funds. Nor can banks continue to reap monopoly rents from bank charters that naturally endowed them with a considerable degree of market power. Instead, today's more competitive banking environment is causing banking institutions to evaluate carefully the risks and returns involved in serving the needs of the public.

49

Various groups of individuals are particularly interested in evaluating bank performance. First, and foremost, bank shareholders are directly affected by bank performance. Investors take advantage of bank information to develop expectations concerning future performance that can be used to price common shares appropriately (in addition to capital notes and debentures that may be issued by the bank). Second, bank management traditionally is evaluated on the basis of how well the bank performs relative to previous years and compared with similar (or peer group) banks. Hence, employees' salaries and promotions frequently are tied to the performance of the bank. Bankers also need to be informed about the condition of other banks with which they have dealings. Loan purchases and participations from poorly managed institutions may be suspect; moreover, Fed funds sold and repurchase agreements with other banks require that some knowledge of their performance be obtained to prevent loss of funds in the event of their failure and subsequent closure by regulatory authorities. Third, regulators concerned about the safety and soundness of the banking system and the preservation of public confidence monitor banks using on-site examinations and computer-oriented ''early warning systems'' to keep track of bank performance.

Fourth, depositors may be interested in how well the bank is doing, especially if they hold deposits in excess of the insured amount (e.g., each depositor is allowed federal insurance up to $100,000). Fifth, and last, the business community and general public should be concerned about their banks' performance to the extent that their economic prosperity is linked to their success or failure.

The present chapter is organized into two parts. The first part provides a general framework for evaluating bank performance. This framework helps to conceptualize the nature of bank behavior, in addition to pointing out possible interactions between various aspects of performance. In this section we discuss the internal and external performance factors that need to be evaluated by bank management.

The second part of the chapter discusses a variety of key financial characteristics that can be calculated from bank accounting statements known as Call Reports of Income and Condition, including profitability, capitalization, asset quality, operating efficiency, liquidity, taxes, and more.

A FRAMEWORK FOR EVALUATING BANK PERFORMANCE

Like any corporation, the ultimate measure of a bank's performance is the value of its common shares. Maximization of shareholder wealth is a complex issue that involves both internal and external management factors. Internal factors are areas of bank management that the officers and staff of the bank have under their immediate control. By contrast, external factors are environmental aspects of the bank's market over which management has no direct

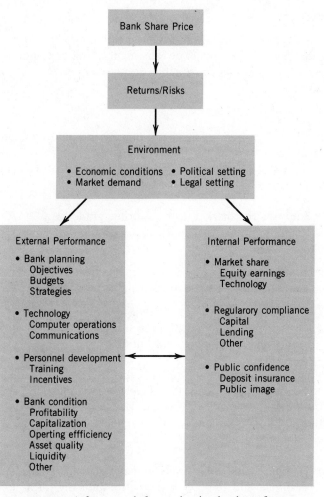

FIGURE 3.1   A framework for evaluating bank performance.

control. Figure 3.1 shows the interrelationship between these two performance factors. The problem that bank management faces is allocating scarce resources (i.e., land, labor, and capital equipment) to the different performance dimensions shown there in order to maximize the total value of the bank. In this regard, interactions between different performance areas must be carefully considered. For example, increasing the bank's market share and competitiveness may compromise the bank's financial condition, because operating expenses have to be increased. In turn, regulatory compliance and public confidence may be affected. Of course, changes in the bank's environment can alter the investment decisions of management with regard to the internal and external performance areas shown in Figure 3.1.

Internal Performance

In this section we discuss three aspects of internal performance: bank planning, technology, and personnel development. Bank condition is another dimension of internal performance, which is discussed in more detail in the second part of this chapter.

Bank Planning

As a first step in planning, bank objectives should be stated. Obviously, the ultimate objective of the bank (as mentioned earlier) is the maximization of owners' equity. Other bank objectives serve to reach this result. Some examples of bank objectives are the following:

- Improve the market share of prime grade loans.
- Upgrade the quality of management expertise in the area of high technology lending.
- Expand the financial services being offered to retail customers to increase the size and diversification of the deposit base.
- Implement an automated delivery system for payment services.
- Diversify the loan portfolio to a greater extent in terms of both different assets and geographic distribution.

Once the objectives of the bank are developed, they can be translated into specific, quantifiable goals. Goals clearly communicate the results that management seeks in both the short- and long-term planning horizon. For example, with reference to the market share objective given earlier, the following goals may be adopted:

- Expand prime grade loans to manufacturing companies by 15 percent the first year and 10 percent thereafter annually for a period of 4 years.
- Maintain retail business lending at the same pace as in the past.
- Trim lending in other areas of the bank by 5 percent per year across the board for the next 5 years.

By quantifying goals, management formalizes the planning process. This step in bank planning should involve all levels of management in order to ensure that reasonable goals are established and are understood by everyone. Also, personal involvement in the process of setting goals may improve morale, increase communication between departments, and help to coordinate bank operations.

Budgets, or profit plans, are in-depth statements of the objectives that are intended to bring objectives down to the departmental level of the bank. Budgets allocate estimated labor and capital resources to various departments with the goals of the bank in mind. Typically, budgets are for a 1-year period and contain monthly and quarterly refinements. The specific results expected of each department are defined in the budget, which enables periodic reviews to monitor progress toward goals. In general, budgets are used to exercise internal control over the bank's operations.

By contrast, strategic planning seeks to anticipate emerging internal and external factors that could affect the bank's achievement of goals in the long run. Rather than being mechanical like budgeting, it is creative in nature. It is more concerned with effectiveness in achieving goals, whereas budgeting focuses on cost efficiency. Also, strategic planning is more general than a budget plan in its content, and thus provides guidance for the future as well as a blueprint for managing the bank's environment. However, this planning must be compatible with the bank's annual budget.

The way in which the planning process is managed by officers and staff will have a major influence on the performance of the bank. Increasing competition has tended to accentuate the importance of careful planning. Institutions that do not implement comprehensive planning procedures will undoubtedly have lower share prices on average and be at greater risk of failure than other banks.

Technology

Automation of operations can improve internal performance in a number of ways. For example, more up-to-date and accurate information can be supplied to customers and managers alike. New financial services, such as automatic bill paying, can be offered to the public. Also, at least in the long run, the operating costs of the bank may be reduced, as capital investment in computer and communications equipment is substituted for labor. Especially for small banks, automation may not be feasible because of low public demand for electronically produced financial services or lack of internal informational needs. In this case cooperative relationships with correspondent banks, bankers' banks, and joint ventures (including franchising relationships, network sharing, and other third-party business arrangements) can be employed. Large banks typically lease or purchase equipment and spread the cost among subscribing smaller banks. However, large banks may benefit from cooperative relationships also.

Computer and communications technology are dominant fixed expense items for automated banking services. These expenses can be considerable, especially for small banks, and may be reduced by cooperative relationships as mentioned previously. Because rapid obsolescence of technology is a major problem with investing too heavily in automated equipment, many banks weigh leasing against purchase of automated equipment. Also, large banks frequently spread the costs of automation by selling automated services to smaller, subscribing banks. In general, banks need to control automation expenses.

Personnel Development

Because commercial banks are labor-intensive, it is essential that attention be focused on personnel development. Human resources play a critical role in the achievement of bank goals and objectives.

Challenges. Two major challenges facing today's banks are the greater emphasis on personal selling of financial services and the trend toward geographic expansion in banking. The wide variety and complexity of today's banking services require interpersonal skills to communicate and sell them to customers. Thus, existing officers and staff need to be involved in sales training and marketing techniques. Moreover, geographic expansion in banking has been gathering momentum over the past decade. As a bank expands throughout its state and across state lines, employees need continued training to develop the skills necessary to adapt to the changing geographical diversification of the institution.

Job Satisfaction. Effective management of human resources is also needed to satisfy the pursuits of individuals in the organization. The bank can contribute to the attainment of employees' personal satisfaction through job enrichment programs and training, for example. On a more basic level, compensation for work that is well done is necessary to maintain motivation. Wages and salaries should be sufficient to attract and retain quality personnel. Furthermore, salary structures should be flexible enough to recognize different levels of merit due to outstanding work, as well as the acquisition of new skills. The fringe benefits program should also reflect differences among individuals. In summary, appropriate nonmonetary and monetary compensation for employees is consistent with maximizing job performance.

From a management standpoint, the success of personnel development programs should be assessed periodically. This requires that some degree of employee program monitoring be conducted over time. Changes should be implemented, if it is believed that they would improve bank performance.

External Performance

External performance is reflected in the ability of the bank to cope successfully with competitors, regulators, and the public. This section briefly overviews each of these market participants.

Market Share

Market share is the proportion of assets, deposits, and loans held by a bank in its business region relative to other banks. Failure to meet market demands normally will result in a decline in market share.

Earnings. Market share can affect the earnings of the bank. For example, given that the bank's rate of return on assets did not change, if its asset size declined, then earnings per share would decline. This is because the number of shares does not change while the total earnings of the bank are falling in line with the erosion of the asset base. Conversely, growing too fast can also lower equity returns, because assets are expanded but not profitably. For example, if the bank's assets grew by 20 percent but the net income after taxes decreased by 10 percent (because higher deposit rates had to be offered to the public to attract sufficient funds to finance the relatively rapid rate of asset expansion), the earnings per share of the bank would decline. Furthermore, growth may not only affect profitability but it may change the perceived riskiness of the bank by the financial market (perhaps because of increased credit risk), which would also result in a loss of share value. Thus, growth for the sake of growth alone is not a suitable goal. Bank managers should set market share goals with the internal performance of the bank in mind.

Technology. A well-worn phrase in modern business organizations is that "technology is the future." By implementing new technologies, banks promote the perception that they are up-to-date and progressive. Hence, technology is a marketing tool that can attract customers. Another reason to offer the latest technology to the public is to improve the competitiveness of the bank. Technology enables the bank to reach out to customers beyond the traditional market boundaries. It also serves to enhance the convenience of using the bank's financial services; that is, an implicit service return is paid to customers, which increases the attractiveness of the bank. The best examples of this type of technology are credit cards, debit cards, and automated teller machines (ATMs). These products give the bank a presence in a wide geographic region (e.g., throughout a number of states) and allow customers more flexibility in their transactions activities. Another example is the growing use of communications technology to provide telephone bill-paying services, point-of-sale (POS) payment services, and other remote payment services. These automated devices are more generally known as electronic funds transfer systems (EFTS).

   As already mentioned, automation can reduce the fixed costs of plant and equipment (or "brick-and-mortar"). It is possible, however, that operating costs are increased by EFTS. In this case the added operating costs must be weighed against the potential benefits in terms of improved competitiveness.

Regulatory Compliance

Another dimension of external performance is regulatory compliance. All banks must heed the laws and regulations of the relevant federal and regulatory authorities. Failure to comply will prompt some form of supervisory action. Such action could take the form of a simple letter explaining a problem with compliance that can be easily rectified by the bank, or it could take the form of a full-blown audit of the bank in an attempt to determine the extent of a major problem. Requests for a plan of action by the bank to overcome the problem(s) could be made and then monitored over time to assess the progress of the bank. Of course, as regulatory interference increases, the costs of compliance increase for the bank.

Public Confidence

Public confidence relates to the market's *perception* of a bank's safety and soundness. No matter how well capitalized a bank is, a loss of public confidence can cause a run on deposits and subsequent closure by regulatory authorities. A case in point is the failure of Hartford Federal, a thrift institution in Hartford, Connecticut, in the early 1980s. By coincidence, news that the Federal Savings and Loan Association (FSLIC) had placed Hartford Federal on its watch list appeared in the local paper on the same day that the movie "The Night the Money Stopped" aired on a national TV network. The timing of these two events touched off a run that lasted for a week and ended in the closure and sale of the thrift by the FSLIC. Clearly, public confidence is necessary to maintain bank solvency.

ANALYZING BANK PERFORMANCE WITH FINANCIAL RATIOS

Financial ratios are constructed by forming ratios of accounting data contained in the bank's Reports of Income (i.e., profit and loss) and Condition (i.e., balance sheet). This is done by adjusting absolute dollar amounts for various accounts by dividing by a number that allows comparisons over time and between banks. A wide variety of financial ratios can be calculated to assess different characteristics of financial performance. To evaluate a particular financial ratio for a bank, comparisons with peer group banks are recommended. Also, it is beneficial to track the ratio over time relative to other banks. Even without comparison with other banks, ratio trends over time may provide valuable information about the bank's performance. A potential shortfall of financial ratio analysis is that other factors are held constant. To overcome this problem a number of financial ratios should be calculated that provide a broader understanding of the bank's financial condition. The remainder of this chapter discusses key ratios commonly used by bank analysts to evaluate different dimensions of financial performance, including profitability, capitalization, asset quality, operating efficiency, liquidity, and interest sensitivity. The Report of Income and Report of Condition data shown in Tables 3.1 and 3.2, respectively, are used to demonstrate the calculation of financial ratios for a hypothetical institution named US Bank.

Profit Ratios

ROE

The rate of return on equity (ROE) is a good starting point in the analysis of a bank's financial condition for the following reasons: (1) if the ROE is relatively low compared with other banks, it will tend to decrease the bank's access to new capital that may be necessary to expand and maintain a competitive position in the market; (2) a low ROE may limit a bank's growth because regulations require that assets be (at a maximum) a certain number of times equity capital; and, (3) ROE can be broken down into component parts that help to identify trends in the bank's performance. ROE indicates the rate of return on

TABLE 3.1
REPORT OF CONDITION: US BANK

Report of Condition Items	Year End (in millions of dollars)	
	1986	1987
Cash and due from depository institutions	280	295
U.S. Treasury securities	53	56
Obligations of other U.S. government agencies	25	24
Obligations of state and political subdivisions	80	80
All other securities	21	25
Federal funds sold and securities purchased	40	44
Total cash and securities	502	524
Loans	718	759
Lease financing receivables	13	15
Bank premises, furniture, and fixtures	16	18
All other assets	75	78
Total assets	1,324	1,394
Demand deposits	229	230
Time and savings deposits	369	390
Deposits in foreign offices	110	115
Deposits of U.S. government	2	2
Deposits of state and political government	51	53
All other deposits	245	265
Total deposits	1,006	1,055
Federal funds purchased and securities sold	121	141
Interest-bearing demand notes and other borrowings	39	45
Mortgage indebtedness	2	2
All other liabilities	75	80
Total liabilities	1,243	1,323
Subordinated notes and debentures	5	5
Preferred stock—par value	1	1
Common stock—par value	30	17
Surplus	20	20
Undivided profits and capital reserves	25	28
Total equity capital	81	71

equity capital. Because the ultimate objective of bank management should be to maximize shareholder wealth, this ratio is particularly important.

Defining equity capital as the sum of common and preferred stock, paid-in surplus (above the book value at the time of issuance), undivided profits (or retained earnings), and reserves for future contingencies, the ROE for US Bank

TABLE 3.2
REPORT OF INCOME: US BANK

Report of Income Items	Year End (in millions of dollars)	
	1986	1987
Interest and fees on loans	100	101
Interest on balances with depository institutions	17	18
Income on federal funds sold and securities purchased	6	6
Interest on U.S. Treasury and other agencies' securities	8	8
Interest on obligations of state and political subdivisions	6	6
Interest on other securities	1	1
Income from direct lease financing	1	1
Income from fiduciary activities	2	2
Service charges on deposit accounts	2	2
Other service charges	5	5
Other operating income	4	4
Total operating income	152	154
Salaries and employee benefits	16	17
Interest on CD's of $100,000 or more	19	20
Interest on deposits in foreign offices	35	36
Interest on other deposits	18	18
Interest on federal funds purchased and securities sold	16	17
Interest on demand notes and other borrowings	4	4
Interest on subordinated notes and debentures	1	1
Occupancy, furniture, and fixed expenses	5	5
Provision for possible loan losses	3	3
Other operating expenses	9	9
Total operating expenses	126	130
Income before taxes and securities transactions	26	24
Applicable income taxes	13	12
Income before securities gains or losses	13	12
Securities gains, net of taxes	−1	−1
Net income	12	11
Cash dividend	8	8
Undivided profits	4	3
Recoveries credited to provision for possible loan losses	2	0
Losses charged to provision for possible loan losses	−4	−3

using the data in Tables 3.1 and 3.2 is calculated as follows (numbers are in millions of dollars):

$$\text{Rate of return on equity } (\%) = \frac{\text{Net income}}{\text{Total equity capital}} \times 100 \qquad (3.1)$$

	1986	**1987**
US Bank	$12/76 \times 100 = 15.8\%$	$11/66 \times 100 = 16.7\%$
Peer Group	15.0%	15.0%

US Bank's equity earnings rate increased from 15.8 percent in 1986 to 16.7 percent in 1987. Assuming that banks of similar size in its market had average ROEs of 15.0 percent in both 1986 and 1987, on the surface at least, it appears that the bank has above average profitability and has recently improved its profitability. As we will see, this interpretation of the bank's performance is premature. Further analyses are necessary before any conclusions can be reached.

ROA

The rate of return on assets (ROA) measures the ability of management to utilize the real and financial resources of the bank to generate returns. ROA is commonly used to evaluate bank management. For US Bank, ROA can be calculated as follows:

$$\text{Rate of return on assets } (\%) = \frac{\text{Net income}}{\text{Total assets}} \times 100 \qquad (3.2)$$

	1986	**1987**
US Bank	$12/1{,}324 \times 100 = 0.9\%$	$11/1{,}394 \times 100 = 0.8\%$
Peer Group	1.0%	1.0%

As can be seen, the rate of return on assets actually declined from 0.9 percent to 0.8 percent. Since the average bank in the US peer group had an ROA of 1.0 percent in both 1986 and 1987, it is obvious that the profitability of the bank was slightly below average. Also, profitability declined recently, whereas other similar banks did not experience a similar loss of earning power. These results suggest that there are problems with profitability that should be examined more fully through further ratio analyses.

Unraveling Profit Ratios

In the preceding ratio analyses we found that US Bank had relatively low ROAs compared with its peer group, but that its ROEs were relatively high. This difference can be shown to be attributable to the low percentage of equity used by US to finance its assets. To see this, consider the following formula:

$$\text{ROE} = \text{ROA} \times \text{Equity multiplier}$$

$$\frac{\text{Net income}}{\text{Total equity}} = \frac{\text{Net income}}{\text{Total assets}} \times \frac{\text{Total assets}}{\text{Total equity}} \qquad (3.3)$$

This formula shows the return on equity ratio as the product of ROA and a ratio indicating the extent to which the bank is using financial leverage, known as the equity multiplier. In the present example the ROE of US Bank can be broken down as follows (where some degree of rounding error is allowed):

	1986	**1987**
US Bank	15.8% ($\approx$ .9 $\times$ 17.4)	16.7% ($\approx$ .8 $\times$ 21.1)
Peer Group	15.0% ($\approx$ 1.0 $\times$ 15.0)	15.0% ($\approx$ 1.0 $\times$ 15.0)

It is clear that the equity multiplier for US Bank increased from 1986 to 1987 and was responsible for the increase in ROE (since ROA declined during this 2-year period). Moreover, US Bank was more highly leveraged than other banks in its peer group, which increases its riskiness.

Another useful formula for unraveling profits is as follows:

$$\text{ROE} = \text{Profit margin} \times \text{Asset utilization} \times \text{Equity multiplier}$$

$$\frac{\text{Net income}}{\text{Total equity}} = \frac{\text{Net income}}{\text{Operating income}} \times \frac{\text{Operating income}}{\text{Total assets}} \times \frac{\text{Total assets}}{\text{Total equity}} \quad (3.4)$$

Notice that this formula breaks down ROA into the product of profit margin and asset utilization. The profit margin ratio provides information about the ability of management to control expenses, including taxes, given a particular level of operating income. The asset utilization ratio represents the ability of management to employ assets effectively to generate revenues. Together, these two ratios enable the bank analyst to gain insight into the derivation of ROA.

For US Bank, equation (3.4) can be used as follows:

	1986	**1987**
US Bank	15.8% ($\approx$ .079 $\times$ .115 $\times$ 17.4 $\times$ 100)	16.7% ($\approx$ .071 $\times$ .110 $\times$ 21.1 $\times$ 100)
Peer Group	15.0% ($\approx$ .083 $\times$ .120 $\times$ 15.0 $\times$ 100)	15.0% ($\approx$ .085 $\times$ .118 $\times$ 15.0 $\times$ 100)

These figures show that both the profit margin and the asset utilization of US Bank have declined and jointly contributed to its decline in ROA. Although peer group banks experienced a decline in asset utilization, an increase in profit margins because of improved expense control offset this decline. Thus, the increase in ROE for US Bank was caused by greater use of financial leverage, as opposed to better expense control or asset utilization by bank management.

Other Profit Measures

A number of other profit measures are commonly used in banking, which provide further insight into a bank's financial performance. One of these is the net operating margin (NOM):

$$\text{Net operating margin } (\%) = \frac{\genfrac{}{}{0pt}{}{\text{Total operating}}{\text{income}} - \genfrac{}{}{0pt}{}{\text{Total operating}}{\text{expense}}}{\text{Total assets}} \times 100 \quad (3.5)$$

where total operating income is total interest and noninterest income, and total operating expense is total interest and noninterest expenses plus the provision for possible loan losses. For US Bank we have:

	1986	**1987**
US Bank	$[(152 - 126)/1{,}324] \times 100 \simeq 2.0\%$	$[(154 - 130)/1{,}394] \times 100 \simeq 1.7\%$
Peer Group	2.2%	2.2%

Because NOM excludes taxes and securities gains (losses), it is normally considered to be an indicator of bank operating earnings. As the preceding calculations suggest, US Bank's operating earnings declined between 1986 and 1987 and were below the level of peer group banks.

Another profit measure is the net interest margin (NIM), which is defined as follows:

$$\text{Net interest margin } (\%) = \frac{\genfrac{}{}{0pt}{}{\text{Total interest}}{\text{income}} - \genfrac{}{}{0pt}{}{\text{Total interest}}{\text{expense}}}{\text{Total assets}} \times 100 \quad (3.6)$$

where total interest income is on a *pretax* basis (i.e., municipal bond interest income must be "grossed up" by dividing by 1 minus the marginal tax rate of the bank to convert it to a pretax equivalent amount). Given the pretax equivalent interest earned for US Bank was $6/(.5) = $12 in both 1986 and 1987, the NIM is:

	1986	**1987**
US Bank	$[(144 - 93)/1{,}324] \times 100 = 3.9\%$	$[(146 - 96)/1{,}394] \times 100 = 3.6\%$
Peer Group	4.2%	4.2%

Because interest income and expenses make up the lion's share of total operating income and expenses, respectively, NIM is well worth calculating. As indicated earlier, much of the decline in profitability at US Bank was due to the decrease in the net-interest margin.

A profit measure that is closely related to NIM is the yield spread, defined as

$$\text{Yield spread } (\%) = \genfrac{}{}{0pt}{}{\text{Average rate}}{\text{earned on assets}} - \genfrac{}{}{0pt}{}{\text{Average rate paid on}}{\text{interest-bearing liabilities}} \quad (3.7)$$

Once again, the earnings rate on municipal securities needs to be grossed up by the tax factor as a preliminary step. The average yield for each type of asset (liability) is multiplied by its respective proportion of total assets to obtain a weighted average rate of interest on assets (liabilities). The difference in rates earned and paid, or yield spread, represents the bank's role as financial intermediary in the financial marketplace. If the yield spread is high compared with peer group banks, strong interest rate management is indicated. The only potential drawback of earning relatively high yield spreads is that other financial institutions may be induced to enter the bank's market. Conversely, a relatively low yield spread would tend to lower share values, inhibit the growth of the bank, and possibly slow down economic growth in the community. In general, the appropriate level of the yield spread is determined by many factors, including competition, market demand, and bank management.

Risk Ratios

Capitalization

As shown in equation (3.3), capitalization directly influences the rate of return on equity. The leverage ratio can affect the growth rate of the bank also. For example, if the policy of the bank was to keep the equity multiplier equal to 10, then each dollar of retained earnings could be used to support $10 of assets, because $9 could be borrowed by the bank to maintain the same equity multiplier. It should be obvious that a high equity multiplier can increase both ROE and the growth rate of the bank as long as ROA is positive.

On the downside, if ROA were negative, ROEs would be magnified in a negative direction. Also, in the preceding example bank asset size would need to decline tenfold for every dollar lost to keep the equity multiplier constant. In the extreme, if losses exceeded bank capital, the bank would be insolvent and subject to closure by the chartering agency.

Asset Quality

Asset quality can only be assessed indirectly using financial ratios. On-site inspection of the bank's outstanding individual loans is certainly the best way to evaluate asset quality. In the absence of this opportunity, some financial ratios can provide at least an historical account of the credit worthiness of a particular bank's loan portfolio.

Loss Rate. The loss rate gives the actual losses on loans net of recoveries as a proportion of loans. It is calculated as follows:

$$\text{Loss rate (\%)} = \frac{\begin{matrix}\text{Gross loan losses} \\ \text{charged to PLL}\end{matrix} - \begin{matrix}\text{Gross recoveries on} \\ \text{loans charged to PLL}\end{matrix}}{\text{Total loans}} \times 100 \quad (3.8)$$

where PLL denotes the provision for possible loan losses. For US Bank the loss rate was as follows:

	1986	1987
US Bank	$[(4 - 2)/718] \times 100 \simeq .3\%$	$[(3 - 0)/759] \times 100 \simeq .4\%$
Peer Group	.2%	.3%

This ratio suggests that US Bank has experienced greater net losses on loans than similar banks. The ratio of gross loan losses to total loans may also be calculated, which in the present example would show that US Bank's increasing loss rate was caused by rising credit risks rather than recovery problems. Furthermore, the ratio of net loan losses to PLL plus equity capital may be useful for evaluating the overall ability of the bank to absorb losses. Because US Bank's equity capital declined from $81 million in 1986 to $71 million in 1987, its ability to use equity to absorb loan losses has declined.

Loan Risk. The loan ratio indicates the extent to which assets are devoted to loans as opposed to other assets, including cash, securities, and plant and equipment. The ratio and results for US Bank are as follows:

$$\text{Loan ratio } (\%) = \frac{\text{Total loans}}{\text{Total assets}} \times 100 \qquad (3.9)$$

	1986	1987
US Bank	$(718/1,324) \times 100 = 54.2\%$	$(759/1,394) \times 100 = 54.5\%$
Peer Group	48.0%	48.0%

These data suggest that the higher loss rate of US Bank compared to its peer group was likely associated with its relatively greater exposure to loan (or credit) risk.

Operating Efficiency

A key management area that many studies have found to be the primary factor distinguishing high and low profit banks is operating efficiency. Operating efficiency deals with the production of outputs, such as deposit and loan accounts and securities services, at minimum cost per dollar (or account).

A number of ratios can be calculated to provide information on cost control by simply dividing various expense accounts by total operating expenses. The following figures are percentages of total operating expenses for different expense categories:

Expense Ratio	1986		1987	
	US Bank	Peer Group	US Bank	Peer Group
Interest expenses	73.8%	73.1%	76.8%	73.1%
Noninterest expenses				
Wages and salaries	12.7	14.0	13.1	14.0
Occupancy	4.0	3.5	3.8	3.5
PLL	2.4	2.4	2.3	2.4
Other	7.1	7.0	6.9	7.0
Total	100.0	100.0	100.0	100.0

Interest expenses as a percentage of total operating expenses increased between 1986 and 1987 for US Bank and exceeded peer group expenditures, which were stable over this period of time. Thus, higher interest expenses as compared with similar banks were at least partially responsible for US Bank's relatively low net interest margin (NIM). It is also likely that paying relatively higher interest rates on deposit and nondeposit funds has contributed to the increase in US Bank's asset size. This example demonstrates the earlier caution that growth should not be undertaken for the sake of growth alone. Unprofitable growth tends to lower bank capital and impair future growth prospects.

Wages and salaries (and related fringe benefits) are normally the largest noninterest expense item. US Bank is below its peer group in this regard; however, this is not necessarily a good way to control operating costs. Underpaid personnel or understaffed departments could eventually cause losses in profitability and market share. Assuming that this is not the case, US Bank is controlling this category of expenses. With reference to the level or changes in wages and salaries, it may be desirable to calculate ratios using the level or change in revenues in the denominator in order to assess labor productivity.

The occupancy expense ratio indicates the level of fixed expenses that the bank is carrying. Relatively high fixed expenses are not always an indicator of poor expense control. In the 1960s and 1970s, for example, banks operated branch offices in part as a means of providing greater convenience to customers (assuming state laws permitted branching). Because Regulation Q prevented banks from paying market rates of interest on deposit accounts at times, branch offices represented an added (implicit) service return to customers. However, the phase-out of Regulation Q in the 1980s has caused many banks to trim their branch office facilities to reduce expenses (as interest expenses began to rise dramatically). New electronic technology is also causing many banks to reshuffle the structure of their expenses. More funds are being allocated to ATMs and other means of delivering services, causing wage expenses to fall (as capital is substituted for labor) as well as on-premise occupancy expenses for buildings and furniture. Assuming no significant differences in automated and branch office services, US Bank's occupancy ratio is slightly higher than its peer group.

The provision for loan losses to total operating expenses ratio is also subject to some degree of interpretation. On the one hand, if this ratio is relatively high, both profitability and capital growth (i.e., retained earnings) would be lowered. At the same time, however, a strong provision for loan loss ratio provides good coverage of loan losses and tends to lower taxes because PLL is expensed from taxable income. The opposite relationships hold in the event this ratio were relatively low. One way to evaluate this ratio is with respect to the bank's particular financial condition. If a bank's profitability and capital growth are relatively lower than its peer group, then a higher provision for possible loan loss ratio would probably be needed to ensure that the bank can safely absorb loan losses. Also, the PLL expense should be compared with the actual amount of charge-offs that the bank (and its peer group) has experienced. In regard to these considerations, US Bank's PLL as a percentage of total operating income is comparable with its peer group, but its profitability and capital are below average, and its net charge-offs on loans (as discussed earlier) are higher than its peer group. Thus, US Bank would appear to have lower PLL expenses than its peer group after taking into consideration other aspects of its financial condition.

Liquidity

Liquidity can be defined as the extent to which the bank has funds available to meet cash demands for loans and deposit withdrawals. Banks require different amounts of liquidity depending on their growth rate and variability in lending and deposit activities.

One problem in measuring liquidity is that liability management has been gradually replacing asset management as the way to fund liquidity needs. That is, over the last 20 years banks have been decreasing the quantity of liquid assets they hold for the purpose of meeting loan demands and deposit withdrawals (i.e., asset management) and increasing their usage of deposit and nondeposit sources of funds paying market rates of interest (i.e., liability management). These trends have tended to affect banks in the following ways:

- Gross rates of return on assets have increased because longer-term assets normally have higher rates of return than short-term assets (due to upward sloping yield curves).
- U.S. Treasury security holdings have declined.
- Credit risk has increased in many banks as liquid assets have been replaced by loans.

The shift away from money market assets and toward more lending was motivated in large part by the rising costs of funds in the latter 1970s and early 1980s as Regulation Q ceilings on deposits were phased out and competition for deposit funds intensified. These asset and liability changes have dramatically altered the management of bank liquidity in the last decade.

Even though liability management is becoming more prevalent as an approach to meeting liquidity needs, it is still meaningful to calculate financial ratios that focus on the asset liquidity of the bank. If a bank suffered financial distress for any reason, it is likely that other banks and the market in general would reduce their lending to the institution. In this situation the bank would need to rely on its asset liquidity to a greater extent. Thus, asset liquidity is a reserve that the bank can draw upon in the event its access to purchased funds is reduced. Another reason for banks to hold liquid assets is to fund loans when interest rates are relatively high. Assuming loan demand was fairly strong, short-term assets bearing little price risk may be a less expensive source of funds than relatively high interest rate deposits. In essence, liquid assets are an alternative source of funds that at times may be cheaper than using liability management methods to raise funds.

Cash on Hand. The simplest liquidity ratio is the cash to total assets ratio, which is calculated as follows:

$$\text{Cash ratio } (\%) = \frac{\text{Cash and balances due from depository institutions}}{\text{Total assets}} \times 100 \qquad (3.10)$$

where cash is currency and coin plus balances due from depository institutions, including both interest- and noninterest-bearing balances. A drawback of using cash to measure liquidity is that it includes cash items in the process of collection, which represents checks presented to the bank for payment that are written on other institutions but not yet credited as such. These cash balances are available to the bank only until the checks clear.

For US Bank the data in Table 3.1 yield the following:

	1986	**1987**
US Bank	$(280/1{,}324) \times 100 = 21.1\%$	$(295/1{,}394) \times 100 = 21.1\%$
Peer Group	15.0%	15.0%

The relatively higher cash ratio for US Bank compared with its peer group suggests either that its cash needs are exceptional or that cash is not being managed effectively. Because the opportunity cost of idle funds equals the rate of return on loans and securities, a high cash ratio can lower bank revenues and, in turn, reduce profit rates. This may not be the case, however, if in fact cash balances held at other depository institutions are interest bearing or correspondent services are received as payments in kind.

Cash and Securities. Marketable securities are the major source of asset liquidity in banking. The most comprehensive measure of asset liquidity, therefore, is the cash plus securities to total assets ratio, which can be calculated as follows:

$$\text{Cash and securities ratio} = \frac{\text{Cash plus securities held}}{\text{Total assets}} \times 100 \quad (3.11)$$

where securities held include U.S. Treasury securities, other U.S. government securities, state and local government (or municipal) securities, other securities, federal funds sold, and securities purchased under agreement to resell (or repurchase agreements). For US Bank we have:

	1986	**1987**
US Bank	$(502/1{,}324) \times 100 = 37.9\%$	$(524/1{,}394) \times 100 = 37.6\%$
Peer Group	38.0%	38.0%

Notice that US Bank's cash and securities ratio did not change much between 1986 and 1987. Because the asset size of the bank increased during the period, we can infer that the bank expanded its asset liquidity in proportion to the increase in its asset base. Given the fact that peer group banks had similar ratios, this evidence suggests that the bank's asset liquidity is being managed appropriately.

It should be noted that a ratio including only money market instruments maturing in less than 1 year may also be calculated. This is because investment securities with maturities longer than 1 year are purchased more for their income than for liquidity purposes. Furthermore, investment securities have more price risk, defined as the change in price associated with a change in interest rates, which causes their market values to vary from book values more than in the case of money market securities. To the extent that interest rates have changed from the time securities are purchased, the cash and securities ratio will be in error, such that appropriate adjustments for price risk are recommended when data permit.

Other Financial Ratios

Many more financial ratios than those discussed previously are conceivable. The analyst may construct other financial ratios, if it is believed that they will help to reveal the strengths and weaknesses of the bank under study. For example, two areas that may be useful to explore are the ability of the bank to minimize taxes and the interest sensitivity of its mix of sources and uses of funds.

Taxes. The tax exposure of the bank can be assessed by using the following ratio:

$$\text{Tax rate } (\%) \; = \; \frac{\text{Total taxes paid}}{\text{Net income before taxes}} \times 100 \qquad (3.12)$$

where total taxes paid includes the tax consequences of security gains and losses. The tax rate for US Bank was as follows:

	1986	1987
US Bank	$(13/26) \times 100 = 50.0\%$	$(12/24) \times 100 = 50.0\%$
Peer Group	50.0	50.0

In general, the marginal tax rate (i.e., the tax rate applicable to the last dollar of income earned) for most banks is the maximum statutory rate.

One way that banks traditionally lowered their tax burden was to purchase municipal bonds, which are exempt from federal income tax. Under the Tax Reform Act of 1986, this tax reduction technique is substantially lessened because interest expenses incurred on deposits subsequently invested in tax-exempt obligations can no longer be deducted from income for tax purposes. An exception to this new law is the purchase of tax-exempt securities (excluding private activity bonds, such as industrial development bonds) issued by municipalities offering $10 million or less of government obligations.

Another means of lowering taxes in the past was to deduct larger provisions for loan losses from income than anticipated charge-offs would suggest. According to the new tax law, however, deductions are allowed only as loans are actually charged off.

Effective July 1, 1987, the following three-bracket tax structure was applicable to income earned by banks (and corporations in general):

Taxable Income	Rate (in percent)
Less than $50,000	15
$50,000–$75,000	25
More than $75,000	34

Income between $100,000 and $335,000 is exposed to a 39 percent tax rate, and beyond $335,000 a flat tax rate of 34 percent applies to all income.

Interest Sensitivity. Interest sensitivity is the responsiveness of liability costs and asset returns to changes in interest rates. The difference between the quantities of interest-sensitive assets and liabilities is known as the dollar gap. To compare the interest sensitivity of different banks, the following dollar gap ratio can be calculated:

$$\text{Dollar gap ratio } (\%) = \frac{\substack{\text{Interest rate-} \\ \text{sensitive assets}} - \substack{\text{Interest rate-} \\ \text{sensitive liabilities}}}{\text{Total assets}} \times 100 \quad (3.13)$$

where rate sensitive is roughly defined as short-term assets and liabilities with maturities of less than 1 year. To obtain a more complete picture of interest sensitivity, it is normally recommended to calculate gap ratios for assets and liabilities of different maturity ranges (e.g., 0–90 days, 90–120 days, and 120 days–1 year). By structuring assets and liabilities in terms of maturity ranges, or "buckets," the analyst can determine the extent to which a change in interest rates would affect bank profitability. If interest rates increased (decreased) in the future, positive gap ratios would cause the bank's profitability to increase (decrease). The opposite effects would correspond to negative gap ratios. Chapter 14 discusses interest rate sensitivity and gap management in more detail.

In the case of US Bank, assuming that all securities, one-half of loans and lease financing receivables, and all deposits have maturities of less than 1 year, and excluding cash and due from the calculations, the gap ratio is as follows:

	1986	**1987**
US Bank	$[(587.5 - 1{,}127)/1{,}324]$ $\times 100 = -40.7\%$	$[(616 - 1{,}196)/1{,}394]$ $\times 100 = -41.6\%$
Peer Group	-5.0%	-6.0%

The large negative gap ratio for US Bank relative to its peer group suggests that its profitability will be affected much more than its peers by a change in interest rates within the next year. If interest rates increase (decrease) in the near future, US Bank's profitability will decrease (increase) dramatically because of the negative gap ratio. It is true that some amount of interest sensitivity may be desirable to take advantage of anticipated movements in interest rates, but excessive sensitivity, as in the present instance, may well be considered "betting the bank" and, therefore, is not prudent management.

With reference to the mix of assets and liabilities, it is also informative to look more closely at the changing composition of the balance sheet. If the bank is shifting from consumer and real estate loans to commercial loans, for example, there will likely be an increase in credit risk. At the same time, however, the liquidity of the loan portfolio might increase, as commercial loans may be sold more readily to other banks than retail types of loans. On the liability side of the balance sheet, if the bank is decreasing its use of demand deposits and increasing its use of interest-bearing deposits, it may expect to have higher interest expenses but an increased ability to meet liquidity needs through liability management. Moreover, the interrelationships between assets and liabilities have important implications to successful bank performance (See Box 3.1 for a discussion of how some banks achieve top financial performance.)

TRENDS IN BANK PERFORMANCE

Table 3.3 shows the return on equity (ROE) for all insured U.S. commercial banks, broken down by asset size and by year for the period 1980 through 1986.

BOX 3.1

COMMERCIAL BANKS WITH TOP FINANCIAL PERFORMANCE

A study by Robert Clair at the Federal Reserve Bank of Dallas was conducted to identify financial strategies of banks in the Eleventh Federal Reserve District, which tended to be associated with top performance. Because strategies under the control of bank management were of primary interest, the study focused on asset and liability structure, especially reserve management, capitalization, growth, and off-balance sheet activities. Some variables that are, to a more limited extent, within the control of management were also considered, including loan losses and expense control.

The performance criterion chosen was the average annual return on assets (ROA) over the period 1981–1985, where net income excluded extraordinary income. Banks were classified into three groups: (1) small banks, with between $25 million and $100 million of assets, (2) mid-sized banks, with between $100 million and $250 million of assets, and (3) large banks, with more than $250 million of assets. Banks with ROAs in the top 10 percent of institutions in their asset group were defined as top performers. Banks with ROAs below the median level were defined as low performers.

Four types of strategies in particular were examined by the study. The proxies used to measure each strategy were as follows:

1. *Investment strategy:* percentage of total assets allocated to eight categories of loans and two categories of assets. The related ratios of loan interest income to total income were calculated also.

2. *Funding strategy:* percentage of total assets funded by transactions deposits, savings and small time deposits, large time deposits, foreign deposits, and borrowed funds.

3. *Growth strategy:* overall growth of total assets.

4. *Off-balance sheet strategy:* percentage of total assets allocated to loan and lease commitments and letters of credit and to commitments on forward, future, and option contracts. These measures were intended to capture management's usage of noninterest, service income, which was also directly measured as the ratio of noninterest income to total income.

The following results of comparisons between top and low performing banks were obtained:

- Two successful financial strategies were the commercial real estate strategy and the conservative strategy. The former involved rela-

BOX 3.1 (*Continued*)

tively higher lending in commercial real estate, lower lending in commercial and industrial loans, and higher lending to consumers. The conservative strategy was associated with low credit risks and strong asset liquidity.

- A third group of top performers did not use any distinct financial strategy but did tend to control their expenses better than other banks.
- Regardless of financial strategy, top performers had lower loan losses than low performers.
- Among small banks, top performers acquired larger (smaller) proportions of funds from transactions accounts (small savings and time deposit accounts) than low performers.
- Among large banks, top performers tended to use a lower proportion of borrowed funds than low performers.
- Financial strategies are affected by cyclical changes in business conditions (e.g., the success of the commercial real estate strategy is related to the growth of the commercial construction business). As such, banks should adapt their strategies based on economic forecasts of the future.

Source: Robert T. Clair. "Financial Strategies of Top-Performance Banks in the Eleventh District," *Economic Review*, Federal Reserve Bank of Dallas (January 1987), pp. 1–13.

During this period, Regulation Q interest rate ceilings on small deposit accounts were phased out among depository institutions. As shown in section B of Table 3.3, the return on assets for banks under $1 billion in asset size declined throughout the 1980–1986 period, whereas billion-dollar banks experienced a decline in asset earning rates between 1982 and 1984 (caused by losses on international loans) and then rebounded to previous earnings' levels by 1985 at the latest. Part of this difference in earnings performance can be attributed to the fact that interest rate deregulation did not affect billion-dollar banks as much as smaller institutions, because the former's deposit base is composed of large wholesale deposits, most of which have been unaffected by retail-level regulatory changes. Another reason for the difference in earnings is that the agricultural sector suffered severe losses throughout the first half of the 1980s. Because billion-dollar banks had a much smaller proportion of their assets devoted to farm loans than smaller banks, they were less affected by the credit risk problems in agriculture. Billion-dollar banks, however, have been seriously affected by LDC (less-developed countries) debt. In the second half of 1987, most large banks with sizable LDC debt holdings dealt with this growing

TABLE 3.3

RETURN ON EQUITY AND ITS COMPONENTS FOR ALL INSURED U.S. COMMERCIAL BANKS BY ASSET SIZE: 1980–1986

	A. Return on Equity (ROE)[a]						
Asset Size	1980	1981	1982	1983	1984	1985	1986
Under $25 million	13.2%	12.9%	10.1%	7.9%	5.0%	3.1%	0.9%
$25–100 million	14.7	14.1	13.1	11.7	10.3	9.0	7.5
$100–300 million	14.1	13.4	12.3	12.2	12.4	11.9	10.4
$300 mil–$1 billion	13.9	13.3	11.9	11.9	13.1	11.4	9.9
$1–5 billion	13.5	13.5	7.4	11.9	13.3	14.5	13.4
Over $5 billion	14.5	14.2	12.0	10.1	9.0	11.8	13.4
All banks	14.0%	13.8%	12.1%	11.2%	10.6%	11.5%	10.5%

	B. Return on Assets (ROA)[a]						
Asset Size	1980	1981	1982	1983	1984	1985	1986
Under $25 million	1.24%	1.24%	0.98%	0.78%	0.50%	0.31%	0.09%
$25–100 million	1.20	1.18	1.08	0.96	0.84	0.74	0.61
$100–300 million	1.04	1.01	0.90	0.89	0.91	0.87	0.76
$300 mil–$1 billion	0.95	0.92	0.80	0.80	0.89	0.81	0.67
$1–5 billion	0.79	0.79	0.42	0.69	0.79	0.88	0.84
Over $5 billion	0.60	0.59	0.52	0.47	0.45	0.60	0.59
All banks	0.82%	0.81%	0.71%	0.67%	0.65%	0.71%	0.65%

	C. Equity Capital as a Percentage of Total Assets[a]						
Asset Size	1980	1981	1982	1983	1984	1985	1986
Under $25 million	9.38%	9.64%	9.75%	9.88%	9.95%	9.88%	9.60%
$25–100 million	8.16	8.34	8.26	8.18	8.18	8.25	8.16
$100–300 million	7.38	7.52	7.34	7.30	7.31	7.32	7.28
$300 mil–$1 billion	6.83	6.91	6.75	6.70	6.79	7.08	6.75
$1–5 billion	5.84	5.85	5.71	5.78	5.92	6.05	6.29
Over $5 billion	4.13	4.16	4.32	4.65	4.98	5.08	5.21
All banks	5.84%	5.86%	5.87%	6.00%	6.14%	6.20%	6.21%

Sources. Adapted from Ross Waldrop, "Commercial Bank Performance in 1985," *Banking and Economic Review,* Federal Deposit Insurance Corporation (April 1986); and Ross Waldrop, "Commercial Bank Performance in 1986," *Banking and Economic Review,* Federal Deposit Insurance Corporation (March/April 1987).

[a] Total equity and total assets figures based on the average for the year.

problem by significantly increasing their previous provisions for loan losses. Subsequently, many large banks issued new capital stock to cover the losses on writing off LDC debt.

Despite declining asset profitability among banks with assets less than $1 billion, section C of Table 3.3 indicates that capital as a percentage of assets did not change. Thus, these banks either reduced dividends to shareholders or asset size, or both, in order to comply with regulatory capital adequacy requirements. Billion-dollar banks' equity capital ratios on average increased between 1983 and 1986, in all likelihood due to higher capital requirements imposed by regulators (to be discussed in more detail in Chapter 12).

In general, return on equity (ROE) figures in section A of Table 3.3 mimic the time pattern of return on asset (ROA) figures in section B. Notice that for banks with over $100 million assets, even though ROA's tended to decline as asset size increased, ROE's were about the same as asset size increased. Of course, the reason for this is that equity capital as a proportion of total assets decreased as asset size increased.

According to financial theory, the expected return per unit risk should be the same for all financial assets. Because the ROE's of banks with assets in excess of $100 million are fairly comparable with one another, one would expect that the risk of these different-sized banks would also be similar. Although many types of risk can affect bank performance, asset quality is a basic dimension of balance-sheet risk that can be readily measured. In this regard, average loss rates (i.e., net charge-offs to loans and leases) shown in section A of Table 3.4

TABLE 3.4

ASSET QUALITY AND EARNINGS LOSSES FOR ALL INSURED U.S. COMMERCIAL BANKS BY ASSET SIZE: 1980–1986

Asset Size	A. Loss Rate (Net Charge-Offs to Loans and Leases)[a]						
	1980	1981	1982	1983	1984	1985	1986
Under $25 million	0.45%	0.54%	0.82%	0.95%	1.22%	1.78%	1.86%
$25–100 million	0.40	0.43	0.67	0.85	0.90	1.32	1.45
$100–300 million	0.38	0.41	0.63	0.67	0.70	0.89	1.06
$300 mil–$1 billion	0.43	0.42	0.65	0.70	0.62	0.81	1.07
$1–5 billion	0.48	0.47	0.48	0.62	0.81	0.79	0.92
Over $5 billion	0.32	0.27	0.48	0.62	0.81	0.79	0.92
All banks	0.38%	0.37%	0.57%	0.68%	0.77%	0.85%	0.99%

Asset Size	B. Percentage of Insured Banks with Earnings Losses						
	1980	1981	1982	1983	1984	1985	1986
Under $25 million	5.68%	6.93%	12.4%	16.9%	22.3%	26.2%	29.6%
$25–100 million	1.74	3.49	5.2	7.5	10.0	12.7	16.1
$100–300 million	1.56	4.44	6.2	6.0	6.3	8.5	11.7
$300 mil–$1 billion	1.70	2.93	4.6	5.4	4.5	6.7	11.3
$1–5 billion	0.35	2.99	3.7	5.9	4.7	3.3	5.9
Over $5 billion	2.70	—	4.4	9.4	6.1	1.4	6.0
All banks	3.71%	5.14%	8.3%	11.0%	14.0%	16.7%	19.7%

Sources. Adapted from Ross Waldrop, "Commercial Bank Performance in 1985," *Banking and Economic Review*, Federal Deposit Insurance Corporation (April 1986); and Ross Waldrop, "Commercial Bank Performance in 1986," *Banking and Economic Review*, Federal Deposit Insurance Corporation (March/April 1987).

[a] Total loans and leases are based on the average for the year.

indicate that the asset quality of different-sized banks with assets of more than $100 million was fairly similar from 1980 to 1986.

Additional information about the riskiness of different-sized banks is provided in section B of Table 3.4. In particular, the table compares the percentage of insured banks with earnings' losses for banks of different size. No clear trends emerge from these comparisons, except perhaps in 1985 and 1986, in which billion-dollar banks appeared to have significantly lower percentages of banks with negative earnings than smaller banks. In general, therefore, it appears that, excluding small banks with assets of less than $100 million, there are no apparent differences in either returns on equity or asset risk of different-sized banks.

REGULATORY MONITORING OF BANK FINANCIAL CONDITION

EWS

In the 1970s federal bank regulators began using financial ratios to monitor banks' condition between routine on-site examinations. Dubbed ''early warning systems'' (EWSs), these interim analyses were intended to detect changes in condition between bank examinations or bank holding company inspections. Thus, the purpose of these EWSs was to do surveillance that would help regulators allocate resources more efficiently and reduce the number of bank failures.

The first step of the EWS is to screen banks to identify low performing institutions. To do this, one or more of the following procedures is applied (depending on the regulator):

- Compare the bank's performance for each ratio relative to a peer group of banks.
- Compare the bank's performance for each ratio relative to a critical value set by the regulator.
- Form a composite score by combining a number of ratios and comparing the score with other banks.

Table 3.5 shows the financial ratios used by federal bank regulators in 1981 in their EWS procedures. As can be seen, different regulators used different ratios to screen banks. In terms of procedures, the Federal Deposit Insurance Corporation (FDIC) used critical values in their screening procedures, as denoted by ''C'' for most of its ratios. The Federal Reserve Board (FRB) and the Office of the Comptroller of the Currency (OCC) used composite scores in their screening procedures. Bank regulators periodically alter the financial ratios they use in their screening procedures to upgrade EWS models.

In general, EWS models have been a cost efficient and convenient way to keep track of a bank's condition between examinations. Numerous studies

TABLE 3.5

FINANCIAL RATIOS USED BY FEDERAL BANK REGULATORS IN EWS PROCEDURES

Financial Ratio	FRB	FDIC	OCC
Capital			
(1) Equity capital decrease		X	
(2) Equity capital/Total assets		C	X
(3) Retained earnings/Average equity capital			X
(4) Equity capital/Adjusted equity capital	X		
(5) Gross capital/Adjusted risk assets	X		
Profitability			
(1) Net Operating income/Average total assets		C	
(2) Net income/Assets			X
(3) Interest expense on deposits and federal funds purchased and borrowings/Total operating income		C	
(4) Adjusted return on assets			X
(5) Net income/Total assets-cash items	X		X
(6) Total other earnings/Average assets			X
Asset Quality			
(1) Gross loan losses/Net operating income + Provision	X		
(2) Provision for possible loan losses/Average assets			
(3) Gross charge-offs—Recoveries/Average loans		C	
Liquidity			
(1) Net borrowings-Mortgages/Cash and due from banks + Total securities maturing in one year or less		C	
Interest Sensitivity and Liabilities for Borrowed Money			
(1) $100,000 or more time deposits + Net borrowings/Total loans		C	
(2) Interest-sensitive funds/Total sources of funds	X		
Efficiency ratios			
(1) Total operating expenses/Total operating income			
(2) Noninterest expense/Total operating income-Interest expense	X		
(3) Cost of savings deposits/Total savings deposits			
(4) Net interest earnings/Average assets			
Change Ratios			
(1) Change in asset mix			X
(2) Change in liability mix			X
(3) Change in loan mix			X
(4) Cash dividends on common and preferred stock/Net income		C	
(5) Cash dividends/Net income	X		
Other Ratios			
(1) Commercial and industrial loans/Total loans, gross	X		

Source. Barron H. Putnam, "Early Warning Systems and Financial Analysis in Bank Monitoring," *Economic Review*, Federal Reserve Bank of Atlanta (November 1983), pp. 9–10.

have shown that these statistical models can identify most banks about to fail within 2 years prior to their actual collapse. Beyond 2 years, forecasting accuracy has proven much less reliable.

EWSs are not without their drawbacks. For example, there is no consensus of opinion on exactly which financial ratios are the best indicators of bank performance. Also, when many variables are used at one time to get a composite score, there is no clear-cut rationale for utilizing one combination of variables over any other combination. Indeed, perhaps the next-best approach is simply to use as many ratios as possible because each ratio contributes additional information about overall bank condition. It should be obvious that ratio analysis is an inexact science and, as such, should be supplemented by on-site observations whenever possible.

CAMEL

All three bank regulatory agencies employ the same rating system for on-site examinations of banks. Known as the CAMEL rating system, individual banks are scored from 1 (best) to 5 (worst) for each of the following five criteria: (1) Capital adequacy, (2) Asset quality, (3) Management, (4) Earnings, and (5) Liquidity. In the case of bank holding companies, however, there is no uniform rating system.

A potential drawback of financial statement risk measurement techniques is the difficulty in identifying fraud, embezzlement, and insider abuses. Table 3.6 shows that 31.4 percent of 124 failed U.S. commercial banks in the period 1971–1982 collapsed for these reasons. These data indicate that theft or defalcation is a significant problem in the banking system. One way to improve the

TABLE 3.6
PRIMARY CAUSES OF FAILURE AMONG U.S. COMMERCIAL BANKS: 1971–1982 (As a Percent of the Total Number of Bank Failures)

Cause of Failure	1971–1982	1980–1982
Low credit quality		
Loans	61.3%	67.3%
Inside loans	14.5%	9.6%
Poor funds management		
Interest rate risk	4.8	5.8
Liquidity	2.4	1.9
Fraud and embezzlement		
Internal	11.3	11.5
External	5.6	3.8
Number of cases	124	52

Source. Staff, *Deposit Insurance in a Changing Environment,* Federal Deposit Insurance Corporation, Washington, D.C. (April 15, 1983).

ability of regulators, bankers, and others to spot these kinds of problem situations is to increase the disclosure of information about the bank's activities.

Currently, all national, state member, and insured nonmember commercial banks are required quarterly to file a Report of Condition and a Report of Income with their federal supervisory agency. Commercial banks with more than $300 million total assets must also file a Large Bank Supplement each quarter with more detailed schedules of key asset, liability, income, and expense accounts. In 1984 banks were further classified in terms of reporting requirements as follows: (1) banks with foreign offices have the most detailed reports; (2) banks with only domestic offices and assets of $100 million or more have no foreign detail requirements; and (3) banks with less than $100 million in total assets have simpler reports (which are even more streamlined for banks under $25 million assets). More important, the supporting schedules required by regulators were expanded considerably. For example, as of December 31, 1982, a report of the amounts of delinquent and renegotiated loans and lease financing receivables was required on a quarterly basis. Moreover, beginning June 30, 1983, schedules for information concerning the bank's sensitivity to interest rate changes and off-balance sheet transactions were required. These added reporting requirements provide regulators with more accurate information concerning the acquisition and allocation of bank funds and aid in uncovering misappropriations of funds. Notably, the Uniform Bank Performance Report (UBPR) is created from the resulting data by the FDIC and distributed for use by examiners of all three federal banking agencies and by bankers and others interested in analyzing bank financial performance.

SUMMARY

The evaluation of bank performance is a complex process involving interactions between the environment, internal operations, and external activities. The ultimate objective of management is to maximize the value of the bank's equity shares by attaining the optimal mix of returns and risks. In this respect bank management needs to develop a comprehensive plan in order to identify objectives, goals, budgets, and strategies that will be consistent with the maximization of share values. Planning should encompass both internal and external performance dimensions. The primary method of evaluating internal performance is by analyzing accounting statements. Financial ratios of accounting items permit an historical sketch of bank returns and risks. External performance is best measured by evaluating the bank's market share, regulatory compliance, and public confidence. Because of increasing innovation and deregulation in the financial services industry, internal and external competitiveness is becoming much more important than in the past.

IMPORTANT CONCEPTS

asset quality	market share
asset utilization	net interest margin
budgets	net operating margin
CAMEL rating systems	objectives
capitalization	operating efficiency
cash and securities ratio	planning
cash ratio	profit margin
dollar gap	profitability
deposit insurance	provision for possible loan losses (PLL)
employee compensation	public confidence
EFTS	rate of return on assets (ROA)
equity multiplier	rate of return on equity (ROE)
EWS	regulatory compliance
goals	share valuation
interest sensitivity	strategies
leverage ratio	tax rate
liquidity	technology
loan ratio	Uniform Bank Performance Report
loss rate	yield spread

REFERENCES

Bovenzi, John F., James A. Morino, and Frank E. McFadden. "Commercial Bank Failure Prediction Models," *Economic Review,* Federal Reserve Bank of Atlanta, November 1983, pp. 14–26.

Clair, Robert T. "Financial Strategies of Top-Planning Banks in the Eleventh District," *Economic Review,* Federal Reserve Bank of Dallas, January 1987, pp. 1–13.

Putnam, Barron H. "Early Warning Systems and Financial Analysis in Bank Monitoring," *Economic Review,* Federal Reserve Bank of Atlanta, November 1983, pp. 6–12.

Sinkey, Joseph F., Jr. *Problem and Failed Institutions in the Commercial Banking Industry.* Greenwich, Conn.: Jai Press, 1979.

Urnikus, Marian S. "The New Tax Law: What It Means for Your Bank," *ABA Banking Journal,* November 1986, pp. 56, 59, 63, 65.

Waldrop, Ross. "Commercial Bank Performance in 1985," *Banking and Economic Review,* Federal Deposit Insurance Corporation, April 1986, pp. 19–24.

Waldrop, Ross. "Commercial Bank Performance in 1986," *Banking and Economic Review,* Federal Deposit Insurance Corporation, March/April 1987, pp. 11–18.

QUESTIONS

3.1. Discuss the difference between bank goals and bank objectives in the planning process. What is the ultimate objective of the bank?

3.2. Why is conserving costs by keeping employee salaries, wages, and fringe benefits down not necessarily a good idea?

3.3. Define bank growth. Why might super growth be a problem for a bank?

3.4. Give at least three reasons for staying up-to-date with bank technology.

3.5. Why do you think banks are sensitive about news reports concerning them in the financial press?

3.6. ROE and ROA are two key measures of bank profitability. Discuss the importance of these ratios to (a) insured depositors, (b) bank shareholders, and (c) bank management.

3.7. If a bank has a relatively low ROA but a relatively high ROE, what factor would explain this difference? Show an equation to demonstrate your answer.

3.8. In calculating the net interest margin, why does municipal bond interest earnings have to be grossed up?

3.9. If federal regulators require that bank capital be increased to at least 7 percent of total assets, how would bank growth be affected?

3.10. Do loan losses reduce bank profit?

3.11. What have bank studies found to be the primary factor distinguishing high and low profit banks? Discuss why this factor logically can affect profit.

3.12. What has been the trend in bank liquidity over the last 20 years? What implications to different kinds of bank risk does this trend have?

3.13. How did the Tax Reform Act of 1986 affect interest deductions on deposits?

3.14. If the dollar gap ratio is negative and interest rates are expected to rise in the near future, what will happen to bank profitability, provided that all else is the same?

3.15. Why have billion dollar banks been less affected by deposit rate deregulations than smaller, retail banks?

3.16. Define EWS and CAMEL in terms of their regulatory purposes.

PROBLEMS

3.1. (a) Exhibits 3.1 and 3.2 provide year-end Reports of Condition and Income for Z-Bank in 1986 and 1987. Exhibit 3.3 shows a list of financial ratios for Z-Bank's peer group. Calculate these financial ratios for Z-Bank. Round your answers to the hundredths place. For the dollar gap ratio assume that all securities, one-half of loans and lease financing receivables, and all deposits have maturities less than one year, and exclude cash and due from the calculation of this ratio.

EXHIBIT 3.1
REPORT OF CONDITION: Z-BANK

Report of Condition Items	Year-End (in millions of dollars)	
	1986	1987
Cash and due from depository institutions	200	205
U.S. Treasury securities	50	40
Obligations of other U.S. government agencies	20	17
Obligations of state and political subdivisions	70	68
All other securities	20	18
Federal funds sold and securities purchased	35	30
Total cash and securities	395	378
Loans	700	600
Lease financing receivables	10	10
Banks premises, furniture, and fixtures	15	16
All other assets	70	65
Total assets	1,190	1,069
Demand deposits	267	138
Time and saving deposits	350	250
Deposits in foreign offices	100	100
Deposits of U.S. government	2	2
Deposits of state and political government	50	45
All other deposits	100	170
Total deposits	869	705
Federal funds purchased and securities sold	140	180
Interest-bearing demand notes and other borrowings	30	40
Mortgage indebtedness	5	5
All other liabilites	70	65
Total liabilities	1,114	995
Subordinated notes and debentures	5	5
Preferred stock—par value	1	1
Common stock—par value	40	40
Surplus	10	10
Undivided profits and capital reserves	20	18
Total capital	76	74

EXHIBIT 3.2
REPORT OF INCOME: Z-BANK

Report of Condition Items	Year-End (in millions of dollars)	
	1986	1987
Interest and fees on loans	120	100
Interest on balances with depository institutions	15	13
Income on federal funds sold and securities purchased	5	4
Interest on U.S. Treasury and other agencies' securities	7	7
Interest on obligations of state and political subdivisions	5	5
Interest on other securities	1	1
Income from direct lease financing	2	2
Income from fiduciary activities	1	1
Service charges on deposit accounts	3	2
Other service charge	6	5
Other operating income	4	3
Total operating income	169	143
Salaries and employee benefits	20	18
Interest on CD's of 100,000 or more	15	13
Interest on deposits in foreign offices	35	37
Interest on other deposits	8	14
Interest on federal funds purchased and securities sold	18	23
Interest on demand notes and other borrowings	3	3
Interest on subordinated notes and debentures	1	1
Occupancy, furniture, and fixed expenses	6	6
Provision for possible loan losses	4	4
Other operating expenses	10	10
Total operating expenses	120	129
Income before taxes and securities transactions	49	14
Applicable income taxes	23	7
Income before securities gains or losses	23	7
Securities gains, net of taxes	−1	−1
Net income	22	6
Cash dividends	12	6
Undivided profits	10	0
Recoveries credited to provision for possible loan losses	1	1
Losses charged to provision for possible loan losses	−3	−7

(b) Discuss the profitability of Z-Bank by comparing its performance in 1986 and 1987 and by comparing it to its peer group in these years. Break down ROE in your analysis of profitability and discuss the influence of components of ROE on Z-Bank's profitability.

(c) Discuss Z-Bank's risk ratios over time and relative to its peer group. What are Z-Bank's strengths and weaknesses?

(d) If interest rates rise in the future, what implication is there to Z-Bank's profitability.

EXHIBIT 3.3

FINANCIAL RATIOS FOR Z-BANK'S PEER GROUP

Financial Ratios	1986	1987
Profit Ratios:		
Return on equity(ROE)	20.00%	18.00%
Return on assets(ROA)	1.00%	0.90%
Profit margin	7.00%	6.50%
Net operating margin	2.40%	2.30%
Net interest margin	5.20%	5.00%
Asset utilization		
Risk Ratios:		
Capital		
Equity multiplier	16.00	15.50
Asset Quality		
Loss rate	0.35%	0.45%
Loan ratio	55.00%	53.00%
Operating Efficiency		
(% of total assets)		
Interest expense	6.50%	6.55%
Wages and salaries	1.72%	1.74%
Occupancy	0.48%	0.49%
PLL	0.30%	0.32%
Other expenses	0.85%	0.85%
Liquidity		
Cash ratio	17.00%	17.00%
Cash and securities ratio	36.00%	37.00%
Other Financial Ratios		
Tax rate	50.00%	50.00%
Dollar gap ratio	−15.00%	−10.00%

APPENDIX

THE UNIFORM BANK PERFORMANCE REPORT

The Uniform Bank Performance Report (UBPR) is published by the Federal Financial Institutions Examination Council, which is composed of representative federal regulators from the Board of Governors of the Federal Reserve System, Federal Deposit Insurance Corporation, Federal Home Loan Bank Board, National Credit Union Administration, and Office of the Comptroller of the Currency. Produced quarterly beginning in December 1981, the UBPR provides comprehensive Call Report data from Reports of Income and Condition for all insured U.S. commercial banks, bank holding companies, and insured mutual savings banks. Information regarding savings and loan associations and credit unions can be acquired from their respective federal regulatory authorities. In December 1986, the UBPR became available to all insured commercial banks and was made available for sale to the public.

TABLE A3.1
UBPR NATIONAL DATA FOR ALL INSURED U.S. COMMERCIAL BANKS

	12-31-86	12-31-85	12-31-84	12-31-83	12-31-82
Number of banks in nation	14,188	14,406	14,483	14,469	14,455
Earnings and Profitability					
As a Percent of Average Assets:					
Net interest income	4.56	4.80	4.74	4.84	5.03
+ Noninterest income	0.74	0.74	0.73	0.67	0.65
− Overhead expense	3.46	3.46	3.37	3.36	3.39
− Provision: loan/lease losses	0.72	0.66	0.46	0.37	0.32
= Pretax operating income	1.07	1.37	1.58	1.73	1.90
+ Securities gains (losses)	0.09	0.04	0.00	0.00	0.00
= Pretax net operating income	1.24	1.46	1.58	1.74	1.89
Net operating income	0.73	0.86	0.93	1.02	1.10
Adjusted net operating income	0.80	0.98	1.03	1.09	1.15
Adjusted net income	0.75	0.90	0.95	1.01	1.08
Net income	0.74	0.87	0.94	1.02	1.10
As a Percent of Average Earning Assets:					
Interest income	10.78	11.93	12.68	12.31	13.70
Interest expense	5.81	6.68	7.47	6.96	8.13
Net interest income	5.02	5.30	5.25	5.39	5.61
Loan & Lease Loss, Reserve and Noncurrent Loans and Leases					
Net loss to average total loans/ leases	1.31	1.08	0.76	0.65	0.57
Earnings coverage of net loss(X)	4.87	6.19	8.75	9.46	10.30
Loss reserve to net loss(X)	2.25	2.40	3.06	3.17	3.20
Loss reserve to total loans & leases	1.48	1.29	1.09	1.03	1.00
% noncurrent loans & leases	2.79	2.67	2.32	2.16	2.12
Liquidity and Rate Sensitivity					
Volatile liability dependence	−12.94	−10.92	−10.45	−11.44	−10.61
Net loans & leases to assets	50.43	52.02	52.44	49.95	49.73
Net assets repricable in 1 year or less to assets	−6.33	−1.26	−2.00	−0.04	N/A

TABLE A3.1 (*Continued*)

	12-31-86	12-31-85	12-31-84	12-31-83	12-31-82
Capitalization					
Member primary capital to average assets[a]	9.11	9.22	9.16	9.04	9.03
Nonmember primary capital to average assets[a]	9.10	9.20	9.16	9.04	9.03
Cash dividends to net income	36.83	34.54	34.28	32.12	31.26
Retained earnings to average total equity	4.25	5.45	6.28	7.41	8.31
Growth Rates					
Assets	7.36	7.28	8.51	10.60	9.87
Total equity capital	5.19	6.96	7.54	9.07	9.57
Net loans & leases	4.66	6.49	14.48	11.19	9.03
Volatile liabilities	3.90	11.33	22.96	1.78	15.82

Source. Federal Financial Institutions Examination Council, *Uniform Performance Report*, Washington, D.C. (1986).

[a] Primary capital is equal to the sum of equity capital plus loan and lease loss reserves, permanent and convertible debt, minority interests in consolidated subsidiaries, less intangible assets (see Chapter 12 for further discussion). Effective June 1985, the Federal Reserve Board's definition of primary capital, which it applies to member banks, differs somewhat from the FDIC's definition, which applies to nonmember banks.

The UBPR is a valuable source of both individual bank and aggregated data that can be used by bank examiners, financial analysts, bank managers, and others to analyze commercial bank performance. Aggregated data can be obtained for state or peer group averages (e.g., 25 different peer groupings are available that consider differences in asset size, location in a metropolitan/nonmetropolitan area, and branching/nonbranching status). The following sections are contained in the UBPR:

SUMMARY RATIOS

INCOME INFORMATION
   Relative income statement and margin analysis
   Noninterest income and expense ratios
   Foreign office trends (if applicable)

BALANCE SHEET INFORMATION
   Balance sheet—percent composition of assets and liabilities
   Analysis of loan loss reserves and loan mix
   Analysis of past due, nonaccrual, and restructured loans and leases
   Analysis of repricing opportunities

LIQUIDITY ANALYSIS
   Investment portfolio and capital analysis
   Commitments and contingencies

Table A3.1 is a reproduction of the UBPR summary ratios for all insured commercial banks as of December 31, 1986. Many of the ratios shown are self-explanatory; however, in some instances it would be advisable to refer to the UBPR User's Guide.

LIQUIDITY MANAGEMENT

Managing liquidity is becoming increasingly complex for commercial banks. One general area of liquidity management is the **estimation** of funds' needs, which is related to deposit inflows and outflows and varying levels of loan commitments. Deregulation of interest rate ceilings on deposits in the early 1980s tended to increase the intensity of competition in deposit markets. Moreover, large banks are facing increased competition for loans from other financial institutions and from nonfinancial firms. Many banks, therefore, are finding it more difficult to estimate liquidity needs.

The second general area of liquidity management involves **meeting** liquidity needs. Two types of liquidity are available to meet potential liquidity requirements—asset liquidity and liability liquidity. Asset liquidity simply concerns the conversion of liquid assets to cash. Liability liquidity is more complicated and involves estimating outside sources of discretionary funds (e.g., Fed funds, repurchase agreements, certificates of deposit, and other borrowings). Because use of these sources of liability liquidity has been growing in recent years, it could be misleading to use financial ratios based on accounting statements alone to gauge bank liquidity.

ESTIMATING LIQUIDITY NEEDS

The first step in any analysis of bank liquidity is the estimation of liquidity needs. These needs arise from deposit withdrawals and loan demands, and to estimate them, the bank must forecast the level of future depository activities and loan commitments. Although loan growth generally will not exceed deposit growth in a community, differences can arise temporarily. Forecasting month-to-month or seasonal liquidity needs is a process based normally on the experience of the bank, with appropriate adjustments for specific future events that would alter typical liquidity needs. Admittedly, considerable subjectivity is involved in forecasting the future. Consequently, it is prudent to adjust the estimated need upward to some extent to avoid a cash shortage, which could result in lost lending opportunities, reduced depositor confidence, and/or regulatory agency suspicions concerning safety and soundness.

Forecasts should break down assets and liabilities into controllable and non-controllable categories. Most kinds of loans, as well as demand deposits and interest-bearing retail deposit accounts, are not under the direct control of bank management. Securities in the investment portfolio purchased to comply with regulatory restrictions and discretionary sources of funds (e.g., Fed funds and certificates of deposit) are generally beyond direct control also. Among non-controllable items, the difference between assets and liabilities indicates the liquidity need of the bank. Controllable assets and liabilities can then be employed to meet this need.

Sources and Uses of Funds Method

One method of estimating future liquidity needs is to develop a sources and uses of funds statement. To do this, bank management must unravel uncontrollable assets and liabilities to examine each balance sheet account. For example, the loan portfolio would have to be divided into its component parts—commercial and industrial real estate loans, residential real estate loans, and other loans. The demand for funds by businesses and individuals in these different lending areas could be estimated from economic projections. Commercial and industrial loan demand, for instance, would be influenced by both the production and growth expectations of the business sector, in addition to the internal profitability of business firms. Moreover, if businesses demand external funding, many firms opt to bypass the banking system and access the financial markets directly through investment banks. Although it is not easy to forecast the amount of bank financing needed by business firms, experience and judgment are often sufficient guides to follow in obtaining a final estimate of loan demands.

Similarly, deposit levels are influenced by economic and competitive market conditions. As interest rates rise, corporate treasurers move funds out of demand deposits and into interest-bearing assets and, therefore, banks will tend to experience increasing competition for deposit funds from nonbank financial service companies such as money market mutual funds. Other variables may periodically influence deposit levels also, such as changes in monetary policy and international financial markets.

Table 4.1 gives a hypothetical sources and uses funds statement for a bank over a 6-month period. The expected increase in total loan demand in the spring and subsequent decline in early summer is a common seasonal trend in agricultural banking. When loan demands increase, deposit balances often decline, as many bank customers obtain both deposit and loan services from the same bank. Notice that decreases in loans and increases in deposits are sources of funds. Increases in loans and deposit withdrawals are uses of funds, and thus subtracting deposit changes from loan changes yields an estimate of liquidity needs.

To estimate the figures presented in Table 4.1, past seasonal trends were reviewed by bank management. Next, these trends were adjusted for cyclical movements in economic and financial conditions. For example, a bank having a large proportion of its assets invested in commercial and industrial loans needs to adjust loan estimates downward if a recession in the business sector is forecasted. Although loan demand will fall and therefore ease liquidity needs, rising unemployment will tend to depress deposit balances, offsetting the decline in loans. A bank with a relatively high proportion of residential real estate loans would be particularly affected by movements in interest rates. As interest

TABLE 4.1
ESTIMATING LIQUIDITY NEEDS BASED ON A SOURCES AND USES OF
FUNDS STATEMENT

End of Month	Estimated Total Loans	Estimated Total Deposits	Estimated Change		Estimated Liquidity Needs
			Loans	Deposits	
December	$68,000	$85,000	$ —	$ —	$ —
January	70,000	90,000	2,000	5,000	(3,000)
February	79,000	86,000	9,000	(4,000)	13,000
March	89,000	83,000	10,000	(3,000)	13,000
April	96,000	78,000	7,000	(5,000)	12,000
May	95,000	79,000	(1,000)	1,000	(2,000)
June	88,000	85,000	(7,000)	6,000	(13,000)

rates rise, loan demand can be expected to fall at some point, because many applicants can no longer qualify to meet the higher interest expenses.

Local and regional economic factors must also be evaluated and used to adjust estimated liquidity needs. A dramatic example of such a factor is the decline in energy prices in the early 1980s, which created "pockets" of economic doldrums, especially in the South and Southwest, where many oil and gas companies were driven out of business or forced to cut production severely. The resultant decline in loan demand was greater than the decline in deposits associated with the downturn, which caused some banks in these regions to have excess liquidity. For others, the subsequent decline in economic activity caused severe deposit losses, which caused these banks to suffer a liquidity squeeze. Thus, local and regional business conditions can have a significant impact on the sources and uses of bank funds.

Structure-of-Deposits Method

Another way to estimate liquidity needs is the structure-of-deposits method. The basic idea of this approach is to list the different types of deposits that the bank is using to acquire funds and then assign a probability of withdrawal to each type of deposit within a specific planning horizon. High risk, or unstable, deposits require substantial liquidity to support, whereas low risk, or stable, deposits require relatively less liquidity. The major strength of the structure-of-deposits method is that it centers management attention on the probable cause of liquidity pressures (i.e., deposit withdrawals). On the other hand, its main weakness is ignoring other liquidity demands stemming from loans. Despite this drawback, as well as the subjectivity of the deposit classification process, the structure-of-deposits method is a useful technique for controlling liquidity risk.

As a simple example, bank management might have structured its deposit sources as follows:

	Amount Held (in millions)	Probability of Withdrawal in Next 3 Months
Short-term (unstable):		
Demand deposits	2	.90
Other transactions accounts	10	.60
Medium-term:		
Small time and savings deposits	50	.30
Long-term (stable):		
Large time deposits	10	.20

As indicated, the bank has relatively low amounts of short-term and long-term deposits. The major deposit source is medium-term small time and savings deposits, which are relatively stable. In this case liquidity demands from deposit withdrawals should be fairly modest. Of course, this same structuring method may be applied to nondeposit funds sources also, especially if these sources are particularly important to the bank.

ASSET LIQUIDITY

Historically, asset liquidity was the primary means by which banks met cash demands. Money market instruments, such as treasury bills and short-term obligations of state and political subdivisions (municipal securities), are ''liquid'' in the sense that they can be sold readily with minimal loss of capital. Relatively large loan demands and deposit withdrawals were typically met by liquidating these near-money instruments. Other liquidity needs could be covered by cash assets, including vault cash, bank deposits at Federal Reserve banks, bank deposits at other banks, and other available cash (e.g., cash items in the process of collection, in addition to cash and due from banks, which are holdings of other banks' certificates of deposit). This approach to liquidity management traditionally fell under the rubric of ''asset management.''

Asset management was the dominant method of bank management until the 1960s, when ''liability management'' became popular as an alternative means of meeting cash needs. Liability management involves the acquisition of deposit and nondeposit sources of funds as liquidity needs arise. As discussed later in this chapter, liability management substantially altered the role of liquidity management in banking.

Role of Asset Liquidity

There are two basic roles of asset liquidity management in modern banking. First, liquid assets serve as an alternative source of funds for the bank; the bank can use either assets or liabilities to meet cash needs. Its selection of sources of funds will depend heavily on their relative costs. If it is less costly to sell off some liquid assets than to issue certificates of deposit (CDs), asset liquidity will be favored over liability liquidity to acquire funds. Consider a situation in which interest rates are relatively high and are expected to continue to rise in the near future. Increased loan demand at this time might be better met by selling treasury bills and absorbing a modest capital loss than by issuing CDs, which would have to be rolled over at higher interest rates in the future. Although the rates on money market instruments and CDs would be about the same, as rates rise in the future, the switch from lower-earning treasury bills to higher-earning assets such as commercial loans will boost bank profitability.

The second role of asset liquidity management is as a reserve. If the financial market loses confidence in a bank's safety and soundness, it is likely that borrowed sources of funds would become inaccessible. In this case, the bank would have to rely upon its liquid assets to maintain business operations. Thus, asset liquidity is a reserve to forestall problems that threaten bank solvency. In keeping with this rationale, regulators impose **primary reserve** requirements that apply to cash held in their vaults and on deposit at a Federal Reserve district office. **Secondary reserves** are near money financial instruments that have no formal regulatory requirements and provide an additional reserve of liquid assets to meet cash needs. Finally, one should note that use of liability management increases bank asset size and so requires appropriate increases in capital reserves to stay within regulatory guidelines. By contrast, liquidating money market assets does not change bank size and, therefore, does not affect bank capital reserves.

Primary Reserves

Most primary reserves are cash assets held to satisfy legal reserve requirements. Banks seek to minimize cash accounts because there is an opportunity cost to holding idle funds. Thus, total cash reserves generally equal legal reserves. To the extent that legal reserves exceed the cash reserves banks would hold in the absence of these requirements, banks are *taxed* by the government. Taxation is an appropriate interpretation here because the Federal Reserve invests banks' deposits held at its district banks in treasury securities, and most of the resultant earnings are transferred to the U.S. Treasury to help pay the fiscal budget. In this regard, an exodus of member banks from the Federal Reserve system occurred in the 1960s and 1970s, as bankers complained of relatively high reserve requirements imposed on member compared with nonmember banks.

In 1980 the Monetary Control Act was passed under Title I of DIDMCA. This legislation requires all depository institutions to carry legal reserves set by the Federal Reserve under Regulation D. It eliminated any reserve requirement incentive for banks to leave the system, while establishing uniform reserve rules for banks. Moreover, it tightened the linkage between reserves and money supply and thus served to facilitate monetary control (because reserve requirements are a fulcrum used by the central bank in an attempt to achieve its monetary and economic objectives). To further enhance its ability to control the money stock and so rein in inflation, in 1984 the Federal Reserve began using contemporaneous reserve requirement accounting methods (CRR) on transactions deposits rather than lagged reserve requirement accounting (LRR). Figure 4.1 compares these two accounting techniques.

Lagged Reserve Requirements

Under LRR, there was a 1-week computation period beginning on Thursday and ending on Wednesday. Banks summed reservable deposits (i.e., deposits subject to reserve requirements) and vault cash for the week and divided by five to get daily average deposits. A 14-day lag occurred from the beginning of the computation period to the beginning of the maintenance period. The mainte-

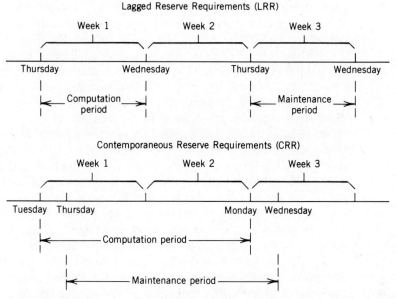

FIGURE 4.1   A comparison of lagged and contemporaneous reserve accounting techniques.

nance period was also 1 week, running from Thursday to Wednesday. During this period the bank had to carry sufficient reserves to cover reserve requirements on deposits held during the computation period. Excesses or deficiencies in reserves within 2 percent of requirements could be carried over to the next maintenance week. A deficiency of more than 2 percent would be penalized by the opportunity cost of these funds equal to the discount rate plus 2 percent multiplied by the excess deficiency.

Contemporaneous Reserve Requirements

The new CRR rules, as illustrated in Figure 4.1, are contemporaneous in that the computation and maintenance periods overlap to a great extent. The computation period begins Tuesday and ends 14 days later on Monday. The maintenance period begins 2 days after the beginning of the computation period on Thursday and ends 2 weeks later on Wednesday. Thus, there is only a 2-day lag between the ends of the computation and maintenance periods.

These CRR rules apply to transaction deposit accounts. For nonpersonal time deposits and Eurocurrency liabilities, there is a 30-day lag between the end of the 2-week computation period and the end of the 2-week maintenance period. These deposits, therefore, are subject to LRR rules that are more lagged than previously.

As before, CRR rules allow banks to use Federal Reserve deposits and vault cash to meet reserve requirements during the maintenance period; however,

CRR changed the accounting for these items. Deposits at the Fed during the maintenance period are applicable, whereas vault cash is counted in the 14-day period ending 30 days *before* the end of the current maintenance period.

CRR tends to shift the burden of reserve adjustment away from the Fed and toward the banking system. With LRR, as the end of the maintenance period neared, banks essentially were provided reserves by the Fed through discount window borrowing. If demand for reserves was high before the close of the maintenance period, the federal funds rate would rise significantly, causing banks to go to the window to satisfy reserve requirements. Banks purchased or sold federal funds to adjust for shortages or excesses, respectively, in legal reserves. This approach to monetary policy implied that the level of bank deposits determined bank reserves (equal to the sum of nonborrowed and borrowed reserves). CRR forces banks to adjust their reserve positions on an ongoing basis throughout the maintenance period. Because there is less reliance by banks on the discount window to meet reserve requirements, bank reserves more directly influence the level of deposits. This accounting approach is consistent with the Fed's shift in monetary policy in October 1979, from federal-funds targeting to targeting of monetary aggregates. From a management standpoint, it is more difficult to manage the reserve position of the bank under CRR than under LRR. Also, it is likely that a higher level of reserves is needed with CRR because there is less certainty about the target level of reserves.

Managing the Money Position

Managing the money position of a bank relates to minimizing cash holdings. Because legal reserve requirements exceed bank preferences in general, the money position is synonymous with reserve management. Table 4.2 shows an example of how a bank would calculate its required reserves. The three basic categories of deposits shown in Table 4.2 are defined as follows:

Transactions Accounts. All deposits are included on which the account holder is permitted to make withdrawals by negotiable or transferrable instruments, payment orders of withdrawal, and telephone and preauthorized transfers (in excess of three per month) for the purpose of making payments to third persons or others. Examples of these types of deposit accounts are: demand deposits, NOW accounts, and share draft accounts (offered by credit unions).

Nonpersonal Time Deposits. These deposits are time deposits, including savings deposits, that are not transactions accounts and that in general are not held by an individual. However, certain transferrable time deposits held by individuals and other obligations are included. For example, MMDA (and similar accounts) with no more than six preauthorized, automatic, or other transfers per month (of which no more than three can be checks) are included.

Eurocurrency Liabilities. These funds represent net borrowings from related foreign offices, gross borrowings from unrelated foreign depository institutions, loans to U.S. residents made by overseas branches of domestic depository institutions, and sales of assets by U.S. depository institutions by their overseas offices. Eurocurrencies (or so-called Eurodollars) are used mainly by large banks as an alternative source of deposit funds.

Total reserves required according to the calculations in Table 4.2 are $3,918,000. Because the bank has an average daily vault cash balance of $418,000 (which is based on the 2-week period ending 30 days prior to the end of the 2-week maintenance period under CRR), it needs $3,830,000 on deposit at its Federal Reserve district bank. If it has excess reserves, it can carry over the greater of 2 percent of the average daily minimum reserve balance or $25,000 to the next maintenance period. If it has deficient reserves, it must offset this shortfall in the next maintenance period.

If the bank had a deficiency (or excess) in reserves, the federal funds market is the most likely source (use) of funds. Sometimes unexpected payments on loans and deposits will cause cash balances to increase substantially above legal requirements. In this case, the money manager would seek first to evaluate the nature of this increase. If it is clearly a temporary matter, short-term money market instruments (such as treasury bills, bankers' acceptances, or commercial paper) could be purchased to earn interest on the excess cash. If

TABLE 4.2
CALCULATING RESERVE REQUIREMENTS FOR COMMERCIAL BANKS

Type of Deposit and Deposit Interval	Average Dollar Amount (in millions) in Computation Period	Percentage Reserve Requirement[a]	Effective Date[a]	Average Dollar Reserves Required (in millions) in Maintenance Period
Net transactions accounts				
$0–$36.7 million[a]	$29.8	3%	12-30-86	$0.894
Over $36.7 million	20.2	12%	12-30-86	2.424
Nonpersonal time deposits by original maturity				
Less than 1.5 years	15.0	3%	10-06-83	0.450
1.5 years or more	10.0	0%	10-06-83	—
Eurocurrency liabilities				
All types	5.0	3%	11-13-80	0.150
Total reserves required				3.918
Less vault cash				(0.418)
Federal Reserve District Bank				$3.830

[a] The Monetary Control Act of 1980 requires that the amount of transactions accounts against which the 3-percent requirement applies be modified annually by 80 percent of the percentage increase in transactions accounts held by all depository institutions, determined as of June 30 of each year.

the increase in cash appears to be more permanent, the money manager would consider longer-term investment opportunities, such as capital market securities (e.g., longer-term government securities, including municipal securities, and corporate bonds) and loans. On the other hand, significant drains on cash balances could be met either by selling short-term, liquid securities or by raising funds in the deposit markets. The deregulation of interest rate ceilings on deposits has made the latter strategy more feasible than it was in the past, because posting relatively competitive deposit rates can rapidly attract funds from across the nation.

Small and large banks generally differ in their approach to managing their money positions. During the beginning of the reserve maintenance period, small banks will tend to run a surplus volume of reserves at the Federal Reserve. After this point, they will sell their excess reserves in the federal funds market. By contrast, large banks tend to experience an increasing shortfall in reserves as the maintenance period proceeds. They become purchasers of Fed funds later in the maintenance period, which are supplied primarily by small banks. This general pattern of reserve holdings at large banks does not always occur, however. It may be altered because of anticipated Fed funds rates—for example, if a money manager believed interest rates in the Fed funds market were going to rise substantially near the end of the maintenance period (perhaps because of tight money conditions), it would be less costly to purchase Fed funds at the beginning of the maintenance period and to sell any surplus at the end of the period. Alternatively, larger banks may experience relatively volatile reserve levels throughout the maintenance period because of changes in loan demands and deposit activity that occur as the bank reacts aggressively to changing market conditions.

Secondary Reserves

Once future liquidity needs have been estimated, the bank must decide what sources of liquidity will be tapped to cover these needs. Excess cash reserves are a primary consideration because of the interest opportunity cost involved with holding them. If deposits are forecasted to decline in the near future, some amount of cash reserves is likely to become available for use because reserve requirements will decline. Remaining liquidity needs must be covered either with liquid assets or discretionary funds.

Assuming liquid assets are to be used, banks normally seek to match the maturities of their assets with specific future liquidity needs. This **money market approach** enables the bank to avoid transactions costs, as well as price risk, while maximizing interest revenues. Table 4.3 gives a brief description of the principal money market instruments used by banks for liquidity purposes.

Cyclical monetary policies to restrain strong inflationary pressures can cause liquidity pressures that force banks to rely more on their asset liquidity than on their liability liquidity. This possibility influences the decision concerning the choice of liquid assets to hold. For example, Treasury bills (and notes

TABLE 4.3
PRINCIPAL MONEY MARKET INSTRUMENTS

Treasury Bills (T-bills) are direct obligations of the U.S. government that have an original maturity of 1 year or less. T-bills are discount instruments that are sold at a weekly auction. The minimum denomination is $10,000, with larger denominations available in multiples of $5,000 above this minimum. Original maturities of T-bills are 3 months, 6 months, and 1 year.

Federal Agency Securities are issued by various government agencies (e.g., Federal Land Banks, Federal Home Loan Banks, Banks for Cooperatives, Federal National Mortgage Association, and Tennessee Valley Authority). These securities have little or no default risk, because the issuing agencies are acting in the public interest to finance sectors of the economy that the government wishes to support (e.g., housing, agriculture, and small business); some agencies are backed directly by the federal government, whereas others carry the implicit assumption of government support. Agency securities are interest-bearing instruments with varying maturities and minimum denominations of $50,000 or more.

Repurchase Agreements (RPs or repos) are securities purchased (sold) under agreement to resell (repurchase) with a securities dealer. RPs may or may not have a set maturity date, but generally their term does not exceed 3 months. They have low default risk because T-bills are normally pledged as collateral. Interest is paid on transactions that involve at least $1 million.

Bankers' Acceptances are time drafts used in international trade that are "accepted" by a large bank. For example, an importer may obtain a letter of credit from a bank, which is used by the exporter to draw a draft on the bank for payment of goods. Upon accepting the draft, the bank can market it if it wishes. Maturities normally extend throughout the transit period for shipment of goods (i.e., from 30 to 180 days).

Negotiable Certificates of Deposit (CDs) are interest-bearing liabilities of banks and other depository institutions that may be sold to third parties and carry minimum denominations of $100,000. Maturities range from about 1 to 18 months, and rates may or may not vary with interest rate conditions. Eurodollar CDs are dollar-denominated securities issued by foreign branches of major U.S. banks and foreign-owned banks. Yields on CDs can differ depending on the size and risk of issuing banks and exceed treasury yields on instruments of equal maturity.

Federal Funds (Fed funds) are immediately available funds that represent interbank loans of cash reserves, either held on deposit at Federal Reserve district banks or elsewhere (including correspondent banks). Government intervention may cause Fed fund rates to move sharply in response to monetary policy operations of the Federal Reserve. Fed funds "sold" are liquid assets of the lending institution that appear as Fed funds "purchased" on the borrowing institution's liability side of the balance sheet. Fed funds are not considered deposits and, therefore, do not require that reserves be held against them. Most Fed funds' transactions are "overnight loans" and expire in a single day. Typically, Fed funds flow from small respondent banks with excess liquidity to larger correspondent banks with liquidity demands.

Commercial Paper is a short-term, unsecured promissory note issued by major U.S. corporations and nonfinancial companies. Denominations normally are in multiples of $1,000, with a minimum of $25,000. Maturities range from 3 days to 9 months. Commercial paper may or may not be a discount instrument, and rates closely track the prime rate quoted by major U.S. banks. Little or no secondary market exists for this security.

and bonds nearing maturity) are most liquid because of a strong secondary market. By contrast, commercial paper has a weak secondary market. Bankers' acceptances and negotiable certificates of deposit (CDs) have a good secondary market and, thus, fall somewhere between these two extremes. Of course, the bank must trade off liquidity risk against interest earnings in selecting the asset securities it will purchase.

Although timing securities to mature in order to meet liquidity demands is the most common approach to managing asset liquidity, there may be an opportunity to take advantage of yield curve relationships by using an *aggressive* liquidity approach. For example, if the yield curve were upward-sloping and expected to remain at the same level in the near future, the purchase of longer-term securities would not only offer higher yields than shorter-term securities but also could offer the realization of capital gains if they were sold before maturity to meet liquidity needs. Capital gains are possible because, as time passes and the securities' maturities shorten, their interest rate declines in line with the upward slope of the yield curve. These potential earnings' gains would have to be weighed against transactions costs and risks associated with this aggressive approach.

LIABILITY LIQUIDITY

An alternative approach to liquidity management is to purchase the funds necessary to meet loan demands and deposit withdrawals. This approach falls under the more general heading of liability management, a topic that is covered in detail in Part 4 of this text. In this section our purpose is to discuss liability management briefly in the context of liquidity.

There are substantial differences between small and large banks in their use of liability liquidity. Large banks that are active in the money market have a natural advantage over smaller banks in terms of their ability to cost-effectively raise funds through federal funds, repurchase agreements, negotiable CDs, Eurocurrency deposits, and other types of purchased funds. By contrast, smaller banks often obtain purchased funds in the money market through their larger correspondent banks. Because smaller banks tend to have deposits in excess of loan demands, they will deposit excess funds at correspondents in exchange for money market services. Correspondent balances thus serve as an additional source of asset liquidity for smaller banks and as an additional source of liability liquidity for larger banks.

The primary advantage of liability management is that assets can be shifted from lower-earning money market instruments to higher-earning loans and longer-term securities. Greater asset diversification also may be possible in this instance.

On the downside, there are risks involved in liability management. If interest rates increase suddenly, the cost of funds could rise substantially as purchased funds come due and must be rolled over at higher rates. If the bank's assets are less sensitive to interest rate changes than its liabilities are, profit margins would suffer and capital may become inadequate. As profit margins decline, the bank might have to sell off assets to reduce its need for purchased funds and improve its capital ratios. Capital losses on the sale of assets might further squeeze profit margins, however. Because liquid assets would minimize capital losses, larger banks need to carry some amount of money market instruments to help offset interest rate risk. Furthermore, in the event that the public loses confidence in the bank's safety and soundness, deposit withdrawals may increase temporarily, and liquid assets will help absorb these withdrawals. Thus, **interest rate risk** is increased under liability management of liquidity.

Liability management also increases the bank's financial risk. As discussed in Chapter 12, **financial risk** is the increase in the variability of earnings per share that is associated with an increase in debt as a proportion of total assets (i.e., financial leverage). Bank managers thus need to consider the risk preferences of shareholders when using liability liquidity.

One of the greatest difficulties in using liabilities to meet liquidity needs is estimating the availability of external funds. The quantity of deposit and nondeposit funds depends on many factors, including monetary policy actions by the Federal Reserve, economic conditions, and the bank's financial strength. These uncertainties require that banks have more than sufficient access to different kinds of liabilities to make sure that liquidity needs are safely covered. Chapter 11 provides detailed discussion of different sources of bank funds.

FUNDS MANAGEMENT OF LIQUIDITY

As suggested by the preceding discussion, management of liquidity is best handled by combining asset liquidity and liability liquidity, or a **funds management** approach. Funds management involves comparing total liquidity needs with total liquidity sources.

Liquidity Ratios

From the standpoint of bank analysts, bank liquidity can only be roughly estimated using Call Reports of Condition. Three common ratio measures of bank liquidity are loans/deposits, loans/liabilities, and liquid assets/liabilities. The two former ratios are inversely related to liquidity, whereas the latter ratio is positively related to liquidity. None of these three measures, however, considers either expected future liquidity needs or the ability of the bank to obtain liquidity from borrowed funds. Nevertheless, they are easy to calculate and they can be useful in evaluating changes in liquidity over time. To illustrate, Table 4.4 gives the average values of these ratios for all U.S. insured commercial banks from 1978 to 1986. Both the loans/deposits and loans/liabilities ratios increased noticeably in 1979 and again in 1984. The 1979 increase does not appear to have been necessarily caused by a decline in asset liquidity, however,

TABLE 4.4

LIQUIDITY RATIOS OF ALL INSURED COMMERCIAL BANKS OVER TIME[a]

Liquidity Ratio	1978	1979	1980	1981	1982	1983	1984	1985	1986
Loans/Deposits	.66	.72	.72	.73	.70	.69	.77	.77	.76
Loans/Liabilities	.56	.62	.61	.61	.58	.56	.64	.64	.63
Liquid Assets[b]/ Liabilities	.29	.28	.28	.28	.26	.26	.22	.21	N/A[c]

[a] Data collected from consolidated reports of condition published by the FDIC.

[b] Liquid assets is defined here as cash and due from depository institutions plus U.S. treasury securities and obligations of other U.S. agencies and corporations.

[c] Data were not available to calculate this ratio.

because the liquid assets/liabilities ratio only declined slightly. Instead, we can infer that banks moved funds from securities investments to loans. By contrast, the proportionate increase in lending in 1984 was offset for the most part by a decline in the liquid assets/liabilities ratio, which can be interpreted to mean that asset liquidity declined to some degree in that year.

A better approach to measuring liquidity is to account for changes over time in both liquidity needs and sources. To do this, the following ratio can be calculated on a period-by-period basis:

$$\frac{\text{Liquid assets and liabilities in period } t}{\text{Estimated liquidity needs in period } t} \tag{4.1}$$

Table 4.5 calculates this ratio for a hypothetical bank using the estimated liquidity needs from Table 4.1 and other information on the bank's liquid assets and estimated liability liquidity (i.e., detailed information of this kind is probably

TABLE 4.5

EVALUATING BANK LIQUIDITY BY COMPARING LIQUIDITY NEEDS AND SOURCES OVER TIME

End of Month	Estimated Liquidity Needs[a]	Asset Liquidity	Estimated Liability Liquidity	Total Liquidity	Bank Liquidity Ratio
January	(3,000)	5,000	10,000	15,000	−5.00[a]
February	13,000	6,000	10,000	16,000	1.23
March	13,000	7,000	10,000	17,000	1.31
April	12,000	7,000	10,000	17,000	1.42
May	(2,000)	4,000	10,000	14,000	−7.00[a]
June	(13,000)	3,000	10,000	13,000	−1.00[a]

[a] Negative liquidity need causes the bank liquidity ratio to be negative, which can be interpreted to mean that the bank has sufficient liquidity.

only available internally to bank management). Notice that estimated liability liquidity stays the same from month to month. It is possible, however, that changing economic and financial market conditions could affect the ability of the bank to access purchased funds over time. Asset liquidity is under greater management control and can be varied to ensure that adequate total liquidity is available to meet deposit and loan needs. As shown in Table 4.5, the bank has negative liquidity needs (or excess liquidity) in January, May, and June, such that negative liquidity ratios result in these months. In the other months the ratio exceeded one, indicating that sufficient liquidity was available to meet normal operating needs. If the ratio had been in the range between zero and one, the bank could experience a potential liquidity problem.

Optimum Bank Liquidity

A question that bank management must ultimately face is whether the liquidity ratio is optimal. One facet of optimality is that the liquidity ratio needs to be high enough to meet even *unexpected* changes in liquidity needs and sources. On the other hand, the liquidity ratio should not be too high because there is an opportunity cost of excessive liquidity. Also, liquidity management can conflict with other management goals in areas such as interest sensitivity management, loan management, and portfolio management. Thus, the bank must trade off the cost of maintaining liquidity and the cost of insufficient liquidity. As shown in Figure 4.1, at some point an optimum liquidity level is reached at which liquidity costs are minimized.

Because of the reliance on forecasted needs and sources, a reasonable margin for error should be built into any assessment of bank liquidity. Estimates of the amount of uncertainty inherent in evaluating liquidity needs and sources should be at least informally considered. Greater uncertainty tends to increase the potential costs of maintaining liquidity, as well as the potential costs of insufficient liquidity. As such, the optimum quantity of bank liquidity is increased by greater uncertainty. To evaluate uncertainty and its effects on bank liquidity more formally, a graphical comparison of the probability distributions of both liquidity needs and sources could be constructed as shown in Figure 4.2. The shaded area is proportional to the probability that the bank will use up all of its liquidity. As the amount of overlap in these two distributions increases, it becomes more likely that the bank will be illiquid at some point during the period of time under consideration.

It should be obvious that liquidity management is a complex balancing of risks and returns. Banks today differ considerably not only in their liquidity needs and sources but also in the extent to which they use different liquidity management strategies. As banks expand their asset base, changes in liquidity management should be considered. Also, changes in bank condition may require bank management to modify its approach to liquidity.

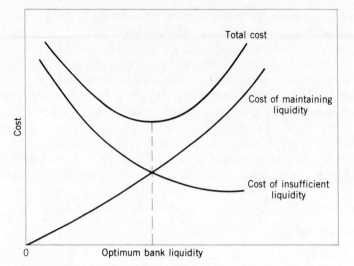

FIGURE 4.2 Trading off the costs of maintaining liquidity against the cost of insufficient liquidity.

Regulatory View of Bank Liquidity

Regulators are concerned with the adequacy of a bank's liquidity, in contrast to the least cost liquidity strategy. The criteria used by the three federal regulatory agencies (Federal Reserve, Comptroller of the Currency, and FDIC) under the 1978 Uniform Interagency Bank Rating System to evaluate bank liquidity are as follows:

Among the factors in evaluating liquidity are the availability of assets readily convertible into cash, the bank's formal and informal

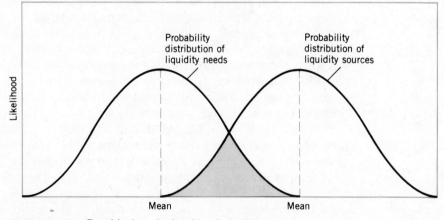

FIGURE 4.3 Graphical analysis of bank liquidity.

commitments for future lending or investment, the structure and volatility of deposits, the reliance on interest-sensitive funds including money market instruments and other sources of borrowing, and the ability to adjust rates on loans when rates on interest-sensitive sources of funds fluctuate. The examiner-analyst will review the frequency and level of borrowings and include judgments of the bank's ability to sustain any level of borrowings over the business cycle or to attract new sources of funds.[1]

The Uniform Bank Performance Report (UBPR) published by the Federal Financial Institutions Examination Council gives liquidity analyses of individual banks, as well as different groupings of banks. Table 4.6 shows selected figures from UBPR liquidity analyses for all insured U.S. commercial banks during the period 1982 to 1986. Temporary investments are money market instruments, core deposits are relatively stable sources of deposits normally under $100,000, and volatile liabilities are large CDs and purchased deposits (i.e., certificates placed by brokers) and nondeposit sources of funds. Banks with larger percentage holdings of temporary investments and core deposits, and lesser percentage holdings of volatile liabilities, would generally be considered more liquid than otherwise. Applying these criteria to Table 4.6, it would appear that liquidity has increased recently, especially between 1985 and 1986. The liquidity ratios confirm this trend. The lower portion of Table 4.6 shows percentage change information from year to year. Notice that the variability over time of securities over 1 year and volatile liabilities is particularly pronounced. This is because these sources of funds are often utilized to meet unexpected liquidity demands.

Although not shown in Table 4.6, regulators also consider the loan mix of the bank in judging liquidity, as well as other potential factors that could be relevant. For example, a bank with a relatively risky loan portfolio financed by brokered deposits would be suspected of extreme liquidity risk in the sense that it is "reaching" for interest income on risky loans with "hot" deposits, which are relatively expensive and can disappear overnight. If either loan problems occur or the brokered deposits cannot be rolled over, the bank would suffer a severe liquidity crisis. It is therefore important to distinguish between operational liquidity and crisis liquidity management. The former term applies to liquidity practice in normal everyday operations, whereas the latter type of liquidity relates to a problem situation that threatens the bank's solvency. Referring to the preceding example, the bank may be considered operationally liquid but relatively illiquid in a crisis situation.

The variety of data collected by federal regulators to gauge bank liquidity is indicative of the fact that it is a multidimensional concept. No single index is currently available that captures all of the factors included in an evaluation of

---

[1] Federal Reserve Bank of New York, "A New Supervisory System for Rating Banks," *Quarterly Review*, Summer 1978, p. 50.

TABLE 4.6
UBPR LIQUIDITY ANALYSIS OF ALL INSURED U.S. COMMERCIAL BANKS

Percent of Total Assets	*12/31/82*	*12/31/83*	*12/31/84*	*12/31/85*	*12/31/86*
Temporary investments	19.23%	18.48%	18.80%	19.13%	20.37%
Core deposits	77.31	78.73	77.72	77.70	78.68
Volatile liabilities	12.38	11.07	12.12	12.30	11.69
Liquidity Ratios:					
Temporary investments to volatile liabilities	238.47	271.53	255.37	260.75	292.92
Temporary investments less volatile liabilities to assets	6.70	7.21	6.61	6.76	8.54
Net loans and leases to deposits	56.93	56.85	59.49	58.76	56.62
Net loans and leases to core deposits	65.57	64.71	68.82	68.45	65.56
Net loans and leases to assets	49.73	49.95	52.44	52.02	50.43
Percent Change In:					
Temporary investments	24.16	13.11	17.56	15.53	19.99
Securities over 1 year	9.85	13.52	−5.62	11.30	8.41
Net loans and leases	9.03	11.29	14.48	6.49	4.66
Core deposits	9.91	12.98	7.64	7.56	8.86
Volatile liabilities	15.82	1.78	22.96	11.33	3.90
Total assets	9.87	10.60	8.51	7.28	7.36

Source. Adapted from Federal Financial Institutions Examination Council, *Uniform Bank Performance Report,* 1986.

liquidity, including the liquidity of assets, stability of liabilities, access to borrowed funds, and liquidity needs. Instead, each bank must be analyzed on an individual basis.

SUMMARY

Liquidity management involves estimating future expected liquidity needs and then planning to meet those needs by converting assets to cash, acquiring external funds, or both. To estimate liquidity needs the sources and uses approach can be used to evaluate the effects of deposit inflows and outflows and changing loan demands on bank liquidity. The structure-of-deposits method is another way to estimate liquidity needs, and focuses on the stability of deposits as a source of funds.

Once liquidity needs are estimated, bank management must plan to meet those needs. Asset liquidity is a traditional approach, and liability liquidity is a more modern approach. One advantage of asset liquidity over liability liquidity is that it offers a reserve to cover unexpected liquidity problems. In line with this thinking, the Federal Reserve requires under Regulation D that cash reserves be carried by banks. Contemporaneous reserve requirement (CRR) accounting procedures must be used for transactions deposits, whereas lagged reserve requirement (LRR) procedures must be applied to nonpersonal time deposits and Eurocurrency liabilities. Banks also hold secondary reserves of money market instruments that may be quickly converted to cash with little or no capital loss. Use of cash and short-term financial instruments to meet liquidity needs does not affect the capital position of the bank, whereas liability liquidity can affect the bank's capital position, which must be sufficient to satisfy regulatory requirements.

Liability liquidity enables the bank to shift funds from lower-earning money market instruments to higher-earning loans and investment securities. It also tends to increase the financial flexibility of the bank in dealing with liquidity needs. If it is cheaper to acquire funds than it is to liquidate assets to finance new loans, the former should naturally be used, barring the influence of other factors in the decision. Liability management of liquidity needs is not without risks, however. Debt interest obligations rise as a percentage of total assets, which tends to increase the bank's exposure to interest rate risk, as well as its financial risk because of increased financial leverage.

Optimally, bank managers must weigh the cost of maintaining liquidity against the cost of insufficient liquidity in an attempt to minimize the total costs of liquidity management. By contrast, regulators are more concerned with the adequateness of the bank's liquidity, as measured in the Uniform Bank Performance Report (UBPR) and by bank examiners.

IMPORTANT CONCEPTS

asset liquidity

bank liquidity ratio

bankers' acceptance

capital adequacy

capital market securities

commercial paper

computation period

contemporaneous reserve accounting

controllable assets

controllable liabilities

correspondent banks

Eurocurrency deposits

Eurocurrency liabilities

federal agency securities

federal funds

federal funds rate

financial risk

funds management

interest rate risk

lagged reserve accounting

liability liquidity

liquidity risk

maintenance period

money market approach

municipal securities

negotiable certificates of deposit

nonpersonal time deposits

noncontrollable assets

noncontrollable liabilities

primary reserve requirements

primary reserves

repurchase agreements

reservable deposits

secondary reserve requirements

secondary reserves

sources and uses of funds method

sources and uses of funds statement

Uniform Bank Performance Report (UBPR)

vault cash

REFERENCES

Binder, Barrett F. et al., *Assets/Liability and Funds Management at U.S. Commercial Banks,* A Research Report Prepared for the Bank Administration Institute's Accounting and Finance Commission, Rolling Meadows, Ill.: Bank Administration Institute, 1982.

Bradley, Stephen P. and Dwight B. Crane, *Management of Bank Portfolios,* New York.: Wiley, 1975.

Goodfriend, Marvin, "The Promise and Pitfalls of Contemporaneous Reserve Requirements for the Implementation of Monetary Policy," *Economic Review,* Federal Reserve Bank of Richmond, May/June 1984, pp. 3–12.

Rose, John T., "An Analysis of Federal Reserve System Attrition Since 1960," Staff Study No. 93, Washington, DC: Board of Governors of the Federal Reserve System.

Rose, Peter S. and Donald R. Fraser, *Financial Institutions,* Second Edition, Plano, TX: Business Publications, Inc., 1985.

QUESTIONS

4.1. What is the first step in any bank liquidity analysis? Discuss two methods of accomplishing this first step.

4.2. Why has asset management been less emphasized over the last 20 years?

4.3. When would asset liquidity be preferred to liability liquidity?

4.4. Why are legal reserves considered a tax on banks?

4.5. What are lagged reserve requirements? If there is a deficiency of legal reserves, what is the penalty?

4.6. What are contemporaneous reserve requirements? How is vault cash counted in maintaining reserves using CRR?

4.7. How are reserve requirements calculated for MMDAs?

4.8. How do small and large banks differ in the management of their money positions?

4.9. What is the "money market approach" to liquidity management?

4.10. Discuss the risks and returns associated with using liability management to handle liquidity needs.

4.11. What is funds management? What does it seek to do?

4.12. Discuss optimality in bank liquidity management. How does uncertainty affect optimal bank liquidity?

4.13. How do regulators evaluate bank liquidity? How much liquidity is adequate?

4.14. How does operational liquidity differ from crisis liquidity management?

4.15. If liquid assets and liabilities in period t divided by estimated liquidity needs in period t is between zero and one, might there be a problem with bank liquidity?

EXHIBIT 4.1
SOURCES AND USES OF FUNDS STATEMENT

End of Month	Estimated Total Loans	Estimated Total Deposits
June	$180,000	$190,000
July	190,000	180,000
August	210,000	190,000
September	240,000	200,000
October	200,000	210,000
November	180,000	200,000
December	170,000	190,000

PROBLEMS

4.1. (a) From the Sources and Uses of Funds Statement in Exhibit 4.1 calculate the estimated changes in loans and deposits from month-to-month, as well as the estimated liquidity need.

(b) Given the results of part a above, in which months does the bank have excess or deficient liquidity? If there is a deficiency, what sources of liquidity are there to meet the liquidity need? In the month(s) in which there is excess liquidity, what uses of funds are there to avoid holding too much idle cash?

(c) Given the information in Exhibit 4.2, calculate the bank's ratio of estimated liquidity sources to liquidity needs. Is there a possibility that the bank will have a liquidity problem at some time in the coming months?

EXHIBIT 4.2
ESTIMATED LIQUIDITY NEEDS AND SOURCES OF LIQUIDITY

End of Month	Estimated Liquidity Needs	Asset Liquidity	Estimated Liability Liquidity
June	$ 0	3,000	5,000
July	(10,000)	4,000	10,000
August	20,000	4,000	5,000
September	10,000	3,000	3,000
October	30,000	2,000	5,000
November	(10,000)	3,000	10,000
December	(10,000)	4,000	10,000

4.2. Given the following deposit data, calculate the total reserves required:

	Average Dollar Amount (in millions) in Computation Period
Net transactions accounts	
0-$50.0 million	$45.0
Over 50.0 million	30.0
Nonpersonal time deposits	
Less than 1.5 years (maturity)	20.0
1.5 years or more (maturity)	5.0
Eurocurrency liabilities	
All types	2.0

INVESTMENT MANAGEMENT

As a general rule, investment securities are held by commercial banks to produce income in the form of interest paid and capital gains, rather than to provide liquidity. Hence, investment securities are a residual commitment, funded after the bank has adequately met primary and secondary reserves' needs. This residual characteristic is most evident in the cyclical nature of purchases and sales of investment securities. During recessionary periods when demand for commercial credit is relatively low, investment securities are a good alternative source of income. As economic recovery proceeds and loan demand increases, maturing investment securities can be rolled over into loans, or shorter-term securities may be sold to fund higher-earning loan or investment security opportunities. To some extent, therefore, it is fair to say that investment securities provide a tertiary reserve of funds to meet the liquidity needs of banks.

Aside from this residual role, investment securities play other roles in bank management. For example, they may be pledged as collateral on public deposits of federal, state, and local governments, borrowing from Federal Reserve banks, and securities sold under agreement to repurchase. They may also be used to reduce federal income taxes. Because municipal securities issued by state and local governments are exempt from federal income taxes, they provide a means of reducing bank taxes. Investment securities may also be purchased to increase the diversification of the bank's total asset portfolio or to take advantage of an upward-sloping yield curve, both of which are portfolio adjustments that attempt to maximize return per unit risk. In the present chapter we overview investment policies and goals, types of investment securities, evaluating investment risk, and investment strategies.

DEVELOPING INVESTMENT POLICIES AND GOALS

Bank investment policy should be formally established so that managers can make decisions that are consistent with the overall goals of the organization. In general, bank policy should be to maximize the return per unit risk on the investment portfolio of securities, although regulatory requirements, lending needs, tax laws, liquidity sources, and other factors that could limit return/risk performance constrain maximization to some extent. Bank policy should have sufficient flexibility to enable it to shift investment goals in response to changes in financial and economic conditions and competition from rival institutions. For example, the bank must decide how to divide assets between liquidity and securities investment. Higher asset liquidity reduces the risk of missing profitable lending opportunities because of a shortfall of available funds; however, higher returns on foregone investment opportunities are normally sacrificed. Liability management tends to decrease the emphasis on asset liquidity (as discussed in the previous chapter), which implies that investment securities are more likely to comprise a significant part of the asset base of today's banks. Furthermore, the volatile interest rate environment of the 1970s and early 1980s caused the potential risks and returns on investment securities to increase substantially in comparison with the rest of the post-World War II era. Investment policies, therefore, can have a significant influence on overall bank profitability.

The investment policy should be written out as a guide to managers in allocating responsibilities and setting investment goals. The size and general composition of the investment security portfolio will influence the number and qualifications of bank personnel involved in investment operations. Managers should establish written goals that can subsequently be reviewed to evaluate portfolio performance.

Large banks with assets of more than $300 million or so need to devote greater effort toward developing investment policies and goals than do smaller institutions. One reason for this is simply the relatively larger amount of funds committed to investment securities. Another reason is that many smaller banks follow the investment recommendations of larger, correspondent banks, in addition to subscribing to the many investment services these larger banks may offer (e.g., safekeeping of financial instruments, trading services, and computer portfolio analyses). Thus, larger institutions have more than their own portfolios at stake in the securities investment area.

TYPES OF INVESTMENT SECURITIES

Investment securities can be arbitrarily defined as those securities with maturities exceeding 1 year. Two categories of securities dominate over 90 percent of bank investment portfolios—U.S. government and agency securities, and obligations of states and political subdivisions, or municipal securities. Other bonds and equity securities are heavily restricted by regulations (e.g., high-quality corporate bonds are allowed but are subject to restrictions, and common stock investment is not permitted under the Glass–Steagall Act, a part of the 1933 Banking Act).

U.S. Government and Agency Securities

U.S. Treasury Securities

Most Treasury notes and bonds purchased by banks have maturities ranging from 1 to 5 years, so it is likely that these securities are purchased as a residual commitment of funds to meet expected future liquidity needs. Unlike Treasury bills, which are sold at a discount and pay no coupon interest, Treasury notes and bonds are coupon-bearing instruments, consistent with their income function. Because the market for Treasuries in the 1- to 5-year range is relatively deep and broad, these securities provide an extra measure of bank liquidity. Additionally, these securities serve to secure both deposits of public monies (e.g., tax and loan accounts of the U.S. Treasury) and loans from Federal Reserve banks, and they are widely accepted for use in repurchase agreements.

Agency Securities

Many federal agencies issue securities that are not direct obligations of the U.S. Treasury but nonetheless are federally sponsored or guaranteed. Some examples of federal agencies are the Government National Mortgage Association (GNMA), Federal Home Loan Mortgage Corporation (FHLMC), Federal Housing Administration (FHA), Veterans Administration (VA), Farm Credit Administration (FCA), Federal Land Banks (FLB), and Small Business Administration (SBA). Ginnie Mae's (GNMAs), for instance, represent a claim against interest earnings on a pool of FHA and VA mortgages issued by private mortgage institutions. The principal and interest on these so-called pass-throughs are guaranteed by the full faith and credit of the U.S. government. Similar securities issued by the Federal National Mortgage Association (Fannie Mae's, or FNMAs) and the Mortgage Guarantee Insurance Corporation (Maggie Mae's, or MGICs) and other agencies represent claims on mortgage pools; however, because FNMA is a federally sponsored agency and MGIC is a private mortgage bank, FNMA securities have lower interest rates than do MGIC securities.

In recent years banks have increased their purchases of agency securities as a percentage of total U.S. government securities. The major reason for this trend is that agencies earn a slightly better yield than do Treasuries without sacrificing much liquidity, because secondary markets for agencies have become fairly well developed over the last 20 years.

Municipal Securities

Municipal securities are issued by state and local governments to finance various public works, such as roads, bridges, schools, fire departments, parks, and so on. They normally offer higher yields than do U.S. governments and agency securities because they are exposed to default risk. General obligation municipal bonds (GOs) are backed by the "full faith and credit" of the taxing governmental unit. Revenue bonds are somewhat riskier than GOs because they are backed by the earning power of a public project, such as a toll road. The supply of revenue bonds has risen in recent years because of the desire by communities to borrow funds and thereby defer taxation.

Taxes

The primary advantage of "munis" compared with other securities is their exemption from federal income taxes (as well as from state income taxes if issued by a governmental unit within the state). To compare a municipal security to a government security, the pretax equivalent rate of return on a municipal security can be calculated as follows:

$$\text{Pretax equivalent rate of return} = \frac{\text{Municipal bond yield to maturity}}{1 - \text{marginal tax rate of investor}} \tag{5.1}$$

For example, if the yield-to-maturity on a 5-year municipal bond were 6 percent and the bank's marginal tax rate (applicable to the last taxable dollar earned) were 40 percent, the pretax equivalent rate of return would be $6/(1 - .4) = .10$, or 10 percent. It should be noted, however, that under the Tax Reform Act of

1986 not all munis are exempt from taxes (e.g., private activity bonds are taxable).

Municipal bond investment can be used to reduce bank income taxes. For example, consider the following short-form income statement for a bank:

Total interest on securities	$1,000[a]
Municipal bond interest	600
Other securities' interest	400
Total interest on loans	2,000
Total operating income	3,000
Total interest expenses	(2,100)
Total noninterest expenses	(300)
Total operating expenses	(2,400)
Net operating income	600
Less municipal bond interest	(600)
Taxable income	0
Less taxes	(0)
Net income after taxes	0

[a] In thousands.

Notice that net operating income (NOI) is just offset by municipal interest earnings such that the bank does not have any taxable income. If NOI were less than municipal interest earned, the bank would obtain no benefit from the tax exemption on munis. This type of situation occurred for many U.S. banks in the 1980s, because profit margins narrowed due to deregulation, regional economic doldrums, and farming sector problems. Under the Tax Reform Act of 1986, however, banks are now subject to more stringent minimum corporate taxes, which are designed to ensure taxation of profitable businesses (including banks). Consequently, some amount of municipal bond income may be subject to taxes under the new tax law.

Of course, at least from a tax management perspective, bank management should not hold municipal securities beyond the point at which interest earnings of munis exceed net operating income. For various reasons, such as liquidity needs and lending opportunities, management may opt to hold smaller quantities of municipal securities than needed to eliminate taxes. In this case taxes can possibly be reduced by other means, including utilizing leasing, making loans subject to foreign tax credits, timing loan and security losses, and accelerating depreciation.

Finally, the Tax Reform Act of 1986 has made the purchase of municipal securities somewhat less attractive than in the past. Prior to the Act, 80 percent of municipal bond interest expense was exempt from federal taxes. Under the new law this deduction is eliminated.

Corporate Bonds

A corporate bond is a long-term debt security issued by a private corporation. Because the historical failure rate of corporations far exceeds the default rate by state and local governments on their debt obligations, it is necessary to evaluate carefully the default risk of this type of bond. Moody's and Standard & Poor's publish letter grades (similar to those discussed previously for municipal bonds) that are useful in gauging corporate bonds' credit quality. Further financial analysis of the firm's accounting statements over the last 5 years can provide additional information about a corporation's credit risk.

Prior to the 1980s, commercial banks did not purchase corporate bonds unless their yield exceeded the pretax equivalent yield on a municipal bond. As a bank continues to purchase municipal bonds, at some point its marginal tax rate will fall below the full statutory tax rate, which normally causes the corporate yield to exceed the pretax munis yield. Increased purchases of corporate bonds in recent years indicate that this has happened to many banks.

Recent Portfolio Composition

Table 5.1 shows the composition of the securities portfolio of all insured U.S. commercial banks at year end during the 5-year period 1982–1986. Securities with maturities over 1 year comprised about 20 percent of total assets, which was approximately equal to the percentage of temporary investments, defined as interest-bearing bank balances, federal funds sold, trading accounts assets,

TABLE 5.1

COMPOSITION OF SECURITIES PORTFOLIO FOR ALL U.S. COMMERCIAL BANKS: 1982–1986

Balance Sheet Composition	1982	1983	1984	1985	1986
A. As a Percent of Total Assets					
Total loans	50.82%	50.13%	52.34%	53.23%	52.06%
Securities over 1 year	20.28	20.73	19.19	17.82	18.13
Temporary investments	18.58	18.78	18.20	18.72	19.79
B. As a Percent of Total Securities					
U.S. Treasury and agency securities	63.30%	63.38%	69.67%	67.44%	68.17%
Municipal securities	34.84	29.42	27.18	28.53	24.54
All other securities	0.45	0.51	0.73	0.90	3.49
Securities under 1 year	31.91	34.01	37.36	34.51	32.83
Securities 1 to 5 years	47.43	47.87	45.54	46.54	43.49
Securities 5 to 10 years	12.64	11.81	10.84	12.62	14.04
Securities over 10 years	6.86	4.04	3.42	3.41	6.31

Source. *Uniform Bank Performance Report,* Federal Financial Institutions Examination Council, Washington, D.C., 1987.

and debt securities with maturities of less than 1 year. The mix of total securities was dominated by U.S. Treasury and agency securities, which normally accounted for 63 to 70 percent of total securities during this 5-year period. Municipal securities accounted for 25 to 35 percent of total securities. In this regard, banks held more municipal securities in 1982 (which was marked by a recession) and gradually decreased their holdings of munis during the steady but slow economic expansion from 1983 to 1986. All other securities, which are corporate bonds for the most part, were less than 1 percent of total securities in all years, except 1986, in which this category jumped to about 3.5 percent. This sudden change seems to indicate that commercial banks were attempting to increase their portfolio yields by shifting from municipal securities to corporate bonds.

Of total securities held, about 32 to 37 percent had maturities of less than 1 year and, therefore, were purchased primarily for liquidity purposes. The majority of securities, about two-thirds, had maturities exceeding 1 year and may be considered the investment portfolio. Of these securities, about 75 percent had maturities in the range of 1 to 5 years. Thus, most investment securities will mature at different times within one business cycle. This provides banks with some degree of flexibility in their allocation of funds throughout the business cycle.

EVALUATING INVESTMENT RISK

The investment risk involved in purchasing securities can be evaluated either on an individual security basis or in the context of the total asset portfolio of the bank. Thus, both security-specific and portfolio considerations should be taken into account to understand the risk of investment securities.

Security-Specific Risk

Default Risk

Default risk is the probability that promised payment of interest and principal will not be made on time. In general, municipal and corporate bonds (and some agency bonds) have greater credit risk than do federal government securities. As already mentioned, Standard and Poor's and Moody's both provide credit-risk ratings that indicate the long-run probability of timely payment of promised interest and principal. Bonds are assigned letter ratings by Moody's/S&P's as follows:

Aaa/AAA   Highest-grade bonds that have almost no probability of default

Aa/AA   High-grade bonds having slightly lower credit quality than triple-A bonds

A/A	Upper-medium-grade bonds that are partially exposed to possible adverse economic conditions
Baa/BBB	Medium-grade bonds that are borderline between definitely sound and subject to speculative elements, depending on economic conditions

Junk bonds

Ba/BB	Lower-medium-grade bonds that bear significant default risk should difficult economic conditions prevail
B/B, Caa/CCC, Ca/CC, C/C	Speculative investments of varying degree that have questionable credit quality
DDD, DD, D	Bonds with these ratings are in default and differ only in terms of their probable salvage value

Except in rare instances (e.g., a bond may have been downgraded subsequent to its purchase), banks restrict themselves to investment-grade securities, which fall within the "prudent-man" rule of law.

Bond prices move inversely to credit risk, which means that lower-quality bonds have higher yields on average than do higher-quality bonds. This difference in yield between low- and high-quality bonds (or yield spread) tends to vary with economic conditions. During recessionary periods, when default is perceived to be most likely to occur, yield spreads are greater than they are during economic expansions. For bank management, this cyclical behavior of yield spreads implies that lower-quality bonds offer relatively favorable yields per unit of risk during recessionary periods (when loan demand is depressed and the bank may have excess cash to invest). Municipal bonds purchased during an economic downturn could be timed to mature at different points in the future in order to provide added liquidity throughout the expansionary phase of the business cycle.

Bank managers need to consider the effect of default risk on bond prices to assess the yield-to-maturity being offered. The pricing equation for a typical bond can be stated as follows:

$$P = \sum_{t=1}^{m} \frac{\text{Promised coupon payments}}{(1 + YTM)^t} + \frac{\text{Promised par}}{(1 + YTM)^m} \tag{5.2}$$

where P = the current market price of the bond maturing in period m, and YTM = the promised yield-to-maturity. The promised coupon payment is equal to the coupon rate stated in the bond indenture agreement multiplied by the par (or principal) value of the bond. Notice that the yield-to-maturity is the rate of return that sets the present value of promised cash flows equal to the current price of the bond. Thus, yield-to-maturity is mathematically derived from the contractural terms of the bond.

To evaluate the effect of default risk on bond prices (and, therefore, on yields-to-maturity), equation (5.2) needs to be recast in expected value terms. In this respect, equation (5.2) can be equivalently written as:

$$P = \sum_{t=1}^{m} \frac{\text{Expected coupon payments}}{[1 + E(R)]^t} + \frac{\text{Expected par}}{[1 + E(R)]^m} \qquad (5.3)$$

where $E(R)$ = the expected rate of return. Expected coupon payments can be defined as $P_t \times$ (Promised Coupon Payment) + $(1 - P_t) \times$ (Liquidation Value of the Promised Coupon Payment), with P_t = the probability of receiving promised payments in period t, $(1 - P_t)$ = the probability that the bond will default. The expected par value can be calculated in a similar way by substituting the promised par value of the bond and the liquidation value of the promised par in the preceding expression. It is clear from equation (5.3) that, as the probability of payment declines, causing expected cash flows to decrease, bond prices should decline. In turn, the expected rate of return, as well as the yield-to-maturity, increase as default risk increases.

The difference between the yield-to-maturity with positive default risk and the yield-to-maturity on a riskless bond similar in all other respects is known as the yield spread. The pricing equation for a riskless security such as a U.S. Treasury security can be written as:

$$P = \sum_{t=1}^{m} \frac{\text{Riskless coupon payments}}{(1 + r_f)^t} + \frac{\text{Riskless par}}{(1 + r_f)^m} \qquad (5.4)$$

where r_f = the riskless rate of return as proxied by the U.S. Treasury yield-to-maturity. Given that the value of bond, or P, is the same in the preceding equations, the yield spread for a bond with default risk is $YTM - r_f$. Thus, yield spread has two components: the difference $YTM - E(R)$ is attributable to default risk itself, and the difference $E(R) - r_f$ is due to risk-averse behavior by investors (i.e., $E(R) = r_f$ for investors that are indifferent to risk). These components suggest that in purchasing bonds with default risk, bank management should consider not only the default risk of particular bonds under consideration, but also their preference for bearing default risk.

As a simple example, assume that a 1-year risky bond promises to pay $100 coupon at year end, par value is $1,000, and its market price is $900. Using equation (5.2), we have $980 = ($100 + $1,000)/(1 + YTM). Solving for the yield-to-maturity, we get YTM = 12.24 percent. If the probability of receiving promised coupon and par payments is estimated by bank management to be .90, and there is therefore a probability of .10 that the bond will default and that investors will instead receive the liquidation value of the bond equal to $700, the expected value of these cash flows can be calculated as .90 ($1,100) + .10

($700) = \$1,060. Using equation (5.3), we have \$980 = \$1,060/[1 + E(R)]. Solving for the expected rate of return, we now get $E(R) = 8.16$ percent. If the 1-year Treasury rate is 7.00 percent, then the yield spread, or $YTM - r_f$, equals 12.24 percent − 7.00 percent = 5.24 percent. The portion of this yield spread that is due to default risk, or $YTM - E(R)$, equals 12.24 percent − 8.16 percent = 4.08 percent, and the portion attributable to the risk preferences of investors, or $E(R) - r_f$, equals 8.16 percent − 7.00 percent = 1.16 percent.

Price Risk

Price risk refers to the inverse relationship between changes in the level of interest rates and the price of securities. This relationship is particularly relevant to bank managers of investment securities, because securities purchased when there is slack loan demand and interest rates are relatively low may need to be sold later at a capital loss (to meet loan demand) in a higher interest rate environment. In light of this potential pitfall, securities should be timed to mature during anticipated future business-cycle periods of increased loan demand. Bonds maturing beyond 5 years normally fall outside of this range and so are not generally emphasized in the investment portfolio. Moreover, because the yield curve tends to be upward-sloping and to flatten out after about 5 years, there is typically little income incentive to purchase securities beyond the 5-year range.

When interest rates are relatively high and the expansionary phase of the business cycle is peaking out, purchasing securities with terms longer than 5 years may well be justified. At such times loan demand is beginning to fall as business firms decide that interest rates are so high that borrowing would not be profitable (i.e., the net present value of projects declines as interest rates rise and expectations for future business revenues fall). The next-best income-producing alternative is to purchase long-term securities. Earning high yields for an extended period of time is clearly one benefit of purchasing such securities, because interest rates will probably decline during a downturn in business activity. Another (although perhaps less obvious) benefit is that if these long-term securities are later sold to meet load demand (for example), a capital gain could be realized, because interest rates will likely be lower than they were when the securities were originally purchased. The longer the term-to-maturity of the securities that are sold, the larger this capital gain would be. Thus, longer-term securities may be purchased as an aggressive approach toward price risk. Such an approach is not without its potential pitfalls, because there are uncertainties in forecasting both expected future interest rates and business cycle movements. Bank management needs to weigh the expected returns against the expected risks in order to evaluate price risk properly in this situation.

To evaluate the amount of price risk on a bond, it is necessary to consider not only the expected change in interest rates but also the duration of the bond. As discussed in Chapter 2, duration is a measure of bond maturity that considers the timing of cash flows. The change in price, or ΔP, caused by a change in the level of interest rates, or Δi, equals $P \times D \times \Delta i$, where P is the original price of the bond, and D is the duration of the bond. Thus, if a bond currently selling for \$1,000 has a duration of 5 years and interest rates are expected to increase by 2 percent in the coming year, the bond's price will decline by approximately \$100 (i.e., \$1,000 $\times$ 5 $\times$ .02). Because high-coupon bonds have shorter durations than do low-coupon bonds of the same yield and term-to-maturity, high-coupon bonds have relatively less price risk.

A prerequisite to utilizing the concept of duration to evaluate the price of securities in the investment portfolio is the estimation of expected future changes in interest rates. In this regard, it is helpful to examine the yield curve. Figure 5.1 shows the yield curve for U.S. Treasury securities as of June 30, 1986.

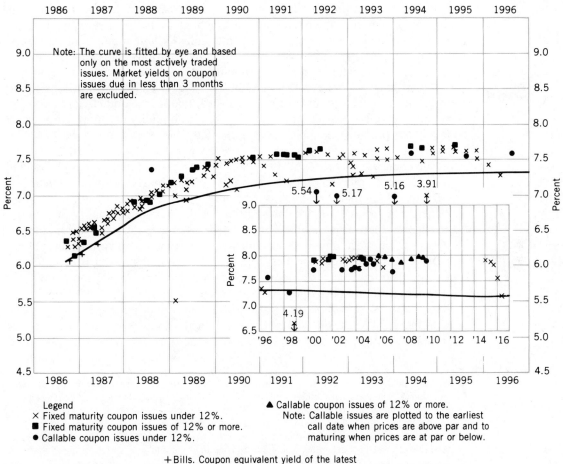

FIGURE 5.1 Yields of Treasury securities, June 30, 1986 (based on closing bid quotations). *Source*. U.S. Treasury Bulletin, Washington, D.C.

According to the **expectations theory** of the yield curve, the following geometric average relationship is hypothesized to hold between long- and short-term interest rates over time:

$$(1 + {}_0R_2) = \sqrt{(1 + {}_0R_1)(1 + {}_1r_2)} \tag{5.5}$$

where ${}_0R_2$ is the 2-year (spot) rate at the present time, ${}_0R_1$ is the 1-year (spot) rate at the present time, and ${}_1r_2$ is the 1-year (future implicit) rate that will exist 1 year from now. Given that ${}_0R_2 = 10$ percent and ${}_0R_1 = 9$ percent, then the rate ${}_1r_2$ can be calculated to be 11 percent; that is $(1 + .10)^2/(1 + .09) = 1 + .11$. Thus, 1-year interest rates can be expected to increase by about 2 percent within the next year.[1]

It is advisable to adjust the interest rate forecast based on the expectations theory for other possible influences on yields over time. One factor is the **liquidity preference** of lenders in the financial market. Risk-averse lenders prefer to lend funds for short periods of time, unless a premium is paid for foregoing greater liquidity and lending funds for longer periods. This added return, or premium, is known as a liquidity premium.[2]

Many analysts believe that liquidity premiums cause expectations theory forecasts to be biased upward or downward; that is, the actual yield curve is a summation of the expectations yield curve plus liquidity premiums. For example, in our previous example, ${}_0R_2 = $ expected yield on 2-year bonds + liquidity premium. If the liquidity premium were 0.5 percent, the expected 2-year rate would equal 9.5 percent (i.e., $10 = .095 + .005$). Substituting this adjusted long-term rate into equation (5.5), the new forecast for the 1-year rate next year is 10 percent, which means interest rates can be expected to increase by 1 percent, rather than 2 percent before accounting for the potential liquidity premium.

Another factor that could affect yields over time is the relative supplies and demands for short- and long-term financial instruments by various market participants, especially government and institutional investors. It is generally acknowledged that there are **segmented markets** in the financial system because there are different participants in the money and capital markets. Commercial banks, the Federal Reserve, and corporations requiring inventory and other working capital are the key participants in the money market, whereas life insurance companies, pension funds, and corporations demanding capital funds

---

[1] The geometric average relationship between long- and short-term interest rates shown in equation (5.5) holds because of the arbitrage activities of investors. Arbitrage would take place, for example, if the 2-year rate, or ${}_0R_2$, was greater than 9 percent. Now investors could earn higher returns by purchasing the 2-year bond, as opposed to purchasing 1-year securities in two consecutive years. Investors would sell 1-year bonds and purchase 2-year bonds. As this process proceeds, the price of the 1-year securities would fall, causing their yield to rise, and the price of the 2-year bond would rise, causing its yield to rise. Eventually, an equilibrium would be reached in which it would no longer be advantageous to purchase 2-year bonds. At this point equation (5.5) would hold once again.

[2] See J. R. Hicks (1946) for more complete discussion of liquidity premiums.

for investment projects dominate the long-term bond market. Generally speaking, short-term interest rates tend to be more volatile than long-term rates. Consequently, short-term rates will have the greatest influence on the shape of the yield curve and, therefore, on forecasts of expected future interest rates. Adjusting for liquidity preferences, for example, we earlier estimated 1-year interest rates to increase by about 1 percent next year. This forecast could be adjusted further for anticipated changes in Federal Reserve monetary policy, corporate working capital needs, and commercial bank effects on the supply and demand for money.

In sum, interest rate forecasts should account for market expectations, liquidity preferences, and market segmentation. Forecasts of potential future changes in interest rates enable investment managers to evaluate the influence of these changes on security prices. These estimates can be valuable in making purchase and sale decisions, particularly if the bank is seeking aggressively to manage the investment portfolio throughout the business cycle.

Marketability Risk

Not all bonds can be sold quickly without loss of principal. If the bank has to sell investment securities to meet liquidity demands, it will likely sell U.S. government securities before municipal and corporate bonds because the secondary market for the former securities is deeper and broader than for the latter bonds. Viewed from another perspective, to guard against marketability risk, investment managers should evaluate the likelihood of liquidity demands exceeding secondary (or liquid) reserves and then purchase investment securities with this potential added liquidity need in mind. In this regard, if municipal bonds are sold at the end of an expansion when money is tight and interest rates are relatively high, marketability risk is less than at other times because of increased interest in munis on the part of wealthy individuals in high tax brackets at such times. Note also that corporate bonds would probably not be more marketable at the peak of an expansion than they would be at other points in the business cycle and thus they can be considered to be less marketable than municipal bonds at such times.

Call Risk

Municipal and corporate bonds issued when interest rates are at relatively high levels commonly have a call provision in their indentures. The call provision gives the borrowing firm or institution the right to redeem the bond prior to maturity. The bond is callable only if the call deferment period has expired and the current price of the bond has risen to at least the call price, which exceeds the original price of the bond. As interest rates decline over time, the bond's price rises and eventually "strikes" the call price. If the call deferment period has lapsed, the bond can be redeemed. The bank's call risk in this situation is the reinvestment of the par value in bonds bearing lower interest yields. As compensation for this reinvestment risk, the indenture will state a call premium (i.e., an added "sweetener" paid to the bondholder) payable on various dates in the future. When bonds are called early, the call premium is higher, which offsets in part or whole the call risk.

When banks attempt to purchase bonds during high interest rates periods and then sell them for sizable capital gains as rates fall, call risk is especially worth evaluating. Because callable bonds have an additional element of uncertainty, they tend to offer higher yields than other bonds.

Portfolio Risk

The riskiness of investment securities should also be evaluated in a portfolio context. In this way the effect of investment securities on the risk of the bank's total portfolio of assets can be considered.

To evaluate portfolio risk, it is necessary to estimate expected rates of return and the potential variability of rates of return. The expected rate of return for an asset can be estimated by the following calculation:

$$E(R_j) = \sum_{i=1}^{n} P_i R_{ji} \tag{5.6}$$

where P_i = the probability that a particular (random) state of nature will occur (with a total of n states of nature considered), and R_{ji} = the rate of return on asset j in the ith state of the nature. Table 5.2 gives some hypothetical data and demonstrates the calculation of $E(R_j)$ using equation (5.6); that is $E(R_j) = 7$ percent.

Measuring Variability

To measure the risk of the security, the variability of the rates of return can be proxied by their standard deviation, or σ. The standard deviation is calculated

TABLE 5.2
HYPOTHETICAL CALCULATION OF THE EXPECTED RATE OF RETURN

State of Nature	P_i = Probability	R_{ji}	$P_i R_{ji}$	$R_{ji} - E(R_j)$	$[R_{ji} - E(R_j)]^2$	$P_i[R_{ji} - E(R_j)]^2$
1	.10	.05	.005	−.02	.0004	.00005
2	.20	.06	.012	−.01	.0001	.00001
3	.40	.07	.028	—	—	—
4	.20	.08	.016	.01	.0001	.00001
5	.10	.09	.009	.02	.0004	.00005
	1.00		$E(R_j) =$ .070			$\sigma^2(R_j) =$ .00012
						$\sigma(R_j) \cong$ .011

by taking the square root of the variance of returns, or $\sigma^2(R_j)$, where

$$\sigma^2(R_j) = \sum_{i=1}^{n} P_i \, [R_{ji} - E(R_j)]^2 \tag{5.7}$$

and

$$\sigma(R_j) = [\sigma^2(R_j)]^{1/2} \tag{5.8}$$

Based on these equations, Table 5.2 shows that the standard deviation of rates of return is about 1.1 percent.

Assuming that rates of return are normally distributed, $E(R_j)$ and $\sigma(R_j)$ can be used to understand the risk and return characteristics of a security. Figure 5.2 graphically depicts the probability of certain rates of return on the vertical axis and rates of return themselves on the horizontal axis. Notice that 65 (95) percent of the normal distribution falls within one (two) standard deviations of the mean, or $E(R_j)$. Given $E(R_j) = 7$ percent and $\sigma(R_j)$ 1.1 percent, we can infer that 65 percent of the time the security's rate of return will fall within the range of 5.9 to 8.1 percent, and 95 percent of the time it will be from 4.8 to 9.2 percent.

Portfolio Effects

With these risk and return concepts in hand, consider the effect of security j on the expected return and risk of the bank's assets. We define the expected return

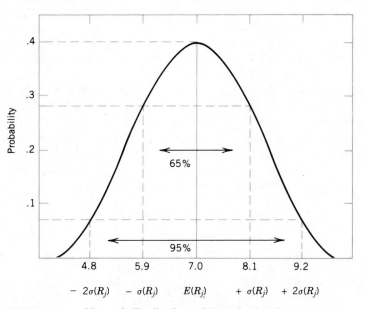

FIGURE 5.2   Normal distribution of hypothetical investment op-portunity.

and standard deviation of the bank's existing portfolio of assets *before* considering security j as $E(R_p)$ and $\sigma(R_p)$. The bank's expected rate of return and variance of rates of return can be calculated as follows:

$$E(R_{bank}) = aE(R_j) + (1 - a)\ E(R_p) \tag{5.9}$$

where a = the proportion of funds invested in security j with expected rate of return $E(R_j)$, and $(1 - a)$ = the proportion of funds invested in the existing portfolio of assets with expected rate of return $E(R_p)$, and

$$\sigma^2(R_{bank}) = a^2\sigma^2(R_j) + (1 - a)^2\sigma^2(R_p) + 2a(1 - a)COV(R_j, R_p) \tag{5.10}$$

where $COV(R_j, R_p)$ = the covariance of the rates of return of security j and portfolio p, or

$$COV(R_j, R_p) = \sum_{i=1}^{n} P_i[R_{ji} - E(R_j)]\ [R_{pi} - E(R_p)] \tag{5.11}$$

Table 5.3 shows a hypothetical example of how security j might affect the expected rate of return and risk of the bank's portfolio of assets. The existing assets are calculated to have $E(R_p)$ = 6 percent and $\sigma(R_p) \simeq 1.8$ percent. If security j were added to the asset portfolio of the bank, then $E(R_{bank})$ = 6.1 percent and $\sigma(R_{bank})$ = 1.5 percent. Thus, security j would not only increase the bank's total expected rate of return, it would also reduce the bank's risk by decreasing the standard deviation of rates of return. Note that bank risk declines both because the security's standard deviation was less than the existing portfolio's standard deviation and because the covariance term was negative. Hence, we can infer that the effect of a security on the risk of the bank's portfolio of assets is not a simple weighted average of the assets' risks (where weights are the proportional investment); instead, an adjustment must be made for the relationship of the security's pattern of rates of return to the existing portfolio's rates of return in different states of nature (i.e., the covariance term affects the bank's portfolio risk).

To elaborate on this convariance adjustment, we can redefine the last term in the variance formula shown in equation (5.10) as

$$2a(1 - a)\ COV(R_j, R_p) = 2a(1 - a)\ \rho_{jp}\sigma(R_j)\sigma(R_p) \tag{5.12}$$

where ρ_{jp} = the correlation of security j with portfolio p. If $\rho_{jp} = 1$, we say that the two patterns of rates of return are perfectly positively correlated. If $\rho < 1$, the variance measures of risk is reduced, with maximum variance reduction occurring at $\rho = -1$, which is called perfect negative correlation. The reduction of variance caused by less than perfect positive correlation is technically known as **diversification**.

TABLE 5.3
HYPOTHETICAL EXAMPLE OF HOW A SECURITY AFFECTS THE RISK AND RETURN OF THE BANK PORTFOLIO

State of Nature	P_i = Probability	$a = 10\%$ R_{ji}	$(1-a) = 90\%$ R_{pi}	$P_i[R_{pi} - E(R_p)]^2$	(1) $R_{ji} - E(R_j)$	(2) $R_{pi} - E(R_p)$	(3) (1) × (2)	P_i × (3)
1	.10	.05	.10	.00016	-.02	.04	-.0008	-.00008
2	.20	.06	.08	.00008	-.01	.02	-.0002	-.00004
3	.40	.07	.06	—	—	—	—	—
4	.20	.08	.04	.00008	.01	-.02	-.0002	-.00004
5	.10	.09	.02	.00016	.02	-.04	-.0008	-.00008

$$E(R_j) = .07 \qquad E(R_p) = .06 \qquad \sigma^2(R_p) = .00032 \qquad COV(R_j,R_p) = -.00024$$
$$\sigma(R_p) \cong .018$$

$$E(R_{bank}) = aE(R_j) + (1 - a)E(R_p)$$
$$= (.10)(.07) + (.90)(.06)$$
$$= .061$$

$$\sigma^2(R_{bank}) = a^2\sigma^2(R_j) + (1 - a)^2\sigma^2(R_p) + 2a(1 - a)COV(R_j, R_p)$$
$$= (.10)^2(.00012) + (.90)^2(.00032) + 2(.10)(.90)(-.00024)$$
$$= .0002172$$
$$\sigma(R_{bank}) \cong .015$$

A. Perfect positive correlation: $\rho_{12} = 1$

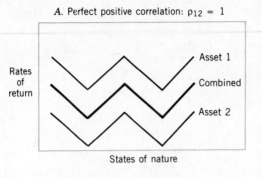

B. Perfect negative correlation: $\rho_{12} = -1$

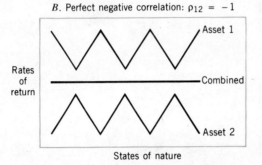

C. Positive but not perfect correlation: $0 < \rho_{12} < 1$

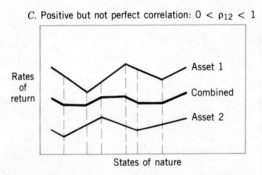

FIGURE 5.3 Assets correlation and risk reduction.

Figure 5.3 graphically depicts these different correlation possibilities and their effects on risk. The rates of return patterns for two assets of equal value considered separately in different states of nature are shown by thin lines, and their combination is shown with a bold line. The variability, or risk, of each rate of return pattern can be visually compared by observing the amount of its movement up and down over different states of nature. Figure 5.3-*A* shows that combining perfectly positively correlated assets does not reduce risk. At the other extreme, Figure 5.3-*B* shows the total elimination of risk by combining perfectly negatively correlated assets. In the real world correlations between financial assets are normally positive but not perfectly so. Figure 5.3-*C* shows that risk is reduced by combining assets with this type of correlation; that is, the combined pattern is flatter in states of nature in which the rate of return on one asset is rising while the other asset's rate is declining.

Because bank assets are restricted to debt instruments, such as bonds, commercial loans, and mortgages, and these assets' yields tend to follow interest rate changes, the correlations among bank assets' rates of return are usually highly positive. Recent evidence reported by the Federal Reserve,[3] for example, has indicated that securitization of loan markets by commercial banks and other financial institutions has caused mortgage rates to follow treasury rates more closely. A partial offset to this trend is that differences in maturity cause prices (and, therefore yields) of bank assets to be less than perfectly positively correlated as interest rate levels change over time. Because investment securities are longer term than most other bank assets, they tend to have a significant diversification effect on the bank's asset portfolio.

INVESTMENT STRATEGIES

Investment strategies should be guided by the principle that income be maximized within the context of regulations, taxes, liquidity needs, correspondent banking relationships, management expertise, and various types of investment risk. Management can choose between passive strategies that do not require active management and aggressive strategies that are specially designed to take advantage of prevailing or expected market conditions.

Passive Strategies

Two passive strategies used in managing the investment portfolio are the spaced-maturity, or ladder, approach and the split-maturity, or barbell, approach. Smaller banks commonly use these methods because they are simple to implement, and thus conserve management resources. Also, the investment goals of many small banks are often of secondary importance because the majority of their excess funds is transferred upstream to larger correspondent banks in return for financial services.

Spaced-Maturity Approach

Otherwise known as the "ladder approach," the spaced-maturity investment strategy involves spreading available investment funds equally across a specified number of periods within the bank's investment horizon. For example, if the bank wanted an investment portfolio of $10 million, and its investment horizon was 5 years, then it would purchase $2 million of 1-year securities, $2

---

[3] See Thomas D. Simpson (1988).

million of 2-year securities, and so on until the $10 million was evenly distributed over the 5-year planning period.

This strategy is not only simple to set up but also to maintain, as principal redeemed on 1-year securities coming due would be rolled over into 5-year securities to keep an evenly spaced maturity of securities over 5 years. Other advantages of this approach are that trading activity (and, therefore, transactions costs) are kept at a minimum, and an average rate of return is earned because investment securities are spread out evenly along different points in time on the yield curve. The major drawbacks of this approach are that the bank is passive with respect to interest rate conditions and that liquidity is sacrificed to some extent should loan demands exceed short-term investment securities.

Split-Maturity Approach

Another relatively conservative strategy is to purchase larger proportions of short and long-term securities and smaller proportions of intermediate-term securities. This so-called barbell approach offers a balance of higher income on the long-term securities (assuming the yield curve is upward-sloping) and good liquidity through substantial purchases of short-term securities. One way to maintain the barbell strategy is to reinvest matured short-term securities in the longest-maturity, short-term securities and sell shortest-maturity, long-term securities and reinvest in the longest-maturity, long-term securities. The periodic sales of securities result in modest capital gains or losses depending on changes in the level or shape of the yield curve. Of course, there is a trade-off here between transactions costs versus liquidity and income benefits from using the barbell strategy relative to the space-maturity strategy. Variations on the barbell strategy include holding no longer-term securities, which is known as a "front-end loaded approach," and holding no shorter-term securities, or a "back-end loaded approach." These strategies may be implemented by the bank to stress either liquidity or income, respectively, in the investment strategy.

Aggressive Strategies

Larger banks with sizable investment portfolios and more volatile loan demands than smaller banks, typically engage in one or more aggressive strategies intended to maximize their investment income. Because these strategies require a certain level of management expertise and trading activity, management must weigh the added costs against the potential benefits when selecting an appropriate strategy. In general, aggressive strategies may be classified into two groups—yield-curve strategies and bond-swapping strategies.

Yield-Curve Strategies

"Playing the yield curve" is a widely used phrase that means the bank is attempting to take advantage of expected future changes in interest rates by coordinating investment activities with the shape and level of the yield curve. When the yield curve is at a relatively low level and is upward-sloping, short-term securities are usually purchased. As interest rates rise in the months (or years) ahead, the securities are repeatedly rolled over into higher earning assets. At the same time, they provide added liquidity should investment securities be needed to meet loan demands. When the yield curve is at a relatively high level and is flat or downward-sloping in shape, the bank would switch to longer-term securities. This strategy provides higher yields to maximize interest income as well as a tax loss on the sale of shorter-term securities (to the extent that the relatively higher level of interest rates has pushed the market price of shorter-term securities below their original purchase price). Liquidity is not as relevant at this point in the business cycle because it is expected that loan demand will decline because of the high interest rates. As interest rates decline in future periods, capital gains are earned on these long-term securities because of favorable price risk. When interest rates are believed to have bottomed out, the long-term securities are sold and the principal and capital gains are rolled over into short-term securities.

This **switching** strategy in playing the yield curve is not without its potential problems, however. Market timing is pivotal to success. For example, if interest rates continued to rise after the maturity of investment securities is lengthened (in anticipation of a decline in rate levels), the bank would be forced to meet liquidity needs either by purchasing funds at increasingly higher costs or selling the long-term securities at a capital loss (plus transactions costs). Such a mistake could have a significant impact on the bank's profitability. Thus, it is recommended that some amount of short-term securities not be rolled over into longer-term securities, so that an element of liquidity is maintained in the investment portfolio.

Another approach to playing the yield curve is known as "riding the yield curve." For this strategy to work: (1) the yield curve must be upward-sloping, and (2) the level of interest rates must not be expected to move upward as much as indicated by the shape of the yield curve in the near future. According to this strategy, the investment manager would purchase securities with a longer time horizon than the investment horizon of the bank. With an upward-sloping yield curve, as the term of these long-term securities nears the investment horizon, their price would increase because shorter-term securities have lower yields, and therefore higher prices, than do longer-term securities.

To estimate the holding period yield of riding the yield curve, the following formula can be used:

$$Y_h = Y_0 + \frac{T_r(Y_0 - Y_m)}{T_h} \tag{5.13}$$

where Y_h = the holding period yield, Y_0 = the original yield on the security purchased, Y_m = the security's market yield at the end of the holding period when it is sold, T_r = the remaining maturity of the security when sold, and T_h =

the holding period equal to the lapsed time between the purchase and sale of the security. As long as the yield on the security declines from its original yield on the purchase date such that $Y_m < Y_0$, the second term on the right-hand side of equation (5.13) gives an estimate of the approximate capital gain caused by riding the yield curve. On the other hand, if interest rates increased in line with the expectations theory of the yield curve, then $Y_m = Y_0$ and $Y_h = Y_0$, or the holding period yield is the same as the original yield. Also, if interest rates increased more than expected, then $Y_m > Y_0$ and $Y_h < Y_0$, or a capital loss would cause the holding period yield to fall short of the original yield.

Obviously, playing the yield curve by using the switching strategy or by riding the yield curve requires considerable market forecasting expertise. According to expectations theory, the expected return is identical across all maturities for any holding period. Thus, playing the yield curve involves forecasting changes in interest rates that are not expected by the market as a whole. In this regard, although "outguessing" the market is surely possible, such as aggressive strategy may well be imprudent on a large scale. For this reason, playing the yield curve is a strategy that should not be overemphasized in investment management and should be coupled with one or more other investment strategies.

Bond-Swapping Strategies

Exchanging one bond for another for return and risk reasons is known as a *bond swap*. A swap may be undertaken in anticipation of future changes in interest rates or simply because the swap would clearly be a superior choice. For example, management may perform a **tax swap** if the corporate bond yield is higher than the pretax equivalent municipal bond yields currently held by the bank. If the municipal bond is sold at a capital loss, a tax savings equal to the bank's marginal tax rate multiplied by the capital loss is realized. Thus, even if the corporate and municipal pretax yields are comparable, a tax swap may still be inititated to lower the bank's tax burden. Alternatively, if the bank's marginal tax rate declined for some reason (e.g., a decline in earnings or change in applicable tax laws), the bank might choose to swap municipal bonds for corporate bonds. Opposite reasoning would apply to swapping corporate for municipal bonds.

A **substitution**, or **price**, **swap** entails selling securities comparable to the ones being purchased because the latter have a higher yield. In an efficient market, where securities' prices reflect all publicly available information, it is not common to find imbalances of this sort, but it is possible to find mispriced securities at times (i.e., a temporary market disequilibrium).[4] Trading banks that have day-to-day market operations in various securities are most likely to execute substitution swaps. A trading account must be maintained for regulatory purposes, and the resultant trading profits (and losses) must be reported as

---

[4] Fischer Black (1975) gives an excellent discussion of the implications of an efficient market to bank management in general.

a separate account in the bank's operating earnings. It should be mentioned that other portfolio profits (and losses) and associated taxes on securities are reported after net operating earnings are adjusted for federal income taxes.

A **yield-pickup**, or **coupon**, **swap** involves the exchange of a low-coupon bond for a high-coupon bond, or vice versa. The trade-off between coupon earnings and capital gains in such a swap could be influenced either by interest-rate risk (duration) differences or tax differences.

Finally, a **spread**, or **quality**, **swap** implies the exchange of two bonds with unequal risk. As in the case of substitution swaps, and abnormally low or high price for a security must prevail for this swap to be profitable. The bank would seek to sell (buy) securities that are overpriced (underpriced) and purchase (sell) securities that are correctly priced in the market. When market equilibrium is restored, the reverse market purchase and sale activities would be executed.

SUMMARY

Investment securities provide an alternative source of income for commercial banks, especially when loan demand is relatively low during slowdowns in economic activity. Bank policy should aim to maximize the return on the securities portfolio per unit of risk within regulatory and market constraints. In this regard, bank management needs to consider the tax implications of municipal securities, default risk and call risk of municipal and corporate bond securities, interest rate risk of longer-term securities, and marketability of securities. The effects of investment policy on the risk and return of the bank's total assets should also be evaluated in a portfolio context, where diversification benefits may be gained by purchasing securities with return patterns that are not perfectly positively correlated with the return patterns of other bank assets.

Once bank policy is established, an investment strategy needs to be chosen. Passive strategies, such as the spaced-maturity, or ladder, approach and the split-maturity, or barbell approach, do not require much expertise, conserve management resources, and are inexpensive to implement. Aggressive strategies, such as playing the yield curve and bond swapping, require more management expertise, involve more trading activity, and are riskier in nature than passive strategies but offer higher earnings potential.

IMPORTANT CONCEPTS

agency securities	call premium
aggressive investment strategies	call price
back-end loading approach	call provision
barbell approach	corporate bonds
bond-swapping strategies	correlation

coupon payment
coupon swap
covariance
default risk
deferment period
diversification
duration
expectations theory of yield curve
expected value of coupon payments
FHA
FHLMC
FNMAs
front-end loading approach
GNMAs
investment grade bonds
investment risk
investment securities
junk bonds
liquidity preference
market segmentation
marketability risk

MGICs
municipal bonds
par value of bond
passive investment strategies
pass-through certificates
playing the yield curve
portfolio risk
pretax equivalent rate of return
price risk
spread swap
substitution swap
switching strategy
tax swap
Treasury bills
Treasury bonds
Treasury notes
VA
yield curve strategies
yield-pickup swap
yield spread
yield-to-maturity

REFERENCES

Black, Fischer. "Bank Funds Management in an Efficient Market," *Journal of Financial Economics* 2, 1975, pp. 323–339.

Hicks, J. R. *Value and Capital,* 2nd ed. London: Oxford University Press, 1946.

Van Horne, James C. *Financial Market Rates and Flows,* 2nd edition. Englewood Cliffs, NJ: Prentice-Hall, 1984.

Simpson, Thomas D. "Developments in the U.S. Financial System Since the Mid-1970s," *Federal Reserve Bulletin,* Board of Governors of the Federal Reserve System, January 1988, pp. 1–13.

QUESTIONS

5.1. Why are Treasury bills not considered to be investment securities?

5.2. Why might agency securities be preferred to Treasury notes and bonds?

5.3. How do municipal bonds reduce taxes for a bank?

5.4. What do bond ratings indicate? How does bond yield vary with these ratings?

5.5. Why is investment policy affected by the interest rate cycle?

5.6. Why do most investment securities have maturities in the range of one-to-five years?

5.7. Why do banks generally avoid junk bonds?

5.8. Discuss two components of bond risk premiums.

5.9. Define price risk. How can a bank take advantage of price risk in a relatively high interest rate period?

5.10. Why might forecasts of future interest rates using the expectations theory of the yield curve be wrong? How would you adjust for other interest rate influences?

5.11. Why do bonds issued in relatively low interest rate periods have low call risk?

5.12. Why is call risk an important factor for an investment manager purchasing bonds in a relatively high interest rate period?

5.13. How does diversification affect portfolio return? How does it affect portfolio risk?

5.14. Show a graph of two assets that offer no diversification benefit. Also draw graphs illustrating both partial and complete diversification of risk.

5.15. What is the key to diversification?

5.16. Why might the split maturity approach to investment management be preferred to the spaced maturity approach?

5.17. What does "playing the yield curve" mean? How is it different from "riding the yield curve?"

5.18. Briefly discuss four kinds of bond swaps.

PROBLEMS

1. (a) Given a five-year municipal bond yielding 10 percent, a comparable five-year corporate bond yielding 15 percent, and a tax rate of 34 percent facing the bank, which bond should be preferred by the bank?

   (b) Given the following income statement information, calculate the bank's net income after taxes. Assume a tax rate of 34 percent on taxable income.

	(in thousands)
Total interest on securities	$2,000
Municipal bond interest	500
Other securities' interest	1,500
Total interest on loans	4,000
Total operating income	6,000
Total interest expense	(4,100)
Total noninterest expense	(900)
Total operating expense	(5,000)

2. (a) A two-year bond paying $50 coupons at the end of each year and a par value of $1,000 has a yield-to-maturity of 10 percent. Calculate the market price of the bond.

   (b) Assume that the probability of payment of coupons and par value for the bond in part (a) is as follows:

	Probability of Payment
Coupon payment at end of first year	.95
Coupon payment at end of second year	.90
Par value paid at end of second year	.90

   Assume also that coupon interest and par value are zero in default. Calculate the expected rate of return on the bond from this information and the information in part (a) above.

   (c) If the two-year Treasury rate is 6 percent, what is the yield spread, in addition to the portion of the yield spread due to default risk and the portion due to risk aversion?

3.   Given the following information about security j in the state of nature i:

State of Nature	P_i = Probability	R_{ji}
1	.10	.08
2	.25	.10
3	.30	.12
4	.25	.14
5	.10	.16

   (a) Calculate the mean and variance of security j's rate of return.

   (b) Given further the rate of return on the bank's portfolio of assets is as follows:

State of Nature	P_i	R_{pi}
1	.10	.16
2	.25	.14
3	.30	.12
4	.25	.10
5	.10	.08

   Find the mean and variance of the rates of return on the bank's portfolio of assets.

   (c) If the bank invests funds in security j such that 10 percent of its funds are allocated to security j and 90 percent of its funds are allocated to its previous portfolio of assets, what will be the mean and variance of rates of return for the bank?

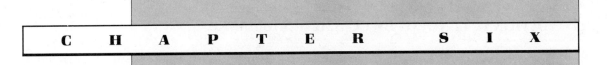
PRINCIPLES OF COMMERCIAL LENDING

This chapter examines lending activities at commercial banks and some of the practices they use in making commercial loans. Additional information about commercial lending is presented in Chapters 7 and 8. Chapters 9 and 10 deal with mortgage lending and consumer lending, respectively. International lending is the subject of Chapter 17.

TRADITIONAL LENDING BY COMMERCIAL BANKS

The first chartered commercial bank in the United States was founded in Philadelphia by Robert Morris in 1781. It was called the Bank of North America and it made loans to the federal government and to merchants. By the end of the Civil War in 1865, there were about 1,800 commercial banks. Banks in the nineteenth century typically made short-term, self-liquidating loans to businesses and provided a place for safekeeping depositor's funds. **Self-liquidating** means that the funds from the loan are used to buy, say, inventory. When the inventory is sold, the proceeds are used to repay the loan. This view of banking is presented in the following excerpts taken from lectures given at Harvard University in the late 1800s.

> "The leading wants to be provided for by banks are first, loans upon considerable scale, required by individuals embarking in enterprises beyond their own means; and second, the temporary employment of money which is not required by the owner for immediate use, or at least the means of safely keeping it.
>
> Security of the principal and the rate of return are therefore the essential considerations in the selection of investments. . . . Commercial banks must, in addition, endeavor to keep themselves in a highly liquid condition at all times. Most of the conditions of the case are best answered by the "discount" of commercial paper. . . . The time for which such obligations have to run varies . . . but in most cases is short enough to imply early repayment to the bank."[1]

The lectures went on to say that when commercial loans could not be granted in sufficient quantity, banks could invest some of their funds in U.S. government bonds and other high-quality bonds. However, bankers were cautioned not to invest in corporate stocks because stock prices were too volatile, and not to invest in mortgages because they might be difficult to sell when banks needed money. Thus the traditional view was that banks held liquid deposits and should invest those funds in short-term liquid assets.

CURRENT LENDING ROLE
OF COMMERCIAL BANKS

The current view of lending is different. As shown in Table 6.1, commercial banks today engage in a wide variety of short- and long-term lending activities. Nevertheless, three types of loans account for 87 percent of the total loans

[1] Charles F. Dunbar and Oliver M. W. Sprague. *The Theory and History of Banking,* 3rd. ed. New York: Putnam, 1922, pp. 2–29.

TABLE 6.1
TOTAL LOANS AND LEASES AT ALL COMMERCIAL BANKS
December 1987 (billions of dollars)

Type	Amount	Percentage
Commercial and industrial	$ 571.1	33.7
Real estate	577.4	34.1
Individual	322.7	19.1
Security	33.5	2.0
Nonbank financial institutions	31.8	1.9
Agricultural	31.3	1.8
State and political subdivisions	51.1	3.0
Foreign banks	8.6	0.5
Foreign official institutions	5.1	0.3
Lease financing receivables	24.1	1.4
All other loans	35.7	2.1
Total	$1,692.4	99.9%[a]

Source. Federal Reserve Bulletin, March 1988, p. A16.
[a] Figures may not add to total due to rounding.

made by banks. They are commercial and industrial loans, real estate loans, and individual loans.

Commercial and Industrial Loans

Commercial and industrial loans are loans made to business concerns to finance their day-to-day activities (e.g., inventories) and to finance their longer-term needs (e.g., plant and equipment). The maturity of these loans ranges from 1 day (called overnight loans) to 10 years or longer. More will be said about various types of commercial and industrial loans shortly.

Real Estate Loans

Real estate loans are loans for the acquisition, construction, and development of land and buildings as well as mortgage loans. **Construction and development loans** are used by real estate developers to finance the building phase of real estate projects, such as office buildings, shopping centers, and housing developments. Construction and development loans are considered temporary financing, and they may have maturities of up to 2 years or more, depending on the length of time necessary to complete the project. Once the construction phase is completed, permanent financing is obtained for the project. **Permanent financing,** or long-term financing for large commercial real estate projects is provided by some banks as well as by life insurance companies and pension plans. Many banks require the borrower to obtain a commitment for permanent financing from a long-term lender before they will make a construction loan.

This avoids the problem of the bank becoming the long-term lender if no one else will take the loan. As a general rule, life insurance companies and pension plans are longer-term investors than commercial banks.

Banks also lend money to people to buy houses. These loans are called **home mortgages**. Many home mortgage loans have an original maturity of 25 years or longer. The term *original maturity* was used because the maturity of mortgage loans declines as they are paid off over time. In addition, banks often sell their mortgage loans to other investors such as the Federal National Mortgage Association (FNMA), a government sponsored, privately owned corporation that buys and sells mortgages.

Individual Loans

Loans to individuals are frequently called **consumer loans** because the funds are used to buy consumer goods such as automobiles, appliances, and other durable goods—products that are supposed to last a long time. In addition, individuals use consumer loans to pay for vacations, medical bills, and for anything else that they can buy.

Other Loans

The remaining types of loans listed in Table 6.1 reveal that banks engage in a wide range of lending activities. They make loans to finance securities' brokers and dealers, loans to foreign banks and foreign governments, leasing and other types of loans. It can be said that banks will make any type of loan, provided (1) the funds are used for lawful purposes, (2) the loan is expected to be profitable, and (3) if the size and type of loan meet the bank's needs. A particular bank, however, may choose not to make certain types of loans as a matter of policy. Loans to foreign dealers in firearms is one example.

TYPES OF COMMERCIAL AND INDUSTRIAL LOANS

Commercial and industrial loans are used to finance the assets of business concerns. As shown in Figure 6.1, the total assets of a firm can be divided into two categories—permanent assets and temporary assets. Permanent assets include plant and equipment as well as the portion of working capital (cash, accounts receivable, and inventory) that will be sustained over time. Temporary assets include the portion of working capital that fluctuates with periodic changes in sales and revenues. For example, the inventory of Happy Days Toy Store is expected to increase before Christmas. When the toys are sold, the inventory will be reduced but the accounts receivable will increase. As these are collected and the cash is used elsewhere, working capital will be reduced.

Figure 6.1 also shows that temporary assets should be financed with temporary loans and permanent assets with permanent loans. Violating this concept

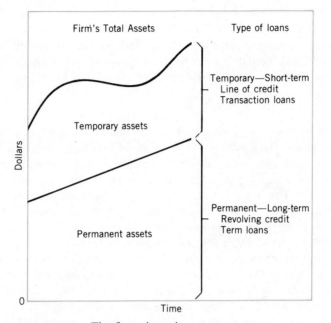

FIGURE 6.1   The financing mix.

has resulted in financial problems for both business concerns and bankers alike. For example, it does not make sense for Happy Days Toy Store to borrow funds for 5 years to finance its inventory of toys for one Christmas season. Nevertheless, some businesses attempt to do just that and some banks are willing to go along with it. This kind of a mismatch usually happens when funds are borrowed to finance both temporary and permanent assets, and the two become blended together in one package rather than being treated as separate loans. Let's examine specific types of loans, or **credit facilities** as they are called by bankers. The loans being described can be used for temporary or permanent financing, depending on their terms.

Line of Credit

A **line of credit is** an agreement between a customer and the bank, that the bank will entertain requests for a loan from that customer, but it is *not* obligated to make the loan. Under most circumstances, however, banks honor their lines of credit. A line of credit is established when the bank gives a letter to the customer stating the dollar amount of the line, the time it is in effect, and other conditions or provisions. The line of credit is the maximum amount that can be borrowed under the terms of the loan. Borrowing on lines of credit is used to finance temporary or seasonal increases in inventory and accounts receivable. When the inventory is sold, receivables are collected, and the funds are used to reduce the loan. Frequently, lenders require inventory or receivables as collateral. The line of credit is usually for 1 year, but loans made under it may be repaid on demand, in 90 days after the loan is made, or some other terms.

Sometimes short-term loans are rolled over or refinanced so often that both the firms and the banks view them as a form of long-term financing. When that occurs, long-term financing should be considered by both parties.

Revolving Loan

Revolving loans are generally used to finance borrowers' temporary and seasonal needs. They are similar to a line of credit, except that the bank *is* obligated to make the loans up to the amount of the commitment (the maximum amount of the loan) if the borrower is in compliance with the terms of the agreement. The borrower may repay the loans, and then borrow them again, up to the amount of the commitment. Revolving loans usually have a maturity of 2 years or more. Revolving loans that are automatically renewed for longer periods of time are called **evergreen facilities**. The renewal is at the option of the bank and depends on the borrower's financial condition at that time. Sometimes revolving loans are converted into term loans, which are discussed next. The provision of the loan agreement explains all the details of the loan, including commitment fees (which will be explained shortly), methods of repayment, interest rates, **compensating balances** (a percentage of the loan that must be left on deposit at the bank), **restrictive convenants** (terms limiting the borrower's actions or use of funds), and other conditions.

Term Loan

A **term loan** is usually a single loan for a stated period of time, or a series of loans on specified dates. They are used to for a specific purpose, such as acquiring machinery, renovating a building, refinancing debt, and so forth. They should not be used to finance day-to-day operations. Term loans may have an original maturity of 5 years or more. The maturity of the loan should *not* exceed the economic life of the asset being financed if that asset is being used as collateral or security for the loan. And the amount of the loan should be less than the value of the asset it is financing. The difference between the value of asset and the amount being financed is the borrower's equity. In this case, the borrower has some of his or her own funds committed to the asset, and it provides the bank a ''cushion'' in the event of default. Equally important, in the event of default, the value of the asset should exceed the amount of the loan.

Term loans generally are repaid out of the cash flow (earnings plus depreciation) being financed, and the loan may be repaid on an amortized basis or at one time. These rules can be summarized as follows: *loans can be repaid only from income or assets.* Therefore, one should determine whether there is sufficient income and/or assets before making a loan. These ''rules to good lending'' are illustrated in the top section of Figure 6.2. The point of these rules is that they help protect the bank's ''security interest'' in the loan.

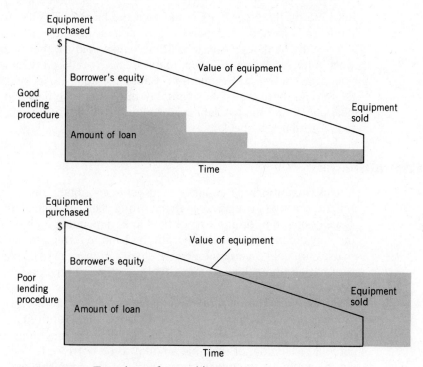

FIGURE 6.2 Term loans for machinery.

The lower section illustrates improper lending procedures—a loan that exceeds the value of the asset it is financing. In addition, the maturity of the loan exceeds the life of the asset. If the borrower defaults, when the value of the equipment exceeds the value of the loan, the bank will incur a substantial loss on this loan.

Overdrafts

An overdraft occurs when a check is written on uncollected funds. If a bank pays on a check written against uncollected balances, it is extending an unsecured loan. The loan can be for less than 1 day (**daylight overdraft**) when a check is written or funds transferred out by wire in the morning and the deposit to cover that check or wire transfer in is not received until that afternoon, or for 1 or more days.[2]

Suppose that a firm located in New York City deposits a check drawn on a bank located in El Paso, Texas. It will take about 2 days for the check to be

[2] For additional details see David L. Mengle, David B. Humphrey, and Bruce J. Summers. "Intraday Credit: Risk, Value, and Pricing," *Economic Review*, Federal Reserve Bank of Richmond, January/February 1987, pp. 3–14.

collected by the New York bank from the bank in Texas. Although the New York firm's balance has increased, it cannot use those funds to write checks without the bank's permission. Many banks analyze their customer's "out of town" checks and permit them to write checks only on their average collected balances. Under the Competitive Banking Equality Act of 1987 (Public Law 100-86), no more than 1 business day may intervene between the deposit of a local check and the availability for withdrawal of those funds, and 4 business days for nonlocal checks.

Loan Commitments

A **loan commitment** is an agreement between a bank and a firm to lend funds under terms that are agreed upon in writing. The agreements may or may not be "legally binding" on the part of the bank, depending on how they are written, and may contain clauses that permit the bank to terminate the agreement. Such clauses are called **material adverse change** *clauses* (MAC) clauses. Additional information about loan commitments of various types is presented in Chapter 18.

Firms often pay a **commitment fee** to banks for the privilege of having revolving credit facility or to make a loan at some future date, even though no funds are actually borrowed. The commitment fee may range from 0.25 to 0.50 percent per annum of the total amount to be borrowed. For example, assume that $5 million is the unused portion of the commitment, and the commitment fee is 0.50 percent per annum computed on a 360-day basis. The commitment fee for 45 days is $3,125.00.

Commitment $\times$ 0.50%

$$\$5,000,000 \times 0.005 = \$3,125.00$$

Daily fee = total fee/360

$$\$25,000/360 = \$69.444$$

Fee for 45 days = daily fee $\times$ 45 days

$$\$69.444 \times 45 = \$3,125.00$$

Banks may compute the fee on a 365-day basis. Using 365 days, the daily fee is $68.493 and the total fee for 45 days is $3,082.19. The bank is better off using 360 days.

The commitments specify the amount of the commitment fee and the amount of funds to be borrowed, but the cost of borrowing depends on the prevailing rates at the time the loan is made. However, the cost is usually specified when the commitment as made in terms of the **prime rate** (the base rate on corporate loans) plus a certain percent, such as prime plus two percentage points when the funds are borrowed. Payment of the commitment fee assumes that the customer can get funds when they are needed, and the bank earns the fee without having to make an investment at the time the agreement is made.

Leasing

Although this chapter concerns loans, commercial banks make leases that are an alternative to commercial loans. Leases are a popular source of **asset-based lending**—the financing of tangible long-term assets such as planes and ships. Asset-based lending is also widely used to finance inventories and accounts receivable. Asset-based lending is discussed in the appendix to this chapter. A **lease** is a contract that enables a user—the **lessee**—to secure the use of a tangible asset over a specified period of time by making payments to the owner—the **lessor**. The contract also specifies the details of the payments, the disposition of income tax benefits, provisions for maintenance, renewal options, and other clauses that permit the contract to qualify as a true lease under the Internal Revenue Code. Three categories of leases are of concern here—operating leases, financial leases, and leverage leases.

Operating leases are short-term leases used to finance equipment such as computers, where the term of the lease is a fraction of the economic life of the asset. That is, the asset is not fully amortized over the term of a lease. Operating leases may be canceled.

Financial leases are used in connection with financing long-term assets and have a term that is equal to the economic life of the asset. For example, a communications satellite may be leased for 12 years. Such leases usually are not canceled.

A **leveraged lease** is a special type of lease that is used to finance large transactions. It involves at least three parties: a lessee, a lessor (called the equity participant), and a long-term lender (called the debt participant). In a leveraged lease, the equity participant may only provide, say, 10 percent of the funds, with the remainder provided by debt participants on a nonrecourse basis. However, the equity participant may get all of the tax benefits (tax credits and depreciation) and the debt participants get interest and loan payments if they are paid. Banks can be either equity or debt participants.

COLLATERAL

The best security behind a loan is the borrower's willingness and ability to repay it. Nevertheless, sound banking practices require that certain types of loans be backed by collateral. **Collateral** refers to an asset pledged against the performance of an obligation. In other words, if the borrower does not pay off the loan, the bank takes the collateral. Thus, collateral reduces the bank's risk when it makes a loan because it can sell the collateral in the event of default. In addition, collateral reduces the cost of borrowing to the borrower, because it reduces the bank's risk, which in turn reduces its costs and lending rates. The use of collateral increases the costs to the bank, however, because of increased documentation and the costs of monitoring the collateral. Nevertheless, without collateral some borrowers could not obtain loans, and thus collateral benefits both borrowers and lenders in certain types of loans. In other types of loans collateral is not used. For example, a large creditworthy corporation borrowed $20 million for 1 day until it sold its own commercial paper. The minimal risk and the large volume of paperwork to obtain liens against specific assets mitigated the need for collateral in this case.

Characteristics of Good Collateral

The five factors listed in the following paragraphs determine the suitability of items for use as collateral. The suitability depends in varying degrees on standardization, durability, identification, marketability, and stability of value.

Standardization

Certain types of grains have been graded by the U.S. Department of Agriculture. For example, soybeans are graded as No. 1 yellow, No. 2 yellow, or No. 3 yellow. These grades indicate the quality of the beans. Similarly, other types of commodities and merchandise have been graded to facilitate their use in trade and as collateral. The point is that there is no ambiguity between the borrower and the lender as to the nature of the asset being used as collateral.

Durability

This refers to the ability of the asset to withstand wear, or to its useful life. Durable goods make better collateral than nondurables; in other words, a truck makes better collateral than fresh flowers.

Identification

Certain types of assets are readily identifiable because they have definite characteristics or serial numbers that cannot be removed. Two examples are a large office building and an automobile that can be identified by make, model, and serial number.

Marketability

In order for collateral to be of value to the bank, the collateral must be marketable. Large pieces of equipment that have one limited use are not as desirable as collateral as trucks that have multiple uses.

Stability of Value

Bankers prefer collateral whose market values are not likely to decline dramatically during the period of the loan. Wheat, for example is not as desirable as real estate for collateral.

Types of Collateral

Virtually anything can be used as collateral if a lender is willing to accept it. Some of the most common types of collateral that are used in commercial lending are examined here.

Accounts Receivable

Accounts receivable can be used as collateral in three ways. They are pledging, factoring, and bankers' acceptances.

Pledging. A borrower can **pledge** accounts receivable with his or her bank. In this case the borrower retains ownership of the receivables, and usually there is **no notification** made to the buyer of the goods for which the receivables have been pledged.

Before accepting the receivables, the bankers evaluate the credit rating of the firm owing the receivables. Accounts receivable from firms with weak credit ratings or those that are overdue may not be acceptable as collateral.

The percentage of face value of the accounts receivable that the banker is willing to advance depends on the size, number, and quality of the receivables. Most bankers prefer to advance funds from a few well-established firms that usually do not return the merchandise they purchased.

Factoring. Factoring is the sale of accounts receivable to a **factor** that is usually a bank or finance company. When the receivables are sold, the **buyer** of the goods is usually **notified** to make payments to the factor. Like pledging, factors prefer receivables from well-established firms. One important difference between the two methods is that factors frequently buy receivables on a **nonrecourse** basis. This means that the factor accepts the credit risks for the receivables that they purchase. Accordingly, the factor may advance only 80 or 90 percent of the face value; the remainder is held in reserve until the receivables are collected or until some predetermined date. In addition, the factor charges a commission ranging from 1 to 3 percent of the total face value, and monthly interest charges on the advances. For example, suppose that Southern Mill Outlet wants to factor $100,000 in receivables. The factor holds a reserve of 10 percent (advances 90 percent), charges a 3-percent commission, and a 2-percent monthly interest charge. The Southern Mill Outlet receives $85,260 and the factor earns $4,740 plus what they can earn on investing the reserve.

Face value of the accounts receivable	$100,000
Reserve held by factor (10%)	10,000
Commission (3%)	3,000
Funds that may be advanced	87,000
Less monthly interest charge (2%)	1,740
Funds available to Southern Mill Outlet	$85,260

Banker's Acceptance. A banker's acceptance arises from foreign trade. Suppose that an American exporter sells computers to a French concern. The French importer agrees to pay for the computers 30 days after they have been delivered. The means of payment is a **time draft**, which is similar to a predated check. The American manufacturer can send the time draft (which, from the American's point of view, is the same as an account receivable) to the French importer's bank and have it **accepted**. This means that the French bank becomes responsible for the payment of the draft, and will collect the funds from the importer when the draft becomes due. In other words, the French bank is guaranteeing payments of the French importer's obligation. The accepted draft is called a **banker's acceptance**. It is a negotiable instrument that can be traded in the securities market. Therefore the American manufacturer can sell the banker's acceptance at a discount (i.e., below face value) to compensate investors who bought it, but cannot collect the full value until it matures.

Inventory

Inventory is widely used as collateral against commercial loans. The characteristics of good collateral that were discussed previously—standardization, durability, identification, marketability, and stability of value—determine its desirability as collateral. Five common ways that inventory is used as collateral are explained in the following sections. The first three methods (floating lien, trust receipt, and chattel mortgage) permit the borrower to maintain possession of the inventory. The latter two methods (terminal warehouse and field warehouse) place the control of inventory in the hands of a third party.

Floating Lien. A floating lien or continuous lien is used to cover all of a firm's inventory—raw material through finished goods. The floating lien has two advantages from the borrowers viewpoint. First, it enables the entire inventory to be pledged, although part of it may have some undesirable characteristics. Second, the borrower can sell finished inventory in the ordinary course of business because the lien does not follow each item. The major disadvantage is that banks may lend only 50 percent of the value of such inventory because of its undesirable characteristics.

Depending on the size of the firm and the type of inventory involved, some banks connect inventory and account receivables together as collateral. This is because when the inventory is sold, the firm receives cash or receivables.

Trust Receipts. Trust receipts, or **floor planning** as it is commonly called, is used to finance automobiles, trucks, airplanes, and consumer durable goods such as televisions. The title for the inventory is held by the lender and the borrower assumes the role of trustee for the goods. When the inventory is sold, the borrower repays the lender who then releases the title to the property. For example, Nissan sells 20 new cars to a dealer in the United States who floor plans them with a local bank. The bank pays Nissan, retains title to the cars, and permits the dealer to display and sell them under the terms of the trust receipt security agreement. When a car is sold, the bank is paid with the proceeds from the sale and releases the title.

Trust receipts provide greater security for lenders than floating liens, but the method is not perfect. Some unscrupulous borrowers have used titles from wrecked cars as physical proof of their existence to borrow from lenders. This is why lenders must make periodic physical audits of the items being floor planned.

Chattel Mortgage. A **chattel mortgage**, or security agreement as it is sometimes called, gives the lender a lien on tangible personal property. The property must be clearly identified by serial number or some other means, so that it can be registered with the appropriate government authority. Frequently automobiles that are floor planned have chattel mortgages. When the items are sold, the appropriate government authority is notified to release the lender's claim and provide a clear title.

Warehouse Receipts. Banks have the greatest control and security when inventory that is used as collateral is held in a bonded public warehouse, which is commonly called a **terminal warehouse**. Under this arrangement, the inventory is stored in a public warehouse and the receipt is held by the lender. Inventory can be released only when proper receipts are presented at the warehouse. The receipts may be either negotiable or nonnegotiable. Negotiable receipts are commonly used to finance inventories of commodities, (e.g., corn), which are traded actively. Most lenders prefer nonnegotiable receipts because it gives them greater control.

Sometimes the borrower and lender agree to establish a **field warehouse** on the borrower's premises. A certain area of the borrower's premises is set aside and segregated by a fence or some other security arrangement. The advantage to the borrower is having the inventory at a convenient location. In either case, public or field warehousing, the borrower must pay for the cost of storage and security.

From the lender's point of view, warehouse receipts and field warehousing provide greater security than floating liens; however, there are still opportunities for fraud. Because there is some risk involved, lenders may offer only up to 85 percent of the book value of the inventory.

Order Bills of Lading. Finally, there are some ways in which inventories are used that are unique to particular industries. Common carriers, for example, use order bills of lading (which are a special kind of receipt) as collateral on commodities that are in transit.

Livestock and Crops

Livestock (cattle, hogs, etc.) is widely used as collateral, and credit is extended on it through all stages of the production process. Credit is also extended for planting crops. Such loans normally are payable when the crops are harvested.

Marketable Securities

Marketable securities, including corporate stocks and bonds, certificates of deposit, U.S. Treasury securities, and others, may be used as collateral for business loans. The amount of credit extended on such securities varies widely. Always keep in mind that the market value of stocks and bonds can vary widely from day-to-day.

Natural Resources

Natural resources, such as oil and gas reserves, are used as collateral. The value of the natural resources depends on estimates by qualified engineering firms. The lender, however, can tell the engineering firms what price assumptions and discount rates apply to the reserves. The borrower, of course, pays for the estimate. The engineering estimates are subject to errors about the size of the reserves, and the banker should keep this in mind when making a loan.

Real Property and Equipment

Real property refers to real estate that includes houses, office building, shopping centers, factories, and so on. Such property is widely used as collateral. In addition, equipment of various sorts may be used. Equipment includes trucks, forklifts, drill presses, robotics, and other items.

Guarantees

Bankers can improve their security by having a third party guarantee the payments. The third party may be an individual, insurance company, or U.S. government agency such as the Small Business Administration. For example, a parent company may guarantee a loan made by a subsidiary. Without the guarantee, the loan would not have been made. With the exception of the government agencies, the quality of the guarantee depends on the financial strength of the guarantor. Guarantees are discussed in more detail in Chapter 8.

In summary, most banks require some kind of collateral or guarantee when they make business loans. Small businesses frequently use the personal assets of the principals as collateral. Personal assets include real estate, cars, the surrender value of life insurance policies, or anything else of value.

BOX 6.1

THE EFFECT OF DERIVED DEMAND ON THE VALUE OF COLLATERAL: THE CASE OF THE BIG SHIPS

Derived demand means that the demand for one product affects the demand for another. For example, the demand for new cars affects the demand for tires and glass. The concept of derived demand is important to keep in mind when evaluating the suitability of an asset as collateral. Consider the case of VLCCs (very large crude carriers), or supertankers that carry crude oil. The VLCCs carry 200,000 deadweight tons or more. The term **deadweight ton** (dwt.) is a measure of a vessel's cargo capacity. The VLCCs possess some characteristics of good collateral. They are durable and easy to identify; however, their value depends on derived demand. Specifically, it depends on the demand for oil and its price. In 1970, the price of Arabian light crude oil was $1.39 per barrel.[a] By 1975, the price had increased to $11.51 per barrel, and then it soared to $34.00 per barrel in 1981. Similarly, oil production in the Middle East increased dramatically until the early 1980s when surplus capacity caused downward pressure on market prices. During the 1970s there was increased demand for VLCCs to carry crude oil, and banks were anxious to finance crude oil tankers. In fact, "young bankers from Continental Illinois were busy thrusting money at the industry like sailors on shore leave . . .," and they made about $1 billion in ship loans (Continental Bank failed in 1984).[b] Other banks joined in the lending spree, too. After all, the demand for oil *was* strong and many lenders assumed that oil prices would continue to rise and ships would be needed to carry the oil.

They were wrong. The rising cost of oil induced oil users to conserve oil and to use alternative sources of energy such as coal and nuclear power. Surpluses of oil developed, and then Middle East oil prices declined in the early 1980s. These were some of the factors that contributed to the reduced (derived) demand for VLCCs. Owners of some oil tankers found it profitable to scrap their ships for as little as 15 cents on the dollar of the original purchase price. Others could not afford the cost of fuel to sail the ships to the scrapyards. The result was foreclosures and losses for both shipowners and the banks that lent to them.

There is an important lesson to be learned here. The market value of some collateral is affected by derived demand. When the price of oil soared, the demand for VLCCs increased. When oil prices fell, the demand for VLCCs declined to such an extent that both lenders and borrowers suffered.

[a] *Middle East Oil and Gas*, Exxon Corporation, 1984, p. 27.
[b] Jack Willoughby, "Shipwreck," *Forbes*, July 29, 1985, p. 119.

THE DOLLAR SIZE OF COMMERCIAL LOANS

The general perception held by the public is that most commercial loans are made for relatively large dollar amounts, which is correct but misleading. According to surveys made by the Board of Governors of the Federal Reserve System of short-term commercial and industrial (C&I) loans made by banks, about 80 percent of the total C&I loans are for $1 million or more.[3]

Although these large loans account for most of the **dollar volume** of loans made, they account for a less than 5 percent of the total **number** of loans made.

The average size of these large loans is about $6 million. Almost half of these large loans have a 1-day maturity. Most of the 1-day loans are made by large commercial banks to large corporations that finance part of their operations with commercial paper. When redemptions of commercial paper exceed sales, these corporations finance the difference by borrowing from banks until new commercial paper can be sold. The cost of bank loans is frequently 200 basis points higher than the cost of commercial paper.

The largest **numbers** of C&I loans are made for smaller dollar amounts. Most of the loans are made for less than $50,000.

FEDERAL LIMITS ON THE SIZE OF BANK LOANS

Relative Size of Bank Loans

Federal law dictates the relative size of a loan or extension of credit that national banks can make to one borrower. This includes outstanding loans as well as loans that are guaranteed by the borrower. Under the Garn-St Germain Depository Institutions Act of 1982, national banks were permitted to lend up to 15 percent of their primary capital and surplus for an unsecured loan, and an additional 10 percent for loans fully secured by marketable collateral.[4] Therefore, 25 percent of capital and surplus is the maximum that can be loaned to any one borrower. Before the Garn-St Germain Act, the limit was 10 percent.

To understand how the 25-percent limit affects the size of loans, consider Table 6.2, which shows the maximum dollar amount of a loan that can be made to one borrower. The current regulatory minimum ratio of total capital-to-assets is 6 percent. Some banks, however, have a ratio of 9 percent or more. As shown in the table, a small bank with $50 million in assets and a 6-percent capital ratio can lend a maximum of $750,000 to one borrower. If the ratio were

---

[3] "The Survey of Terms of Bank Lending" is conducted quarterly and reported in the *Federal Reserve Bulletin*, Table A70.

[4] Primary capital includes common stock, perpetual preferred stock, capital surplus, undivided profits, contingency and other capital reserves, securities convertible into common and perpetual reserves, allowances for loan and lease losses, and minority interest in the equity accounts of consolidated subsidiaries. Secondary capital includes limited life preferred stock (including related surplus), bank subordinated notes and debentures and unsecured long-term debt of the parent company and its nonbank subsidiaries.

TABLE 6.2
MAXIMUM DOLLAR AMOUNT OF A LOAN TO ONE BORROWER FOR VARIOUS SIZE
BANKS AND CAPITAL RATIOS[a]
(millions of dollars)

Asset Size of Bank	Capital/Asset Ratio	
	6%	9%
$50 (small bank)	$0.750	$1.125
$500 (medium bank)	7.500	11.250
$1,000 (large bank)	15.000	22.500

[a] The maximum loan to one borrower is 25 percent of capital.

9 percent, the maximum size loan is $1,125,000. Most banks would not consider it prudent to lend 25 percent of their capital to one borrower, and thus the amounts shown in the table exceed what occurs in practice. This means that a small bank with the minimum required capital-to-asset ratio has a relatively small lending limit. At the other end of the size spectrum, a large bank with $1 billion in assets and the minimum required amount of capital has a lending limit of $15 million, enough to satisfy most borrowers.

Exceptions to the Limit

There are exceptions to the 25 percent of capital lending limit imposed by the Garn-St Germain Act. One exception is for loans that are secured by bonds, notes, CDs, U.S. Treasury securities, or securities that are fully guaranteed by the U.S. government. Other exceptions involve loans backed by deposits in the lending bank, by commercial paper, bankers' acceptances, and bills of lading. Special interest groups also received some relief from the 25-percent limit. One group is the Student Loan Marketing Association—a U.S. government organization. Other groups that benefited are livestock ranchers and dairy cattlemen. Certain loans or extensions of credit arising from the sale of livestock and dairy cattle are exempted.

THE LENDING DECISION

The decision to allocate funds among commercial and industrial loans, real estate loans and consumer or other types of loans depends on a variety of factors, including the size and location of the bank, economic conditions, risk, and funding.

Bank's Size and Location

The largest commercial banks are headquartered in downtown major metropolitan areas. These banks were probably organized when downtown was the center of economic commercial and industrial activity. Over the years, both the downtown banks and the metropolitan areas grew and prospered. As the population migrated to the suburbs, it was followed by new banks or branches of existing ones. So for historical reasons, the large urban banks usually served the large downtown businesses and the new, smaller suburban banks and branches served the needs of consumers and small business concerns. Today we call banks that specialize in business loans **wholesale banks** and those that specialize in consumer loans **retail banks**, although most banks blend both types of trade.

Size is important because large banks can make bigger loans than small banks. This is why large business concerns that borrow millions of dollars prefer to deal with large banks that can handle their needs, both domestic and foreign.

Services

Along this line, the number of personnel of large commercial banks enables them to offer specialized services, such as an international banking department, which some smaller banks cannot offer. In other words, the big banks have **economies of scope**, referring to their ability to offer a wide range of products at relatively low costs. It is not surprising, therefore, that the loan portfolios of large commercial banks emphasize large-size commercial and industrial loans. It follows that smaller banks without the same lending capabilities usually make loans to smaller business concerns.

Participations

Participations, however, make it possible for small banks to share in making large loans. A **participation** is a part of a lending arrangement. Suppose that AmSouth makes a $100 million loan but wants to retain only $20 million of it because they want to spread their funds over a larger number of loans. The remainder is divided into smaller amounts and sold to other banks. AmSouth is a large, regional bank. If the loans are sold to smaller banks, the participations are said to be sold **downstream**. Conversely, if AmSouth sells them to larger banks, such as Citibank—one of the nation's largest banks—the participations are sold **upstream**.

Economic Conditions and Credit Risk

Economic conditions refer to the level of economic activity today and in the future, as well as the outlook for interest rates. Many banks are located in areas where the level of economic activity is dominated by one large firm or industry, such as automobiles, mining, or forest products, which are **cyclical industries**— their revenues fluctuate with the business cycle. Although banks can diversify their loan portfolios by using participations, their primary business comes from the communities they serve.

Suppose that a bank is located in an area dominated by forest products, and the economic outlook is bleak when forest product sales decline. In addition, revenues for firms that supply goods and services to the forest product industry decline also, and unemployment in the region increases. Some business concerns and individuals may be unable to repay their loans on time. Faced with this situation, bank managers have to make difficult decisions. If they withhold additional loans from the distressed firms, the firms may go bankrupt and the bank might lose money on the outstanding loans. If they make additional loans, there is still the chance that some firms will go bankrupt, and the bank's losses would increase. Unfortunately, there is no simple solution to this dilemma. Bankers must weigh the credit risks against the expected returns. **Credit risk** is the risk of losing money on a loan. One aspect of weighing the credit risk is credit analysis of existing and potential customers. Credit analysis is examined in the next chapter.

Interest Rates and Credit Risk

The outlook for interest rates also affects the degree of credit risk that banks face. Consider the case of Bob Hayden, the owner of Bob's Tool Leasing Company, which bought heavy machine tools such as drills and presses, and leased them to manufacturing concerns. Throughout most of our economic history, short-term interest rates have been lower than longer-term interest rates. Therefore, it costs less to borrow short-term funds than it does to borrow long-term funds. Bob understood the logic of this and borrowed heavily from his bank to invest in machine tools. He arranged fixed lease payments for the 3-year term of the leases with the manufacturers, and then he bought the machine tools, which he financed with 6-month loans. The reason for using 6-month loans was that the interest cost on them was lower than the interest cost on longer-term loans. The bank gave him 6-month loans at the prime rate plus 2 percentage points. Thus, Bob's cost of funds changed whenever market rates of interest and the prime rate changed. The prime at the time the loan was made was 10 percent, so Bob's interest cost was 12 percent. The leases provided Bob a 16-percent return. Bob's gross profit was the 4 percentage points, the difference between his return and the cost of funds. Things went well for Bob and the bank until interest rates increased sharply and the prime rate increased to 18 percent. Then Bob's cost of funds was 20 percent, but his return from the lease payments was 16 percent, giving him a loss of 4 percentage points. Because the lease payments he received could not be increased, Bob could not cover the increased cost of his loan, and he went bankrupt.

Although Bob went bankrupt, the bank minimized its losses on the loans because the machine tools were used as collateral. When Bob could not pay off his loans, the bank took ownership of the machine tools and then sold them to another lessor.

Bob could have avoided bankruptcy by financing the permanent assets (the machine tools) with permanent funds. The loan should have been structured to match the maturity of the loan with the maturity of the funding and lock in a spread (difference) between the lease and loan payments.

Interest Rate Risk

Interest rate risk refers to the change in the market value of assets that is due to a change in market rates of interest. Recall from Chapter 2 ("Bank Investments") that there is an inverse relationship between market rates of interest and the market price of outstanding bonds. That is, when interest rates go down, the price of bonds goes up. Similarly, the price of long-term mortgage loans and other long-term loans is affected in the same way. Bank managers must therefore take the outlook for interest rates into account when they review the long-term loans they hold and when they make additional long-term loans. For example, suppose that interest rates are expected to increase over the next 3 months, which means that the market value of the mortgage loans that the bank holds will decline. The bankers must decide (1) if they want to sell the mortgage loans before they decline in value or continue to hold them, and (2) if they should make additional mortgage loans at the current rates.

Lending and Funding Strategies

Lending and funding strategies are inexorably linked together in order to obtain a positive **spread** between the interest earned on loans and interest expense. The term **funding** means borrowing. One strategy to keep a positive spread between borrowing and lending rates is to make all commercial loans on a **floating-rate** basis. A floating rate means that the interest rate charged on the loan changes whenever some index rate, such as the bank's 90-day CD rate, changes. It may not be possible or desirable to "float" all of the loans all of the time. Let's examine some other strategies that illustrate the linkages between lending and borrowing in the context of the business cycle, which is depicted in Figure 6.3. The business cycle has four phases: recovery, prosperity, recession, and depression. The figure also shows that interest rates follow the course of business activity. Interest rates generally increase as business activity increases during the recovery and prosperity phases of the cycle and then decline as business activity slows down. Unfortunately, the precise turning points of both business activity and interest rates are more difficult to predict than is suggested in the figure. Nevertheless, the relationships between business activity and interest rates shown in the figure are sufficient for our purposes.

During the recovery phase of the business cycle, banks should make loans with floating interest rates, which can increase as interest rates increase. It follows that they should avoid making long-term loans at low fixed rates at the trough of the cycle. In order to maximize their spread between interest earned on loans and interest expense, they should borrow long-term at low fixed rates.

During the prosperity phase, when interest rates are approaching their peak.

it is time to make long-term, fixed rate loans to lock in the high yields. Because interest rates will decline as business activity slows, floating-rate loans should be avoided. On the other side of the balance sheet, now is also the time to avoid borrowing long-term fixed rate funds at high interest rates because interest rates will fall.

Falling interest rates during the recession phase of the business cycle suggest that banks should make long-term, fixed rate loans while interest rates are still high. These loans should be financed by borrowing short-term to take advantage of declining costs.

As the business cycle approaches the trough, the long-term fixed rate loans (such as mortgages) that were made at higher rates during the prosperity and recession phases can be sold at a profit to supplement income. Also, this is the time to increase floating-rate loans in anticipation of the recovery phase of the business cycle. Because interest rates are low now, it is time to borrow long-term at fixed rates.

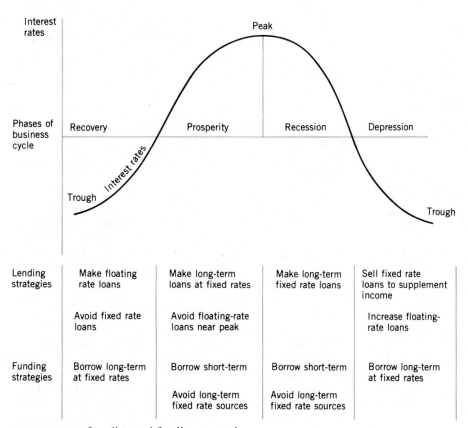

FIGURE 6.3 Lending and funding strategies.

WRITTEN LOAN POLICY

The Board of Directors of a bank has the ultimate responsibility for all of the loans made by the bank. Because the Board delegates the task of making loans to others, it is common practice to have a **written loan policy** establishing general guidelines and principles for the bank's lending activities. It is important to understand that the policies are guidelines; they are not inflexible rules carved in granite.

Written policies vary widely from bank to bank. The policies of a small bank that lends primarily to farmers will differ from that of a large bank specializing in international lending. Nevertheless, some items that are present in many written loan policies are presented here.

General Policy

The general policy outlines the bank's lending objectives in terms of profitability and risk. For example, the policy may state that the bank is in the business of making sound and profitable loans. An important part of this goal is that all loans should have a plan of liquidation at the time these loans are made. The general policy section may also include statements concerning the organizational structure for supervising lending activity.

Risk

By definition, lending funds involves some degree of risk, and we know that risk is related to returns. The higher the risks the higher the expected returns. The degree of risk that a bank is willing to face may be expressed in the following way.

> The bank is not an investor and should limit its risk to that which is commensurate with the return usually available to it as a lender. The yield on a customer's total relationship should meet the bank's earning objectives after allowing for the cost of funds, risk factors, and the cost of administration.

Loan Supervision

The Board of Directors establishes policies regarding the lending authority of individual loan officers and the approval process for particular types of loans of various sizes. Figure 6-4 shows the structure of lending authority for Western Bankshares, a holding company with $4.8 billion in assets. Smaller banks have fewer layers of management and a simpler approval process than the one shown here. In this case, the loans are divided into five categories: secured, unsecured, overdrafts, insiders, and employees. The maximum loan limits for individual loan officers are $250,000 for secured loans and about half that

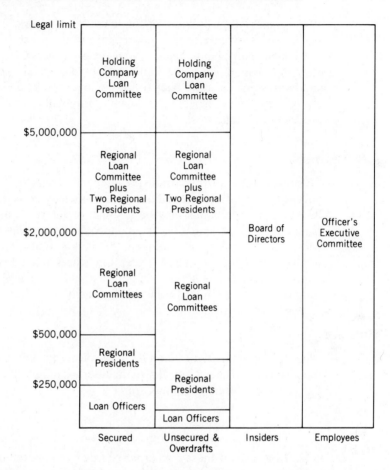

Regional Loan Committee: Regional Officers and Directors
Holding Company Loan Committee: Holding Company Officers and Directors

FIGURE 6.4   The Lending Authority for Western Bankshares ($4.8 billion assets).

amount for unsecured loans and overdrafts. A $2-million secured loan, for example, would require approval from the holding company's regional president and regional loan committee. Larger loans require additional approval. This bank considers a customer's **total relationship** when evaluation a loan. The total relationship includes all loans made or guaranteed by the same customer. For example, a customer with outstanding loans of $500,000 and $20,000, who cosigns for a $10,000 loan would have a total relationship of $530,000. The $10,000 is treated as though it were $530,000 as far as the approval process is concerned.

Insider loans and employees loans receive special treatment in this bank. The Financial Institutions Regulatory and Interest Rate Control Act (FIRA) of

1978 requires Board approval for loans to directors, executive officers, and stockholders owning 10 percent or more of the stock.

Finally, many banks have a **loan review process**. This is an audit of loans after they have been made to determine whether all of the laws, regulations, and bank's policies have been followed, and if the bank if facing risks that it did not perceive with respect to the loans. More will be said about the loan review process in Chapter 8.

Geographic Limits

To some extent, a bank's trade area depends on its size. Small banks generally have a local trade area, medium-size banks may consider themselves regional banks, and large banks may be national or international in scope. Thus, one bank's policy may state that "sound local loans are one of the most satisfactory and profitable means of employing the bank's funds. Therefore, it is the intent of the Board that with few exceptions the bank's loans are limited to the metropolitan area we serve." In contrast, another bank's policy is "to concentrate our lending efforts in the Pacific Basin."

Credit Policies

This section deals with administration of credit files and documentation that must be kept on each loan. It also includes a listing of the types of loans that the bank desires. Some examples are:

1. Loans to business concerns on a short-term basis against a satisfactory balance sheet and income statement.
2. Loans to business concerns secured by a chattel mortgage on marketable business equipment to be amortized over a period of not more than 10 years.
3. Personal loans secured by second mortgages on personal homes.

This section of the policy also contains a listing of **undesirable loans**. For example:

1. Capital loans to a business where the loan cannot be repaid within a reasonable period except by liquidation of the business.
2. Loans to persons whose integrity or honesty is questionable.
3. Loans secured by stock in a closed corporation where there is no ready market.

Finally, this section of the policy may cover loans to officers and directors, collateral, procedures for collection of past-due accounts, charge-offs, and overdrafts.

In summary, the written loan policy explains how the Board of Directors wants the bank's lending operations to be conducted. It should be sufficiently complete and clear so that loan officers know what they must do in order to help the bank grow profitably.

As mentioned previously, loan policies are guidelines, not inflexible rules. Good loan officers try to find ways to grant loans that violate the loan policy. For example, suppose that a prospective small business borrower does not have a satisfactory balance sheet and income statement. Based on the loan policy, a loan may be denied. A creative loan officer, however, might get the principals of the business to include their homes as part of the collateral for a loan. Now there is adequate security and the bank can approve the loan.

SUMMARY

The role of lending at U.S. commercial banks has changed dramatically over the years. In the distant past, short term, self-liquidating loans were the standard. Today, banks provide loans of all maturities and methods of repayment. The principal categories of loans are: commercial and industrial, real estate, and individual (consumer) loans. Commercial and industrial loans are used to finance temporary and permanent business assets. Lines of credit and transaction loans are used for temporary assets, and revolving loans and term loans are used for permanent assets. The purpose of collateral was introduced, as well as the characteristics of good collateral and various types of collateral. Accounts receivable, inventory, and real property and equipment are the most commonly used types of collateral for commercial and industrial loans.

Most of the commercial loans made by commercial banks are for less than $50,000. The maximum amount that national banks can lend to any one customer is limited to 25 percent of their equity capital, but most banks will not risk that much on one customer. The amount that they will loan depends on their size, geographic location, and the risk they are willing to face. Some of these limits and others are explained in banks' written loan policies. The Board of Directors of the bank, who have the ultimate responsibility for all loans that are made, use the written loan policy as a guideline for those involved in the lending process.

IMPORTANT CONCEPTS

asset-based lending	construction and development loan
bankers' acceptances	consumer loans
chattel mortgage	credit facility
collateral	credit risk
commercial and industrial loans	cyclical industries
commitment fee	daylight overdraft
compensating balance	downstream

economies of scope	material adverse change clause
evergreen facility	nonrecourse
factor	notification
field warehouse	participation
floating lien	permanent financing
floating rate (loan)	pledging (receivables)
floor plan	real estate loans
funding	retail bank
Garn-St Germain Act	revolving loan
interest rate risk	self-liquidating loan
lease	terminal warehouse
lessee	term loan
lessor	total relationship
leveraged lease	upstream
line of credit	warehouse receipt
operating lease	wholesale bank
order bill of lading	written loan policy

REFERENCES

Dunbar, Charles F., and Oliver M. W. Sprague. *The Theory of History of Banking,* 3rd. ed. New York: Putnam, 1922.

Mengle, David L., David B. Humphrey, and Bruce J. Summers. "Intraday Credit: Risk, Value, and Pricing," *Economic Review*, Federal Reserve Bank of Richmond, January/February 1987.

QUESTIONS

6.1. What is a self-liquidating loan?

6.2. Are home loans considered consumer loans? Why or why not?

6.3. Distinguish between interim construction on development loans and permanent financing in business real estate lending.

6.4. Why is it important to have temporary versus permanent financing available on commercial and industrial loans?

6.5. What are the differences between a line of credit and a revolving loan? What are evergreen facilities?

6.6. Term loans are made for what purpose? What is the borrower's equity in an asset financed by a term loan? What is the bank's security interest in such a loan?

6.7. When does an overdraft occur? Why is it a loan? Under the Competitive Banking Equality Act of 1987, what is the minimum time between the deposit and withdrawal of funds using both local and out-of-town checks?

6.8. What are MAC clauses in loan commitments? Why are firms willing to pay commitment fees?

6.9. Why are leasing arrangements considered to be asset-based financing? Briefly distinguish between the three major types of leases.

6.10. How does collateral benefit both the borrower and the lender? What five factors affect the suitability of collateral?

6.11. Distinguish between pledging and factoring accounts receivables.

6.12. What is a bankers' acceptance? What reasons are there for explaining the widespread use of bankers' acceptances in international trade?

6.13. Briefly define the following terms:

(a) Floating lien.

(b) Trust receipts.

(c) Chattel mortgage.

(d) Warehouse receipts.

(e) Order bills of lading.

6.14. How did the Garn-St Germain Depository Institution Act of 1982 affect bank lending limits?

6.15. What are wholesale versus retail banks? How might participations cause these two kinds of banks to interact? How might participations geographically diversify credit risk for the banks involved?

6.16. Why is matching the maturity of the loan with the maturity of the asset or lease important?

6.17. How does the business cycle affect loan maturities? Lending volume?

6.18. Why is a written loan policy important? What are some of the main features of a loan policy?

APPENDIX

ASSET-BASED LENDING AT COMMERCIAL FINANCE COMPANIES AND COMMERCIAL BANKS*

Asset-based lending practiced by commercial finance companies such as Heller Financial, CIT, Commercial Credit, GECC, and others normally is quite different than asset-based lending practiced by commercial banks. In fact, only when a bank acquires a commercial finance company and allows that entity to operate autonomously can it be said that the practices are alike. This appendix explains some of the differences between the two.

* Robert N. Stone, University of Alabama, coauthored this appendix.

The typical borrower for an asset-based loan is a firm doing between $1 and $10 million in annual sales. As with most businesses, that firm will approach a bank for financing. If the bank chooses not to service the loan request, then the firm may be a viable candidate for the commercial financier.

Commercial finance companies, traditionally building their business through bank referrals, championed the term **asset-based lending**. These loans were predicated on the liquidating value of the collateral pledged to secure a loan; financial statements are examined but are a secondary factor in a loan review. On the other hand, although a bank may "secure" a loan with assets, loan approval is, for the most part, based on the firm's balance sheet and its associated ratios; collateral, even though pledged to "secure" the loan, is not the primary factor that forms the basis for loan approval.

Why would a bank refer a business to a commercial finance company? First, loans are referred because they are considered too risky for the bank. The risk may have been determined because the firm was having financial problems, or conversely, the firm was doing so well it had outpaced its capital base and the balance sheet did not merit, under bank scrutiny, loan approval. Second, most commercial finance firms try to make their clients bankable. When that happens, the bank obtains a client, either new or returning, that otherwise may have been forced into bankruptcy without the help of the commercial financier.

ASSET-BASED LENDING

Asset-based lending is a form of commercial lending where the assets of a company are used to secure the company's obligation to the lender. In the broadest sense, all secured loans could be classified as asset-based loans. However, the financial community has defined asset-based lending to include only those loans that have as their collateral base accounts receivable, inventory, machinery and equipment and real estate, singly or packaged in various combinations (i.e., receivables and inventory; receivables and machinery, etc.).

A further distinction between asset-based loans and other secured loans resides in the amount of policing or monitoring required to ensure the existence, value, and integrity of the collateral. All asset-based loans require a higher level of monitoring than do nonasset-based loans. Commercial finance firms do this policing; banks rarely police a loan to the same degree. It is this monitoring and the constant collateral appraisal process that differentiates asset-based loans from other "secured" commercial loans. A borrower may have $100,000 of receivables pledged to secure a loan. If the account debtors who owe this amount differ on Tuesday from those of Monday, the secured lender views the quality of Tuesday's loan as potentially different from the quality of Monday's. A bank typically will look at Monday's and Tuesday's loans as the same, each based on $100,000 of receivables.

ASSET VALUES

Before making a loan, commercial finance companies determine lendable values for assets. In the case of accounts receivable, agings are reviewed for the quality of the receivables. Receivables over 90 days old usually are not part of the lending base; disputed items as confirmed by account debtors are not allowed; contra-accounts, where an account both buys from and sells to the client firm, are not allowed; consignment sales are not, and so forth. In short, anything that could negatively effect the collectibility of a receivable is eliminated from the borrowing base. Each month, a percentage of the firm's account debtors is contacted by the commercial finance house either by phone or mail to verify account balances. In the case of machinery and equipment, the commercial finance company asks machinery and equipment dealers or auctioneers to determine how much such equipment would bring at auction. Accurate liquidating value is thereby determined and a percentage of this value becomes available for borrowing purposes. Inventory financing is often the most difficult collateral to lend against. The age of the inventory must be considered as is the resale value of it. The commercial finance firm is concerned with a potential market for the inventory that may come into their possession. Thus, for example, even white paint is of questionable collateral value, because there are hundreds of shades of white paint, each brand shaded sightly differently by respective manufacturers to lock in a customer base. Liquidating this collateral (i.e., finding a buyer for resale) may be impossible.

When reviewing a loan request, banks take factors other than liquidation value into account. For example, banks consider the total banking relationship. This relationship includes all loans and guarantees made by, or related to, the borrower. Banks are also concerned about potential business that customers can generate for the bank, such as payroll and personal checking account relationships, trust accounting relationships, and various installment loan possibilities. Because of their important role in their respective communities, banks are far less likely than commercial finance companies to foreclose on a loan or engage in a lawsuit, because this might tarnish the bank's reputation. Although the commercial finance company is prepared to foreclose on the collateral if necessary, banks try to avoid this alternative.

Once the commercial finance company determines that adequate value can be obtained from the pledged assets, and that this amount will help the firm, the loan is made. "Help the firm" means that the initial loan will materially reduce payables, allow the firm to take advantage of purchase discounts, take on new inventory lines, and so forth. Commercial finance firms may lend up to 40 or 50 percent of the **market (liquidating) value** of inventories and up to 80 percent on accounts receivable under 90 days old. Banks, on the other hand, may lend an average of 60 percent or more on the **book value** of the inventory and average of 80 percent on the **book value** of accounts receivable.

ACTIVE PARTICIPATION

From the time the loan is made until it is paid off, the commercial finance company becomes an active participant in the management of the loan. The "policing" by the commercial financier focuses on the maintenance of the integrity of the collateral that secures the loan. Collections, for example, may be sent directly to the commercial finance company's lockbox rather than collected by the borrower. Invoices, probably those over $100, may be sent to the commercial finance company for review. Account debtor credit limits are mutually set by the lender and his or her borrowing client and, in this process, the commercial finance firm will provide the client with ongoing credit information on current and prospective customers. Accounts receivable agings are reviewed monthly, and a percentage of the receivables is confirmed each month by the commercial finance company contacting account debtors. Such confirmation is usually done by phone calls from an independent accounting firm owned by the commercial financier; confirmations may also be done by mail. Inventory levels are monitored periodically by the commercial finance company to the point of physical inspection for maintenance of record keeping and physical quality as well. Finally, the borrower's accounting policies are "beefed up," and record-keeping processes are reviewed and improved if possible. In each of these cases, the commercial finance firm will advise the client that actions are to protect collateral values.

Such participation requires human resources. In a commercial finance company, an operations officer (not the lending officer who "booked" the account) typically handles about 10 loan accounts with an outstanding balance of $300,000 per account. The commercial finance firm usually goes to great lengths to separate their marketing aspects of bringing in new accounts with their day-to-day monitoring of those accounts. Different officers handle each phase of the lending relationship. In contrast, some commercial bank lending officers may manage 15 to 20 loan accounts with outstanding balances of $2.5 million per account. Moreover, the finance company usually assigns three or more people to administer an account, whereas banks do not commit such human resources.

Commercial finance firms do *not* become involved in the general management of the customer's business. This is because in the event of a bankruptcy, the commercial finance firm wants to be certain that the court does not set aside its security interest in the assets of the subject company. This could happen if attorneys argued that the demise of the firm was a consequence of that firm following the advice of their commercial financier.

PRICING

Commercial finance companies price asset-based loans at prime plus 3 to 4 or more points in order to cover cost of supervision and assistance given to customers, as noted previously. In contrast, banks charge less (prime plus 1.75–2.25), because they have lower labor costs associated with the loans and because they have the opportunity to obtain other revenue from the client.

SUMMARY

Commercial finance companies are more aggressive asset-based lenders than commercial banks. They lend relatively more to "risky" firms than would a bank, not because they want a riskier portfolio but because they believe they can commit the resources to keep abreast of the changing collateral (i.e., manage the risk). Their efforts result in a tremendous benefit to clients, for the questions asked by the commercial financier to their borrowers result in borrowers becoming more astute businesspeople. Although the commercial financier avoids direct participation in a client's business, the indirect involvement via collateral administration is the ingredient that helps a client improve their financial position to such an extent that banks will want them as a customer. Such monitoring costs are higher than those of banks, and thus higher rates of interest are charged by commercial finance firms.

THE PROCESS OF COMMERCIAL LENDING

Commercial lending is a process involving various steps over time by both the borrower and the lender. This is the first of two chapters that gives a step-by-step overview of that process.

ASKING FOR A COMMERCIAL LOAN

Loan Request

Today, banks actively solicit loans in local and distant markets. Loan officers visit prospective customers to offer loans and services provided by their respective banks. This type of sales effort is typical of large banks seeking me-

GALAXY STEREO, INC.
283 Melody Lane
Houston, Texas 77001

January 3, 1988

Ms. Vivian Belmont,
Vice President
Western National Bank

Dear Ms. Belmont,

The purpose of this letter is to request a $4 million revolving credit agreement secured by the firm's accounts receivable and inventory. The funds will be used as working capital to finance our expansion. We intend to repay the loan on a quarterly basis as the receivables are collected over the next three years.

As you know, Ms. Belmont, Galaxy Stereo was acquired from Kangsai Electronics three years ago. The firm is a wholesale distributor of stereo equipment. We design our own stereo equipment, build most of it in the Orient, and then sell our own brand and private brand labels to retail distributors throughout the United States and Canada. We have been able to expand rapidly because we offer favorable credit terms to the retail distributors. Currently we have 1,241 retail distributors, up from 158 when we began operations. Our goal is to reach 1,500 by year end.

Since we began operating in Houston, we have maintained our payroll account at Western National Bank, but we have never borrowed money from your institution. Now we are consolidating our banking relationships, which is why we are giving you the opportunity to grow with us.

For your information, I have enclosed a business plan, a résumé of our officers, audited financial statements, and a pro forma statement for next year.

I would like to meet with you next Thursday to discuss the loan. Please let me know what time will be convenient for you.

I look forward to hearing from you.

Sincerely,

Maurice Isaac

Maurice Isaac
President

BWI/MI
Enclosures

FIGURE 7.1   Loan request.

dium- and large-size firms as customers. However, the process of commercial lending usually begins when someone asks for a loan. From the borrowers' point of view, there is an art to asking for a loan. Many potential borrowers are denied loans or do not get the type of loan they need because they do not make effective loan presentations. Some borrowers, for example, do not know what type of loan (i.e., line of credit, term loan) will meet their financial needs, or what type of collateral (i.e., accounts receivable, bill of lading, second mortgage) is suitable for their loans. The following example illustrates the proper steps to follow in asking for a commercial loan.

Maurice Isaac, president of Galaxy Stereo, began the lending process by sending a letter to his bank asking for $4 million (Figure 7.1). The letter also included a brief history of the firm and other pertinent information. In addition,

TABLE 7.1
FINANCIAL STATEMENTS

GALAXY STEREO, INC.
Financial Statements ($000)

	1985	1986	1987
Assets			
Cash	$ 680.00	$ 411.00	$ 794.00
Accounts receivable	550.00	1,479.00	5,776.00
Inventory	1,262.00	2,629.00	6,073.00
Prepaid expenses	180.00	114.00	415.00
Deferred tax charges	0.00	0.00	173.00
Total Current	2,671.00	4,633.00	13,231.00
Plant & equipment	3,185.00	5,235.00	10,170.00
Other	5,579.00	177.00	336.00
Total Assets	$ 5,862.00	$ 10,045.00	$23,737.00
Liabilities and Equity			
Notes payable	$ 782.00	$ 901.00	$ 2,114.00
Accounts payable	3,078.00	3,555.00	7,688.00
Accrued expenses	438.00	1,173.00	1,959.00
Current long-term debt	479.00	525.00	474.00
Taxes	0.00	0.00	87.00
Total Current	4,779.00	6,154.00	12,322.00
Long-term debt	219.00	2,679.00	3,015.00
Long-term leases	475.00	250.00	224.00
Deferred taxes	0.00	0.00	173.00
Equity			
Common stock	75.00	79.00	93.00
Additional paid in capital	3,345.00	4,109.00	7,305.00
Retained earnings	−3,031.00	−2,863.00	968.00
Less Treasury shares at cost	0.00	−363.00	−363.00
Total Equity	389.00	962.00	8,003.00
Total Liabilities & Equity	$ 5,862.00	$ 10,045.00	$23,737.00

TABLE 7.1 (*Continued*)

	1985	1986	1987
		December 31	
Income and Expenses			
Sales	$ 12,950.00	$ 22,367.00	$54,120.00
Other revenue	228.00	516.00	1,421.00
Total	13,178.00	22,883.00	55,541.00
Cost of goods sold	11,190.00	14,581.00	38,101.00
Depreciation		671.50	1,004.00
Sales	2,117.00	3,818.00	7,732.00
General & administrative	822.00	1,512.00	2,944.00
Research & development	724.00	1,192.00	1,351.00
Interest	230.00	539.00	935.00
Total	3,893.00	7,061.00	12,962.00
Taxes	0.00	60.00	1,545.00
Extraordinary items	191.00	60.00	1,458.00
Net income from operations	−1,905.00	1,181.00	2,933.00
Net income	−1,714.00	1,241.00	4,391.00
Shares outstanding, fully diluted	7,000,000	7,900,500	9,310,250
Earnings per share	−0.24	0.16	0.47

Maurice inclosed résumés of the firm's officers, financial data, and a business plan. He also requested a meeting with the banker.

Financial Data

Galaxy Stereo sent the bank its balance sheet and income statements for the 3 years of its existence. Five years of data would have been preferable, but Galaxy was only 3 years old. A quick glance at the financial statements shown in Table 7.1 reveals that Galaxy experienced rapid growth. In the most recent year, it had total revenues of $55.5 million and a net income of $4.4 million. Total assets amounted to $23.7 million.

Galaxy also sent the bank the pro forma statement of revenues and expenses, depicted in Table 7.2. The purpose of this statement is to project monthly revenues and expenses for the next year. The usefulness of pro forma statement depends on the accuracy of the projections and the assumptions that are made constructing it. For example, this pro forma statement projected that revenues will increase 5 percent monthly at the beginning of the period and then at a decreasing rate for the remainder of the year. Total revenues for the year are expected to be $69.9 million, up from $55.5 million in the previous year. Galaxy assumed, for example, that cost of goods sold would be 65 percent of sales, and they made other assumptions about costs. If the projections and assumptions are correct, the statement is a useful tool for both the firm and the bank. Otherwise, its usefulness depends on the degree to which it errs. The

TABLE 7.2
PRO FORMA STATEMENT OF REVENUES AND EXPENSES

GALAXY STEREO, INC.
Pro forma Statement ($000)

	Jan.	Feb.	Mar.	Apr.	May	Jun.	Jul.	Aug.	Sep.	Oct.	Nov.	Dec.	Total
Revenues													
Total sales	$4,612	$4,843	$5,036	$5,238	$5,447	$5,665	$5,892	$6,127	$6,373	$6,627	$6,893	$7,168	$69,921
Other	138	145	151	157	163	170	177	184	191	199	207	215	2,098
Total	$4,750	$4,988	$5,187	$5,395	$5,611	$5,835	$6,069	$6,311	$6,564	$6,826	$7,099	$7,383	$72,019
Expenses													
Cost of goods sold	2,998	3,148	3,274	3,405	3,541	3,682	3,830	3,983	4,142	4,308	4,480	4,659	45,449
Depreciation	369	387	403	419	436	453	471	490	510	530	551	573	5,594
Selling & administrative	876	920	957	995	1,035	1,076	1,119	1,164	1,211	1,259	1,310	1,362	13,285
R & D	92	97	101	105	109	113	118	123	127	133	138	143	1,398
Interest	92	97	101	105	109	113	118	123	127	133	138	143	1,398
Taxes	138	145	151	157	163	170	177	184	191	199	207	215	2,098
Total	$4,428	$4,649	$4,835	$5,028	$5,229	$5,439	$5,656	$5,882	$6,118	$6,362	$6,617	$6,882	$67,124
Net Income	323	339	353	367	381	397	412	429	446	464	482	502	4,894

bank's credit analysts should make their own projections and compare the results.

Some firms provide banks with cash budgets, which are projections of inflows and outflows of cash. This is especially useful to banks because loans are repaid out of cash, and the figures provide additional information that they will use when they evaluate the loan request. The pro forma statement shown in the figure includes sales for credit and noncash expenses such as depreciation. Thus, the cash available to repay loans each month is not the same as the net income.[1]

Business Plan

A business plan serves two purposes. First, it is a document used to raise money.[2] It describes a firm's past and current operations and explains how the funds that are being raised will be used to further the firm's goals, to reward the firm's investors, and to repay the loans. Second, a business plan is used internally to provide operating guidelines to managers so they know what is expected of them. Some key elements that appear in business plans are:

- The goals and objectives of the business.
- A description of the business, including its history and comments on products, services, and markets. Included here is an analysis of management's skills and weakness, and the financial condition of the firm.
- An analysis of the competition as well as threats to and opportunities for the firm.
- Strategies that the firm will use to compete.
- An operating plan to carry out the goals and strategies.
- A process to monitor the progress of the plan and to revise it if necessary.

Galaxy Industries provided a five-page summary of their business plan to the bank. Maurice Isaac knew that the most effective business plans used to raise funds were short ones. Most bankers do not want to read 50- to 100-page business plans.

Initial Interview

The bank uses the initial interview with prospective borrowers to obtain all of the information necessary to make a loan decision. That interview may be the

---

[1] For commentary on cash flows and how they should be calculated, see Leopold A. Bernstein and Mostafa M. Masky, "Again Now: How Do We Measure Cash Flow from Operations?" *Financial Analysts Journal,* July/August 1985. pp. 74–77. For problems interpreting cash flows, see Benton E. Gup and Michael T. Duggan, "Cash Flow: The Tip of An Iceberg," *Business Horizons,* September/October 1988.

[2] Business plans used for this purpose are described in Joseph R. Mancuso, *How to Start, Finance, and Manage Your Own Business,* Englewood Cliffs, NJ: Prentice-Hall, 1978, and William R. Osgood, *How to Plan and Finance Your Business,* Boston: CBI Publishing, 1980.

only time that the borrower and banker meet face-to-face. The interview may take place at the bank or at the prospective borrower's place of business. Many banks require their loan officers to complete reports about the initial interview. When a borrower's business plan is not available, the bank wants to know about the current state of the business and its prospects. Banks also want a brief history of the business, its officers, and financial statements for the past 5 years if they are available. Typical questions that bankers ask prospective borrowers during initial interviews are: Is your business a sole proprietorship, a partnership, or a corporation? Is its trade area local, national, or international? Do you have loans outstanding now, and what are the terms of the loans? If your other bank treated you so well, why are you coming to us now? Specific questions with respect to the loan are:

- What is the amount of the loan?
- When are the funds needed?
- How are the funds going to be used?
- When is the loan going to be repaid?
- How is the loan going to be repaid?
- What collateral will be pledged?

When a firm provides the bank with a business plan, the bank may use the initial interview to clarify certain aspects of the plan and to discuss the terms of the loan.

EVALUATING A LOAN REQUEST

The next step in the process of commercial lending is for the bank to evaluate the loan requests. The evaluation involves the so-called 5 Cs of credit, which are:

Character (personal characteristics of the borrower and attitudes about willingness to pay debts)

Capacity (ability to pay debts)

Capital (financial condition)

Collateral (pledged assets)

Conditions (economic conditions)

The 5 Cs are used to determine (1) whether the borrower can and will repay the loan and (2) the degree of risk associated with the loan. Risk, used in this context, refers to the likelihood of default. Default may mean failure for the firm and potential losses and negative public relations for the bank.

In addition to the 5 Cs, other factors must be considered before granting a loan. The other factors involve the type of business requesting the loan and the composition of the bank's loan portfolio.

Character

The term **character** refers to a combination of qualities that distinguishes one person or group from another. To some extent, the words **character** and **reputation** overlap in meaning. We are using character to refer to a borrower's honesty, responsibility, integrity, and consistency to determine their willingness to repay loans. Evidence of these traits can be found in a firm's credit record, which reveals whether it pays bills on time and takes trade discounts. Credit records may contain information about legal actions against the firm concerning payment of bills and other information that is pertinent to bankers. Credit records may be obtained from other banks, from credit bureaus, and from credit agencies such as Dun and Bradstreet. Figure 7.2 contains a typical Dun and Bradstreet credit report. It gives vital data about the firm, with particular emphasis on its history of payments and its financial condition. A history of the president and the operations of the firm are also provided.

Banks also exchange information concerning their customers. Box 7.1 presents Robert Morris Associates' code of ethics concerning the exchange of commercial credit information between banks. All of the credit information considered collectively should indicate the borrowers' willingness to pay.

Capacity

Capacity relates to the borrowers' financial ability to pay their obligations. Their financial ability to pay is determined by current and expected income and expenses. Financial analysis of the borrowers' financial statements gives some insight into their capacity. Recent audited financial statements are preferred for this purpose.

Borrowers' capacity may be affected by economic or business conditions over which they have no control. For example, suppose that a builder borrowed funds to construct an apartment building. Neither the lender nor the builder was aware that other builders were raising funds to build apartments nearby. All of the builders obtained their funds and built apartments. The result was excess capacity of apartments in that area. This, in turn, led to intense competition and lower than expected rental income. Several builders who were unable to meet their projected incomes went bankrupt. The point is that external factors over which the borrower and lender have no control can turn otherwise sound projects into failures; and vice versa.

Capacity also refers to one's legal capacity to borrow funds. That is, a borrower representing a corporation or partnership must have their written authorization to make a loan on their behalf. This is part of the representations that will be discussed shortly.

Financial Analysis

Financial analysis consists of evaluating a firm's current financial condition and then comparing that firm's ratios with those of similar firms. Table 7.3 illustrates financial ratios for Galaxy Stereo. The ratios were calculated by the

```
        Dun & Bradstreet, Inc.              This report has been prepared for

     BE SURE NAME, BUSINESS AND        ANSWERING        SUBSCRIBER: 008-001042
     ADDRESS MATCH YOUR FILE           INQUIRY

        THIS REPORT MAY NOT BE REPRODUCED IN WHOLE OR IN PART IN ANY MANNER WHATEVER

     CONSOLIDATED REPORT                              {FULL REVISION}
```

```
DUNS: 06-647-3261            DATE PRINTED              SUMMARY
RETTINGER PAINT CORP.        AUG 13, 197-      RATING         CC2

727 WHITMAN WAY              WHOL PAINTS &     STARTED        1950
BENSON, MI  48232            VARNISHES         PAYMENTS       DISC-PPT
     TEL 313 961-0720                          SALES        $ 424,612
                            SIC NO.            WORTH        $ 101,867
                            51 98              EMPLOYS        5
CARL RETTINGER, PRES.                          HISTORY        CLEAR
                                               CONDITION      GOOD
                                               TREND          STEADY


SPECIAL EVENTS   Business burglarized July 3 but $18,000 loss is fully insured.


PAYMENTS  {Amounts may be rounded to nearest figure in prescribed ranges}
REPORTED  PAYING       HIGH        NOW      PAST     SELLING      LAST SALE
          RECORD       CREDIT      OWES     DUE      TERMS        WITHIN
07/7-     Disc         30000       17000    -0-      2 10 30      1-2 mos.
          Disc         27000       14000    -0-      1 10 30      2-3 mos.
          Disc-Ppt     12000       4400     200      2 10 30      1 mo.
          Ppt          9000        8000     -0-      30           1 mo.
06/7-     Disc         16000       7500     -0-      2 10 30      2-3 mos.
05/7-     Disc         9000        3800     -0-      2 10 30      1 mo.
          Ppt          1500        -0-      -0-      30           1-2 mos.


FINANCE
06/22/7-        Fiscal statement dated May 31, 197-:
           Cash          $ 20,623        Accts Payable        $  47,246
           Accts Rec       55,777        Owing Bank              34,000
           Merchandise     92,103        Notes Pay {Trucks}       7,020
                         ---------                             ---------
             Current      168,503          Current               88,266
           Fixts. & Equip. 13,630        Common Stock            35,000
           Trucks           8,000        Earned Surplus          66,867
                         -------                               ---------
           Total Assets   190,133          Total               190,133
           SALES {Yr}: $424,612.  Net profit $17,105.  Fire ins. mdse $95,000;
        equipt $20,000.  Mo. rent: $3500.  Prepared by Steige Co., CPAs, Detroit, MI.

                              --0--
           06/22/7- Lawson defined monthly payments: $3000 to bank, $400 on notes.
        Admitted collections slow but losses insignificant.  Said inventory will drop
        to $60,000 by December.  Expects 5% sales increase this year.
PUBLIC FILINGS
03/25/7-        March 17, 197- financing statement A741170 named subject as debtor and
        NCR Corp., Dayton, O. as secured party.  Collateral: equipment.
05/28/7-        May 21, 197- suit for $200 entered by Henry Assoc., Atlanta, Ga. Docket
        A27519.  Involves merchandise which Lawson says was defective.
BANKING
06/25/7-        Account, long maintained, carries average balances low to moderate five
        figures.  Unsecured loans to moderate five extended and now open.
HISTORY
06/22/7-  CARL RETTINGER, PRES.              JOHN J. LAWSON, V PRES.
          DIRECTORS:  The Officers
                Incorporated Michigan February 2, 1950.  Authorized capital 3500 shares,
        no par common.  Paid in capital $35,000, officers sharing equally.
                RETTINGER, born 1920, married.  Employed by E-Z Paints, Detroit 12 yrs,
        five as manager until starting subject early 1950.
                LAWSON, born 1925, married.  Obtained accounting degree 1946 and then
        employed by Union Carbide, Chicago until joining Rettinger at inception.
OPERATION
06/22/7-        Wholesales paints and varnishes {85%}, wallpaper and supplies.  500
        local accounts include retailers {75%} and contractors.  Terms: 2 10 30.  Peak
        season spring thru summer.  EMPLOYEES: Officers active with three others.
        LOCATION: Rents 7500 sq ft. one-story block structure, good repair.
```

FIGURE 7.2   A Credit Report.

BOX 7.1

RMA CODE OF ETHICS

Robert Morris Associates developed the following Code of Ethics for the exchange of credit information between banks. The articles of the Code are:

1. There are two cardinal principles in the exchange of credit information: confidentiality and accuracy of inquiries and replies. This includes the identity of inquiries and sources which cannot be disclosed without their permission. Adherence to these and the other principles embodied in the Code is essential, since offenders jeopardize their privilege to participate further in the exchange of credit information.

2. Each inquiry should indicate its purpose and amount involved.

3. Responses should be prompt and disclose sufficient material facts commensurate with the purpose and amount of the inquiry. Specific questions should be given careful and frank replies.

4. It is not permissible when soliciting an account to make an inquiry to a competitor without frankly disclosing that that subject of the inquiry is a prospect. Reply is at the discretion of the bank of account.

5. A request for information based on actual or contemplated litigation shall be clearly identified as such. Reply is at the discretion of the bank of account.

6. All credit correspondence, including form letters, should bear the manual signature of a responsible party.

7. The sharing of credit information on a mutual customer should not be more frequent than annually, unless a significant change in the relationship requires an earlier revision.

8. When multiple inquiries are made simultaneously on the same subject, the inquirer should clearly state that information from the bank's own files is sufficient.

Source: Robert Morris Associates, *Code of Ethics*, Philadelphia, Pa., 1980.

TABLE 7.3
FINANCIAL ANALYSIS

GALAXY STEREO, INC.
Financial Statements ($000)

| | December 31 | | | Percent of Sales | | |
	1985	1986	1987	1985	1986	1987
Income and Expenses						
Sales	$ 12,950.00	$ 22,367.00	$54,120.00	100.00%	100.00%	100.00%
Other revenue	228.00	516.00	1,421.00	0.02	0.02	0.03
Total	$ 13,178.00	$ 22,883.00	$55,541.00	1.02	1.02	1.03
Cost of goods sold	11,190.00	14,581.00	38,101.00	0.86	0.65	0.70
Depreciation		671.50	1,004.00	0.00	0.05	0.08
Expenses						
Sales	2,117.00	3,818.00	7,732.00	0.16	0.17	0.14
General & administrative	822.00	1,512.00	2,944.00	0.06	0.07	0.05
Research & development	724.00	1,192.00	1,351.00	0.06	0.05	0.02
Interest	230.00	539.00	935.00	0.02	0.02	0.02
Total	$ 3,893.00	$ 7,061.00	$12,962.00	0.30	0.32	0.24
Earnings	−1,782.00	168.00	3,918.00	−0.14	0.01	0.07
Taxes	0.00	60.00	1,545.00	0.00	.00	0.03
Extraordinary items	191.00	60.00	1,458.00	0.01	.00	0.03
Net income from operations	−1,905.00	1,181.00	2,933.00	−0.15	0.05	0.05
Net income	−1,714.00	1,241.00	4,391.00	−0.13	0.06	0.08
Shares outstanding, fully diluted	7,000,000	7,900,500	9,310,250			
Earnings per share	−0.24	0.16	0.47			

| | | | | Percent of Assets | | |
	1985	1986	1987	1985	1986	1987
Assets						
Cash	$ 680.00	$ 411.00	$ 794.00	0.12	0.04	0.03
Accounts receivable	550.00	1,479.00	5,776.00	0.09	0.15	0.24
Inventory	1,262.00	2,629.00	6,073.00	0.22	0.26	0.26
Prepaid expenses	180.00	114.00	415.00	0.03	0.01	0.02
Deferred tax charges	0.00	0.00	173.00	0.00	0.00	0.01
Total Current	2,671.00	4,633.00	13,231.00	0.46	0.46	0.56
Plant and equipment	3,185.00	5,235.00	10,170.00	0.54	0.52	0.43
Other	5,579.00	177.00	336.00	0.95	0.02	0.01
Total Assets	$ 5,862.00	$ 10,045.00	$23,737.00	1.00	1.00	1.00
Liabilities and Equity						
Notes payable	782.00	901.00	2,114.00	0.13	0.09	0.09
Accounts payable	3,078.00	3,555.00	7,688.00	0.53	0.35	0.32
Accrued expenses	438.00	1,173.00	1,959.00	0.07	0.12	0.08
Current long-term debt	479.00	525.00	474.00	0.08	0.05	0.02
Taxes	0.00	0.00	87.00	0.00	0.00	0.00
Total Current	4,779.00	6,154.00	12,322.00	0.82	0.61	0.52
Long-term debt	219.00	2,679.00	3,015.00	0.04	0.27	0.13
Long-term leases	475.00	250.00	224.00	0.08	0.02	0.01

TABLE 7.3 (*continued*)

	December 31 1985	1986	1987	Percent of Sales 1985	1986	1987
Deferred taxes	0.00	0.00	173.00	0.00	0.00	0.01
Equity						
Common stock	75.00	79.00	93.00	0.01	0.01	0.00
Additional paid in capital	3,345.00	4,109.00	7,305.00	0.57	0.41	0.31
Retained earnings	−3,031.00	−2,863.00	968.00	−0.52	−0.29	0.04
Less Treasury shares at cost	0.00	−363.00	−363.00	0.00	−0.04	−0.02
Total Equity	389.00	962.00	8,003.00	0.07	0.10	0.34
Total Liabilities & Equity	$ 5,862.00	$ 10,045.00	$23,737.00	1.00	1.00	1.00
Market Data						
Cash dividends/share	0.00	0.00	0.00			
Dividend payout ratio	0.00	0.00	0.00			
Price/share (high)	2.25	7.75	4.50			
Market value equity	15,750,000	61,228,875	41,896,125			

	1985	1986	1987
Ratios:			
Profitability			
Earnings per share	−0.24	0.16	0.47
Return on equity	−4.41	1.29	0.55
Return on assets	−0.29	0.12	0.18
Internal growth rate	−4.41	1.29	0.55
Profit margin	−0.13	0.06	0.08
Tax rate	0.00	0.05	0.35
Activity			
Sales per day	35.48	61.28	148.27
Days receivables outstanding	15.50	24.14	38.95
Days inventory outstanding	35.57	42.90	40.96
Days cash outstanding	19.17	6.71	5.35
Days payable outstanding	1.18	0.69	0.28
Capital expenditures		917.00	5,903.00
Change in capacity		0.18	0.58
Number of dealers	410	679	1303
Sales per dealer	31.59	32.94	41.53
Liquidity			
Quick ratio	0.26	0.50	0.53
Current ratio	0.56	0.75	1.07
Leverage			
Long-term debt/equity	1.78	3.04	0.40
Interest coverage	−6.75	1.31	5.19

TABLE 7.3 (*continued*)

	1985	1986	1987
Bankruptcy Model, Z Ratio			
X1 Market value of equity	15,750,000	61,228,875	41,896,125
X2 Current assets/total assets	0.46	0.46	0.56
X3 Retained earnings/total assets	−0.52	−0.29	0.04
X4 EBIT/total assets	−0.26	0.07	0.20
X5 X1/book value of debt	3.15	6.93	2.73
X6 Asset turnover	2.25	2.28	2.34

$$Z = 1.2\ X2 + 1.4\ X3 + 3.3\ X4 + 0.6\ X5 + 0.99\ X6$$

	1985	1986	1987
Z =	3.07	6.80	5.36

Z Score >3 = bankruptcy not likely
Z Score >1.8 and <3 = Not defined
Z Score <1.8 = bankruptcy characteristics

bank's credit analysts on a personal computer, using an electronic spreadsheet. Western National Bank developed its own format for financial analysis, although commercial versions are available. The table shows income and expense items expressed as a percent of sales, and balance sheet items expressed as a percent of total assets. In addition, various ratios and indicators were computed dealing with market data, profitability, activity, liquidity, and leverage. Finally, a model used to predict the likelihood of bankruptcy was calculated. The definitions of the measures used in Table 7.3 appear in Table 7.4.

The credit analysis is based on quarterly or annual data provided by the firm. Because it may take a month or more after the quarter has ended to get the data to the bank, the current financial condition of the firm may differ significantly from what appears on their financial statements. Equally important, audited financial statements may differ from those used for internal control. These are reasons why loan officers must keep abreast of current developments with their customers.

The most important part of financial analysis is interpreting the data. Credit analysts look for trends and problem areas and then assess firms' ability to repay loans. A detailed explanation of the financial ratios and indicators is beyond the scope of this book. Nevertheless, examining some of Galaxy's data is worthwhile. For example, the credit analyst noticed that the number of days of accounts receivable outstanding more than doubled in the 3-year period under review. She wondered whether Galaxy was selling stereos, but not collecting on the sales—a condition that can cause serious cash flow problems. However, a review of the business plan provided the answer: Galaxy recently began offering credit terms to dealers. The dealers have 30 days to pay for their purchases. The increased receivables contributed to higher liquidity ratios for

TABLE 7.4
DEFINITIONS OF RATIOS

Market Data	**Equations**
Cash dividends/share	Cash dividends/number of shares
Dividend payout ratio	Cash dividends/net income
Price/share (high)	From company reports
Market value equity	Market price $\times$ number of shares

Ratios:
Profitability

Earnings per share	Net income/number of shares
Return on equity	Net income/total equity
Return on assets	Net income/total asset
Internal growth rate	(1-dividend payout ratio) $\times$ return on equity
Profit margin	Net income/sales
Tax rate	Taxes/net income

Activity

Sales per day	Sales/365 (NOTE: understates total revenue/ day)
Days receivables outstanding	Accounts receivable/sales per day
Days inventory outstanding	Inventory/sales per day
Days cash outstanding	Cash/sales per day
Days payable outstanding	Accounts payable/sales per day
Capital expenditures	From company reports
Change in capacity	Capital expenditures/plant and equipment
Number of dealers	From company reports
Sales per dealer	Sales/number of dealers

Liquidity

Quick ratio	(Cash + accounts receivable)/current liabilities
Current ratio	Current assets/current liabilities

Leverage

Long-term debt/equity	(Long-term debt + leases)/equity
Interest coverage	Earnings before interest and taxes (EBIT)/ interest

Bankruptcy Model, Z Ratio

X1 Market value of equity	Market price $\times$ number of shares
X2 Current assets/total assets	Current assets/total assets
X3 Retained earnings/total assets	Retained earnings/total assets
X4 EBIT/total assets	EBIT/total assets
X5 X1/book value of debt	Market value of equity/book value of debt
X6 Asset turnover	Total revenue/total assets

the firm. She also noted that the firm had relatively little debt and easily covered its interest payments. Also, Galaxy paid its short-term obligations on time—maybe too fast.

Next she compared Galaxy's ratios to those of other firms. She obtained the data for other firms from *RMA Annual Statement Studies*.[3] Robert Morris Associates (RMA) is a national association of commercial loan and credit officers that provides information and other services for commercial bankers. The *RMA Annual Statement Studies* provide comparative financial data on more than 300 lines of business. Dun and Bradstreets' *Key Business Ratios in 800 Lines* is another valuable source of information.[4] Finally, many trade groups publish financial data concerning their members. For example, the National Restaurant Association publishes the *Restaurant Industry Operations Report,* and the American Trucking Association publishes *Financial and Operating Statistics*.[5]

Industry Analysis

Evaluating "capacity" also involves an analysis of the firm's industry and business. Some of this information is provided by the firm itself in the business plan. Additional information about specific industries is available from a variety of sources, including U.S. Department of Commerce, *U.S. Industrial Outlook,* and Standard & Poor's *Industry Surveys*. In the case of Galaxy, the credit analyst knows that there is intense competition from other wholesale distributors and excess production capacity overseas. This suggests that there will be substantial price cutting, which may affect Galaxy's projections of revenues. In addition, she knows from experience with distributors, that they have had problems controlling the dealers that handle their lines. Much of Galaxy's growth came from sales to new dealers, and she believed that the rate of growth would slow appreciably.

Capital

Capital represents the amount of equity capital that a firm has, which can be liquidated for payment if all other means of debt collection fail. Equity capital is equal to total assets less total liabilities and is also referred to as book value. There may be considerable differences between the book value of assets and their liquidation value—the amount that one would receive in a forced sale. In any case, bankers consider equity capital as a cushion of assets in the event of a loan default.

---

[3] Published annually be Robert Morris Associates, Philadelphia National Bank Bldg., Philadelphia, Pa. 19107.

[4] Dun and Bradstreet, Inc., 99 Church Street, New York, N.Y., 10007.

[5] National Restaurant Association, 1850 K Street, N.W., Washington, DC 20006; American Trucking Association, Inc., 1616 P St., N.W., Washington, DC 20036.

Collateral

Collateral refers to assets that are pledged for security in a credit transaction. As mentioned in Chapter 6, bankers prefer collateral that is tangible, durable, and easily identifiable, such as a shopping center. Accounts receivable and inventories are also widely used as collateral, and that is what Galaxy wants to use. Galaxy's inventory consists of stereos and compact disc players, and their accounts receivable are from more than 1,200 retail distributors, which are mostly small firms. Based on Galaxy's financial analysis (Table 7.3), most of the distributors are paying on time. Nevertheless, Western National Bank's experience with small retail distributors of electronic goods has not been good; they have a high mortality rate.

Conditions

Conditions refers to external factors that are beyond the control of a firm, but may affect their ability to repay debts. Import restrictions on electronic equipment such as stereos is one example of an external factor that could affect Galaxy. Changes in tax laws, regulations, energy prices, and technology are other factors that affect some firms. In a previous example, excess capacity in apartments caused some builders to go bankrupt.

Other Considerations in Lending

Even if a prospective borrower satisfies the 5 Cs of credit, the bank may decide to deny the loan. One reason for denying the loan is that the bank may not want to make loans to particular types of businesses or to foreign businesses. For example, Western National Bank has a policy against lending to mining operations in South Africa. The bank also limits the dollar amount of loans that it will lend in Central America and Africa. In addition, Western National Bank believes in diversification, and does not permit more than 5 percent of its total commercial loans to be concentrated in any one industry.

Small banks located in areas dominated by one firm or industry have more difficulty diversifying their loan portfolios. In the mid-1980s, for example, many small agricultural banks in Iowa had financial trouble because some farmers were unable to repay their debts. The problem loans were concentrated among those who borrowed large sums to buy farmland that appreciated in value during the 1970s. Lower farm income during the early 1980s' recession resulted in operating losses for some farmers, and they were unable to cover the interest payments on their loans. At the same time, the value of Iowa farmlands declined in reaction to the prospects for lower earnings. Accordingly, some farmers were unable to sell their land at prices sufficient to cover their debts. The result was that agricultural banks in Iowa had to charge-off (write off as a loss) a large 1.31 percent of their loans in the first half of 1985 compared to 0.72 percent at other agricultural banks in the United States. Agricultural banks in Iowa and elsewhere accounted for more than half of the bank failures in 1985. Most of the failed banks were relatively small, with average assets of $22 million.[6]

STRUCTURING COMMERCIAL LOAN AGREEMENTS

When a bank decides to make a loan, all of the terms of the loan are put into a contract called a loan agreement. All commercial loan agreements have three basic elements: (1) the amount to be borrowed, (2) the method of repayment, and (3) the fees to be paid by the borrower to the banker. The structuring of a loan refers to the essential provisions of loan agreements that specify the obligations and responsibilities of both the borrower and the banker. Most commercial loans are designed to meet the needs of a particular borrower; therefore the provisions of loan agreements may be different. Nevertheless, some provisions that are common to commercial loan agreements are presented here.[7]

Amount and Terms of Credit Facilities

Type and Amount

The loan agreement states the type of credit facility (i.e., revolving loan) and the amount that may be borrowed. Recall that Galaxy asked for a $4-million revolving loan. The bank may limit the amount of the loan outstanding to, say, the lesser of $4 million or 70 percent of the value of the eligible collateral. In addition, Galaxy may be required to borrow in increments of $100,000. Some banks require an annual clean-up of their revolving loans. This means that the bank might require a certain period (i.e., 30 days) when there is no loan outstanding. The purpose of the annual clean-up is to show the bank that the loan is used to meet seasonal needs and is not being used as permanent financing.

Collateral Documentation

If a loan is secured by collateral, it is necessary to get proper documentation granting the bank a security interest or lien in that collateral. Perfecting a security interest or lien may entail a land survey, title search, executing pledge agreements and other documents, and filing them with the proper legal authorities. Unless the documentation is done according to the letter of the law, the banker may have no legal claim on the collateral. The documentation should be completed before the loan is made.

---

[6] Emanuel Melichar, Division of Research and Statistics, Board of Governors of the Federal Reserve System, ''Farm Financial Experience and Agricultural Banking Experience.'' Statement before the Subcommittee on Economic Stabilization of the Committee on Banking, Finance, and Urban Affairs, U.S. House of Representatives, October 23, 1985.

[7] For additional details of loan provisions, see Roger Tighe, *Structuring Commercial Loan Agreements,* Boston: Warren, Gorham & Lamont, 1984.

Repayment

The repayment of loans can vary from 1 day to 3 years or longer. The entire amount can be due on 1 day, or repaid in a series of installments. As discussed in Chapter 6, the payment schedule should be related to the economic life of the assets being financed.

The loan agreement may provide for the prepayment of all or part of the loan. The prepayment (paying the loan before it is due) may be at the borrower's discretion or required by the banker if the borrower does not comply with certain provisions of the loan. For example, the entire balance is due in 30 days if the borrower sells the factory that is pledged as collateral.

In order to extend the period of financing, banks may have a revolving loan followed by term loan. That is, when the revolving loan is due, the bank extends a term loan for the amount outstanding. Loans that are "rolled over" by using revolving/term loans, evergreen facilities, or by some other means may represent "permanent" financing for the borrower. Generally speaking, banks should not provide permanent financing.

Interest Rates and Fees

The interest charged on loan balances may be computed at a fixed rate of interest or at a variable rate of interest. The loan agreement states the interest rate that will be charged for fixed rate loans (i.e., 15 percent), or the basis for floating-rate loans. For example, a floating-rate loan may be priced at the bank's prime rate (or some other index) plus 2 percentage points per annum. If the bank's prime rate is 12 percent at the time the loan is made, the borrower will be charged 14 percent. When the prime rate changes, however, the interest rate charged the borrower will also change.

Representations

In a loan agreement, a **representation** is the statement of facts made by a borrower to induce a banker to make a loan. Galaxy provided Western National Bank with information about its legal status as an organization, its authority to borrow funds, its financial condition and creditworthiness, about its business, and other important information that may affect the financial relationship between the two.

Bankers know that some corporate bylaws and regulations limit their ability to borrow. For example, a division of a large corporation may have limited borrowing authority. Proper documentation of the division's authority to borrow is required prior to making a loan.

Representations are supposed to be true at the time the loan is made. Misrepresentations may violate criminal codes and subject the borrower to both civil and criminal proceedings in the event of default.

Covenants

In order to obligate the borrower to maintain certain conditions, the loan agreement may contain covenants. A **covenant** is a promise by the borrower in a loan agreement to take, or not to take, certain actions. Covenants help protect the bank's investment by providing guidelines for the operation of the borrower's business, and by providing information about the borrower. If the borrower fails to comply with the covenants, the bank can take appropriate actions to restrict additional loans or to recover the amounts due.

Affirmative Covenants

Promises to take actions are called affirmative covenants. Requiring borrowers to maintain their properties, keep them insured, pay their obligations, comply with the law, and provide periodic financial statements are examples of affirmative covenants.

Negative Covenants

Promises not to take actions are called negative covenants. They usually concern the borrowers' operations and prohibit them from taking certain actions in the ordinary course of business. For example, as long as the loan agreement is in effect, the borrower might be prohibited from selling bonds without the consent of the bank. Prohibiting the borrower from pledging or encumbering any of its real assets, or paying cash dividends, or selling its assets (other than inventory) are examples of restrictive covenants.

Financial Covenants

The borrower may be required to provide the bank with periodic financial statements. These may be used to monitor the borrower's financial condition. In addition, the bank may require that the borrower maintain certain financial ratios. For example, Galaxy may be required to maintain a current ratio (current assets/current liabilities) of 1.0 or more and a long-term debt-to-equity ratio of less than 0.75.

Default

Borrowers are in default when they do not comply with the covenants. Being in default permits the bank to take certain remedies to protect its investment. The bank may require the borrower to correct the problems within a stated period of time, or take whatever action is necessary to collect its funds. The extreme case is forcing the borrower into bankruptcy.

LOAN PRICING

One key element in the process of commercial lending is loan pricing—determining what interest rate to charge the borrower and how to calculate that rate. The interest rate can be determined by using a loan pricing model. The purpose of loan pricing models is to determine the minimum price that a bank should charge on a commercial loan. Before we examine loan pricing, let's consider the effective yield.

How to Calculate the Effective Yield

There is a difference between the nominal interest rate—the interest rate stated in the loan agreement—and the effective yield that takes the payment accrual basis and the payment frequency into account. The method for calculating effective yields will be explained after some terms have been defined.

Payment Accrual Basis

The **payment accrual basis** refers to the number of days used in the interest rate calculation. One part of the calculation involves the number of days in a year. Interest may be calculated on the basis of a 365-day year or a 360-day year. To illustrate the difference, consider a $1-million loan at a 10-percent nominal rate of interest. The daily interest payment (interest income to the bank and interest expense to the borrower) of the loan is determined by multiplying the amount of the loan by the nominal interest rate and then dividing by the appropriate number of days (365 or 360), and multiplying that figure by the amount of the loan. Accordingly, the cost of a $1-million loan at 10-percent interest is $273.97 on a 365-day basis and $277.78 on a 360-day basis. These calculations will be presented shortly.

Another part of the calculation involves the number of days that the loan is outstanding. One can use the *actual* number of days the loan is outstanding, or a 30-day month base can be used.

Payment Frequency

The final variable is the frequency of interest payments. Typically, term loans are structured with monthly, quarterly, or annual payments. Because of the time value of money (money is worth more today than if the same amount is received in the future), frequent payments are favored by bankers but are harder to sell to borrowers.

Effective Yield

To illustrate the effective yield, let's consider a 345-day term loan beginning on January 1 and ending on December 11. The principal amount is $1 million and the interest rate is 10 percent. The calculations for a 360-day year and 30-day month are as follows:

1.	$1,000,000	Principal amount
2.	× 0.10	Annual interest rate
3.	$100,000	Annual interest amount
4.	360	Divide by number of days in year (360 or 365)
5.	$277.78	Daily interest payment
6.	× (30 days × 11 months + 11 days)	Times 11, 30-day months plus 11 days (341 days) or the actual number of days
7.	$94,722.22	Total interest paid

$$\text{Effective yield} = \frac{\text{Total interest paid}}{\text{Principal amount}} \times \frac{365}{\text{Term of loan in days}} \quad (7.1)$$

$$= \frac{\$94,722.22}{\$1,000,000.00} \times \frac{365}{345} = 10.02\%$$

The same process (with the appropriate number of days in lines 4 and 6) may be used to calculate the effective yields for 360-day years with actual number of days and 365-day years with actual number of days. The effective yield for the three methods are:

	Effective Yield
360-day year/30-day month	10.02%
360-day year/actual number of days	10.14%
365-day year/actual number of days	10.00%

Loan-Pricing Models

Naive Model

The purposes of a loan-pricing model are (1) to help establish the minimum rate that a bank should charge on a loan and (2) to determine whether the income from a loan covers all of the expenses plus a profit. Unfortunately, no single loan-pricing model is suitable for all types of loans. Accordingly, a bank may use different methods for pricing different types of loans. For example, an overnight "federal funds" loan would not be priced in the same way as a construction loan to build a shopping center. Moreover, a loan-pricing model that is suitable for a large bank may not be appropriate for a small bank. Keeping this in mind, let's examine several different loan-pricing models. The general notion of a loan-pricing model is expressed in equation (7.2).

$$\text{Rate of return (\%)} = \frac{\text{Net income (\$)}}{\text{Loan (\$)}} \quad (7.2)$$

This equation gives us the rate of return on the loan, which is the interest income charged on a loan divided by the amount of the loan. Suppose a bank makes a loan for $100 and wants a minimum rate of return of 12-percent interest. Using equation (7.2) to solve for net income, the bank must earn $12 in order to obtain a 12-percent rate of return.

$$12\% = \frac{\$12}{\$100}$$

Return on Net Funds Employed

The loan-pricing model we are going to examine works in the same fashion. The bank establishes the required rate of return that it wants to earn on the loan, and then it has to determine the net income from the loan. If the loan cannot generate sufficient net income to earn the required rate of return, the bank should consider rejecting the loan.

We will now examine each of the components of the model, and then solve for loan income.

Marginal cost of funds + Profit goal

$$= \frac{(\text{Loan income} - \text{Loan expense})}{\text{Net bank funds employed}} \quad (7.3)$$

Required Rate of Return

In this model, the required rate of return is equal to the marginal cost of funds plus a profit goal. The marginal cost of funds is the bank's short-term cost of funds. The 90-day CD rate is frequently used as a proxy for the marginal cost of funds. The profit goal is a markup over the cost of funds, and it reflects the degree of risk involved in the loan. For example, a low risk loan might be priced at the marginal cost of funds plus, say, 2 percentage points per annum. The markup will increase as the risk increases. Thus, the highest risk loan that the bank is willing to make has a markup of 5 percentage points.

The percentage return that the bank charges on its loans must also take into account the rate of return required by the bank's shareholders. Like any other business, the financial objective of management is to maximize shareholder wealth.

Loan Income

Net income is loan income less loan expense. Loan income comes from interest charges and fees. The fees include commitment fees, origination fees (for setting up the loan), and fees for other services.

Loan Expense

Loan expense includes all direct and indirect costs associated with making, servicing, and collecting the loan; however, it does not include the bank's cost of funds. Making effective cost estimates to be used in the model is difficult to do. To illustrate the difficulty, suppose that a loan officer spent 35 hours' working time trying to attract a new loan customer. Let's consider just the officer's time, which is worth $100 per hour. The cost is $3,500. If the customer borrows $10,000 for 90 days, the equation suggests that the bank would have to charge more than $3,500 (35 percent) to cover that cost alone. Obviously the bank would not attempt to charge that amount. Nevertheless, someone has to pay for the loan officer's time. This is done by using cost accounting data and trying to make reasonable estimates of the cost of making, servicing, and collecting loans.

Net Bank Funds Employed

The net bank funds employed is the average amount of the loan over its life, less funds provided by the borrower, net of Federal Reserve reserve requirements. Borrowers provide funds in the form of compensating balances or other balances held at the bank. The bank cannot use the entire amount on deposit because the Federal Reserve System requires that it maintain a specified amount of reserves against those balances.

To illustrate the use of equation (7.3), let's make the following assumptions:

1. Marginal cost of funds is 10 percent.
2. Profit goal is 2 percent.
3. Loan expense is $2,000.
4. Net bank funds employed is $100,000.

Given these assumptions, we use equation (7.3) to solve for loan income, which works out to $14,000.

$$(10\% + 2\%) = \frac{(\text{Loan income} - \$2,000)}{\$100,000}$$

$$\text{Loan income} = \$14,000$$

The $14,000 is the amount of income this loan must generate in order for the bank to earn its required rate of return. This figure understates the correct amount because it does not take the time value of money into account. Nevertheless, it is a good "ball-park" estimate of the income that is needed.

This loan-pricing model is best suited for banks that have effective cost accounting data and that can estimate the other data that are required. If this model is used to price variable rate loans, the rate of return to the bank will change whenever the loan rate changes. This problem is resolved in the next model.

Minimum Spread

Some banks price loans by determining the minimum spread they will accept between their lending rate and their costs plus a profit margin. For example, assume that a bank's costs are 12 percent. If the bank wants to encourage lending, it will accept a smaller profit margin and charge borrowers 13 percent. If the bank wants to retard lending, it will increase the spread and charge borrowers 15 percent. Encouraging and discouraging lending is common practice and reflects banks' changing financial needs. Banks know that many large commercial loans are repriced every day or every 30, 60, or 90 days, and that large borrowers regularly shop around for the lowest rates. A bank that increases its lending rate in one period to discourage a borrower may decide to make the loan the next time it is repriced. Loans to finance corporations waiting to sell commercial paper are an example of loans that are repriced frequently. As mentioned in Chapter 5, such loans account for about half of the total dollar volume of all commercial loans made.

Average Cost Versus Marginal Cost

The costs used in this model include the cost of funds and operating costs. Here, too, problems arise in determining the relevant costs. Because operating costs have been discussed previously, let's focus on the cost of funds. Should the bank use the average cost of funds or the marginal cost of funds? To illustrate this problem, suppose that a large firm wants to borrow $1 million for 90 days. The bank's lending rate is the cost of funds plus 1 percentage point per annum. The bank raised $0.5 million by selling a 90-day CD at 12 percent. The bank raised an additional $0.5 million in other interest-bearing deposits that cost 8 percent. The average cost of funds, which is determined by dividing total interest cost by total deposits and borrowed funds, is 10.0 percent. The marginal cost of funds, or the 90-day CD rate, is 12 percent.

Should the bank use the average cost of funds or the marginal cost of funds to price the loan? When market rates of interest are rising, the bank should use the marginal cost of funds because it is higher than the average cost of funds. When market rates of interest are falling, however, it should use the average cost of funds, which is higher than the marginal cost.[8]

Another consideration is how the loan is funded. If the $1-million, 90-day loan was **match funded** by selling a $1-million 90-day CD, the CD rate should be used. On the other hand, if the bank views all of its deposits as a "pool" of funds used to finance loans, the answer is still the marginal rate. In theory, the marginal loan (the next loan to be made) should be charged the marginal cost of funds.

All of the examples used here suggest that in order to make a profit, a bank's lending rate should be greater than its cost of funds. As explained in the appendix, however, there are exceptions to that rule.

---

[8] The relationship between the prime rate and the marginal cost of funds is discussed in Brian C. Gendreau, "When Is the Prime Rate Second Choice?" *Business Review,* Federal Reserve Bank of Philadelphia, May/June 1973, pp. 13–23. The relationship between the prime rate and the average cost of funds is discussed in Michael A. Goldberg, "The Pricing of the Prime Rate," *Journal of Banking and Finance,* June 1982, pp. 277–296.

Prime Rate

The **prime rate** is the base rate on corporate loans. In the past, the prime rate was the lowest commercial rate, but that is no longer the case. Today it is an index, and loans may be priced above or below the prime rate. Examples of loans priced below the prime rate include government guaranteed or insured loans, loans secured by the lending banks's CDs, loans made under commitments at lower rates, loans that have been renegotiated (i.e., loans in default that are being worked out), and student loans.[9]

The prime rate can vary from bank to bank. The prime rate that is published in *The Wall Street Journal,* for example, is for large money center U.S. commercial banks. The published prime may differ from the prime rate at other banks because of differences in costs of funds and markets.

The Price of Loans

Table 7.5 lists the average size, maturity, and interest charged on short-term, fixed rate commercial and industrial loans.[10] The data reveal that large short-term loans have lower interest rates than smaller longer-term loans. The largest category of loans has an average size of $7,865,000, 15 days maturity, and an interest rate of 7.62 percent. The smallest category of loans has an average size of $7,000, 111 days maturity, and an interest rate of 11.5 percent. There are several explanations for this. About half of the loans for $1 million or more are "overnight" loans with a maturity of 1 day. They are used by large, credit-worthy corporations to provide funds until they can sell commercial paper. These loans are treated more like securities transactions than loans. They have relatively little credit risk, despite the size of the loans. Moreover, the administrative costs of making large loans is lower than making an equivalent dollar amount of small loans. Also, it can be argued that the small-size loans are riskier than the large-size loans. There is some evidence to support that view. At the time these data were collected, the prime rate was 8.5 percent. Using this number as a reference, the rate charged by banks declined from 11.50 percent for small loans ($1,000 − $24,000) to 7.62 percent for larger-size loans, a spread of 388 basis points, reflecting both risk and administrative costs.

A case can be made that administrative costs associated with handling a large number of small loans are greater than the administrative costs of handling a few large ones, especially the 1-day loans that are treated more like securities transactions than loans. Accordingly, small borrowers were charged more than large borrowers.

---

[9] For an interesting article on this subject, see Gerald C. Fischer, "The Prime Rate Controversy: There Is Light at the End of the Tunnel," *The Journal of Commercial Bank Lending,* November 1984, pp. 13–22.

[10] For an in-depth analysis of loan-pricing, see Thomas R. Brady, "Changes in Loan Pricing and Business Lending at Commercial Banks," *Federal Reserve Bulletin,* January 1985, pp. 1–13.

TABLE 7.5
AVERAGE TERMS OF FIXED-RATE COMMERCIAL AND
INDUSTRIAL LOANS MADE FOR UNDER 1 YEAR,
FEBRUARY 1988

Size Category ($1,000)	Average Size ($1,000)	Maturity (days)	Loan Rate (percent)
$1–24	7	111	11.50
25–49	33	130	10.92
50–99	63	104	11.09
100–499	206	128	9.92
500–999	691	43	8.44
1,000+	7,865	15	7.62

Source. Federal Reserve Statistical Release E.2: "Survey of Terms of Bank Lending Made During February 1–5, 1988," March 11, 1988.

SUMMARY

The process of commercial lending begins with the request for a loan. Prospective borrowers provide the bank with detailed information about the business, and how the borrowed funds are going to be used and repaid. The information may be presented in a business plan or when the borrower is interviewed by the banker. Then the bank must evaluate the loan request. The evaluation involves the 5 Cs of credit: character, capacity, capital, collateral, and conditions. The bank also considers the composition of its loan portfolio. If the bank agrees to make a loan, it structures a loan agreement that specifies all of the terms and conditions for both the borrower and the lender. The loan agreement includes the interest rate that will be charged the borrower. The interest rate can be determined by using different loan-pricing models, depending on the needs of the bank and the borrower.

IMPORTANT CONCEPTS

affirmative convenant	5Cs of Credit
annual clean-up	initial interview
average cost of funds	loan-pricing model
business plan	marginal cost of funds
capacity	negative covenant
character	nominal interest rate
collateral	payment accrual basis
collateral documentation	prepayment
conditions	prime rate
covenant	representation
default	risk
effective yield	structuring a loan agreement
financial covenant	

REFERENCES

Bernstein, Leopold A., and Mostafa M. Masky. "Again Now: How Do We Measure Cash Flow from Operations?" *Financial Analysts Journal,* July/August 1985.

Brady, Thomas R. "Changes in Loan Pricing and Business Lending at Commercial Banks," *Federal Reserve Bulletin,* January 1985.

Fischer, Gerald C. "The Prime Rate Controversy: There Is Light at the End of the Tunnel," *The Journal of Commercial Bank Lending,* November 1984.

Gendreau, Brian C. "When Is the Prime Rate Second Choice?" *Business Review,* Federal Reserve Bank of Philadelphia, May/June 1973.

Goldberg, Michael A. "The Pricing of the Prime Rate," *Journal of Banking and Finance,* June 1982.

Gup, Benton E., and Michael T. Duggan. "Cash Flow: The Tip of An Iceberg," *Business Horizons,* September/October 1988.

Mancuso, Joseph R. *How to Start, Finance, and Manage Your Own Business.* Englewood Cliffs, NJ: Prentice-Hall, 1978.

Melichar, Emanuel. Division of Research and Statistics, Board of Governors of the Federal Reserve System, "Farm Financial Experience and Agricultural Banking Experience." Statement before the Subcommittee on Economic Stabilization of the Committee on Banking, Finance, and Urban Affairs, U.S. House of Representatives, October 23, 1985.

Osgood, William R. *How to Plan and Finance Your Business.* Boston: CBI Publishing, 1980.

Robert Morris Associates. *RMA Annual Statement Studies.* Philadelphia National Bank Building, Philadelphia, Pa. 19107.

Tighe, Roger. *Structuring Commercial Loan Agreements.* Boston: Warren, Gorham & Lamont, 1984.

QUESTIONS

7.1. What kinds of financial data should be submitted in a loan application?

7.2. What areas should a business plan cover?

7.3. List the 5 C's of credit. How might one assess a loan applicant's character? Why is character so important? Why might collateral suddenly disappear near the time of financial collapse for a firm?

7.4. When one uses financial data to evaluate capacity, why is it important to make comparisons of data over time and with other similar firms?

7.5. Why is capital a deterrent to firm failure?

7.6. Are economic conditions easily predicted for a firm? If they are crucial to the success of a loan or group of loans, does this increase credit risk?

7.7. What are the three basic elements of a loan agreement? What is a representation? What if statements made in the representation are false?

7.8. What are loan covenants? What kinds of covenants are there?

7.9. When a firm defaults in a loan, what options are available to the bank?

7.10. Define the following terms:
    (a) payment accrual basis.
    (b) nominal interest rate.
    (c) effective yield.

7.11. How should the required rate of return on a loan be calculated? How can estimates of the components of this rate be derived?

7.12. What is the difference between average and marginal costs of funds for banks?

7.13. How is the prime rate used in pricing loans? Might other interest rate indexes be used in pricing commercial loans?

7.14. Should small loans be priced differently from large loans? Why or why not?

PROBLEMS

7.1. Given the following data, calculate the effective yield:

$$
\begin{aligned}
\text{Principal} &= \$50,000, \\
\text{Annual interest rate} &= 12 \text{ percent}, \\
\text{Payment accrual basis} &= 360 \text{ days}, \\
\text{Loan term} &= 272 \text{ days}.
\end{aligned}
$$

7.2. (a) Evaluate the loan request by Galaxy Stereo, Inc., by using the information in Figure 7-1 and Tables 7-1 to 7-4. Finalize your evaluation with a loan decision.

    (b) Next, assuming the prime rate is 10 percent, what rate seems appropriate on the loan? How is this rate affected by the bank's cost of funds and desired profit margin?

7.3. (a) How is it possible for a bank to borrow funds at a rate greater than its lending rate and still make a profit?

    (b) Use the data in Table 7A-1, and determine, if principal was changed to $2,000,000, what would be the profit (or loss) on the loan?

    (c) What is the annualized breakeven rate? Calculate this rate.

APPENDIX
BORROWING AND LENDING RATES

The conventional wisdom is that banks must borrow funds at low cost and lend them at higher rates in order to make a profit. However, this appendix explains how banks can borrow longer-term funds at high rates, lend them shorter-term

TABLE 7A.1
PROFITABLE TRADING WITH PERVERSE BORROWING AND LENDING RATES

Bank borrows funds for 180 days	$t_1 = 180$
Bank lends them for 90 days	$t_2 = 90$
$t_1 - t_2 = t_3$	$t_3 = 90$
180 days borrowing rate 16%	$r_1 = 16\%$
90-day lending rate 15.5%	$r_2 = 15.5\%$
Principal $1 million	$P = \$1,000,000$

Interest due for 180 days

$$1,000,000 \times 0.16 \times \frac{180}{360} = \$80,000$$

Lend for t_2 (90 days) @ r_2 (15.5%)

$$1,000,000 \times 0.155 \times \frac{90}{360} = \underline{38,750}$$

Interest due for t_3

$$\$80,000 - \$38,750 = 41,250$$

Annualized break-even rate b

$$\frac{\text{Interest due in } t_3}{\text{Principle at beginning of } t_3} \times \text{No. of periods}$$

$$\frac{\$41,250}{\$1,038,750} \times \frac{360}{90} = 15.88\%$$

$$b = \frac{r_1\left(\frac{t_1}{t_3}\right) - r_2\left(\frac{t_2}{t_3}\right)}{1 + \frac{r_2 t_2}{360}}$$

Assume reinvestment rate at r_3 (15.95%)

$$\$1,038,750 \times 0.1595 \times \frac{90}{360} = \$41,420$$

Profit = interest earned − interest cost

$$(\$41,420 + \$38,750) - \$80,000 = \$170$$

Profit will occur where

$$\frac{t_1}{t_3} - \frac{\frac{r_2 t_2}{360}}{r_1 t_3} \leq 1$$

at lower rates, and make a profit. The reason for profit is that the returns from the shorter-term loans are reinvested and the returns are compounded. The following example will illustrate the point.

For simplicity, assume that there are no taxes or transactions costs. Furthermore, assume that funds can be borrowed and lent at the rates stated. Suppose that a bank borrows $1 million for 180 days at 16 percent. The bank's cost of funds for the 180 days is $80,000.

$$\$1,000,000 \times 0.16 \times 180/360 = \$80,000$$

Then the bank lends the $1 million for 90 days at 15.5 percent, and earns $38,750 on that loan.

$$\$1,000,000 \times 0.155 \times 90/360 = \$38,750$$

Now the bank has the $1 million plus the $38,750 interest that it earned to lend for the next 90-day period. If the bank lends those funds at, say 15.95 percent (still below their borrowing cost), for the 90 days, it will earn $41,420.

$$\$1,038,750 \times 0.1595 \times 90/360 = \$41,420$$

The total interest earned in both periods is $80,170—a profit of $170!

Total interest = $38,750 + $41,420 =	$80,170
Interest cost	80,000
Profit	$ 170

Table 7A.1 shows the additional details of these transactions as well as the annualized break-even rate, which is the minimum interest rate that the bank must earn in the second lending period in order to break even. It also shows the necessary conditions for profit to occur.[1] When perverse borrowing and lending rates occur within the framework discussed here, profits are the largest at higher levels of interest rates and longer terms to maturity. When the assumptions are relaxed, there is the possibility that banks may not be able to reinvest their funds at or above the break-even rate. However, there are ways to hedge that risk, which are not presented here.

The concept of reinvestment rates and compound interest is generally understood but rarely applied to the portfolios of banks. By taking this into account in their portfolio positions, some banks may improve their earnings.

---

[1] The equations were developed by T. H. Mattheiss, The University of Alabama.

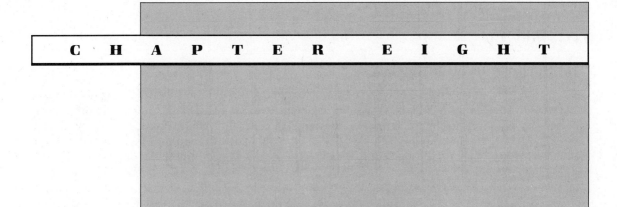

THE PROCESS OF COMMERCIAL LENDING, CONTINUED

It has been said that anyone can make a loan, but it takes a banker to collect it. Therefore the process of commercial lending does not end when a loan is made, because four things can happen to the loan: it can be (1) repaid, (2) renewed, (3) it go into default and the bank may sustain losses, or (4) the bank may sell the loan to someone else. In order to reduce loan losses and increase profits, banks engage in a loan review process. They also obtain guarantees for some loans and sell others.

LOAN REVIEW

The Purpose of Loan Review

The purpose of loan review is to minimize loan losses by reviewing outstanding loans to identify potential problems with specific loans, and to identify weaknesses in procedures or personnel in general. Loan review serves as an internal audit system for the lending and credit analysis functions of a bank. In order to carry out their audit, reviewers must answer the following questions:

1. Did the loan officer conform to the bank's written loan policies? If not, did the loan officer document the reasons for deviating from the loan policy?
2. Is the documentation complete?
3. Was there an adequate financial analysis of the borrower at the time the loan was made?
4. What is the current financial condition of the borrower? Are there potential problems?
5. What immediate corrective actions, if any, should be taken?

The Loan Review Function at Banks

Each bank performs the loan review function differently, depending on its size and needs. The needs of a large money center bank are different than those of a small farm bank. Similarly, the needs of a unit bank are different than those of a bank with intrastate and interstate branches. Nevertheless, there are some common areas of concern that are presented here.

How to Organize Loan Review

The task of reviewing the work of loan officers and credit analysts is politically sensitive because reviewers expose errors and problems in someone else's work. A senior loan officer may not like a reviewer finding fault with the way he or she handled documents or some other aspect of a loan. The loan officer may try to persuade the reviewer to overlook minor infractions of policy, or look for a job elsewhere. To avoid potential conflicts of interest and political pressure in the organization, the loan review department or area should be staffed by people who are not working in areas of the bank that are being reviewed. In addition, loan review personnel should report to senior bank officers who are outside the lending area being reviewed.

What Will they Do?

Each bank must specify what loan review should look for when examining loans. Should the emphasis be placed on adhering to the bank's written loan policy, on documentation, on financial analysis to determine possible problem loans, or looking for frauds? A lot of time and money can be spent reviewing documents, loan agreements, and analyzing financial statements. Although computers have reduced some of the workload of financial analysis, it still requires time and money to enter the data and then have someone interpret it. Because human resources are costly, it is necessary to limit the scope and depth of loan reviews.

Scope of Loans to Be Reviewed

Although this part of the book deals with commercial loans, the scope of loan review may include all types of loans made by the bank, including real estate, consumer, loans to governments, and so on. The scope of loans also refers to the number of loans to be reviewed. The review may include all loans made, or all loans above a specified dollar amount (e.g., $50,000), or a sample of loans. Along this line the bank may review selected aspects of loans from a sample and do a detailed review of all loans for $250,000 or more.

A related issue is frequency of reviews. Loans can be reviewed continuously, quarterly, semiannually, or annually. Each bank must compare the risk of loan losses because of inadequate reviews with the costs of the review process. No single "correct" answer applies to all banks. Nevertheless, the answers to the questions raised here will help determine the number of people that are involved in loan review and how it is organized in the bank.

PROBLEM LOANS[1]

Banks do not intentionally make loans that they know will become **problem loans**—loans in default because the borrower violated some aspect of the loan agreement. Although banks do not know in advance which loans will become problems, they expect a certain number of these loans. A bank that has no problem loans is being too conservative in its lending policies and foregoing profitable lending opportunities. Conversely, a large number of problem loans suggests that bank managers increased their risk in hopes of earning high returns. Their expectations may not be satisfied if the problems are not resolved to their satisfaction.

In a well-diversified loan portfolio, a few problem loans will not put the bank in jeopardy. The key phrase here is "diversified loan portfolio." From the bank's point of view, it means that the loan repayments are not perfectly positively correlated; that is, if one loan goes bad, others will not go bad for the same reasons. Thus a bank that lends primarily to farmers producing wheat is

---

[1] This section benefited significantly from comments on problem loans made by Gordon B. Trulock, Executive Vice President, First Alabama Bancshares, Inc., at the 39th Annual Bank Forum, Montgomery, AL, December 5, 1985.

more likely to be in jeopardy if the prices of wheat and farmland fall than a bank that makes loans in a variety of industries and geographic locations.

Most borrowers start out intending to adhere to the terms of the credit agreement and repay the loan. But circumstances change and the borrower may be unable or unwilling to comply with the loan agreement. Usually, the changes occur over time and astute loan officers recognize the symptoms of potential problem loans.

Symptoms of Problem Loans

In this section we are going to examine the symptoms of problem commercial loans. Some of these symptoms may apply to consumer loans and other types of loans.

Changes in the Borrower's Financial Behavior

Changes in the financial behavior of the borrower may be indications of impending problems. Late loan payments and the use of overdrafts are two examples of changed behavior. **Overdrafts** are checks or wire transfers of funds drawn against an account in amounts exceeding the funds available in that account. The bank may, or may not, extend credit to cover the overdrafts.

Do not confuse overdrafts with the cash management technique of *not* depositing funds to cover checks until they are expected to be drawn. For example, Highland Lumber Company gives its employees their payroll checks on Friday afternoon after the banks close for the weekend, but does not deposit the funds to cover those checks until Monday morning. This practice permits Highland Lumber to earn interest on the employee payroll funds until they are drawn on Monday. If Highland did not deposit sufficient funds on Monday when the payroll checks are cashed, there would be overdrafts.

Writing checks against **uncollected funds** is another trend that may indicate a customer is in financial trouble, or a very astute cash manager. Uncollected funds are checks that have been deposited by the customer in the bank, but the bank has not received payment for those checks. This is sometimes called **clearing float** or just **float.**

If a check is written against uncollected funds, the bank is extending credit until the funds are collected. To avoid extending credit in this manner, many banks specify the number of business days between the date of deposit and the date when funds are available for withdrawal. Under the Competitive Banking Act of 1987, by September 1, 1990, most local checks must be available for withdrawal in 1 business day and nonlocal checks in 4 business days. There are some exceptions for very large checks and checks believed to be uncollectable.

Material changes in financial statements and credit reports may be indicators of potential problems. For example, is the borrower selling goods at wholesale prices, instead of retail prices, to obtain funds to pay off short-term debts? Are accounts receivables growing out of proportion to sales, suggesting that the borrower is selling goods but is not getting paid for them? Is the borrower switching suppliers because old suppliers will not extend more trade credit? Did the borrower change tax accountants to get more liberal interpretations? In order to answer these and other questions, loan officers must monitor their loans and know their customers.

Changes in the Borrower's Organization and Life-style

Frequent changes of top management and key personnel may suggest a management problem. Similarly, extravagant spending by the borrower's officers may be a warning flag, too. Did the borrower buy a new plane to tour the country and go on vacations, or was it to reduce the costs of transportation and make more efficient use of their time?

Changes in the Account Relationship

Borrowers who are having problems may want to renegotiate loan agreements to ease the covenants and forestall making payments. They may also be unwilling to supply the bank with current financial data and may not answer the loan officer's calls.

Assess the Problem

Once a problem loan is recognized, the bank must take corrective action to minimize potential loan losses. It should not be coerced into taking hasty action, however. The loan did not become a problem overnight, and the problem will not be solved immediately. Each problem loan is different and requires a unique solution. Some problems are temporary and can be resolved easily, whereas others are long-term, requiring complex solutions. Some problems involve small sums, whereas others involve large sums, guarantors, stockholders, and other debtors. Finally, some problems cannot be solved and the loans must be written off as a loss.

Workout

Workout is banking jargon for trying to resolve a problem loan. In order to develop a workout program, the bank must assess the problem loan and determine its credit exposure.[2] If the problem loan is fully collateralized, has guarantors, and there is little or no credit exposure, the bank's workout program will be different than if it has a large credit exposure.

[2] For additional information see Joseph R. Eyring, "Five Key Steps for a Successful Workout Program," *The Journal of Commercial Bank Lending,* December 1984, pp. 28–35.

Credit Exposure

Credit exposure is the amount of money the bank can lose. A bank's claims on the borrower depend on correct documentation, legal filings, and specification in the loan agreement. Therefore, a review of all items affecting the loan is required.

Financial Condition of the Borrower

The current financial condition of the borrower is one of the major determinants of a successful resolution of a problem loan. Accurate and up-to-date financial information is essential. Some banks use their own credit departments or outside accounting firms to obtain the information. Then the bank must analyze the data to determine the likelihood of salvaging the loan.

Attitude

A positive, cooperative attitude by both the borrower and the bank is helpful. The bank can make recommendations to the borrower to help resolve the problem. For example, the bank may recommend hiring an accountant to keep records and collect receivables. It may also recommend putting inventory that is being used as collateral in a field warehouse. The bank may also ask for additional collateral and guarantees from a third party. If the borrower agrees, the bank can renegotiate certain parts of the loan to facilitate its payment.

Litigation

If the borrower is unwilling or unable to work out the problem loan, the bank may sue. If this happens, there is no guarantee that a judge or jury will find for the bank. In addition, there is the possibility of a countersuit by the borrower, charging that the bank did not live up to its lending agreement, or by withholding additional funds, the bank caused the borrower to go bankrupt, as an example. Thus the bank stands to lose the amount of the loan, or more, plus the cost of litigation. Lawsuits should only be brought as a last resort.

Problem loans may also result in the borrower suing the bank for alleged violations of the loan agreement, or a tort (a wrongful act resulting in injury). Such **lender liability** lawsuits are becoming more prevalent. Box 8.1 is one example of such a lawsuit.

LOAN LOSSES

Charge-Offs

Some problem loans cannot be salvaged and are charged off as a loss. The recommendation for a charge-off occurs when a loan officer seriously doubts the ability of a borrower to repay the loan. Although the loan officer makes the

---

BOX 8.1

ROTTEN APPLES/LENDER LIABILITY

When a loan goes bad, a bank can cut off additional credit to the borrower to minimize its loss. There may be some risk in cutting off credit, however, as the following case illustrates.

For many years, Bank of America had a lending relationship with George Jewell, a farmer who sold apples to the James E. O'Connell Company (O'Connell) for processing. Bank of America also loaned money to O'Connell and to Sebastopol Cooperative Cannery, which was O'Connell's local competitor. When the apple market entered a slump in the mid-1970s, and O'Connell could not repay its loans, Bank of America cut off their credit. Jewell borrowed money from Bank of America, which he then lent to O'Connell to keep them in business, in exchange for control of the firm. He wanted O'Connell to remain in business in order to prevent the Sebastopol Cooperative from fixing apple prices. He did not know that O'Connell had delinquent loans at Bank of America since 1973. In the late 1970s, when the apple market deteriorated further and interest rates reached record levels, O'Connell went bankrupt and Bank of America cut off Jewell's credit, which at one time totaled more than $2 million. Jewell sued, claiming that Bank of America allowed him to fail so the bank could protect its $18-million loans to the cooperative. Jewell won, and a jury awarded him $22 million in punitive damages against Bank of America for deliberately forcing him out of business. Since then, the cooperative failed, too.[a]

[a] Based on Philip Sudo, "Court Upholds $22 Million Damages Against Bank of America in Farm Case," *American Banker*, October 28, 1985, pp. 1–30.

---

recommendation, the final decision to charge off a loan rests with the Board of Directors. Bank examiners also have the authority to require loans to be charged off if they deem them uncollectable.

Each bank is examined periodically by federal or state examiners. Part of the examination process is to evaluate the quality of loans, and the ratings on loans are frequently changed. Loans that do not have problems are classified as "not rated." Loans that have problems are classified as "Other Loans Especially Mentioned" (OLEM), "substandard," "doubtful," or "loss," depending on severity of the problem.

When a loan is charged off, it is removed from the loan portfolio and charged against income or a reserve for loan losses. For example, the accounting for a $100,000 charge-off is:

Reserve for loan charge-off	$100,000	
Commercial loans		$100,000

The charge-off has no effect on the bank's earnings because the earnings were reduced previously when provisions for loan losses were added to the reserve. Banks are permitted to reduce their current taxes by transfers to a reserve for loan losses. The amount that can be transferred (after 1988) is based on their actual loss experience.

The ratio of net charge-offs to average loans and leases for all banks was 0.89 percent in 1987, up from 0.57 percent 5 years earlier. The increased rate of charge-offs reflects problems with agriculture, real estate, and energy loans. The rate of charge-offs is also related to the size of banks. Banks with assets under $100 million had a charge-off rate of 1.14 percent, whereas the 10 largest U.S. banks had a 0.67 charge-off rate.[3]

Loan Loss Recovery

The fact that a loan has been charged off does not mean that it is a total loss; the bank may be able to recover all or part of the funds charged off. Consider the case of a $200,000 loan to finance part of a large apartment building. The bank accepted the borrower's share of ownership in the building as her collateral. When the borrower defaulted on the loan, the bank could not force the sale of the building to liquidate the collateral because the other owners had no financial obligation to the bank. Twelve years later, the building was sold and the bank recovered its funds.

The recovery of a charged-off loan has a direct effect on the bank's income. The income recovered was not generated by assets on the balance sheet and there was no risk in obtaining it. The income can be thought of as "pure profit" in the period in which it was recovered. The accounting for the amount recovered is:

Cash	$200,000	
Other income, recovery of charged-off loans		$200,000

Many banks do not pay adequate attention to this source of income. One reason is that the loan officers who made the charged-off loans may have changed jobs. Other loan officers are rewarded for making new loans, and prefer not to deal with someone else's mistakes. To avoid this problem, some banks have specialists in recovering funds from loans that have been charged off.

[3] "The FDIC Quarterly Banking Profile," Fourth Quarter 1987, preliminary data.

PRIVATE FINANCIAL GUARANTEES

Guarantees—having a private party or government guarantee payments in the event that a borrower defaults on a contract—are becoming increasingly popular among borrowers and lenders. Borrowers, such as municipalities that obtain guarantees for payment of their bond's interest and principal, benefit in lower-cost financing and greater market acceptance of guaranteed issues. Lenders, such as banks, benefit because guarantees of loan payments or leases reduce their risk—at least some of the time.

Types of Private Financial Guarantees

Private financial guarantees (not backed by government) take a variety of forms. The most common guarantees are surety bonds and standby letters of credit. **Surety bonds** are obligations of insurance companies to make payments if, for example, a borrower defaults on a loan agreement. **Standby letters of credit** are obligations of banks to pay in the event a customer defaults on a contract. Banks use standby letters of credit to compete with insurance companies for their surety business. A typical charge for a standby letter of credit is a fixed dollar amount (i.e., $100) plus an annual percentage of the face amount (i.e., 2 percent). Thus, the cost of a 1-year standby letter of credit for $1 million is $20,100. Additional information on standby letters of credit is presented in Chapter 18.

Some financial guarantees are complex and include recourse and collateral agreements that eliminate the true transfer of risk. Consider the arrangement between Citibank and Travelers Indemnity Company, which is depicted in Figure 8.1.[4] Citibank sold loans to Chatsworth Funding Corporation, a firm created solely to buy Citibank's high-quality, 90-day loans. Chatsworth funded the purchases of loans by selling commercial paper that was guaranteed by Travelers. If there is a default, Citibank had a recourse agreement to reimburse Travelers for 10 percent of the loans.

The Controller of the Currency ruled that Citibank could not take the loans sold to Chatsworth off its books because it retained a liability for them through the recourse agreement; therefore, it did not represent a true sale. And the Securities and Exchange Commission expressed concern about banks selling their strongest assets to special purpose companies like Chatsworth without advising their stockholders.

---

[4] This section draws on examples from a series of articles by Lynn Brenner, which appeared in the *American Banker:* "The Illusory World of Guarantees: Good Can Look Bad, and Bad Good," June 25, 1985, pp. 1, 27, 29; "Booming Financial Guarantees Market Generates Profits—and Some Questions," June 24, 1985, pp. 1, 17, 18, 23; "Regulators Worry About Guarantees, June 26, 1985, pp. 1, 15; "The Financial Guarantee Business Presents a Challenge to Regulators, June 27, 1985, pp. 1, 18.; and from other sources not cited.

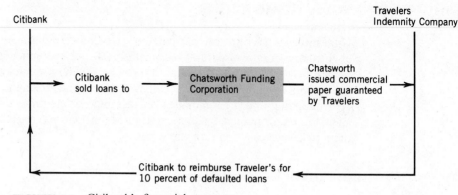

FIGURE 8.1   Citibank's financial guarantee.

Caveat Emptor—Let the Buyer Beware

Financial guarantees do not eliminate default risk or the riskiness of loan port-folios. In fact, they may contribute to increased risk as banks substitute finan-cial guarantees for high credit standards or higher rates charged on risky loans. Some guarantors who want to earn premium income may guarantee risky credits. For example, a real estate syndicator obtained financial guarantee insurance from Glacier General Assurance Company and Pacific American Insurance Company for mortgage-backed securities that were sold to financial institutions throughout the United States. Bank America was the trustee and escrow agent for the mortgage pools. When it was discovered that the proper-ties underlying the mortgages were overvalued, and that the insurers could not pay their claims, Bank of America, as trustee for the mortgage pools, had to pay $95 million to the financial institutions holding the mortgages.[5]

One important lesson to be learned from Bank of America's experience is that financial guarantees do not relieve a bank from doing a thorough job of credit analysis if they have a credit exposure. Another lesson is that not all insurers are equal. Like bonds, Standard & Poor's rates insurance companies on their ability to pay claims; AAA is the highest quality rating. Standard & Poor's did not rate Glacier General Assurance Company and Pacific American Insurance Company; in fact, they never heard of them.

Even insurance from AAA-rated insurance companies is not risk free. Insur-ance companies make financial guarantees on obligations where they foresee

---

[5] For additional details on the insurance companies, see Mike Carroll, "California Places Gla-cier Under Conservatorship," *American Banker,* March 6, 1985, pp. 1, 7. This article points out that an audit revealed that Glacier had $121 million in liabilities, $85 million in assets, and a negative equity of $36 million.

no risk, consequently the premiums are small in comparison with the underwriting exposure or risk they face. If an insurance company foresees a potential loss, it probably will not make the financial guarantee. The insurer is presumed to have perfect foresight and will stay in business long enough to pay off over the life of the guarantee. The practice of a premium based on no risk is in sharp contrast to casualty and life insurance, where there is a relationship between premiums and risk. For example, the insurance premium on a $50-million municipal bond issue may be half the difference between the 12-percent interest rate on an uninsured bond and 11-percent interest rate on a guaranteed bond, or 50 basis points. That guarantee extends for the 15- or 20-year life of the bond. If catastrophic changes occur in the economy that were unforeseen by the insurer, it may cause massive defaults and they may be unable to satisfy their obligations from their reserves built from investing the small premium.

There is also a risk of litigation. Fireman's Fund Insurance Company paid a $55-million settlement in connection with two financial guarantees that had limits of $12 million. In another case, Lloyd's of London gave financial guarantees to leasing firms for lease payments of cancelable operating leases on computers. The lessee had the right to cancel the lease after a certain number of payments, and the insurance protected the lessor by guaranteeing lease payments until maturity of the contract. When IBM announced a new computer, there were large numbers of cancellations of leases on old computer equipment, which resulted in $250 million in claims on Lloyd's. Two prominent leasing firms, OPM Leasing Company and Itel Corporation, went bankrupt, despite their insurance coverage by Lloyds'.[6]

Parent Company Guarantees

Loans of subsidiary companies may be guaranteed by the parent corporation. As demonstrated in the Bank of America case, a guarantee is only as good as the guarantor. Similarly, the quality of the parent corporation must be considered in assessing the value of their guarantee at the time the loan is made as well as over the course of the loan. The guarantees may be written or oral. PepsiCo gave oral guarantees on a $40-million bank loan for another firm that purchased its old, unused bottles. PepsiCo did not want to use a written guarantee because it might have raised questions about the accounting treatment of the sale. In addition, PepsiCo did not tell its auditors about the guarantee. The Securities and Exchange Commission was concerned about the disclosure by the banks and guarantors of oral guarantees.[7]

---

[6] James S. Schallheim and John J. McConnell, "A Model for the Determination of 'Fair' Premiums on Lease Cancellation Insurance Policies," *The Journal of Finance*, December 1985, pp. 1439–1457.

[7] Lee Berton and Bruce Ingersoll, "SEC Is Likely to Caution Accountants: Disclosure of Corporate Loan Guarantees Is Sought," *The Wall Street Journal*, December 12, 1985, p. 6.

Government Loan Guarantees

Federal government loan guarantees play important roles in housing, agriculture, commerce, and education, and in other sectors of the economy. In September 1987, the government had $731.4 billion guaranteed or insured loans outstanding. To put the primary amount of government guaranteed loans in perspective, it is equal to 43 percent of total loans outstanding at all commercial banks. Loan guarantees and insurance in the housing sector of the economy account for more than 79 percent of the total government guarantees. Let's examine several of the government agencies that impact banking, beginning with those involved with housing.

Federal Housing Administration

The FHA is a government agency created by the National Housing Act of 1934 to stimulate home building by **insuring** mortgage loans. It operates under the Department of Housing and Urban Development (HUD). The primary functions of this agency are to aid in the expansion of the residential mortgage market and to improve housing standards. These functions are accomplished by the FHA's insurance programs and by the physical standards it sets for insured properties. The FHA insures loans for construction, purchase, improvement, and repair of residential properties. If the borrower defaults, the FHA insurance is paid to the mortgage lender. By insuring against default, the FHA encourages lenders to make loans they might not otherwise make, and borrowers to take advantage of relatively low-cost loans.

Government National Mortgage Association

GNMA, or Ginnie Mae as it is commonly called, operates under HUD. One function of GNMA is to improve the liquidity of home mortgage loans. It does this by guaranteeing the payment of interest and principal on securities backed by pools of FHA/VA mortgages. The securities are issued by GNMA-approved financial institutions (such as banks) and are fully guaranteed by the U.S. government. Technically, they are called "fully guaranteed pass-through securities." The securities are sold to securities dealers and brokers who, in turn, sell them to investors, which may be private individuals or other banks.

Veterans Administration

The VA **guarantees** home mortgage loans and manufactured home loans (mobile homes) to assist veterans in acquiring and improving homes on relatively liberal terms. The guarantee means that if the borrower defaults on a VA loan, the VA purchases the property in question, or, in some cases, refinances the loan (under the Veterans' Housing Foreclosure Assistance Act of 1983). Because both FHA and VA loans are government backed, they are readily sold and accepted in the secondary mortgage market—the market for outstanding mortgages.

Farmers Home Administration

The FmHA is a credit agency of the U.S. Department of Agriculture. This credit agency is considered a lender of last resort to farmers. Through the Rural Development Act of 1972, the FmHA is authorized to guarantee certain farm loans made by commercial lenders. These loans include emergency loans, rural rental housing loans, soil and water loans, Indian tribal loans, and business and industrial loans. This credit agency, and other agricultural lenders, were affected adversely by the deteriorating farm credit conditions in the mid-1980s.[8]

Commodity Credit Corporation

The CCC is a credit agency of the U.S. Department of Agriculture. Its primary role is to support prices of selected farm commodities (grains, cotton, soybeans). Farmers who participate in government commodity support programs may pledge their crops as collateral for nonrecourse loans from the CCC. When the market price of the pledged commodities is below the CCC's loan rate per bushel or pound, farmers use the CCC. For example, if the market price of cotton is below the loan rate, farmers will store their cotton in an approved warehouse. Then they take the warehouse receipts to the CCC, which will advance them funds. The loan may be for 10 months or longer. If a farmer cannot sell his or her crop at a better price in the market during the period of the loan, the CCC buys the cotton at the agreed price. When the market price is higher than the loan rate, farmers sell their commodities elsewhere.

Student Loan Marketing Association

SLMA, or Sallie Mae, provides liquidity to banks and other eligible lenders engaged in their program by buying insured student loans from them, and by making advances secured by the insured loans.

Small Business Administration

The SBA assists small businesses by making direct loans to them, or by guaranteeing all or parts of loans made by banks and other private lenders. When the SBA makes part of a loan and guarantees the remainder that is made by a

---

[8] For discussions of the farm credit crunch and the farm credit system, see *Economic Perspectives,* Federal Reserve Bank of Chicago, November/December 1985. The *farm credit system* includes Federal Land Banks, Federal Intermediate Credit Banks, and Banks for Cooperatives. They extend credit for farm production, farm equipment, and real estate. Also see Frederick T. Furlong and Randall J. Pozdena, ''Agricultural Credit Conditions, *FRBSF Weekly Letter,* Federal Reserve Bank of San Francisco, August 30, 1985.

private lender, it is called an "immediate participation." SBA's share of the loan cannot exceed $150,000. The SBA can guarantee up to 90 percent of other qualified loans for a maximum amount of $500,000. The loans can be used for working capital, inventory, equipment and supplies, and for building construction and expansion.

By law, the SBA cannot make or guarantee a loan if a business can obtain funds at a reasonable cost from a bank or private lender. In order to qualify for a loan, a small business must be independently operated for profit, and must meet certain standards with respect to size, employment, and income. The definition of **small business** varies from industry to industry. For example, a manufacturing firm can employ from 500 to 1,500 persons, whereas the employment in a wholesale firm cannot exceed 500. The maximum annual receipts range from $3.5 to $13.5 million in retail industries, from $3.5 to $14.5 in service industries, and $17 million in construction. Thus, the term **small business,** is relative, and some small businesses are quite large.

LOAN SALES AND PARTICIPATIONS

Investment Banking

Some commercial banks are evolving into investment bankers. The term **investment banker** typically refers to firms in the securities industry that provide other firms with advice and assistance in selling securities. **Securities** is used in the broad sense of the word, and includes pools of mortgages, loans, and so on. Merrill Lynch, Morgan Stanley, First Boston, and Salomon Brothers are examples of traditional investment bankers. In recent years, banks have been performing some similar services by packaging and selling loans as well as securities. One reason for this trend is that large corporations are placing increased reliance on securities markets to raise funds instead of borrowing from commercial banks. For example, some large corporations are selling commercial paper instead of making short-term bank loans. As mentioned in Chapter 6, the largest dollar volume of commercial and industrial loans is for corporations that are waiting to sell commercial paper. Because of the loss of these customers (AAA- or AA-rated industrial firms) to the credit markets, banks have made riskier (BBB-rated) loans at higher rates. However, the money center banks may be unable to keep up their own credit ratings and fund the riskier loans profitably. Therefore, they are selling all or part of the riskier loans to institutions that do find them profitable; and the money center banks are performing investment banking functions.

Investment bankers bring together those organizations that need funds with those that have funds to invest. Their function includes providing advice and services concerning the borrower's financial needs, and underwriting the borrower's securities or brokering their loans. The term **underwriting** means buying securities (i.e., bonds) from a borrower at one price and selling them to investors at a higher price. The difference between the two prices is the underwriter's gross profit. The underwriter is a principal in the transaction because it takes ownership of the securities it sells. Consequently, underwriters incur some risk because they may be unable to sell the securities at a profit. In contrast, when investment bankers act as **brokers,** they are the borrower's agents and receive a commission for selling securities they do not own. Investment bankers in the securities markets cannot act as agent and principal in the same transaction. However, the market for loans is not regulated like the securities market. Some banks underwrite loans for business concerns and sell them on a nonrecourse basis to other banks. They may also "broker" loans.

The banks can sell all or part of the loans. If they sell part of the loan to other banks, it is called a **participation.** Money center banks generally sell participations downstream to smaller banks, thrifts, and other types of financial institutions.

Benefits of Selling Loans and Participations

In broad terms, selling loans helps to allocate financial resources where they are needed throughout the world. Narrowing the focus, selling loans provides specific benefits to both the seller and buyer. Keep in mind that loans sold without recourse are removed from the selling bank's balance sheet, whereas those sold with recourse remain on the balance sheet. When loans are sold without recourse, total assets are reduced by a similar amount. Therefore, the existing equity capital provides a higher capital/asset ratio than before. Bank regulators prefer high capital/asset ratios. Banks frequently sell loans without recourse to earn fees from originating the loans and servicing them. Loans sold with recourse are one method of funding portfolios. Additional reasons for selling loans are:

Liquidity

Banks can improve their liquidity by selling part of their loan portfolios. The price reflects the quality and risk of the loans being sold. Banks should not reduce the overall quality of their loan portfolios by selling off their best credits to increase their liquidity.

The fact that there is a demand for loans from banks with excess liquidity makes the sale of loans possible. Such banks may be located in areas where loan demand is slack or the bank wants other types of loans for diversification or some other reason. For example, by buying participations, small agricultural banks can participate in industrial loans that are not available in their local markets.

Special Needs

Some banks buy loans to satisfy a particular need in their loan portfolios. When oil prices rose in the late 1970s, Continental Illinois Bank and Trust Company wanted to participate in energy, and thus bought oil loans from Penn Square Bank. When oil prices declined in the early 1980s, many of the oil loans defaulted. This example illustrates how Continental satisfied its particular need to invest in oil loans. It also illustrates the risk associated with oil loans, because they contributed significantly to the failure of Continental Bank. Making or acquiring loans is a risky business.

Some customers have specialized financial needs that a bank may be unable to handle. When that happens, the bank can participate with a specialized lender, such as General Electric Credit Corporation, get the benefits of GECC's size and expertise, and serve their customer at the same time. The customer also benefits because the blended interest rate charged by both lenders may be lower than the cost of borrowing from GECC alone.

Attracting Large Loans

As mentioned in Chapter 6, banks are prohibited from making loans in excess of 25 percent of their capital to one customer. Although few banks would lend that much to one customer, some banks may have the opportunity to make large loans that they cannot or do not want to handle alone. When this is the case, they can sell all or part of the loan, and still serve their customer.

SUMMARY

Commercial lending is a process that begins when a customer asks for a loan and ends when the loan is repaid, renewed, sold, or when the attempted recovery ceases for funds that were charged off as a loss. In order to reduce possible loan losses, banks engage in a loan review process. Although the process varies from bank to bank, it is an attempt to detect potential loan problems before they occur. This is accomplished by reviewing new and existing loans. Nevertheless, some loans will become problem loans, that may be worked out or charged off as a loss. Even then, some funds may be recovered.

Another way to reduce the risk of lending is to obtain financial guarantees from private parties or from government. Private financial guarantees reduce, but do not eliminate, the risk of default. Government financial guarantees are provided by various government organizations in housing, agriculture, education, commerce, and other areas.

Finally, banks can sell commercial loans or participations in loans to other lenders. This adds a significant dimension to the management of loan portfolios by allowing banks to acquire loans they might not otherwise obtain or to sell loans as the need arises.

IMPORTANT CONCEPTS

brokers
Commodity Credit Corporation
credit exposure

Farmers Home Administration (FmHa)
Federal Housing Administration (FHA)
float

government loan guarantees

Government National Mortgage
Association (GNMA)

investment banking

lender liability

loan review

overdraft

participations

private financial guarantees

problem loans

small Business

Small Business Administration (SBA)

standby letter of credit

Student Loan Marketing Association (SLMA)

surety bond

uncollected funds

underwriting

Veterans Administration (VA)

workout

REFERENCES

Berton, Lee, and Bruce Ingersoll. "SEC Is Likely to Caution Accountants: Disclosure of Corporate Loan Guarantees Is Sought," *The Wall Street Journal,* December 12, 1985.

Brenner, Lynn. Series of articles in the *American Banker,* June 24 to 27, 1985.

Carroll, Mike. "California Places Glacier Under Conservatorship," *American Banker,* March 6, 1985.

Economic Perspectives, Federal Reserve Bank of Chicago, November/December 1985.

Eyring, Joseph R. "Five Key Steps for a Successful Workout Program," *The Journal of Commercial Bank Lending,* December 1984.

Furlong, T. and Randall J. Pozdena. "Agricultural Credit Conditions, *FRBSF Weekly Letter,* Federal Reserve Bank of San Francisco, August 30, 1985.

Schallheim, James S. and John J. McConnell. "A Model for the Determination of 'Fair' Premiums on Lease Cancellation Insurance Policies," *The Journal of Finance,* December 1985.

QUESTIONS

8.1. What questions should a loan review address?

8.2. How can the risk of problem loans be reduced? What symptoms of potential problem loans should bank managers recognize?

8.3. If a potential problem loan is identified, what actions might the loan officer take to help minimize potential losses? Is there any risk to the bank of taking corrective actions?

8.4. What classifications might a problem loan have?

8.5. When a loan is charged off, how does it affect bank earnings? Explain your answer. Is a loan loss a total loss?

8.6. What are surety bonds and standby letters of credit? Do financial guarantees eliminate default risk on loans?

8.7. How are premiums on financial guarantees provided by an insurance company set? How good are such guarantees?

8.8. Why does the government have such a massive loan guarantee program?

8.9. When was the FHA created? What are its primary functions? How does GNMA differ in function?

8.10. What is FmHA? What is CCC? How do they differ?

8.11. What is an ''immediate participation'' by the SBA? What restrictions on SBA loan contract terms are there?

8.12. What does an investment banker do? What does underwriting mean? Is there risk involved in underwriting?

8.13. Why might a bank sell loans and participations?

REAL ESTATE LENDING

Following commercial and industrial loans, real estate loans usually account for the second largest dollar volume of loans made by commercial banks.[1]

As shown in Table 9.1, mortgage loans outstanding at commercial banks amounted to $563 billion in 1987, with most of the loans being for 1- to 4-family residential properties and commercial properties. The data for commercial properties include loans for land, construction and development, and commercial properties.

[1] Unless stated otherwise, data cited in this chapter were obtained from the *Federal Reserve Bulletin,* monthly; U.S. Department of Commerce, *Statistical Abstract of the United States,* annual; United States League of Savings Institutions, *Savings Institution Source Book,* annual.

TABLE 9.1
MORTGAGE LOANS
OUTSTANDING AT
COMMERCIAL BANKS, 1987,
3rd Quarter
(billions of dollars)

Type of Loan	
1- to 4-family	$265
Multifamily	31
Commercial	253
Farm	14
	$563

Source. Federal Reserve Bulletin, Board of Governors of the Federal Reserve System, March 1988, p. A39.

In addition to making new residential mortgage loans, commercial banks buy and sell outstanding residential mortgage loans in the secondary mortgage market. Finally, some bank holding companies have mortgage banking and real estate investment trust affiliates, which engage in real estate finance. We will explore each of these areas in this chapter.

SELECTED CHARACTERISTICS OF RESIDENTIAL REAL ESTATE

New Private Housing Starts

A basic axiom of real estate is that everyone lives somewhere. Where one lives depends on the number of people in the family unit, their current and expected levels of income, the level of interest rates, the cost of housing, inflation, and other factors. Because all of the factors mentioned change over time, the aggregate demand for housing and mortgage loans fluctuates from year to year. By way of illustration, consider the number of new private housing starts shown in Figure 9.1. The heavy line at the top of the figure represents total private housing starts and shows the cyclical nature of the construction trade. Notice that housing starts declined sharply during the Depression years (1930s), and during World War II (1940s). After the war, housing starts rebounded, but there was a change in the composition of housing, with multifamily units (shown as "other" in the figure) becoming increasingly important. In addition, beginning in the 1970s, there were large changes in the total level of housing starts, which fluctuated between one- and two-million units per year. These fluctuations were caused by substantial changes in level of real economic activity, inflation, and interest rates. Against this background, let's examine some characteristics of individual homes.

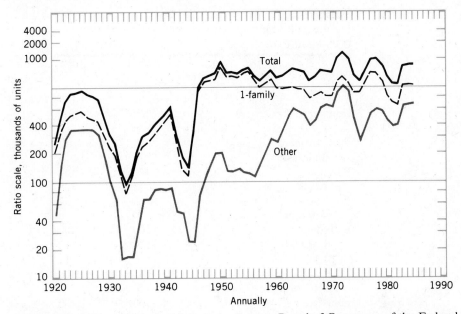

FIGURE 9.1   New private housing starts. *Source*. Board of Governors of the Federal Reserve System.

Purchase Price

During the 1970–1985 period, the average purchase price of a new home financed with a **conventional mortgage** (one not backed by the FHA or VA) increased from $35,500 to $105,000. Although it is true that housing prices increased because of inflation and other factors, the extent of the price increase is misleading for a number of reasons.

Changes in quality is the first reason that price of new homes is higher. Differences in the quality of housing are reflected in the data presented in Table 9.2, which contrasts selected characteristics of single-family homes completed in 1970 with those completed in 1985. The data reveal that newer houses were larger, had more bathrooms, more were air-conditioned, and had features that the earlier homes did not have. Although not shown in the table, the newer homes contained items such as microwave ovens, washer and dryer, and other features that may not have been included in the purchase prices of the earlier homes. In the past, many of these consumer durable goods were acquired separately.

A second reason why the average purchase price is misleading concerns regional differences in prices. On average, the price of housing in the Northeastern part of the United States is higher than in the Midwest. In 1985, for example, the median price of a family home was $88,900 in the Northeast and $58,900 in the Midwest. There are also vast differences among cities, reflecting different market conditions. For example, the median value (1985) of a house in

TABLE 9.2
CHARACTERISTICS OF NEW, PRIVATELY OWNED,
ONE-FAMILY HOMES

Characteristic	1970	1985
Floor area		
Average square feet	1,500	1,785
Number of stories (%)	100	100
1	74	52
2 or more	17	42
Split level	10	6
Bedrooms (%)	100	100
2 or less	13	25
3	63	57
4 or more	24	18
Bathroom (%)	100	100
1 or less	32	13
1 1/2	20	11
2	32	48
2 1/2 or more	16	29
Foundation (%)	100	100
Full or partial basement	37	35
Slab	36	48
Crawl space	27	18
Heating fuel (%)	100	100
Electricity	28	44
Gas	62	49
Oil	8	3
Other	1	4
Central air-conditioning (%)	100	100
With	34	70
Without	64	30
Parking facilities (%)	100	100
Garage	58	70
Carport	17	5
No garage or carport	25	25

Source. U.S. Department of Commerce, *Statistical Abstract of the United States,* 1987, Table 1273.

Anaheim–Santa Ana, Caifornia, was $136,200, whereas the median value of a house in Tampa–St. Petersburg–Clearwater, Florida, was $58,400.

The third reason why the average price is misleading concerns differences between first-time home buyers and repeat home buyers. In 1985, for first-time buyers the median purchase price of homes was $75,100, and $106,200 for buyers who had previously owned homes. Those who previously owned homes benefited from inflation, which increased the equity value of their homes, and thus they could afford higher-priced housing. They may also have been older than first-time buyers, which suggests they had higher incomes, too.

Financing

Eighty-one percent of the newly completed single-family homes in 1985 were financed with mortgage loans. The remainder were paid for in cash or with some other asset. Of those homes that were financed with borrowed funds, 57 percent were financed with conventional mortgages and the remainder with government-backed mortgages. The average maturity of conventional mortgage loans on new homes was 27.0 years and the average loan to price ratio was 77.1 percent. The **loan to price ratio** is the percentage of the purchase price that is lent. (The ratio for existing homes was lower, 75.7 percent, reflecting slight differences in risk from the lenders' perspective). This means that the new-home buyer had to deposit 22.9 percent of the purchase price. Recall that the average purchase price of a new home in 1985 was $105,000. Thus, a new buyer was required to make a down payment of $24,045. The relatively high cost of housing and the high down payment excluded lower-income buyers from the housing market and many purchased mobile (manufactured) homes or live in apartments.

Mobile homes are a substitute for houses. Mobile home shipments were 33 percent of single-family housing starts in 1970 and 28 percent in 1985. Part of the reason for the decline in the percentage is the increased number of apartment units available. The fact that high-income individuals and repeat buyers could afford to buy new homes, and many low-income individuals were excluded from the new home market, tended to put an upward bias on the purchase price of new homes. High-income individuals buy high-priced homes.

Collateral

Residential real estate makes good collateral for mortgage loans. The collateral is durable, easy to identify, and in most cases the borrower cannot move the land or structures elsewhere. Despite these fine qualities, the value of real estate can go up or down. During periods of inflation, residential real estate appreciated in value in many parts of the country, thereby enhancing its value as collateral. During deflation, however, housing in some areas depreciated in value.

The fact that real estate has a fixed geographic location is both good and bad. It is good in the sense that the collateral cannot be removed. It is bad in the sense that its value is affected by adjacent property. If a toxic waste dump site were to locate in what was previously a golf course, the value of the adjacent residential property would decline. Finally, real estate is illiquid; that is, it is difficult to sell on short notice at its fair market value. These comments on residential real estate also apply to commercial real estate.

RESIDENTIAL MORTGAGE LOANS

The variability of interest rates in the late 1970s and early 1980s and the deregulation of financial institutions contributed to the increased use of adjustable rate loans, as mortgage lenders attempted to keep the returns on their assets higher than the costs of their funds. Thus, adjustable-rate mortgages (ARMs) became increasingly popular and accounted for almost half of the mortgage loans made in 1985. ARMs permit lenders to vary the terms of the mortgage loan when market rates of interest change. Fixed rate mortgages, where the terms of the mortgage do not change, accounted for the remainder of mortgage loans made in that year.

Fixed Rate Mortgages

Before the advent of ARMs, fixed rate, fully amortized, level payment mortgages were the predominant form of financing home loans. **Fixed rate, fully amortized, level payment mortgage** means that the interest rate does not change and the debt is gradually extinguished through equal periodic payments on the principal balance. In other words, the borrower pays the same dollar amount each month until the mortgage loan is paid off. **Partially amortized, fixed rate mortgages** are also used for financing home loans. In this case, only a portion of the debt is extinguished by level periodic payments and the unamortized amount is paid in a lump sum—a **balloon payment**—or refinanced when the loan matures. Generally, partially amortized loans finance 60 percent or less of the appraised value of the pledged property, and they have relative short maturities (e.g., 5 years).

Monthly Mortgage Payments

The dollar amount of monthly payments depends on the size of the loan, the interest rate, and the maturity. Table 9.3 shows the monthly mortgage payments for a $1,000 mortgage loan with selected annual interest rates and maturities. A close examination of the table reveals two important facts. First, the dollar amount of the monthly mortgage payment increases as the interest rate increases. For example, the monthly mortgage payment for a loan with 10 years to maturity ranges from $11.10 when the interest rate is 6 percent, to $16.76 when the interest rate is 16 percent. Second, the dollar amount of the monthly

TABLE 9.3
MONTHLY MORTGAGE PAYMENTS FOR A $1,000 MORTGAGE LOAN

Annual Interest Rates %	Years to Maturity				
	10	15	20	25	30
6	$11.10	$ 8.44	$ 7.16	$ 6.44	$ 6.00
8	12.13	9.56	8.36	7.72	7.34
10	13.22	10.75	9.65	9.09	8.78
12	14.35	12.00	11.01	10.53	10.29
14	15.35	13.32	12.44	12.04	11.85
16	16.76	14.69	13.92	13.59	13.45

TABLE 9.4

MONTHLY MORTGAGE PAYMENT COMPARISONS

Rates	\$80,000	\$82,000	\$84,000	\$86,000	\$88,000	\$90,000	\$92,000	\$94,000	\$96,000
					25-Year Mortgage Loan Amounts				
10.00%	726.96	745.14	763.31	781.48	799.66	817.83	836.01	854.18	872.35
10.25	741.11	759.63	778.16	796.69	815.22	833.74	852.27	870.80	889.33
10.50	755.35	774.23	793.11	812.00	830.88	849.76	868.65	887.53	906.42
10.75	769.67	788.92	808.16	827.40	846.64	865.88	885.13	904.37	923.61
11.00	784.09	803.69	823.29	842.90	862.50	882.10	901.70	921.31	940.91
11.25	798.59	818.56	838.52	858.49	878.45	898.42	918.38	938.35	958.31
11.50	813.18	833.50	853.83	874.16	894.49	914.82	935.15	955.48	975.81
11.75	827.84	848.54	869.23	889.93	910.62	931.32	952.02	972.71	993.41
12.00	842.58	863.64	884.71	905.77	926.84	947.90	968.97	990.03	1,011.10
12.25	857.39	878.83	900.26	921.70	943.13	964.57	986.00	1,007.44	1,028.87
12.50	872.28	894.09	915.90	937.71	959.51	981.32	1,003.13	1,024.93	1,046.74
12.75	887.24	909.42	931.60	953.78	975.97	998.15	1,020.33	1,042.51	1,064.69
13.00	902.27	924.82	947.38	969.94	992.49	1,015.05	1,037.61	1,060.16	1,082.72
13.25	917.36	940.29	963.23	986.16	1,009.10	1,032.03	1,054.96	1,077.90	1,100.83
13.50	932.52	955.83	979.14	1,002.45	1,025.77	1,049.08	1,072.39	1,095.71	1,119.02

mortgage payment declines as the maturity of the loan is extended. When the interest rate is 6 percent, the monthly mortgage payment declines from \$11.10 when the maturity is 10 years maturity, to \$6.00 when the maturity is 30 years.

Maturity

Don't be misled by lower monthly payments. For a given interest rate, the *total* cost of the loan is higher with longer maturities (smaller monthly payments) than shorter maturities (higher monthly payments). The total cost is determined by multiplying the mortgage payment per \$1,000 of loan for each interest rate by the dollar amount of the loan (in thousands) and the number of months. By way of illustration, consider an \$80,000 mortgage loan at 12 percent with a maturity of 10 years. The monthly payment is \$1,148 (\$14.35 × 80 = \$1,148) and the total cost over the life of the loan is \$137,760 (\$1,148 × 120 months = \$137,760). If the maturity were 25 years, the monthly payment would be reduced to \$842.40, but the total cost would be \$252,720, which is \$114,960 more than the cost of the shorter-term loan.[2]

Amount and Interest Rate

Table 9.4 provides another perspective on size of monthly mortgage payments. The table shows the monthly payments for a 25-year mortgage for selected

[2] The monthly mortgage payment for an \$80,000 loan at 12 percent for 25 years shown in Tables 9.4 and 9.5 is \$842.58. The difference between \$842.58 and \$842.40 is due to computer rounding in different programs.

dollar amounts and interest rates. The size of the payment in this table depends on the amount of the loan and the interest rate. Large loans and high interest rates increase the size of monthly payments. As noted previously, the monthly mortgage payment for an $80,000 mortgage at 12 percent is $842. If the amount borrowed were $96,000, the monthly payment would be $1,011. If the interest rate on an $80,000 loan were increased from 12 percent to 13.5 percent, the monthly payment would increase from $842 to $933.

Principal and Interest

Let's examine the monthly mortgage payment in greater detail and consider the amount that is allocated to principal and to interest. Table 9.5 shows the breakdown between principal and interest for an $80,000 loan at 12 percent for 25 years. The striking feature of this table is the disproportionate amount of the monthly payment that is applied to interest. Total mortgage payments amounted to $10,110.96 during the first 12 months of the loan. Of that amount, $9,570.93 went to interest and only $540.03 was used to reduce the principal amount of the loan.

Additional Costs

This section describes various techniques lenders use to increase or maintain their returns on mortgage loans.

TABLE 9.5
MORTGAGE AMORTIZATION, $80,000 AT 12
PERCENT FOR 25 YEARS
(months 1–12)

Month	Principal	Interest	Balance
1	$ 42.58	$ 800.00	$79,957.43
2	43.01	799.57	79,914.41
3	43.44	799.14	79,870.98
4	43.87	798.71	79,827.11
5	44.31	798.27	79,782,80
6	44.75	797.83	79,738.05
7	45.20	797.38	79,692.85
8	45.65	796.93	79,647.20
9	46.11	796.47	79,601,09
10	46.57	796.01	79,554.51
11	47.03	795.55	79,507.49
12	47.51	795.07	79,459.98
Totals	$540.03	$9,570.93	

Points

In addition to paying interest on the borrowed funds, lenders charge both fixed rate and adjustable rate mortgage borrowers additional fees or points to increase their income, and to cover the costs of originating and closing mortgage loans. A point is 1 percent of the principal amount of a mortgage loan (e.g., one point on a $80,000 mortgage is $800). Closing costs on residential mortgage loans are normally one to two points or more. The points are usually paid by the borrower at the time of the closing. They may be deducted from the face amount of the loan or paid as a cash cost. If they are deducted from the face amount of the loan, a one-point closing cost on an $80,000 mortgage loan would result in a disbursement of $79,200 to the borrower.

Points increase the **effective interest rate** of a mortgage loan. The effective interest rate is contract interest rate plus points and other costs amortized over the payback period of the loan. As a rule of thumb, each point (1 percent) increases the interest charge by one-eighth (1/8) of 1 percent. The 1/8 factor corresponds to a **payback period** (number of years until the loan is paid off) of about 15 years. If the loan is paid off in 5 years, the factor increases to 1/4. For example, suppose that the contract interest rate on a mortgage loan is 13 percent and four points are charged at the closing. The effective interest rate for a 15-year payback is 13.5 percent ($13\% + 0.125 \times 0.04 = 0.135$). If the payback were in 5 years, the effective interest rate would be 14 percent.

The payback period may be shorter than the original maturity of the mortgage loan because of the mobility of our population. According to the 1980 Census, about 48 percent of the U.S. population had moved from one home to another in the previous 5 years.

Buydown

A buydown occurs when the seller pays an amount to the lender to permit the home buyer to obtain a lower interest rate or monthly payment. The lower payments may facilitate the sale of the house. In order to cover the cost of the buydown, the seller generally raises the selling price of the house.

Late Charges

Borrowers are required to make their monthly payments by a certain date or pay a late charge. Late charges cover the costs of handling delinquent accounts and add to the lender's income.

Prepayment Penalty

Some mortgage loans contain a penalty for early prepayment of the loan. The purpose of a prepayment penalty is to permit the lender to retain the earning asset for a minimum period of time.

Due-on-Sale Clause

Some mortgage loans contain a **due-on-sale clause,** which means that the mortgage loan is not transferable to the new buyer, and the balance of the loan must be paid to the lender when the house is sold. Other loans, however, are **assumable,** which means that the mortgage loan can be transferred to the buyer, if he or she meets the lender's credit requirements and pays a fee for the assumption.

Mortgage Insurance

Private mortgage insurance for conventional mortgage loans is available to borrowers. It enables them to purchase more expensive homes with smaller initial investments; that is, they get higher loan to value ratios. It also reduces the risk to the lender by insuring against loss on a specified percentage of the loan, usually the top 20 to 25 percent.

ADJUSTABLE RATE MORTGAGES (ARMs)

Special Features of ARMs

Index

The purpose of ARMs is to permit lenders to maintain positive returns on their mortgage loans when market rates of interest and their cost of funds change. This is accomplished by linking the mortgage rate to an *index,* such as the 1-year Treasury security rates, which are an indicator of the lender's cost of funds.

As an inducement to borrowers, lenders offer lower interest rates on ARMs than on fixed rate loans. In December 1986, the effective interest rates on fixed rate loans and ARMs were 10.13 percent and 8.81 percent, respectively.

Adjustments

When the index changes, the lender can (1) make periodic changes in the borrower's monthly payments, (2) keep the monthly payment the same and change the principal amount of the loan, (3) change the maturity of the loan, or (4) any combination of the preceding. The best adjustment, from the lender's point of view, depends on whether interest rates are expected to rise or fall over the life of the mortgage. If they are expected to rise, increased monthly payments will increase the lender's cash flow. If they are expected to fall, option (2) will permit the lender to more or less maintain their spread between earning assets and costs of funds. The **adjustment period**—when the changes occur—varies from bank to bank and can be monthly, annually, or any other time period.

Caps

Some ARMs have **rate caps** that limit how much the interest rate can change at each adjustment period or over the term of the loan; or **payment caps** that limit how much the payments can change within each adjustment period or over the term of the loan. For example, the rate cap is that the interest rate may change no more than 2 percentage points annually nor more than 5 percentage points over the life of the loan. An example of a payment cap is that although the interest rate has increased, the borrower's payments cannot increase more than $50 per year. When there are caps, **negative amortization** can occur when the increased payments on the loan do not cover the increased interest costs, and the unpaid interest is added to the unpaid balance of the loan.

Margin

Margin is the number of percentage points that the lender adds to the index rate to determine the rate charged on the ARM during each adjustment period. The equation for the ARM rate that is charged is:

$$\text{ARM interest rate} = \text{index rate} + \text{margin} \qquad (9.1)$$

Suppose the index rate is 10 percent and the margin is 2 percent. The interest rate that will be charged on the ARM is 12 percent (10% + 2% = 12%). The margin usually remains constant over the life of the loan. The size of the margin, however, can vary from lender to lender.

Discounts

Lenders (or the seller using a buydown) may offer prospective home buyers a lower interest rate or lower payments for the first year (or less) of the mortgage loan to induce the buyer to use an ARM (or to buy the house). The lower ARM rate or payment is called the **discount.** After the discount period, the ARM rate or payment will be adjusted to reflect the current index rate.

Conversion

Some ARMs are convertible into fixed rate mortgages at designated times. When the conversion occurs, the new rate is determined by the current rate of interest on mortgage loans. As a rule, the ARM rate on convertible mortgages is higher than the rate on nonconvertible ones.

Risk

By using ARMs, lenders have shifted some of the interest rate risk of holding mortgage loans from themselves to borrowers. The lenders, however, may have traded reduced interest rate risk for increased default risk and lower income. There is evidence that some lenders consider ARMs riskier than fixed rate mortgages because they generate less interest income during periods of declining interest (which was the case from 1981–1985).[3]

Lenders also believe that ARMs have higher default risk than fixed rate mortgages. One reason for this is that if interest rates increase sufficiently, the borrower's ability to repay the loan may be diminished. These risks are no doubt reflected in the relatively narrow spread between the effective rates changed on fixed rate mortgages and ARMs, which was mentioned earlier.

Private mortgage insurance companies also consider ARMs riskier than their fixed rate counterparts, and thus they raised the insurance premiums on ARMs to 30 percent or more above the premiums for fixed rate mortgages. In addition, they increased the ratio of income to initial loan payments for new ARM borrowers to reduce their risk.[4]

Alternative Mortgage Instruments

Alternative mortgage instruments and ARMs are generic terms that cover a variety of mortgage instruments, where the terms of the contract can change or where they differ from the traditional fixed rate mortgage loan. Listed in the following sections are the principal types of alternative mortgage instruments and ARMs.

Variable Rate Mortgage

The VRM permits the lender to vary the interest rate and or payments on the mortgage loan on a periodic basis, depending on the movement of the index rate. The VRM may or may not have caps.

Graduated Payment Mortgage

Because of the high cost of housing, many young buyers cannot afford large monthly mortgage payments. GPMs address this problem by making a fixed rate loan whereby monthly payments are low at first and then rise over a period of years. For example, the FHA-insured GPMs have five different rates of increase. The payments can increase 2 1/2 percent, 5 percent, 7 percent annually for 5 years, or they may increase 2 or 3 percent annually for 10 years.

Because the monthly payments on GPMs are so low in the early years, there is negative amortization. Also, during periods of rising interest rates, negative amortization could be a significant problem for borrowers. For example, if the borrowers decided to sell the home in a few years and it did not appreciate in value, the principal balance on the loan would have increased because of nega-

[3] Michael J. Stutzer and William Roberds, "Adjustable Rate Mortgages: Increasing Efficiency More than Housing Activity," *Quarterly Review*, Federal Reserve Bank of Minneapolis, Summer 1985, p. 12.

[4] John L. Goodman, Jr. and Charles A. Luckett, "Adjustable-Rate Financing in Mortgage and Consumer Credit Markets," *Federal Reserve Bulletin*, November 1985, p. 829.

tive amortization. In other words, they would owe more than they originally borrowed on the house, and the sale of the mortgaged house might not provide sufficient funds to pay off the loan.

Shared Appreciation Mortgage

A SAM is a mortgage loan arrangement whereby the borrower agrees to share in the increased value of the property (usually 30 to 50 percent) with the lender in return for a reduction in the fixed-interest rate at the time the loan is made. The increased value is determined at some specified date in the future when the loan can be refinanced or when the property is sold. Sharing a decline in value may not be part of the agreement.

Growing Equity Mortgage

GEMs are 15-year fully amortized home mortgage loans. They are made a fixed rate and the initial payments are calculated on a 30-year schedule. They are paid off more rapidly, however, because there is a 4-percent annual increase in the monthly payments, all of which goes to reduce the principal balance of the loan. In addition, the interest rate is made below the prevailing rate for 30-year loans. Borrowers who can afford the increased payments can save thousands of dollars in interest payments.

Reverse Annuity Mortgage

The RAM is designed for senior citizens who own their homes free and clear and want to increase their incomes by borrowing against the equity in their homes. In this case, the lender pays the homeowner a fixed annuity based on a percentage value of the property. The homeowner would not be required to repay the loan until his or her demise, at which time the loan would be paid from the proceeds from the estate, or when the home is sold. The interest rate on the loan may be adjustable and the loan may have a refinancing option.

Balloon Payment

Balloon loans are relatively short-term loans (e.g., 5 years). At the end of that period, the entire amount of the loan comes due and a new loan is negotiated. The initial payments are usually based on a 20- to 30-year amortization. This is similar to the **Canadian rollover mortgage** or **renegotiable mortgage**—where the maturity is fixed, but the interest payments are renegotiated every 3 to 5 years. This method was widely used in the early 1980s, when interest rates were soaring and lenders did not want to be locked into long-term mortgage loans.

Second Mortgage

Many homeowners use a second mortgage when they need funds for business or some other purpose. A second mortgage is made in addition to the first mortgage and uses the same property as collateral. Second mortgages usually have short maturities—3 to 5 years. Second mortgages have an inferior claim to the first mortgage if the real estate is foreclosed. A second mortgage created for the purpose of helping to finance the sale of real estate is sometimes called a **purchase-money mortgage.** This type of mortgage is commonly used to finance land and real estate developments.

A **seller take-back** first or second mortgage may involve interest payments only during the life of the loan and then a balloon payment when the principal is due at maturity. To illustrate a seller take-back second mortgage, suppose that a person wants to buy a house for $170,000. The seller owes $80,000 on a 10-percent mortgage. The buyer assumes the first mortgage and makes a $40,000 down payment, and the seller gives the buyer a second take-back mortgage for $50,000 for 5 years at 14 percent, well below the market rate. The monthly interest payments on the second mortgage are $583.33 and the $50,000 principal amount will be due in 5 years.

If the seller take back is arranged as a private mortgage between the buyer and seller, sellers must collect the monthly payments and cannot receive their equity before the full term of the mortgage. If the mortgage is arranged by an institutional lender, however, and it meets certain conditions, the seller may be able to sell the second mortgage.

A **wraparound mortgage** is another version of a second mortgage, which was widely used when interest rates were high in the early 1980s. Wraparounds arise when a home is sold. The term **wraparound** is used because the new mortgage loan includes the first mortgage loan—a second mortgage is "wrapped around" the first mortgage loan. Generally, the wraparound has a higher interest rate and longer term to maturity than the first mortgage loan. Under a wraparound plan, the lender often assumes the payments on the existing mortgage loan, then issues another mortgage to the new buyer.

For example, suppose that a house costs $120,000 today. The existing mortgage balance on the house is $48,000 at 7 percent. The new home buyer makes a down payment of, say, $24,000 and receives a $96,000 loan from the seller at 13 percent, which is below the market rate of 14.5 percent. The lender of the wraparound receives 13 percent and pays out 7 percent on the older first mortgage loan. The lender's profit is the difference between the two rates, plus the potential profit from the sale of the property being financed. This is possible only with existing mortgages that are assumable by the buyer. All FHA and VA mortgages are assumable.

FEDERAL LAWS IN RESIDENTIAL REAL ESTATE LENDING

Federal laws prescribe certain terms and conditions under which lenders can make residential real estate loans. Selected highlights of the principal laws are presented here. Some of these laws also apply to consumer loans.

Title 12, U.S. Code 371

National banks have certain restrictions concerning real estate lending imposed on them by Title 12, U.S. Code 371 that do not apply to other lenders. For example, they can lend no more than 66.67 percent of the appraised value of unimproved real estate. If there are offsite improvements, such as streets, water, and sewer, they can lend up to 75 percent of the appraised value. If the property includes buildings, they can lend up to 90 percent of the appraised value. In addition, the maturity of the loans cannot exceed 30 years. However, these restrictions do not apply to loans that are fully insured or guaranteed by state or federal government agencies.

Real Estate Settlement Procedures Act of 1974 (RESPA)

Settlement is the process by which the ownership of real estate, which is represented by the title, passes from the seller to the buyer. The intent of RESPA is to provide buyers and sellers with information about the settlement process. RESPA covers most residential real estate loans, including lots for homes or mobile homes. Certain real estate transactions are exempted, including loans to buy 25 acres or more, construction loans on lots already owned, home improvement loans, and loans to finance property for immediate resale.

When a buyer applies in writing for a loan covered by RESPA, the lender must send the borrower estimates of the settlement costs within three business days and a special information booklet describing the settlement and charges. One day before settlement, the borrower has the right to see the completed Uniform Settlement Statement that will be used.

RESPA prohibits anyone from taking or giving a fee (a kickback) for referrals, such as recommending a title company to do the title search, or for taking fees where no service has been performed. In addition, RESPA limits the amount of monthly escrow payments. An **escrow** is a reserve of funds that is held aside to make future payments for taxes, insurance, and other items. The monthly payments must not exceed 1/12th of the annual amount needed to cover such payments, plus an amount that will maintain a 1/6th reserve. No interest is paid on the escrow accounts.

Fair Housing Act of 1968

The Fair Housing Act, which is Title VII of the Civil Rights Act of 1968, as amended by the Housing and Community Development Act of 1974, prohibits discrimination on the basis of race, color, religion, sex, or national origin in connection with the sale or rental of most housing and vacant land offered for sale for residential construction. The Act applies to credit transactions involving housing and also prohibits discrimination by appraisal and brokerage services.

Home Mortgage Disclosure Act of 1975

This law was enacted to prohibit home mortgage lenders from denying real estate credit on the basis of a borrower's race, color, or national origin. The Act requires that mortgage lenders provide information about their lending practices both to individuals and public officials in order to monitor their lending activities in that regard.

Community Reinvestment Act of 1977

The Community Reinvestment Act is directed at federally regulated lenders that take deposits to extend real estate credit. Such institutions are required to serve the needs of people in the community. Section 804 of the Act directs federal financial supervisory agencies to assess the extension of real estate credit to the entire community, including low- and moderate-income neighborhoods. The intent is for depository institutions to provide capital for local housing and economic development.

The Secondary Mortgage Market

The **secondary mortgage market,** in which mortgage loans are purchased and sold, increases the liquidity of residential mortgages and lessens the cyclical disruptions in the housing market. In addition, the secondary mortgage market has attracted investors from outside the traditional mortgage investment community by selling securities backed by mortgage loans. The three major participants in the secondary market are the Federal National Mortgage Association, the Government National Mortgage Association, and the Federal Home Loan Mortgage Association. These three organizations were created by Congress to develop a secondary mortgage market. Some private organizations also operate in the secondary mortgage market.

Federal National Mortgage Association

The **Federal National Mortgage Association** (FNMA or Fannie Mae) was chartered in 1938 to create a secondary market for home mortgages. Under the Housing Act of 1954, FNMA was restructured so that its secondary market operations would eventually be privately owned. The secondary market operations were converted to a private corporation on September 30, 1968 in conformance with the National Housing Act (12 U.S.C. 1716, et seq.). Since then, FNMA has been a government sponsored, privately owned corporation whose stock is traded on the New York, Pacific, and Midwest Stock Exchanges. Although it is a privately owned corporation, the President of the United States appoints 5 of the 15-member board of directors, and it is subject to government supervision and regulation. Equally important, FNMA can borrow from the Treasury, which gives it a privileged status among privately owned corporations. Therefore, it is more like a quasi-governmental agency than a privately owned company, which is completely independent of the federal government. FNMA provides liquidity to the mortgage market by providing a market and buying mortgages and through it Mortgage-Backed Security guaranty activities. FNMA deals in single- and multifamily conventional mortgages, government backed mortgages, adjustable rate mortgages, and second mortgages. FNMA also deals in mortgage loans for hospitals and certain publicly financed projects.

Commitments

For a fee, FNMA makes commitments or contracts with mortgage lenders to buy a specific dollar volume of mortgages of specific types within a certain period of time. The fee, which varies from time to time, was 85 basis points at the end of 1985. Most commitments obligate the lender to sell mortgages to FNMA at the agreed-upon prices.

Mortgage-Backed Securities

FNMA packages pools of mortgages in **Fannie Mae Guaranteed Mortgage Pass-Through Certificates** and guarantees the payment of principal and interest. Because the full title of these securities is cumbersome, they are called mortgage-backed securities (MBS). The mortgages come from FNMA's own portfolio or from lenders who pool them. FNMA issues and guarantees the MBS, which are backed by these loans. The size of an MBS ranges from $1 million to $1 billion or more. Most MBS's are sold to mortgage lenders. In FNMA's jargon, mortgage lenders *swap* their mortgages for an MBS. This type of swap should not be confused with interest rate swap, which is explained in Chapter 18. The lenders can retain MBS or split them in smaller amounts and sell them to other investors.

Mortgage-backed bonds are a second type of mortgage-backed security. Mortgage-backed bonds are obligations of the issuer. The mortgages used as collateral are reported as assets on the issuer's financial statements and the mortgage-backed bonds are reported as liabilities. Typically, the cash flows from the mortgages used as collateral for mortgage-backed bonds are not dedicated to the payment and interest and principal of the bonds. Those bonds that do dedicate the cash flows from the mortgages to the payment of interest and principal are known as **pay-throughs.** The bonds usually have a maturity ranging from 5 to 12 years.[5]

[5] For additional details, see Christine Pavel, ''Securitization,'' *Economic Perspectives,* Federal Reserve Bank of Chicago, July/August 1986, pp. 16–31. This article deals with ''securitization,'' the pooling and repackaging of otherwise illiquid loans into securities and then selling them to investors. More is said about this in Chapter 18.

Government National Mortgage Association

The **Government National Mortgage Association** (GNMA or Ginnie Mae) was created by the National Housing Act in 1968 to handle some of the functions previously performed by the Federal National Mortgage Association. GNMA is a government-owned corporation that operates within the Department of Housing and Urban Development (HUD). It has three major activities: (1) GNMA guarantees the timely payment of principal and interest on their own version of mortgage-backed securities; (2) GNMA has a Special Assistance Function under which it purchases mortgages on low-income housing projects and other mortgages; and (3) it is responsible for managing and liquidating a portfolio of mortgages owned by the federal government.

GNMA guaranteed mortgage-backed securities are pools of FHA/VA mortgages issued by private mortgage lending institutions, and the MBS's are backed by the full faith and credit of the U.S. government. The MBS's are issued on government insured or guaranteed single-family level payment mortgages, growing equity mortgages, graduated payment mortgages, and manufactured home loans. In the past, MBS's were also issued on certain multifamily public project loans, multifamily construction loans, and buydown loans.

The GNMA securities are **modified pass-through** securities. This means that GNMA pays to the holders of the MBS monthly interest and principal at the rate shown on the securities plus the principal scheduled on the pooled mortgages, whether such payments are collected or not. GNMA also pays unscheduled payments from early payoffs of mortgage loans. When interest rates declined in the early 1980s, many mortgage loans were paid off or refinanced at lower rates, resulting in large unscheduled payments to holders of GNMA securities. The issuer of the mortgage loan is responsible for any shortfalls in the mortgage payments.

Figure 9.2 illustrates how the GNMA MBS program works. The process begins when a lender, such as a bank, applies to GNMA for approval as an issuer of MBS's, and at the same time for a guaranty of a security; then, GNMA approves the issuer and issues a commitment for the MBS. With that approval and commitment, the issuer acquires a pool of mortgage loans. In addition, the issuer may also arrange with a securities dealer to make a market in the MBS when it becomes available. Other arrangements must be made for a custodian to hold the mortgages and other documents as well as holding the principal and interest (P&I) and tax and insurance (T&I) funds. When all of this is done, the issuer submits the paperwork to GNMA for final approval. When the approval is granted, GNMA instructs its transfer agent to deliver the certificates to the issuer, who can hold them, or sell them to investors.

Federal Home Loan Mortgage Corporation

The **Federal Home Loan Mortgage Corporation** (FHLMC or Freddie Mac, or the Mortgage Corporation) was created by the Emergency Home Finance Act of 1970 to strengthen the existing secondary mortgage market. It is owned by

HOW THE "GNMA MORTGAGE-BACKED SECURITIES PROGRAM" WORKS

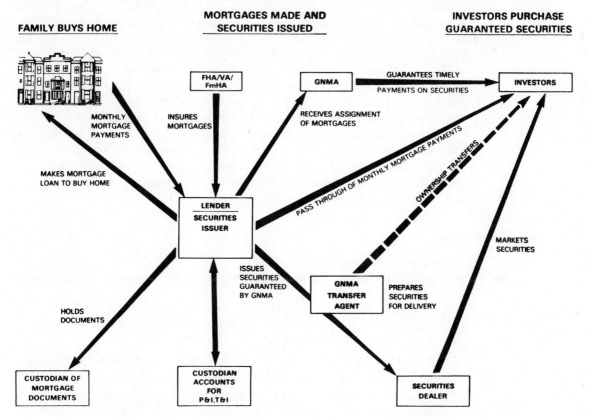

FIGURE 9.2   How the "GNMA mortgage-backed securities program" works.

the Federal Home Loan Bank System and deals mainly with savings and loan associations. FNMA purchases FHA/VA and conventional first and second mortgages from qualified mortgage lenders, and repackages them to sell to investors. The FHLMC's mortgage-backed securities are called **Mortgage Participation Certificates (PCs)**. To help finance its operations, the FHLMC sells **Collateralized Mortgage Obligations** (CMOs), which are debt obligations secured by conventional mortgage loans.

REMICS

The Tax Reform Act of 1986 created a new type of mortgage obligation called a Real Estate Mortgage Investment Conduit, or REMICS. Under prior tax laws, trusts were established to market interest in mortgage pools. However, income tax problems arose with some trusts. To avoid corporate taxes, all of the beneficiaries of the trust had to have an undivided interest in it and equal pass-through of the benefits. This condition was not possible when one class of beneficiaries received payments faster than another, or accepted a different amount of default risk. If the trusts were taxed as corporations, the amounts paid to the beneficiaries were considered dividends for tax purposes.[6]

To avoid this and other problems with trusts, CMOs were developed. Because they are debts of the issuers, payments to their interest holders are considered interest for tax purposes. Moreover, CMOs remain as liabilities on the balance sheet of the issuer, and they are taxed as corporations.

In an effort to solve these problems, Congress created REMICS, which are multiple-class real estate mortgage-backed securities that are treated as pass-through entities for tax purposes. Because of their tax treatment, they are expected to become the dominant vehicle in the secondary mortgage market, and CMOs will cease to be issued.

Private Participants

Private organizations were developed to make a profit in the secondary mortgage market by buying and selling mortgages. Some of the leading participants are:

- The Home Mortgage Access Corporation, established by the National Association of Homebuilders.
- Sears Mortgage Securities Corporation, which is part of the Sears Financial Network established by Sears, Roebuck and Company.
- Mortgage Guaranty Insurance Corporation (MGIC), a private mortgage insurer.
- General Electric Credit Corporation (GECC), a division of General Electric Corporation, is one of the nation's largest diversified financial and leasing organizations.
- Residential Funding (RFC), a division of Norwest Mortgage Inc., which is part of Norwest Corporation, a diversified financial services organization.

Although this list is not complete, it does show the variety of private organizations that participate in the secondary mortgage market.

COMMERCIAL MORTGAGE LOANS

As mentioned at the beginning of this chapter, commercial mortgages include loans for land, construction, and real estate development, and loans on com-

---

[6] For details see Thomas P. Vartanian and John F. Coverdale, "Remics Provide New Vehicle for Secondary Mortgage Market," *American Banker,* November 14, 1986, pp. 4, 6, 21; also see *Explanation of the Tax Reform Act of 1986,* Chicago: Commerce Clearing House, 1986, pp. 409–417.

mercial properties, such as shopping centers, office buildings, or warehouses. Frequently commercial real estate loans are linked to commercial loans. For example, suppose a delivery firm wants to expand, buy new trucks, and build a warehouse. The bank would make a term loan to finance the trucks, a construction loan to build the warehouse, and then refinance it with a mortgage loan when it is completed. The mortgage loan on the warehouse cannot be pooled and sold like home mortgage loans. Nevertheless, it is a profitable loan. It is financed on a floating-rate basis for 7 years, and it is cross-collateralized with the trucks.

A common practice for life insurance companies that make large commercial real estate loans is to share in the equity or profits from the real estate venture. National banks are not allowed to share in the equity, but they may share in the income or earnings of the borrower. This may be done to reduce the interest cost (and increase the ultimate earnings to the bank).[7]

Construction Loans

Construction loans require the bank to make irregular disbursements to the borrower/builder. One method of making the disbursements is based on completion of certain phases of construction. For example, 30 percent may be paid when the foundation is completed, 30 percent when the project is under roof and the plumbing and wiring have been completed, and the remainder when the structure is completed and ready for occupancy. Another method is to pay the builder upon presentment of bills from suppliers and subcontractors as the building progresses. Construction loans have to be flexible to meet the needs of the borrower and the lender.

Construction loans are considered "interim" financing; that is, the loans are in effect only during the development and construction phase of the real estate project. When the project is complete, the builder is expected to get "permanent," long-term financing. In the case of home loans, the permanent financing will be provided when the homes are sold and the buyers obtain mortgage loans. In the case of commercial property, long-term financing can be obtained from life insurance companies, pension and retirement plans, as well as banks and savings and loan associations.

During the development and construction phase of development, the land and partially completed structures serve as collateral for the loan. If the developer/builder is unable to complete the project for any reason, and defaults on the loan, the lender may take possession of the partially completed structure. Then the lender has to consider finishing the structure or liquidating it. Because considerable risk may be involved with interim financing, the interest rates charged are relatively high for some borrowers.

Interest rates on construction loans are frequently priced at the prime rate plus 1 or more percentage points, depending on the risk involved. In addition, an **origination fee of** 1–3 percent of the amount of the loan may be charged.

---

[7] Code of Federal Regulations 7.7312.

This fee is charged to cover the cost of the paperwork involved and to increase the effective yield on the loan to the bank.

MORTGAGE BANKING COMPANIES

Bank holding companies are permitted by the Federal Reserve (Section 4(c)8, Regulation Y) to engage in mortgage banking. The term *mortgage banking* is misleading because mortgage bankers are not banks. The principal functions of mortgage bankers are to originate mortgage loans and then sell the loans to others, while they service the payments of principal and interest.

Origination of Mortgage Loans

To **originate** mortgage loans means that the mortgage banker finds a borrower (i.e., a home buyer), completes all of the mortgage documents, and uses its own funds to close the real estate transaction. A mortgage loan is **closed** when the mortgage banker consummates the transaction by exchanging a deed for consideration. The origination process includes appraising the property, doing a title search, negotiating the terms of the loan, and recording the documents in accordance with applicable real estate laws. The mortgage banker may charge the seller points on the mortgage loans. They may also charge an origination fee of 1 to 5 percent of the amount of the loan for their service, which is paid by the borrower.

When sufficient amounts of closed mortgage loans are accumulated, they are pooled and sold in the secondary mortgage market or directly to investors. To avoid the risks of rising interest rates while organizing a pool, mortgage bankers may obtain commitments from investors to buy the pools at agreed upon terms.

Servicing Mortgage Loans

Servicing mortgages means collecting payments of principal and interest, escrows for taxes and insurance, and foreclosing on the loans if necessary. The mortgage bankers receive a fee for this service, which is attractive to their investors who may be in a different part of the county and may be unwilling or unable to collect on their mortgage loans. A typical fee for servicing is 3/8ths of 1 percent of the principal amount.

Carry

The difference between the interest rate earned on the mortgage loans held by mortgage bankers and the cost of borrowing to finance that inventory is called the **carry.** If the returns from the mortgages exceed the cost of borrowing, there is a positive carry. If the returns from the mortgages are less than the cost of borrowing, there is a negative carry.

REAL ESTATE INVESTMENT TRUSTS

In 1960, Congress enacted Section 856 of the tax code to provide the public with the opportunity to invest in professionally managed real estate portfolios. Accordingly, real estate investment trusts (REITs pronounced "reets") could sell stock to investors and borrow additional funds to invest in real estate. Shares of publicly-held REITs are traded on major stock exchanges and in the over-the-counter market. These shares provide a means for some investors who lack funds and experience to invest in a managed real estate portfolio. For banks, REITs provide another way to engage in the real estate business. Some banks own or control REITs.

The REITS management group serves as an adviser, and receives a fee of 1 to $1\frac{1}{2}$ percent or more of the assets under management.

REITs qualify for special tax provisions if they meet certain tax code requirements. The principal requirements are: (1) 95 percent or more of the income must be distributed to shareholders, (2) 75 percent or more of the assets must consist of real estate or real estate loans or real estate mortgages, and (3) 75 percent of the income must be real-estate related.

REIT's Portfolios

REITs can own real estate as well as make real estate loans of all types. The composition of particular REIT's portfolios varies widely, depending on their geographic location and other factors. For example, BRE Properties, formerly BankAmerica Realty Investors, has primary emphasis on income-producing real estate investments in California and West Coast real estate. Their investments include shopping centers, office buildings, hotels, and other properties. In contrast, Federal Realty Investment Trust invests nationwide and has its primary emphasis on shopping centers; L & N Housing Corporation emphasis is on rental housing in the Sunbelt; and Lomas & Nettleton Mortgage Investors has its primary emphasis on short-term construction loans.

SUMMARY

This chapter examined real estate lending with particular emphasis on residential mortgage loans. The chapter began with an overview of new private housing starts and the cost of financing. The cost of financing to the borrower—or the income to the lender—depends on the level of interest rates, term to maturity, and whether the mortgage is fully amortized and has fixed or adjustable rates. In recent years, ARMs have become increasingly popular because lenders can alter the returns on their mortgage loans when their cost of funds changes.

Federal laws concerning residential real estate lending deal mostly with prohibiting discrimination on any basis other than the creditworthiness of the borrower.

The secondary mortgage market is a relatively recent financial innovation designed to improve the liquidity of mortgage loan. The major participants in the market are FNMA, GNMA, and the FHLMC.

Commercial banks also make commercial mortgage loans. These include loans for land, construction, and longer-term loans. Frequently, commercial mortgage loans are tied in with a commercial loan agreement.

Banking organizations also engage in real estate lending and ownership through mortgage banking and real estate investment trust companies.

IMPORTANT CONCEPTS

adjustable-rate mortgages
adjustment period
balloon payment
buydown
Canadian rollover mortgage
Caps
carry
Collateralized Mortgage Obligations (CMOs)
commitment
Community Reinvestment Act of 1977
construction loan
conversion
discount
due-on sale clause
effective interest rate
escrow
Fair Housing Act of 1968
Fannie Mae guaranteed pass-through certificates
Federal Home Loan Mortgage Corporation (FHLMC)
Federal National Mortgage Association (FNMA)
fixed rate, fully amortized, level payment mortgage
Government National Mortgage Association (GNMA)
graduated payment mortgage (GPM)
growing equity mortgage (GEM)

Home Mortgage Disclosure Act of 1975
index
late charges
loan to price ratio
margin
mortgage-backed bonds
mortgage-backed securities
mortgage banking company
mortgage insurance
Mortgage Participation Certificates (PCs)
originate loans
origination fees
partially amortized, fixed rate mortgage
payback period
payment cap
pay-throughs
points
prepayment penalty
purchase-money mortgage
rate cap
Real Estate Investment Trust (REIT)
Real Estate Mortgate Investment Conduits (REMICS)
Real Estate Settlement Procedures Act of 1974 (RESPA)
renegotiable mortgage
reverse annuity mortgage (RAM)
secondary mortgage market
second mortgage

seller take-back

service (loans)

settlement

shared appreciation mortgage (SAM)

Title 12, U.S. Code 371

variable rate mortgage (VRM)

wraparound mortgage

REFERENCES

Goodman, John L., Jr., and Charles A. Luckett. "Adjustable-Rate Financing in Mortgage and Consumer Credit Markets," *Federal Reserve Bulletin*, November 1985.

Pavel, Christine. "Securitization," *Economic Perspectives*, Federal Reserve Bank of Chicago, July/August 1986.

Stutzer, Michael J. and William Roberds. "Adjustable Rate Mortgages: Increasing Efficiency More than Housing Activity," *Quarterly Review*, Federal Reserve Bank of Minneapolis, Summer 1985.

Vartanian, Thomas P. and John F. Coverdale. "Remics Provide New Vehicle for Secondary Mortgage Market," *American Banker*, November 14, 1986.

QUESTIONS

9.1. Why are housing prices considerably higher today compared with the 1960s?

9.2. Why is residential real estate good collateral for a loan? Why is it bad collateral?

9.3. What type of home loan has a balloon payment?

9.4. What factors affect monthly payments on home loans? Briefly explain their effects on payments.

9.5. Define the following terms: (a) points, (b) effective interest rate, (c) buydown, (d) prepayment penalty, and (e) due-on-sale.

9.6. What advantage to borrowers do ARMs have compared with conventional, fixed-rate loans? To lenders?

9.7. Regarding ARMs, what are(is): (a) rate caps, (b) payment caps, (c) negative amortization, (d) margins, and (e) discounts?

9.8. How have interest rate risk and default risk been altered by using an ARM instead of a fixed-rate mortgage?

9.9. Briefly distinguish between the following types of mortgages: (a) VRMs, (b) GPMs, (c) SAMs, (d) GEMs, (e) RAMs, and (f) balloon loans.

9.10. Why do homeowners use a second mortgage? Name three versions of second mortgages.

9.11. Briefly describe the purposes of the following federal laws: (a) Title 12, U.S. Code 371, (b) RESPA, and (c) Fair Housing Act of 1968.

9.12. What are the three major participants in the secondary mortgage market?

What are their basic functions and securities with which they are involved?

9.13. What are REMICs? CMOs?

9.14. Distinguish between "interim" and "permanent" financing in the home loan market.

9.15. Discuss the functions of mortgage banking companies. What is the carry?

9.16. What is a REIT? Why form a REIT?

9.17. Discuss the advantages and disadvantages of home ownership compared with renting.

CONSUMER LENDING

In November 1987, commercial banks had $272.2 billion in consumer install-ment credit outstanding, which was 45 percent of total consumer installment credit outstanding. **Consumer installment credit** refers to loans to individuals that are scheduled to be repaid in two or more installments and for personal, household, or family consumption. Consumers have the right to pay the loans in full, however, if they choose to do so. Consumer installment credit is also issued by finance companies, credit unions, retailers, savings and loan associa-tions, gasoline companies, and mutual savings banks.

CONSUMER LOANS AT COMMERCIAL BANKS

Portfolio Considerations

Consumer loans differ from other types of loans in several respects. Consumer loans usually have an original maturity of 5 years or less and they are for relatively small dollar amounts. The greatest risk associated with them is default risk—the risk that the borrower will not repay the loan. Defaults tend to increase with the size of the loan, with longer-term maturities, and are inversely related to the value of the collateral relative to the size of the loan.

Because consumer loans are highly regulated and competitive, the interest rates charged on them do not increase with default risk. Instead, the market has segmented consumer loans. Historically, the highest-risk consumers borrowed from finance companies and the lowest-risk consumers borrowed from banks. Finance companies, in turn, charged higher rates than banks. Although the historic difference in lending rates has eroded in recent years, consumer lenders establish the degree of default risk they are willing to take and consider it and other factors when setting their lending rates. This is particularly evident in credit cards where the nominal rates (i.e., 18 percent) are the same; but some banks will issue cards only to customers with low expected default risk, whereas other banks are willing to take more risk.

Because the loans tend to be short-term and are generally small to average size, the administrative costs are high relative to the amounts outstanding. Nevertheless, consumer installment loans can be profitable. In 1985, the latest date for which data are available, the average net return before tax was 2.4 percent on consumer installment credit and 1.9 percent on credit cards. This compares with 2.3 percent on real estate loans and 2.8 percent on commercial and industrial loans.[1] Equally important, a study of profitability of large commercial banks during the 1982–1986 period revealed that high-quality consumer loans were the primary reason that banks had persistently high returns on assets in each of the years reviewed.[2]

Installment Loans

Automobile Loans

As shown in Table 10.1, **automobile loans** accounted for 38.9 percent of the consumer installment loans at commercial banks. This category includes loans made directly by banks for new and used automobiles as well as indirect loans made by automobile dealers and then purchased by banks. Such indirect loans

[1] Glenn B. Canner and James T. Ferfgus, "The Economic Effects of Proposed Ceilings on Credit Card Interest Rates," *Federal Reserve Bulletin*, January 1987, pp. 1–2.

[2] Benton E. Gup and John R. Walter, "Profitability of Large Commercial Banks: The Secret of Their Success," *Midland Corporate Finance Journal*, Winter, 1988, pp. 24–29.

TABLE 10.1

CONSUMER INSTALLMENT CREDIT HELD BY
COMMERCIAL BANKS, NOVEMBER 1987

Type of Credit	Amount ($ millions)	Percent
Automobile	$105,910	38.9%
Revolving	93,014	34.2
Mobile home	8,406	3.1
Other	64,910	23.8
Total	$272,240	100.0%

Source. Board of Governors of the Federal Reserve
System, *Federal Reserve Bulletin,* March 1988,
p. A40.

are called **dealer paper.** Because automobile sales are cyclical, the proportion
of automobile loans varies widely from time to time.

Automobile loans may have an original maturity of 48–60 months and some
banks will finance 90–100 percent of the cost. Such terms are commonly offered in **lease-a-like loans.** These are balloon loans with a repurchase agreement
that makes them "look like" a closed-end lease from the customer's point of
view. Closed-end leases will be discussed shortly. Under a repurchase agreement, the bank (or some other third party) will repurchase the automobile at the
end of the term of the loan, at the customer's option, for a price that is equal to
the balloon obligation. In other words, the bank takes the automobile instead of
the final payment. Suppose that the amount borrowed for the loan is $12,000
and the automobile is expected to have a value of $4,000 at the end of the loan
period—which is the same amount as the balloon. At the end of the loan
period, the customer can:

1. Sell or trade-in the car and pay off the balance of the loan.

2. Keep the car and pay off or refinance the balance.

3. Exercise the repurchase agreement instead of paying off the loan.

The repurchase agreement stipulates that the vehicle must be within certain
standards for mileage and wear and tear. For example, the mileage limit may be
15,000 miles per year and the buyer is required to provide normal maintenance.
The trade-in value of the automobile is usually supported by an insurance
policy, thereby reducing the risk to the bank. As discussed in Chapter 8, private
financial guarantees are only as good as the quality of the guarantor.

The monthly payments on balloon loans are often 300–500 basis points
higher than the monthly payments on a lease because the lender does not get
the tax advantage of the depreciation from the vehicle.

Like mortgage loans, automobile loans can be pooled and sold to investors.
Salomon Brothers, an investment banking firm, calls their product CARS—

Certificates of Automobile Receivables. This is part of the trend toward securitization, which permits banks to increase the liquidity of otherwise illiquid assets.

Revolving Loans

Revolving loans, or **open-end credit,** are those in which the borrower has a line of credit up to a certain amount, and may pay off the loans and credit charges over time. The terms of repayment are flexible, and are largely at the discretion of the borrower. Most revolving loans charge interest on the amount borrowed only if the borrower pays less than the full amount of the loan at the end of a grace period of 30 days or less. This does not apply to cash advances, which may incur finance charges beginning on the transaction date. Revolving loans have no definite maturity. Bank credit cards, such as VISA and MasterCard, account for about 90 percent of the revolving loans. **Check overdraft** accounts that permit borrowers to write checks for more than their actual bank balance account for most of the remainder.

Bank Credit Cards

All bank credit cards have the following common features:

1. The credit card holder has a prearranged line of credit with a bank that issues credit cards. Credit is extended when the credit card holder buys something and signs (or approves) a sales draft at a participating retail outlet. The retail merchant presents the sales draft to the bank for payment in full, less a **merchant's discount** that is based on:

    (a) the retail outlet's volume of credit card trade

    (b) the average size of each credit card sale

    (c) the amount of compensating balances kept at the bank

    (d) some combination of the preceding factors

The merchants' discounts range from nothing to 6 percent or more. If the credit is presented for payment at the merchant's bank, which may not be the bank that issued the credit card, the merchant's bank will get part of the merchant's discount for handling the transaction and routing it to the bank that issued the card. Finally, the issuing bank presents the sales draft to the credit card holder for payment.

2. The credit-card holder can pay for the draft in full within a grace period (e.g., 30 days), and not be charged interest on the outstanding balance—depending on the method used to compute interest charges—or pay some minimum amount each month on an installment basis. Banks depend on interest income earned on these credit balances as the major source of income from their credit-card operations. They also charge an annual fee (e.g., $30) for the privilege of using a credit card.

3. The final feature is the plastic credit card itself, which serves special purposes. First, it identifies the customer to the merchant. Second, it is used to transfer account information to the sales draft by use of an imprinting machine. Finally, the card may be encoded with a magnetic strip or computer chip that provides additional information about the cardholder's financial condition. The cards with the computer chips are called "smart cards."

About 40 percent of the credit-card debt outstanding is **convenience use,** where the cardholder uses the credit card instead of cash or checks and pays the amount owed in full when billed, thereby avoiding interest charges.[3] Thus, the dollar amount of revolving credit shown in Table 10.1 overstates the amount of interest-bearing revolving loans.

Three types of credit card plans are available to banks. The first type of plan utilizes a single principal bank to issue the credit card, maintain accounts, bill and collect credit, and assume most of the other functions associated with credit cards.

In the second type of plan, one bank acts as a limited agent for the principal bank. The principal bank issues the card, carries the bulk of the credit, and performs the functions described in the first plan. The functions of the agent bank are to establish merchant accounts and accept merchant sales drafts; it receives a commission on the business it generates without incurring costs of a credit card operation. The limited agent bank may have its own name and logo on the card. Cardholders assume that the card is issued and managed by that bank, but that is not the case.

In the third plan, a bank affiliates with one of the major **travel and entertainment card** (T&E) plans such as American Express. A travel and entertainment card is not a credit card; cardholders must pay the amount owed when billed; they do not have the option of making small payments over time. Banks affiliating with T&E cards do not set up a credit card system, but offer T&E cardholders an optional line of credit. The cardholders can pay the travel and entertainment card bill through the bank and borrow directly from the bank against a preestablished line of credit. In this plan, the bank becomes involved with the transactions only if the cardholder decides to pay the bill in installments or uses the line of credit.

Mobile Home Loans

Mobile home loans include direct and indirect loans made to individuals to purchase mobile homes. A mobile home is a movable dwelling unit, 10 feet or more in width and 35 feet or more in length, which may be moved on its own chassis. They are not considered the same as travel trailers, motor homes, or modular housing. In the case of indirect loans, banks may require the dealers from whom they purchased loans to stand behind them in the event of default. This can be accomplished by the dealer keeping a reserve account at the bank

---

[3] Charles A. Luckett and James D. August, "The Growth of Consumer Debt," *Federal Reserve Bulletin,* June 1985, pp. 389–402.

Box 10.1

HISTORY OF CONSUMER CREDIT IN THE UNITED STATES

During the eighteenth century and first half of the nineteenth century, the principal nonbank agencies that extended credit were small merchants, physicians, and pawnbrokers. The Industrial Revolution brought about changes in credit demands and institutions. Industrialization made more goods available for consumers and created a class of wage earners that was bolstered by large-scale immigration into the United States. The credit needs of the industrial wage earners differed from the credit needs of farmers, who generally borrowed on "open-book" accounts (without formal agreements) and paid off their debts with the crops that were sold. In contrast, industrial wage earners received steady incomes and could pay their debts on a regular basis throughout the year. Accordingly, the concept of installment credit evolved, because many workers received low wages and required credit to raise their standard of living above subsistence levels. These credit needs were partially satisfied by **small-loan companies,** which concentrated on making personal loans secured by personal property and wage assignments. Those who could not obtain credit from legitimate small-loan companies borrowed from **loan sharks,** individuals who charged excessive rates of interest—sometimes in excess of 200 percent—and sometimes required the borrower's physical well being as collateral. Today such interest rates are a violation of the federal extortion and credit statutes (Title 18, U.S.C. 891–896).

By the turn of the twentieth century, installment credit and loan sharks were widespread throughout the United States. The first legislation concerning installment credit and the abuses of loan sharks was enacted in Massachusetts in 1911. This law permitted lenders to make loans of up to $300 and charge an interest rate of 42 percent per year. Other states enacted similar legislation. A direct result of the effort to curb and regulate loan sharks was the development of consumer finance companies.

After World War I, new types of credit institutions developed. The availability of consumer durables such as automobiles and washing machines expanded the demand for consumer credit. Sales finance companies, which buy consumer installment credit contracts from retail dealers and provide wholesale financing to those dealers, grew from this demand. Commercial banks were the next institution to enter the consumer loan field. The National City Bank of New York opened the first personal loan department in 1928. Revolving retail credit appeared when John Wanamaker, a large Philadelphia department store, introduced it in 1938. The next major innovation was the development of the credit card. In 1951, Franklin National Bank (New York) issued the first bank credit card. This plastic money was the forerunner of the credit cards issued by banks, retailers, oil companies, and others.

until the loan is repaid. Additional protection for the lender can be obtained in the form of insurance.

Mobile home loans with maturities of 12 years or less may be guaranteed by the FHA or VA. Mobile (manufactured) home loans that are backed by FHA/VA qualify as collateral in GNMA mortgage-backed securities.

Other Loans

The "other" type of credit is a catchall category that includes all other consumer loans made to individuals. Loans for boats, vacations, debt consolidation, and for other purposes are included here.

Noninstallment Loans

Commercial banks also make noninstallment consumer loans, which are loans that are scheduled to be repaid in a lump sum. The largest component of the noninstallment loans are **single-payment loans** that are used to finance the purchase of one home while another home is being sold. This type of loan is commonly called a **bridge loan.** Other noninstallment loans are used to finance investments, and for other purposes.

Leases

Leasing is an alternative method of financing consumer durables such as automobiles, airplanes, and boats. Under a lease, the bank owns the automobile and "rents" it to the customer. The lease may be **open-end,** in which case the bank is responsible for selling the automobile at the end of the lease period. If the amount received is less than a previously agreed-upon residual value, the customer pays the difference. If it is more than the residual value, the customer receives the difference. Under a **closed-end** lease, the bank assumes the risk of the market value being less than the residual value of the automobile. National banks must have insurance on the residual on closed-end leases. The monthly payments for closed-end leases are higher than those for open-end leases because the bank has a greater risk. Because the bank owns the automobile and gets the tax benefit (depreciation), however, the monthly payments may be less than that of a loan of an equivalent amount to buy the automobile outright.

Under the Consumer Leasing Act of 1976 (and Federal Reserve Regulation M), consumer leases must meet the following criteria:

- A lease of personal (not real) property
- The term of the lease must exceed 4 months
- It must be made to a natural person (not a corporation)
- The total lease obligation must not exceed $25,000
- It must be for personal, family, or household purposes

FINANCE AND INTEREST CHARGES

The Truth in Lending Act (Title I of the Consumer Protection Act of 1968), which is implemented by Federal Reserve **Regulation Z,** requires lenders of consumer loans to provide borrowers with written information (before they sign a loan agreement) about finance charges and annual percentage rates so they may compare credit costs. The extent to which consumers use the information to make intelligent decisions is not clear. Few consumers have the time or the knowledge to compare the nuances of the costs of financing. As we will see shortly, costs are not always what they appear to be on the surface. Stated otherwise, some methods of calculating costs result in higher profits for lenders than others.

Finance Charge

The **finance charge** is the **dollar amount** paid for the use of credit. It is the difference between the amount repaid and the amount borrowed. Finance charges do *not* include charges that would be paid under cash transactions, such as sales tax. The finance charge includes interest, service charges, origination fees, guarantee insurance premiums, appraisal fees, credit report fees, and other fees that charged the borrower as a condition of or incident to the extension of credit. For example, suppose that a customer borrows $1,000 for 1 year and pays $80 in interest, a $10 service charge, and a $10 origination fee. The finance charge is $100.

There are some exceptions to the general definition of finance charge. For example, premiums for property insurance purchased in connection with a credit transaction may be excluded from the finance charge. Similarly, premiums for credit life, accident, or loss-of-income may be excluded if the creditor discloses in writing that such insurance is optional. In addition, in loans secured by real estate, fees for title searches, credit reports, and so on are excluded.[4]

Finance Charges on Revolving Credit

Four methods of assessing finance charges on revolving credits are presented here. As previously mentioned, some methods of computing charges result in higher profits than others. To illustrate the differences in potential profits, or costs to the consumer, consider the following transactions.

On June 5, Lincoln David receives a statement with the total amount of $100

---

[4] Kenneth Spong, *Banking Regulation: Its Purposes, Implementation, and Effects,* 2d ed., Federal Reserve Bank of Kansas City, 1985, p. 132.

due for the billing period ending May 31. There will be no finance charge if the balance is paid by June 30. On June 1, Lincoln made a $100 purchase that will appear on his next monthly statement. On June 15, he made a $20 payment on the loan. The interest rate charged on the unpaid balance is $1\frac{1}{2}$ percent monthly (18 percent annually).

Adjusted Balance Method

Using this method, the finance charge is applied against the amount that has been billed less any payments made prior to the due date. The amount billed in this example is $100 and the payment was $20, resulting in $80. The finance charge is $1\frac{1}{2}$ percent times $80, which amounts to $1.20.

Previous Balance Method

According to this method, the finance charge is applied against the original amount billed and no consideration is given to the $20 payment. The finance charge is $1\frac{1}{2}$ percent times $100, which amounts to $1.50.

Average Daily Balance Method Excluding Current Transactions

According to this method, the finance charge is based on the average daily balance outstanding over the current 30-day period, but does not include current transactions. The average daily balance is $90 ($100 for 15 days and $80 for 15 days) and the finance charge is $1.35 ($90 $\times$ $1\frac{1}{2}$% = $1.35).

Average Daily Balance Method Including Current Transactions

According to this method, the finance charge is based on the average daily balance outstanding during the current 30-day period, including new purchases made during that time. The average daily balance is $200 for the first 15 days ($100 from April and $100 purchased on June 1) and the $180 for the last 15 days ($200 less $20 = 180), so the average balance for the entire period is $190. The finance charge is $1\frac{1}{2}$ percent times $190, which amounts to $2.85.

In review, by using different methods for determining the unpaid balance, finance charges on the same transaction based on an 18-percent annual interest rate ($1\frac{1}{2}$% monthly) ranged from a low of $1.20 to a high of $2.85!

Annual Percentage Rate

The **annual percentage rate** (APR) is the percentage cost of credit on an annual basis. The APR may be used to compare credit costs of loans of various sizes and maturities. For example, suppose that you borrow $1,000 for 1 year. The finance charge is $54.56, to be repaid together with the principal amount at the end of the year. In this example, you have had the use of $1,000 for the entire year. The APR is 5.46 percent ($54.56/$1,000 = 5.46%).

Now let's change the example and assume that you are required to make 12 monthly payments of $87.88 each. The finance charge is the same as the preceding, $54.56, but you do not get the use of $1,000 for the entire year because of the monthly payments. In fact, you get to keep less and less of the $1,000 each month. In this case, the APR is determined by the following equation:[5]

$$P = PMT \left[\frac{1 - (1 + i)^{-n}}{i} \right] \tag{10.1}$$

where P = original principal amount ($), PMT = periodic payments ($), i = periodic interest rate (%), and n = number of periodic payments (number).

Readers who are familiar with financial management will recognize that the APR is the **internal rate of return** (IRR)—the rate of interest that equates the present value of the periodic payments with the principal amount of the loan. The APR can be calculated easily by calculators programmed to calculate the IRR, by computer programs, or with greater difficulty by using present value of annuity tables. In addition, the equation can be used to determine the periodic payments when the interest rate and principal amount are known.

Using equation (10.1), we determine that the periodic rate is

$$\$1,000 = \$87.88 \left[\frac{1 - (1 + i)^{-12}}{i} \right] = 0.82690$$

Because the periodic rate is monthly, we determine the nominal annual rate by multiplying the periodic rate by 12. Accordingly, the APR in this example is 9.92 percent ($12 \times 0.82690 = 9.92\%$)—about 10 percent.

Add-on Rate

In some states, the maximum interest rate that may be charged on consumer loans is stated as an **add-on rate.** The term **add-on** means that the interest is added on to the amount borrowed. Consider a $1,000 loan for 1 year at 10 percent add-on interest. The $100 interest ($1,000 \times 10\% = \$100$) is added on to the amount borrowed, so that the total amount owed is $1,100. The monthly payments are determined by dividing the total amount owed by 12 ($1,100/12 =

---

[5] An alternate form of equation shown is

$$P = \sum_{t=1}^{n} \frac{PMT}{(1 + i)^n}$$

This equation does not provide the flexibility of equation 10-1, especially when computing *PMT*.

$91.67). Using equation 10.1, the APR is 17.97 percent, almost double the add-on rate (10 percent).

$$P = PMT \left[\frac{1 - (1 + i)^{-n}}{i} \right]$$

$$\$1,000 = \$91.67 \left[\frac{1 - (1 + i)^{-12}}{i} \right]$$

$$i = 1.498$$

$$APR = 12 \times i = 12 \times 1.498 = 17.97 \text{ percent}$$

Discount Rate

In a discount loan, the creditor deducts the finance charge from the principal amount of the loan and the borrower receives the difference. Consider a $1,000 loan discounted at 10 percent. The creditor deducts $100 from the $1,000 principal amount and the borrower receives $900. Nevertheless, the borrower must repay $1,000 in 12 monthly payments of $83.33 ($1,000/12 = $83.33). When calculating the APR on discount loans, the amount received by the borrower is set equal to the discounted monthly payments. The APR for the discount loan is 19.90 percent.

$$P = PMT \left[\frac{1 - (1 + i)^{-n}}{i} \right]$$

$$\$1,000 = \$83.33 \left[\frac{1 - (1 + i)^{-12}}{i} \right]$$

$$i = 1.6528$$

$$APR = 12 \times 1.6528 = 19.90 \text{ percent}$$

Table 10.2 summarizes the APRs for the four methods of computing interest on a $1,000 loan. From the bank's point of view, the discount method produces the highest returns followed by the add-on method. The single payment note at the end of the period provides the lowest returns.

TABLE 10.2
APRs ON A $1,000, 1-YEAR LOANS

Method of Computing Interest	Finance Charge	APR
Single payment of principal and interest at end of year	$ 54.56	5.46%
Monthly amortization	54.56	9.92
Add-on, monthly amortization	100.00	17.97
Discount, monthly amortization	100.00	19.90

Adjustable Rate Consumer Loans

Adjustable rate consumer loans (ARCs) permit banks to adjust their interest income when their cost of funds changes in order to maintain a positive spread between returns and interest costs. Stated otherwise, they want to match cash inflows with cash outflows. This is accomplished by indexing the interest rate charged on ARCs to a market rate, such as treasury bills, or the bank's cost of funds. Periodic adjustments (e.g., monthly) are made in the rate charged on ARCs to reflect changes in the index rate. By using this mechanism, banks transfer most of the interest rate risk associated with lending to their customers. The amount of interest rate risk that is transferred may be limited by **rate caps,** which limit the upward movement of interest rates charged on loans, and **floors,** which specify the lowest rate charged on loans.

Interest Rate Differentials

Banks offer ARCs to borrowers at lower interest rates than fixed rate loans to entice them to take on additional risk. The difference between the initial rate charged on fixed and adjustable rate loans is the premium that banks charge for assuming interest rate risk. Initial rate differentials on ARCs range from $\frac{1}{2}$ to $1\frac{1}{2}$ percent, with 1 percent being the most common amount.[6]

Repricing

When the index rate changes, the bank can reprice the loan (a) by changing the periodic payments or (b) by permitting the payments to remain the same and extending the maturity of the loan (or making a balloon payment at the end of the loan). Extending the maturity of loans is the most common method of repricing. When using this method, the bank adjusts the proportion of the payment being applied to principal and interest. By way of illustration, suppose that a monthly payment of $100 is divided equally between interest and principal. If the index rate increases, the bank would increase the interest portion of the payment to, say, $55 and reduce the amount going to principal to $45. The bank's income statement would reflect an additional $5 in interest income. However, the actual dollar of interest collected (cash inflows) by the bank did not change—it was an accounting entry. Thus, the bank did not achieve its objective for using ARCs—to match cash inflows to cash outflows. In addition, extending the maturity of loans increases their default risk. Long-term loans are riskier than short-term loans.

The Cost of Prepayment

Many borrowers pay off installment loans before they are due. The amount they have to pay depends on the method used for determining the unpaid

---

[6] John L. Goodman, Jr. and Charles A. Luckett, "Adjustable-Rate Financing in Mortgage and Consumer Credit Markets," *Federal Reserve Bulletin,* November 1985, pp. 832–835.

balance. Banks use two methods—the actuarial method and the rule of 78s. It is important to recognize that these two methods do not divide the interest evenly over the maturity of the loan. Instead, interest charges are computed so that a larger amount is collected if the loan is prepaid.

Actuarial Method

The actuarial method measures the exact amount of credit that a borrower has used computed at the APR stated in the contract and applies it to the declining balance of the loan. In other words, borrowers are charged for what they used. As illustrated in the following section, the difference between this method and the rule of 78s is relatively small, except when interest rates are high and the loan is long-term.

Rule of 78s

The rule of 78s, sometimes called the **sum of the digits method,** is calculated in the following manner. Suppose that Goldy borrows $1,000, which is to be repaid in 12 monthly installments, and the annual finance charge is $100. Goldy decides to repay the entire loan as soon as possible. To determine the amount of interest to be paid, add all of the whole numbers between 1 and 12 (1 + 2 + 3 . . . + 12 = 78) and the sum is 78. If the loan were for 18 months, the sum would be 171 (78 + 13 + 14 . . . + 18 = 171). The sum for other maturities is calculated in the same manner or by using the following equation.

$$\text{Sum of digits} = N/2 \times (N + 1)$$

where N = the number of payments.

By way of illustration, if the loan is for 18 months, $N = 18$, and the sum of the digits is

$$171 = 18/2 \times (18 + 1)$$

Getting back to Goldy, if the loan is repaid after 1 month, the bank will collect 12/78ths of the total finance charge ($15.38). If the loan is repaid after 2 months, the bank will collect 23/78ths of the total interest (12/78 + 11/78 = 23/78 = $29.49). After 3 months, the bank collects $42.31 (12/78 + 11/78 + 10/78 = 33/78 = $42.31). Using this method, the bank collects most of the interest if the loan is paid off early.

The method used to calculate the unpaid balance is significant when large loans with long-term maturities are involved. Assume, for example, that a $4,000 automobile loan repayable in 3 years at an APR of 12 percent is repaid in full at the end of 1 year. The unpaid balance using the rule of 78s is $2,835.93, and the unpaid balance using the actuarial method is $2,822.34. The difference is $13.59.

Now consider a $15,000 mobile home loan repayable in 15 years at an APR of 12 percent and the loan paid in full at the end of 5 years. The unpaid balance using the rule of 78s is $13,846.31 and the unpaid balance using the actuarial method is $12,547.85. The difference is $1,298.46.[7] Thus, banks receive substantially more income using the rule of 78s than using the actuarial method. The rule of 78s method is prohibited in some states.

CONSUMER CREDIT REGULATION

Congress enacted numerous laws designed to protect consumers. Some of the laws, listed in chronological order are:

- The Consumer Protection Act of 1968 (includes Truth in Lending Act, Federal Reserve Regulation Z)
- The Fair Credit Reporting Act (1970)
- The Fair Credit Billing Act (1974)
- The Equal Credit Opportunity Act (1974)
- The Real Estate Settlement Procedures Act (1974)
- The Home Mortgage Disclosure Act (1975)
- The Consumer Leasing Act (1976)
- The Fair Debt Collection Practices Act (1977)
- The Right to Financial Privacy Act (1978)
- The Electronic Funds Transfer Act (1978)

This partial listing gives some indication of the scope of federal consumer credit legislation. Because it is not feasible to cover the entire range of consumer credit regulation, we will focus on the Truth-in-Lending Act and the Equal Credit Opportunity Act.

Truth in Lending

The purpose of the Truth-in-Lending Act is for creditors to disclose to individual consumers who are borrowers (not business borrowers) the amount of the finance charge and the annual interest rate (APR) they are paying to facilitate the comparison of finance charges from different sources of credit. Finance charges and APR were discussed earlier in this chapter. The law requires that the disclosures be clear and conspicuous, grouped together, and segregated from other contractual matters to make it easier for consumers to understand.

The law also protects consumers against unauthorized use of credit cards in the event they are lost or stolen. The maximum amount a consumer must pay

---

[7] U.S. Congress, Senate, Committee on Banking, Housing and Urban Affairs, *Consumers Guide to Banking,* 94th Congress, 2nd session, April 1976, pp. 20–21. This study contains useful information about financing costs.

for unauthorized credit charges made by someone else is $50 before the credit card issuer is notified of the loss. The credit card holder is not liable for unauthorized use after notifying the credit card issuer.

The law also regulates the advertising of terms of credit. The intent here is to provide full disclosure of financing terms so that consumers can make intelligent decisions. Finally, the law gives consumers the right to cancel within 3 business days credit transactions in which their primary residence is used as security. This gives consumers time to think about the transaction and decide whether they want to go ahead with it. This right does not apply to first mortgage loans, but is applicable to second mortgage loans, used to obtain funds for remodeling and other purposes.

The Equal Credit Opportunity Act

The purpose of the Equal Credit Opportunity Act (ECOA) is to ensure that credit is made available fairly and impartially, based on the creditor's tests of creditworthiness. It prohibits discrimination against any applicant for credit because of race, color, religion, national origin, sex, marital status, or age, or because the applicant is receiving income from public assistance programs or Social Security.

Lenders may still evaluate credit applicants on the basis of their willingness and ability to repay loans. This is generally based on the applicant's character, capacity, and collateral. Creditors use various combinations of these factors in reaching their decisions, and some set higher credit standards than others. Thus, creditors may ask questions about the applicant's occupation, length of employment, length of residence, and whether the applicant rents or owns. Although some creditors rely on their judgment in making credit decisions, others use statistical "credit scoring" systems to evaluate applicants. More will be said about credit scoring shortly.

Age is given some special consideration. The applicant must be old enough to sign a binding contract (18 or 21 years old, depending on state laws). At the other end of the age spectrum, an older applicant may not qualify for an unsecured, large, long-term loan with a small down payment, but may qualify for a smaller, shorter-term loan with a large down payment and secured with good collateral.

Creditors cannot ask such questions as the applicant's religion, national origin, or sex (except for mortgage loans). Questions about the applicant's birth control practices or plans to have children are prohibited unless they are part of a medical history. The federal government requires mortgage lenders to ask the sex of the applicant, but the applicant is not required to answer the question. Nevertheless, the creditors may ask related questions in order to estimate the applicant's ability to pay. The related questions may concern the number of children that the applicant must support, their ages, and other relevant questions. Figure 10.1 is a typical application for a line of credit, and it illustrates the information that may be asked.

I/we want a Line of Credit in the amount you approve. Send me/us, immediately, a cash advance of $ _____

SEND CHECK TO: ☐ Home ☐ Business

NAME

| First Name | Middle Initial | Last Name |
| Date of Birth | Social Security No. | Home Phone ( ) |

RESIDENCE

Street Address		How Many Yrs.
City	State	Zip
Previous Street Address		How Many Yrs.
City	State	Zip
☐ Own ☐ C/O Parents/Relatives ☐ Rent ☐ Other	Monthly Rent Payment $	Street Address
Rent Payment Made to:		
City	State	Zip

EMPLOYMENT

Employer		Occupation
Employer's Street Address		
City	State	Zip
No. Yrs. Employed	Annual Income $	Business Phone ( )
Previous Employer		No. Yrs. Employed
Previous Employer's Address		

OTHER INFORMATION

Annual amount and source of other income—include alimony, child support or separate maintenance only if you wish to have it relied upon for this application. $ _____

Have you had any Judgments against you? ☐ No ☐ Yes
Have you ever Filed Bankruptcy? ☐ No ☐ Yes

CO-APPLICANT

If any other person will use or will be contractually liable as co-maker for this account, please complete this section.

First Name	Middle Initial	Last Name
Social Security No.	Date of Birth	Relationship	If Applicant's Spouse, No. Yrs. Married
Residence Street Address		
Employer	Occupation	Number Yrs. Employed	Annual Income $
Employer's Street Address		Business Phone ( )
City	State	Zip

REVOLVING

ASSETS—DESCRIPTION

Market Value				Account No.
$	Cash on Hand and in Banks			
	☐ Checking Bank Name	Address		Account No.
	☐ Savings Bank Name	Address		Account No.
$	IRAs, Keoughs, Annuities, Vested Pension Cash Value			
$	U.S. Gov't. Securities (Type)			
$	Stocks (Name, Number of Shares, In Name of)			
$	Bonds			
$	Residence	Purchase Price $		
$	Other Real Estate (Type of Property and Address, Title in Name of) (Please Give Details on a Separate Sheet if Necessary)		Purchase Price $	
$	Value of Medical/Dental/Professional Practice or Business	Medical/Dental Equipment Value $	Accounts Receivable $	
$	Auto (Do not include leased autos) Yr., Make, Model	Auto Yr., Make, Model		
$	Other Assets (Please Give Details on a Separate Sheet if Necessary)			
$	**This figure represents my TOTAL ASSETS**			

LIABILITIES—NAME AND ADDRESS OF CREDITOR

Balance Owed	Monthly Payment		Account No.
$	$	Mortgage or Liens on Residence	
$	$	Other Mortgages or Liens on Real Estate (Property Description) (Please Give Details on a Separate Sheet)	
$	$	Margin Accounts	
$	$	Auto Loan or Leasing Company	
$	$	Auto Loan or Leasing Company	
$	$	Personal Loan	
$	$	Credit Card ☐ Visa ☐ Mastercard	
$	$	Installment Purchase	
$	$	Department Store	
$	$	Education Loans	
$	$	All Unpaid Taxes (Specify)	
$	$	Total Indebtedness Owed on Professional Practice Creditor's Name	
$	$	All other indebtedness or liabilities including Charge Cards not listed above (Please Give Details on a Separate Sheet)	
$	$	Travel/Entertainment Cards ☐ American Express ☐ Diners ☐ Carte Blanche	
$	$	Co-Signer, Guarantor or Endorser	
$	$	Amount You Pay for Alimony or Child Support	
$	$	**This figure represents my TOTAL LIABILITIES**	

To reach me quickly call _____ between the hours of _____ AM and PM

Area Code / Phone Number

NOTICE: Please read other side of this application and sign where indicated. (If more space is needed to list all assets or liabilities, use a separate sheet.)

FIGURE 10.1 Credit application.

If Credit Is Denied

Credit cannot be denied on the basis of sex, marital status, or age. The denial must be based on the creditworthiness of the applicant.

If credit is denied, the creditor must notify the applicant within 30 days. The notification must be in writing and must explain the reasons for the denial. Frequently, the denial is based on information received from a **credit bureau**— a firm that provides credit information for a fee to creditors. Credit bureaus obtain their information from creditors, and sometimes errors are made or information is out of date. For example, bankruptcies must be removed from credit histories after 14 years (10 years after October 1979) and suits, judgments, tax liens, and arrest records must be removed after 7 years.

Under the Fair Credit Reporting Act, applicants have the right to examine the credit file and correct errors or mistakes in it. The credit bureau is required to remove any errors which the creditor that supplied the information admits are there. If a disagreement still remains, the applicant can include a short statement in the file, stating his or her side of the story.

Uniform Consumer Credit Code

In an attempt to make the credit laws of several states uniform, a Uniform Consumer Credit Code has been adopted by various states. This model code sets maximum annual percentage rate ceilings of 21 percent on revolving charge accounts and 36 percent on small loans and sales credit. The designers of the code set the maximum interest rates artificially high in hopes that the actual rates charged will be determined by the forces of supply and demand and will be substantially less than the ceiling rates.

The intent of the Uniform Consumer Credit Code can be depicted in graphic terms. As shown in Figure 10.2, i_2 represents the artificially high ceiling interest rate. At that rate, the amount of credit demanded (Q_2) is less than lenders are willing to supply (Q_3), and the interest rate that clears the market is i_1. However, there is another situation that should not be overlooked. If the ceiling interest rate (i_3) is lower than the market-clearing interest rate, the amount of credit supplied (Q_3) will be less than the amount demanded (Q_4). This was the case in the late 1960s, when market interest rates exceeded the ceiling set by state usury codes and lenders were unwilling to make certain types of loans. **Usury codes** specify the maximum interest rates that can be charged on certain types of loans.

Holder-in-Due-Course

When banks buy dealer paper (such as automobile loans) in good faith and without contractual defects, they become the holder-in-due-course. This means that customers having problems with the automobile (or other merchandise) may not withhold payment because they are financially obligated to pay the

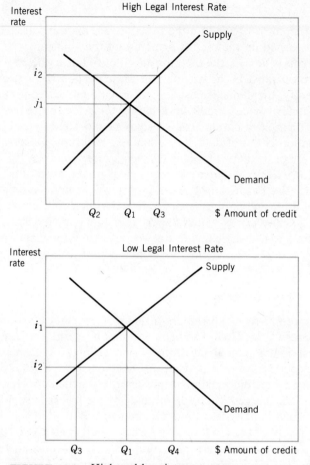

FIGURE 10.2   High and low interest rates.

bank. Widespread abuses to customers led to restrictions in the use of the holder-in-due-course doctrine in various states, and the Federal Trade Commission wants to abolish it as an unfair trade practice in consumer credit transactions.

THE CREDIT DECISION

Two methods used to evaluate consumer credit decisions are based on judgment and statistical techniques. The former is subject to wide variations in decisions, because the judgment of one loan officer may differ from that of another. In addition, taking the credit application and interviewing the prospective borrower is time-consuming and costly. The statistical technique described in a later section standardizes the criteria used to make credit decisions, which are made by computer programs. The statistical techniques are widely used with credit card applications. Neither method is perfect.

Judgment

A prospective borrower may meet face-to-face with a loan officer or fill out a credit application. In either case, the bank must review the data on the application and make a credit decision. The evaluation may include a review of the prospective borrower's past credit performance and other relevant data. This process works best when the loan is for high-priced durable goods, such as automobiles, where the bank requires collateral for the loan. For relatively small loans (e.g., under $500), the administrative cost of taking an application may not justify the return. Another alternative is to make the loan on a credit card.

Credit-Scoring Systems

Credit-scoring systems are statistical techniques that use the information given in a credit application to discriminate among those who are likely to be good borrowers and repay their loans and those who are not likely to repay their loans.[8] A certain number of "points" or weights are given to factors such as the length of employment, whether one rents or owns a home, the level of income, and so on. If the sum of the points is above a critical value (e.g., 160 points), the applicant is granted credit. Credit-scoring systems are especially useful for evaluating large numbers of applications at relatively low cost per application—such as evaluating applications for credit cards.

However, there are costs to be considered when using credit scoring systems and other systems to make credit decisions.[9] These costs are:

1. Acceptance cost, which includes bad debts that may be incurred, the average cost of financing the loans, and the average collection cost.

2. Rejection costs because the bank rejected some loans that it could have made. Some good customers may be rejected.

3. Cost of additional information that may be required before a decision is made plus the cost of making an additional decision. For example, suppose that an application is rejected because it was not filled out correctly or completely. The prospective borrower may correct the information, or provide additional information, which increases the processing cost.

[8] See Edward I. Altman, Robert B. Avery, Robert A. Eisenbeis, and Joseph F. Sinkey, Jr., *Application of Classification Techniques in Business, Banking and Finance,* Greenwich, CT: JAI Press, 1981. Chapter IV deals with credit scoring applications.

[9] Deleep Mehta, "The Formulation of Credit Policy Models," *Management Science,* **15,** 1986, pp. B30–B50.

SUMMARY

Consumer lending is a major activity of commercial banks. Consumer loans are divided into two categories—installment and noninstallment. Installment loans account for most of the loans. This category includes loans that are repaid on an installment basis. About 40 percent of the installment loans are for automobiles. Banks can make automobile and other consumer loans directly to customers or indirectly through dealer loans that they purchase. Installment loans also include revolving loans, bank credit cards, mobile home loans, and other types of consumer loans. Noninstallment loans are those that are scheduled to be repaid in one payment. In addition to lending, banks also engage in leasing automobiles and other items to consumers.

Under the Truth-in-Lending Act, banks and other lenders are required to disclose to borrowers the dollar amount of the finance charge and the annual percentage rate charged on loans. Nevertheless, adjustable rates, add-on rates, discount rates, and the rates charged on revolving loans can be confusing and sometimes misleading. Prepayment penalties can add to the confusion and cost of loans.

To protect consumers, Congress has passed laws covering various aspects of consumer credit. The laws deal with disclosure, billing and debt collection practices, and discrimination. Credit decisions must be based on the creditworthiness of the borrower. This may be determined by judgment or a credit-scoring system. The laws also specify what happens when credit is denied.

IMPORTANT CONCEPTS

actuarial method

add-on rate

adjustable rate consumer loans

adjusted balance method

annual percentage rate (APR)

automobile loans

average daily balance method excluding current transactions

average daily balance method including current transactions

bank credit card

bridge loan

check overdraft

closed-end lease

consumer installment credit

credit bureau

credit-scoring systems

dealer paper

discount rate

Equal Credit Opportunity Act

finance charge

floor (for rates)

holder-in-due-course

internal rate of return (IRR)

lease-a-like-loans

leasing

merchant's discount

mobile home loans

noninstallment loans

open-end credit

open-end lease

previous balance method   single payment loan
rate cap   sum of the digits method
Regulation Z   travel and entertainment card
repricing   Truth-in-Lending Act
revolving loans   Uniform Consumer Credit Code
rule of 78s

REFERENCES

Altman, Edward I., Robert B. Avery, Robert A. Eisenbeis, and Joseph F. Sinkey, Jr. *Application of Classification Techniques in Business, Banking and Finance.* Greenwich, CT: JAI Press, 1981.

Canner, Glenn B., and James T. Ferfgus. "The Economic Effects of Proposed Ceilings on Credit Card Interest Rates," *Federal Reserve Bulletin,* January 1987.

Goodman, John L. Jr., and Charles A. Luckett. "Adjustable-Rate Financing in Mortgage and Consumer Credit Markets," *Federal Reserve Bulletin,* November 1985, pp. 832–835.

Gup, Benton E. and John R. Walter. "Profitability of Large Commercial Banks: The Secret of Their Success," *Midland Corporate Finance Journal,* Winter, 1988, pp. 24–29.

Luckett, Charles A., and James D. August. "The Growth of Consumer Debt," *Federal Reserve Bulletin,* June 1985.

Mehta, Deleep. "The Formulation of Credit Policy Models," *Management Science,* **15,** 1986.

Spong, Kenneth. *Banking Regulation: Its Purposes, Implementation, and Effects,* 2d ed., Federal Reserve Bank of Kansas City, 1985.

U.S. Congress, Senate, Committee on Banking, Housing and Urban Affairs, *Consumers Guide to Banking,* 94th Congress, 2nd sessions, April 1976.

QUESTIONS

10.1. How do consumer loans differ from other types of loans in general?

10.2. What is dealer paper? Lease-a-like loans? Securitized automobile loans?

10.3. Define the following terms: (a) revolving loans, (b) noninstallment loans, (c) bridge loans, (d) open-end leases, and (e) ARCs.

10.4. What factors affect the merchant's discount on credit card purchases?

10.5. Briefly describe three types of bank credit card plans.

10.6. What is the finance charge on a consumer loan? APR?

10.7. What is add-on interest? How does it affect the APR?

10.8. As the index rate changes, the bank can reprice an ARC in what ways?

10.9. How do the actuarial method and rule of 78s differ in terms of costs of prepayment?

10.10. Briefly discuss the Truth in Lending Act and Equal Credit Opportunity Act.

10.11. What is a credit bureau? Do individuals have the right to examine and attempt to correct errors in their credit file?

10.12. What are usury rates? What is good and bad about usury rates?

10.13. What are two ways to make consumer credit decisions? Contrast their advantages and disadvantages.

10.14. What is a loan shark? What financial institution developed as a result of the desire to curb and regulate loan sharks? How did sales finance companies evolve?

PROBLEMS

10.1. David purchased a $300 VCR using revolving credit on September 20. The billing period ends September 30, and no finance charges are incurred if the balance is paid by October 31. On October 28 David makes a $50 payment on the loan. If the interest rate is $1\frac{1}{2}$ percent monthly, calculate the finance charge for October using the following methods:

(a) Adjusted balance method.
(b) Previous balance method.
(c) Average daily balance method excluding current transactions.
(d) Average daily balance method including current transactions.

10.2. Given the following information on a car loan:

$$\text{Principal amount} = \$10,000$$

$$\text{Periodic payments} = \$300$$

$$\text{Number of periodic payments} = 48$$

(a) Calculate the APR for this loan.
(b) If add-on interest of $10 per month were charged on this loan, what would the APR be?
(c) If the loan was discounted at 5 percent (and there was no add-on interest), what would the APR be?

10.3. Given the car loan information in problem 2 above and an APR of 10 percent, and assuming the loan is repaid in full at the end of two months, calculate the unpaid balance due using the following:

(a) Rule of 78s.
(b) Actuarial method.

PART THREE

LIABILITIES AND EQUITY

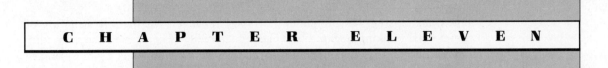

Managing Bank Liabilities

Inflationary surges in the 1960s and 1970s, competition in the financial services industry, and deregulation of deposit rates in the 1980s spurred banks to innovate many new sources of funds, which have dramatically transformed the liability side of their balance sheets. In this chapter an overview of the changing structure of bank liabilities is provided. Various aspects of bank liabilities management are covered also, including pricing and cost control.

STRUCTURE OF BANK LIABILITIES

Demand deposits have historically dominated the liability structure of commercial banks. Savings and time deposits normally played a significant but secondary role in the acquisition of deposit funds, and nondeposit borrowings were almost nonexistent. Beginning in the 1960s, however, the liability structure of commercial banking began to change substantially. For example, by the mid-1960s, time and savings deposits surpassed demand deposits as the primary source of bank funds. In the 1970s nondeposit borrowings grew rapidly and emerged as a major new source of funds for larger banking institutions. Additionally, the variety of deposit and nondeposit accounts and securities offered to the public by commercial banks greatly expanded. In this section deposit and nondeposit sources of bank funds are overviewed, as well as the historical developments that shaped the new liability structure of commercial banking.

Deposit Sources of Funds

Bank deposits may be categorized as either core deposits or purchased deposits. Core deposits are typically deposits of regular bank customers, including business firms, government units, and households. Purchased deposits are acquired on an impersonal basis from the financial market by offering competitive interest rates. Core deposits provide a more stable, long-term source of funds than purchased deposits, whereas the latter serve as a liquidity reserve that may be tapped when needed.

Extensive use of purchased deposits may expose a bank to liquidity problems. In contrast to core deposits, a large proportion of purchased deposits may not be insured by the Federal Deposit Insurance Corporation (FDIC). Also, unlike core deposits that normally provide both explicit interest earnings and implicit service returns, purchased deposits provide only explicit interest earnings. These differences cause purchased deposits to be much more sensitive to both changes in bank risk and interest rates than core deposits. If the financial market perceives a decline in a bank's safety and soundness, its purchased deposits would have to be rolled over at higher rates and may even cease to be available (as depositors shy away from placing liquid assets in institutions that may become insolvent). Thus, the risks and returns of core deposits and purchased deposits differ considerably from one another.

Deposit accounts can be categorized as follows: demand deposits, small time and savings deposits, and large time deposits. As a consequence of deposit rate deregulation over the last decade (see Box 11.1), both small and large time deposits can serve the dual roles of core and purchased deposit sources of funds.

Box 11.1

DEPOSIT RATE REGULATION, BANK INNOVATION, AND DEREGULATION

Financial crises in the late 1800s, and particularly the Great Depression in the 1930s, motivated Congress to pass the Glass–Steagall Act as part of the 1933 Banking Acts. Under Glass–Steagall, payment of interest on

Box 11.1 (*Continued*)

demand deposits was prohibited. It was believed that interest payments caused intense competition between banks that induced them to make riskier loans in an effort to pay the high costs of deposits. The same logic was applied to a 1935 extension of the Glass–Steagall Act that gave the Board of Governors of the Federal Reserve System the power to set deposit rate ceilings (Regulation Q) affecting all federally insured banks.

Deposit rate ceilings led to a series of "credit crunches" in the 1960s and 1970s. In 1966, for example, market rates rose above deposit rate ceilings. On previous occasions ceiling rates were increased; however, the Fed did not change the ceiling rate this time. Large CD sales dropped considerably causing bank credit to dry up. Similar episodes of high interest rates in the periods 1969–70 and 1973–74 likewise caused credit contractions.

In an attempt to meet credit demands during these periods, banks and other depository institutions began innovating around deposit rate barriers. In 1966, for example, large banks acquired time deposit funds from the Eurodollar market. Subsequent extension of Regulation Q to these deposits led large banks in 1969 to make greater use of nondeposit sources of funds, including nonbank federal funds, repurchase agreements, and commercial paper issued by holding companies. These sources of funds did not play as large a role in the 1973–74 credit crunch, as rate ceilings on large CDs had been eliminated by then.

Banks also began innovating new transactions accounts. As the general level of interest rates edged upward in the 1960s and 1970s, they began to offer payments in kind and to indirectly pay interest on demand deposit balances. Payments in kind involved nonprice benefits such as free checking and branch facilities offering greater convenience. Indirect payments of interest were offered in the form of gifts for opening new accounts and "sweep" accounts for large depositors that automatically transferred checking balances over some amount to repurchase agreements, money market funds, and other short-term, interest-bearing assets at the end of the day. Smaller depositors were offered automatic transfer service (ATS) accounts that allowed them to minimize transactions balances by automatically transferring funds from their interest-bearing savings account to their checking account as overdrafts occurred.

Bank innovation and rising competition for consumer deposits prompted Congress to deregulate applicable deposit rate ceilings. A summary of this deregulation is as follows:

Depository Institutions Deregulation and Monetary Control Act (DIDMCA of 1980):

Authorized all depository institutions to sell NOW (negotiable order of withdrawal) accounts to individuals and nonprofit organizations

BOX 11.1 (*Continued*)

in December, 1980, as well as automatic transfer service (ATS) accounts. A six-year phaseout of interest rate ceilings on time and savings deposits was planned.

Garn-St Germain Depository Institutions Act of 1982

Authorized all depository institutions to issue money market deposit accounts (MMDAs) in December, 1982 with no interest rate restrictions and limited check-writing privileges.

Depository Institutions Deregulation Committee (DIDC)

Established by DIDMCA of 1980, the DIDC authorized Super-NOW accounts effective January, 1983, reduced minimum balance requirements on MMDAs, Super-NOWs, and time deposits of 7–31 days maturity to $1,000 in January, 1985, and eliminated the aforementioned requirements in January, 1986, in addition to rate ceilings on NOW accounts and passbook savings accounts. The DIDC was dissolved at the end of March, 1987, as originally intended under DIDMCA of 1980.

Remaining Regulatory Restrictions

No interest payments on demand deposits or regular checking accounts are allowed and NOW and Super-NOW accounts cannot be offered on commercial accounts. Minimum early withdrawal penalties are required on time deposits. A maximum $150,000 limit on nonpersonal savings deposits is still in effect. Finally, reserve requirements under Regulation D apply to transactions accounts and nonpersonal time and savings deposits.

In today's deregulated deposit market two important factors affecting deposit interest costs are FDIC deposit insurance and competition. Some experts believe that deposit insurance premiums charged by the FDIC (i.e., $\frac{1}{12}$th of 1 percent of deposits) are too low for the risk involved. This underpricing causes the cost of insured deposits to be lower than if they were not insured. In turn, banks have an incentive to increase their use of financial leverage, which must be restricted by regulatory capital standards. However, competition tends to drive up interest costs and can act to offset this insurance benefit. For example, problems at savings and loan associations throughout the 1980s have caused these thrift institutions to aggressively bid for deposit funds and cause overpricing of deposits for banks in some regions of the country at times. This overpricing is a temporary phenomenon, but it underscores the importance of the effect of competition on deposit costs.

Source: Robert Craig West, "The Depository Institutions Deregulation Act of 1980: A Historical Perspective," *Economic Review*, Federal Reserve Bank of Kansas City, February 1982, pp. 3–13.

Checking Deposits

Checking deposits, including demand deposits, are transactions balances requiring relatively higher reserve requirements than other types of deposits. They may be classified into three categories: (1) consumer demand deposits, (2) corporate demand deposits, and (3) government deposits. Consumer demand deposit accounts may or may not be interest-bearing. Interest-bearing demand deposits—known as NOW (or negotiable order of withdrawal) accounts—were authorized nationwide in January 1981 under DIDMCA of 1980.[1] NOW accounts originally offered rates of interest up to $5\frac{1}{2}$ percent on balances held at commercial banks. First introduced in 1972 in the New England region, NOWs were instrumental in curtailing outflows of deposit funds to money market mutual funds (MMMFs) when interest rates rose above Regulation Q ceilings at various times in the 1970s and 1980s.

The "NOW experience" of banks has indicated that these interest-bearing accounts are not much more costly than regular checking accounts. For example, in New England, during the period 1976 to 1982, one researcher[2] found that NOW accounts averaged 6.89 percent compared to 5.42 percent for regular checking accounts. It was observed that regular checking accounts had relatively higher **implicit,** or noninterest, service costs than NOW accounts and that banks had increased service charges on NOW accounts to offset some of the differences in interest costs. From the customer's standpoint, the mix of implicit, or noninterest, and **explicit,** or interest, pricing offered by banks influences the type of transactions account that is opened. From the perspective of bank management, both operational costs and consumer demands must be evaluated to price transactions accounts correctly.

Starting in January 1983, depository institutions were permitted to offer Super-NOWs (SNOWs) with unregulated rates on balances equal to or exceeding $2,500. Unlike NOWs, SNOWs had limited check-writing privileges. Like NOWs, SNOWs were subject to reserve requirements, albeit lower ones than applied to NOW balances. SNOWs enabled depository institutions to compete more effectively with MMMFs for household deposits. Even though SNOWs were at a disadvantage with MMMFs to the extent that reserve requirements were a tax, they were eligible for federal deposit insurance, which was not available for MMMF accounts. In early 1986, interest rate restrictions on NOWs were relaxed, so that there is no longer any distinction between NOWs and SNOWs.

Corporate demand deposit accounts are still prohibited from paying interest. Most of these deposits are compensating balances that are required by banks in return for various commercial services, such as coin and currency services, check-clearing services, and credit services. As interest rates rose in the latter

---

[1] NOWs are available not only to consumers but to government agencies, nonprofit organizations, and single proprietorships, in which there is no distinction between the person and the firm.

[2] See Herb Taylor, "The Return Banks Have Paid on NOW Accounts," *Business Review,* Federal Reserve Bank of Philadelphia, July/August 1984, pp. 13–23.

part of the 1970s and early 1980s, corporate treasurers complained of the higher opportunity costs of compensating balances. To accommodate corporate customers, banks began unbundling the costs of various financial services. Service fees were viewed by corporations as a more accurate way to price services than compensating balances in the high and volatile interest climate of the times. Also, service fees are tax deductible as a business expense, whereas income lost by maintaining noninterest-bearing compensating balances is not. In terms of bank management, however, it is more difficult to use fees as opposed to balances. The cost of providing each product and service must be carefully examined to properly price each one. Also, service fee and compensating balance options must be negotiated with each customer.

Small Time and Savings Deposits

Small deposits of less than $100,000 may be acquired through time deposits (otherwise known as savings certificates, or retail CDs) and savings deposits. Small time deposits can be offered with denominations as low as $1,000. These deposits have fixed maturities and yields that approximate those of Treasury securities of equal maturity. A slight premium is normally required by depositors over the Treasury yield, however, because these deposit instruments are nonnegotiable and have early withdrawal penalties attached to them. Small time deposits are normally categorized by maturity as 7 to 31 day, 32 day to 1 year, and greater than 1 year.

As deregulation of interest rate ceilings proceeded in the early 1980s, public demand for retail CDs steadily increased. Many large banks sought to take advantage of this **consumerism** movement by pricing retail CDs at yields slightly higher than Treasury yields.

Savings deposits are interest-bearing deposits that do not have fixed maturities. Savings deposits can be set up periodically to cover overwithdrawals of transactions accounts (called ATS, or automatic transfer service) or to provide transactions funds by means of limited check-writing privileges. A good example of the latter type of savings account is the money market deposit account (MMDA). MMDAs have no rate restrictions and allow consumers to make up to six transfers (three by check) per month. Authorized under the Garn-St Germain Act of 1982, MMDAs were designed to compete with money market mutual funds (MMMFs). The accounts were highly successful, surpassing the $218 billion held by MMMFs only 1 year after their introduction in December 1981. Although their growth has been less spectacular since then, they represent a major source of savings deposits in banking today.

Large Time Deposits

Time deposits issued in denominations in excess of $100,000 are known as negotiable certificates of deposit (CDs). Large, or "jumbo," CDs are marketable securities with maturities ranging from 14 days to 18 months. First issued by First National City Bank of New York (now Citibank) in February 1961,

NCDs were quickly offered by other money center banks and dealers, causing the volume of NCDs to expand rapidly. By 1966 these CDs were second only to Treasury bills among outstanding money market instruments.

Originally, large CDs were issued by New York banks in an attempt to retain corporate demand deposits that paid no interest. Rising short-term interest rates in the post-World War II period motivated corporate treasurers to draw down demand deposits and buy Treasury bills, commercial paper, and repurchase agreements with dealers. To stem this deposit outflow and retain their share of credit flows, large banks designed the CD to appeal to corporate depositors. Initially subject to Regulation Q interest rate ceilings, rate ceilings were removed on large CDs by May 1973.

Later, large CDs became the primary source of funds for liability management. Most CD buyers are still nonfinancial corporations, but other market participants, such as MMMFs, now buy CDs also. Because CDs are commonly issued in denominations exceeding the $100,000 FDIC insurance limit (e.g., a round lot in the secondary market is usually $1 million), the default risk of the issuing bank can affect rates of interest on these CDs. Indeed, a tiered CD market has evolved in which money center and large regional banks tend to offer CDs at lower rates than smaller banks.

Eurodollar Deposits

A Eurodollar deposit is a dollar-denominated deposit in a bank office outside the United States. Originally dominated by European-based bank offices, the term still applies to out-of-country dollar deposits in general.

Large banks normally tap Eurodollar deposits through their foreign branch offices. For example, foreign branches sell Eurodollar CDs, which are dollar-denominated negotiable CDs. These funds are then loaned to domestic offices. Because the secondary market is smaller compared with domestic CDs, and FDIC deposit insurance is unavailable, Eurodollar CDs usually have higher yields than domestic CDs. An advantage of Eurodollar CDs, however, is that they are generally free from reserve requirements. In this regard, Eurodollar borrowing has historically been greatest during high interest rate periods in which foreign dollar deposits are used to meet domestic reserve requirements. Such deposits are also used to make loans to nonbank corporations operating abroad.

Brokered Deposits

Brokered deposits are small and large time deposits obtained by banks from middlemen seeking insured deposit accounts on behalf of their customers. Deposit brokers appeared in the early 1980s when depositors began to face increased risk of loss because of bank failure. An often-cited example of this risk was the failure of Penn Square Bank in July 1982. For the first time since the Great Depression, federal regulators liquidated a large bank, rather than allowing the bank to be merged or acquired by a solvent bank with no loss to depositors. Depositors that were not insured (because their balances exceeded the $100,000 FDIC limit) suffered large losses, as evidenced by the fact that only 55 percent of uninsured claims were covered by year end 1985.

Because interest rates on large, negotiable CDs in denominations of $100,000 were unregulated, and rates on smaller, retail-level CDs were deregulated for the most part by year end 1982, brokers entered deposit markets to bring together depositors (sellers) seeking insured accounts with banks and other depository institutions (buyers) demanding lower-cost, insured deposit funds. Electronic funds transfer technology enabled brokers to cost-effectively "split" $1 million (for example) into ten $100,000, fully-insured, deposit accounts at 10 different depository institutions. Alternatively, brokers can offer smaller depositors better yields by pooling their deposits and selling "shares" in "participating" large CDs offering higher yields than smaller CDs.

Federal regulators have opposed the use of brokered deposits. In April 1982, for example, the FDIC announced that brokers could obtain only $100,000 of deposit insurance per bank, as is the case for any depositor. It was believed that, because insured depositors are less likely to "discipline" bank management by withdrawing their funds or charging higher rates on deposits, bank safety and soundness might be compromised to the extent that banks used nationally brokered deposits to grow excessively or to take excessive loan risks. However, the FDIC's rule on brokered deposits was struck down by a court decision in June 1984. At present, banks with fully insured brokered deposits in excess of either their total capital (including reserves) or 5 percent of their total deposits must provide monthly reports of the volume, interest rates paid, and usage of such deposits to the FDIC. In this regard, recent evidence suggests that banks with low supervisory ratings tend to use more brokered deposits than higher-rated institutions.[3]

IRA and Keogh Plans

IRA and Keogh plans are personal pension plans that individuals may use to defer federal income taxes on contributions and subsequent investment earnings. Keogh plans have been available to self-employed individuals since 1962. They allow up to 25 percent of earned, nonsalaried income but not greater than $30,000 to be deposited in a tax-deferred account. Individual Retirement Account (IRA) plans were allowed for all individuals under the Economic Recovery Tax Act of 1981. IRAs enable individuals to set aside earnings for retirement up to an allowable maximum per year. IRS rules determine how much of these contributions can be deducted from income (if any). Both of these personal retirement accounts are subject to a 10-percent tax penalty if withdrawn before age $59\frac{1}{2}$.

IRAs and Keoghs have become a major source of long-term, stable deposit

---

[3] See Panos Konstas, "Brokered Deposits," *Banking and Economic Review*, Federal Deposit Insurance Corporation, May 1986.

funds for banking institutions. One problem with these new accounts is the intensity of market competition. IRAs can be offered by banks, savings institutions, brokerage firms, insurance companies, mutual funds, and employers with qualified pension, profit-sharing, or savings plans. To be competitive, banks must offer attractive interest rates and good service, both of which trim profit margins. Even so, these accounts are a source of deposits that should not be overlooked.

Nondeposit Sources of Funds

Nondeposit sources of funds are money market liabilities that are purchased for relatively short periods of time to adjust to liquidity demands. Because they are typically used in liability management, they are often referred to as "managed liabilities." The use of purchased funds came about as a consequence of tight money periods in which deposit rate ceilings caused banks to develop alternative sources of funds. Unlike deposit funds, nondeposit funds typically are exempt from federal reserve requirements, interest rate ceilings, and FDIC insurance assessments.

Federal Funds

In general, federal funds are short-term, unsecured transfers of immediately available funds[4] between depository institutions for use in one business day (i.e., overnight loans). About 20 percent of the federal funds have maturities longer than 1 day. Banks typically either purchase or sell "fed" funds, depending on their desired reserve position, which is normally based on legal reserve requirements. Because Federal Reserve open market operations directly affect the quantity of bank reserves, Fed funds rates are relatively more volatile than other money market rates. Also, in the last few days of the reserve maintenance period, the Fed funds rate may jump significantly, if relatively low supplies of excess reserves are in the banking system.

Overnight loans usually are booked by verbal agreements between corresponding officers of depository institutions. Written contracts or brokers, or both, may be employed if the parties are unfamiliar with one another. Overnight loans may be put on a continuing-contract basis in which they are automatically renewed unless otherwise notified. Such contracts are often arranged between large correspondent banks and smaller respondent institutions, and tend to lower transactions costs (e.g., brokers' fees and funds transfer charges).

---

[4] Immediately available funds can be defined as those bank funds that can be withdrawn or used for payment by the public on any given business day. They consist of the collected liabilities of commercial banks plus the deposit liabilities of Federal Reserve banks.

Repurchase Agreements

Nonbank depositors supply funds to banks through repurchase agreements (RPs, or repos). An overnight RP can be defined as a secured, 1-day loan in which claim to the collateral is transferred. Multiple-day RPs can be arranged for a fixed term ("term RPs") or on a continuing basis. An RP is created by the sale of securities in exchange for immediately available money with the simultaneous promise to buy back the securities at a specific date at a set price within the next year. The repurchase price is typically the initial sale price plus a negotiated rate of interest. U.S. Treasury and federal agency securities are normally used as collateral (which allows the institutions to avoid reserve requirements), but CDs, mortgage-backed securities, and other securities may be used on occasion. The transaction is known as a reverse RP (or matched sale-purchase agreement) from the perspective of the purchaser of the securities.

Because RP purchasers acquire title to the securities for the term of the agreement, they may use them to create another RP or to meet the delivery of a forward or futures contract, a short sale, or a maturing reverse RP. This flexibility makes the RP a low-risk money market instrument that dealers can use to meet diverse liquidity needs among investors, including business firms, depository institutions, state and local governments, and other financial institutions. Although RPs usually are available in denominations of at least $1 million (wholesale market), smaller denominations under $100,000 (retail market) have appeared in recent years. Retail RPs must have maturities of 89 days or less and, like wholesale RPs, are not subject to interest rate ceilings. However, deposits obtained from retail RPs are not federally insured.

Discount Window Advances

Banks can borrow funds from the 12 regional Federal Reserve banks by means of a "discount window advance." Advances can be used by banks to meet unanticipated reserve deficiencies. Funds cannot be borrowed, however, either to "arbitrage profits" through acquiring higher-earning financial assets with advances or to supplement bank capital. Discount window borrowings normally are overnight loans that are deposited in the bank's reserve account at its Federal Reserve district bank. Advances must be secured by approved collateral, such as U.S. Treasury securities and government agency securities, municipal securities, one- to four-family home mortgages, short-term commercial notes, and other marketable securities. Also, interest and principal are due at maturity.

Prior to the Monetary Control Act of 1980, only Federal Reserve System member banks could use the discount window for reserve management purposes. However, this Act enabled all depository institutions with transactions balances or nonpersonal time deposits (except bankers' banks) to access the discount window.

Bankers' Acceptances

A banker's acceptance is a time draft drawn on a bank by either an exporter or an importer to finance international business transactions. The bank may discount the acceptance in the money market to (in effect) finance the transaction.

An example perhaps best explains how banks use acceptances to acquire loanable funds. A U.S. importer (buyer) may obtain a letter of credit in their behalf from their bank. The letter of credit authorizes the foreign exporter (seller) to draw a draft on the bank in payment of goods. The exporter can discount the draft at their foreign bank, which then forwards the draft and shipping documents to the U.S. bank issuing the letter of credit (perhaps through its U.S. correspondent bank). If everything is in order, the issuing bank stamps "accepted" on the face of the time draft, and a negotiable instrument known as a banker's acceptance is created. The acceptance can be discounted by the issuing bank for the account of the foreign bank. At this point the acceptance is a financial asset of the bank and a liability of the importer. Normally, however, the issuing bank also sells the acceptance in the secondary market. In this case the acceptance is being used as a source of funds in the sense of recouping funds committed to the foreign bank.

It is noteworthy that all parties concerned benefit from the acceptance transaction. Exporters receive payment for goods at the time of shipment, importers receive credit for the transit period of the goods, foreign banks usually obtain service fees, domestic banks obtain a new source of funds to finance loans (plus service fees), and money market participants have another interest-bearing instrument in which to invest funds temporarily.

The maturities on bankers' acceptances range from 30 to 180 days and are timed to coincide with the transit (and disposal) of goods. Market yields are only slightly above that of U.S. Treasury bills, as issuing banks are large institutions with good international reputations. Banks earn not only the discount on the acceptance from corporate borrowers but a fee equal to a minimum of $1\frac{1}{2}$ percent (i.e., $\frac{1}{8}$ of 1 percent per month), depending on the credit rating of the borrower.

Commercial Paper

Commercial paper is a short-term, unsecured promissory note sold by large companies with strong credit ratings. Banks can use their holding companies to issue commercial paper and acquire loans and investments from them. Bank holding companies (BHCs), therefore, are another channel through which funds can be raised. Banks have also established independent companies, which are not holding companies, to issue commercial paper and then funnel the proceeds to one or more subsidiary banks by purchasing bank loans and investments.

Commercial paper, or notes, is sold in $1,000 denominations with maturities normally ranging from 30 to 270 days. There is little or no secondary market for commercial paper; however, some dealers may redeem notes prior to maturity. Most BHCs sell their notes directly to institutional investors (i.e., "direct paper") as opposed to using a securities dealer to make a public sale (i.e., "dealer paper").

Capital Notes and Debentures

Banks can purchase long-term funds by issuing capital notes and debentures, or senior debt capital. During the Great Depression, distressed banks raised much-needed funds by selling these kinds of debt issues. The stigma of this experience prompted the Comptroller of the Currency to discourage national banks from issuing senior debt securities until the 1960s. To provide banks more flexibility in managing their capital, the Comptroller ruled in 1962 that these debt securities could be counted as part of (unimpaired) capital in calculating lending limits on unsecured loans to any one borrower. Many banks quickly moved to sell notes and debentures for this reason.

Changing definitions of bank capital and associated regulatory requirements (e.g., see Chapter 12) have caused banks to use notes and debentures sparingly. An interesting development in recent years has been the proposal by some industry experts to force banks to issue some minimum quantity of senior debt securities. Because capital notes and debentures are uninsured, it is believed that the marketplace would price these issues according to risk and, therefore, provide some amount of "market discipline." Additionally, bank regulators could use bank debt prices as another way to detect possible problem situations.

Capital notes and debentures are subordinated, or second in order of claims, to bank deposits in the event of bank failure. Issues are made in a wide assortment of denominations and maturities in order to tailor them for sale to specific bank customers, including correspondent banks of the issuing bank. Normally, senior debt securities are issued by large banks, because small banks do not have as ready an access to the capital markets, and transactions costs are relatively high for smaller issues.

Changing Structure of Bank Liabilities

Table 11.1 provides information on the basic changes that have taken place from 1960 to 1981 in the structure of bank liabilities for all insured U.S. commercial banks. As indicated, the proportion of liabilities acquired from deposit sources declined from about 97 percent in 1960 to about 81 percent by 1981. Borrowed funds, by comparison, increased from only about 0.2 percent of total liabilities in 1960 to about 12 percent in 1981.

The most significant trend in the structure of bank liabilities was the shift of funds from demand deposits to time and savings deposits. In 1960 transactions balances accounted for 66 percent of total liabilities, but this source of low-cost funds fell to about 25 percent by 1981. Time and savings deposits, on the other hand, increased from about 31 percent of total liabilities in 1960 to about 57

TABLE 11.1
SOURCES OF BANK FUNDS OVER TIME: ALL INSURED U.S. COMMERCIAL BANKS
(As a Percentage of Total Liabilities)

Year	Total Deposits	Transactions Deposits	Time and Savings Deposits	Borrowed Funds
1960	97.2%	66.1%	31.1%	0.1%
1961	97.1	64.7	32.3	0.2
1962	96.0	60.0	36.0	1.3
1963	95.9	56.9	38.9	1.2
1964	96.4	56.3	40.1	0.8
1965	96.0	53.3	42.7	1.3
1966	95.0	51.7	43.3	1.2
1967	95.0	50.6	44.4	1.3
1968	93.8	49.4	44.4	1.9
1969	88.0	49.0	39.9	3.7
1970	90.4	46.4	43.9	3.6
1971	90.9	44.3	46.6	4.4
1972	90.1	43.3	46.7	5.5
1973	88.0	40.0	48.0	7.5
1974	87.9	37.0	50.9	6.6
1975	88.5	36.5	52.0	6.5
1976	88.5	35.7	52.9	8.1
1977	87.8	31.6	51.9	8.5
1978	85.8	33.9	51.9	10.6
1979	83.6	33.1	50.6	11.4
1980	83.0	30.2	52.8	9.5
1981	81.2	24.6	56.6	12.2

Source. Adapted from *Federal Reserve Bulletin,* Board of Governors of the Federal Reserve System, Washington, DC, selected issues.

percent in 1981. Another important trend is the increase in borrowed funds from only 0.1 percent in 1960 to 12.2 percent in 1981 (due in large part to negotiable CDs). These major shifts have increased the costs of funds for commercial banks and, in turn, have substantially changed the way in which banking organizations are managed.

Table 11.2 focuses attention on the liability structures of all insured U.S. commercial banks for the more recent period 1982 to 1986. During this time, demand deposits as a percentage of total assets declined from 18.8 percent to 14.2 percent. Time deposits under $100 million and other small savings deposits also declined noticeably. Offsetting these declines was an increase in interest-bearing checking accounts (i.e., NOW, ATS, and Super-NOW accounts) from 5.95 percent in 1982 to 9.33 percent in 1986. MMDA savings accounts also helped to offset declines in other kinds of retail deposits. Indeed, gains in these new, interest-bearing checking accounts increased core deposits to a certain extent in recent years.

Managed, or volatile, liabilities, by contrast, declined somewhat in recent

TABLE 11.2

LIABILITY STRUCTURE OF ALL INSURED U.S. COMMERCIAL BANKS: 1982–1986

Liabilities	As a Percentage of Total Assets				
	1986	1985	1984	1983	1982
Demand deposits	14.16%	14.60%	15.45%	16.69%	18.77%
All NOW and ATS accounts	9.33	8.34	8.14	7.49	5.95
Super NOWs included in above	NA	3.36	2.90	1.86	NA
MMDA savings	13.55	12.66	11.48	8.73	NA
Other savings deposits	6.81	6.61	7.39	9.90	12.39
Time deposits under $100 million	32.33	33.60	33.84	34.11	38.41
Core deposits	77.61	77.17	77.58	78.19	76.39
Time deposits over $100 million	10.81	10.86	10.19	9.41	10.60
Deposits in foreign offices	5.61	6.62	7.50	8.99	9.84
Federal funds purchased and repurchase agreements	0.25	0.42	0.62	0.72	1.41
Other borrowings	0.14	0.16	0.19	0.17	0.15
Volatile liabilities	12.33	12.53	12.05	11.33	13.04
Acceptances and other liabilities	1.16	1.32	1.38	1.34	1.45
Total liabilities (including mortgages)	91.45	91.32	91.30	91.21	91.22

Source. Federal Financial Institutions Examination Council, *Uniform Bank Performance Report*, Washington, DC (1986).

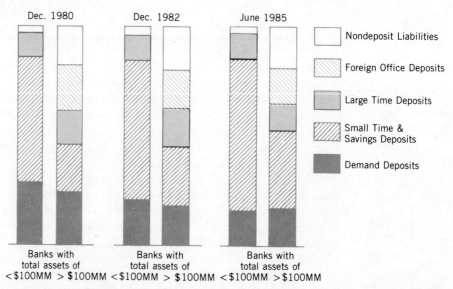

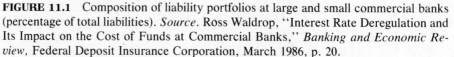

FIGURE 11.1   Composition of liability portfolios at large and small commercial banks (percentage of total liabilities). *Source.* Ross Waldrop, "Interest Rate Deregulation and Its Impact on the Cost of Funds at Commercial Banks," *Banking and Economic Review,* Federal Deposit Insurance Corporation, March 1986, p. 20.

years. As shown in Table 11.2, the use of deposits in foreign offices, as well as fed funds and RPs, declined between 1982 and 1986. Thus, banks have recently shifted away from wholesale sources of funds and moved toward greater use of retail funding.

Naturally, the structure of liabilities is different for banks of different size. Figure 11.1 compares the composition of liabilities for banks with less than $100 million in assets with that of banks having more than $100 million in assets. As shown, larger banks have a more balanced mix of sources of funds, including demand deposits, small time and savings deposits, large time deposits, foreign office deposits, and nondeposit liabilities. Smaller banks rely much more heavily on small time and savings deposits than larger banks because of their relatively greater retail orientation. Notice also that smaller banks had larger percentage declines in demand deposits than did larger banks from year end 1980 to mid-year 1985. For smaller banks, the decline in demand deposits was offset almost exactly by an increase in small time and savings deposits. For larger banks, small time and savings deposits increased by more than the percentage decline in demand deposits, as deposits from foreign offices and large time deposits decreased on a proportionate basis.

Although core deposits rose as a percentage of assets in response to deposit rate deregulation, which can be considered a stabilizing factor in the banking industry, interest costs increased also. Figure 11.2 indicates that interest expenses for both small and large banks increased significantly from about year end 1980 to mid-year 1982. This upward trend in interest costs occurred despite declines in 3-month CD rates from over 18 percent in early 1981 to a range of about 8 to 9 percent by mid-year 1982. Thus, new interest-bearing checking accounts caused interest expenses to increase significantly as deposit rate deregulation began in the early 1980s, a short-term result that many industry observers attribute to initial promotional efforts by depository institutions seeking to establish market shares.

Another apparent trend in Figure 11.2 is a gradual narrowing in the difference in interest expenses between small and large banks. Small banks' interest costs rose in response to deposit rate deregulation, whereas large banks actually experienced a decline in interest costs. The reason for this opposite effect of deregulation is that small banks have traditionally relied more on regulated deposits than large banks. Furthermore, large banks were able to reduce interest costs by substituting lower-cost retail deposits for relatively more expensive foreign and large time deposits. These changes in funds' sources have narrowed the gap in interest costs between small and large banks.

Changing interest expenses have also differentially affected net interest margins (i.e., total interest income minus total interest expenses divided by total assets) of small and large banks. Table 11.3 indicates that rising interest expenses decreased interest margins from 5.28 percent in 1980 to 4.46 percent in 1986 for banks with less than $25 million in assets. Banks with over $5 billion in assets, however, increased their net interest margins from 3.12 percent to 4.01 percent during this period. This narrowing of net interest margins between

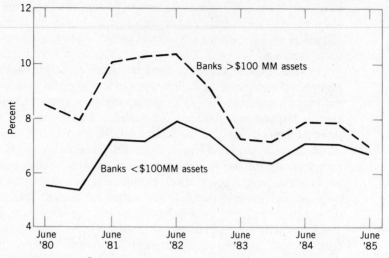

FIGURE 11.2   Interest expense as a percent of earning assets. *Source*. Ross Waldrop, "Interest Rate Deregulation and Its Impact on the Cost of Funds at Commercial Banks," *Banking and Economic Review,* Federal Deposit Insurance Corporation, March 1986, p. 21.

TABLE 11.3
NET INTEREST MARGINS OF ALL INSURED U.S. COMMERCIAL BANKS: 1980–1986

	Net Interest Margin						
Asset Size	*1980*	*1981*	*1982*	*1983*	*1984*	*1985*	*1986*
Under $25 million	5.28%	5.56%	5.06%	4.92%	4.93%	5.05%	4.46%
$25–100 million	5.06	5.19	4.67	4.54	4.56	4.71	4.51
$100–300 million	4.83	5.02	4.49	4.35	4.47	4.58	4.68
$300 million–$1 billion	4.74	4.86	4.40	4.32	4.43	4.62	4.51
$1–5 billion	4.18	4.39	4.08	4.00	4.17	4.27	4.22
Over $5 billion	3.12	3.12	3.10	3.13	3.38	3.57	3.54
All banks	4.07%	4.15%	3.87%	3.81%	3.95%	4.09%	4.01%

Sources. Adapted from Ross Waldrop. "Commercial Bank Performance in 1985," *Banking and Economic Review,* Federal Deposit Insurance Corporation, April 1986; and Ross Waldrop, "Commercial Bank Performance in 1986," *Banking and Economic Review,* Federal Deposit Insurance Corporation, March/April 1987.

small and large banks, therefore, appears to be directly attributable to deposit rate deregulation.

MANAGING BANK LIABILITIES

Dismantling of Regulation Q and rising competition for deposit funds has resulted in a wide variety of deposit products and associated services. This growing diversity of liability services has caused banks to use product differentiation as a way of distinguishing themselves from competitors. Table 11.4, for example, compares the pricing strategies of five Philadelphia area banks for NOW, Super-NOW, and MMDA accounts as of January 1, 1985 (minimum balance requirements of $1,000 on the latter two accounts were in effect at that time). The total pricing strategy is a combination of convenience (e.g., ATMs, or automated teller machines), service charges, minimum balances to avoid service charges or earn interest (or both), and other unique characteristics of particular accounts. In general, these pricing features are traded off against one another; for instance, banks with low service charges either had higher minimum balances or lower numbers of ATMs. Of course, the pricing strategy of individual banks is also influenced by their desired liability mix (see Box 11.2 for a discussion of how bank preferences have adversely affected basic banking services for lower-income families). In this section we discuss different aspects of the pricing decision that should be considered in the management of bank liabilities, in addition to the control of costs involved in acquiring funds.

Box 11.2
BASIC BANKING SERVICES[a]

One problem that has arisen as a result of the recent deregulation of depository institutions has been complaints from low-income individuals (or families) that basic financial services are either too expensive or are unavailable to them. Explicit pricing of transactions services is viewed by some people to be unfair, because banks have priced deposit accounts to attract higher-income individuals and are less concerned with lower-income individuals. Indeed, some industry observers believe lower-income individuals' accounts are overpriced at times both to discourage their patronage and partially subsidize intense competition for high net worth customers. Because some depository institutions have tied credit availability to deposit services since deregulation, a significant percentage of lower-income customers have complained that they are finding it more difficult to obtain credit than previously.

These service shortfalls have moved federal regulatory authorities to issue public notices that call for trade associations and individual depository institutions to support the offering of "basic financial services." Public debate on the subject, however, has not reached any consensus of opinion concerning the definition of these services, nor has there been any federal legislation passed in this area (although several bills have been introduced in recent years). The Federal Financial Institutions Examination Council (FFIEC) has commented that the following features constitute *minimum* consumer needs:

BOX 11.2 *(Continued)*

- the need for a safe and accessible place to keep money
- the need for a way to obtain cash (including, for example, the cashing of government checks)
- the need for a way to make third-party payments (including, for example, checking accounts)

The FFIEC has stated that these needs could be met by cooperation with the deposit services industry, rather than through imposing restrictive regulations or drafting legislative mandates. Nonetheless, a number of states have adopted laws that require financial institutions to offer certain basic financial services. Most of these laws pertain to reducing service charges on savings and checking services to anyone 65 years of age or older, as well as to individuals under 18 years of age in some cases.

Consumer surveys sponsored by federal regulatory agencies have revealed an increase in the proportion of Americans with no deposit account held at a financial institution. Also, research by the Federal Reserve Board has indicated that service fees charged on transactions accounts (but not minimum balance requirements) have increased at a more rapid rate than the general level of interest rates in recent years. These trends have generally been modest but are cause for at least some concern. Further research into the reasons families did not hold a deposit account has provided the following explanations: affordability of banking services, and insufficient income or transactions to warrant maintaining an account. Interestingly, few families cited high service charges and high minimum balance requirements as problems inhibiting deposit account ownership. Instead, they pointed to inconvenient locations and operating hours as the main difficulties. These results call into question exactly what is meant by basic banking services. Definitional issues aside, it does appear that deregulation has lessened the amount and quality of financial services available to lower-income families in some instances.

a This discussion draws heavily from the following work: Glenn B. Conner and Ellen Maland, "Basic Banking," *Federal Reserve Bulletin*, Board of Governors of the Federal Reserve System, April 1987, pp. 255–269.

The Pricing Committee

The pricing committee should be staffed by employees from throughout the bank. Because pricing decisions greatly affect the deposit base, they must be coordinated with other bank activities, including lending, marketing, accounting, data processing, operations, and trust services. Top management should appoint members to the pricing committee and periodically review its performance.

TABLE 11.4
PRICING NEW DEPOSIT ACCOUNTS

Bank	No. of ATMs Phila/ Phila MSA	Service Charges		Minimum Balance to Avoid Service Charges		Minimum Balance to Earn Interest		Additional Restrictions on MMDAs
		NOW	SNOW	NOW	SNOW	SNOW	MMDA	
I	80/280	$3/mo $.25/ck 25c/ATM transaction	$3/mo $.25/ck 25c/ATM transaction	$1000	$2500	$1000 (5.25)	$1000 (5.25)	No more than 6 automatic, pre-authorized, or ATM withdrawals or transfers per month
II	80/280	$5/mo $.15/ck $.10/ATM transaction	$1/mo $.15/ withdrawal	$1000	$15,000	$2500 (5.25)	$2500 (5.25)	No more than 6 withdrawals per month
III	32/60	$1.50/mo $.25/ck $.20/ATM transaction	$3/mo $.25/ck $.20/ATM transaction	$1200	$5000	$2500	$2500	No more than 6 transfers/mo to checking account
IV	80/280	$7/mo	$7/mo	$1000	$2500	$2500 (5.25)	$1000 (5.25)	$.50 per transaction over 10/mo
V	26/44	$6/mo $.10/ck	$4/mo $.25/ck	$1200	$3500 (AB)	$1000 (5.25)	$1000 (5.25)	No checks

Source. Adapted from Paul Calem, "The New Bank Deposit Markets: Goodbye to Regulation Q," *Business Review*, Federal Reserve Bank of Philadelphia, November/December 1985, p. 24.

Notes. (AB) denotes average balance requirement.
(5.25) denotes rate earned when MMDA or SNOW balance falls below minimum.

Committee assignments should address the primary objectives of deposit maintenance, market competitiveness, cost minimization, and adequate funding to meet lending goals. Information pertaining to these objectives must be gathered and reviewed periodically. Subsequent changes in pricing existing products need to be monitored for their effects on costs and deposit flows. Also, the committee should play a major role in the development and introduction of new products.

Components of the Pricing Decision

The Federal Reserve Bank of New York[5] conducted a series of interviews with senior commercial and savings bankers at the end of 1986 and beginning of 1987 on the pricing of their institutions' deposits. Bankers were asked what factors they considered in pricing consumer deposit products. The following key factors were identified:

- wholesale cost of funds
- pricing strategy of competitors
- interest elasticity (or responsiveness) of consumer demand
- past deposit flows for various kinds of consumer accounts
- maturity structure of deposits

The wholesale cost of funds, or large CD rates, was viewed by bankers as an alternative cost of money. Adjustments for differences in maturity (e.g., MMDAs, NOWs, and savings deposits that can be immediately withdrawn and have no fixed maturity), reserve requirements, and servicing were made to estimate retail costs of funds.

Various market factors influenced the pricing decision. The pricing strategy of competitors was monitored regularly, as well as the deposit flows of their own institution regarding various types of accounts. Additionally, the interest elasticity of demand for different deposit accounts was estimated to assess the potential influence of price changes on deposit flows.

Bankers also reviewed the maturity structure of their institution's deposits to determine what deposits were maturing and when they would come due. In general, bankers indicated that they did not consider the bank's short-term funding needs in making pricing decisions for consumer deposits. Such liquidity needs were met for the most part by wholesale deposits. This pricing behavior suggests that retail deposits are perceived primarily as core deposits.

Pricing decisions were reviewed on a weekly basis by most of the banks surveyed. Of course, changes in pricing were implemented less frequently. For

---

[5] This discussion is based on the following article: Richard G. Davis, Leon Korobrow, and John Wenninger, "Bankers on Pricing Consumer Deposits," *Quarterly Review,* Federal Reserve Bank of New York, Winter 1987, pp. 6–13.

example, even though large CD rates may have changed, the rate on MMDAs may not have been changed because MMDAs are less interest sensitive than CDs (presumably because MMDAs are shorter-term and tend to be used by customers as temporary accounts to "park cash" until it can be reinvested). Savings accounts were believed to be relatively insensitive to interest rate changes also. Rates on consumer CDs, however, were changed more frequently following a change in large CD rates. Generally, among revisions that were made, bankers observed that changes in implicit prices were seldom implemented, perhaps only once a year. Thus, most pricing changes involved explicit interest, service charges, and fees.

Formulating Pricing Policy

The pricing policy is a written document that contains the pricing details of deposit services. One banking consultant[6] recommended that the following areas be covered in the bank's pricing policy:

- service fees versus minimum balance requirements
- deposit costs and volumes and their relationship to profits
- credit availability and compensating balances
- customer relationship pricing
- promotional pricing of new products
- other marketing elements such as product differentiation

Obviously, the pricing process is based on a large number of variables that require experience and judgment to evaluate effectively. Forthcoming discussion touches upon the previously mentioned pricing factors in greater detail.

Deposit Pricing Matrix

In banking, both explicit and implicit pricing of products and services are used. Explicit pricing relates to interest expenses, whereas implicit pricing concerns noninterest expenses, such as free services, which are payments in kind. Figure 11.3 is a pricing matrix that gives some examples of explicit and implicit pricing of bank liabilities and their effects on bank revenues and costs.

Deregulation of deposit accounts has caused banks to move toward greater use of explicit pricing and decreased use of implicit pricing. This shift has been the result of unbundling costs, which means simply using explicit pricing to reflect more closely the true costs of producing specific products and services. Prior to deregulation, free checking was normally available as an implicit payment of interest to customers. Free checking was justifiable, because no inter-

[6] See L. Biff Motley, *Pricing Deposit Services: A Decision Making Handbook*, Boston, MA: Bankers Publishing Co., 1983, pp. 202–203.

FIGURE 11.3 Deposit pricing matrix

Effect on Bank Cash Flows \ Pricing Strategy	Explicit Prices	Implicit Prices
Bank Costs	• Interest payments • Gifts (e.g., appliances) • Compounding interest (e.g., daily)	• Below cost provision of services (e.g., free checking) • Added convenience (e.g., branch offices, ATMs, business hours)
Bank Revenues	• Service charges (e.g., charge per check) • Fees (e.g., overdrafts)	• Minimum balance requirements • Restrictions (e.g., limited check-writing privileges)

est could be earned on transactions balances, and individuals included some amount of savings balances in their transactions accounts for the sake of convenience. Deregulation of deposit rates allowed retail depositors to choose from alternative new accounts, some of which had predominantly checking features (e.g., NOW accounts), savings features (e.g., MMDA accounts), or a mixture of both (e.g., Super-NOW accounts). Naturally, banks priced each type of deposit account differently to distinguish them from one another. Further deregulation has subsequently eliminated the distinction between NOWs and Super NOWs and reduced differences between MMDAs and passbook savings accounts. In general, banks are continuing to adjust the explicit and implicit dimensions of their pricing strategies, as they learn more about operating in a deregulated deposit rate environment.

Profitability and Deposit Pricing

The goal of bank management should be to maximize deposit revenues and minimize deposit costs in an effort to maximize bank profitability. **Cost/revenue analysis** is one way in which managers can better understand how deposit pricing decisions are affecting bank profitability.

Figure 11.4 shows a hypothetical cost/revenue analysis for a bank as it expands its deposit base. Total bank costs equal fixed costs of land, buildings, and equipment, plus variable costs of deposits and other activities. Total bank revenues include deposit revenues, loan and security portfolio revenues, and other revenues. Profit maximization requires the following: (1) minimization of total costs at each output level; (2) maximization of total revenues at each output level; and (3) marginal total costs equal marginal total revenues (i.e., the cost of an additional dollar of deposits equals the revenue it would provide when invested by the bank). The latter marginal cost/revenue condition is represented in Figure 11.4, where the slopes of the total costs and total revenue curves are equal. Upper and lower breakeven points occur where costs and

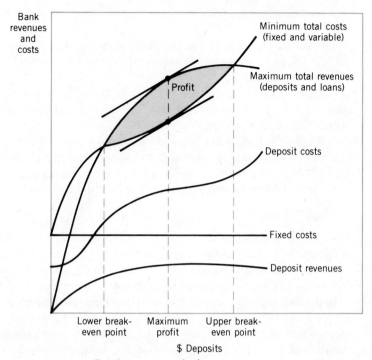

FIGURE 11.4   Cost/revenue analysis.

revenues equal one another in absolute (rather than marginal) terms. These points describe the output range within which the bank can profitably operate.

Notice that profit is maximized where the differences between deposit costs and deposit revenues, or *net* deposit costs, are maximized for a particular deposit level. Once an optimal deposit level is estimated, the minimization of net deposit costs for the target deposit base is the task of the pricing committee. Some of the ways in which banks have been reducing deposit costs in recent years are: (1) check truncation (i.e., cleared checks are not returned to customers); (2) stricter penalties for early withdrawal on time deposits; (3) reducing the number of products to avoid spreading resources too thin; (4) using weekly or monthly interest compounding instead of daily compounding; and (5) waiting for customers to ask for higher interest products rather than automatically moving their funds into these products. Obviously these cost-cutting techniques are not always successful because customers may become dissatisfied with the bank's service and withdraw their deposits.

Lending and Deposit Costs

Deposit costs can be affected by bank loan policies. For example, most loans require that compensating (deposit) balances be maintained by the borrower. Such balances are inexpensive to maintain because they usually pay no interest, require no promotional expenditures, and have minimum transactions costs (e.g., customer information is already on file). Another advantage of compensating balances is that they are relatively stable sources of deposits that are less likely to be withdrawn than other deposits, thus lowering the cost **per unit risk** of deposits.

Another way in which loan policy can lower deposit costs is through tie-in arrangements between deposit and loan services. Those customers that have deposit accounts could be provided greater access to credit. For instance, farm operators hold deposit accounts at rural banks not so much to earn interest but to establish a banking relationship that would enable them to obtain loans when needed. Thus, the credit function can be used by banks not only to raise deposit funds (i.e., compensating balances) but to reduce deposit costs.

Customer Relationship Pricing[7]

"Relationship banking" is an expression that includes the *total* financial needs of the public rather than just *specific* needs. It also includes fulfilling long-term needs, as opposed to immediate needs, such as cashing a check. Patrons are viewed as clients, as opposed to customers, according to this viewpoint.

In deposit pricing using relationship banking, each client is provided a package of financial services that is priced to reflect his or her individual needs. Thus, some degree of flexibility is required in pricing policies to enable bank management to develop stronger, more comprehensive relationships with clients.

As an example, consider a small businessperson who needs cash management services, retirement accounts, variable-rate loans, financial planning services, insurance, and trust services. Deposit services would comprise a relatively small part of the total package of financial services that this individual may be interested in buying. If this person came in simply requesting deposit services, it would be advantageous to **cross-sell** a variety of services by providing them at lower costs and greater convenience than if they were sold separately. This kind of tie-in arrangement often enables the bank to obtain cost-reducing benefits from economies of scale (i.e., the unit costs of each service decline as total output increases) and economies of scope (i.e., the unit costs of two or more services are lower when produced jointly, rather than separately, because inputs such as labor and capital are being more fully employed than otherwise). These operating cost savings can be passed along in whole or part to clients in the form of either lower prices or increased services.

Promotional Pricing

Promotional pricing is used occasionally to introduce new products. An excellent example is the pricing behavior of depository institutions during the intro-

---

[7] This section is based in part on the following book: Leonard L. Berry, Charles M. Futrell, and Michael R. Bowers, *Bankers Who Sell: Improving Selling Effectiveness in Banking,* Homewood, IL: Dow Jones-Irwin, 1985.

duction of MMDA accounts in December 1982 under the Garn Bill. These accounts were heavily advertised and offered rates well above market rates in an effort to attract deposits lost earlier to money market mutual funds because of Regulation Q deposit rate ceilings. As shown in Figure 11.5, within 6 months of their introduction, MMDA accounts grew to about $360 billion, in large part due to the promotional efforts of depository institutions. After the accounts were established, rates offered on MMDAs dropped to market levels.

More frequently, promotional pricing is used to support or rejuvenate demand for existing products. Some of the potential reasons for such promotions include increasing market share, modifying existing products, developing brand recognition or overall bank image, and targeting particular market segments of the population in certain geographic areas.

Other Marketing Elements Related to Pricing

Product Differentiation. Designing products and services to meet the needs of specific market segments is known as product differentiation. As mentioned earlier, banks typically must price their liabilities in different ways to compete effectively for funds. For example, if Bank One charged high service charges per check but had a low minimum balance requirement for earning market rates of interest, rival Bank Two would likely price its accounts to have lower per-check charges and higher minimum balance requirements than Bank One. Cus-

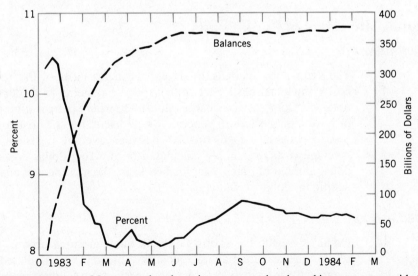

FIGURE 11.5 Money market deposit accounts—levels and interest rates paid. *Source.* Herbert Baer, Gillian Garcia, and Simon Pak, "The Effect of Promotional Pricing on Dynamic Adjustment in the Markets for MMMFs and MMDAs," *Proceedings of a Conference on Bank Structure and Competition,* Federal Reserve Bank of Chicago, April 23–25, 1984, p. 156.

tomers with lower incomes would tend to favor Bank One, whereas higher-income individuals would tend to prefer Bank Two. This is just one example of how banks can use pricing to seek the patronage of a particular market segment. Many other pricing combinations can be instituted to develop distinctive financial products and services. If banks did not differentiate their products, and instead competed side-by-side for the same customers, many customers might be forced to purchase products that are not priced to fit their needs.

Distribution. Another part of the pricing decision that bank managers should consider is the physical delivery of deposit services to the public. The problem here is one of logistics—namely, how to optimize the time and place preferences of customers, while minimizing bank operating costs net of associated revenues.

Banks have two basic distribution channels from which to choose. **Retail** channels distribute services to the general public, whereas **wholesale** channels distribute large volume services to corporate enterprises and government units. Banks may utilize alternative facilities to distribute retail and wholesale services, including full- or limited-service facilities, different kinds of paying and receiving stations (e.g., drive-in teller windows and ATMs), and various kinds of electronic communications equipment (e.g., pay-by-phone services). The exact components of the distribution network are dependent on customer numbers, types, locations, and buying habits, in addition to the product channels being employed by competing institutions.

Estimating the Costs of Bank Funds

Cost Definitions

The acquisition of bank funds entails incurring both financial and operating costs. Financial costs pertain to explicit payments to lenders minus revenues obtained from service charges and fees, whereas operating costs arise in the provision of services in general. When discussing the costs of bank funding, it is also necessary to distinguish between average costs and marginal costs. **Average costs** are simply calculated by dividing dollar costs of funds by the dollar amount of funds. **Marginal costs** are the incremental costs of acquiring an additional dollar of funds.

Weighted Average Costs

On an aggregate basis, costs of bank funds are measured in weighted average terms. The weighted average cost of funds can be calculated by summing the average (or marginal) cost of each source of funds times the proportion of total funds raised from each respective source of funds. According to financial theory, because profit-maximizing firms will seek to minimize their costs of funds, the weighted-average cost of funds should be equal to the marginal cost of funds. We may write this marginal cost of funds as follows:

$$CT = C_1 \frac{F_1}{TF} + C_2 \frac{F_2}{TF} + \cdots + Cn \frac{Fn}{TF} \qquad (11.1)$$

where CT = the marginal (weighted average) cost of funds, Cn = marginal cost of the nth source of funds, Fn = funds acquired from the nth source of funds, and TF = total funds acquired by the bank. Theoretically, the marginal costs of the individual sources of funds, or Cn, are equal to one another as well as to CT, **after adjusting for differences in risk.** This must be so because the bank would naturally acquire funds from the cheapest source until its cost rose to the marginal cost of other funds' sources.

The marginal (weighted average) cost of funds can also be interpreted as the minimum yield on bank investments in loans and securities that must be earned to avoid a loss in equity share values. This interpretation is based on the notion that funds should continue to be acquired and invested as long as shareholders earn yields in excess of the minimum required rate of return.[8]

Purposes of Cost Analyses

Performance Reports. Table 11.5 provides historical cost data for different sources of funds (excluding equity) that could be included in a performance report. Funds available for investment are less than the amount of funds acquired by the amount of reserves required (because of either legal requirements or management preferences). Financial costs equal total interest costs net of service revenues, and operating costs are based on allocated expenses for labor, premises, occupancy expenses, and other operations associated with physically-producing accounts.[9] The total cost of funds is divided by funds available for investment to obtain the average cost of each type of fund. Notice that reserve requirements raise the *effective* cost of funds, which is associated with funds usable for investment purposes. The final step is to calculate the weighted average cost of funds by applying equation (11.1). As shown in Table 11.5, this historical cost equaled 7.18 percent.

The information displayed in Table 11.5 may be used by the pricing committee to identify both problems and opportunities. For example, public deposits were costing an average of 10 percent more than any other type of funds, even though the risk associated with these funds is relatively low (because government accounts are a fairly stable source of deposits). Thus, management could work on reducing the cost of public deposits. On the other hand, the average

---

[8] See Franco Modigliani and Merton H. Miller, "Corporate Income Taxes and the Cost of Capital: A Correction," *American Economic Review,* June 1963, pp. 433–443.

[9] Interest costs and allocated operating costs of various sources of funds, in addition to cost breakdowns of various asset categories, are available through the Federal Reserve System's Functional Cost Analysis (FCA) service. Banks can voluntarily participate in this program by providing necessary data. Alternatively, many banks are implementing in-house cost accounting systems to collect data.

TABLE 11.5
HISTORICAL COST ANALYSIS (in thousands of dollars)

Source of Funds[a]	(1) Funds Acquired	(2) Funds Available for Investment	(3)= (1)/100,000 Proportion of Funds Acquired	(4) Financial Cost[b]	(5) Operating Cost[c]	(6)= (4)+(5) Total Cost	(7)= (6)/(2) Avg. Cost of Funds	(3) × (7) Weighted Avg. Cost of Funds
Deposit Sources								
Demand deposits	$20,000	$17,600	0.20	−$10	$200	$190	1.08%	0.216%
NOW accounts	8,000	7,040	0.08	480	40	520	7.39	0.591
Passbook savings	5,000	4,850	0.05	350	20	370	7.63	0.382
MMDAs	7,000	7,000	0.07	525	30	555	7.93	0.555
Retail CDs	14,000	14,000	0.14	1,120	20	1,140	8.14	1.140
Large CDs (≥$100,000)	25,000	24,250	0.25	2,125	60	2,185	9.01	2.253
Public deposits	10,000	8,800	0.10	800	80	880	10.00	1.000
Nondeposit Sources								
Fed funds & repos	4,000	4,000	0.04	360	30	390	9.75	0.390
Other borrowed money	5,000	5,000	0.05	450	30	480	9.60	0.480
Notes and debentures	2,000	2,000	0.02	140	30	170	8.50	0.170
Total	$100,000	$94,540	1.00	$6,340	$540	$6,880	Wtd. Avg. = 7.18 percent Cost	

[a] The following simplified reserve requirements are assumed to apply to various sources of funds: transactions accounts (12%), nonpersonal time deposits (3%), personal time and savings deposits (0%), and nondeposit funds (0%).

[b] Financial costs equal interest expenses minus revenues from service charges and fees.

[c] Operating costs equal total expenses involved in physically producing accounts.

cost of demand deposits was only about 1 percent, well below the cost of other kinds of funds. Bank management could increase promotional expenses, lower service charges and fees, or increase implicit service returns (by increasing operating expenses) to expand this relatively inexpensive source of funds. This kind of historical overview of costs can help guide bank management in minimizing the costs of funds in the future. In turn, cost minimizing behavior of bank managers causes the marginal costs of all sources of funds to remain about the same, including the cost of equity funds, on a risk-adjusted basis.

Investment Decisions. Care must be taken *not* to use the marginal cost of any particular source of funds as the cutoff rate in investment decisions. This approach to investment decisions is short run in nature and ignores the long-run implications involved in intermediating savings flows from different sources to investment in different loans and securities. Instead, it is the marginal cost of the entire *mix* of funds that must be used as a cutoff criterion in investment decisions. Table 11.6 shows the marginal cost of each type of funding, which is equal to the incremental percentage cost of acquiring an additional dollar of

TABLE 11.6
MARGINAL COST ANALYSIS

Source of Funds	Funds Acquired	Proportion of Funds Acquired	Marginal Cost[a,b]	Marginal Weighted Average Cost of Funds
Deposit Sources				
Demand deposits	$20,000	0.18	6.50%	1.170%
NOW accounts	8,000	0.07	7.80	0.546
Passbook savings	5,000	0.05	7.90	0.395
MMDAs	7,000	0.06	8.10	0.486
Retail CDs	14,000	0.13	8.30	1.079
Large CDs ($\geq$$100,000)	25,000	0.23	8.40	1.932
Public deposits	10,000	0.09	8.00	0.720
Nondeposit Sources				
Fed funds and repos	4,000	0.04	8.20	0.328
Other borrowed money	5,000	0.04	8.30	0.332
Notes and debentures	2,000	0.02	8.50	0.170
Equity	10,000	0.09	20.00	1.80
Total	110,000	1.00	Marginal cost = 8.79 percent	

[a] Marginal cost is based on total financial and operating costs per dollar of funds available for investment. Marginal costs of funds vary according to the risk(s) of these funds.

[b] The marginal cost of equity is on a before-tax basis in order to compare it with debt forms of funding. The marginal tax rate of the bank is assumed to be .34, such that the required rate of return by shareholders is 13.20 percent.

funds from that source. The weighted average of these costs, where the weights are the proportions of each source of funds in the long run, is the marginal cost of funds to be used in bank investment decisions. In Table 11.6 the marginal cost is calculated to be 8.79 percent. In order to be worthwhile to shareholders, an investment would have to yield 8.79 percent or more.

The greatest difficulty in applying the marginal cost concept to real-world investment decisions is the estimation of individual marginal costs for different sources of funds. The earnings/price ratio for common stock is a good proxy for the after-tax marginal cost of equity funds (see note *b* in Table 11.6 concerning the distinction between before-tax and after-tax equity costs). Unfortunately, most banks do not have actively traded common stock. In this case, some multiple of book value must be used to estimate market value. Neither are liabilities' marginal costs readily calculable in many cases. Although marginal financial costs can be estimated fairly accurately from market and internal information, marginal operating costs of acquiring an additional dollar of deposit funds may be difficult to assess. Experience and judgment are the best resources that can be used to avoid this problem. Thus, even though there are some drawbacks to marginal cost analysis in investment decisions, management expertise normally is sufficient to make appropriate estimates.

Finally, the marginal cost of funds may not be appropriate in making *long-run* investment decisions. For such decisions a weighted-average of the marginal cost of long-term funds can be used to calculate what is known as the marginal cost of capital. The marginal cost of capital can serve as a hurdle rate in capital budgeting decisions involving the purchase of nonfinancial assets, such as bank office buildings, equipment, and furniture, as well as long-term financial assets, such as corporate and municipal bonds. In general, long-term funds have maturities greater than 1 year and, therefore, are acquired from the capital market rather than the money market. Capital funding sources for banks are notes, debentures, and equity, including capital stock and retained earnings. Because bank assets are primarily short-term or have yields that can be adjusted more than once a year, the marginal cost of funds is relatively more important than the marginal cost of capital in financial decision making.[10]

SUMMARY

Sources of bank funds have changed substantially over the last two decades because of recurring inflation, rising competition, and deregulation of deposit rates. During this period, banks increased their usage of nondeposit funding and, conversely, decreased deposit funding. More important, in large part because of changing customer needs, banks shifted away from demand deposits and toward greater reliance upon time and savings deposits. In this regard, brokered deposits have been symptomatic of increasing risk in the banking

---

[10] By contrast, because nonfinancial, private business firms have substantial long-term investments, the marginal cost of capital is emphasized in the administration of funds.

industry, in addition to the national-level competition for deposit funds. The wide variety of retail deposit accounts that have been introduced within the last decade or so—such as NOWs, Super NOWs, ATSs, MMDAs, and retail CDs—have transformed the liability side of banks' balance sheets. This transformation has been appropriately referred to as the consumerism movement.

The pricing committee is responsible primarily for the management of bank liabilities, and is composed of employees throughout the bank.

IMPORTANT CONCEPTS

arbitrage profits	IRA
ATS accounts	Keogh plan
bankers' acceptance	large time deposits
bank holding companies (BHCs)	managed liabilities
basic financial services	marginal cost of capital
brokered deposits	marginal cost of funds
capital notes and debentures	matched sale-purchase agreement
CD	MMDAs
check truncation	MMMFs
commercial paper	NCD
compensating balances	net interest margin
consumer demand deposits	nondeposit funds
consumerism movement	noninterest costs
core deposits	NOW account
corporate demand deposits	overnight loan
cost/revenue analysis	payment in kind
cross-selling	pricing policy
dealer paper	product differentiation
demand deposits	promotional pricing
DIDC	purchased deposits
DIDMCA	Regulation Q
direct paper	retail CD
discount window advances	reverse RP
economies of scale	RP
economies of scope	savings certificates
Eurodollar deposits	savings deposits
explicit costs	senior debt capital
federal funds	service costs
FFIEC	small time deposits
Garn–St Germain Act	Super-NOW accounts
Glass–Steagall Act	sweep accounts
implicit costs	term RP

tie-in arrangement
unbundling costs
volatile liabilities

weighted average cost of funds
wholesale funding

REFERENCES

Baer, Herbert, Gillian Garcia, and Simon Pak. "The Effect of Promotional Pricing on Dynamic Adjustment in the Markets for MMMFs and MMDAs," *Proceedings of a Conference on Bank Structure and Competition,* Federal Reserve Bank of Chicago, April 23–25, 1984, pp. 153–177.

Berry, Leonard L., Charles M. Futrell, and Michael R. Bowers. *Bankers Who Sell: Improving Selling Effectiveness in Banking.* Homewood, IL: Dow Jones-Irwin, 1985.

Calem, Paul. "The New Bank Deposit Markets: Goodbye to Regulation Q," *Business Review,* Federal Reserve Bank of Philadelphia, November/December 1985, pp. 19–29.

Conner, Glenn B., and Ellen Maland. "Basic Banking," *Federal Reserve Bulletin,* Board of Governors of the Federal Reserve System, April 1987, pp. 255–269.

Davis, Richard G., Leo Korobrow, and John Wenninger. "Bankers on Pricing Consumer Deposits," *Quarterly Review,* Federal Reserve Bank of New York, Winter 1987, pp. 6–13.

Goodfriend, Marvin and William Whelpley. "Federal Funds: Instrument of Federal Reserve Policy," *Economic Review,* Federal Reserve Bank of Richmond, September/October 1986, pp. 3–11.

Konstas, Panos. "Brokered Deposits," *Banking and Economic Review,* Federal Deposit Insurance Corporation, May 1986, pp. 4–5.

Lumpkin, Stephen A. "Repurchase and Reverse Repurchase Agreements," *Economic Review,* Federal Reserve Bank of Richmond, January/February 1987, pp. 15–23.

Modigliani, Franco and Merton H. Miller. "Corporate Income Taxes and the Cost of Capital: A Correction," *American Economic Review,* June 1963, pp. 433–443.

Motley, L. Biff. *Pricing Deposit Services: A Decision Making Handbook.* Boston, MA: Bankers Publishing Co., 1983.

Taylor, Herb. "The Return Banks Have Paid on NOW Accounts," *Business Review,* Federal Reserve Bank of Philadelphia, July/August 1984, pp. 13–23.

Waldrop, Ross. "Interest Rate Deregulation and Its Impact on the Cost of Funds at Commercial Banks," *Banking and Economic Review,* Federal Deposit Insurance Corporation, March 1986, pp. 19–22.

Waldrop, Ross. "Commercial Bank Performance in 1985," *Banking and Economic Review,* Federal Deposit Insurance Corporation, April 1986, pp. 19–24.

Waldrop, Ross. "Commercial Bank Performance in 1986," *Banking and Economic Review,* Federal Deposit Insurance Corporation, March/April 1987, pp. 11–18.

West, Robert Craig. "The Depository Institutions Deregulation Act of 1980: A Historical Perspective," *Economic Review,* Federal Reserve Bank of Kansas City, February 1982, pp. 3–13.

QUESTIONS

11.1. Define core deposits of a bank. Also define purchased deposits.

11.2. Why are purchased deposits generally considered to be more risky than core deposits?

11.3. What does the Glass–Steagall Act have to do with deposit rate regulation? What is the rationale for this regulation?

11.4. Are commercial accounts still subject to Reg Q? Would a corporate client prefer compensating balances or service fees on a loan, all else the same?

11.5. Does FDIC deposit insurance tend to increase bank risk-taking? What specific kind of risk increases?

11.6. What are "basic financial services?" What two reasons explain why many Americans do not own a deposit account?

11.7. What are explicit and implicit deposit costs?

11.8. What advantage does a MMDA possibly have over a money market mutual fund (MMMF) account?

11.9. What is the "consumerism movement?"

11.10. Why is there a tiered CD market?

11.11. Is a dollar held in a bank office in Hong Kong a Eurodollar deposit? Are such deposits eligible for FDIC insurance?

11.12. What are brokered deposits? Why do regulators oppose the practice of deposit brokering?

11.13. What are "managed liabilities?" Give three differences between deposit funds and managed liabilities.

11.14. List and briefly discuss four sources of nondeposit liabilities.

11.15. How do the deposit compositions of small and large banks differ?

11.16. Pricing deposit accounts is a complex process. Give at least four factors affecting the pricing of consumer deposits.

11.17. Is there an optimal level of bank deposits in the sense of maximizing bank profitability? Use a graph to illustrate your answer and to discuss your graph.

PROBLEMS

11.1. (a) Given the data in Exhibit 11.1 showing the amounts and costs of funds for ABC Bank, calculate its weighted average cost of funds.
   (b) Which sources of funds had average costs that exceeded the weighted average cost of funds?

(c) Does it appear that some sources of funds are relatively costly considering their risk?

11.2. (a) Given the data in Exhibit 11.2, calculate the marginal weighted average cost of funds for ABC Bank.

(b) For what purpose can bank management use the marginal cost result in part a?

(c) Why do various costs of funds differ? Under what conditions would they be equal?

EXHIBIT 11.1

AVERAGE COSTS OF FUNDS FOR ABC BANK IN 1988

Sources of Funds	*(in millions of dollars)*	
	Average Amount Available for Investment	Average Cost
Deposits		
Demand deposits	15	5.00%
Interest-bearing checking	30	7.00
Passbook savings	10	8.00
Small CDs	20	9.00
Large CDs	30	10.00
Eurodollar CDs	5	10.40
Nondeposits		
Fed funds	6	8.00
Repos	10	8.50
Discount window advances	4	7.50
Other liabilities	12	10.00
Stockholders equity	12	15.00

EXHIBIT 11.2

MARGINAL COSTS OF FUNDS FOR ABC BANK IN 1988

Sources of Funds	Funds Acquired	Marginal Cost
Deposits		
Demand deposits	18	6.00%
Interest-bearing checking	33	7.25
Passbook savings	11	8.30
Small CDs	20	9.15
Large CDs	32	10.15
Eurodollar CDs	5.5	10.55
Nondeposits		
Fed funds	6	8.40
Repos	10	8.80
Discount window advances	4	7.90
Other liabilities	12	10.50
Stockholders equity	12	15.00

BANK CAPITAL MANAGEMENT

Declines in bank earnings in the 1980s have heightened interest in capital management among bankers and regulators. From the bankers' perspective, using less capital is a way to magnify (or lever) asset earnings and so earn higher equity rates of return. By contrast, regulators prefer that banks increase their capital to ensure their safety and soundness in the event earnings become negative. In general, bank shareholders and regulators have differing viewpoints of bank capital management.

This chapter defines bank capital and discusses its role in managing both bank operations and financial risk. The issue of capital adequacy is then discussed from the differing viewpoints of bank regulators and bank shareholders. Capital trends for U.S. commercial banks are covered also.

DEFINITION OF BANK CAPITAL

Like nonfinancial firms, capital in banking includes equity plus long-term debt. Equity is a residual account in the sense that it is the difference between total assets on the left-hand side of the balance sheet and total liabilities on the right-hand side of the balance sheet. Unlike nonfinancial firms, however, bank capital also includes reserves that are set aside to meet anticipated bank operating losses.

Equity

Equity is comprised of common stock, preferred stock, surplus, and undivided profits. The book value of common (and preferred) equity is equal to the number of shares outstanding multiplied by their par value. Surplus is the amount of paid-in capital in excess of par value realized by the bank upon the initial sale of stock. Finally, undivided profits equal retained earnings, which are the cumulative net profits of the bank that are not paid out in the form of dividends to shareholders.

An alternative way to measure equity is in terms of the market value of common and preferred stock. Market values reflect not only historical book values of equity but also the expected future returns and risks of the bank. Thus, market value is both an **ex post** and **ex ante** concept, whereas the Report of Condition is strictly an **ex post** valuation of equity.

As an example, suppose that a newly chartered bank sold one million common shares with a par value of $9 per share for $10 per share. During the first 3 years of business, the bank had undivided profits of $100,000, $110,000, and $120,000, respectively. Equity capital, as indicated in the Report of Condition, would be as follows:

Preferred stock	$ 0
Common stock	9,000,000
Surplus	1,000,000
Undivided profits	330,000
Total equity	$10,330,000

Normally, the market value of equity would exceed the *ex post* book value of equity, because most banks expect to have positive earnings per unit of risk in the future. Unfortunately, the equity stock of most banks is not traded in the open market either because it is closely held by a small group of investors or because trading activity is too low to warrant listing on a stock exchange. In this case the accounting (or book) value serves as a benchmark in comparing the equity positions of different banks.

Long-Term Debt

Notes and debentures are sources of long-term debt that banks can utilize to raise additional external funds. Because this debt is second in priority to depositor claims in the event of liquidation arising from bank failure, it is said to be "subordinated." Banks use far less long-term debt than do nonfinancial firms because most of their debt is in the form of short- and intermediate-term deposit funds, which essentially are money market sources of funds. Nonetheless, long-term bank debt increased substantially in the 1960s, especially among large banks. This increase was motivated by a change in regulatory requirements that allowed notes and debentures (with maturities of at least 7 years) to be used to meet capital standards for national banks.

A major advantage of using debt capital (as opposed to equity capital) is that interest payments are tax deductible, whereas equity earnings are fully exposed to federal income taxes. Consequently, debt is a less-expensive after-tax source of external capital than is equity in general.

For small banks the use of long-term debt is much more costly than it is for large, billion-dollar banks. Fixed transactions costs can raise the marginal cost of small debt issues to an unreasonably high level. Moreover, small issues normally are less liquid than larger issues, causing investors to demand a higher rate of return, which raises the cost of borrowing for small banks. Most notes and debentures, therefore, are issued by large banks.

Reserves

Banks set aside earnings for loan (and lease) loss reserves. When a loan defaults, the loss does not reduce current earnings because it can be deducted from the reserve account. To establish reserves to meet anticipated loan losses, banks expense an account known as the *provision for loan losses* (PLL) in the income statement. By expensing PLL, banks reduce their tax burden.[1] In the past banks used either the experience method or the percentage method to calculate their PLL. The experience method involved using the average loan losses over the previous 6 years. The percentage method simply takes 0.6 percent of eligible loans outstanding. Under the Tax Reform Act of 1986, however, larger banks can only deduct partially or wholly worthless loans from income. Industry observers believe that this new approach will cause large banks with more than $500 million in assets to accelerate charging off bad debts. The PLL account is considered part of capital by regulatory authorities.

---

[1] It is important not to confuse the provision for possible loan losses with the allowance for possible loan losses. The allowance is a valuation reserve because it indicates the balance of the bank's bad-debt reserve. The allowance is carried as an asset item on the balance sheet. Net loans on the balance sheet represents gross loans minus this allowance. To calculate the allowance, the balance from last year is added to recoveries on loans and this year's PLL. Next, actual losses on loans are subtracted to obtain this year's balance in the allowance account.

Also, capital reserves that appear in the capital portion of the balance sheet are counted by regulators. Capital reserves include amounts set aside to pay dividends or retire stocks and bonds outstanding. Finally, regulators also include as reserves certain funds set aside as contingency reserves to meet unexpected losses, which otherwise do not appear on the balance sheet.

ROLE OF BANK CAPITAL

Bank capital serves two basic roles. The first, and most obvious, is that it is a source of funds. A new bank requires funds to finance start-up costs of capital investment in land, plant, and equipment. Established banks require capital to finance their growth, as well as to maintain and modernize operations. They normally rely upon internal capital (retained earnings) to a much greater extent than external capital (long-term debt and equity stock). However, external capital is often used to finance major structural changes, such as acquisitions and mergers.

The second function of capital is to serve as a cushion to absorb *unexpected* operating losses. For example, the depth of the economic downturn in the agricultural and oil industries in the early and mid-1980s caught most experts by surprise. Relatively high loss rates on loans in these sectors surpassed the loan loss provisions of many banks, causing them to use capital to absorb unanticipated losses. Banks with insufficient capital are declared insolvent by their regulatory agency and are handled by the Federal Deposit Insurance Corporation (to be discussed in greater detail later in this chapter).

It should be recognized that long-term debt instruments are a capital source of funds that cannot be used to absorb losses except in a liquidation of a failed institution. Thus, in contrast to equity sources of capital, long-term debt only weakly satisfies the role of capital as a cushion to absorb losses. As we will see, this is why bank regulators distinguish between equity and debt sources of capital.

Causes of Bank Failure

Table 12.1 lists the primary causes of commercial bank failure during the period 1971–1982. The data are broken down by bank size to reflect differences between small and large banks. Loan losses were consistently the most important reason for failure for banks of all sizes. In this regard, insider loans that were made for the personal gain of bank officers accounted for between 31 and 67 percent of the failures. Thus, illegal uses of funds are important in terms of explaining bank failures also.

Another key factor associated with bank failure was liquidity. For large banks, liquidity problems accounted for 51 percent of failures. For smaller banks, this factor was responsible for between 24 and 36 percent of failures. This difference can be explained by the fact that large banks normally carry a

TABLE 12.1
CAUSES OF COMMERCIAL BANK FAILURE BY SIZE DECILE, 1971–1982[a]

	Size Decile					
Cause of Failure	1 (Small)	2–3	4–5	6–7	8–9	10 (Large)
Loans	83%	77%	81%	60%	57%	86%
Insider loans	31	26	38	67	43	33
Rate sensitivity	14	10	24	13	14	48
Liquidity	35	36	24	33	29	57
Number of cases (including assistance cases)	29	31	21	15	7	21

Source. Federal Deposit Insurance Corporation. *Deposit Insurance in a Changing Environment*, Washington, DC: FDIC, 1983, pp. 11–17.

[a] Causes are shown as a percentage of the number of failures for each size group.

relatively low percentage of liquid assets compared with small banks. Because large banks make greater use of liability management to meet liquidity needs than small banks, it is not surprising that interest sensitivity accounted for 48 percent of large bank failures, which is far greater than 10 to 24 percent among smaller bank failures.

CAPITAL ADEQUACY

As mentioned earlier, bank regulators and bank shareholders tend to have differing views about the adequacy of capital. Regulators normally are concerned about the downside risk of banks; that is, they focus on the lower end of the distribution of bank earnings. By contrast, shareholders are more concerned with the central part of the earnings distribution, or the expected return available to them. Both regulators and shareholders also consider the variability of bank earnings, albeit from different perspectives once again. Regulators perceive earnings variability in the context of the likelihood that earnings will fall so much that capital is eliminated and the bank becomes insolvent. Shareholders require higher earnings per share as the bank profitability becomes more variable. Thus, shareholders receive compensation for bank risk, whereas regulators do not.

Regulators' Viewpoint

From the viewpoint of regulators, financial risk increases the probability of bank insolvency. Greater variability of earnings after taxes means that interest and noninterest expenses are more likely to exceed bank earnings and that capital will be required to absorb potential losses. If there is insufficient capital to absorb losses, regulators must close the bank due to capital impairment.

Alternatively, regulators close banks that are insolvent, which means that if assets were liquidated in an orderly fashion, their market value would be inadequate to cover noncapital liabilities.

The problem faced by regulators is that, although requiring banks to maintain higher capital tends to lower financial risk, such requirements may inhibit the efficiency and competitiveness of the banking system; that is, capital requirements that exceed unregulated levels act as a constraint on the lending operations of banks. In this instance, banks may not allocate loanable funds in the most efficient way. The productivity of the economic sector could therefore be lessened by this constraint on the financial system. Regulatory restrictions on bank capital could also hinder their competitiveness relative to other sellers of financial services. For example, relatively high capital requirements tend to constrain the rate at which bank assets may be expanded. Unable to grow as rapidly as other financial service companies, banks would be at a competitive disadvantage. Thus, regulatory policy regarding capital adequacy must weigh the potential benefits of safety and soundness against the potential costs of efficiency and competitiveness.

Capital Standards

In general, regulators favor added capital as a buffer against insolvency to promote the safety and soundness of the financial system. "Safety and soundness" in this instance implies protecting depositor funds and preventing financial panics through the provision of a stable money supply. Regulators historically have maintained different standards for capital adequacy and have changed those standards many times. For example, because deposit runs were the major threat to bank soundness in the early 1900s, the Office of the Comptroller of the Currency (OCC) required banks to have capital-to-deposit ratios of 10 percent or more. In the 1930s, the newly formed FDIC began employing a capital-to-asset ratio to measure capital adequacy, because risky assets (e.g., defaults on loans) were perceived to be the major cause of failure. During World War II, banks accumulated large proportions of default-free government securities to help finance federal debt, which caused regulators to utilize a capital-to-risk-asset ratio, where risk assets was defined as total assets minus cash and government securities.

Over the last 40 years, a wide variety of methods for assessing capital adequacy has been applied by regulators. In the 1950s, for example, the Federal Reserve Board (FRB) began using the Form for Analyzing Bank Capital (FABC) to classify assets into different risk categories. Banks were required to hold a different percentage of capital against each asset category (e.g., 0.4 percent capital against U.S. Treasury bills and 10 percent capital against business loans). Also, smaller banks had higher capital requirements because of the perception that their portfolio diversification was less than larger banks. Because OCC standards applied to national banks, FRB standards applied to state member banks and banks affiliated with holding companies, and FDIC stan-

TABLE 12.2
COMPONENTS OF PRIMARY AND SECONDARY CAPITAL

Item	Description
Primary Capital	
Common stock	Aggregate par or stated value of outstanding common stock.
Perpetual preferred stock	Aggregate par or stated value of outstanding perpetual preferred stock. Preferred stock is a form of ownership interest in a bank or other company, which entitles its holders to some preference or priority over the owners of common stock, usually with respect to dividends or asset distributions in a liquidation. Perpetual preferred stock does not have a stated maturity date and cannot be redeemed at the option of the holder. It includes those issues that are automatically converted into common stock at a stated date.
Equity capital: Surplus	Amount received from the sale of common or perpetual preferred stock in excess of its par or stated value.
Undivided profits	Accumulated dollar value of profits after taxes that has not been distributed to shareholders of common and preferred stock as dividends.
Capital reserves	Contingency and other capital reserves. Reserves for contingencies include amounts set aside for possible unforeseen or indeterminate liabilities not otherwise reflected on the bank's books and not covered by insurance. Capital reserves include amounts set aside for cash dividends on common and preferred stock not yet declared and amounts allocated for retirement of limited-life preferred stock and debentures subordinated to deposits.
Plus:	
Mandatory convertible instruments[a]	Debt issues that mandate conversion to common or perpetual preferred stock at some future date; they must meet the following conditions to be included in primary capital:

1. The securities must mature (convert to common or preferred stock) in 12 years or less.
2. The aggregate amount of mandatory convertible securities counted as primary capital may not exceed 20 percent of primary capital net of mandatory convertible securities.
3. The issuer may redeem the securities before maturity only with the proceeds of the sale of common or perpetual preferred stock.
4. The holder of the security cannot accelerate the payment of principal except in the event of bankruptcy, insolvency, or reorganization.

TABLE 12.2 (Continued)

Item	Description
	5. The security must be subordinated in right of payment to all senior indebtedness of the issuer.
Reserves for loan and lease losses	Amount set aside to absorb anticipated losses. All charge-offs of loans and leases are charged to this capital account, and recoveries on loans and leases previously charged off are credited to this capital account.
Minority interest in consolidated subsidiaries	The sum of the equity capital of the subsidiaries in which the bank has minority interest multiplied by the percentage ownership of the bank in the subsidiaries.
Minus:	
Equity commitment notes	Debt obligations that the issuer must repay only from the proceeds of the sale of common or perpetual preferred stock. These notes are included in mandatory convertible instruments, but are excluded from primary capital.
Intangible assets[b]	Generally these assets represent the purchase price of firms that have been acquired in excess of their book value.
Secondary Capital	
Limited-life preferred stock[c]	Preferred stock with a maturity date.
Plus:	
Subordinated notes and debentures[c]	Debt obligations of issuer, with fixed maturity dates, that are subordinated to depositors in case of insolvency. Subordinated notes and debentures issued by depository institutions are not insured by the federal deposit insurance agencies.
Mandatory convertible instruments not eligible for primary capital[d]	See mandatory convertible instruments definition given previously.

[a] Only up to 20 percent of primary capital excluding mandatory convertible instruments.

[b] The FDIC and OCC subtract all intangible assets except for purchased mortgage servicing rights. The Fed subtracts only the "goodwill" portion of intangible assets.

[c] The limited-life preferred stock and subordinated notes and debentures included in secondary capital must have an original weighted average maturity of at least 7 years. All three federal banking agencies limit the aggregate amount of secondary capital to less than 50 percent of a bank's primary capital.

[d] The amount that exceeds 20 percent of primary capital excluding mandatory convertible instruments; equity commitment notes excluded from primary capital.

dards applied to state-chartered banks, the capital adequacy of any individual bank was determined to a certain degree by its particular regulatory agency.

Another problem with capital standards has been their enforceability. In the past, regulators relied primarily upon persuasion to enforce capital standards. Seldom were cease and desist orders employed to obtain compliance, because regulators were not supported by force of law. This problem was solved by the International Lending Supervision Act of 1983. This Act gave regulators the legal authority to establish minimum capital requirements and enforce them. Normally, the regulator requires violating banks to submit a plan to correct the capital shortfall, which is now enforceable in the courts.

Yet another problem with previous capital standards is the question of equity. In the past, small banks had more restrictive capital requirements than large banks. Presumably bank size was directly related to safety and soundness according to this dichotomy. However, the historical evidence on bank failures in the United States has not proven failure risk to be positively related to asset size.

Uniform Capital Requirements. In 1981 federal bank regulators established minimum primary capital-to-asset ratios. The FRB and OCC adopted a 6-percent minimum for banks with less than $1 billion in assets and 5 percent for banks over $1 billion assets. The FDIC applied a 5-percent minimum ratio to all banks. Multinational banks, which are the 17 largest banks in the United States, were evaluated on a case-by-case basis. Under the 1983 International Lending and Supervision Act, however, multinationals were required also to meet the 5-percent minimum primary capital requirement.

Further improving uniformity, in 1985 the three federal bank regulators settled on a 5.5-percent primary capital ratio for all banks. In this regard, regulators established zones for billion-dollar banks that consider ranges of primary and total capital ratios, as well as asset quality and other factors that are relevant to capital risk. Finally, if a bank is judged to be undercapitalized, it must make up the shortfall under the supervision of its regulatory agency. Progress toward compliance with capital standards is monitored over time.

In response to this uniform capital/asset ratio measurement of capital adequacy, undercapitalized, larger banks have generally raised new capital, reduced their holdings of liquid assets, and increased off-balance-sheet activities (because only booked assets are counted in the calculation of the capital ratio). Some larger institutions, forced to increase capital, have also sought to cut operating costs, raise service prices, and make riskier loans. These changes have more than offset the advantage of added capital in many cases and so have tended to defeat the capital adequacy goals of regulators.

Risk-Adjusted Capital Requirements. In 1987, U.S. federal regulatory agencies, in conjunction with the Bank of England and authorities from 12 leading industrial countries, agreed to release for public comment a proposed risk-based capital framework.[2] The major rationale for this proposal was that histor-

---

[2] The proposal was adopted in 1988 by the Basle Committee on Banking Regulations and Supervisory Practices, which is comprised of representatives of the central banks and supervisory authorities of Belgium, Canada, France, West Germany, Italy, Japan, Netherlands, Sweden, Switzerland, United Kingdom, United States and Luxembourg. The Committee has been working for several years on strengthening the capital resources of international banks.

ical evidence indicated no clear-cut relationship between bank capital and failure risk. In the Great Depression, for example, capitalization was not linked directly to failure. Since that time, as discussed earlier, illegal practices, loan losses, and liquidity have been most responsible for bank failures. Not only would the proposed standards be more closely related to failure risks, they would also promote convergence of supervisory policies on the adequacy of capital among countries with major banking centers.

Intended to supplement, rather than replace, the current capital requirements, a weighted-average measure of total assets is to be used to calculate capital requirements, where the weights would correspond to different categories of assets grouped according to their risk. The key measure of capital adequacy is risk asset ratio to be calculated as follows:

$$\text{Risk asset ratio} = \frac{\text{Adjusted primary capital}}{\text{Weighted risk asset base}} \qquad (12.1)$$

where the **weighted risk asset base** is the sum of the categories of "on-balance sheet" risk assets, as shown in Table 12.3, weighted by the appropriate percentage—0, 10, 20, 50, and 100 percent, and **adjusted primary capital** is primary capital minus intangible assets, bank holdings of other banks' capital instruments, and some other capital items. Off-balance sheet activities would also be included in the calculation of total risk-adjusted assets. No minimum has been established, but it has been proposed that a 7.25-percent ratio be required after 3 years and an 8-percent requirement after a 5-year transition period. Higher standards could be established at the discretion of supervisory authorities in different countries. Individual banks' requirements set by the different regulators would be affected by on-site examinations of banks' quality and diversification of assets, interest rate risk, liquidity, earnings level and stability, management control of risk, and other factors. Thus, the new approach to capital adequacy attempts to link capitalization to bank exposure to risk, with emphasis on loan risk in particular and probability of default in general. It is expected that risk-adjusted capital ratios will exceed current capital requirements for most banks, especially for smaller institutions.[3]

FDIC. The Federal Deposit Insurance Corporation (FDIC) has a vested interest in bank capital adequacy. It insures deposits held by approximately 98 percent of all U.S. commercial banks. Banks are required to pay premiums equal to 1/12th of 1 percent to insure deposit accounts up to $100,000. Rebates are paid to sound institutions at the end of the year that in total equal 60 percent of the FDIC's collections minus disbursements and operating expenses.

---

[3] For more in-depth discussions of risk-adjusted capital, see James Chessen, "Risk-Based Capital Comes to the Fore," *Issues in Bank Regulation,* Spring 1987, pp. 3–15; and Janice M. Moulton, "New Guidelines for Bank Capital: An Attempt to Reflect Risk," *Business Review,* Federal Reserve Bank of Philadelphia, July/August 1987, pp. 19–33.

TABLE 12.3
SUMMARY OF RISK CATEGORIES FOR PROPOSED RISK-ADJUSTED
CAPITAL REQUIREMENTS[a]

Weight	General Description
On-Balance Sheet Assets	
0%	(a) Cash
	(b) Balances at and claims on domestic central banks
	(c) Loans to domestic central governments
	(d) Securities issued by domestic central governments
	(e) Loans and other assets fully collateralized by cash or domestic central government securities or fully guaranteed by domestic central governments
20%	(a) Claims on domestic and foreign banks with an original maturity of under 1 year
	(b) Claims on domestic banks with an original maturity of 1 year and over and loans guaranteed by domestic banks
	(c) Claims on foreign central governments in local currency financed by local currency liabilities
	(d) Cash items in process of collection
0, 20, or 50%	(a) Claims on the domestic public sector, excluding central government (at national discretion) and loans guaranteed by such institutions
50%	(a) Loans to owner-occupiers for residential house purchase fully secured by mortgages
100%	(a) Claims on the private sector
	(b) Cross-border claims on foreign banks with an original maturity of 1 year or more
	(c) Claims on foreign central governments
	(d) Claims on commercial companies owned by the public sector
	(e) Premises, plant and equipment and other fixed assets
	(f) Real estate and other investments
	(g) Capital instruments issued by other banks
	(h) All other assets

Off-Balance Sheet Items

Credit risk due to such items is considered by multiplying a credit conversion factor, which is an estimate of the likely size and occurrence of actual credit exposure due to off-balance sheet commitments by the bank, by the weights applicable to the asset category of the counterparty for an on-balance sheet transaction.

Credit Conversion Factors

100%	(1) Direct credit substitutes (e.g., general guarantees of indebtedness, including standby letters of credit and acceptances)
	(2) Sale and repurchase agreements and asset sales with recourse, where credit risk remains with the bank
	(3) Forward purchases, forward deposits, and partly-paid shares and securities, which represent commitments with certain drawdown

TABLE 12.3 (Continued)

Weight	General Description
50%	(1) Certain transaction-related contingent items (e.g., performance bonds, bid bonds, warranties, and standby letters of credit related to particular transactions)
	(2) Note issuance facilities and revolving underwriting facilities
	(3) Other commitments (e.g., formal standby facilities and credit lines) with an original maturity exceeding 1 year
20%	(1) Short-term, self-liquidating, trade-related contingencies (e.g., documentary credits collateralized by the underlying shipments)
0%	(1) Similar commitments with an original maturity of less than 1 year, or which may be canceled at any time

[a] Foreign exchange and interest rate related items are subject to special treatment because banks are not exposed to credit risk for the full face value of the contract, but only to the potential cost of replacing the cash flow if the counterparty defaults. Adapted from Joint News Release, Comptroller of the Currency, Federal Deposit Insurance Corporation, and Federal Reserve Board, December 10, 1987.

Created in 1933, the FDIC has two policy objectives. First, deposit insurance is intended to protect depositors of modest means against bank failures. Second, the insurance is supposed to protect communities, states, or the nation from the economic consequences of a breakdown in the payments system. The record shows that since its inception the FDIC has effectively met these objectives, with 100-percent recovery of insured deposits and about 99-percent recovery of total deposits.

When a distressed bank situation arises, the FDIC handles it in one of five ways: (1) depositor payoff, (2) purchase and assumption, (3) provision of financial aid, (4) charter of a Deposit Insurance National Bank, or (5) reorganization. In a depositor payoff, each insured depositor receives up to $100,000 from the FDIC within 1 week. Liquidated proceeds from the bank are used for this purpose, and remaining funds are used to pay off other deposit and nondeposit claims, as well as the FDIC itself. It is normally less costly, however, for the FDIC to use the purchase and assumption (P&A) method of disposition. Under this approach, the bank is merged with a healthy bank. The FDIC accepts the lower-cost bid for the bank and pays off part (or all) of the acquiring bank's losses in the merger.

If the closure of a bank would severely disrupt banking services to a community or cause creditors to suffer extraordinary losses, the FDIC can choose among the latter three approaches cited previously. Financial aid can be used temporarily to assist a distressed bank. A Deposit Insurance National Bank (DINB) can be chartered by the FDIC to take over operations until the bank is either closed or acquired by another bank. Finally, the major creditors can reorganize the bank with or without intervention. Of these five alternative approaches, liquidations and mergers are the most commonly used.

Deregulation of financial institutions over the last decade has caused new problems for the FDIC. Deregulation has enabled banks to choose among a broader opportunity set of risks and returns in their liability and asset management. Intuitively, it is inappropriate for all banks to pay the same deposit insurance costs. Indeed, it is believed that some banks are taking excessive risks in an attempt to exploit the mispricing of deposit insurance by the FDIC. For these reasons, the FDIC is currently considering a risk-based premium schedule that would be based on banks' financial condition. It is also considering the application of market discipline to control bank risk taking—for example, the bank would be required to issue uninsured bonds that would be publicly traded and, therefore, would act to signal regulators and others of bank problems perceived by the financial marketplace (see Box 12.1 for further discussion).

Box 12.1
RISK-BASED DEPOSIT INSURANCE PREMIUMS

The FDIC is currently considering the use of risk-based deposit insurance premiums to control bank risk taking. The present fixed-rate deposit insurance pricing charges premiums equal to $\frac{1}{12}$ of 1 percent of bank deposits and rebates excess FDIC insurance funds on a pro rate basis to sound banks at the end of the year. It is believed that this pricing scheme gives banks incentive to increase their risk taking. One way that banks could exploit this fixed-rate pricing is to increase their debt by expanding their deposit base. As we discuss in the text, the proposed risk-based capital requirements should prevent this type of exploitation. In effect, capital requirements that vary with bank risk force the shareholders to "co-insure" the bank (in the sense that the FDIC and equityholders share the burden of bank operating losses).

Other ways that banks can take advantage of fixed-rate deposit insurance pricing is to increase their credit risk, interest rate risk, and liquidity risk. It is true that risk-based capital requirements could take these risks into account. However, at the present time, as is indicated by Table 12.3, risk-based capital requirements primarily focus on credit risk. It is not yet clear how other risks could be worked into a capital requirement formula.

The FDIC has proposed to *explicitly* price bank risks, as opposed to *implicitly* price them using capital requirements. Two measures of risk assessment are to be utilized. One measure is the CAMEL rating of the bank as determined by periodic examiner review. As explained in Chapter 3, CAMEL ratings grade five dimensions of bank performance from 1 (best) to 5 (worst): (C) capital adequacy, (A) asset quality, (M) management ability, (E) earnings, and (L) liquidity. Banks rated 4 and 5 are included on the FDIC's problem-bank list.

BOX 12.1 (*Continued*)

The second measure of bank risk is a risk index developed from statistical regression methods. The risk index is calculated as follows:

$$I = .818 - .151 \text{ (primary capital/total assets)}$$
$$+ .211 \text{ (loans more than 90 days past due/total assets)}$$
$$+ .265 \text{ (nonaccruing loans/total assets)}$$
$$+ .177 \text{ (renegotiated loans/total assets)}$$
$$+ .151 \text{ (net loan charge-offs/total assets)}$$
$$- .347 \text{ (net income/total assets)} \tag{1}$$

where all ratios are in percent (annualized) terms. The risk index I indicates the probability of being a problem bank. Notice that if all ratios are zeros, the I equals .818, which is a high probability of being a problem bank.

CAMEL ratings and the risk index I would be used to assign banks to one of two risk classes. If I is positive *and* the CAMEL rating is 3, 4, or 5, the bank is judged to be above-normal risk. All other banks are considered to be normal risk. Above-normal risk banks would be required to pay premiums equal to $\frac{1}{6}$ of 1 percent of deposits. Normal risk banks would continue to pay the current premium rate.

Critics of the FDIC's proposal point out that measuring bank risk is not without some degree of arbitrariness. On the other hand, proponents argue that, since investors price risk in the financial marketplace, the FDIC can similarly price risk. As a compromise solution, some experts have recommended that banks be forced to issue notes and debentures. The prices of such uninsured securities would provide "market discipline" because risky banks would suffer price declines. Also, regulators could use this price information both as a check on their risk assessments of banks and as an early warning indicator of potential bank problems. Although there are clearly benefits of using market discipline to control bank risk, some industry observers believe small banks would suffer higher costs of funds than large banks because they would have marketability difficulties (causing them to discount their bonds more than large banks).

It is likely that the FDIC's risk-based deposit insurance proposal will undergo modifications before it is actually implemented. Despite differences in opinion on how to implement it, there is a consensus opinion that new regulatory techniques of controlling bank risk-taking are needed to ensure safety and soundness and to protect public confidence in the banking system.

Source: Robert B. Avery and Terrence M. Belton, "A Comparison of Risk-Based Capital and Risk-Based Deposit Insurance," *Economic Review*, Federal Reserve Bank of Cleveland, fourth quarter, 1987, pp. 20–30.

Shareholders' Viewpoint

Shareholders view bank capitalization in a substantially different way than regulators. Shareholders seek an optimal mix of debt and equity finance to maximize the value of their common stock. Because share values are a function of both expected future cash flows available to equity owners and their associated risks, shareholders focus on the expected value of rates of return on equity and their variability. In this section we review some of the major factors that typically influence capital structure decisions of bank shareholders.

Financial Risk

Financial risk is associated with borrowing funds to finance assets. As a bank substitutes debt (including both deposit and nondeposit liabilities) for equity, there is less margin for error in lending, liability management, investment, and other bank operations. This financial risk is reflected in the variability of earnings per share (EPS). Table 12.4 gives an example of the effect of financial risk on EPS. It is clear from the results there that greater use of debt (i.e., financial

TABLE 12.4
FINANCIAL RISK AND VARIABILITY OF EARNINGS PER SHARE (EPS)

	(in thousands of dollars)					
	Low Debt			*High Debt*		
	Bad	*Ex- pected*	*Good*	*Bad*	*Ex- pected*	*Good*
Net earnings before interest expenses	$9,000	$10,000	$11,000	$9,000	$10,000	$11,000
Interest expenses	(7,000)	(7,000)	(7,000)	(9,000)	(9,000)	(9,000)
Net earnings	2,000	3,000	4,000	–0–	1,000	2,000
Taxes (@ 40%)	(800)	(1,200)	(1,600)	–0–	(400)	(800)
Earnings after taxes	$1,200	$ 1,800	$ 2,400	–0–	$ 600	$ 1,200
	Common shares outstanding = 1 million					
Earnings per share (EPS)	$1.20	$1.80	$2.40	$0	$.60	$1.20
Percentage change in net earnings before interest expenses relative to expected outcome	−10%	0%	+10%	− 10%	0%	+ 10%
Percentage change in EPS relative to expected outcome	−33%	0%	+33%	−100%	0%	+100%

leverage) causes the percentage change, or variability, of EPS to increase. The relationship between debt usage and EPS variability can be written simply as:

$$\% \text{ change in EPS} = \% \text{ change in EBIT} \times \frac{\text{EBIT}}{\text{EBIT} - \text{Interest}} \qquad (12.2)$$

where EBIT equals net operating earnings before interest expenses.

Although shareholders must bear more variation in earnings if they use greater financial leverage, tax deductions on interest payments lower the costs of making loans. For example, suppose debt and equity rates were equal to 10 percent (after adjusting for risk differences) and the bank's marginal tax rate was 40 percent. The after-tax cost of debt to the bank would be only 6 percent because of the tax deductibility of interest expenses (i.e., $10\% \times [1 - .40]$). The relatively lower cost of debt compared to equity on an after-tax basis tends to cause a preference for debt financing by shareholders.

In nonfinancial corporate enterprises, shareholders cannot necessarily increase their wealth by using debt to obtain tax deductions beyond some leverage point. As compensation for the increased probability that the firm will be unable to pay the higher debt load, debt claimants can be expected to raise the required interest rate that the firm must pay. Also, debtors may place limits on the extent to which corporations can borrow in the future, as well as on the kinds of debt that can be used. At some level of financial leverage, the tax gains on leverage are offset by higher interest payments and restrictions on debt usage.

In banking, however, because of deposit insurance, the debt usage of shareholders normally is not limited by debtors, who generally are bank depositors. Depositors of insured banks generally do not require a higher rate of interest depending on the bank's leverage, nor do they place restrictions on the issuance of new debt. In the absence of these forms of market discipline, regulators must control bank leverage by setting standards and imposing compliance costs on banks that violate these standards. Thus, bank capital structure is determined by the interaction between shareholder preferences for low-cost deposits and regulatory barriers that constrain the use of leverage.

Ownership Control

Another reason that shareholders might prefer to use debt rather than equity to finance bank assets is to avoid dilution of ownership. Use of equity to finance assets, for example, increases the number of shares of common stock outstanding. If the expected future earnings of the bank are held constant (i.e., its asset size is unchanged), earnings per share decline as the number of outstanding shares increases. To overcome this problem, most shares are endowed with preemptive rights that enable owners to maintain their proportionate ownership of the firm's equity stock. With fewer owners, the bank can be controlled more easily by the remaining shareholders. Indeed, most small and medium-sized banks in the United States are said to be "closely held" by a small number of owners.

Management Control

It is possible that greater debt usage increases stockholders' control of management. In other words, ownership control tends to enhance management control. In closely-held banks, because the owners are often the executive officers, minimal conflicts of self-interest arise. In banks that are not closely held, however, it is possible that (for example) managers may make decisions to protect and enhance their careers at the expense of shareholders.

Although shareholder meetings should normally resolve conflicts of this kind, management might dominate such meetings under some circumstances.[4] For example, if equity ownership is diluted among a large number of owners, individual owners might view themselves as having a negligible effect on the outcome of stockholder meetings. Faced with the costs of collecting information necessary to vote intelligently on issues raised at meetings, many owners may opt out of bank control. This does not necessarily mean that bank managers can act imprudently. Poor performance will tend to stir interest among shareholders concerning management capability. Also, the bank may become a takeover target—that is, if its shares are undervalued, well-managed banks might seek to purchase a controlling interest in the bank and remove existing management. If shareholders finance bank assets with greater proportionate amounts of debt, individual owners have a greater vested interest in stockholder meetings and, therefore, management control is more easily achieved.[5]

Market Timing

Cyclical price movements in the debt and equity markets can affect bank financing decisions. If the level of interest rates is relatively high and debt prices are depressed, it may be cheaper to use equity financing, even accounting for the tax deductibility of interest. Thus, general market conditions may at times favor equity over debt. Alternatively, if inflation is expected to increase in the near future, debt may be preferred over equity because interest payments could be made in "cheaper" dollars (due to the decline in the nominal value of currency).

Bank income can also affect debt usage by banks. For example, the marginal

[4] See Joseph E. Stiglitz, "Credit Markets and the Control of Capital," *Journal of Money, Credit, and Banking,* May 1985, pp. 133–152.

[5] For banks using large amounts of nondeposit liabilities, it is possible that the degree of financial leverage employed by shareholders could be limited. Uninsured debtholders seeking to protect their claims from new debtholders' claims as well as from potential bankruptcy costs incurred in failure can be expected to require debt covenants that place an upper bound on bank leverage. To the extent that this occurs, concentration of ownership would tend to be reduced, as well as the associated control of bank management by shareholders.

tax rate of the bank may be sufficiently low to warrant the use of equity over debt. This might occur because of considerable income earned from municipal bonds not exposed to ordinary income taxes, loan losses, depreciation, and other noncash expenses. Alternatively, marginal tax rates may decline because of low net operating income.

Asset Investment Considerations

Bank asset and capitalization decisions are interrelated to some extent. For example, under the Garn Bill of 1982 banks can lend no more than 15 percent of their capital, plus an additional 10 percent of loans secured by marketable collateral, to any individual borrower (i.e., the previous limitation was 10 percent of capital). Restrictions also exist on the purchase of various securities investments. Additionally, as asset risk increases, more bank capital is needed to absorb potential losses. By properly diversifying their portfolio of assets, banks can operate safely with less capital than would be required in the absence of diversification. Third, the proposed risk-based capital guidelines of regulators (see Table 12.3) plan to tie capital closely to the risks of different assets held by banks.

Dividend Policy

Shareholders usually desire the payment of some proportion of bank earnings in the form of cash dividends. This is because they either wish to consume part of their investment income or because they want to diversify their investment holdings. Most owners also want regular and predictable dividend payments. A sudden decrease in dividends would likely raise questions among shareholders concerning the bank's profitability and cause share prices to decline. Thus, bank management should establish and maintain a dividend policy.

In developing a dividend policy, the bank needs to determine its payment strategy. One strategy is to use fixed dividend payments. This strategy satisfies shareholder demands for consistent returns, but if earnings decline, this approach may force the bank to raise external debt and equity to finance operations, regardless of their costs. Alternatively, a fixed payout ratio strategy could be implemented, which means that a specific percentage of net income is distributed to owners. This strategy does not constrain the bank's financing choices as much as the fixed dividend strategy; however, it causes dividends to vary with net income over time.

Unfortunately, considerable controversy surrounds the question of why shareholders wish to receive income in the form of dividends instead of capital gains. If shareholders sold shares of stock to consume income or diversify more fully, they could do so when they wished to rather than when the firm distributed dividends. Also, receiving income in capital gains form defers income taxes until such gains are realized, which is a clear advantage relative to receiving periodic dividends. Despite these (and perhaps other) disadvantages of dividends, it is generally true that a sizable proportion of earnings is paid out as dividends to shareholders. A long-standing rationale for this is that individuals simply prefer to receive cash returns sooner rather than later because of risk aversion concerning uncertainty in the future. Alternatively, some individuals may prefer the convenience of regular dividends, which involve no transactions costs. In general, differences in individuals' preferences cause "clienteles" to exist, which firms attempt to attract by setting dividend policy appropriately. A more recent argument is that firms pay dividends as a way to signal shareholders of expected future changes in earnings. Obviously, the "optimal" dividend policy in the sense of maximizing share price remains somewhat of a puzzle.

Debt Capacity

It is generally preferable to avoid using the maximum amount of debt possible in order to increase financial flexibility. If a bank borrowed to the limit of capital regulations, for example, it may be unable to take advantage of an unexpected investment opportunity. Also, some amount of borrowing capacity provides slack that can be used to meet unanticipated liquidity problems. Thus, some amount of debt capacity is desirable as a reserve to help cover potential cash shortages.

Transactions Costs

Costs of issuing securities can affect bank financing plans. The acquisition of debt is normally much more costly for nonfinancial corporations than it is for banking institutions. Banks have easier access to credit markets than do nonfinancial firms, mainly because of their intermediary role as depository institutions and their access to insured deposits.

In contrast to most nonfinancial firms, however, all but the largest banks would find the transactions costs of equity issues relatively high. This is because bank issues of equity stock are smaller on average than nonfinancial, corporate issues. Transactions costs, including registration with the Securities and Exchange Commission (SEC), underwriting expenses, legal fees, and other expenses, have a large fixed component that raises the per-share cost of smaller issues. Thus, scale economies in transactions costs make public offerings of equity fairly expensive for most banks. To sidestep the costs of public offering, many banks use private sales to raise new equity capital. No SEC registration is required and underwriter fees can be avoided in a private issue of stock.

Mergers and Acquisitions

External growth through mergers and acquisitions generally requires raising new capital to purchase a controlling equity interest in the target institution(s). The mix of debt and equity used to finance external growth is complicated by the existing capital structures of the bank itself and the target institution(s). The consolidated banking organization must meet regulatory capital requirements, be consistent with the desires of the acquiring (and possibly the target) shareholders, and fulfill other management criteria previously discussed. For example, a common-for-common exchange in an acquisition would dilute the earnings per share of the acquirer, if the acquiree's stock had a relatively higher price/earnings ratio. If an acquirer could use excess debt capacity plus cash to purchase the acquiree's shares, however, no dilution of earnings per share would occur.[6] Obviously, capital decisions for the purpose of external expansion are quite complex, so many banks hire professional specialists to obtain consulting advice.

On the other hand, banks anticipating a takeover attempt by another institution may repurchase equity. By repurchasing equity and increasing concentration of ownership, the ability of outsiders to seize voting control through buying publicly available shares (known as a "hostile takeover") is mitigated. However, such a capital strategy could compromise other factors influencing the capital position of the bank, such as excessive financial risk due to higher leverage.

Internal Expansion

The rate at which a bank can internally expand its assets and still maintain its capital ratio is known as the internal capital generalization rate (ICR). This rate can be calculated as follows:

$$
\begin{array}{c} \text{Internal} \\ \text{Capitalization} \\ \text{Rate (ICR)} \end{array} = \frac{1}{\begin{array}{c}\text{Capital}\\\text{ratio}\end{array}} \times \begin{array}{c}\text{Return}\\\text{on}\\\text{assets}\end{array} \times \begin{array}{c}\text{Earnings}\\\text{retention}\\\text{ratio}\end{array} \qquad (12.3)
$$

where the capital ratio = total equity/total assets, return on assets = net income after taxes/total assets, and earnings retention ratio = net income available to shareholders minus preferred and common stock dividends/net income available to shareholders.

According to the ICR ratio, decreasing the capital ratio allows a more rapid expansion of bank assets.[7] Conversely, higher capital requirements force banks to *earn* their growth by using internally generated profits to expand assets size, as opposed to *borrowing* their growth by purchasing debt in the market. Management's approach to finance asset growth is a function of regulatory rules concerning capital adequacy, competitive pressures, financial market conditions, and various internal factors (such as shareholder preferences for debt).

---

[6] If capital requirements are binding (or exceed unregulated capital levels), it follows that those banks with strong capital positions and excess debt capacity will be better able to take advantage of geographical deregulation in the near future.

[7] We should add here that higher capital requirements are favored for this same reason (i.e., rapid rates of growth increase the risk of bank failure according to historical evidence).

TRENDS IN BANK CAPITAL

Table 12.5 shows the trends in the ratio of equity capital to total assets for all insured U.S. commercial banks during the period 1970 to 1986. In the early 1970s, capital ratios declined from about 6.5 to below 6 percent and remained there more or less until 1982. Probably in response to the new uniform capital guidelines initiated in December 1981, capital ratios increased in 1982 to about 7 percent in 1983. Since 1984 capital ratios have gradually declined to the low 6 percent range.

TABLE 12.5
EQUITY CAPITAL RATIOS AND CAPITAL AND ASSET GROWTH RATIOS
OVER TIME FOR ALL INSURED U.S. COMMERCIAL BANKS

Year	Ratio of Equity Capital to Total Assets	Growth in Equity Capital	Growth in Total Assets
1970	6.58%	7.8%	10.8%
1971	6.32	8.6	13.0
1972	5.95	10.0	16.8
1973	5.67	10.9	16.5
1974	5.65	10.0	10.4
1975	5.87	8.8	4.7
1976	6.11^a	12.4^a	8.0
1977	5.92	9.7	13.3
1978	5.80	10.3	12.6
1979	5.75	11.2	12.2
1980	5.80	10.6	9.7
1981	5.83	10.0	3.3
1982	6.98	7.6	8.7
1983	7.32	13.9	7.1
1984	6.46	−5.5	8.7
1985	6.37	7.2	13.9
1986	6.26	12.0	14.3

Source. Consolidated Reports of Condition, *Federal Reserve Bulletin,* Board of Governors of the Federal Reserve System: Washington, DC, selected issues.

^{a} Figures may have been affected by an accounting change in the measurement of equity capital in 1976.

Table 12.5 also shows the growth rates of equity capital and total assets over time. These two growth rates follow one another for the most part. This strong association highlights the fact that bank asset growth is constrained by equity capital growth. As an example, if a bank sought to increase its size by 10 percent, it would have to raise capital by 10 percent to maintain the same capital ratio. Thus, a bank's ability to increase capital directly affects its ability to expand its asset base.

TABLE 12.6

AVERAGE INTERNAL CAPITAL GENERATION RATE FOR ALL INSURED U.S. COMMERCIAL BANKS[a]

Ratios	1978	1979	1980	1981	1982	1983	1984	1985	1986
1/Capital Ratio	16.70	17.13	17.11	17.02	16.97	16.76	16.26	16.11	16.10
Return on Assets	0.77%	0.81%	0.80%	0.77%	0.71%	0.67%	0.63%	0.67%	0.61%
Earnings Retention Rate	.65	.65	.64	.61	.56	.51	.52	.53	.57
Internal Capital Generation Rate	8.36%	9.02%	8.76%	7.99%	6.75%	5.73%	5.33%	5.72%	5.60%

[a] Based on consolidated Reports of Income and Condition published by the Federal Deposit Insurance Corporation.

Table 12.6 shows the average internal capital generation rate for all insured U.S. commercial banks for the years 1978 to 1986. As indicated there, this rate declined sharply from 8.76 percent in 1980 to 7.99 percent in 1981 and continued to decline until 1984, after which it has risen somewhat. Lower returns on assets and lower retention rates (as banks tended to maintain dividend levels despite earnings declines) explain most of this downward trend. Thus, in general, the rate at which banks can grow without decreasing their capital ratios declined significantly in the 1980s compared with the recent past.

Historically, there have been considerable differences in the capital ratios of small and large banks. Table 12.7 shows primary capital ratios for banks grouped into six asset categories. Notice that, as asset size decreases, capital ratios rise. The main reason for these differences has been capital regulation. However, current uniform guidelines adopted in December 1981 have tended to decrease differences in capital ratios between large and small banks.

TABLE 12.7

PRIMARY CAPITAL/TOTAL ASSETS FOR DIFFERENT SIZES OF COMMERCIAL BANKS

Asset Size	1982	1983	1984	1985	1986
Under $25 million	10.24%	10.39%	10.58%	10.62%	10.43%
$25–100 million	8.80	8.72	8.78	8.93	8.90
$100–300 million	7.95	7.86	7.90	8.00	8.03
$300 million–$1 billion	7.37	7.22	7.38	7.73	7.53
$1–5 billion	6.37	6.31	6.51	6.71	6.99
Over $5 billion	4.94	5.31	6.10	5.97	6.20
All banks	6.47%	6.59%	6.98%	6.97%	7.07%

Source. Ross Waldrop, "Commercial Bank Performance in 1986," *Banking and Economic Review,* Federal Deposit Insurance Corporation, March/April 1987.

SUMMARY

Bank capital management is a controversial subject because regulators and shareholders have differing viewpoints concerning the adequacy of capital. Regulators consider bank capital as a cushion to absorb operating losses. Bank capital for regulatory purposes has two components: primary capital and secondary capital. Uniform federal capital guidelines effective in 1981 have caused many large banks with inadequate capital to decrease their holdings of liquid assets and resort to off-balance sheet activities that are not subject to the guidelines. Because evidence has indicated that bank failures historically have not been related to capitalization, and that bank risk is the main cause of failure, federal regulators have recently proposed that risk-based capital requirements be used in the future.

Shareholders view capitalization (or the mix of debt and equity funds used to finance the bank's assets) from the standpoint of maximizing the value of their ownership claims. Although added debt increases the interest burden of the bank and also increases the probability of failure, the tax deductibility of interest expenses lowers the cost of debt financing relative to equity financing. Whereas in nonfinancial, corporate enterprises debtors would require higher interest rates as financial leverage increases (or would impose limitations on corporate borrowing), banks obtain a large proportion of their funds from federally insured depositors, who are not exposed to default risk and, therefore, do not monitor bank borrowing. As such, regulatory requirements are the main limitations on borrowing faced by banks. Given the regulatory requirements on capital adequacy, bank shareholders need to consider the following areas in making capital structure decisions: (1) financial risk, (2) ownership control, (3) management control, (4) market timing, (5) asset investment considerations, (6) dividend policy, (7) transactions costs, (8) mergers and acquisitions, and (9) internal expansion.

IMPORTANT CONCEPTS

bank capital	equity commitment notes
bank equity	FABC
book value of equity	FDIC
capital adequacy	financial leverage
capital impairment	fixed dividend payment strategy
capital reserves	fixed dividend payout ratio strategy
common stock	FRB
contingency reserves	hostile takeover
deferred tax reserves	intangible assets
DINB	internal capital generalization ratio
EPS	International Lending Supervision Act

limited-life preferred stock

mandatory convertible instruments

market value of equity

minority interest in consolidated
subsidiaries

OCC

perpetual preferred stock

preemptive right

primary capital

private stock issue

provision for loan losses (PLL)

risk asset ratio

SEC

secondary capital

subordinated notes and debentures

subordination

surplus

total capital

undivided profits

REFERENCES

Avery, Robert B., and Terrence M. Belton. "A Comparison of Risk-Based Capital and Risk-Based Deposit Insurance," *Economic Review,* Federal Reserve Bank of Cleveland, fourth quarter 1987, pp. 20–30.

Buser, Stephen A., Andrew H. Chen, and Edward J. Kane. "Federal Deposit Insurance, Regulatory Policy, and Optimal Capital Structure," *Journal of Finance,* March 1981, pp. 51–60.

Chessen, James. "Risk-Based Capital Comes to the Fore," *Issues in Bank Regulation,* Spring 1987, pp. 3–15.

Gilbert, R. Alton, Courtenay C. Stone, and Michael E. Trebing. "The New Capital Adequacy Standards," *Review,* Federal Reserve Bank of St. Louis, May 1985, pp. 14–15.

Lash, Nicholas A. *Banking Laws and Regulations: An Economic Perspective,* Englewood Cliffs, NJ: Prentice-Hall, 1987.

Mitchell, Karlyn. "Capital Adequacy at Commercial Banks," *Economic Review,* Federal Reserve Bank of Kansas City, September/October 1984, pp. 17–30.

Moulton, Janice M. "New Guidelines for Bank Capital: An Attempt to Reflect Risk," *Business Review,* Federal Reserve Bank of Philadelphia, July/August 1987, pp. 19–33.

Stiglitz, Joseph E. "Credit Markets and the Control of Capital," *Journal of Money, Credit, and Banking,* May 1985, pp. 133–152.

Talley, Samuel H. *Bank Capital Trends and Financing,* Staff Study No. 122, Board of Governors of the Federal Reserve System, Washington, DC, February 1983.

Waldrop, Ross. "Commercial Bank Performance in 1986," *Banking and Economic Review,* Federal Deposit Insurance Corporation, March/April 1987, pp. 11–18.

QUESTIONS

12.1. Define bank capital. Why are reserves to cover losses on loans counted as capital?

12.2. Is the balance sheet an accurate source of information in calculating bank capital?

12.3. What are the two key functions of bank capital?

12.4. Why are notes and debentures considered bank capital?

12.5. What are the major causes of bank failure according to historical evidence?

12.6. How much capital is "adequate?"

12.7. Why is measuring adequate capital from a regulatory viewpoint so difficult?

12.8. Define primary and secondary capital. Why make this distinction?

12.9. Explain the problems of using uniform capital requirements.

12.10. Why has there been a switch to risk-based capital requirements?

12.11. How would a risk-based capital requirement be calculated?

12.12. What five options does the FDIC have in handling a distressed bank?

12.13. What changes is the FDIC considering in regard to its deposit insurance system? How might market discipline supplement deposit insurance pricing to control bank risk?

12.14. What are the advantages of debt finance to bank shareholders?

12.15. What are the disadvantages of debt finance to bank shareholders?

12.16. Why are the capital ratios of small and large banks different? Will this change in the future?

12.17. What is the PLL account? How is it calculated for small and large banks? How does it differ from the allowance for possible loan losses?

PROBLEMS

12.1. Given the following information, calculate primary and secondary capital:

	(in thousands)
Common stock	$ 30,000
Perpetual preferred stock	5,000
Surplus	2,000
Undivided profits	100,000
Capital reserves	1,000
Reserves for loan and lease losses	5,000
Intangible assets	1,000
Subordinated notes and debentures	2,000

If the bank has total assets (in thousands) of $2,840,000, does it have adequate capital under 1985 regulatory standards?

12.2. Given the following information, calculate the risk asset ratio measure of capital adequacy:

	(in thousands)
Vault cash	$ 5
Cash balances at district Federal Reserve Bank	10
U.S. government securities	25
Repurchase agreements	30
Federal funds	20
Corporate bonds	10
Municipal bonds	80
Home loans	100
All other loans	800

Also given is that primary capital equals $80,000 and intangible assets equal $5,000.

12.3. Suppose Bank One has earnings before interest and taxes (EBIT) equal to $10 million and interest expenses equal to $8 million. There are 1 million shares of common stock outstanding. If EBIT increased by 10 percent, what would be the percentage change in earnings per share (EPS)?

12.4. Calculate the internal capitalization rate using the following information:

Net income	$ 100
Dividends	40
Total equity	800
Total assets	10,200

What does this rate mean to the bank?

If the regulatory standard for capital was 7 percent, what is the maximum asset growth rate implied for the bank?

How would a higher capital standard affect the bank's asset growth?

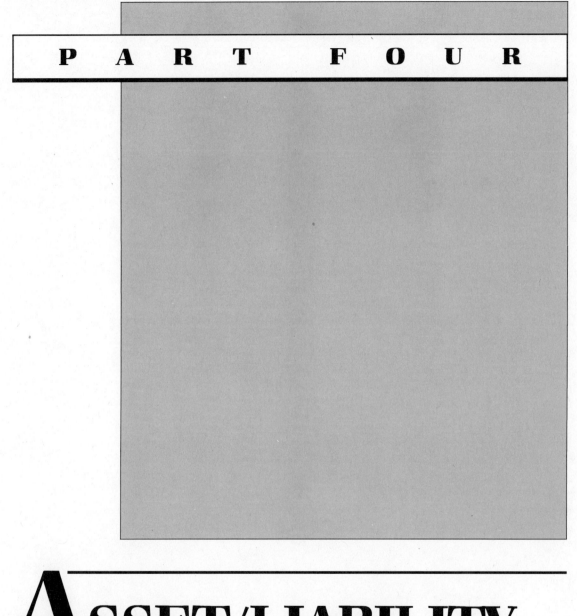

ASSET/LIABILITY MANAGEMENT

CHAPTER THIRTEEN

AN OVERVIEW OF ASSET/LIABILITY MANAGEMENT

The previous chapters have dealt with the management of specific components of the balance sheet of commercial banks, including the management of securities and the loan portfolio. Although effective management of each of these balance sheet components is necessary for the financial institution to achieve its goals, it is vitally important that the management of the components is coordinated so that they jointly contribute to the goals of the organization. Overall, coordinated management of the entire portfolio of a financial institution is referred to as asset/liability management and is normally placed under the control of the asset/liability management committee (ALCO).

Asset/liability management is an integral part of the planning process of commercial banks and other financial institutions. In fact, asset/liability management may be considered as one of the three principal components of a planning system. Asset/liability management is generally viewed as short-run in nature, focusing on the day-to-day and week-to-week balance sheet management necessary to achieve near-term financial goals. Slightly longer term, annual profit planning and control looks at a detailed financial plan over the course of a fiscal or calendar year. Finally, as the third component of the planning process, strategic planning focuses on the long-run financial and nonfinancial dimensions of the institution's performance. Annual profit planning and long-run strategic planning provide a framework for the formulation and implementation of short-run asset/liability management.

Perhaps the best way to understand the role of asset/liability management is to view it within the context of the overall sources and uses of funds. As shown in Figure 13.1, banks draw their funds from a variety of different sources and allocate those funds to a number of different uses. Funds are obtained from transactions deposits (demand deposits, NOW accounts, and Super NOW accounts), savings deposits, time deposits (both consumer certificates of deposits and large, "jumbo" CDs), short-term borrowings such as federal funds' borrowings, longer-term borrowings such as through selling subordinated notes and debentures, and equity capital. The average cost of funds and their stability will be determined by the mix of sources chosen by management.

From this pool of funds, bank management must make choices about acquiring assets that serve the needs of the bank for meeting legal requirements, earning income, and providing liquidity. Reserve requirements imposed by the Federal Reserve must, of course, be met prior to purchasing earning assets; although, as discussed earlier, reserve requirements must be met only on a daily average basis. The amount of investable funds, therefore, is the amount of total sources less the amount that must be held in the form of noninterest-

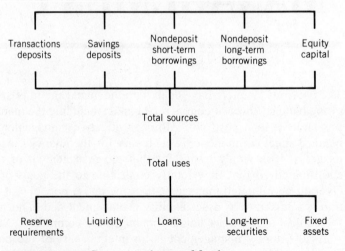

FIGURE 13.1   Sources and uses of funds.

earning vault cash and deposits at the Federal Reserve. These funds may then be invested to produce liquidity, which could mean acquiring short-term assets such as treasury bills or selling funds in the overnight interbank market (i.e., the federal funds market). Funds available after meeting reserve requirements and liquidity needs can then be invested to produce income for the bank. Both loans and longer-term securities provide income, although the amount of income per dollar invested and the liquidity characteristics vary. Of course, banks must also make decisions about commitments of funds to fixed assets such as buildings, computer equipment, and other "real" rather than financial assets.

The flexibility of managing the sources and uses of funds varies considerably depending upon the time horizon of management. In the short run, the number of different sources and uses that may be changed in order to achieve the objectives of the bank are relatively limited. The amount of funds available from transactions deposits, savings deposits, and small consumer certificates of deposit is not subject to change quickly. Similarly, shifting the loan portfolio and even much of the longer-term securities portfolio is difficult in the short run. Over a more extended period, the flexibility available to management is increased, although long-run portfolio management may more properly be considered within the context of strategic planning than traditional asset/liability management.

THE FOCUS OF ASSET/LIABILITY MANAGEMENT

Asset/liability management focuses on the net interest income of the institution. Net interest income is the difference between the dollar amount of interest received from loans and investments and the dollar amount of the interest paid for deposits and other liabilities, as shown in equation (13.1).

$$\text{Net interest Income} = \$ \frac{\text{Interest}}{\text{revenue}} - \$ \frac{\text{Interest}}{\text{expense}} \qquad (13.1)$$

This difference between the total dollar interest revenue and the total dollar interest expense is referred to as the dollar net interest income. Expressing this dollar amount as a percentage of earning assets allows us to express the net interest income as a percent or margin. Total dollar net interest income obviously is not comparable between institutions of substantially different size, whereas net interest margin (expressed as a percentage) may be meaningfully compared among institutions.

This equation can be rewritten as equation (13.2)

$$\text{Net interest margin} = \frac{\text{Net interest income}}{\text{Earning assets}} \qquad (13.2)$$

or as equation (13.3)

$$\text{Net interest margin} = \text{Interest yield (percent)} \\ - \text{Interest cost (percent)}$$

(13.3)

Net interest margins vary substantially for banks of different sizes, as shown in Table 13.1. Smaller banks (those with total assets under $100 million) traditionally have enjoyed larger (in fact, considerably larger) net interest margins than the money center banks or other banks with total assets over $1 billion. As shown in Table 13.1, in 1985, the smallest size group of banks had net interest margins that averaged 4.74 percent, whereas the nine money center banks had net interest margins that averaged only 2.93 percent. These differences depend, to a considerable extent, on the different markets from which small and large banks draw their funds and on differences in the rates paid for funds and earned on loans. Smaller banks historically have been able to gather funds at lower cost and earn more on their loan portfolios. However, with the elimination of deposit-rate ceilings and with the increase in competition in both deposit and loan markets, the gap between net interest margin at small and large banks has narrowed. Net interest margins have declined at the smaller banks, making improved asset/liability management particularly important for those banks.

ASSET/LIABILITY MANAGEMENT IN HISTORICAL PERSPECTIVE

Coordinated asset/liability management is a relatively recent phenomenon. From the end of World War II until the early 1960s, most commercial banks obtained their funds from relatively stable (and interest-free) demand deposits and from small time deposits. Interest rate ceilings (Regulation Q) limited the extent to which banks could compete for funds. Opening more branches (where permissible by law) in order to attract funds through greater customer conven-

TABLE 13.1

NET INTEREST MARGIN FOR U.S. INSURED COMMERCIAL BANKS (PERCENT) 1981–1985

Type of Bank	Year				
	1981	1982	1983	1984	1985
All insured commercial banks	3.53	3.66	3.60	3.73	3.88
Banks with less than $100 million in total assets	4.93	4.96	4.82	4.66	4.74
Banks with $100 million to $1 billion in total assets	4.46	4.53	4.42	4.42	4.55
Nine money center banks	2.25	2.49	2.53	2.83	2.93
Large banks other than money center banks	3.31	3.42	3.35	3.56	3.80

Source. Federal Reserve *Bulletin.*

ience or committing more funds to the advertising budget was one of the few ways to attract more funds. As a result, most sources of funds were "core" deposits (not sensitive to interest rates), which increased with the growth of the national and local economy. Moreover, the volatility of interest rates was quite small. In this environment, bank funds management concentrated on the control of assets. Bank financial management principally was *asset* management. Liability management as it is known today did not exist.

During the 1960s, especially after the Vietnam War became a significant economic and political event in 1966, the demand for bank loans accelerated. The growth in loan demand pressed upon the ability of commercial banks to fund the loans from existing deposit sources. As a result, banks sought to expand faster than their core deposit growth would allow by reaching out for additional funds. As they did this, liability management was created. With liability management, commercial banks bought funds from the financial markets whenever necessary—either to meet loan demand, to purchase securities, or to replace reductions in other sources of their funds. The management of liabilities then became an active part of bank financial management.

Liability management could be accomplished with any sources of funds that were available from the financial markets, provided that Regulation Q did not constrain the bank from offering market rates to attract funds. Since (especially during the 1970s) deposit rate ceilings as established by Regulation Q limited banks to offering noncompetitive interest rates for many of their deposits, liability management, or purchased money as the process is sometimes known, concentrated on *non*deposit sources that were not subject to Regulation Q. The purchase of funds in the interbank or federal funds market represents perhaps the most widely used source of funds for liability management. Many large banks used the Eurodollar market extensively for funds, however. In addition, during periods when market rates of interest were below Regulation Q ceilings (or when the regulations lifted those ceilings), banks were able to rely upon deposit sources in their liability management.

Liability management fundamentally changed the asset/liability problem facing commercial bank management. With liability management, banks had two sources of funds—core deposits and purchased funds—with quite different characteristics. These differences are illustrated in Figure 13.2. Section (*a*) shows that, for core deposits, the volume of funds is relatively insensitive to changes in interest rate levels; that is, the demand for core deposits by bank customers is relatively interest inelastic. From the perspective of bank management, core deposits offer the advantage of stability. Within relatively large variations in interest rate levels, the amount of core deposits does not change greatly. However, core deposits have the disadvantage of not being overly responsive to management needs for expansion. If the bank experiences a sizable increase in loan demand, it cannot expect to fund the loan growth with core deposits.

For purchased funds, however, as shown Figure 13.2*b*, the bank can obtain all the funds that it wants (within some reasonable limit) if it is willing to pay the

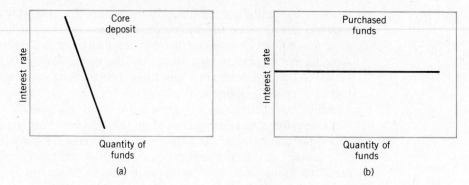

FIGURE 13.2   Interest elasticity of core deposits and purchased funds.

market-determined price. Unlike core deposits, where the bank determines the price, the interest rates on purchased funds are set in the national money market. The bank is a price taker in the purchased funds market, whereas it is a price setter in the core deposit market. The purchased money market gives the bank flexibility in the amount of funds available, with the bank able to raise whatever funds it wants in order to fund its loan demand (provided that interest rate ceilings do not constrain it). However, the purchased money market has two significant risks that the core deposit market does not have. First, the interest rate may be highly volatile, with the demand curve shown in Figure 13.2*b* shifting upward or downward frequently and sometimes by large amounts. Second, purchased money may be unavailable for banks perceived to be in financial difficulty. This availability risk is particularly significant for banks that finance a large share of their assets with purchased money. Any perception that the quality of the assets is poor may cause the demand curve in Figure 13.2*b* to disappear. Then the bank would shift, perhaps overnight, from a position in which it could raise almost unlimited funds at the going market interest rate to that in which it could raise no funds. Given that most purchased money sources of funds are short term, often overnight, the change in funds' availability can quickly cause a crisis that may, in an extreme situation, cause the bank to fail. Continental Illinois faced this situation in 1984 and had to be rescued by a joint effort of the bank regulatory agencies.

Liability management became the dominant method of funding asset/liabilities needs (especially for large banks) in the 1970s. Many banks significantly reduced their liquid assets and depended almost entirely on purchased funds. With highly unstable interest rates in the early 1980s, and with financial distress and failure felt by a large number of banks, many banks have moved away from exclusive reliance on liability management. Management of the bank's portfolio today thus involves managing both assets and liabilities.

THE INFLUENCE OF RATE, VOLUME, AND MIX

Changes in net interest income are the principal determinants of the ultimate profitability of banks. Net interest income itself is basically determined by (1) the interest rates earned on assets and paid for funds, (2) the volume of funds, and (3) the mix of funds (also referred to as portfolio composition). Other things equal, an increase in the interest rates earned on assets will increase the net interest income, whereas an increase in the interest rate paid on funding sources will reduce net interest income. Other things equal, an increase in the volume of funds raised and invested (e.g., by doubling the size of the bank) will increase net interest income (note that it may not change the net interest margin). Also, other things equal, a shift toward more higher yielding assets or less costly sources of funds will increase net interest income. Other things are seldom constant, however. Hence, changes in net interest income usually reflect changes in each of these three factors.

In order to isolate the effects of one of the factors that influences the net interest income, it is necessary to hold all the other factors constant. For example, if the concern involves determining the effects of interest rate changes, then the impact of volume and mix (i.e., portfolio composition) must be held constant. The effect of interest rate changes can be determined by estimating the amount of revenue that would have been earned (paid) in the period under consideration with the same volume of assets and the same mix of assets (and liabilities if the concern is with interest paid) in the earlier period. Similarly, the volume variable is computed by holding the earning asset mix and interest rates constant and varying the volume of the assets (and liabilities). The mix variance is, in a sense, the residual change in net interest income due after the changes caused by volume and rate have been accounted for, and reflects changes in the mixes of sources and uses of funds, or in the composition of the portfolio.

Table 13.2 provides an interest variance analysis for a hypothetical bank. From 198X-1 to 198X, net interest income increased by $123,170,000. This increase in net interest income was the result of a $146,962,000 increase in total interest income, which more than offset a $23,792,000 increase in total interest expense. But why did total interest income grow more rapidly than total interest expense? Was it because of interest rate changes or asset growth? In fact, as Table 13.2 shows, the expansion was due entirely to volume growth. If the total assets of the bank had remained the same, net interest income would have fallen.

Looking at the bottom of Table 13.2, the increase in net interest income due to volume expansion was $150,124,000, more than fully accounting for the entire change in net interest income. Interest rates declined from 198X-1 to 198X, with interest revenue on assets (especially loans) falling more rapidly than interest revenue on liabilities. Also, a change in the mix of assets and liabilities contributed to a slight reduction in net interest income, principally

TABLE 13.2
INTEREST VARIANCE ANALYSIS

	198X vs. 198X-1 (in thousands)			
	Rate	Volume	Mix	Total
Interest Income				
Money market investments	$ (4,282)	$ 11,892	$(2,634)	$ 4,976
Investment securities	(8,876)	81,716	(5,492)	67,348
Loans	(126,668)	220,386	(19,080)	74,638
Total interest income	(148,946)	163,476	(31,044)	146,962
Interest Expense				
Interest-bearing deposits	(71,276)	113,940	(15,008)	27,656
Short-term borrowings	(43,232)	59,824	(10,404)	6,188
Long-term borrowings	(8,204)	(2,058)	210	(10,052)
Total interest expense	(127,196)	176,828	(25,840)	23,792
Net Interest Income	$(21,750)	$150,124	$(5,204)	$123,170

reflecting a decline in interest revenue due to a shift into loans on which interest revenue declined with falling open-market interest rates.

MEASURING INTEREST-RATE SENSITIVITY

GAP Analysis

The most commonly used measure of the interest sensitivity position of a financial institution is **GAP analysis.** Under this approach, all assets and liabilities are classified into two groups—interest-rate sensitive or noninterest-rate sensitive—according to whether their interest return (in the case of assets) or interest cost (in the case of liabilities) varies with the general level of interest rates. Note that the focus of gap analysis is on the **interest return or cost** of the asset or liability, not on the effect of interest rate changes on the capital value of the asset. Gap analysis essentially classifies assets or liabilities according to the following decision rule.

$$\text{Interest-rate sensitive assets} \quad r > 0$$
$$\text{Interest-rate nonsensitive assets } r = 0 \tag{13.4}$$

where r is the correlation coefficient between some index of market interest rates and the interest return or cost on the asset. In short, interest-rate sensitive assets (liabilities) are those whose interest revenues (costs) vary (are correlated with) interest-rate movements and noninterest-rate sensitive assets (liabilities) are those whose interest revenues (costs) do not vary (are not correlated with) interest-rate movements.

Classification of Assets and Liabilities

Table 13.3 illustrates the classification of the assets and liabilities of a financial institution according to their interest-rate sensitivity. Those assets and liabilities whose interest return or costs vary with interest rate changes over some given time horizon are referred to as rate-sensitive assets (RSA) or rate-sensitive liabilities (or RSL). Those assets and liabilities whose interest return or costs *do not* vary with interest-rate movements over the same time horizon are referred to as nonrate-sensitive (NRS). (Another way of explaining this concept is with use of the term **repriceable.** Those assets and liabilities that reprice within the time horizon are rate sensitive.) Note that the selection of the time period over which to measure the interest sensitivity of the asset or liability is crucial. An asset or liability that is interest-rate sensitive in one time period may not be rate sensitive in a shorter time period. Over a sufficiently long time period virtually all assets and liabilities are interest-rate sensitive. As the time period (or planning horizon) is shortened, however, the ratio of rate-sensitive to nonrate-sensitive assets and liabilities falls. At some sufficiently short time period (1 day, for example) virtually all assets and liabilities are noninterest-rate sensitive.

In the classification of assets and liabilities used in Table 13.3, short-term securities and short-term deposits are those with a maturity of 1 year or less. Under this criterion, interest-rate sensitive assets are all those assets with a maturity of 1 year or less (short-term securities and short-term loans) *and* variable rate loans (assuming that the rates on those loans adjust with interest rate changes within a year). All other assets are noninterest-rate sensitive. Those include vault cash, long-term securities, long-term loans, and other assets. Interest-rate sensitive assets in Table 13.3 thus total $75 and noninterest-rate sensitive assets total $120. Hence, rising or falling interest rates will have relatively limited impact on the interest revenue for the financial institution.

TABLE 13.3
CLASSIFICATION OF ASSETS AND LIABILITIES BY INTEREST SENSITIVITY

Assets			*Liabilities and Capital*		
Vault cash	NRSA	$ 20	Demand deposits	NRSL	$ 5
Short-term securities	RSA	15	NOW accounts	NRSL	5
Long-term securities	NRSA	30	Money market deposits	RSL	20
Variable rate loans	RSA	40	Short-term savings	RSL	40
Short-term loans	RSA	20	Long-term savings	NRSL	60
Long-term loans	NRSA	60	Federal funds borrowings	RLS	55
Other assets	NRSA	10	Equity	NRS	10
		$195			$195

Note. NRSA = Nonrate-Sensitive Assets
  RSA   = Rate-Sensitive Assets
  NSRL = Nonrate-Sensitive Liabilities
  RSL   = Rate-Sensitive Liabilities

The total effect of any change in the general level of interest rates on the net interest income of a financial institution depends *both* on the effects on interest revenue *and* interest expense. The effect on interest expense depends, in turn, on the interest sensitivity of liabilities. In the example given in Table 13.3 interest-rate sensitive liabilities are short-term savings deposits, money market deposits (whose interest rates are generally adjusted each week), and federal fund borrowings (whose rates change daily with the federal fund rate). Noninterest-rate sensitive liabilities are demand deposits (whose interest rate is fixed at zero by federal law), NOW accounts (checking accounts that pay a positive interest rate but whose interest rate changes infrequently), and long-term savings, such as 3- or 4-year certificates of deposit. Interest-rate sensitive liabilities thus total $115, whereas noninterest-rate sensitive liabilities total $70. Hence, changes in interest rates will have a substantial impact on the interest costs of this institution.

Definition of the Gap

The total effect of interest rate changes on profitability can be summarized by its *gap*. The gap is the difference between the amount of interest-rate sensitive assets (RSAs) and interest-rate sensitive liabilities (RSLs). The gap may be expressed in a variety of ways. The simplest expression of the gap is the dollar gap, which as shown in equation (13.5) is simply the difference between the dollar amount of interest-rate sensitive assets and the dollar amount of interest-rate sensitive liabilities.

$$\text{Dollar GAP} = \text{RSA(\$)} - \text{RSL(\$)} \qquad (13.5)$$

Comparison of the interest sensitivity position of different financial institutions using the dollar gap is not meaningful because of differences in the size of the institutions. Such a comparison requires some type of "common size" gap measures. Those are as follows:

$$\text{Relative GAP ratio} = \frac{\text{GAP \$}}{\text{Total assets}} \qquad (13.6)$$

$$\text{Interest-rate sensitivity ratio} = \frac{\text{RSA \$}}{\text{RSL \$}} \qquad (13.7)$$

The relative gap ratio as given in equation (13.6) expresses the dollar volume of the gap (dollar RSAs − dollar RSLs) as a percentage of total assets. The interest-sensitivity ratio expresses the dollar volume of RSAs as a fraction of the dollar volume of RSLs.

TABLE 13.4
SUMMARY OF INTEREST-RATE SENSITIVITY
MEASURES

Asset Sensitive	
Dollar gap	Positive
Relative gap ratio	Positive
Interest-rate sensitivity ratio	>1
Liability Sensitive	
Dollar gap	Negative
Relative gap ratio	Negative
Interest-rate sensitivity ratio	<1

Asset and Liability Sensitivity

A financial institution at a given time may be **asset or liability sensitive.** If the financial institution were asset sensitive, it would have a positive gap, a positive relative gap ratio, and an interest-sensitivity ratio greater than 1. Conversely, an institution that was liability sensitive would have a negative gap, a negative relative gap ratio, and an interest-sensitivity ratio less than 1. (See Table 13.4).

Financial institutions that are asset sensitive will experience an increase in their net interest income when interest rates increase and a decrease in their net interest income when interest rates fall. In contrast, financial institutions that are liability sensitive will experience a decrease in their net interest income when interest rates increase and an increase in their net interest income when interest rates fall. The financial institution in Table 13.3 is liability sensitive. Because rising interest rates will raise the cost of its funding sources faster than the increase in interest earnings in its asset portfolio, the net interest income of the institution will drop with an increase in interest rates (although it would increase with a drop in interest rates).

Gap, Interest Rates, and Profitability

The effects of changing interest rates on net interest income with different gap positions is illustrated in equation (13.8).

$$E(\Delta \text{NII}) = \text{RSA\$}(\Delta i) - \text{RSA\$}E(\Delta i)$$
$$= \text{GAP \$} (\Delta i) \tag{13.8}$$

where $E(\Delta \text{NII})$ = expected change in the dollar amount of net interest income, and $E(\Delta i)$ = expected change in interest rates.

TABLE 13.5
GAP, INTEREST RATES, AND NET INTEREST INCOME

Gap	Change in Interest Rate	Change in Net Interest Income
Positive	Increase	Increase
Positive	Decrease	Decrease
Negative	Increase	Decrease
Negative	Decrease	Increase
Zero	Increase	Zero
Zero	Decrease	Zero

An example may help to illustrate the effects of changing interest rates on the net interest income of a financial institution. Suppose a financial institution has RSAs of $55 million and RSLs of $35 million, and thus has a GAP of $20 million. If interest rates were to rise from 8 to 10 percent, the net interest income of the institution would rise by $4 million. Of course, the effect of this interest rate change on net interest margin (which is net interest income divided by earning assets) depends upon the previous level of net interest income as well as the size of earning assets of the financial institution. Conversely, if RSAs of the institution were $35 million and RSLs were $55 million, the institution would have a negative gap and would be liability sensitive. An increase of 2 percentage points in interest rates would, in this situation, *lower* net interest income by $4 million.

The effects of changing interest rates on net interest income may be summarized as shown in Table 13.5. For commercial banks with a positive gap, net interest income will rise or fall as interest rates rise or fall. For banks with a negative gap, net interest income will rise or fall inversely with interest rate changes; that is, net interest income will increase with falling interest rates and fall with rising interest rates. In contrast, banks with a zero gap should experience no change in their net interest income because of changing interest rates.

Incremental and Cumulative Gaps

The gap between interest-rate sensitive assets and interest-rate sensitive liabilities may be measured either incrementally or in cumulative terms. The incremental gap measures the difference between rate-sensitive assets and rate-sensitive liabilities over increments of the planning horizon. The cumulative gap measures the difference between rate-sensitive assets and liabilities over a more extended period. The cumulative gap is the sum of the incremental gaps. Of course, if there is only one planning horizon, the incremental gap and the cumulative gap are the same.

Table 13.6 illustrates the calculation of incremental and cumulative gaps, with a 1-year planning horizon broken down into four increments: 0–30 days, 30–90 days, 90–180 days, and 180–365 days. Note that over the entire 365-day

TABLE 13.6
INCREMENTAL AND CUMULATIVE GAPS

	Assets Maturing Within or Repriceable Within	Liabilities Maturing Within or Repriceable Within	Incremental Gap	Cumulative Gap
0–30 days	$ 50	$ 30	+20	+20
30–90 days	25	20	+ 5	+25
90–180 days	0	20	−20	+ 5
180–365 days	0	5	− 5	0
	$ 75	$ 75		

period the bank has interest-sensitive assets equal to interest-sensitive liabilities; it is neither asset nor liability sensitive. However, the zero gap position over the entire 365-day period is somewhat misleading. For the first 30 days, the bank has a large (+20) positive gap. Even for the first 90 days, the bank has a positive incremental gap. The cumulative gap peaks at 90 days, and then begins to decline as the incremental gap is negative for the next two periods.

Most banks measure and manage their asset/liability position over more than one period, indicating the importance of incremental and cumulative gaps. This creates flexibility for management. For example, bank management may expect interest rates to rise sharply over the next 30 days, then level off, and then fall. The gap positions in Table 13.6 are consistent with this interest rate expectation.

The Gap at Major Banks

Table 13.7 shows the actual gap position at a number of major banks as of the last quarter of 1983 and the first three quarters of 1984. The gap is defined as interest-sensitive assets minus interest-sensitive liabilities. For purposes of the calculations in Table 13.6, interest-sensitive assets include all assets that are repriced within 1 year and comprise loans and leases, debt securities, and other interest-bearing assets. Interest-rate sensitive liabilities are all liabilities that are repriced within 1 year, and include time CDs of $100,000 or more, all other domestic time deposits, total deposits in foreign offices, money market deposit accounts, Super NOWs, and demand notes issued to the U.S. Treasury. A negative gap (interest-sensitive assets less interest-sensitive liabilities) indicates that the net interest income would decline as interest rates increased and rise as interest rates fell. In contrast, a positive gap (interest-sensitive assets greater than interest-sensitive liabilities) indicates that the net interest income would increase as interest rates increased and fall as interest rates declined.

As shown in Table 13.6, considerable variation existed at the major banks in the size of their gaps. The largest gap in the fourth quarter of 1983 was a

TABLE 13.7

RATE SENSITIVITY GAP AS A PERCENTAGE OF TOTAL ASSETS[a] (20 large banks)

	1983	1984		
	Fourth Quarter	First Quarter	Second Quarter	Third Quarter
Bank of America	−11.4	−10.5	−13.8	−12.1
Bank of New York	6.6	7.2	5.8	0.8
Bankers Trust Company	3.9	5.9	− 1.1	1.7
Chase Manhattan Bank	9.0	− 2.7	− 3.5	− 5.0
Chemical Bank	1.9	2.2	− 2.8	− 1.0
Citibank	− 1.8	− 3.1	− 2.9	− 3.6
First Interstate Bank, California	− 1.8	− 1.8	− 0.3	− 0.2
First National Bank of Boston	− 0.9	− 2.5	− 1.1	− 0.4
First National Bank of Chicago	− 4.1	− 9.0	− 6.9	− 8.6
Interfirst Bank, Dallas	− 4.2	− 5.3	− 2.5	− 5.0
Irving Trust Company	− 4.0	2.5	4.7	2.0
Manufacturers Hanover Trust Company	5.9	5.4	4.6	2.7
Marine Midland Bank	− 1.9	− 7.5	− 5.8	− 4.2
Mellon Bank	− 3.2	2.0	4.3	4.2
Morgan Guaranty Trust Company	− 2.4	− 1.4	− 0.7	− 4.0
National Bank of Detroit	0.8	− 0.2	0.7	1.0
North Carolina National Bank	− 2.1	3.2	2.2	2.2
RepublicBank, Dallas	2.4	3.6	1.2	2.1
Security Pacific National Bank	− 4.1	− 4.7	− 4.6	− 6.8
Wells Fargo Bank	− 1.9	− 5.7	− 5.9	− 4.9
Average	− 0.3	− 1.1	− 1.4	− 1.9

Source. Elijah Brewer, "Bank Gap Management and the Use of Financial Futures," Federal Reserve Bank of Chicago *Economic Perspectives,* March/April 1985, p. 14.

[a] One-year rate-sensitivity gap.

Rate-sensitive assets include all assets repricing or maturing within 1 year and comprise loans and leases, debt security, and other interest-bearing assets.

Rate-sensitive liabilities are all those liabilities scheduled to reprice or mature within 1 year and include domestic time CDs of $100,000 or more, all other domestic time deposits, total deposits in foreign offices, money market deposit accounts, Super NOWs, and demand notes issued to the U.S. Treasury.

negative 11.4 percent at Bank of America. In contrast, Chase Manhattan Bank had a positive 9.0-percent gap for that quarter.

Most banks maintained a consistent positive or negative gap during the four quarters shown in the table. For example, Bank of America had a negative gap throughout the period, as did Citibank, Morgan Guaranty Trust Company, Security Pacific National Bank, and Wells Fargo Bank. However, the size of the gap as a percentage of total assets generally was small. Few banks had gaps (positive or negative) that exceeded 10 percent. In fact, the gap at most banks was less than 5 percent. Limitations of the gap, of course, limit the influence of interest rate changes on the net interest margin.

ASSET/LIABILITY MANAGEMENT, INTEREST-RATE RISK, AND CREDIT RISK

The focus of asset/liability management is on interest-rate risk. As discussed in Chapter 1, however, bank management is concerned with managing the entire risk profile of the institution, including interest-rate risk, credit risk, liquidity risk, and other dimensions of risk. If those risks were unrelated (i.e., uncorrelated), then management could concentrate on one type of risk, making appropriate decisions, and ignoring the effects of those decisions on the other types of risk. However, there does appear to be considerable interrelationships between the different types of risk, with a particularly significant connection between interest rate and credit risk, especially if commercial banks use their loan portfolio as the principal vehicle to adjust their interest rate risk exposure.

A simple example may best illustrate the relationship between interest-rate risk and credit risk. Suppose, for example, that asset/liability management strategy concludes that the bank should increase its emphasis on variable rate loans. Suppose also that interest rates increase dramatically after a large amount of these loans has been made. Rising interest rates lead to higher payments for borrowers, especially if the loans are long term, such as home mortgages. The heavier cash outflow burden might reasonably be expected to produce a greater number of defaults in the bank's loan portfolio. The converse situation would arise if asset/liability strategy increased the emphasis on fixed rate loans and interest rates fell dramatically. Unless borrowers were able to refinance these loans at acceptable costs, the incidence of defaults would be likely to increase substantially. And even if refinancing were easy enough to reduce the default rate, the bank would still find its asset/liability management strategy thwarted because assets that were considered fixed rate would in fact be rate sensitive.

SUMMARY

Asset/liability management refers to short-run balance sheet management designed to achieve near-term financial goals. The focus of asset/liability management is generally on the net interest income defined as the difference between total dollar interest income and total dollar interest expense. Expressed in relative terms, the focus is on net interest margin, where net interest income is divided by the volume of earning assets. Active and aggressive asset/liability management is a relatively recent phenomenon and reflects the increase in volatility of interest rates, the elimination of interest rate ceilings on deposits, and the growth of purchased money (as opposed to "core" deposits).

Net interest income is affected by the interest rates earned on assets and paid on liabilities, by the volume of assets and liabilities, and by the mix of assets and liabilities. Changes in net interest income (and margin) from one period to the next may be partitioned into those caused by interest rate changes, those caused by changes in the volume of funds, and those caused by changes in the mix of assets and liabilities. Asset/liability management generally focuses on the effects of interest rate changes on net interest income.

The most commonly used measure of a bank's interest sensitivity position is its gap, defined as the difference between the volume of interest-sensitive assets and interest-sensitive liabilities. Interest-sensitive assets and liabilities are those whose interest earnings or costs change with the general movement of interest rates within some planning horizon. The focus of this analysis is on the profitability and costs of assets and liabilities rather than on the value of those assets and liabilities. If a bank has more interest-sensitive assets than liabilities, it is said to be asset sensitive and will usually experience an increase in net interest income as interest rates rise (and a decrease in net interest income as interest rates fall). If a bank has more interest-sensitive liabilities than interest-sensitive assets, it is said to be liability sensitive, and will usually experience a decline in net interest income when interest rates increase (and an increase in net interest income when interest rates fall).

IMPORTANT CONCEPTS

core deposits

cumulative GAP

income

incremental GAP

net interest income

net interest margin

purchased funds

non rate sensitive assets/liabilities

rate, volume, mix and net interest income

rate sensitive assets/liabilities

repriceable assets/liabilities

REFERENCES

Angotti, A. A., and M. L. Mauer. "Slope and Spread: A Tool for Strategic Performance," *Magazine of Bank Administration,* August 1980, pp. 28–34.

Baker, J. V., Jr. "Why You Need a Formal Asset/Liability Management Policy," *Banking,* June 1978, pp. 33–43.

Binder, B. F. "Asset/Liability Management," *Magazine of Bank Administration,* Parts 1–3, November/December 1980, January 1981.

Brewer, Elijah. "Bank Funds Management Comes of Age—A Balance Sheet Analysis," *Economic Perspectives.* Federal Reserve Bank of Chicago, May/June 1980, pp. 13–18.

Galvin, W. M. *Asset/Liability Management: A Handbook for Commercial Banks.* Rolling Meadows, Ill.: Bank Administration Institute, 1982.

McKinney, G. W., Jr. "A Perspective on the Use of Models in the Management of Bank Funds," *Journal of Bank Research,* Summer of 1977, pp. 122–127.

Olson, R. L., and H. M. Sollenberger. "Interest Margin Analysis: A Tool of Current Times," *Magazine of Bank Administration,* May 1978, pp. 45–51.

Stigum, M. and R. Brand. *Managing Bank Assets and Liabilities.* Homewood, Ill.: Dow-Jones, Irwin, 1983.

QUESTIONS

13.1. What is asset/liability management? What are its goals? How does it relate to other portions of the planning function of a commercial bank? Is it more important now than in past decades? If so, why?

13.2. What is net interest income? Net interest margin? Are they related to bank size?

13.3. How has deregulation of deposit rates affected net interest margin?

13.4. How has increased interest rate volatility in financial markets affected net interest margins?

13.5. Has the mix of core deposits versus purchased funds changed at commercial banks? If so, why? What have been the consequences of the change?

13.6. What risk is there in aggressively using liability management?

13.7. Briefly explain the influences of rate, volume, and mix on net interest income?

13.8. What is the GAP? Why is it important? What role do repriceable or rate sensitive assets and liabilities play in the measurement of the GAP?

13.9. What is meant by the term asset-sensitive? Liability-sensitive? Why are they important?

13.10. Distinguish between the incremental gap and the cumulative gap. Why is this distinction important?

13.11. What information is needed to predict the effects of a change in interest rates on the net interest income of a commercial bank? Is this information available to an analyst outside the bank?

13.12. How would an increase (decrease) in interest rates affect a bank with a positive dollar gap? Negative dollar gap?

13.13. How might interest rate risk management affect credit risk management?

PROBLEMS

13.1. Given the following information:

Assets	$	Rate	Liabilities and Equity	$	Rate
Rate sensitive	$3000	10.0%	Rate sensitive	$2000	8.0%
Nonrate sensitive	1500	9.0	Nonrate Sensitive	2000	7.0
Nonearning	500		Equity	1000	
	$5000			$5000	

(a) Calculate the expected net interest income at current interest rates and assuming no change in the composition of the portfolio. What is the net interest margin?

(b) Assuming that all interest rates rise by one percentage point, calculate the new expected net interest income and net interest margin.

13.2. Assume the following for Bank A:

Assets: $20 million in one-year fixed rate commercial loans
$10 million in one-year fixed rate consumer loans
Liabilities: $30 million in 180-day CDs.

Calculate the 3-month, 6-month, and 1-year cumulative GAP:

13.3. Given the following:

Total assets   = $200
Rate sensitive assets   = $100
Rate sensitive liabilities = $50
Existing interest rates = 8%
Expected interest rates = 10%

Calculate the following:
(a) Relative gap ratio
(b) Interest rate sensitivity ratio, and
(c) Expected change in net interest income.

13.4. Calculate the influence of volume and rate changes for the following data:

Time period	t	$t + 1$
Total Liabilities	150	180
Rate (%)	8%	10%

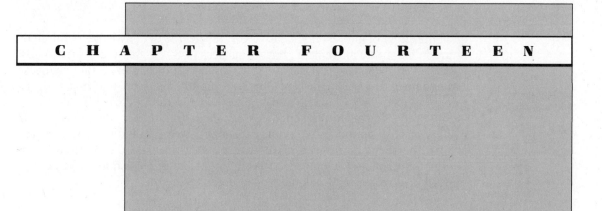

TECHNIQUES OF ASSET/LIABILITY MANAGEMENT: DOLLAR GAP AND DURATION GAP

The principal purpose of asset/liability management traditionally has been to control the size of the net interest income. This control may be *defensive* or *aggressive*. The goal of defensive asset/liability management is to insulate the net interest income from changes in interest rates; that is, to prevent interest rate changes from decreasing or increasing the net interest income. In contrast, aggressive asset/liability management focuses on *increasing* the net interest income through altering the portfolio of the institution.

Both defensive and aggressive asset/liability management relate to the management of the interest-sensitivity position of the asset and liability portfolio of a financial institution, and the success or failure of both strategies depends upon the effect of interest rates. However, the degree of knowledge required of future interest rate movements for the success of the aggressive asset/liability management depends upon the ability to forecast future interest rate changes. For example, a strategy that anticipates rising interest rates and that restructures the portfolio to benefit from the anticipated rate increase would fail if interest rates remained unchanged or declined. In contrast, defensive asset/liability management does not require the ability to forecast future interest rate levels. The focus of the defensive strategy is to insulate the portfolio from interest rate changes, whether the direction of the interest rate movement is upward or downward, predictable or unpredictable.

INSTRUMENTS USED IN ASSET/LIABILITY MANAGEMENT

A commercial bank may use any of the financial instruments currently on its balance sheet or potentially on the balance sheet in adjusting its assets and liabilities. Most commonly in the short run, however, the bank will use money market instruments in order to adjust its asset and liability portfolio. The principal types of assets that the bank will use to alter the interest sensitivity of its entire asset portfolio include federal funds, short-term treasury securities, federal agency securities, Eurodollar time deposits and certificates of deposit, domestic negotiable certificates of deposit, and repurchase agreements. **Federal funds** are overnight interbank loans. Shifting funds into federal funds sale tends to shorten the maturity of the bank's assets and makes the assets more interest sensitive. **Short-term treasury** (or agency) securities allow the bank to earn interest on highly liquid, credit-risk free securities that are available in a wide variety of maturities. Bank management can also vary the interest sensitivity of assets by making deposits at other banks in domestic or Eurodollar **certificates of deposit.** And a bank may buy a short-term security such as a treasury bill with the obligation to sell it back in the near term as a means of adjusting the maturity of its assets.

On the liability side of the balance sheet, the bank may issue certificates of deposit in various sizes and maturities or may borrow in the federal funds market. Federal funds borrowings, or overnight funds, are the most interest sensitive and least stable source of funds. Shifting from CDs to federal funds shortens the maturity of the liability side of the balance sheet, makes it more interest sensitive, and increases the risk of the bank's portfolio.

APPROPRIATE DEGREE OF INTEREST-RATE RISK

One of the most difficult decisions that bank managers face is determining the appropriate degree of interest-rate risk to take. At one extreme, referred to as a defensive interest-rate risk management, the bank would attempt to structure its assets and liabilities in order to eliminate interest-rate risk. The other extreme would bet the bank on expectations of interest rate changes (i.e., an aggressive strategy, in fact, an extremely aggressive strategy). Few banks follow either extreme, with most banks taking some but very limited interest-rate risk. In making decisions about the appropriate amounts of interest-rate risk, bank management should consider the following.

The profitability of a bank that does not take interest-rate risk may be inadequate. If the bank matches the interest sensitivity of its assets with the interest sensitivity of its liabilities, the spread between the costs of its funds and the amounts that can be earned by investing the funds may be inadequate. Large banks in particular may be unable to earn an adequate return in the extremely competitive loan markets that they operate within unless they accept both credit *and* interest-rate risk.

A policy of eliminating interest-rate risk may be incompatible with the desires of the bank's loan customers. Suppose that loan customers want fixed-rate loans at a time when the bank wants to increase the amount of interest-sensitive assets on its books, or customers want long-term deposits at a time when the bank wants to issue short-term deposits. The bank could ignore the desires of its customers, but if it did so, it would face substantial risk of them taking their entire banking relationship elsewhere. Within reasonable limits, the bank must accommodate the wishes of its customers. Adjustments to the interest sensitivity of its portfolio must then be made elsewhere.

The expertise and risk preference of management also are significant in affecting the aggressive/defensive position of the bank. Managing the assets and liabilities of a bank to achieve a desired risk position often requires extensive knowledge of sophisticated financial market instruments such as futures, options, and swaps. It also requires a management that is comfortable with accepting interest-rate risk. Many bankers feel less comfortable in assessing and managing interest-rate risk than in dealing with credit risk.

DOLLAR GAP MANAGEMENT

Aggressive Management

The management of a bank may choose to focus on the gap in controlling the interest-rate risk of its portfolio. With an aggressive interest-rate risk management program, such a strategy would involve two steps. First, the direction of future interest rates must be predicted. Second, adjustments must be made in the interest sensitivity of the assets and liabilities in order to take advantage of the projected interest rate changes. The prediction of rising interest rates generally results in shifting to a positive gap, whereas the prediction of falling interest rates generally results in shifting the portfolio to a negative gap position. This is illustrated in Table 14.1.

TABLE 14.1

GAP MANAGEMENT UNDER AN AGGRESSIVE PORTFOLIO MANAGEMENT POLICY

Predicted Interest Rate Change	Appropriate Gap Position	Portfolio Change
Increase	Positive	Increase RSA
		Decrease RSL
Decrease	Negative	Decrease RSA
		Increase RSL

Rising Interest Rates

If interest rates were expected to increase, a financial institution with a positive gap (i.e., more rate-sensitive assets than rate-sensitive liabilities) would experience a rising interest income. Net interest income would increase because short-term rate-sensitive assets would increase in interest return more than the liabilities would increase in their cost.

A financial institution that expected interest rates to increase but was not in a positive gap position would need to make adjustments in its portfolio. It might, for example, shorten the maturity of its assets by selling long-term securities and using the funds to purchase short-term securities. It could also make more variable rate loans. Either of these actions would increase the volume of rate-sensitive assets and would thereby allow the higher level of interest rates to be reflected in higher interest income. Another strategy that could be used either as a substitute for the asset portfolio shift or a complement to it would be to lengthen the maturity of the liabilities of the financial institution. This could be done, for example, by selling longer-term CDs and using the funds to replace federal funds borrowings. With such a strategy, the impact of rising interest rates on the cost of funds of the institution would be reduced, thereby contributing to an increase in the net interest income and net interest margin.

Falling Interest Rates

Expectation of falling interest rates would produce just the opposite adjustments in the portfolio under an aggressive portfolio management strategy. Management would want to shift to a negative gap position to benefit from the falling rates. The maturity of fixed rate assets should be lengthened and the volume of variable rate assets should be reduced. Relatedly, the gap position could be shifted to a negative one by shortening the maturity of liabilities, through, for example, replacing certificates of deposit with federal funds borrowings.

Defensive Management

The appropriate gap management policy under a defensive policy would be quite different. As discussed earlier, in contrast to an aggressive policy strategy that seeks to profit from anticipated interest rate movements, a defensive strategy attempts to prevent interest rate movements from harming the profitability of the financial institution. An aggressive strategy thus seeks to raise the level of net interest income, whereas a defensive strategy attempts to reduce the volatility of net interest income.

A defensive strategy attempts to keep the volume of rate-sensitive assets in balance with the volume of rate-sensitive liabilities over a given period. If successful, increases in interest rates will produce equal increases in interest revenue and interest expense, with the result that net interest income and the net interest margin will not change. Similarly, falling interest rates will reduce interest revenue and interest expense by the same amount and leave net interest income and the net interest margin unchanged if the amounts of rate-sensitive assets and liabilities are balanced.

A defensive strategy is not necessarily a passive one. Many adjustments in the asset and liability portfolio under a defensive strategy are often necessary in order to maintain a zero gap position. For example, suppose that a variable rate loan was paid off unexpectedly. If the gap was zero prior to the loan payoff, it would be negative afterward. In order to restore a zero gap, the asset/liability manager would have to add to short-term securities or loans or increase the volume of variable rate loans. Similarly, assume that there was a large and unexpected inflow of funds into short-term CDs, thereby shifting the portfolio from a zero gap to a negative gap. Again the asset/liability manager would have to make portfolio adjustments even under a defensive strategy.

Complications of Dollar Gap Analysis

Although widely used in practice, dollar gap management has a number of important deficiencies that have caused its modification and, in some cases, abandonment. The *first complication* concerns the selection of a time horizon. As discussed earlier, separation of the assets and liabilities of a financial institution into rate-sensitive and nonrate-sensitive ones requires the establishment of a time or planning horizon. Although necessary, the selection of time horizon causes problems because it ignores the time at which the interest-sensitive assets are repriced, implicitly assuming that all rate-sensitive assets and liabilities are repriced on the same day. As an example of the problems caused by such an implicit assumption, suppose that a financial institution had a zero gap (rate-sensitive assets = rate-sensitive liabilities), that the maturity of the rate-sensitive assets was 1 day, that the maturity of the rate-sensitive liabilities was 30 days, and that the planning horizon was 30 days. Given these assumptions, interest rate changes clearly would affect the net interest income of the financial institution even though the institution had a zero gap.

One solution to this problem is to divide the portfolio of assets and liabilities into separate subcategories, referred to as "maturity buckets," and to manage each maturity bucket separately. With the maturity bucket approach, gap analysis becomes the analysis of multiple gaps. Balance sheet items are grouped into a number of "maturity buckets" and the gap is computed for each one of these buckets. For example, the gap might be computed for 1 month, 1 to 3 months, 3 to 9 months, and so on. The gap for each maturity bucket is referred to as an incremental gap, and the incremental gaps sum to the total gap. The maturity bucket approach would not fully solve the problem, however, unless the time horizon were shortened to a 1-day period. Further, expansion of the number of maturity buckets itself causes problems, because it becomes very difficult to determine the overall interest-sensitivity position of the institution.

A *second problem* with traditional gap analysis is the implicit assumption that the correlation coefficient between the movement in general market interest rates and in the interest revenue and cost for the portfolio of the financial institution is one; that is, when interest rates in the market rise (or fall) by 10 percent, the interest revenue on rate-sensitive assets and the interest cost for rate-sensitive liabilities will rise (fall) by precisely 10 percent. The estimated change in net interest income from the calculations shown in Chapter 13 will occur only if this assumption implicit in the calculation is correct. Yet there are reasons to believe that the assumption is not correct. For example, many variable rates are not truly variable—that is, do not adjust quickly and fully to changes in market interest rates. Residential real estate loans provide an excellent example of the limitations that often exist in variable rate loans. Variable rate loans usually adjust their interest rates only over an extended period, frequently 2 or 3 years after the adjustment in market interest rates, and usually have a limit or ceilings on how far upward they can adjust regardless of the changes in market interest rates. Similar constraints exist for a variety of other types of loans. As a result, it would be unusual for the interest returns on rate-sensitive assets to change by exactly the amount of the change in the general level of market interest rates.

One method of dealing with the problem of imperfect correlation of interest rates is the use of the standardized gap. This measure of the gap adjusts for the different interest rate volatilities of various asset and liability items. It uses historical relationships between market interest rates and the interest rates of the bank's asset and liability items in order to alter the maturity and therefore interest sensitivity of the portfolio items. For example, a variable rate asset whose interest rate has been shown to be rather insensitive to market interest-rate movements might be considered as a fixed-rate asset for purposes of short-run gap analysis.

The benefits of the standardized gap approach can be illustrated with the use of Figure 14.1. The rate-sensitivity gap shown in that figure is −30 percent (interest-sensitive assets are 20 percent of total assets, whereas interest-sensitive liabilities are 50 percent of total assets). If it is assumed that rate-sensitive assets are $200 and rate-sensitive liabilities are $500, then the dollar gap is −$300. This may be referred to as the "naive" gap, because it ignores the correlation between the interest rate changes of the individual assets and of the market. But if the interest rate-sensitive liabilities are 90-day CDs and the interest rate-sensitive assets are 30-day commercial paper, they may, and prob-

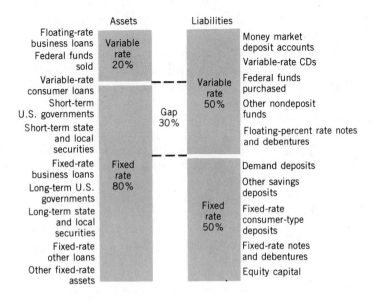

*There can be some trade-off maturity and fix versus variable-rate instruments on bank balance sheets.

FIGURE 14.1   Rate-sensitivity gap.* *Source.* Elijah Brewer, "Bank Gap Management and the Use of Financial Futures," Federal Reserve Bank of Chicago *Economic Perspectives,* March/April 1985, p. 16.

ably will, respond differently to market rate movements. For example, if the CD rate is 105 percent as volatile as the 90-day T-bill, whereas the 30-day commercial paper rate is 30 percent as volatile, then the standardized gap is −$463. This is computed as follows: The standardized volatility of the 90-day CDs is 1.05×500 or 525 and the standardized volatility of the commercial paper is $200 \times .31 = 62$. Comparing the standardized assets with the standardized liabilities produces a standardized gap of −$463. As a result, the potential interest rate risk for this bank is considerably greater than would be indicated by the "naive" gap. An increase in interest rates would produce a much larger fall in net interest margin than the naive gap would indicate.

The *final and perhaps the most significant problem* with the use of traditional gap analysis is its focus on net interest income rather than shareholder wealth. The asset/liability managers of a financial institution may adjust the portfolio of the institution so that net interest income increases with changes in interest rates, but the value of shareholder wealth may decrease. Aggressive asset/liability management based on predictions of interest rate movements increases the risk of loss. Even if asset/liability management does not "bet the bank" through taking extremely high gap positions (negative or positive) and allows the gap to exceed some desired amount, the attempt to restructure the portfolio still will add some degree of risk to the earnings flow of the financial institution. If successful, aggressive gap management may increase the level of net interest income, but it is also likely to add to the volatility of that income. As a result, aggressive gap management may lessen the value of the institution because of its focus on the wrong goal.

Even defensive gap management may produce a decline in shareholder wealth. The main reason would be the possibility that the institution had a zero gap and therefore thought that it was protected from interest rate changes. But, because of the less than perfect correlation between asset earnings, liability costs, and general market interest rate movements, it actually was at risk in its net interest income. A more complex but equally valid problem would arise if the volume of rate-sensitive assets equaled the volume of rate-sensitive liabilities, the volume of nonrate-sensitive assets equaled the volume of nonrate-sensitive liabilities, *but the maturity* of the nonrate-sensitive assets exceeded the maturity of the nonrate-sensitive liabilities. In that case, even if the interest earnings and costs moved precisely with market interest rate movements, the market value of the financial institution would drop if interest rates increased. The market value of the institution would drop with rising rates because, despite a constant net interest income, the market value of the assets of the institution would fall more than the market value of the liabilities. Since ultimately the market value of the equity is equal to the market value of assets less the market value of liabilities, such a policy would lessen the value of the organization to its shareholders.

DURATION GAP ANALYSIS

The deficiencies of traditional gap analysis, especially the focus on accounting income rather than on the market value of the equity, have encouraged a search for alternative approaches to measuring and managing the interest rate exposure of a financial institution. One such approach is **duration gap analysis.** (See Chapter 2 for a discussion of duration.) Duration analysis focuses directly on the market value of the equity of the institution, where market value represents the present value of current and expected future income.[1] With duration gap analysis, the durations of the assets and liabilities of the institution are calculated in order to estimate the effects of changing interest rates on the market value of the assets and liabilities. Once the durations are specified, the effects of changing interest rates on the market value of the equity may be measured simply by taking the sum of the changes in the market value of the assets and liabilities (with appropriate signs).

---

[1] The duration model may also be used to manage net interest income. See the discussion in the article by Toevs listed in the Reference section.

Measurement of the Duration Gap

The interest-sensitivity position of a financial institution with duration gap analysis may be illustrated with the information in Table 14.2. The financial institution whose balance sheet is shown there has three assets: cash, business loans with $2\frac{1}{2}$ years maturity (amortized monthly), and mortgage loans with 30-years maturity (amortized monthly). On the liability side of the balance sheet, the institution has CDs with two different maturities as well as equity capital. It is assumed that the CDs pay interest only once—at maturity. The interest rate on the loans is assumed to be 13 percent, 11 percent on deposits, and the cash assets are assumed to earn no interest.

The duration of each of the assets and liabilities is also given in Table 14.2. Cash is assumed to have a zero duration. The durations of both the business loans and the mortgage loans are shorter than their maturities, because they are amortized. The durations of the CDs are the same as their maturities, because they are single-payment assets.

Interest Rates, the Duration Gap, and Market Value of Equity

Given the preceding information, the duration of the asset portfolio (the weighted duration of the individual assets) is 4.0 years and the duration of the deposits (the weighted duration of the individual types of deposits) is 2.33 years. How will the value of the assets and deposits and (hence the market value of the equity) change as interest rates change?

The effect of changing interest rates on the market value of the equity is related to the size of the duration gap, where the duration gap is measured as in equation (14.1):

$$DGAP = D_a - W\,D_L \tag{14.1}$$

TABLE 14.2
BALANCE SHEET DURATION

Assets	$	Duration (Year)	Liabilities	$	Duration (Year)
Cash	100	0	CD (1 yr.)	600	1.0
Business loans	400	1.25	CD (5 yr.)	300	5.0
				900	2.33
Mortgage loans	500	7.0	Equity	100	
	1000	4.0		1000	

Source. Adapted from George G. Kaufman, "Measuring and Managing Interest Rate Risk: A Primer," Federal Reserve Bank of Chicago *Economic Perspective*, January/February 1984, p. 17.

Note. The duration of assets and liabilities and net worth is a *weighted* average of each of their components.

where DGAP = duration gap, D_a = average duration of assets, D_L = average duration of liabilities, and W = ratio of total liabilities to total assets.

In the example given in Table 14.2, if interest rates were to increase, the market value of the equity would decline. Conversely, if interest rates were to decline, the market value of the equity would increase. For rising interest rates, the value of the assets would drop more than the value of liabilities, and thus the market value of the equity would drop. For falling interest rates the value of the assets would rise more than the value of the liabilities and the market value of the equity would increase.

The change in the market value of the equity can be determined by measuring the size of the duration gap and by specifying the amount of the change in interest rates. In the preceding example, the duration gap may be determined as in equation (14.2).

$$DGAP = 4.0 - (.9)(2.33)$$
$$= 4.00 - 2.10 = 1.90 \text{ Years} \tag{14.2}$$

Equation (14.3) gives an approximation for the expected change in the market value of the equity for a given change in interest rates:

$$\frac{\Delta \text{ Market value of equity}}{\text{Total assets}} = - \text{ DGAP} \left(\frac{\Delta i}{1 + i}\right) \tag{14.3}$$

Suppose that current interest rates are 11 percent, are expected to increase by 100 basis points (1 percentage point), and the duration gap is as given in equation (14.2). Then the percentage change in the market value of the equity will be

$$\% \Delta \text{ in market value of equity} = (-1.90) \left(\frac{1}{1.11}\right) = -1.7 \text{ percent}$$

Defensive and Aggressive Duration Gap Management

If the duration gap is positive (i.e., the duration of assets exceeds the duration of liabilities), then increases in interest rates will reduce the market value of the equity and decreases in interest rates will increase the market value of the equity. Conversely, if the duration gap is negative, with the duration of assets less than the duration of liabilities, rising interest rates will increase the market value of the equity, whereas falling interest rates will lead to a reduction in the market value of the equity. If the duration gap is zero, however, then the market value of the equity is *immunized* from changes in interest rates. Changes in the values of assets because of changes in interest rates will be

TABLE 14.3
DURATION GAP, INTEREST RATES, AND THE MARKET VALUE
OF EQUITY

DGAP	Change in Interest Rates	Change in Market Value of Equity
Positive	Increase	Decrease
Positive	Decrease	Increase
Negative	Increase	Increase
Negative	Decrease	Decrease
Zero	Increase	Zero
Zero	Decrease	Zero

exactly offset by changes in the value of liabilities. (These relationships are summarized in Table 14.3.)

An aggressive interest-rate risk management strategy would alter the duration gap in anticipation of changes in interest rates. For example, if interest rates were expected to increase, management would want to shift from a positive to a negative gap position. It could do this by reducing the duration of assets and/or increasing the duration of liabilities. The expectation of falling interest rates would, of course, produce the opposite type of portfolio management adjustments. Note that the portfolio strategy in response to the expectation of higher interest rates for both duration and dollar gap are similar—more short-term assets and more long-term liabilities. However, such a strategy would produce a *positive* dollar gap, where the gap is measured as the difference between the dollar amount of interest-sensitive assets and liabilities, and a *negative* duration, where the gap is measured as the difference in the number of years of the duration of assets and liabilities.

A defensive interest-rate risk management within this context would seek to keep the duration of assets equal to the duration of liabilities, thereby maintaining a duration gap of zero. As portfolio adjustments occurred at the financial institution because of changes in the demand for loans or in the quantity of CDs, the interest-rate risk manager would make adjustments in the duration of assets and liabilities in order to keep the duration gap at or near zero.

Problems with Duration Gap Management

Although duration gap management does provide additional insight useful to asset/liability managers, it also has a number of problems. For example, the immunization of the market value of equity to interest rate changes will be effective only if interest rates for all maturity securities shift up or down by exactly the same amount (i.e., only if the yield curve moves upward or downward by a constant percentage amount). In fact, yield curves seldom move in this way. In periods of rising interest rates, short-term rates usually move up more than long-term rates, whereas in periods of falling interest rates short-term interest rates usually fall more than long-term rates. In addition, the earlier discussion of the price changes that occur in the value of a financial asset due to interest rate changes was only an approximation. The relationship between interest rate changes and bond price changes is, in reality, not linear, so that the calculation discussed earlier provides only an approximation of the true relationship. If the asset and liability have considerably different duration, comparing the effects of interest rate changes on their values may be unwarranted. Finally, asset/liability managers must deal with the problem of "duration drift." For example, if asset and liability durations are initially matched, so that the portfolio is immunized, the duration gap may drift over time. Assume, for example, that a financial institution finances a long-term (7-year duration) portfolio with a mixture of 5- and 10-year duration deposits. After 3 years the duration of the assets has declined very little, but the duration of the deposits has declined substantially. After 4 years the duration mismatch is even larger. This happens because maturities were not matched initially even though durations were.

Box 14.1

HOW *NOT* TO MANAGE INTEREST RATE RISK

First Pennsylvania Corporation provides an excellent case example of how a bank should *not* manage its interest rate risk. Management of the bank violated one of the basic rules of asset/liability management: Although taking some risk is an acceptable management practice, *never* bet the bank on any interest rate forecasts. Failure to follow this simple principle produced massive losses for the bank, the threat of failure, and ultimately a rescue by the Federal Deposit Insurance Corporation. Existing management was dismissed and, for a considerable period of time, the bank was in effect managed by the FDIC.

In the mid- and late 1970s, First Pennsylvania began to increase markedly their securities portfolio, especially their long-term holdings. Securities as a fraction of total assets ranged from 12 percent in 1972 to 28 percent in 1978. Financially, this expansion in longer-term securities with longer-term sources of funds would not have produced any interest-rate risk problem. However, the buildup in long-term securities was financed primarily with short-term purchased funds. Federal funds purchased (as a percentage of total assets) increased from 8 percent in 1972 to 26 percent in 1978. The bank thus had a large negative gap; it was liability sensitive.

If interest rates had stayed unchanged, First Pennsylvania would have done reasonably well with its strategy of borrowing short and lending

Box 14.1 (*Continued*)

long. If interest rates had fallen, First Pennsylvania would have made large profits. Unfortunately, interest rates exploded upward in late 1979 and 1980 and the negative gap virtually destroyed the bank. Profits turned into losses, the bank experienced a liquidity crisis because it was unable to roll-over its short-term purchased funds. The problem was further intensified by large loan losses that produced an unwillingness on the part of large depositors and other creditors to put funds in the bank. The financial crisis at First Pennsylvania was stemmed only by an FDIC rescue effort in April 1980 that included a $500-million assistance program from the FDIC and a group of private banks.

MANAGING ASSETS AND LIABILITIES OVER THE BUSINESS/INTEREST RATE CYCLE

Although aggressive asset/liability management requires the ability to forecast interest rates, such forecasts are notoriously unreliable. Short-run, month-to-month, or quarter-to-quarter forecasts are more likely to be wrong than right. One way to reconcile the need to forecast interest rates in aggressive asset/liability management and the difficulty in making correct forecasts is to take a slightly longer-run perspective and structure interest sensitivity management around the historical business/interest rate cycle.

Both the level of interest rates and the relationship between short- and long-term rates (i.e., the slope of the yield curve) are closely related to the stages of the business cycle. Table 14.4 provides a simplified view of those relationships. The business cycle is commonly divided into four periods: the expansion phase, when real income, production, and employment are rising; the peak, when the economy reaches its productive capacity; the contraction, when real income, production, and employment are falling; and the trough, at which point the decline ceases and the economy is poised for another expansion. Although no two business cycles repeat themselves exactly and there are distinctive elements to each phase of the cycle, sufficient similarities exist to permit the cycle to be divided into recurring patterns.

TABLE 14.4
THE BUSINESS CYCLE AND THE INTEREST RATE CYCLE

Stage of the Business Cycle	Level of Interest Rates	Term Structure
Expansion	Rising	Moderately upward-sloping
Peak	High	Flat or downward-sloping
Contraction	Falling	Slightly upward-sloping
Trough	Low	Strongly upward-sloping

In the expansion phase of the cycle, interest rates are generally rising. The demand for loanable funds strengthens and the supply of loanable funds is restrained by Federal Reserve monetary policy. The yield curve is moderately upward sloping with long-term rates higher than short-term rates. However, the yield curve is shifting as short-term rates generally rise more than long-term rates, producing a flattening of the yield curve, so the differences between long- and short-term rates narrow. As the economy approaches its peak, interest rates continue to rise, peaking at about the same time as general business conditions do. At or near the peak in general business conditions, the term structure of interest rates may change dramatically. Market participants may expect a drop in rates in the future, and the Federal Reserve may induce exceptional pressures in the money market. As short-term rates continue to increase more than long-term rates, the yield curve continues to flatten until at some point short-term rates exceed long-term rates. At this point, the yield curve becomes downward sloping or inverted.

As the economy passes its peak, interest rates begin to fall. The demand for loanable funds declines as businesses reduce inventory levels and curtail plant and equipment expenditures, consumers reduce their purchases, and state and local governments retrench. The supply of loanable funds is stimulated by an easing of monetary policy and perhaps the rate of inflation declines. Short-term rates usually fall more than long-term rates, and the yield curve begins to return to a positive slope. Finally, as the economy approaches bottom at the depth of the recession, the yield curve becomes sharply upward sloping.

Bank management can use these recurring interest rate patterns in order to increase the net interest margin through appropriate asset/liability management. With a positively sloped yield curve, the possibility of gain through short-funding exists—that is, through borrowing short and lending long. In that case, the dollar gap would be negative because the dollar amount of interest-sensitive assets would be less than the dollar amount of interest-sensitive liabilities. If interest rates begin to rise sharply, however, the bank will need to reduce the size of the dollar gap. Moreover, if the bank was more concerned with the value of its equity than with net interest margin, it would need to maintain a negative duration gap during a period of rising interest rates. As interest rates reached a peak, appropriate asset/liability management would involve both a zero dollar gap and a zero duration gap. As interest rates fall, however, the bank would move back to a negative gap. In this case, with falling interest rates, concern with the market value of equity would suggest a positive duration gap.

Managing the composition of assets and liabilities over the cycle in order to increase net interest income and/or the market value of equity is quite difficult. It requires not only a high level of management skill but also a highly flexible balance sheet. The removal of deposit-rate ceilings has increased balance sheet flexibility at all banks, yet the joint existence of substantial expertise and balance sheet flexibility usually occurs only at large banks. For this reason, most smaller banks may be best advised to concentrate on a zero dollar or duration gap over the cycle.

INTEREST-RATE RISK MANAGEMENT AND THE YIELD CURVE

Chapter 2 discusses the relationship between the yield to maturity on a financial instrument and the maturity or duration of that instrument. This relationship is known as the yield curve. As discussed in that chapter, the yield curve normally is upward sloping so that, other things equal, higher yields are required to get investors to accept the risk that accompanies longer maturities or durations. This normal, positive relationship of yields to maturity or duration produces an incentive for banks to accept interest-rate risk.

Assume that the yield curve is as shown in Figure 14.2. Assume further that the bank were to both borrow and lend with 6-month maturities—that is, the maturity of both its assets and liabilities was 6 months. In that case, at least in the simplified example, it would earn no spread, its cost of borrowing and its earnings on assets (absent credit risk) would be the same. But if it accepted interest rate risk and reduced the average maturity of its liabilities to 3 months, the bank would earn a positive interest rate spread. This spread would be its compensation for accepting interest rate risk. If the yield curve remains unchanged during the planning horizon, the bank will be able to add to its profits.

Bank management must decide whether the risk of borrowing shorter than the maturity of its asset portfolio is worth the potential gain. However, a positively sloped yield curve creates an incentive to maintain a slight liability-sensitive position (rate-sensitive assets less than rate-sensitive liabilities) under most conditions.

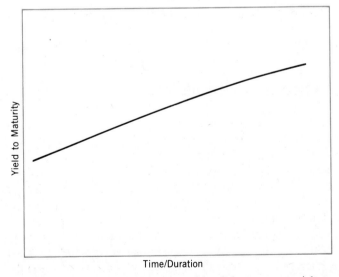

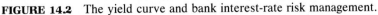

FIGURE 14.2   The yield curve and bank interest-rate risk management.

SIMULATION AND ASSET/LIABILITY MANAGEMENT

The availability of modern computer techniques not only has substantially reduced the mechanical burdens involved in asset/liability management, but also has broadened the scope of possible management techniques. In particular, the existence of computerized asset/liability management models has made possible the simulation of various strategies under differing assumptions.

Simulation or balance sheet models are models that, used with assumptions about interest rate movements and various bank strategies, allow a bank to test or evaluate the balance sheet and income statement implications of alternative strategies. In a sense, simulation models merely allow the bank to examine its total balance sheet and income statement under a wide variety of alternative scenarios. These basic inputs into the models are the nondiscretionary sources and uses of funds. These are then coupled with alternative values of the discretionary sources and uses as selected by bank management.

Properly used, simulation models not only allow bank management to generate a number of balance sheet and income statements, but also provide the necessary information so that management may determine the risk/return trade-offs for different strategies. For example, the bank could generate estimates of its net interest margin under different interest rate and strategy assumptions. It could calculate a probability distribution of net interest margin, including the average or expected value and the variance of the expected values of net interest margins. From the probability distribution generated from alternative strategy assumptions, management will be able to develop at least implicit risk-return trade-offs of different strategies.

Simulations traditionally have been used only at larger banks. Given the cost of such exercises as well as the greater complexities of operations at larger banks, these banks have often found such exercises to be cost-effective. With the expansion of computer technology and the reduction in computer costs, however, as well as the growing complexity of bank operations at small banks, simulation models are increasingly being used by both small and large banks.

INTEREST-RATE RISK AND LIQUIDITY RISK

Interest-rate risk and liquidity risk are different although closely related types of risk. Interest-rate risk management focuses on the effects of alternative portfolio strategies on the net interest margin (or some other goal) of the bank. Liquidity management focuses on the effects of alternative portfolio strategies on the bank's ability to meet its cash obligation to deposits and borrowers. The two are in fact inextricably intertwined. A few examples may assist in understanding the relationship.

Suppose that bank management decides to pursue a liability sensitive position; that is, to have more interest-sensitive liabilities than assets. This interest-rate management strategy necessarily reduces the liquidity position of the bank. More liabilities are coming due in a shorter period, which creates potential funding strains, and fewer short-term highly liquid assets are available to meet those funding needs. Under most circumstances, this mismatch would not be a problem. However, if there is concern about the bank's ability to meet its obligations, a severe funding problem could exist as the liabilities matured.

As another example, suppose that bank management structured the portfolio in order to achieve a positive duration gap—the duration of assets exceeded the duration of liabilities. In that case, the ability to realize liquidity from the assets of the bank has been reduced. Long-duration assets will decline more than short-duration assets if interest rates increase. In that case, the sale of assets to raise funds, although still possible, will cause severe losses, losses that management probably would seek to avoid.

The coordination of interest rate risk and liquidity management is complex, but it is obvious also that they are too interrelated to be managed independently.

SUMMARY

Bank management may adopt a defensive or an aggressive strategy in managing interest-rate risk. With a defensive strategy, the goal is to insulate the net interest margin (or some other measure of bank performance) from fluctuations in interest rates; whereas with an aggressive strategy the goal is to increase the size of the net interest margin (or some other measure of bank performance) by predicting interest rate changes and restructuring the portfolio to benefit from such changes.

If the focus of interest-rate risk management was on net interest margin, a defensive strategy would seek to balance the amount of interest-rate sensitive assets and interest-rate sensitive liabilities. Properly done, interest revenues and interest expenses would rise and fall together with changing interest rates, so that net interest margin would remain unchanged under this dollar gap strategy. With an aggressive dollar gap program, management would establish a positive gap (rate-sensitive assets greater than rate-sensitive liabilities) when interest rates were expected to rise and negative gap when interest rates were expected to fall. If the interest rate forecast was correct, the bank would benefit through a higher net interest margin. Of course, if the interest rate forecast was incorrect, the net interest margin would be reduced.

Although widely used, the dollar gap approach has a number of limitations, including the difficulty in selecting a single, appropriate time horizon; the implicit assumption that interest revenue and costs on rate-sensitive assets and liabilities are perfectly correlated with general interest rate movement; and the myopic focus on net interest margin rather than the goal of maximizing shareholder wealth. Such a limited focus may produce portfolio strategies that, although they increase profitability, may reduce the market value of the equity.

The deficiencies of traditional dollar gap analysis have given rise to an alternative approach that focuses on the market value of the assets, liabilities, and equity of the bank. Under this duration gap analysis, the duration of assets is compared with the duration of liabilities. A defensive duration gap management would balance the duration of assets and liabilities, so that the market value of the equity (although not necessarily the profitability of the bank) would not be affected by interest rate changes. With an aggressive strategy, management would establish a negative duration (duration of assets shorter than the duration of liabilities) if interest rates were expected to increase and a positive duration if interest rates were expected to fall.

IMPORTANT CONCEPTS

Dollar Gap
Aggressive Management
Defensive Management
Standardized Gap
Duration Gap
Business/Interest Rate Cycle
Simulation

REFERENCES

Bierwag, G., G. Kaufman, and A. Toevs. "Duration: Its Development and Use in Bond Portfolio Management," *Financial Analysts Journal,* July–August 1983, pp. 15–35.

Dew, J. "The Effective Gap: A More Accurate Measure of Interest Rate Risk," *American Banker,* June 10, 1981, September 19, 1981, and December 9, 1981.

Flannery, M. "How Do Changes in Market Interest Rates Affect Bank Profits?" *Business Review,* Federal Reserve Bank of Philadelphia, September/October 1980, pp. 13–22.

Grove, M. "On Duration and the Optimal Maturity Strategy of the Balance Sheet," *The Bell Journal of Economics and Management Science,* Autumn 1974.

Kaufman, G. "Measuring and Managing Interest Rate Risk: A Primer," Federal Reserve Bank of Chicago, January-February 1984, pp. 16–29.

Simonson, D., and G. Hempel. "Improving Gap Management as a Technique for Controlling Interest Rate Risk," *Journal of Bank Research,* Summer 1982.

Toevs, A. "Gap Management: Managing Interest Rate Risk in Banks and Thrifts," *Economic Review,* Federal Reserve Bank of San Francisco, Spring 1983, pp. 20–35.

QUESTIONS

14.1. What is the difference between defensive and aggressive asset/liability management?

14.2. Why is it advantageous for banks to accept some amount of interest-rate risk? How much interest-rate risk should a bank take?

14.3. What kind of aggressive gap management would be appropriate if interest rates are expected to fall?

14.4. What problems occur in the practical implementation of gap management? What possible solutions can help to reduce these problems?

14.5. Could a bank with a zero gap still be exposed to interest-rate risk? Give two possible reasons that it might be.

14.6. If a bank has a positive duration gap and interest-rates rise, what will happen to bank equity? Explain your answer.

14.7. What is immunization in the context of bank gap management?

14.8. What assumptions are made in using duration gap analysis?

14.9. How is the business cycle related to interest rate movements? (Divide the business cycle into four periods in your answer.)

14.10. How should bank management change its dollar gap as the yield curve changes?

14.11. What is simulated asset/liability management? What benefit is it to a bank?

14.12. How is interest-rate risk linked to liquidity risk? Give an example.

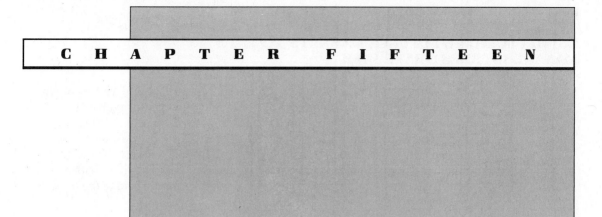

TECHNIQUES OF ASSET/LIABILITY MANAGEMENT: FUTURES, OPTIONS, AND SWAPS

This chapter concentrates on three relatively new techniques used by banks (and other financial institutions) to manage interest rate risk. Although recent in development and application, they have enjoyed explosive growth and have become very significant techniques. Although they are more commonly used in defensive asset/liability management, the techniques may also be used in a more aggressive mode. The chapter discusses each technique separately and then compares and evaluates them as alternative devices for managing interest rate risk.

USING FINANCIAL FUTURES MARKETS TO MANAGE INTEREST-RATE RISK

The adjustments to a bank's portfolio that were discussed in the previous chapter—changing the dollar gap and/or the duration gap—involve alterations in the current cash (or spot) market positions in the portfolio of assets and liabilities. Equivalent adjustments in the interest sensitivity position of the bank can be achieved through transactions in the futures markets. These transactions, in effect, create new or synthetical assets and liabilities with interest sensitivity positions different than those that are currently held in the portfolio.

Nature of Futures

A futures contract is a standardized agreement to buy or sell a specified quantity of a financial instrument on a specified future date at a set price. The buyer of a futures contract agrees to take delivery at a future date of the specified quantity of the financial instrument at today's determined price, whereas the seller agrees to make delivery of that quantity of the financial instrument at the future date at today's established price. The buyer is said to have established a **long position** in the futures market and will benefit if the price of the contract rises. The seller is said to have established a **short position** in the futures market and will benefit if the price of the contract falls. The futures market transaction may be contrasted with a cash or spot market transaction. In the futures markets, pricing and delivery occur at different times, pricing occurs today, delivery occurs at some point in the future. In the cash or spot market, pricing and delivery occur at the same time.

Futures contracts are traded in a number of organized exchanges, with most activity occurring in Chicago and New York. Trading occurs in a large number of different short- and long-term financing instruments, including treasury bills, notes and bonds, domestic certificates of deposit, and Eurodollar time deposits. In each case, the contract traded specifies the precise nature of the financial instrument to be delivered at the maturity of the contract. For example, the treasury bill futures contract traded on the International Monetary Market in Chicago is for a $1 million par value of U.S. Treasury bills with 13 weeks to maturity.

Although futures contracts differ somewhat by type of financial instrument traded and also by exchange, all futures contracts have the following characteristics in common.

First, the contracts are for a specified, standardized amount of a financial instrument, with other identical features, such as the date of delivery. Because the contracts are identical, they are easily traded among market participants at low transaction costs.

Second, the exchange clearinghouse is a counterpart to each contract. Once a futures contract is traded (i.e., the buyer and seller reach agreement on the price), the exchange clearinghouse steps in. The buyer and seller never need to have any relationship with each other. Rather, their relationship is with the exchange clearinghouse. By this device, the risk of default on the contract is minimized because, in effect, the exchange clearinghouse guarantees that each party to the contract will perform as promised.

Third, the contracts may be bought and sold with only a small commitment of funds relative to the market value of the contract itself. This commitment of funds is known as the margin. The margin is actually a performance bond that guarantees the buyer or seller of the contract will fulfill the commitment. The fact that the margin is a small fraction of the contract value creates great "leverage," thereby magnifying the potential gain or loss from a futures market transaction.

Fourth, futures contracts are marked-to-market each day; that is, market participants must recognize any gains or losses on their outstanding futures positions at the end of each day. Gains are added to the margin balance of traders each day and losses are subtracted from the margin balance each day. If the margin balance falls below the exchange mandated minimum, the trader will be required to add funds to the margin account.

Example of a Futures Transaction

Exhibit 15.1 provides an example of a simple futures market transaction. It assumes that the trader buys, on October 2, 1986, one December 1986, treasury bill futures contract at a price of $94.83, or discount yield of 5.17 (100 − 94.83). The trader is now obligated to take delivery (buy) a $1 million (face value) 13-week bill on the maturity date of the contract (December 18, 1986). On the date of the transaction (October 2, 1986), the buyer pays a commission and places down the necessary margin. The buyer will gain if the price of the contract rises (i.e., interest rates fall) but will lose if the price of the contract falls (i.e., interest rates rise).

Suppose that the discount rate on treasury bills *rose* two basis points immediately after the purchase of the futures contract. Because each basis point is equivalent to $25 on the value of the contract, the buyer would lose $50 on the investment. With the practice of marking each contract to market daily, the buyer would have the value of the margin account reduced by $50 at the end of the day (and the seller would have the value of the margin account increased by $50). Marking-to-market will occur as long as the buyer holds the contract or until final maturity of the contract, whichever comes first.

If the buyer holds the contract until maturity, the purchase price at maturity can be determined by the formula given in Exhibit 15.1. If the final index price is $94.81, then the settlement price is $986,880.83. In most cases, however, contracts are closed prior to the delivery date (i.e., the buyer would offset the long position by selling the identical contract), with the result that no delivery actually occurs. In fact, delivery of the underlying financial instrument seldom occurs in most futures market transactions.

EXHIBIT 15.1
EXAMPLE OF A TREASURY BILL FUTURES TRANSACTION

Suppose that on October 2, 1986, a trader buys one December 1986 treasury bill futures contract at the opening price of $94.83. Once the transaction is complete the trader is contractually obligated to buy a $1 million (face value) 13-week treasury bill yielding $100 - 94.83 = 5.17$ percent on a discount basis on the contract delivery date, which is December 18, 1986. At the time of the initial transaction, however, the trader pays only a commission and deposits the required margin with their broker.

Effects of Price Changes. Suppose that the futures prices fell two basis points during that day's trading session, meaning that the discount rate on bills for future delivery rose after the contract was purchased. Since each one basis point change in the T-bill index is worth $25 dollars the trader would lose $50 if he were to sell the contract at the closing price.

The practice of marking futures contracts to market at the end of each trading session means that the trader is forced to realize this loss even though he does not sell the bill; thus, he has $50 subtracted from his margin account. That money is then transferred to a seller's margin account. After the contract is marked to market, the trader is still obliged to buy a treasury bill on December 18, but now at a discount yield of 5.19 percent (the implied futures discount yield as of the close of trading).

Final Settlement. If the trader chooses to hold his contract to maturity, the contract is marked to market one last time at the close of the last day of trading. All longs with open positions at that time must be prepared to buy the deliverable bill at a purchase price determined by the closing futures index price.

The final settlement or purchase price implied by the IMM index value is determined as follows: First, calculate the total discount from the face value of the bill using the formula

$$\text{Discount} = \frac{\text{Days to maturity} \times ((100 - \text{Index}) \times .01) \times \$1{,}000{,}000}{360},$$

where $((100 - \text{Index}) \times .01)$ is the future discount yield expressed as a fraction. Second, calculate the purchase price by subtracting the total discount from the face value of the deliverable bill. Note that this is essentially the same procedure used to calculate the purchase price of a bill from the quoted discount yield in the spot market, the only difference being the use of the futures discount rate implied by the index value in place of the spot market rate.

Suppose that the final index price is $94.81; then, the settlement price for the first delivery day is

$$\$986{,}880.83 = \$1{,}000{,}000 - \frac{91 \times .0519 \times \$1{,}000{,}000}{360}$$

This calculation assumes that the deliverable bill will have exactly 91 days to maturity, which will always be the case on the first contract delivery day except in special cases when a bill would otherwise mature on a national holiday.

Because buying a futures contract during the last trading session is essentially equivalent to buying a treasury bill in the spot market, futures prices tend to converge to the

EXHIBIT 15.1 *(Continued)*

spot market price of the deliverable security on the final day of trading in a futures contract. Thus, the final futures discount yield should differ little, if at all, from the spot market discount yield at the end of the final trading day.

Source. Mark Mark Drabenstott and Anne O'Mara McDonley. "Futures Markets: A Primer for Financial Institutions," Federal Reserve Bank of Kansas City *Economic Review,* November 1984, pp. 17–33.

Techniques in Using Financial Futures

Although futures may be used both to speculate over future interest rate movements and to hedge against interest rate risk, regulatory policies limit bank use of the futures market to a hedging role. A few examples may help in understanding the ways in which banks may use the futures markets.

Using Interest Rate Futures to Hedge a Dollar Gap Position

A long or buy hedge may be used to protect the bank against falling interest rates. For example, suppose that the bank has a positive dollar gap—that is, it has more interest-sensitive assets than liabilities. If interest rates increased, the bank would benefit through higher net interest margins. If interest rates fell, however, the bank's net interest margin would deteriorate. In short, the bank is exposed to interest rate risk. The bank could reduce this interest rate risk by transactions in the spot or cash market such as reducing the interest sensitivity of assets. As an alternative, the bank could engage in a long or buy hedge by purchasing one or more T-bills contracts for future delivery. In that case, if interest rates fell, the reduction in the net interest margin would be offset by the gain on the long hedge in the futures market. Of course, if interest rates increased, the gain in the net interest margin would be offset by the loss on the futures transaction.

A bank may also adjust its interest sensitivity position through the sale of futures contracts (i.e., a short hedge). A short hedge may be used to reduce the interest rate risk associated with a negative dollar gap. If interest rates increased, the unhedged bank would suffer a reduction in its net interest margins. With a short hedge position, however, the bank would experience a gain from the futures hedge that would offset the reduction in the net interest margin. Of course, if interest rates fell, the increased net interest margin would be offset by the loss on the futures contracts.

The number of contracts to be bought (long-hedge) to hedge a position dollar gap or sold (short-hedge) to hedge a negative dollar gap may be calculated using equation (15.1).

$$\text{Number of contracts} = \left(\frac{\$ \text{ Gap}}{2}\right) \times \left(\frac{N}{m}\right) \tag{15.1}$$

where $ Gap = the dollar value of the gap, N = number of months the gap is to be hedged, and m = maturity (in months) of the instruments used to hedge the gap.

Suppose that a bank wishes to hedge a $48 million positive dollar gap over the next month using T-bill futures. The number of futures contracts to be purchased would be

$$8 \quad \text{or} \quad \left(\frac{\$48}{2} \times 1/3\right)$$

Using Interest Rate Futures to Hedge a Duration Gap

Interest rate futures can also be used to hedge a mismatch in the duration of a bank's assets and liabilities. For example, suppose that the bank has a negative duration gap (i.e., the duration of assets is less than the duration of liabilities). In that case, the bank could extend the duration of its assets or reduce the duration of its liabilities, thereby reducing the duration gap. As an alternative, it could establish a long position in the financial futures market. Similarly, if the bank had a position duration gap, it could either reduce the duration of assets, increase the duration of liabilities, or execute a short or sell position in financial futures.

Suppose the bank's portfolio appears as in Table 15.1. It is assumed that the assets are single payment loans repayable in 90, 180, 270, and 360 days and carrying 12 percent interest. It is further assumed that the loans maturing at the end of 90, 180, 270, and 360 days are rolled over for 360, 270, 180, and 90 days, respectively. The loan portfolio is financed with a 90-day CD at 10 percent, providing the bank, initially, with a 2-percentage-point spread. The amount that the bank will owe when the CD matures (3,299.18 or 3221.00 $\times$ 1.10⁴) will be obtained by borrowing for another 90 days.

The bank bears considerable interest rate risk in this example. The duration of its assets is considerably longer than the duration of its liabilities. The duration of the loan portfolio is 0.73 years, whereas the duration of the liabilities is

TABLE 15.1
INTEREST-SENSITIVE ASSETS AND LIABILITIES

Days	Assets	Liabilities
90	$ 500	$3,299.18
180	600	
270	1,000	
360	1,400	

Source. Elijah Brewer. "Bank Gap Management and the Use of Financial Futures," Federal Reserve Bank of Chicago, *Economic Perspectives*, March/April 1985, p. 19.

0.25 years. The bank has a positive duration gap. An increase in interest rates will reduce the value of the equity of the bank; the bank can reduce or eliminate this positive duration gap by a short hedge. Financial futures should be sold until the duration of the assets falls to 0.25, at which point the bank is perfectly hedged.

The duration of a portfolio containing both cash or spot market assets and futures contracts may be calculated with equation (15.2).

$$D_p = D_{rsa} + D_f \frac{N_f FP}{V_{rsa}} \tag{15.2}$$

where D_p = duration of the entire portfolio, D_{rsa} = duration of the rate sensitive assets, D_f = duration of the deliverable securities involved in the hypothetical futures contract from the delivery date, N_f = number of futures contracts, FP = future price, and V_{rsa} = market value of the rate sensitive assets.

The goal is to reduce the duration of the assets to 0.25 years. With this goal, the bank should sell 64 T-bill futures contracts, assuming that T-bills are yielding 12 percent. In that case, the number of T-bill futures contracts to be sold is calculated as shown in equation (15.3)

$$0.25 = 0.73 + 0.25 \frac{N_f \$97.21}{\$3221.50} \tag{15.3}$$

$$N_f = -64$$

Steps Involved in Hedging

Exhibit 15.2 lists the seven steps involved in hedging the interest sensitivity position of the bank, either its dollar gap or its duration gap. These seven steps are:

EXHIBIT 15.2
HEDGING THE INTEREST SENSITIVITY POSITION OF A BANK—SEVEN STEPS

STEP 1. DETERMINE TOTAL INTEREST-RATE RISK.   In March, a financial institution issues a $1 million six-month money market certificate of deposit (MMCD). The institution knows it will roll over the MMCD in September. Through interest-sensitivity analysis, the institution concludes that it will have a negative gap in September because no assets are repriced then. Because the MMCD rollover accounts for most of the gap, the institution decides to hedge the MMCD portion of its negative gap against the risk of higher interest rates.

STEP 2. SELECT A FUTURES CONTRACT.   The institution selects the 90-day treasury-bill futures contract as the hedging medium because price movements between treasury bills and MMCD's are closely correlated. Technically, the hedge is a cross hedge. It is used because the volume of trading is heavier in treasury-bill futures contracts than in the CD futures contracts.

STEP 3. DETERMINE THE NUMBER OF CONTRACTS NEEDED.   The institution calculates the hedge ratio as below:

EXHIBIT 15.2   *(Continued)*

$$\frac{180 \text{ days}}{90 \text{ days}} \cdot \frac{\$1,000,000}{\$1,000,000} \cdot 1 = 2 \text{ contracts}$$

For the purpose of this example, MMCD and treasury bill interest rates are assumed to be perfectly correlated.

STEP 4. DETERMINE THE LENGTH OF HEDGE.   The length of the hedge is six months, to correspond with the rollover of the six-month MMCD.

STEP 5. PLACE THE HEDGE.   The institution places the hedge by selling two 90-day Treasury bill contracts for September delivery. The cash and futures markets positions in March are as shown.

STEP 6. MONITOR THE HEDGE.   A realistic hedging strategy requires that the hedge be closely monitored to determine basis risk and the direction that risk takes. In this example, basis risk is assumed to be zero.

STEP 7. LIFT THE HEDGE.   Interest rates have risen since March. In September, the institution rolls over the MMCD at a rate of 11.64 percent, an increase of 191 basis points. The hedge is offset by buying two 90-day treasury bill contracts for September delivery. The cash and futures market positions then are as shown.

Thus, hedging in the futures market produced a profit to offset the cash market loss, as shown.

The net result also can be examined in terms of annual interest expense. The total MMCD interest expense for March and September issues is $106,850 ($48,650 plus $58,200). Subtracting the $2,950 profit made in the futures market lowers the total expense to $103,900. Thus, hedging lowered the institution's annual interest expense from 10.69 to 10.39 percent.

March

Cash Market	Futures Market
Issues six-month MMCD at a rate of 9.73 percent. Interest expense for six months is $48,650.	Sells two 90-day T-bill contracts for September delivery at a price of 90.87, which implies an interest rate of 9.13 percent.

September

Cash Market	Futures Market
Rolls over six-month MMCD at a rate of 11.64 percent. Interest expense for six months is $58,200.	Buys the 90-day T-bill contracts for September delivery at a price of 89.69, which implies an interest rate of 10.31 percent.

Final Result

Cash Market		Futures Market	
$48,650	March interest expense	90.87	Selling price
−$58,200	Sept. interest expense	89.69	Purchase price
$(9,550)	Net loss	1.18	Net profit

EXHIBIT 15.2   (*Continued*)

Or, 118 basis points at $25 per
basis point = $2,950 net
profit

Source. Mark Drabenstott and Anne O'Mara McDonley. "Futures Markets: A Primer for Financial Institutions," Federal Reserve Bank of Kansas City, *Economic Review,* November 1984, pp. 17–33.

1. Determine the total interest rate risk. Involved here is a micro hedge.
2. Select a futures contract. The futures contract selected should be the one highest correlated with the cash market instrument being hedged. Normally, this would be the same instrument. If the cash market instrument does not have a futures market equivalent, then the bank executes a cross hedge (i.e., a hedge using a futures contract in an asset with the highest correlation with the spot market asset).
3. Determine the number of contracts needed. Step 3 takes into account the less than perfect correlation that may exist between the cash market instrument and the futures market instrument in a cross hedge.
4. Determine the length of the hedge.
5. Place the hedge.
6. Monitor the hedge.
7. Lift the hedge.

Complications in Using Financial Futures

Although financial futures are designed to allow banks to reduce interest rate risk, a number of complications must be considered:

1. The bank must use the futures markets within the limits prescribed by accounting and regulatory guidelines. These guidelines generally limit a bank's financial futures activities to those transactions that relate to a bank's business needs and the bank's capacity to meet its obligations. Exhibit 15.3 provides more details on the accounting and regulatory treatment of futures transactions.

2. For macro hedges, in which the bank is hedging the entire portfolio, the bank cannot, under current guidelines, defer gains and losses from marking the futures contract to market daily. As a result, earnings are likely to be less stable in the short run with the practice of macro hedging. As discussed in Exhibit 15.3, however, if the hedge is a micro one, whereby the hedge is linked directly to a specific asset, then gains and losses can be deferred until the maturity of the contract. Hence, accounting policies favor micro hedge even though a macro hedge is generally more appropriate for portfolio management.

3. The bank faces a number of risks in implementing a hedging strategy using financial futures. Perhaps the most important is basis risk. Basis refers to the difference between the cash and futures price of the financial instrument that is used for the hedge. It is the fact that the cash and futures prices move together that provides an opportunity for risk reduction through hedging. Yet the cash and futures prices are not perfectly correlated. As a result, when the basis changes, as it usually does during the period of the hedge, the ability to reduce interest rate risk is compromised. Interest rate risk may be eliminated only if basis does not change and basis usually does change over the life of the hedge.

4. Bank management also must recognize that the existing gap position of the bank may change due to deposit inflows or loan repayment over which the bank has little control. As a result, a hedge that was appropriate for the portfolio at the time the hedge was created may be inappropriate as the period of the hedge unfolds.

EXHIBIT 15.3
ACCOUNTING RULES AND FUTURES CONTRACTS

Current accounting procedures for futures contracts are set out in a uniform policy on bank contract activity issued by the Federal Reserve Board, the Federal Deposit Insurance Corporation, and the Comptroller of the Currency on November 15, 1979, revised March 12, 1980. Federal regulations give banks the option of carrying futures contracts on a mark-to-market or lower-of-cost-or-market basis. Other rules require all open contract positions be reviewed at least monthly, at which time market values are determined. Futures contracts are valued on either the market or lower-of-cost and market method, at the option of the bank, except that the accounting for trading account contracts and cash positions should be consistent. Underlying securities commitments relating to open futures contracts are not reported on the balance sheet; the only entries are for margin deposits, unrealized losses and, in certain instances, unrealized gains related to the contracts. In addition, banks must maintain general ledger memorandum accounts or commitment registers to identify and control all commitments to make or take delivery of securities. Following monthly contract valuation, unrealized losses would be recognized as a current expense item, and banks that value contracts on a market basis would also recognize unrealized gains as current income. Acquisition of securities under futures contracts is recorded on a basis consistent with that applied to the contracts, either market or lower-of-cost-or-market.

The Financial Accounting Standards Board (FASB), in its ruling effective December 31, 1984, introduced new guidelines for futures contracts. The new rules allow firms to use hedge accounting for future transactions.[a] In hedge accounting, a futures position is defined as a hedging transaction if it can be linked directly with an underlying asset or liability and if the price of the futures contracts is highly correlated with the price of the underlying cash position. If these conditions are met, and if the underlying cash position is not carried at market, futures gains or losses can be **deferred** until the position is closed out. The gains or losses can then become part of the accounting basis of the underlying cash position, to be **amortized** over the remaining life of the asset or liability, and therefore taken into income gradually.

The FASB standards require that banks and other firms formulate their hedged positions in light of their entire mix of assets and liabilities so that macro interest rate exposure is reduced by micro hedges. By insisting that all futures hedges be linked to an identifiable instrument "or group of instruments, such as loans that have similar terms"

EXHIBIT 15.3   (*Continued*)

to qualify for hedge accounting, the FASB is encouraging banks to analyze thoroughly their overall exposure to interest rate risk as well as the components that make up that risk. The FASB standards, however, do not allow hedge accounting for the macro hedging of an overall gap on a bank's balance sheet that cannot be identified with a specific item.

The FASB statements call for the classification of deferred gains and losses as an adjustment to the carrying amount of the hedged items. Bankers should be aware that if such an adjustment is made to appropriate general ledger accounts, the computation of average daily balances for the purpose of determining average yields will be distorted unless special provisions are made. In addition, other FASB statements require that the amortization of the deferred futures gains or losses to interest income or expense start no later than the date that a particular contract is closed out. Profits or losses from the futures position must be taken into the income stream over that time period when the bank expected an adverse impact from interest rates.

[a] Bank regulators reactions to FASB statement, if any, are yet to be determined. As a result, banks futures transactions are still governed by federal banking regulations.

Source. Elija Brewer. "Bank Gap Management and the Use of Financial Futures," Federal Reserve Bank of Chicago, *Economic Perspectives,* March/April 1985.

USING THE FUTURES OPTIONS MARKETS TO MANAGE INTEREST-RATE RISK

Buying and selling options on futures contracts offer an alternative means to manage interest rate risk. Options represent contracts that provide their holders with the right (but not the obligation) to buy or sell a particular financial instrument at a specified price on or before a specified date. In contrast, futures contracts convey both the right *and* the obligation to buy a financial instrument at a specified price on or before a specified date. Options on a number of futures contracts trade on various exchanges (including the International Monetary Market of the Chicago Mercantile Exchange). The most active traded contracts are for treasury bill futures and for Eurodollar time deposit futures.

Characteristics of Options

A **call** option gives the buyer the right (but not the obligation) to buy an underlying instrument (such as a T-bill futures contract) at a specified price (called the exercise or strike price) and the seller the comparable right to sell the underlying instrument at the same price. For this right the buyer and seller pay a fee determined by supply and demand conditions in the options market, which is referred to as a premium.

A **put** option gives the buyer the right (although not the obligation) to sell a specified underlying security at the price stipulated in the contract and the seller the obligation to buy the underlying security. As with calls, the premium is determined by the interplay of supply and demand in the options market.

EXHIBIT 15.4

CONTRACT SPECIFICATIONS FOR OPTIONS ON IMM MONEY MARKET FUTURES

Options on Treasury Bill Futures. IMM treasury bill futures options were first listed for trading in April 1986. The underlying instrument for these options is the IMM 3-month treasury bill futures contract. Expiration dates for traded contracts fall approximately 3 to 4 weeks before the underlying futures contract matures. IMM futures options can be exercised anytime up to the expiration date.

Strike Price Intervals. Strike price intervals are 25 basis points for IMM index prices above 91.00 and 50 basis points for index prices below 91.00. Strike prices typically are quoted in terms of basis points. Thus, the strike prices for traded treasury bill futures options can be 90.50 or 92.25, but not 90.25 or 92.10.

Price Quotation. Premium quotations for treasury bill futures options are based on the IMM index price of the underlying futures contract. As with the underlying futures contract, the minimum price fluctuation is one basis point, and each basis point is worth $25. Thus, a quote of 0.35 represents an options premium of $875 (35 basis points × $25). The minimum price fluctuation for put and call premiums is one basis point. There is no upper limit on daily price fluctuations.

Options on Eurodollar Futures. IMM options on Eurodollar futures began trading in March 1985. Eurodollar options expire at the end of the last day of trading in the underlying Eurodollar futures contract. Because the Eurodollar futures contract is cash settled, the final settlement for Eurodollar options follows the cash settlement procedure adopted for Eurodollar futures.

To illustrate, suppose the strike price for a bought Eurodollar futures call option is 91.00 and the final settlement price for Eurodollar futures is 91.50. Exercising the call option at expiration gives the holder the right, in principle, to place $1,000 in a 3-month Eurodollar deposit paying an add-on rate of 9 percent. But since the contract is settled in cash, the holder received $1,250 (50 basis points × $25) in lieu of the right to place the Eurodollar deposit paying 9 percent.

Strike Price Intervals. Strike price intervals for Eurodollar futures options are the same as treasury bill strike price intervals.

Price Quotation. Premium quotations for Eurodollar options are based on the IMM index price of the underlying Eurodollar futures contract. As with the underlying futures contract, the minimum price fluctuation is one basis point, and each basis point is worth $25.

---

[a] The precise rule used to determine IMM treasury bill futures options expiration dates is as follows. The expiration date is the business day nearest the underlying futures contract month that satisfies the following two conditions. First, the expiration date must fall on the last business day of the week. Second, the last day of trading must precede the first day of the futures contract month by at least 6 business days.

As with futures markets, options contracts are standardized contracts that trade on organized exchanges. Fulfillment of the contract is guaranteed by the market clearing corporation. Unlike futures contracts, however, buyers are not required to put forward a margin (because their loss is limited to the premium paid for the option) although sellers of put and call options must maintain margin positions.

Call and put options on treasury bill and Eurodollar futures are traded on the International Monetary Market. When the contract is exercised, the buyer agrees to take delivery of a T-bill or Eurodollar contract at some future date and the seller agrees to make delivery on a contract. The buyer has a long futures position, whereas the seller has a short futures position. Contract specifications for options in the IMM are given in Exhibit 15.4.

Payoffs For Futures and Futures Options Contracts

In order to provide a comparison of futures options with futures contracts, Figure 15.1 provides the payoff possibilities for both futures and options trans-

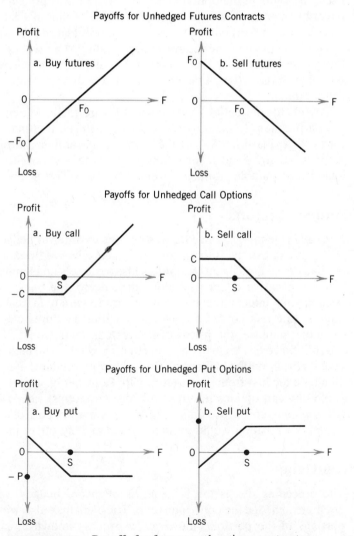

FIGURE 15.1   Payoffs for futures and options contracts.

actions. Figure 15.1a shows the payoff for unhedged long and short futures positions. The horizontal axis measures the price of the futures contract (F), and the vertical axis measures any profits or losses due to changes in the prices of the futures contracts. Because the buyer of a futures contract gains or loses one dollar for each dollar the contract rises or falls, the 45-degree line passed through F_0 in Figure 15.1a provides a representation of the payoff. The payoff from an unhedged short futures position is, of course, the opposite of an unhedged long position.

Figure 15.1b shows the payoff for an unhedged futures call option bought and held until expiration. The buyer pays the amount of the call premium (c), which is the maximum that can be lost. As the value of the futures contract rises, the value of the option increases. At a futures price above F_0, the option buyer has a profit. The logic is reversed for the seller of a call option. The seller receives the call premium. However, the profit from the transaction is diminished as the price of the futures contract falls. At a price of F_0, the loss on the futures contract offsets the receipt of the call premium, whereas at lower prices the seller of the call experiences a loss on the futures contract that exceeds the call premium.

Payoffs for put options are shown in Figure 15.1c. The buyer of a put option pays a premium (P) and receives the right to sell the underlying futures contracts (at strike price S). As the price of the futures contract drops, the premium is recouped and at some (lower) price the buyer of the put has a gain. The logic is comparable although reversed for the seller of a put.

Hedging with Futures Options

Bank management can use futures options in order to hedge interest rate risk, just as it can use the futures contracts themselves. For example, suppose that the bank measured its interest rate-sensitive assets and liabilities and found that it had a negative dollar gap. Without hedging, the bank would experience a declining net interest income if interest rates were to increase. In that case, the interest rate risk could be reduced by selling a futures call option. If interest rates did increase, the prices of futures contracts would fall. Through selling the call, however, the bank has, in effect, locked in the higher price. It can then take its profit on the call option (i.e., the call premium) and use it to reduce or eliminate the loss from the negative gap. Conversely, a bank with a positive gap could buy call options in order to hedge its interest rate risk. If interest rates fall, the bank could lose on its cash or spot market portfolio, but the gain from its options position would partially or completely offset that loss.

Micro and Macro Hedge

The preceding discussion is in terms of macro hedges, where management attempts to hedge the entire portfolio. The bank may also wish to hedge specific portions of the portfolio, however, a process known as micro hedging. For example, suppose that the bank has funded a loan that reprices every 6 months with Eurodollar CDs that reprice every 3 months. In that case, the bank could lose considerably if interest rates increased. To protect itself from such a risk the bank could sell call options on Eurodollar futures. If interest rates increase, the gain from the call options (i.e., the call premium) would offset the loss on the funding of the loan.

INTEREST RATE SWAPS

One of the most recent techniques devised to manage interest rate risk (and also for other purposes) is the interest rate swap. First developed in Europe in 1981, swaps have literally exploded in volume since then and now total over $150 billion. In an interest rate swap, two firms that want to change their interest rate exposure in different directions get together (usually with the help of some financial intermediary) and exchange or swap their obligations to pay interest (just the interest payment obligations are swapped, not the principal).

Assume that one firm has long-term fixed assets financed with short-term variable rate liabilities. Further assume that another firm has short-term variable rate assets financed with long-term fixed rate liabilities. Both firms are exposed to interest rate risk but their exposure is quite different. The first firm gains if interest rates fall, whereas the second firm loses if interest rates decline. Of course, if interest rates increase, the first firm loses and the second firm gains.

For firms having this type of interest rate exposure (e.g., a bank and a savings and loan), the swap of interest payments allows each firm to benefit. The first firm substitutes fixed rate liabilities for its floating rate liabilities and thereby reduces its interest rate risk. The second firm substitutes variable rate liabilities for fixed rate liabilities and also reduces its interest rate risk.

Exhibit 15.5 provides more detailed information on the mechanics of a swap. It deals with a swap between a thrift institution with a large portfolio of fixed rate mortgages and a bank with a portfolio consisting primarily of variable rate loans tied to the London Interbank Offered Rate (LIBOR). On May 10, 1983, the thrift and the bank arrange, through a large investment bank, a swap transaction for $100 million at 7 percent. The thrift agrees to pay the bank a fixed rate of 11 percent per year, payable semiannually. This covers the 11 percent rate the bank is committed to pay on a 7-year bond. The thrift also pays the 2-percent spread incurred by the bank at the time it issued the bond. In return, the bank agrees to make floating rate payments to the thrift at 35 basis points below LIBOR. The investment bank earned a fee of $500,000 for bringing the thrift and the bank together.

The swap of the interest payment obligations reduces interest rate risk for both the bank and the thrift. Although interest rate risk is reduced, it is not eliminated. The floating rate payment that the thrift received is linked to LIBOR, whereas its cost of borrowing is tied more closely to the T-bill rate.

EXHIBIT 15.5

HOW A SWAP WORKS

The following example is based on an actual transaction that was arranged by an investment bank between a large thrift institution and a large international bank; it is representative of many swaps that have been arranged since 1982. "Thrift" has a large portfolio of fixed-rate mortgages. "Bank" has most of its dollar-denominated assets yielding a floating-rate return based on LIBOR (the London Interbank Offered Rate).

On May 10, 1983, the "Intermediary," a large investment bank, arranged a $100 million, 7-year interest rate swap between Thrift and Bank. In the swap, Thrift agreed to pay Bank a fixed rate of 11 percent per year on $100 million, every 6 months. This payment covered exactly the interest Bank had to pay on a $100 million bond it issued in the Eurodollar market. Thrift also agreed to pay Bank the 2 percent underwriting spread that Bank itself paid to issue this bond. In exchange, Bank agreed to make floating-rate payments to Thrift at 35 basis points (.35 percent) below LIBOR. Intermediary received a broker's fee of $500,000.

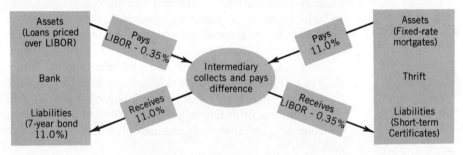

Twice a year, Intermediary (for a fee) calculates Bank's floating-rate payment by taking the average level of LIBOR for that month (Col. 2), deducting 35 basis points, dividing by 2 (because it is for *half* a year), and multiplying by $100 million (Col. 3). If this amount is larger than Thrift's fixed-rate payment (Col. 4), Bank pays Thrift the difference (Col. 5). Otherwise, Thrift pays Bank the difference (Col. 6).

$\boxed{1}$	$\boxed{2}$	$\boxed{3}$	$\boxed{4}$	$\boxed{5}$	$\boxed{6}$
		Floating-rate payment 1/2 (LIBOR-	Fixed-rate payment	Net Payment from Bank	Net Payment from Thrift
Date	LIBOR	0.35%)	1/2 (11%)	to Thrift	to Bank
May 1983	8.98%	—	—	—	—
Nov 1983	8.43%	$4,040,000	$5,500,000	0	$1,460,000
May 1984	11.54%	$5,595,000	$5,500,000	$95,000	0
Nov 1984	9.92%	$4,785,000	$5,500,000	0	$ 715,000
May 1985	8.44%	$4,045,000	$5,500,000	0	$1,455,000

The swap allows both Bank and Thrift to reduce their exposure to interest rate risk. Bank can now match its floating-rate assets priced off LIBOR with an interest payment based on LIBOR, while the fixed-rate interest payments on its bond issue are covered by Thrift. At the same time, Thrift can hedge part of its mortgage portfolio, from which it receives fixed interest earnings, with the fixed-rate payment it makes to Bank. However, the floating-rate payment that Thrift receives is linked to LIBOR while its cost of

EXHIBIT 15.5 (*Continued*)

borrowing is more closely linked to the T-bill rate. Since LIBOR and the T-bill rate do not always move in tandem, Thrift is still exposed to fluctuations in the relation between LIBOR and the T-bill rate.

Source. Jan G. Loeys. "Interest Rate Swaps: A New Tool for Managing Risks," Federal Reserve Bank of Philadelphia, May/June 1985, p. 19.

Because the correlation between movements in T-bill and LIBOR rate is less than perfect, interest rate risk is not fully eliminated.

There are a variety of different participants in the interest rate swap markets. Commercial banks and other financial and nonfinancial organizations use the swap market to reduce their interest rate exposure. In addition, commercial and investment bankers, brokers and dealers in the swap markets arrange swap transactions for others and earn income from creating a market for swaps. Major commercial banks in the United States play a particularly active role in the swap market, as shown in Exhibit 15.6.

EXHIBIT 15.6

FROM ZERO TO $80 BILLION IN THREE YEARS

Interest rate swaps first emerged in the Eurobond market in late 1981.[a] Large international banks, which do most of their lending on a floating-rate basis, were involved in the first swaps so that they could use their fixed-rate borrowing capacity to obtain lower-cost floating-rate funds. Initially, the swapping partners consisted mainly of utilities and lower-rated industrial corporations that preferred fixed-rate financing. During 1982, the first domestic interest rate swap occurred between the Student Loan Marketing Association (Sallie Mae) and the ITT Financial Corp., with Sallie Mae making floating-rate payments to ITT. Since then, the market has grown tremendously; in 1984 about $80 billion in swap agreements were concluded.[b] Any large corporation can now use interest rate swaps as an instrument for asset-liability management.

Both investment banks and commercial banks have been active in arranging interest rate swaps. These intermediaries earn fees by bringing the different parties together, by acting as settlement agent (that is, collecting and paying the net difference in the interest payments), and by serving as guarantor of the agreement. Most intermediaries have recently gone beyond their initial role of merely bringing different parties together and function also as dealers. As a dealer, the intermediary is also the counterparty to each swap it "sells." That is, each party has an agreement only with the intermediary and is totally unaware of who might be on the other side of the swap. This arrangement allows the intermediary to sell one leg of the swap before selling the other and to work with an inventory of as yet unmatched swap agreements. The existence of dealers also facilitates an informal secondary market in swaps, where parties to a swap can sell their position to the intermediary or to another party, thereby increasing the liquidity of this instrument.

A typical swap involves a bond issue for $25 to $75 million with a 3 to 10 year maturity on one side, and a floating-rate loan on the other side. Initially, this floating-rate loan was priced at a fraction over LIBOR, the London Interbank Offered Rate. Recently floating-rate loans have also been using the prime rate, the T-bill rate, or other indices of the cost of short-term borrowing.

EXHIBIT 15.5 *(Continued)*

The most common type of swap is the one described above: a dollar fixed-rate loan swapped for a dollar floating-rate loan, otherwise called the "plain-vanilla" swap. However, several variations on this basic swap have emerged in the market. One such variation is a floating-to-floating swap where parties agree to swap floating rates based on different indices. For example, a bank with assets tied to the prime rate and liabilities based on LIBOR may want to swap the interest payments on its liabilities with payments on a prime-tied, floating-rate loan. Another type of arrangement involves currency swaps such as a swap of a sterling floating-rate loan for a dollar fixed-rate loan. For firms whose assets are denominated in a different currency than are its liabilities, this type of swap may be more appropriate. Finally, rather than exchanging interest payments on liabilities, swaps can also be used to exchange yields on *assets* of different maturities or currencies.

The interest rate swap market has proven to be very flexible in adjusting its product to new customer needs. This innovativeness all but guarantees that swaps will remain a permanent feature of international capital markets.

Source. Jan Loeys. "Interest Rate Swaps, A New Tool for Managing Risk," Federal Reserve Bank of Philadelphia, May/June 1985, p. 20.

[a] For more technical and institutional details on interest rate swaps, see Carl R. Beidleman, *Financial Swaps: New Strategies in Currency and Coupon Risk Management,* (Homewood, Illinois: Dow Jones-Irwin, 1985); and Boris Antl (ed.), *Swap Financing Techniques,* (London: Euromoney Publications Limited, 1983).

[b] Since there are no official reporting requirements on swaps, estimates of the size of this market vary tremendously. The amount of $80 billion, as estimated by Salomon Brothers (see *The Economist,* March 16, 1985, p. 30, Table 16), appears to be somewhere in the middle.

Swaps and Futures

Interest rate swaps provide an alternative to futures (and options) as a bank's device to manage its interest rate risk. Swaps have both advantages and disadvantages when compared with futures. The principal advantages of swaps over futures are twofold. First, swaps may be customized to meet the exact needs of the bank. Because interest rate swaps are negotiated contracts, the terms of maturity and other dimensions of the swap can be tailored to the needs of the bank. Second, the swap can be established for a long-term arrangement—most swaps have maturity of 3 to 10 years. In contrast, financial futures are standardized contracts that have a limited number of specified delivery dates and deliverable types of financial instruments. Most important, futures contracts generally are available only for delivery dates at 3-month intervals that extend only up to $2\frac{1}{2}$ years in the future, making hedging interest rate risk with futures contracts impossible over a long-term period.

Swaps do offer some disadvantages, also relative to futures. Most of these disadvantages stem from the customized nature of the swap contracts. The lack of standardization of swaps increases the search costs of finding counterparts to the swap. In monetary cost terms, also, it is more costly to close out a swap

EXHIBIT 15.7
TOP 25 U.S. BANKS BY NOTIONAL VALUE OF SWAPS OUTSTANDING (IN THOUSANDS)

June 1987 Rank by Notional Value	Rank by Asset Size	Bank	Notional Value June 1987	Notional Value Dec. 1986	Notional Value Dec. 1985
1	1	Citibank	$90,838,000	$66,071,000	$33,380,000
2	5	Chemical Bank	67,253,000	35,531,000	16,051,133
3	7	Bankers Trust	66,828,183	51,565,862	23,541,000
4	6	Manufacturers Hanover Trust	52,550,000	37,956,000	22,413,601
5	4	Morgan Guaranty Trust	50,780,600	40,193,800	21,450,700
6	3	Chase Manhattan Bank	40,051,644	21,948,194	9,994,300
7	8	Security Pacific National Bank	28,457,392	14,739,495	1,328,598
8	9	First National Bank of Chicago	19,381,043	17,722,840	8,458,000
9	2	Bank of America	14,472,000	11,489,000	7,367,000
10	15	First Interstate Bank	13,882,489	11,343,601	7,176,760
11	13	Marine Midland Bank	10,139,480	4,242,480	3,154,600
12	11	Mellon Bank	6,629,518	5,956,720	2,440,046
13	14	Irving Trust	4,898,851	2,437,141	502,400
14	10	Continental Illinois	4,615,319	4,923,875	3,322,362
15	16	Bank of New York	4,534,529	3,573,540	1,216,076
16	19	Bank of New England	2,319,680	1,412,192	312,333
17	22	Philadelphia National Bank	2,281,844	1,210,426	684,000
18	23	Harris Trust	2,117,715	2,109,170	1,603,700
19	20	Citibank South Dakota	2,100,000	945,000	0
20	21	Seattle—First National Bank	1,825,362	1,799,569	754,300
21	12	Bank of Boston	1,819,239	1,931,948	1,482,270
22	24	Comerica Bank—Detroit	1,540,716	1,565,716	1,168,000
23	26	Bank One Columbus	1,524,790	1,362,790	1,607,280
24	25	National City Bank	1,344,218	1,229,218	658,400
25	18	NCNB—North Carolina	1,228,709	689,942	10,000

Source. Steven D. Felgren, "Interest Rate Swaps: Use, Risk, and Prices," Federal Reserve Bank of Boston, *New England Economic Review,* November/December 1987, p. 29.

contract prior to maturity than a futures contract. Equally significant, the bank that enters into a swap agreement faces the possibility that the counterparts may default. Although the bank has no principal at risk, it does have credit risk in the interest payment obligation.

As the swap market has evolved, the importance of these disadvantages has been diminished by the intervention of intermediaries into the market. These intermediaries (generally investment or commercial banks) have been willing (for a fee) to guarantee the payment of interest on a swap contract. Also, to reduce the problems associated with the customized nature of the swap contract, these intermediaries have started to standardize the contract terms, such as the type of floating rate interest, the repricing dates, and collateral requirements. Secondary markets for swaps also have developed, thereby increasing the liquidity of the swap contracts.

SUMMARY

Recent innovations in financial markets have created new instruments that banks can use in managing their interest rate risk. Three in particular have great importance to bank management—futures, options, and swaps. Each allows bank management to alter interest rate exposure, and each has certain advantages and disadvantages when compared with the other. Taken together, however, they give bank managers enormously improved flexibility in managing interest rate risk.

A bank may hedge its interest rate risk in the futures market by taking a position that is the opposite of its existing portfolio position. If, for example, the bank was asset sensitive, it could take a long position in the futures market to hedge risk. If interest rates were to fall, it would suffer a loss with its existing portfolio (because it was asset sensitive) but would incur a gain in its futures position. Conversely, a liability-sensitive bank could protect itself against interest rate movements by establishing a short position in the futures market. Futures market positions could also be used to hedge positive or negative duration gaps.

An alternative way of managing interest rate risk is to buy or sell an option on a futures contract. A call option gives the buyer the right (but not the obligation) to buy an underlying instrument (such as a T-bill futures contract) at a specified price (called the exercise or strike price) and the seller the comparable right to sell the underlying instrument at the same price. A put option gives the buyer the right (although not the obligation) to sell a specified underlying security at the price stipulated in the contract and the seller the obligation to buy the underlying security. Options on futures would be used similarly to the futures themselves in order to hedge interest rate exposure, although options have the advantage of smaller initial outlay in order to accomplish the interest rate risk management.

The third technique for managing interest rate risk without actually altering the existing portfolio is the swap. With a swap, the bank swaps its obligation to pay interest (but not principal) to another party. The bank agrees to pay the interest of the other party (e.g., fixed rate interest), whereas the counterparts agree to pay the bank's interest. Whether asset sensitive or liability sensitive, then, the bank is able through the swap to reduce its exposure to interest rate fluctuations.

IMPORTANT CONCEPTS

call option

call premium

futures options contrast

interest rate futures

interest rate swap

long/short hedge

micro/macro hedge

put option

REFERENCES

Drabenstott, M., and A. McDonley. "Futures Markets: A Primer for Financial Institutions," Federal Reserve Bank of Kansas City, *Economic Review,* November 1984, pp. 17–23.

Felgran, S. D. "Interest Rate Swaps: Use, Risk, and Prices," Federal Reserve Bank of Boston, *New England Economic Review,* November/December 1987, pp. 22–32.

Keen, H. "Interest Rate Futures: A Challenge for Bankers," Federal Reserve Bank of Philadelphia, *Business Review,* November/December 1980, pp. 13–25.

Koch, D., D. Steinhausen, and P. Whigham. "Financial Futures as a Risk Management Tool for Banks and S and L's," Federal Reserve Bank of Atlanta, *Economic Review,* September 1982, pp. 11–29.

Koppenhaver, G. "A T-Bill Futures Hedging Strategy for Banks," Federal Reserve Bank of Dallas, *Economic Review,* March 1983, pp. 15–28.

Koppenhaver, G. "Futures Options and Their Use by Financial Intermediaries," Federal Reserve Bank of Chicago, *Economic Perspectives,* January/February 1986, pp. 18–31.

Loeys, J. "Interest Rate Swaps: A New Tool for Managing Risk," Federal Reserve Bank of Philadelphia, *Business Review,* May/June 1985, pp. 17–25.

QUESTIONS

15.1. What are financial futures contracts? What similarities exist among all futures contracts?

15.2. What is meant by a short position in financial futures? A long position? How is each affected by changes in interest rates?

15.3. Why can buyers and sellers of futures contracts ignore possible default by the other party?

15.4. What does marked-to-market mean?

15.5. Distinguish between a micro hedge and a macro hedge. Are there any inherent conflicts in using both simultaneously in managing interest rate risk?

15.6. How would a bank use interest rate futures to hedge a positive dollar gap? A negative dollar gap?

15.7. How would a bank use interest rate futures to hedge a positive duration gap? A negative duration gap?

15.8. What complications exist in using financial futures to hedge a bank portfolio?

15.9. What is a futures options contract? Compare and contrast a futures options contract with a futures contract.

15.10. Compare and contrast the characteristics of and use of put and call futures options contracts.

15.11. Explain how futures options contracts can be used to hedge interest rate risk.

15.12. What is an interest rate swap? How can it be used to hedge interest rate risk?

15.13. Compare the pros and cons of futures, futures options, and swaps as devices to hedge interest rate risk.

PROBLEMS

15.1. Assume that on April 1 your bank plans to issue a three-month Eurodollar CD in July. On April 1, the bank could issue a three-month Eurodollar CD for 7.02 percent. The corresponding rate for the six-month Eurodollar contract (due in September) was 7.58 percent.

(a) What position should the bank take in the Eurodollar market?

(b) Suppose that the bank took a position in Eurodollar futures on April 1, and that it closes out its position in July when the futures rate is 7.82%. In that situation, has the bank achieved its objective with the hedge?

15.2. Suppose that your bank has a commitment to make a fixed rate loan in three months at the existing interest rate. To hedge against the prospect of rising interest rates, the bank takes a position in the futures options markets. What position should it take? The relevant information is as follows:

    T-bill futures prices 89-1

    Put option 90

    Premium $2500

What will be the net gain to the bank if T-bill futures prices fall to 85? If they increase to 93?

15.3. Given a bank with assets comprised only of one-year loans earning 10 percent and liabilities comprised only of 90-day CDs paying 6 percent. The following cash inflows and outflows during the next year would occur:

			Day		
	0	90	180	270	360
Loans					
Inflows					$1,000
Outflows	$909.09				
CDs					
Inflows	$909.09	$922.43	$935.98	$949.71	
Outflows		$922.43	$935.98	$949.71	$963.65
Net Cash Flows	–0–	–0–	–0–	–0–	$36.35

Notice that for loans $1,000/(1.10) = $909.09. Also notice that CDs are rolled over every 90 days at the constant interest rate of 6 percent [e.g., $909.09(1.06)$^{.25}$, where .25 = 90 days/360 days]. Of course, the positive duration gap of the bank exposes it to the risk that interest rates will rise and CDs will have to be rolled over at higher rates. As a hedge against this possibility, the bank may sell 90-day financial futures with a par of $1,000. In this situation the following entries on its balance sheet would occur over time:

		Day			
	0	90	180	270	360
T-bill futures (sold)					
Inflows		$985.54	$985.54	$985.54	
T-bill (spot market purchase)					
Outflows		$985.54	$985.54	$985.54	
Net Cash Flows		–0–	–0–	–0–	

It is assumed here that the T-bills pay 6 percent and interest rates will not change [i.e., $1,000/(1.06)$^{.25}$ = $985.54].

(a) If interest rates increase by 2 percent in the next year (after the initial issue of CDs), first show the effect on the bank's net cash flows.
(b) Next, show the effect of this interest rate increase on net cash flows from the short T-bill futures position. Does the T-bill futures hedge offset the bank's balance sheet risk?
(c) How might the bank use an option on futures to accomplish this same hedge? How much would the option cost such that the futures gain plus put premium just offsets the loss on the bank's balance sheet (i.e., a perfect hedge is created)? Must the bank maintain a margin on this options contract?

PART FIVE

INTERNATIONAL BANKING

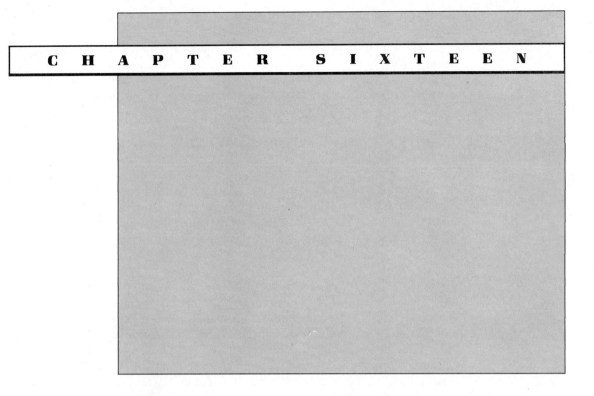

INTERNATIONAL BANKING

The front page of the *American Banker* (February 27, 1986) reported that "The Hospital Corporation of America has arranged a $1.25 billion credit with Chase Manhattan bank as the agent bank and Swiss Bank Corp. as deputy agent." Hospital Corporation of America owns and operates health care facilities in the United States and elsewhere. Foreign banks involved in the revolving credit include the Deutche Bank, Frankfurt; Bank of Nova Scotia, Halifax; Credit Lyonnais, Paris; Lloyds Bank, London; and Bank of Tokyo Trust Company, Tokyo, and others. Selected domestic lenders include Bankers Trust Co., New York; Continental Illinois Bank and Trust Company, Chicago; Bay Bank, Boston; Sun Bank, Orlando; and Metropolitan Federal Savings and Loan Association, Nashville.

Credit facilities such as these are becoming commonplace. The incomplete list of lenders is sufficient to demonstrate the worldwide financial network that exists to facilitate the flow of capital. In this chapter, we will provide an introduction to international banking and selected parts of that network.

DISTINGUISHING FEATURES BETWEEN DOMESTIC AND INTERNATIONAL BANKING

In this section, we examine activities that differentiate domestic from international banking. The principal activities are making foreign loans, dealing in foreign exchange, having facilities in foreign places, and financing international trade. A bank may do any or all of these activities.

Foreign Loans

Differences exist between domestic and international banking. One difference is that international banking involves extending credit to nondomestic (foreign) customers. As shown earlier, Japanese and German banks loaned funds to Hospital Corporation of America. The flow of funds goes the other way, too. Domestic banks make loans to foreign governments and business concerns to finance their capital investment projects and their day-to-day operations. Lending to foreign governments and business concerns contains risks that are not inherent in making loans to domestic borrowers. We will examine these risks in both this chapter and the next one.

Foreign Exchange

International banking also may require dealing in foreign exchange—exchanging one currency for a different country's currency. For example, loans made by a domestic bank to a foreign borrower may be denominated in the United Kingdom's pound sterling or some other currency. Similarly, a domestic bank can buy or sell foreign currencies for its customers. Or a customer may make a **Eurocurrency** deposit, which is a deposit in a currency other than that of the country where the bank is located.[1] The prefix "Euro" means "external" and does not mean that the deposits have to be in Europe; they can be anywhere. A French franc deposited in French bank is a regular deposit. But U.S. dollars, West German deutsche marks, or Japanese yen deposited in a bank located in France are Eurocurrency deposits—they are "external" currencies to the country where they were deposited. The receiving bank will make deposits of equivalent value in banks where the currencies are legal tender. Suppose that General Motors makes a $10 million deposit in a French bank located in Paris.

[1] For additional information on Euromarkets, see Gunter Dufey and Ian Giddy, *The International Money Market,* Englewood Cliffs, NJ: Prentice-Hall, 1978.

The French bank will deposit an equivalent value in the United States for dollar deposits. The risks and problems of dealing in foreign currencies are examined in the next chapter.

BOX 16.1
DEVELOPMENT OF THE EURO-DOLLAR MARKET

The sterling crisis of 1957 precipitated the formation of the Euro-dollar market. The Suez crisis and worsening inflation in Britain put intense downward pressure on the pound sterling and prompted the British government to impose capital controls. The government placed controls on nonresident sterling borrowing and lending by British banks and put restraints on sterling credits granted to countries engaging in third-party transactions. These moves caused a shift away from financing third-party trade with sterling credits and deposits toward the use of dollar financing.

The reduced importance of the pound in comparison to the dollar should have prompted a shift in business from London to New York except that Communist countries preferred to place their dollar deposits in western Europe; they feared that the United States would confiscate those deposits if put in the U.S. Moreover, U.S. regulatory policy indirectly encouraged the development of an Euro-dollar market. Policies such as the U.S. Interest Equalization Tax imposed a substantial levy on the sale of foreign bonds and equities in the U.S. and restrictions on American outward direct investment that virtually forced U.S. companies wishing to expand abroad to have access to Euro-dollar financing.

Furthermore, since 1933, the U.S. government has imposed ceilings on interest rates commercial banks and other depository institutions can pay on their checking and time deposits. These ceilings, specified in the Federal Reserve's Regulation Q, have been maintained in large part to ensure a low-cost source of funds to the main supplier of home mortgages— savings and loan institutions. The Regulation Q ceilings were not applied to deposits booked at U.S. banks' overseas branches, which were also free from reserve requirements. The exceptions allowed U.S. bank branches located abroad to compete with foreign banks not subject to such regulations. Bank branches abroad could offer their corporate customers a competitive rate on time deposits and actually recoup some of the funds lost on domestic deposits. The freedom from reserve requirements and interest rate restrictions, therefore, gave Euro-markets a competitive edge.

While the avoidance of reserve requirements and usury ceilings can explain the growth of the Euro-dollar market, it does not explain how London became the center of that market. According to many observers,

BOX 16.1 (*Continued*)

the competitive edge enjoyed by London stems in large part from its substantial head-start in acquiring the skills for conducting international transactions and its proximity to the European market. These accidents of history and geography were matched by deliberate actions of the British government to grant a substantial latitude to banks operating in London to accept deposits and to make loans in foreign currencies.

Source: Kenneth Bernauer. "The Asian Dollar Market," *Economic Review*, Federal Reserve Bank of San Francisco, Winter 1983, pp. 47–62.

Foreign Places

Some banks dealing in international banking have offshore facilities, and are licensed to operate in London, Japan, the Bahamas, or elsewhere where they can make loans, take deposits, or provide other services. However, it is not necessary to have offshore facilities to engage in international banking.

Financing International Trade

International banks frequently deal in financing international trade. This usually involves letters of credit, and payment or collection of funds upon the receipt of certain documents associated with trade. This aspect of international banking is examined in the next chapter.

HOW U.S. BANKS ENGAGE IN INTERNATIONAL BANKING

This section presents the principal methods used by U.S. banking organizations to participate in international banking. The extent to which banks use these methods depends on whether international banking is an occasional or full-time activity.

Correspondent Banking

Most banks in the United States do not deal in international banking on a regular basis. On those occasions when they have a customer who requires international banking services, they use a correspondent bank that offers such services. Correspondent banks are banks that provide a variety of services to other banks in exchange for fees or deposits. Correspondent banks maintain deposits in domestic and foreign banks, which can be used to facilitate trade by making or receiving payments. Typically, correspondent banks providing international banking services are money center banks (large banks located in New York and other money centers), large regional banks, and foreign banks.

Banks that deal extensively in international trade also use correspondent banks on a regular basis. For example, a U.S. bank may use the Bank of Tokyo Trust Company as its principal correspondent in Japan. Thus, payments to or collections from other banks in Japan will be routed through the Bank of Tokyo Trust Company. Similarly, the U.S. bank maintains correspondent relationships in other money centers of the world. Such networks provide the channels that facilitate the efficient flow of funds in the capital markets throughout the world.

In addition to the services mentioned, correspondent banks make international loans and sell "participations" in those loans to other banks. They deal in "swaps," which was explained in Chapter 15. They deal in foreign exchange, and they also provide investment and other services.

Foreign Branches

Banks have foreign branches in the same fashion that they have domestic branches; that is, a branch represents the parent firm at some distant location. However, some branches are full-service branches offering a full range of banking services to their customers, whereas other branches offer only limited services. The full range of services includes taking deposits, making loans, investments, and trust services as examples.

Under provisions of the Federal Reserve Act, banks that are members of the Federal Reserve System may establish foreign branches with the approval of the Federal Reserve Board.

Eurocurrency deposits in U.S. banks are subject to Federal Reserve reserve requirements, which may differ from the reserve requirements on domestic deposits.

Representative Offices

A representative office is a quasi-sales office. Representative offices cannot book loans or take deposits, but they can develop business for the head office and arrange for these things to be done elsewhere. They also establish a bank's presence in an area where the business is not sufficient to justify the cost of establishing a branch, or where new branch offices are not permitted by local regulations.

Foreign Affiliates

Domestic commercial banks and bank holding companies may acquire an equity interest in foreign financial organizations such as banks, finance companies, and leasing companies. They may own all or part of the stock. The affiliates may be subsidiaries or joint ventures. One advantage of foreign affiliates is that the affiliate is not "foreign" in its own country. This may have tax, political, and marketing advantages. On the other hand, a bank with minority ownership is subject to the same problems as any minority stockholder. Minority stockholders may have little influence in the operating policies of a corporation.

Edge Act Offices

The Edge Act of 1919 (an amendment to the Federal Reserve Act by Senator Walter Edge) permits international banking organizations to have subsidiary corporations, which may have offices throughout the United States to provide a means of financing international trade, especially exports. Their activities include making loans and taking deposits strictly related to international transactions. Accordingly, a California bank can have Edge Act offices located in New Orleans, New York, or Chicago; but those offices are restricted to dealing in business strictly related to international transactions. Edge corporations may also invest in foreign financial organizations such as foreign banks, finance companies, and leasing companies.

Some Edge Act offices are located overseas. They may engage in banking practices permitted in foreign countries, which are not permitted in other types of U.S. banking organizations.

The **International Banking Act of 1978** amended the Edge Act to permit domestic banks to acquire foreign financial organizations. To establish reciprocity, foreign financial organizations were permitted to acquire domestic banks.

International Banking Facilities

In the 1960s and 1970s, offshore banking increased as a means of avoiding reserve requirements, limitations on interest rates placed on time and savings deposits, and other regulations. So-called shell banks were opened in the Bahamas and Cayman Islands, which were nothing more than "name plates," for booking "offshore" transactions that took place in the United States.

Beginning in 1981, the Federal Reserve Board permitted domestic and foreign banks to establish international banking facilities (IBFs) to take deposits and make loans to nonresidents, and serve as a record-keeping facility.[2] In reality, an IBF is a set of accounts in a domestic bank that is segregated from the other accounts of that organization. In other words, an IBF is not a bank, per se, it is an accounting system.

IBF accounts do not have the same reserve requirements as domestic banks. IBFs are granted special tax status by certain states, including California,

---

[2] For additional information on IBFs, see K. Alec Crystal, "International Banking Facilities," *Review*, Federal Reserve Bank of St. Louis, April 1984, pp. 5–11.

Connecticut, Delaware, Florida, Georgia, Illinois, Maryland, New York, North Carolina, Washington, and the District of Columbia. The tax breaks are inducements by the states to encourage the development of international financial centers. By the end of 1986, 540 IBFs were established. About half were located in New York, followed by California and Florida.

IBFs are subject to some restrictions that do not apply to foreign branches of U.S. banks. The restrictions were imposed to minimize their impact on the conduct of monetary policy. They are not permitted to accept deposits or make loans to U.S. residents. They may not issue negotiable instruments, because they might fall into the hands of U.S. residents. Nonbank customers' deposits have a minimum maturity of 2 days so they cannot act as substitutes for domestic demand deposits. The minimum denomination of deposits for nonbank customers is $100,000. Because of the minimum size of the deposits, they are not covered by the FDIC deposit insurance.

Export Trading Companies

The Bank Export Services Act of 1982 permitted bank holding companies, Edge corporations, and others to invest in export trading companies (ETCs), subject to review and limitations set by the Federal Reserve Board. The purpose of ETCs is to combine the financial resources of banks with those of other business concerns to promote the export of goods and services produced in the United States. ETCs may engage in international market research, consulting, insurance, transportation, product research and design, taking title to goods, and other activities. It was hoped that domestic export trading companies would be able to compete with Japanese trading companies that perform similar services in Japan.

FOREIGN BANKS IN THE UNITED STATES

Have you ever heard of Bayerische Vereinsbank? It is one of Germany's major banks, and has offices in New York, Chicago, Los Angeles, Atlanta, and Cleveland. How about Taiyo Kobe Bank? This Japanese bank has offices in New York, Los Angeles, Seattle, Houston, and Chicago. Here are two names that may be familiar to you: Harris Trust and Savings Bank, and the LaSalle National Bank, both of Chicago. Did you know that they are owned by the Bank of Montreal and the Algemene Bank Nederland NV, respectively? Did you know that there are more than 250 foreign banks doing business in the United States with over 900 offices, and about half of those offices are in New York City? We observed that U.S. banks own foreign banks and operate offshore, so it should not be surprising that foreign banks own U.S. banks and operate here.

The International Banking Act of 1978 codified the federal regulation of foreign banking activities in the United States. The Act does not require reciprocity for U.S. banks operating in foreign countries. The regulation and supervision is carried out primarily by the Federal Reserve. However, the Comptroller of the Currency, the FDIC, and state banking authorities may also be involved in their regulation. According to the Act, foreign banks can operate agencies, branches, investment companies, commercial bank subsidiaries, and Edge Act offices in the United States.

Agency

According to the Act, an agency is "any office or any place of business of a foreign bank located in any state of the United States or District of Columbia at which credit balances are maintained, checks are paid, or money lent, but deposits may not be accepted for a citizen or resident of the United States." Agencies are used primarily to facilitate international trade between the United States and the foreign bank's native land.

Branch

The definition for a branch is similar to that of an agency, except a branch "may accept deposits that are incidental to, or for the purpose of carrying out transactions in foreign countries." The branch can do almost anything that the parent bank can do, in exactly the same way domestic branch banks operate.

The foreign parent bank must decide in which state the branch will be located. The parent bank may apply for a state-chartered branch, in which case it must operate under the banking laws of that state. Alternately, it may apply for a federal charter from the Comptroller of the Currency, in which case it will be treated as a member bank of the Federal Reserve System (like all national banks) and be covered by FDIC insurance. State-chartered foreign banks that accept retail deposits (less than $100,000) are required to have FDIC insurance.

A limited branch is an Edge Act office set up outside the home state, or some other facility that does not have all of the powers of the branch bank. Representative offices established by a foreign bank are similar to those described for domestic banks.

Investment Company

Investment companies owned by foreign financial organizations are similar to state-chartered commercial banks with the following exceptions. They can deal in securities such as common stock, whereas banks are not permitted to invest in stocks. In addition, an investment company can lend more than 10 percent of its capital and surplus to one customer, whereas banks have limitations relative to capital on the amount they can lend. Finally, an investment company cannot accept deposits.

Two large foreign investment companies are the Nordic American Banking Corporation and the French American Banking Corporation. The Nordic group is owned by four banks in Denmark, Helsinki, Oslo, and Stockholm. The French organization is owned by the Banque Nationale de Paris.

Do not confuse the foreign investment companies with domestic investment companies (i.e., mutual funds). Although both are called investment companies, they are different types of financial organizations. Domestic investment companies pool investors' funds and invest them in securities to obtain capital gains, income, or some other financial objective. Foreign investment companies make loans and equity investments on behalf of their owners.

Subsidiary

Foreign banks can own U.S. banks, in whole or in part. The banks that they own are subject to the same rules and regulations as any other domestic banks. Several U.S.-chartered banks are at least 50 percent foreign owned, including the Marine Midland Bank NA, Buffalo, New York (Hong Kong and Shanghai Banking Corporation); National Westminister Bank USA, New York, (National Westminister Bank, London); and Union Bank, Los Angeles (Standard Chartered Bank, London).

Several subsidiaries of Japanese banks in California are the Mitsubishi Bank of California, Mitsui Manufacturers Bank, Kyowa Bank of California, Golden State Sanwa Bank, Sumitomo Bank of California, and Bank of Tokyo's California First Bank. This partial listing of foreign-owned subsidiaries suggests that foreign banks play an important role in our banking system.

Finance Companies

Foreign financial organizations may own or operate finance companies. For example, Fuji Bank Ltd., Tokyo, owns Heller Financial, Inc., Chicago. And Barclays Bank Plc, London, owns Barclays American Corporation, Charlotte, North Carolina. Finance companies typically make working capital loans to business concerns and consumer loans. Some of these names, and others mentioned previously, are so familiar to those engaged in banking that one forgets that they are owned by foreign banks. Bank regulators, however, do not forget who owns them. Bank regulation poses some special problems that are addressed next.

REGULATING INTERNATIONAL BANKING

Basle Committee

The Committee on Banking Regulation and Supervisory Practices was created by the governors of the central banks of the Group of Ten (G-10) nations in 1974 to improve the coordination of bank supervision among its members.[3]

---

[3] The information in this section is based on *International Banking, International Coordination of Bank Supervision: The Record to Date,* United States GAO/NSIAD-86-40, February 1986; The 11 countries included in G-10 are: Belgium, Canada, France, Italy, Japan, Luxembourg, the Netherlands, United Kingdom, United States, and West Germany. Another valuable source was *Report on International Developments in Banking Supervision,* Report No. 5, Basle, Switzerland, Bank for International Settlements, September 1986.

The committee is called the Basle Committee because it meets in Basle (pronounced Bäl), Switzerland, about four times each year. The objectives of the committee are (1) to define the responsibilities for supervising international banking, (2) to examine common problems such as foreign exchange positions at bank and monitoring country risk (risks of dealing in a country other than credit risk), and (3) to establish personal contacts to resolve mutual banking problems.

U.S. representatives to the Basle Committee include officials of the Federal Reserve Board, the Federal Reserve Bank of New York, the Office of the Comptroller of the Currency, and the Federal Reserve Deposit Insurance Corporation.

Concordat

In 1983, the Balse Committee made an agreement concerning "Principles for the Supervision of Banks' Foreign Establishments," which collectively with an earlier version is called the revised Concordat. The first principle is that no foreign bank should escape supervision, and the second is that supervision should be adequate. It stressed the need for international collaboration in bank supervision.

There are difficulties in implementing these principles because what is considered a bank in one country may not be considered a bank in another. In 1982, for example, the Italian bank, Banco Ambrosiano, failed, including a subsidiary, Banco Ambrosiano Holdings, which was located in Luxembourg. Governments of these countries assumed no responsibility for the failed subsidiary, which was a "holding company" and not a bank.

The country in which the bank's headquarters is located is called the parent country, and the country where the foreign office of the bank is located is called the host country. To resolve the problem illustrated by Banco Ambrosiano, the Basle Committee gave joint responsibility for bank supervision to the parent and host country's supervisory authorities. In addition, each supervisor (host and parent) can assess the adequacy of the other supervisors. If the host considers the parent authority inadequate, the host should refuse entry to the foreign bank, or limit its operations in the host country. Similarly, parent authorities should be concerned about the adequate supervision of foreign offices of their banks.

Judging the adequacy of foreign supervisory systems may have political and legal ramifications; for example, a negative assessment of another country's supervisory system may not be considered "good politics." In addition, existing laws may not allow applications from foreign banks to be rejected because their supervisory system is "inadequate." Nor would rejection on that basis be consistent with our "open-door" policy.

In the United States, the Board of Governors of the Federal Reserve System has primary responsibility for the supervision of domestic and foreign-owned bank holding companies. The Board is concerned primarily with the domestic operations of foreign holding companies. Accordingly, the Board must approve the application for a foreign bank holding company, it requires annual reports to assess the financial condition of the holding company, it monitors transactions between the subsidiary and the foreign parent organization, and it requires reports on the nonbank activities of the holding company in the United States.

Unresolved Issues

Although the Concordat is a step forward, many problems still face the international regulation of banking. One unresolved issue concerns the financial responsibility of a host country to act as a lender of last resort if a foreign bank is in financial difficulty. Other issues include differences in provisions for loan losses on international loans, foreign exchange risk, and country risk. Thus it is clear that the effective supervision of international banking is a goal, not a reality.

Other Multinational Groups

The Basle Committee is only one of the multinational groups dealing with mutual problems concerning banking. The European Economic Community (EEC) is committed to developing a common banking market, which includes coordinating banking laws.[4]

The Nordic Supervisory Group, which includes Denmark, Finland, Iceland, Norway, and Sweden exchanges information concerning banking legislation. Other regional groups that address banking issues are

Offshore Supervisors Group: Bahamas, Bahrain, Barbados, Cayman Islands, Cyprus, Gibraltar, Guernsey, Hong Kong, Isle of Man, Jersey, Lebanon, Netherlands Antilles, Panama, Singapore, and Vanuatu.

Commission of Banking Supervisory and Regulatory Authorities of Latin America and the Caribbean: All national agencies in the region are included.

SEANZA Forum of Banking Supervisors: Includes national agencies from Southeast Asia and the Pacific Basin.

INSURANCE FOR INTERNATIONAL LOANS

To facilitate international trade and finance, federal government and private organizations work together to provide funds to finance exports and insurance

---

[4] The EEC includes Belgium, France, Germany, Italy, Luxembourg, the Netherlands, United Kingdom, Denmark, Greece, and Ireland.

programs to reduce the risks associated with exporting. Several that affect lending are presented here.

Export-Import Bank

The Export-Import Bank is an independent agency of the U.S. government that was created in 1934 to finance trade with the Soviet Union; it did not extend any loans because no agreement could be reached on the Soviet repayment of old debts owed to the United States. That same year another bank was formed to finance trade to other nations, and the first loan was to Cuba. Both banks were merged in 1936. Today the Export-Import Bank is empowered to engage in the general banking business to facilitate U.S. exports and imports by providing loans, guarantees, and export credit insurance. The Eximbank, as it is called, does not compete with private sources of funds. Instead, it steps in when private funds are not available at rates and terms that permit U.S. exporters to compete with terms available in other countries. The insurance and guarantees obtained by exporters can be assigned to commercial banks, thereby enabling the banks to purchase the exporters' receivables with reduced risks.

Foreign Credit Insurance Association

The FCIA is a group of private casualty and marine insurance companies that acts as agents for the Eximbank, selling and servicing insurance of export credits against nonpayment by foreign debtors due to commercial risks (e.g., changes in demand, technology, etc.), and political risks (e.g., inconvertibility of foreign currency into U.S. dollars, government actions that prevent the import of goods, and war).

Private Export Funding Corporation

PERFCO is owned by U.S. banks and U.S. industrial exporters, and provides private funding that is guaranteed by the Eximbank, to finance U.S. exports. It borrows in the capital markets and relends the funds for exports.

Other Agencies

Guarantees and insurance are also provided by other domestic and international agencies. For example, the Commodity Credit Corporation (CCC) has an export guarantee program for agricultural exports. The Overseas Private Investment Corporation (OPIC), which is part of the International Development Cooperation Agency, has insurance and guarantee programs to encourage U.S. private capital to invest in developing countries.

THE DEBT CRISIS

International lenders face some risks that are different than those of domestic lenders. One such risk was the ''debt crisis,'' which shook the international banking community.[5]

Oil Shocks

An axiom in strategic planning is appropriate here. It is that many of the major factors that influence a firm are beyond its control. So it was in the early 1970s when the Organization of Petroleum Exporting Countries (OPEC) shocked the world with higher oil prices that caused a massive redistribution of world income from industrialized nations to oil-producing nations and less-developed countries (LDCs). Prior to 1973, the average price per barrel of imported crude oil was $1.80. In 1974 the price per barrel was $12.52, and by 1981 it reached a record high of $35 per barrel.

Recylced Petrodollars

The funds paid to the oil-producing nations are called petrodollars. Some of the petrodollars flowed back into the United States, attracted by high interest rates and investment opportunities. In addition, the oil exporters had excess operating capacity in their economies and limited investment opportunities except for more oil production. Thus, the petrodollars were recycled by international banks to nonoil-producing LDCs such as Argentina, Brazil, Mexico, Poland, Korea, and others to help finance their imports.

Total external debt of nonoil-producing LDCs increased from $130 billion to $474 billion from 1973 to 1980. Throughout the 1970s, the debt extended to the LDCs was in balance with the growth in their economies and was considered an acceptable risk. U.S. banks' share of total bank loans to LDCs declined from 55 percent in the early 1970s to about 40 percent by the end of the decade as British, German, Japanese, and other banks intensified competition to make loans.

---

[5] Several summaries of the debt crises and related issues are *The Global Financial Structure in Transition,* Joel McClellan, ed., Lexington, MA.: Lexington Books, 1985, various chapters; Jack M. Guttentag and Richard J. Herring, *The Current Crisis in International Lending,* Washington, DC: The Brookings Institution, 1985; James R. Barth and Joseph Pelzman, *International Debt: Conflict and Resolution,* Fairfax, VA: George Madison University, Economics Department, 1984; Henry C. Wallich, Member of the Board of Governors of the Federal Reserve System, ''The International Debt Situation in an American View: Borrowing Countries and Lending Banks,'' Speech to the Verein fuer Socialpolitik, Frankfurt, Germany, February 8, 1985; Hang-Sheng Cheng, ''Bailing Out Banks?'' FRBSF Weekly Letter, Federal Reserve Bank of San Francisco, July 29, 1983; Hang-Sheng Cheng, ''An LDC Debt Update,'' FRBSF Weekly Letter, Federal Reserve Bank of San Francisco, April 12, 1985.

The international banks of the world seemed to be making two assumptions as a basis for their lending to LDCs. First they assumed that oil prices would continue to rise, or at least not decline. Second, they assumed that inflation would continue, and help debtor nations pay the bank loans. Both assumptions were wrong.

Excess Supply

As oil prices increased, the world's market system reacted in a predictable fashion. Consumption of oil declined as consumers became "energy conscious," and equally important, oil exploration and production increased sharply. Oil from the North Sea, Alaska, and even Mexico began to weaken OPEC's price control of the market. By the early 1980s, the world's supply of oil was increasing relative to demand.

The Bubble Burst

Market interest rates soared to record levels, and the U.S. Treasury bill rate increased from about 7 percent in 1980 to 16 percent in 1981. The increase in interest rates reflected high levels of inflation and expectations of still higher rates of inflation, due, in part, to higher oil prices and accommodative monetary policy. The high levels of interest rates increased the financial burden of debtor nations whose loans were denominated in dollars, and whose loans had floating interest rates.

Recognizing the need to break the back of the inflation, the Federal Reserve tightened monetary policy. By 1982, a deep recession in the United States and other industrialized nations resulted in lower commodity prices and reduced demand for imports. These factors, in turn, contributed to the collapse of the debtor nation's export markets, and they were unable to earn sufficient foreign exchange to repay their loans. Total external debt outstanding for the nonoil-producing LDCs increased from $474 billion in 1980 to $664 billion in 1983! Almost one-third of that amount was loans to Argentina, Brazil, and Mexico. During this period, Poland (1981) and Mexico (1982) rescheduled (delayed payments) of their debts.

Unfortunately, some of the LDCs could not, or would not repay their loans as scheduled. Hence, an international debt crisis occurred.

This overview of the debt crisis does not provide a complete picture of all of the factors affecting a debtor nation's ability to repay loans. For example, Argentina's defeat in the Falklands War resulted in deep political divisions between the military junta and powerful labor unions. When a new president took office in 1984, there was a huge government deficit and the inflation rate in Argentina was over 400 percent per year!

Nor does the overview of the debt crisis reflect the impact on the U.S. economy. For example, Mexico is our third largest trade partner, after Canada and Japan. In 1982, because of its external debt problem, it cut its imports drastically. As a result, our exports to Mexico fell by a staggering 60 percent, and our $4 billion trade surplus with Mexico in 1981 turned into a $4 billion deficit in 1982. Based on an estimate that every $1 billion increase in U.S. exports creates 24,000 new jobs in the U.S. economy, the Mexican debt problem alone appears to have cost the United States 200,000 jobs in 1982.[6]

Illiquid versus Insolvent

The size and scope of the debt crisis created considerable debate about what should be done and who should do it. Part of the debate focused on the difference between illiquid and insolvent countries. Illiquid countries were those that were having temporary liquidity problems, which would be resolved when interest rates fall and worldwide economic activity increases. Then the country's growth would be sufficient to repay its external debts. It was argued that additional funds should be invested in illiquid countries to help them through this difficult period.

An insolvent country is one that is unable to repay its debts now or in the future. In this case, some of the loans made to these countries should be written off (taken as losses).

Deciding whether countries are illiquid or insolvent is a matter of judgment. The view that prevailed was to interpret the world situation from the liquidity perspective, rather than single out particular countries. The banks favored this view because they did not want to write off huge loan losses that would impair their capital. Nevertheless, some banks were reluctant to throw good money after bad, and in the third quarter of 1982, net bank debt outstanding to nonoil-producing LDCs declined.

The international problem required international solutions. The major burden fell on the International Monetary Fund (IMF), which is concerned primarily with monetary stability and balance of payments equilibrium. The IMF provided temporary financial assistance to debtor nations, but there were strings attached. The debtor nations had to curb domestic spending, cut their inflation rates, freeze wages, and take other actions to improve their balance of payments. Such actions were not politically popular with the debtor nations, but most attempted to make the necessary adjustments. The IMF also encouraged, insisted, and coerced international banks to make loans to LDCs to forestall worldwide defaults.

Critics charged that the IMF's actions were Band-Aids designed to bail out international banks at the taxpayer's expense, because the U.S. government contributes to the fund. There is an expression that "a rolling loan gathers no loss." By rescheduling the debts of LDCs, the critics argue that the IMF is postponing the day when banks will have to write off the bad loans. Because the banks made bad loans, the bank's stockholders and not the taxpayers should be made to suffer the consequences.

[6] Hang-Sheng Cheng, "Bailing Out Banks?" 1983.

The supporters of the IMF's actions argue that they are preventing the collapse of the international banking system, which is more important than the profitability of individual banks. In 1982, U.S. bank claims on LDCs far exceeded their capital, and to write off the loans as losses would disrupt the U.S. and world banking systems.

By mid-1986, interest rates were low (treasury bills were about 6 percent), oil sold for $10 per barrel, and the economy was growing, albeit at a slow pace. The debt crisis had evolved into long-term adjustments, austerity, and rescheduling of debts. Countries such as Venezuela and Mexico have fared better than Argentina and Brazil. In early 1987, Brazil suspended payments to foreign banks. In the United States, major banks began to recognize potential losses to LDCs. Citicorp and BankAmerica, for example, raised their reserves for loan losses to $3 billion and $1.1 billion, respectively. The debt problem still exists.

Trade Deficit

The debt problem discussed earlier is part of a larger issue—the trade deficit—which is the difference between our import and our exports. A trade deficit means that we are importing more than we are exporting. The trade deficit is not solely a function of oil prices or other commodities. It is related to other economic factors that are presented in the following accounting identity. This identity shows the relationship between the U.S. government's budget deficit, savings, and trade.[7]

$$\text{Budget deficit} = \text{Net savings} + \text{Trade deficit}$$
$$(G - T) = (S - I) + (M - X)$$

where G = federal government spending including interest on the debt, T = taxes, S = Savings, I = Investment, M = imports, and X = exports.

The identity tells us that a budget deficit (when spending exceeds taxes), must equal the sum of net savings (savings less investment) plus the trade deficit (imports less exports). Stated otherwise, the federal government has two sources of credit: a deficit can be funded by savings or by borrowing from abroad. Alternatively, a deficit can be eliminated by having the government spend less and/or tax more. In 1986, the budget deficit was $204.9 billion, net savings was $99.7 billion, and the trade deficit was $105.2 billion. This is in sharp contrast to 1982, when the $145.9 billion budget deficit was funded from savings ($172.2 billion) and there was a trade surplus of $26.3 billion. The point is that domestic fiscal (taxing and spending) policies affect the trade deficit and the debt crisis.

---

[7] For additional details, see "The Unpleasant Arithmetic of Budget and Trade Deficits," *Federal Reserve Bank of Minneapolis 1986 Annual Report*, Federal Reserve Bank of Minneapolis, 1987.

SUMMARY

International banking is becoming commonplace as the volume of exports and imports of goods, services, and capital increases. International banking usually involves making foreign loans, dealing in foreign exchange, and financing international trade. U.S. banks participate in international banking indirectly by using correspondent banks to handle their transactions. They may participate directly by establishing foreign branches, representative offices, foreign affiliates, Edge Act offices, International Banking Facilities, and Export Trading Companies. These facilities enable banks to deal in international banking and to satisfy various laws and regulations that limit the activities of banks at home and abroad. Similarly, foreign banks have reciprocity and they may have an agency, branch, investment company, subsidiary, and finance company in the United States.

That internationalization of banking has created the need for international regulation of banking activities. The Basle Committee's Concordat is one step toward international regulation.

Various government and private agencies provide insurance and guarantees to promote U.S. foreign trade. These include the Export-Import Bank, the Foreign Credit Insurance Association, Private Export Funding Corporations, and other organizations.

There are risks in international banking that are not present in domestic banking. The debt crisis is one example of a situation that affected international banks and countries throughout the world. The factors that set the stage for the debt crises were the OPEC oil shocks, and the recycling of petrodollars with loans to LDCs. Then record high interest rates and a worldwide recession upset the delicate balance of the LDC's financial structure, and some were unable to repay their loans. The situation required the intervention of the IMF and has yet to be resolved.

IMPORTANT CONCEPTS

agency	Foreign Credit Insurance Association
Basle Committee	foreign exchange
concordat	host country
correspondent bank	international banking facility
debt crisis	investment company
Edge Act office	parent company
Eurocurrency	petrodollars
export-import bank	Private Export Funding Corporation
export trading company	representative office
finance company	subsidiary
foreign affiliate	trade deficit
foreign branch bank	

REFERENCES

Barth, James R., and Joseph Pelzman. *International Debt: Conflict and Resolution.* Fairfax, VA.: George Madison University, Economics Department, 1984.

Cheng, Hang-Sheng. "Bailing Out Banks?" Federal Reserve Bank of San Francisco, July 29, 1983; "An LDC Debt Update," Federal Reserve Bank of San Francisco, April 12, 1985.

Crystal, K. Alec. "International Banking Facilities," *Review,* Federal Reserve Bank of St. Louis, April 1984.

Dufey, Gunter, and Ian Giddy. *The International Money Market.* Englewood Cliffs, NJ: Prentice-Hall, 1978.

Guttentag, Jack M. and Richard J. Herring. *The Current Crisis in International Lending.* Washington, DC: The Brookings Institution, 1985.

International Banking, International Coordination of Bank Supervision: The Record to Date, United States GAO/NSIAD-86-40, February, 1986.

Report on International Developments in Banking Supervision, Report No. 5, Basle, Switzerland. Bank For International Settlements, 1986.

The Global Financial Structure in Transition. Joel McClellan (ed.) Lexington, Mass.: Lexington Books, 1985.

Wallich, Henry C. "The International Debt Situation in an American View: Borrowing Countries and Lending Banks." Speech to the Verein fuer Socialpolitik, Frankfurt, Germany, February 1985.

QUESTIONS

16.1. What are the principal activities of international banking?

16.2. What is a Eurocurrency deposit?

16.3. How are correspondent banks used to engage in international banking?

16.4. Distinguish between the following: (a) foreign branches, (b) representative offices, (c) foreign affiliates, and (d) Edge Act offices.

16.5. What are shell banks? How did they lead to the creation of IBFs?

16.6. What is an ETC?

16.7. How did the International Banking Act of 1978 affect foreign banking in the United States?

16.8. What is the purpose of the Basle Committee? What is the revised Concordat?

16.9. Define the following terms: (a) Eximbank, (b) FCIA, (c) PERFCO, (d) CCC, and (e) OPIC.

16.10. How did the oil crisis contribute to inflation? How did it contribute to the LDC debt crisis?

16.11. What did the Federal Reserve do to reduce inflation associated with the oil crisis? How did the economy react to these actions?

16.12. Distinguish between illiquid and insolvent countries.

16.13. What role does the IMF play in international finance?

16.14. How does the trade deficit affect the budget deficit?

INTERNATIONAL FINANCE AND LENDING

This chapter deals with technical aspects of international lending, some of which are confusing and difficult to comprehend. Nevertheless, they are an integral part of international finance and lending, and understanding them will give you an appreciation of the complexities.

FOREIGN EXCHANGE MARKETS

Foreign exchange refers to exchanging one country's currency for another country's currency. The need to exchange currencies arises when individuals

411

travel abroad or buy foreign goods or services. For example, suppose that you were going to vacation in France where the domestic currency is the **franc.** In order to pay cash for the goods and services you acquire there, you must pay in francs. Similarly, suppose that a company is buying electronic components from a Japanese manufacturing firm. The Japanese firm wants to be paid in **yen.** To deal with these types of financial needs, some commercial banks have developed expertise in dealing with foreign exchange.

Most of the foreign exchange transactions in the United States are handled by a small group of money center banks located in New York, Chicago, San Francisco, and other major cities. These banks have affiliates in London, Frankfurt, Tokyo, and elsewhere throughout the world. Conversely, as noted in the previous chapter, major foreign banks have operations located in the United States. This network of banks forms what is called the **interbank market** where foreign currencies can be bought and sold. The foreign exchange market is the largest financial market in the world!

In addition to the interbank market, there are **foreign exchange brokers** that facilitate the efficient operations of the foreign exchange market. They deal with banks, business concerns, and governments. Even banks that are part of the interbank market use the services of foreign exchange brokers for certain types of transactions.

Commercial banks that are not dealers in foreign exchange can have a correspondent relationship with banks that are active in the interbank market. The correspondent banks handle foreign exchange operations and, for a fee, provide other services for other commercial banks.

Exchange Rates

The foreign exchange market operates 24 hours a day because of time differences throughout the world. When it is 5 A.M. in Chicago, it is 11 A.M. in London, and 8 P.M. of the previous day in Tokyo. Changes in the value of currencies affect governments, corporations with international operations, traders, and speculators throughout the world. Therefore **exchange rates,** the price of one currency in terms of another, can change at any time, except for countries that have a daily fixing of the exchange rate. Some major industrial countries with a daily fixing are France, Germany, Italy, and Japan, and the Scandinavian and Benelux countries.

In theory, any two currencies can be exchanged in a foreign exchange transaction; for example, Swiss francs can be sold for German marks. Such transactions typically occur between banks and their customers. In practice, most transactions in the interbank market involve the purchase or sale of U.S. dollars for a foreign currency. The reasons for this are that the dollar is the principal currency used in foreign trade and investment; and the dollar market for each currency may be more active than the market between Swiss francs and German marks. Let's examine exchange rates first, and then see how different currencies are exchanged in terms of dollars.

The exchange rate between two currencies may be stated in terms of either currency. For example, the exchange rate between the U.S. dollar and the United Kingdom (sterling) pound may be stated as:

Indirect rate = $1 U.S. dollar = 0.5 United Kingdom pounds

or

Direct rate = 1 United Kingdom pounds = $2.0 U.S. dollars

In quoting foreign exchange rates, the **indirect rate** is the U.S. dollar ($1) to the equivalent amount of a foreign currency, and the **direct rate** is one unit of foreign currency to the U.S. equivalent.

Suppose that the indirect rate for German marks (DM) is 0.43478 (marks per dollar). A bank wants to exchange marks for pounds. As mentioned previously, most foreign exchange transactions involve dollars. The rate at which marks and pounds can be exchanged using dollars is called the **crossrate.**[1] It is determined by multiplying the indirect rate for marks times the direct rate for pounds, or

$$\text{Crossrate DM/£} = \text{DM/\$} \times \text{£/\$}$$
$$= 0.43478 \times \$2.00 = 0.86957$$

Returning to the example of dollars and pounds, the direct and indirect exchange rates are reciprocals of the other; therefore, when rates change, they move in opposite directions. For example,

$1 U.S. dollar = £0.6 United Kingdom pounds

£1 United Kingdom pound = $1.67 U.S. dollars.

Foreign Exchange Transactions

In a foreign exchange transaction, the buyer and seller agree to pay each other on a predetermined date called the **value date.** The value date may be the same day as the transaction or at a later date.

Spot Market

Most foreign exchange transactions take place in the **spot market** or where the value date is usually 2 business days after the transaction originated. For exam-

---

[1] These examples of exchange rates do no take into account the small differences between the prices at which currencies are bought and sold. For additional details, see Roger M. Kubarych, *Foreign Exchange Markets in the United States,* revised edition, Federal Reserve Bank of New York, 1983; Rita M. Rodriquez and E. Eugene Carter, *International Financial Management,* 3rd. ed., Englewood Cliffs, NJ: Prentice-Hall, 1984.

ple, on March 5, U.S. bank A buys £1 billion from British bank B at a rate of $2.0 per pound for value on March 7. On the value date, British bank B credits bank A's account in Britain with £1 million, and bank A credits bank B's account in the United States with $2 million. These transactions consist mostly of bookkeeping entries of debits and credits. Except for tourists, currency rarely leaves the country of origin.

Table 17-1 shows the foreign exchange rates for 31 different currencies expressed in units per dollar unless noted otherwise. The prices of most currencies are determined by supply and demand. The prices of others, however, are supported by government actions. In February 1988, for example, the U.S. dollar could be exchanged for 129.17 Japanese yen or 1.6963 West German deutsche marks.

Forward and Futures Markets

Some of the following information duplicates information in other chapters in order to facilitate your understanding of foreign exchange transactions, which can be very complex.

There are differences between the spot market and forward interbank market and the futures market for foreign currencies. The **spot or cash market** is where an actual physical commodity is bought or sold as distinguished from a **futures market,** where futures contracts are traded. In the futures market, standardized transferable legal agreements to make or take delivery of a certain commodity at a known price and time are traded on organized futures exchanges.[2] In the **forward market,** contracts are not standardized nor are they traded on organized exchanges. A **forward contract** is a cash market transaction in which delivery of the commodity (i.e., currency) is deferred until after the contract (a bilateral agreement between buyer and seller) has been made.

The futures market provides future price information about standardized commodity contracts and is a means to transfer risk from hedgers to speculators. In contrast, forward contracts are widely used in day-to-day cash transactions involving loans, leases, real estate, and certain currencies.

Method of Transaction

In the spot and forward interbank market, trading is conducted by telephone or telex between banks, foreign exchange brokers, and corporations that negotiate the terms of the transaction with each other. Thus, participants in the foreign exchange market usually have information about the creditworthiness of each other.

In the futures market, trading is conducted on a commodities exchange such as the International Monetary Market (IMM) and the London International Financial Futures Exchange (LIFFE). Transactions on commodities exchanges

---

[2] Definitions used here are based on those of the Chicago Mercantile Exchange.

TABLE 17.1
FOREIGN EXCHANGE RATES
Currency Units per Dollar

Country/Currency	1985	1986	1987	1987				1988	
				Sept.	Oct.	Nov.	Dec.	Jan.	Feb.
1 Australia/dollar[a]	70.026	67.093	70.136	72.68	71.12	68.60	71.06	71.11	71.40
2 Austria/schilling	20.676	15.260	12.649	12.765	12.674	11.843	11.500	11.635	11.920
3 Belgium/franc	59.336	44.662	37.357	37.657	37.494	35.190	34.186	34.576	35.473
4 Canada/dollar	1.3658	1.3896	1.3259	1.3154	1.3097	1.3167	1.3075	1.2855	1.2682
5 China, P.R./yuan	2.9434	3.4615	3.7314	3.7314	3.7314	3.7314	3.7314	3.7314	3.7314
6 Denmark/krone	10.598	8.0954	6.8477	6.9893	6.9262	6.4962	6.3043	6.3562	6.4918
7 Finland/markka	6.1971	5.0721	4.4036	4.3954	4.3570	4.1392	4.0462	4.0391	4.1159
8 France/franc	8.9799	6.9256	6.0121	6.0555	6.0160	5.7099	5.5375	5.5808	5.7323
9 Germany/deutsche mark	2.9419	2.1704	1.7981	1.8134	1.8006	1.6821	1.6335	1.6537	1.6963
10 Greece/drachma	138.40	139.93	135.47	138.40	138.61	132.42	129.46	131.92	135.56
11 Hong Kong/dollar	7.7911	7.8037	7.7985	7.8035	7.8077	7.7968	7.7726	7.7872	7.7978
12 India/rupee	12.332	12.597	12.943	12.993	12.995	12.972	12.934	13.040	13.065
13 Ireland/punt[a]	106.62	134.14	148.79	147.54	148.72	158.08	162.63	160.64	156.87
14 Italy/lira	1908.90	1491.16	1297.03	1310.86	1302.58	1238.89	1203.74	1216.88	1249.62
15 Japan/yen	238.47	168.35	144.60	143.29	143.32	135.40	128.24	127.69	129.17
16 Malaysia/ringgit	2.4806	2.5830	2.5185	2.5189	2.5308	2.4989	2.4944	2.5400	2.5812
17 Netherlands/guilder	3.3184	2.4484	2.0263	2.0413	2.0267	1.8931	1.8382	1.8584	1.9051
18 New Zealand/dollar[a]	49.752	52.456	59.327	63.352	64.031	61.915	64.664	65.818	66.386
19 Norway/krone	8.5933	7.3984	6.7408	6.6505	6.6311	6.4233	6.3820	6.3538	6.4167
20 Portugal/escudo	172.07	149.80	141.20	142.94	142.82	136.84	133.77	135.87	138.84
21 Singapore/dollar	2.2008	2.1782	2.1059	2.0924	2.0891	2.0444	2.0127	2.0261	2.0185
22 South Africa/rand[a]	45.57	43.952	49.081	48.86	48.79	50.67	51.22	50.62	48.53
23 South Korea/won	861.89	884.61	825.93	810.07	808.47	802.30	798.34	791.31	776.85
24 Spain/peseta	169.98	140.04	123.54	121.34	118.60	113.26	110.80	112.34	114.36
25 Sri Lanka/rupee	27.187	27.933	29.471	29.902	30.347	30.519	30.644	30.825	30.859
26 Sweden/krona	8.6031	7.1272	6.3468	6.3844	6.3560	6.0744	5.9473	5.9749	6.0524
27 Switzerland/franc	2.4551	1.7979	1.4918	1.5029	1.4940	1.3825	1.3304	1.3466	1.3916
28 Taiwan/dollar	39.889	37.837	31.756	30.151	30.036	29.813	29.004	28.628	28.665
29 Thailand/baht	27.193	26.314	25.774	25.765	25.783	25.495	25.249	25.235	25.324
30 United Kingdom/pound[a]	129.74	146.77	163.98	164.46	166.20	177.54	182.88	180.09	175.82
MEMO									
31 United States/dollar[b]	143.01	112.22	96.94	97.23	96.65	91.49	88.70	89.29	91.08

Source. Board of Governors of the Federal Reserve System.
[a] Value in U.S. cents.
[b] Index of weighted-average value of U.S. dollar against the currencies of 10 industrial countries. The weight of the 10 countries is the 1972–76 average world trade of that country divided by the average world trade of all 10 countries combined. Series revised as of August 1978 (see *Federal Reserve Bulletin*, vol. 64, August 1978, p. 700).
Note. Averages of certified noon buying rates in New York for cable transfers.
Data in this table also appear in the Board's G.5 (405) release.

are handled by brokers representing their customers, who may not know each other. The trading takes place in a competitive arena where the amounts bid and offered are known to the market makers. At the end of each trading day, all transactions are "settled" with the exchange's Clearing House, which interposes itself between the two transacting parties and guarantees the contracts.[3]

Contracts

Contracts in the forward market are privately negotiated bilateral agreements that are tailored to meet the needs of the parties involved. They may be any size and in any currency.

Contracts in the futures markets are for a limited number of currencies and the contracts are standardized. The major currencies, such as British pounds, West German deutsche marks, Japanese yen, Swiss francs, and Canadian dollars, are traded on the exchanges, but the Thailand baht and Malaysian ringgit are not traded.

Standardized contracts means that each currency contract that is traded on an exchange has particular characteristics that are known to all market participants. Consider the major features of pound sterling contracts traded on the IMM.

- The unit of trading is 25,000 pounds sterling.
- The minimum price fluctuations shall be in multiples of $0.0005 (five points) per pound sterling.
- There shall be no trading at a price more than $0.0500 above or below the previous day's settling price.
- Trading terminates on the second business day preceding the deliver day of the contract months (March, June, September, December).

The size of contracts for the same currency can very between exchanges. For example, contracts for Swiss francs on the Philadelphia Exchange and Chicago Board Options Exchange are for 62,500 francs and 125,000 francs, respectively.

Margin

Original margin, or **security deposit** is the cash amount of funds that must be deposited with a broker as a guarantee of fulfillment of the futures contracts. The margin requirements for trading a commodity futures contracts are generally 5 to 20 percent of their market value. Thus, the amount of margin that is required on outstanding contracts varies with the market value. Margin is a

---

[3] The stock market "crash" in October 1987 raised questions about the ability of clearing corporations' financial ability to "guarantee" contracts. See Richard Ringer, "Continental Illinois Injects Capital into Recently Acquired Options Unit," *American Banker,* October 26, 1987, pp. 1, 21.

security deposit, and it should not be confused with **stock and bond margins,** which refers to the amount of credit that a broker will extend to buy securities.

In addition to the original margin or security deposit, there is also maintenance margin. The **maintenance margin,** which is usually smaller than the original margin, is the amount that must be maintained on deposit with the broker at all times. At the close of each trading day, open contract positions are adjusted by the commodities exchange for profits or losses. Profits may be withdrawn and losses are collected. This process is called **mark to market.** If a customer's equity in the account drops below the maintenance margin, the broker sends the customer a **margin call** asking the customer to restore the equity to the original margin level.

There are no margin requirements in the forward markets. However, banks may require compensating bank balances.

Delivery

Although 90 pecent of the forward contracts result in the delivery of currencies, usually less than 1 percent of the futures contracts result in delivery. This low percentage is possible because long and short positions can be liquidated or offset. **Offset** is the elimination of a current long or short position by making an opposite transaction; that is, if you own (are long) a contract, you can sell it; or if you don't own a contract that has been sold (short), you can buy one.

Risk

Each party dealing in the forward market must consider the credit risk of the other parties involved in the transactions. Credit risk in the futures markets is minimized, however, because the commodities exchange is the opposite party to each cleared transaction. For example, the IMM has a "Clearing House" where the transactions are settled, and the brokers pay or receive from the Clearing House, which has an excellent credit rating.

Maturity

Maturities of futures and forward contracts can range from days to many months or longer. For example, assume the forward rates for Swiss francs are:

    30-day forward $0.4779
    90-day forward $0.4833
    180-day forward $0.4915

and the spot rate is $0.4751. When the forward rates for a currency exceed the spot rate, the currency is trading at a **premium** in the forward market. The premium may reflect expected price changes or the present value of funds to be received in the future. If the forward rates are less than the spot rate, the currency is trading at a **discount.** In forward transactions, the exchange rate is fixed when the transactions occurs, but no funds exchange hands until the maturity date. Because exchange rates can change between the time the contract is initiated and the time it matures, risks are involved in forward transactions. We will address these risks shortly.

Forward rates frequently are quoted as a percentage deviation from the spot rate on an annual basis. The annual forward (direct) rate, expressed as a premium or a discount, may be determined by using the following equation.

$$\text{Annual forward rate (as a premium or a discount)} = \frac{(F - S) \times 100}{S} \times \frac{360}{n} \qquad (17.1)$$

where F = forward rate, S = spot rate, and n = number of days to maturity.

A financial year in the United States is considered 360 days, but some countries (e.g., England and Belgium) use 365-day financial years. The appropriate number of days should be used in the equation.

To illustrate the use of this equation, the annual forward **direct rate** on the 90-day Swiss franc is

$$\frac{(0.4833 - 0.4751) \times 100}{0.4751} \times \frac{360}{90} = 6.9\% \text{ (premium)}$$

The equation in terms of the **indirect rate** is

$$\text{Annual forward rate} = \frac{(S - F) \times 100}{F} \times \frac{360}{n} \qquad (17.2)$$

$$= \frac{(0.4751 - 0.4833) \times 100}{0.4833} \times \frac{360}{90}$$

$$= 6.8\% \text{ (discount)}$$

Notice that the premium on the direct rate and the discount on the indirect rate have opposite signs (+ −), but are about equal values.

Options

An option is a contract that gives the holder the *right* to buy **(call option)** or sell **(put option)** a specified amount of an asset at a predetermined price **(striking price),** on or before an agreed-upon date. **American options** can be exercised anytime before expiration, but **European options** can be exercised only on the expiration date.[4] Options can be written to buy or sell any asset including

---

[4] American options expire at 5:00 P.M. on the last trading day, which is 2 Fridays before the third Wednesday of the contract months, which are March, June, September, and December. If that Friday is a holiday, the last trading day will be the next business day.

bonds, currencies, real estate, wheat, and so on. The basic form of the options is the same, but the underlying asset is different. Options in foreign currencies, which are examined next, are traded on exchanges in Amsterdam, Chicago, Montreal, and Philadelphia. Options on foreign currency futures are traded on the Chicago Mercantile Exchange. The International Monetary Market (IMM), a division of the Chicago Mercantile Exchange, introduced trading of financial futures in 1972. Since then, the list of financial innovations, including options on futures, has grown substantially.

Option contracts involve a buyer, a seller, the brokers who bring them together, and exchange where the option is traded. The buyer pays the seller a fee called the **premium** for the options acquired. During the life of the option, its market value is called the premium. The premium depends on (1) the relationship between the current price and the striking price, (2) the volatility of the futures price, and (3) the maturity of the contract. The premiums on currency options change in value like any other commodity. The principal factors affecting foreign exchange are balance of payments and governmental influences.

To illustrate the use of a currency option, suppose that a trader believes that the value of the Swiss franc is going to increase. The trader can buy a call option for 62,500 francs at a striking price of 50 cents apiece for a premium of $278. The contract expires in June. If the trader is correct and the price of francs increases to, say, 54 cents, the trader can exercise the contract and buy the francs for 50 cents each, then sell them for 54 cents each, and realize a gross profit of $2,500 ($0.04 × 62,500 = $2,500), which more than covers the cost of the premium and commissions. As shown in Figure 17.1, if the trader was wrong and the price of the franc declined, the loss would be limited to the $278 premium.

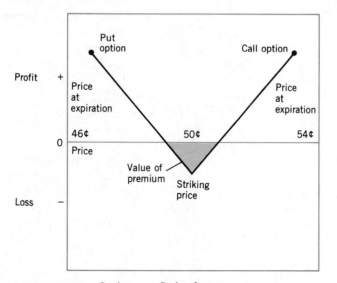

FIGURE 17.1   Options on Swiss francs.

If the value of the Swiss franc was expected to decline, the trader would have purchased a put option. For example, suppose that the price declined to 46 cents per franc. The trader could buy francs in the spot market for 46 cents and then sell them at 50 cents, the striking price of the option, thereby making a profit.

Selling Options

The previous discussion examined some of the rewards and risks of buying options. Now let's examine several reasons for selling options. One reason is to earn the premium income received from the buyers. Suppose that a bank is willing to sell some of its holdings of Swiss francs for the right price. The bank could sell, say, 20 call option contracts and earn $5,560 (20 × $278 = $5,560) in premium income. In addition, the bank is willing to buy some West German marks at 40 cents per mark, or less. It can sell put option contracts and receive a premium of, say, 5 cents per mark. If the mark declines in price, the option will be exercised and the bank's effective cost for the marks will be 35 cents, the 40-cent exercise price less the 5-cent premium. On the other hand, if the price of the marks increases, the bank will have earned $3,125 for each contract of 62,500 marks that it sold.

BOX 17.1
PUT-CALL PARITY

   Though options and forward contracts are distinct instruments, their prices are linked together by the actions of traders who buy and sell both instruments in search of profits. The basic trading strategy for profiting from a price difference between option and forward markets is called a *reversal*. With this strategy, a trader simultaneously buys a call and sells a put, both for the same expiration date and exercise price E. This strategy will give the trader a pattern of gains and losses that duplicates that on a forward contract to purchase the currency on that expiration date at the exercise price E. The trader will, by maturity, gain dollar-for-dollar on the call by the amount the spot price rises above E, or lose dollar-for-dollar on the put by the amount the spot price falls below E, just as he would on a forward contract. The price at which the trader has effectively purchased currency forward, however, should take into account the interest cost of borrowing the difference between the premium C paid for the call and the premium P received for the put (if C is greater than P) over the life of the contracts. Assuming the trader can borrow at an interest rate i, the price at which the trader is buying the currency forward under the reversal will be:

Box 17.1 *(Continued)*

$$E + (C - P)(1 + i) \qquad (1)$$

where C and P are measured per quantity of currency traded.

If the cost of obtaining the currency using this strategy is cheaper than buying it under a forward contract at the going forward rate F, the trader will, by coupling the reversal with a forward sale, earn a profit of π_r:

$$\pi_r = F - E - (C - P)(1 + i) \qquad (2)$$

Alternatively, if the cost of buying currency under a forward contract is cheaper than obtaining it by combining puts and calls, the trader could profit by executing the mirror image trade of the reversal called a *conversion*. Here the trader would create an artificial contract to sell the currency forward by buying a put, selling a call, and investing the difference (if it is positive) between the two premiums in a money market instrument paying a rate of interest i. This strategy will, coupled with a forward purchase, produce a profit of π_c:

$$\pi_c = E + (C - P)(1 + i) - F \qquad (3)$$

As many traders try to take advantage of price differentials between the forward and options markets, they will drive the call prices up and put prices down when executing reversals (and drive call prices down and put prices up in executing conversions) until no more profits can be made with these strategies ($\pi_r = \pi_c = 0$). This implies that in equilibrium the difference between the call and put premiums for an option at an exercise price E will be equal to the difference between the forward exchange rate F and E, discounted to the market interest rate or:

$$C - P = (F - E)/(1 + i) \qquad (4)$$

This relationship is called *put-call parity*. How close does it come to describing the relationship we see in reported option and forward prices? A complete answer requires a careful statistical study, but a rough idea can be obtained by seeing how close the put-call parity theory comes to predicting the actual price differences between puts and calls on one of the Philadelphia Stock Exchanges most active contracts on a recent date. On July 17, 1984, at 10:11 a.m., calls on the Deutsche mark contract with a $.36 striking price and September expiration were trading for $318.75, while puts on that contract were trading for $631.25. These prices are the average bid-offer prices on recent trades, kindly provided by the Financial Options Group, Inc. A 2-month forward contract made on July 17th would be settled on the same date the options expired, and the average bid-offer rate on this contract posted by Citibank's New York office was

BOX 17.1 (*Continued*)

$.3555. The 2-month CD rate, taken here to be a representative interest rate, was 11.63 percent, or 1.85 percent for 2 months.

Inserting the figures for the forward rate, the exercise price, and the interest rate into the put-call parity formula gives a predicted difference between the call and put premiums of −$276.14:

$$\text{Predicted } (C - P) = [(F - E) \times 62{,}500]/(1 + i)$$
$$= [(.3555 - .36) \times 62{,}500]/(1.0185)$$
$$= -\$276.14$$

The difference between the forward price and the exercise price $(F - E)$ was multiplied by the number of Deutsche marks in the Philadelphia Stock Exchange's contract to put these prices in the same units as the premium.

The actual difference between the call and put options on July 17th was −$312.50. So the parity formula used with market data gives a close prediction of what the relationship among call, put, and forward prices was on the date. Could traders have executed reversals and conversions at the time the market data were taken to profit from the price difference? The answer is no: inserting the appropriate bid and offer prices into the reversal condition formulas (equations (2) and (3)) revealed no profit opportunities. In addition, the formulas do not take brokerage costs—which are on the order of $13 to $16 per option—into account. At the time the market data were collected, the September Deutsche mark option with a $.36 striking price was not mispriced relative to the forward market.

Source: Brian Gendreau, "New Markets for Foreign Currency Options," *Business Review*, Federal Reserve Bank of Philadelphia, July–August 1984, pp. 11–12.

Options versus Forwards and Futures

The principal difference between an option and a futures contract is that the option gives the holder the "right" to buy or sell an asset. The holder exercises the option only if it is profitable. The trader exercised the option in Swiss francs because it was profitable to do so. In contrast, forward and futures contracts are obligations to buy or sell an asset whether it is in the holder's best interest or not. Futures contracts and some forward contracts may be fulfilled by delivering the asset or by making offsetting transactions.

Figure 17.2 illustrates another difference between call options and forward and futures contracts. That difference involves the fact that value of both call options and futures contracts declines when the price of the underlying asset

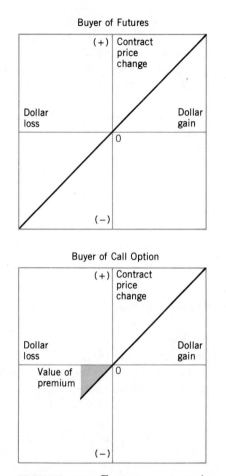

FIGURE 17.2   Fugures versus options.

declines. However, the maximum loss that can be sustained by the holder of the call option is limited to the amount of the premium. The holder of the futures contract has no such limit and the potential loss is greater.

Currency Swaps

Currency swaps are the simultaneous purchase and sale of a foreign currency for **two different value dates.** (This type of swap should not be confused with interest rate swaps that are discussed in Chapter 18.) The transaction takes place with a single counterparty, and there is no risk of exchange rates changing because the contract calls for both the payment and receipt of the same amount of currency at specified rates.[5]

---

[5] Swaps can include more than one counterparty. Also, there is an exchange if the interest to be earned or paid is not covered. This is called **deposit interest cover.**

The following example will clarify how a swap works. On June 8, bank C in the United States "swaps in" 2-month pounds on a spot against a forward transaction with bank D in London. On the first value date, June 10, bank C credits dollars to bank D's account in the United States and bank D credits pounds to bank C's account in London. Both banks can invest those funds until the second value date, August 10, when the transactions are reversed. In essence, bank C has "borrowed" pounds and "loaned" dollars for a 3-month period. Some examples of swaps are explained in connection with risks, which are discussed next.

Foreign Exchange Risks

Dealing in foreign exchange exposes banks to four principal types of risk: exchange rate risk, interest rate risk, credit risk, and country risk.

Exchange Rate Risk

When a bank buys more currency than it sells (it is overbought), it has an **open (long) position.** Conversely, if it sells more than it buys (it is oversold, it has a **short position.** The bank is said to be in a **net covered position** when it buys and sells an equivalent amount in the same currency. When banks have either open or short positions, a change in exchange rates can cause a profit or a loss when the positions are closed out—the **exchange rate risk.** Even if a bank's open position in one currency is offset by its short position in another currency, it can still be exposed to adverse rate movements. Although these comments refer to currency positions, a bank must consider all asset and liabilities denominated in foreign currencies when assessing its total foreign currency exposure.

A bank can limit its trading exposure in foreign currencies by using hedging techniques, by imposing dollar limits on positions in a currency, by imposing dollar limits on regions of the world, and by imposing dollar limits on particular customers. Hedging techniques in the currency market are similar to those discussed in connection with interest rate futures.

Interest Rate Risk

Mismatches in the maturity structure of a bank's foreign exchange position give rise to **interest rate risk.** For example, bank E sells 1 million deutsch marks (DM1 million) on September 15 for value on September 17 to customer X and simultaneously buys DM1 million for value on September 27 from customer Y. The exchange rate is $1 = DM1 2.4, or DM1 = $0.4166. Thus, DM1 million is worth $416,667 to the bank. Nevertheless, the bank charges customer X more than the exchange rate for DM1 million ($416,767) and makes $100 profit on this transaction. Similarly, the bank pays customer Y ($416,567) less than the exchange rate and makes an additional $100 profit.

The bank has a covered position, but on September 17, it must pay DM1 million to customer X and it will not receive the equivalent amount from customer Y until September 27—a mismatch of maturities. To eliminate the risk of adverse interest rate movements during the maturity gap, the bank can arrange for a swap with bank F. Bank E will sell DM1 million spot and buy the same amount for value on September 27. These transactions are summarized below.

| *Exchange rates:* | $1 = DM 2.4 |
| | DM1 = $0.4166 |

Bank E	*Bank F*
September 17 Value date	
Pays DM1 million to customer X	Receives DM1 million
Receives $416,767 from customer X	Pays $416,667
Profit (416,767 − $416,667 = $100)	
September 27 Value date	
Receives DM1 million from customer Y	Pays DM1 million
Pays $416,567 to customer Y	Receives $416,667
Profit (416,667 − $416,567) = $100	
Total profit = $200	

To simplify this example, it was assumed that there was no cost or profit on the swap itself, and that the profit was made by selling and buying DM from customers X and Y. In reality, there are costs to the swap, but that is an unnecessary complication at this point. The illustration demonstrated that the bank could establish a gross profit of $200 on the transactions with customers X and Y, and eliminate exchange risk and interest rate risk. In practice, banks deal with hundreds of customers, and they take advantage of interest rate differential between countries to borrow, lend, or arbitrage to their advantage. Therefore, the swapping process is much more complex than was presented here.

Arbitrage

The term **arbitrage** refers to the purchase of securities (assets) in one market for the **immediate** resale in another market in order to profit from price differences in the two markets. Like speculators in the commodities markets, arbitrageurs provide capital and help to keep the market in balance. For example, suppose that the 3-month secondary rate on domestic certificates of deposits (CDs) is 10.00 percent and the 3-month offer rate on Eurodollar deposits is 10.10 percent. At first glance, it appears that Eurodollar rates are higher than CD rates, but all the relevant costs have not been taken into account. The FDIC insurance amounts to about 0.037 percent per year on assessable domestic deposits.

In addition, the reserve requirements on the CDs and Eurodollars is 3 percent. Using these figures the **effective cost** of the CDs is

$$\frac{10.0\% + 0.37\%}{(1 - 0.03)} = 10.69\%$$

Similarly, the cost of the Eurodollar deposits is

$$\frac{10.10\%}{(1 - 0.03)} = 10.41\%$$

$$\text{Spread} = 10.69\% - 10.41\% = 0.28\%$$

Although the nominal cost of the Eurodollars is higher than the nominal cost of the CDs, the effective cost of the Eurodollars is 28 basis points lower. Therefore, domestic banks will borrow Eurodollars instead of borrowing by using CDs. The type of arbitrage that was just described is called an **inward arbitrage** because the funds are flowing into the United States. The inward arbitrage will continue until upward pressure on the Eurodollar rates and downward pressure on CD rates equalize the effective cost of funds.

An **outward arbitrage** occurs when the effective cost of CDs is less than the effective cost of Eurodollars. The U.S. banks will find it less costly to borrow in the United States than Europe. The increased demand for CDs will bid up the yield until the effective cost of CDs and Eurodollars is equal.

Under normal market conditions, investors should not be able to make arbitrage profits because the premiums or discounts in the various currencies should be exactly offset by the adjusted interest rate differentials. For example, if the short-term interest rates were higher in London than in the United States by 1 percentage point per year (0.5 percentage points for 6 months), the 6-month forward rate for pounds in terms of dollars would be about a 0.5 percentage-point discount from the spot rate. This relationship is known as **covered interest arbitrage** or **interest rate parity.** Because market imperfections do exist, however, there are opportunities for arbitrage profits.

The conditions under which there is no incentive for covered interest arbitrage can be determined by using the following equations, where

S = spot rate (dollars per pound in our example)

F = forward rate (6-month forward exchange rate in dollars per pound in our example)

$p = \dfrac{F - S}{S}$ = premium or discount on the forward pound − expressed in decimal form, where − is the discount and + is the premium

N = short-term interest rate in the United States (per 6 months, expressed in decimal form)

L = short-term interest rate in London (per 6 months, expressed in decimal form)

then

$$1 + N = \frac{1}{S}(1 + L)F \tag{17.3}$$

This equation means that there is no incentive for covered interest arbitrage when one dollar plus the 6-month rate of interest in the United States is equal to one dollar's worth of spot pounds plus the 6-month interest rate in London reconverted into dollars at the forward rate. It follows from the definition of p that $F/S = 1 + p$, and that the equilibrium condition becomes

$$p = N - L - pL$$

Therefore, the precise interest rate parity can be determined by solving

$$p = \frac{(N - L)}{(1 + L)} \tag{17.4}$$

However, because p and L usually are small, an approximation of the interest rate parity condition is

$$p = N - L \tag{17.5}$$

Because of adjustments for FDIC insurance, reserves, and other factors, p is actually a band, sometimes called an **arbitrage tunnel,** within which there is no incentive for arbitrage.

CREDIT RISK

There is **credit risk** in foreign exchange transactions because it is possible that the counterparty (the other bank or broker) in the transaction may be unwilling or unable to meet its contractual obligations.[6]

In 1974, for example, the Bankhouse I.D. Herstatt failed in Germany. Because of differences in time zones, some U.S. banks and others had paid marks to Herstatt early in the day, but Herstatt failed later in the day before completing the other side of the foreign exchange transactions—the U.S. banks did not receive the dollars that were due to them. This particular form of credit risk is called **settlement risk.**

Also consider the case of a bank that buys £1 million for a customer on

---

[6] The credit risk associated with foreign exchange risk is not included in the definition of risk for establishing legal lending considerations (12 U.S. Code 84). It is considered inherent under this code. The only real control on credit risk associated with foreign exchange forward exposure is self-imposed.

January 5 at a rate of $2.0 ($2 million) for value on March 13. In late February, the customer declares bankruptcy and the court-appointed trustee informs the bank that it will not honor the contract. During this time, the price of sterling increases to $2.10, and the bank has to cover its unexpected short position of £1 million at the higher price, resulting in an increased cost of $100,000 to the bank. Of course, the bank can dispute its contract and loss in court, but that is a costly process with no clear outcome.

The point of these examples is that although the intention of dealing in foreign exchange is not to extend credit per se, there are, nevertheless, credit risks in dealing in foreign exchange.

Country Risk

Country risk may be defined as a whole spectrum of risks arising from economic, social, and political environments of a given foreign country having potentially favorable or adverse consequences for the profitability and/or recovery of debt or equity investments made in that country. These risks range from war to confiscation and from branching restrictions to restrictions on earnings remittances.

Country risk is frequently separated into two broad categories—sovereign risk and transfer risk. **Soverign risk** occurs when a national government refuses to permit loans to be repaid or seizes bank assets without adequate compensation. **Transfer risk** occurs when foreign borrowers have problems converting domestic currency into foreign exchange because of foreign exchange controls or for other reasons.[7]

Commercial banks must assess both types of risk. Although cases of expropriation or outright repudiation on loans are rare in the post-World War II period (Cuba and Chile are two examples), cases of debt rescheduling have been commonplace. The restructuring or refinancing is usually preceded by a foreign exchange crisis. **Restructuring debt** usually involves stretching principal and interest payments, whereas **refinancing** usually involves new loans. As one humorist said, refinancings and restructuring of loans are good because "a rolling loan gathers no losses."

Short-term rescheduling problems, such as those that have occurred in Latin America, are frequently associated with fiscal and monetary conditions and inflation. Long-term rescheduling problems, such as those in South Asian countries and Ghana, are associated with other factors, such as the country's debt-service ratio.

International lenders use statistical indicators to help gauge country risk. The data for the indicators are published by the World Bank. Unfortunately, the data are often two or more years out of date by the time they are available,

---

[7] For additional perspectives on country risk analysis, see Edward G. R. Bennett and Leslie E. Grayson, "Country Risk Analysis," in *The Loan Officer's Handbook,* William J. Korsvik and Charles O. Meiburg, eds., Homewood, IL: Dow Jones-Irwin, 1986, pp. 696–715.

so the indicators are of limited value. Three commonly used indicators are the debt-service ratio, current (and cumulative) deficit-export ratio, and the interest-reserve ratio.

Debt-service ratio. Measures foreign exchange earnings used for debt-servicing against total exchange earnings from (current account) exports.

Current deficit-export ratio. The ratio of current account deficit to export earnings from goods and services. When used cumulatively, the ratio gives some indication of the amount and rate of growth of a country's debt burden.

Interest-reserve ratio. Measures net interest payments on external debt to international reserves, indicating a country's short-term ability to make interest payments out of reserves if necessary.

Problems with foreign governments do not always occur far from the United States. In 1982, for example, the Mexican government nationalized the private banking system and established exchange controls. A preferential exchange rate of 50 pesos per dollar was set for certain critical imports and payments of international claims, and another rate of 70 pesos per dollar was set for exports, tourists, and the payment of foreign accounts frozen in Mexican banks.

The extent of a country's risk exposure can be limited by placing dollar limits on investments in foreign countries or regions of the world. In addition, some foreign banks and central governments will guarantee both the principal and interest on certain risks. Finally, the International Monetary Fund provides useful information to bankers about assessing country risk.

INTERNATIONAL LENDING

Some features of international lending are different from domestic lending, which we examined in Chapters 6, 7, and 8. There are some similar practices, also. This section examines only those lending practices that are typically associated with international lending.

Syndicated Loans

The **syndication of large loans** has advantages for both the borrower and the lender. From the borrower's point of view, syndication provides for a larger amount of funds than may be available from any single lender. In addition, the credit terms may be better than for a large number of smaller loans. From the lender's point of view, syndication provides a means of diversifying some of the risks of foreign lending that were discussed previously. It also permits banks of different sizes to participate in international lending.

Another advantage of syndication is that it provides the lead bank with off-balance sheet income. This is particularly important because many foreign banks place restrictions on the growth of their assets/liabilities. Finally, syndication can enhance relations with foreign governments because it is a means of financing their domestic economic activity.

The Syndication Process

There are two types of syndicated bank loans. The first occurs when there is an agreement between the borrower and each lender. The second, which is the one we are concerned with, is a **participation loan,** which is a cross between traditional bank lending and underwriting. In this form of participation, there are three levels of banks in the syndicate-lead banks, managing banks, and participating banks. The lead banks negotiate with the borrower on the terms of the loan and assemble the management group that will underwrite it. They are also responsible for all documentation of the loan (notes, security agreements, legal opinions, etc.). Moreover, they are expected to underwrite a share of the loans themselves, at least as large as that of the other lenders. After the underwriting group has been established, information is sent to other banks that may be interested in participating. For example, the initial telex cables contain the name of the borrower, maturity of the loan, and interest rates. If a bank is interested in participating, it advises a member of the underwriting group and receives additional information that permits it to analyze the credit. Although the loan may be attractive, some banks may reject it because they have already reached their lending limits in that country or region. Finally, syndication does not relieve each participating bank from doing its own credit analysis and assessment of risks.

Loan Pricing

Eurocurrency syndicated loans are usually priced at LIBOR, plus a certain number of points. **LIBOR** is the London interbank offered rate, the rate at which banks *lend* funds to other banks in the Euromarket. LIBOR is usually about $\frac{1}{8}$ to $\frac{1}{4}$ percent above **LIBB**—the London interbank bid—the rate at which they *buy* funds. Accordingly, a syndicated loan may be priced at, say, LIBOR plus $\frac{1}{2}$ percent for the next 5 years. In the Pacific basin, there is **SIBOR,** which is the Singapore intermarket offered rate. Singapore is the center of the Asia dollar market and SIBOR is widely used in Asian trade.

Although LIBOR changes on a daily basis, the interest rates on the loans are usually adjusted every 3 or 6 months. In recent years, many U.S. banks have given some of their domestic customers, especially those that do business overseas, the choice between borrowing at a rate tied either to the prime rate or to LIBOR.

Additional loan costs include commitment fees, underwriting fees, and other charges. Like domestic loans, commitment fees are based on the unused portion of the credit that is available to the firm under the terms of the agreement. For example, the fee may be $\frac{1}{2}$ percent annually of that amount.

Unlike domestic loans, there may be an underwriting fee, which is a one-time front-end cost. Such fees are divided among the lead banks and the other banks in proportion to their participation. These fees for investment banking underwriting are not common in the United States because the Banking Act of 1933 (the Glass–Steagall Act) divorced bank holding companies from the securities business. In recent years, however, the legal barriers between banking and the securities business have been eroding as the courts and the Board of Governors permitted banks certain underwriting activities.

Finally, the loans may also have clauses dealing with foreign taxes and reserve requirements, so that the lenders receive all the payments that are necessary to pay for the principal and interest on the loans.

LETTERS OF CREDIT

Financing international trade is related to but different than dealing in foreign exchange and international lending. International sellers want to be paid for the goods and services they are selling to foreign buyers, whom they may not know or trust. However, the buyers do not want to pay until they have received the goods that were ordered. Differences between national laws, currencies, and customs frustrate the payment process, but payments can be made to the satisfaction of both the seller and the buyer by using commercial letters of credit.

Import Letters of Credit

Commercial letters of credit issued by a domestic bank in favor of a beneficiary in a foreign country are referred to as **import letters of credit.** By way of illustration, we will examine an import letter of credit for Sabra Photos. The mechanics of **export letters of credit** are the same as the illustration, except that the letter of credit is issued by a foreign bank in favor of a beneficiary in this country.

Sabra Photos of Los Angeles wants to import cameras from Shogun Distributors in Japan, but neither has done business with each other before. The manager of Sabra Photos does not want to pay for the goods until they are shipped, and the manager of Shogun Distributors does not want to wait for the goods to arrive before being paid. One solution to this problem is to include a clause in the purchase contract for the cameras, saying that the trade will be financed by a commercial letter of credit. The letter of credit is not the financing instrument, however. It is used to guarantee payment to the exporter if certain conditions are met.

In this situation, the importer's commercial bank can facilitate the payment process between Sabra Photos and Shogun Distributors. The importer's **issuing bank** will issue a **letter of credit,** which is a document agreeing to make payment, from its own account, to the exporter when the conditions of the credit letter are met. In other words, the bank is substituting its own credit for that of the importer. Before issuing the letter of credit, the importer and the bank agree on the terms and conditions under which the bank will make payment to the exporter. These terms and conditions should agree with those in the purchase contract between Sabra Photos and Shogun Distributors, but the bank is bound only by the provisions of the letter of credit.

The issuing bank forwards the letter of credit to the seller's **advising bank** overseas. Depending on the terms of the letter of credit, the advising bank negotiates the documents and, if they are in order, sends them to the issuing bank for payments to be made. The issuer may then pay the seller through the advising (paying) bank. If the advising bank "confirms" the letter of credit, it becomes an obligation of that bank to make payments if the terms of the letter of credit are met. Otherwise, it is acting only as an intermediary between the buyer and seller and will pay only if sufficient funds are available.

Some items that may be found in the letter of credit are:

- The issuing bank will have title to the merchandise.
- The bank is not responsible for the validity, genuineness, or sufficiency of the documents representing title to the merchandise.
- The importer assumes all the risks from legal actions brought by the exporter or those who use the letter of credit.
- The bank is *not* responsible for quality, condition, or value of the merchandise represented by the documents, unless stated otherwise.
- The importer agrees to pay the bank a fee for its services.
- An itemized list of the documents to be delivered to the bank (or its correspondent) by the exporter is included.[8]

If the importer agrees to these and other terms, the bank will issue a letter of credit. The terms and definitions used in connection with letters of credit are published by the International Chamber of Commerce in Paris, France, in the **Uniform Customs and Practices for Documentary Credits,** which has been adopted by many of the world's leading trading countries. The purpose of this document is to provide a common understanding and interpretation of the technical aspects of letters of credit. It includes information on shipping documents, expiration dates, partial shipments, transfers, installment shipments, and other items.

Figure 17.3 is an example of an irrevocable letter of credit to the Taiwan Manufacturing Company, Taipei, Taiwan. The letter explains all the terms and conditions that must be met before payment will be made.

A letter of credit is considered a **contingent liability** of the issuing bank

---

[8] Peter K. Oppenheim, *International Banking,* 3rd. ed., (Washington, DC: American Bankers Association, 1979, p. 78).

IRREVOCABLE
DOCUMENTARY
LETTER OF CREDIT

AmSouth Bank N.A.

1900 5TH AVENUE NORTH, BIRMINGHAM, ALABAMA 35203
TELEX: 596150   CABLE ADDRESS: AMSOUBKBHM

Taiwan Manufacturing Company
No. 17 Chang Chen Road
Taipei, Taiwan

Advised by AIRMAIL/CABLE through:

Bank of Taiwan
P. O. Box 1000
Taipei, Taiwan

WE ESTABLISH OUR **IRREVOCABLE LETTER OF CREDIT NUMBER** IC-4000   **DATED** January 16, 1983 IN YOUR FAVOR

AT THE REQUEST OF   The First Bank of Elmore, P. O. Box 200, Elmore, Kansas, U.S.A. 35000

AND FOR THE ACCOUNT OF   U.S.A. Importing Company, Inc., 1907 Main Street, Birmingham, Alabama
U.S.A. 35000
UP TO THE AGGREGATE SUM OF   Twenty thousand and no/100 U.S. Dollars ($20,000.00 U.S.)

AVAILABLE BY YOUR DRAFT (S) AT   SIGHT DRAWN ON   AmSouth Bank N.A., Birmingham, Alabama

AND ACCOMPANIED BY THE FOLLOWING DOCUMENTS:

Commercial invoices and 4 copies.
Special U.S. Customs invoice and one copy.
Packing list in duplicate.
Insurance policy or certificate in negotiable form covering marine and war risks
   for 110% of CIF value of the goods.
GSP form A in duplicate.
Full set of negotiable clean, "On board" ocean bills of lading made out to order of
   AmSouth Bank N.A., Birmingham, Alabama marked "Notify" Mitchell Customs Broker,
   P. O. Box 100, Mobile, Alabama 36100 and "Notify" U.S.A. Importing Company, Inc.,
   1907 Main Street, Birmingham, Alabama, U.S.A. 35000 and marked "Freight Prepaid".
Container shipments are required.
Latest shipment date on first 5,000 buttons is March 1, 1983; and on remaining
   5,000 buttons is April 1, 1983.
All bank charges other than those of issuing bank are for account of beneficiary.

EVIDENCING SHIPMENT OF   10,000 buttons as per Purchase Order No. 1001 and Sales Confirmation
No. S-5005

FROM   Taiwan   TO   C.I.F. Mobile, Alabama

LATEST SHIPMENT DATE IS   (See above)   (Two only   PARTIAL SHIPMENTS ARE   PERMITTED.)
TRANSHIPMENT IS Not PERMITTED.   INSURANCE IS TO BE EFFECTED BY   Sellers
LATEST NEGOTIATION DATE OF THIS LETTER OF CREDIT IS April 15, 1983
DRAFTS DRAWN AND NEGOTIATED UNDER THIS LETTER OF CREDIT MUST BE ENDORSED HEREON AND MUST BEAR THE CLAUSE:
"DRAWN UNDER THE AMSOUTH BANK, N.A. LETTER OF CREDIT NUMBER   IC-4000   DATED 1/16/83
WE HEREBY ENGAGE WITH BONA FIDE HOLDERS THAT DRAFTS DRAWN STRICTLY IN COMPLIANCE WITH THE TERMS OF THIS CREDIT
AND AMENDMENTS SHALL MEET WITH DUE HONOR UPON PRESENTATION. THIS CREDIT IS SUBJECT TO THE UNIFORM CUSTOMS AND
PRACTICE FOR DOCUMENTARY CREDITS (1974 REVISION), INTERNATIONAL CHAMBER OF COMMERCE PUBLICATION NUMBER XXX
1983   400

(SAMPLE - NOT NEGOTIABLE)
Authorized Signature

WHEN OPENED BY CABLE, THIS CREDIT IS ONLY AVAILABLE IF
ATTACHED TO OUR CORRESPONDENT'S ADVICE OF CABLED
CREDIT, THE TWO CONSTITUTING EVIDENCE OF THE OUTSTAND
ING AMOUNT OF THIS CREDIT.

Authorized Signature

FORM 400-05-2

FIGURE 17.3 Import Letter of Credit

because the actual payment of the credit is not made until the exporter presents the proper documents. Note that the bank is not interested in the merchandise per se; it is interested in the documents.

Bill of Lading

The most important document is the **bill of lading** representing title to the merchandise that was shipped. When the exporter, Shogun Distributor, delivers the cameras to a shipper who will transport the goods, the shipper acknowledges receipt of the goods and details of the shipment with a bill of lading. It also states who is to receive the merchandise and the title to it. Of course, if the goods are damaged and the documents are not in order, the bank will not pay under the terms of the credit agreement.

Other Documents

Other documents that may be required by the bank include the following:

1. An **invoice** describing the items that have been sold, the price, and other information.
2. A **certificate of origin** stating the country where the goods were manufactured or grown.
3. An **inspection certificate,** which is usually issued by an independent third party, stating that the merchandise is what is called for in the purchase agreement.
4. A **draft,** or **bill of exchange,** drawn by the exporter (Shogun Distributors) on the importer's (Sabra Photos) bank for the amount due as stated in the letter of credit. The draft can be drawn so that it is payable *at sight* or at some predetermined *time* (a time draft) after sight.

Most drafts are drawn so that they are payable a certain number of days after sight.

In such cases, if all the documents are presented to the issuing bank and everything is in order, the bank can *accept* the draft by stamping the word ACCEPTED on its face and signing it. The time draft then becomes a **banker's acceptance,** an irrevocable obligation of the bank, and it can be sold by the exporter at a discount in order to obtain the funds due before the date of maturity. The maturity is usually less than 9 months.

To illustrate the use of a banker's acceptance, suppose that the face amount of a time draft is $1 million and that it matures in 6 months. The bank's acceptance charge (commission plus discount rate) is 6 percent per annum. The amount of money to be received by the maker of the draft is $970,000:

(a) 6% × $1 million × 6/12 = $30,000 acceptance charges

(b) $1 million − $30,000 = $970,000 amount received

The acceptance charge is the gross income to the bank. It does not take into account reserve, the cost of funds, or handling costs.

The acceptance is a negotiable instrument, which can be sold by the bank for the account of they payee. Because the acceptance is an obligation of the bank as well as the payee, it is considered a safe investment by investors. Some bankers' acceptances are "eligible" for rediscounting with the Federal Reserve System. There are no reserve requirements on eligible acceptances, but there are reserve requirements on ineligible acceptances.

Confirmed Letters of Credit

In some cases, the exporter of goods may not be satisfied with the financial strength of the importer's advising bank that issued the letter of credit. In this case, the exporter may have his or her bank *confirm* the letter by adding its guarantee that the funds will be paid in accordance with the terms of the credit.

The failure of Penn Square Bank underscores the importance of confirmed letters of credit. Penn Square Bank, N.A., was located in Oklahoma City, Oklahoma. The bank was known as an originator and servicer of energy (oil) loans. It failed in 1982, but before it failed, Penn Square issued irrevocable letters of credit (some are revocable) worth $1.6 million to SGI Holland Inc. and SGI International Holdings.[9]

These letters of credit were not issued in connection with international trade, but served as security for a $1.1-million promissory note made by a local oilman. When the note came due, the oilman did not pay it. The FDIC, which had taken over the bank, refused to honor the letters of credit. The point is that the quality of a letter of credit is only as secure as the quality of the issuer. The failure of Penn Square Bank should serve as a warning that banks can fail, too. Having the endorsement of a second bank reduced the risk. Confirmed letters of credit of this type are also known as **standby letters of credit** which will be discussed in the next chapter.

COLLECTIONS

The term **collection** refers to the process of presenting an item, such as a check, to the maker for payment. In the United States, most items for collection are handled by local clearinghouses or by the Federal Reserve System. However, no similar system exists for collection of international negotiable instruments. Therefore, banks located in one country use correspondent banks or their foreign branches to facilitate the clearing process.

---

[9] "2 Firms, Investors File Penn Square Suits," *Tulsa World*," October 3, 1982, p. B-5.

Clean Collections

Collections are divided into two categories, clean and documentary. **Clean collections** means that there are no documents attached. Traveler's checks and money orders are examples of clean collections. For example, suppose that you were vacationing in Europe and cashed a traveler's check that was drawn on a U.S. bank. The foreign bank in which the traveler's check was deposited would collect on that item by sending it to a correspondent bank in the United States (or its overseas branch) to be credited to the foreign bank's account. The correspondent bank presents the traveler's check to the issuing bank for payment, and when the payment is received, it is credited to the foreign bank's account. In some cases, the correspondent credits the foreign bank's account before the item is collected.

If a check drawn on a foreign bank was deposited in the United States, the reverse process would occur. Because of the length of time necessary to clear the collection item, credit may not be given until the U.S. bank has received the funds or had them credited to its account. Therefore, there may be a substantial difference between the ledger balance of the account and the amount of funds available for use.

Documentary Collections

Drafts, or bills of exchange, were discussed previously in connection with letters of credit. Now consider the case of an exporter that wants to use the **collection method** instead of a letter of credit. In this example, the U.S. exporter has an order to sell auto parts to a South American firm. The parts are shipped, and the exporter takes a copy of the bill of lading, the draft, and other documents to the bank for collection. He or she tells the banker to present the draft and documents to the importer for collection. The U.S. bank will use a South American correspondent to accomplish this. The correspondent works with the importer's bank, and collects the funds and presents the bill of lading and other documents to the importer. This collection method is called **documents against payment.** The bank receives a fee for acting as the exporter's agent in the collection process.

Banks that are actively engaged in such collections may use form letters that give explicit instructions concerning how the payments are to be made, the documents that are involved, and other pertinent information.

Banks are also involved in collections with imports. The U.S. banks present the exporter's draft and documents to the importer for payment. Collections may also be in the form of U.S. dollars or a foreign currency.

The basic difference between the collection method and a letter of credit is that an irrevocable letter of credit is an obligation of the issuing bank, whereas an exporter's draft is drawn on the importer. The collection method is less costly than a letter of credit and is frequently used when the risks to the exporter are relatively small.

SUMMARY

Although there are many similarities between domestic bank operations and international banking operations, there are also many differences. In fact, it is sometimes said that the international banking section of a bank is a bank within a bank because it makes loans, take payments, makes payments, and performs most of the services of a bank. This chapter focused on several aspects of banking that are uniquely international. These included foreign exchange operations, international lending, and collections. Dealing in foreign exchange entails certain risks. To some extent, the exchange rate risk and interest rate risk can be reduced by hedging, swaps, and arbitrage. Credit risk and country risk exposure can be reduced by other means, including diversification of portfolios, lending limits, and government guarantees and insurance.

Many large-scale international loans are syndicated, which is hybrid of investment banking and traditional participation loans. Such loans can be beneficial to both the borrower and the lenders if no problems arise.

Letters of credit are widely used in international trade to facilitate the payment process; the other side of the coin is the collection process. Both are important aspects of international banking.

IMPORTANT CONCEPTS

advising bank

American option

arbitrage

arbitrage tunnel

banker's acceptance

bill of exchange

bill of lading

call option

certificate of origin

clean collection

collection

collection method of payment

commercial letters of credit

confirmed letter of credit

contingent liability

country risk

covered interest arbitrage

credit risk

crossrate

currency swap

current deficit-export ratio

debt-service ratio

direct rate

discount

documents against payment

draft

Edge Act corporations

effective cost

exchange rate

exchange rate risk

exercise price

export letter of credit

foreign bank agencies

foreign exchange

foreign exchange brokers

forward/forward rate (in appendix)

forward market

franc

futures market	options
Glass–Steagall Act	original margin
import letters of credit	outward arbitrage
indirect rate	participation loan
inspection certificate	premium
interbank market	put option
interest rate parity	refinancing
interest rate risk	restructuring
interest-reserve ratio	settlement risk
international banking facility	short position
invoice	SIBOR
inward arbitrage	sight draft
issuing bank	sovereign risk
letter of credit	spot market
LIBB	standardized contracts
LIBOR	standby letter of credit
maintenance margin	striking price
margin call	syndicated loan
mark-to-market	time draft
net covered position	transfer risk
offsets	value date
open position	yen

REFERENCES

Bennett, Edward G. R., and Leslie E. Grayson. "Country Risk Analysis," *The Loan Officer's Handbook,* William J. Korsvik and Charles O. Meiburg (eds.) Dow Jones-Irwin, 1986.

Kubarych, Roger M., *Foreign Exchange Markets in the United States,* revised edition. Federal Reserve Bank of New York, 1983.

Oppenheim, Peter K. *International Banking,* 3rd. ed. Washington, D.C.: American Bankers Association, 1979.

Ringer, Richard. "Continental Illinois Injects Capital Into Recently Acquired Options Unit," *American Banker,* October 26, 1987.

Rodriguez, Rita M., and E. Eugene Carter. *International Financial Management,* 3rd. ed. Englewood Cliffs, NJ: Prentice-Hall, 1984.

QUESTIONS

17.1. What is the interbank market? Foreign exchange brokers?

17.2. Distinguish between indirect and direct exchange rates. How can they be used to calculate a crossrate between Swiss francs and German marks?

17.3. Define the following terms: (a) value date, (b) spot market, (c) futures market, and (d) forward market.

17.4. What is the difference between the margin-security deposit on futures and stock and bond margins? What is the maintenance margin? Margin call?

17.5. Briefly describe the risks in forward transactions.

17.6. Define (a) call options (b) put options, (c) American options, and (d) European options.

17.7. What factors affect premiums on options?

17.8. Which option contract should a purchaser use if the price of a currency is expected to fall in the future? Which option should a seller of options use?

17.9. In what sense are options less risky than futures contracts?

17.10. What is a currency swap? Deposit interest cover?

17.11. What four risks are associated with foreign exchange? Briefly define them.

17.12. Distinguish between inward and outward arbitrage. What is covered interest arbitrage?

17.13. Show an equation for interest rate parity. Can this equation be simplified?

17.14. Briefly discuss two kinds of country risk. What are three measures of country risk?

17.15. What is a letter of credit? Who issues them? How does it facilitate international trade?

17.16. What is a banker's acceptance? Is it a risky investment instrument?

17.17. How does the collection method differ from the use of a letter of credit?

PROBLEMS

17.1. Calculate the annual forward direct rate on 30-day British pounds with a forward rate of $2.20 and a spot rate of $2.00.

17.2. Calculate the crossrate for pounds and marks, given the indirect rate for pounds is .50 and the direct rate for marks is 2.40.

17.3. Suppose that a bank sells a call option to a trader on 10,000 pounds at a striking price of $1.75 each for a premium of $350. The option expires in three months. If the price of pounds increases to $1.85, what would be the profit to the trader upon exercising the call option? What would be the loss to the bank? At what price would both parties break even?

17.4. Bank A has a maturity mismatch in its foreign exchange position. It has sold 5 million Swiss francs on November 13 for value on November 15 to bank X for $2,501,000 and bought 5 million francs for value on November 25 from bank Z for $2,499,000. The exchange rate is $1 = 2 francs or 1 franc = $.50. To eliminate possible interest rate risk during the maturity gap, it arranges a swap with bank B. Write out the transactions of banks A and B on these value dates. What are the profits to bank A of the swap?

17.5. Assuming FDIC insurance costs .40 percent per year on domestic deposits, and the reserve requirement is 3 percent on all deposits, what is the effective cost of three-month CDs paying 9 percent and three-month Eurodollars offering 9.20 percent? Which will banks prefer to borrow? What kind of arbitrage is this?

17.6. Given the following information:

spot rate = $2/pound

six-month forward rate = $2.20/pound

six-month interest rate in the United States = .05

six-month interest rate in London = .04

Is there an opportunity for covered interest arbitrage?

APPENDIX

WHEELING AND DEALING IN THE INTERBANK MARKET[1]

Consider a bank operating in the Eurodollar market when short-term interest rates are higher than long-term interest rates. Typically, the bank will borrow funds from another bank for, say, 6 months at the lower rate and lend those funds to a third bank or customer for 3 months at a higher rate. When the 3-month loan matures, the interest and principal received from the loan can be used to determine the minimum rate of interest that is required to break even on the remaining 3 months of the 6-month loan. This interest rate is called the *forward/forward rate* in the interbank market. the following example illustrates the calculation of the forward/forward rate.

Assumptions:

1. The 180-day Eurodollar rate is 15.50 percent.

2. The 90-day rate is 16.00 percent.

3. The amount of the loan is $1 million for 180 days.

[1] This appendix is based on information that appears in *Inside Eurodollar Futures*. Chicago: International Monetary Market, 1982, pp. 4, 5.

A bank operating in the Eurodollar market borrows $1 million for 180 days at a cost of 15.50 percent. Interest rates are expressed in annual rates. Therefore, the cost of borrowing for 180 days is

$$\text{Cost} = \$1,000,000 \times 15.50\% \times \frac{180 \text{ days}}{360 \text{ days}}$$

$$= \$77,500$$

The bank then lends $1 million for 90 days at 16.00 percent. The interest earned on that loan amounted to

$$\text{Interest} = \$1,000,000 \times 16.00\% \times \frac{90 \text{ days}}{360 \text{ days}}$$

$$= \$40,000$$

The total return to the bank at the end of 90 days is the principal plus the interest, or $1,040,000.

The interest cost on the borrowed funds for the remaining 90 days is determined by subtracting the interest cost received from the 90-day loan from the total amount of interest due.

Interest owed on 180-day loan	$77,500
Interest received	−$40,000
Interest owed for remaining 90 days	$37,000

The annual break-even (forward/forward) rate for lending funds for the last 90 days is determined by dividing the interest owed for the remaining 90 days by the total return from the initial 90-day loan, and multiplying that amount by the number of time periods per year.

$$\text{Break-even rate} = \frac{\$37,500}{\$1,040} \times \frac{360 \text{ days}}{90 \text{ days}}$$

$$= 14.42\%$$

Now the bank has several courses of action from which it may choose.

1. The bank may make another 90-day loan (a rollover loan) at any rate higher than 14.42 percent and make a profit.
2. The bank can close out its position by making a forward deposit.
3. The bank can leave the position open and speculate that interest rates will move in its favor before the position is to be closed.
4. The bank can establish a long hedge for the second 90-day period, thereby protecting itself against falling interest rates. In other words, the bank can

buy a Eurodollar contract that expires at the end of the second 90-day period (when the 180-day loan is due). If interest rates decline, the value of the contract will increase, thereby offsetting lower return on the 90-day rollover loan. There are several advantages to this approach. One is that it requires fewer interbank deliveries and lines of credit. Another is that it does not affect the asset/liability size (footings) of the bank, which do change when a bank borrows and lends.

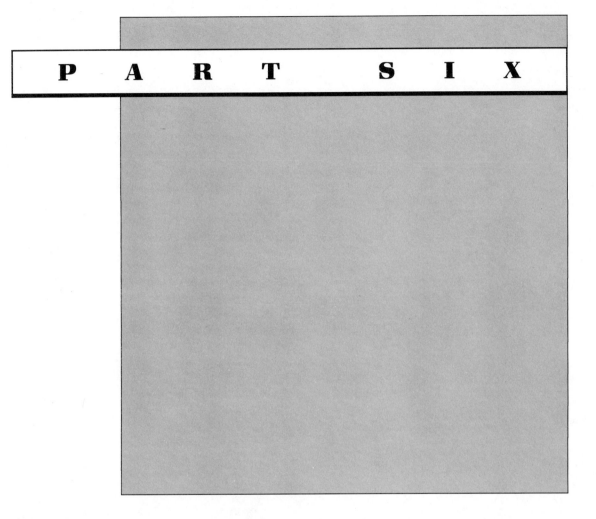

PART SIX

OFF-BALANCE SHEET PRODUCTS AND SERVICES

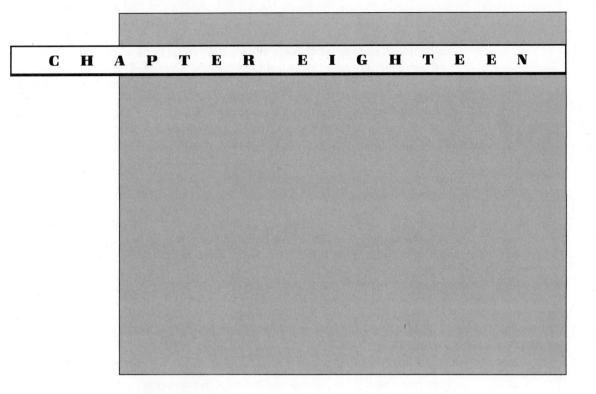

Off-BALANCE SHEET ACTIVITIES

The 1970s and first half of the 1980s were characterized by wild gyrations in market rates of interest, economic booms and busts, and inflation and deflation. In response to these conditions and to satisfy customers' demands and to generate fee income and to increase their capital to asset ratios, banks developed new means of doing business that did not appear on their balance sheets as assets or liabilities—so-called off-balance sheet activities. And in some cases banks acted as brokers (arranging for funds to be provided to borrowers without making loans or raising deposits) rather than dealers (where they make loans).

Two broad groups of off-balance sheet activities are presented in this chapter. The first group involves commitments and contingent claims on the part of

445

the banks. A **contingent claim** is an obligation by a bank to provide funds (i.e., lend funds or buy securities) if a contingency is realized. In other words, the bank has underwritten an obligation of a third party and **currently** stands behind the risk. Default by the party on whose behalf the obligation was written may trigger an immediate loss or may result in the bank acquiring a substandard claim. Because the claims do not appear on the balance sheet until they are exercised, when the loan is made or the securities are purchased, they were not included in the bank regulator's capital-to-risk asset ratios until recently. For convenience, claims are divided into three categories: trade finance, financial guarantees, and investments.[1] The off-balance sheet activities discussed here are the principal ones used primarily by large banks and banks engaged in international finance. A listing of selected off-balance sheet activities is presented in Figure 18.1, which shows Schedule L (Commitments and Contingencies) that banks must supply to bank regulators.

The second group of off-balance sheet activities does not involve contingent claims. This group includes services, such as cash management, that generate fee income for banks of all sizes.

RISKS INHERENT IN FINANCIAL INSTRUMENTS

Before examining off-balance sheet activities involving contingent claims, four types of risk inherent in financial instruments are defined. In addition, other types of risk inherent in banking are mentioned:

1. *Market risk* is the risk that the market price of a financial instrument will change.
2. *Credit risk* is the risk that a counterparty (e.g., a debtor) in a financial transaction will default, resulting in a financial loss to the other party (e.g., a creditor).
3. *Market liquidity risk* is the risk that a financial asset cannot be sold quickly at or near its market value.
4. *Settlement risk* occurs when a bank pays out funds to one participant in a financial transaction before it receives proceeds from that transaction from the counterparty in that transaction. Exchanging foreign currency between banks is one example.

Banks and the banking system face other kinds of risk in addition to those already mentioned. For example, in the discussion of bank loan commitments we will define funding risk. There is also **trading risk** that results from mis-

[1] This breakdown of off-balance sheet activities was developed by James Chessen, "Off-Balance-Sheet Activity: A Growing Concern?" *Regulatory Review,* May 1986, pp. 1–15. Bank "Commitments and Contingencies" are reported on Schedule L of the "Report of Condition" required by bank regulators. Some of the definitions used in this chapter are from the Bank for International Settlements, Committee on Banking Regulations and Supervisory Practices, "The Management of Banks' Off-Balance Sheet Exposures: A Supervisory Perspective," Basle, March 1986.

Schedule RC-L—Commitments and Contingencies

Please read carefully the instructions for the preparation of Schedule RC-L.

Dollar Amounts in Thousands		C360 Bil	Mil	Thou	
1. Commitments to make or purchase loans or to extend credit in the form of lease financing arrangements (report only the unused portions of commitments that are fee paid or otherwise legally binding)	RCON 3423				1.
2. Futures and forward contracts (exclude contracts involving foreign exchange):					
a. Commitments to purchase	RCON 3424				2.a.
b. Commitments to sell	RCON 3425				2.b.
3. When-issued securities:					
a. Gross commitments to purchase	RCON 3434				3.a.
b. Gross commitments to sell	RCON 3435				3.b.
4. Standby contracts and other option arrangements:					
a. Obligations to purchase under option contracts	RCON 3426				4.a.
b. Obligations to sell under option contracts	RCON 3427				4.b.
5. Commitments to purchase foreign currencies and U.S. dollar exchange (spot and forward)	RCON 3415				5.
6. Standby letters of credit:					
a. Standby letters of credit:					
(1) To U.S. addressees (domicile)	RCON 3376				6.a.(1)
(2) To non-U.S. addressees (domicile)	RCON 3377				6.a.(2)
b. Amount of standby letters of credit in items 6.a.(1) and 6.a.(2) conveyed to others through participations	RCON 3378				6.b.
7. Commercial and similar letters of credit	RCON 3411				7.
8. Participations in acceptances (as described in the instructions) conveyed to others by the reporting bank	RCON 3428				8.
9. Participations in acceptances (as described in the instructions) acquired by the reporting (nonaccepting) bank	RCON 3429				9.
10. Securities borrowed	RCON 3432				10.
11. Securities lent	RCON 3433				11.
12. Other significant commitments and contingencies (list below each component of this item over 25% of Schedule RC, item 28, "Total equity capital")	RCON 3430				12.

Memoranda

1. Loans originated by the reporting bank that have been sold or participated to others during the calendar quarter ending with the report date (exclude the portions of such loans retained by the reporting bank; see instructions for other exclusions)	RCON 3431				M.1.
2. Notional value of all outstanding interest rate swaps	RCON 3450				M.2.

FIGURE 18.1 Schedule L. *Source.* Federal Financial Institutions Examination Commission.

matching long and short positions in assets and liabilities. In general terms, we must also keep in mind the overall risk to the stability of the financial system from the increased use of off-balance sheet contingent claims.

TRADE FINANCE

Commercial Letters of Credit

Trade finance includes commercial letters of credit and acceptance participations, both of which are used to finance international trade. Letters of credit, which were explained in Chapter 17, have been used by banks for many years and not considered risky because the bank pays only when the appropriate documents are presented. A letter of credit involves a bank (the **issuer**) that guarantees the bank's customer (the **account party**) to pay a contractual debt to a third party (the **beneficiary**). Letters of credit are contingent liabilities because payment does not take place until the proper documents (i.e., title, invoices, etc.) are presented to the bank.

Acceptance Participations

A banker's acceptance (also discussed in Chapter 17) is created when a bank accepts a time draft (bill of exchange) and agrees to pay it at face value on maturity. The draft normally covers the sale of goods. The banker's acceptance is booked as an asset. Some banks sell participations (called **acceptance participation**) for all or part of the time draft, which reduces the dollar amount shown on their books. However, the accepting bank is still obligated to pay the face amount of the acceptance at maturity. Banks that buy acceptance participations have a contingent liability that does not appear on their balance sheets.

FINANCIAL GUARANTEES

A **guarantee** is an undertaking by a bank (the guarantor) to stand behind the **current** obligation of a third party, and to carry out that obligation if the third party fails to do so. For example, a bank can make a **loan guarantee** whereby it guarantees the repayment of a loan made from party A to party B. The guarantors assume that they are more effective credit analysts than other capital market participants because the ultimate liability of the debt is shifted from the borrower to the guarantor. Assuming the guarantor's credit is better than that of the borrower, the rate of return required by the market on the borrower's obligations is reduced.

Standby Letters of Credit

Standby letters of credit differ from commercial letters of credit in that the bank (issuer) must pay the beneficiary if the account party defaults on a financial obligation of performance contract.[2] Although national banks and most state banks are prohibited from issuing guarantees, standby letters of credit serve the same function and do not violate the law.

Uses of Standby Letters of Credit

Standby letters of credit are commonly used in connection with the issuance of debt obligations (i.e., bonds, notes, commercial paper). For example, the city of Burlington, Kansas, issued $106.5 million bonds with a 7-year maturity to

---

[2] Barbara Bennett, "Off-Balance Sheet Risk in Banking: The Case of Standby Letters of Credit," *Economic Review,* Federal Reserve Bank of San Francisco, Winter 1986, pp. 19–29.; Peter Lloyd-Davies, "Standby Letters of Credits of Commercial Banks," in *Below the Bottom Line,* Staff study of the Board of Governors of the Federal Reserve System, no. 113, January 1982, pp. 17–55; James Chessen, "Standby Letters of Credit," *Economic Outlook,* Federal Deposit Insurance Corporation, November 1985, pp. 13–25; "The Growth of the Financial Guarantee Market," *Quarterly Review,* Federal Reserve Bank of New York, Spring 1987, pp. 10–28.

fund pollution control and improvements. The bonds are to be repaid by payments received by the city from project users. If the payments are not sufficient to cover the interest and principal, the bonds are backed by irrevocable letters of credit from Westpac Banking Corporation (an Australian bank holding company) and The Long-Term Credit Bank of Japan, Limited. In essence, these banking organizations supported the city's ability to borrow funds without the banks raising deposits or making loans.

Another common use of standby letters of credit is in connection with building contractors' obligations to complete a construction project. For example, a contractor (the account party) promises a beneficiary that a hydroelectric plant will be completed on or before a stated date. If the project is not completed before that date, the bank is required to pay the beneficiary. The reason why the project was not completed is not relevant. The only thing that is important is that the account party failed to perform (defaulted) on the obligation to the beneficiary. In this case, the standby letter of credit is a substitute for a surety bond. **Surety bonds** are sold by insurance companies to insure against loss, damage, or default. They are a special type of insurance policy and should not be confused with the debt obligations that are also called bonds.

Standby letters of credit are also used to ensure the delivery of merchandise, to ensure the performance of options or futures contracts, to back other loans, and even to guarantee alimony and child support payments.

Risk

Many banks evaluate account parties that want standby letters of credit in the same way they evaluate commercial loans. Standby letters of credit are considered loans for the purpose of calculating legal lending limits. Because bankers accept only those credits that they believe are least likely to default and be taken down (loans made), they consider their risk minimal. Recall from the discussion of the debt crisis in Chapter 17 that bankers considered the risk of making huge loans to LDCs minimal. However, external factors over which they had no control reduced the ability of the LDCs to repay their debts, giving rise to the debt crisis. Although banks are experts in assessing the creditworthiness of individual borrowers, their track record is suspect with respect to assessing macroeconomic problems, such as the debt crises and deflation.

To further reduce the risk to banks, many standby letters of credit are backed by deposits and/or collateral. Nevertheless, the long-term nature of some of the commitments and risks can change. This is why some banks require periodic renegotiation of the terms of the standby letters of credit.

If and when the standby letter of credit is taken down, the bank may book the unreimbursed balance as a commercial loan.

Finally, banks can manage their risk by limiting the dollar amount of standby letters of credit they issue and by diversifying their portfolio of such letters.

Pricing

Standby letters of credit may have "upfront" and annual fees. For example, the "upfront" fee may be 1 percent of the outstanding and unused guarantee, and the annual fees may range from 25 to 150 basis points lower than the bank would charge for loans of equivalent maturity and risk. The annual fees on standby letters of credit are lower than loan fees, in part, because of the lower administrative cost and other expenses associated with them and because no funding is required.

Bank Loan Commitments

In general terms, a loan commitment represents a bank's promise to a customer to make a future loan(s) or a guarantee under certain conditions. The agreement between the bank and the customer may be informal or formal; however, *some* agreements are not legally binding on the bank or the potential borrower. The major benefits of loan commitments are the assurance of funds to the borrower and fees or compensating balances of equivalent value to the bank. The major drawback is that the bank is acquiring a credit exposure in the future because it may have to make a loan or a guarantee.

Line of Credit

As explained in Chapter 6, a **line of credit** is an agreement between a bank and a customer that the bank will entertain a request for a loan from that customer, and in most cases banks make the loans even though they are not obligated to do so. Lines are frequently informal agreements and the banks do not collect a fee for their service. Accordingly, a line of credit is not a "firm" commitment by the bank to lend funds.

Revolving Loan Commitments

In contrast, a **revolving loan commitment** is a formal agreement between the bank and a customer, which obligates the bank to lend funds according to the terms of the contract. The contract specifies the terms under which loans will be made, including the maximum amounts to be loaned, maturities, and the rates to be charged based on some reference rate such as the prime rate. The customer pays the bank a **commitment fee,** which is also called **facility fee,** for the privilege of being able to borrow funds at a future date. The fee, for example, may be $\frac{1}{2}$ percent per year of the unused balance.

Some revolving loan commitments contain **material adverse change** (MAC) clauses that release the bank from its obligation to make a loan if there has been a material adverse change in the customer's financial condition. Thus, the extent to which loan commitments are unconditional and "legally binding" on a bank varies widely. Nevertheless, in early 1986, over 75 percent of the amount of all commercial and industrial (C&I) loans are made under some form of an agreement.[3]

Funding Risk

The major risk facing banks with loan commitments is that a large number of borrowers will take down their loan simultaneously and the bank may not have sufficient funds to make the loans. This condition is known as **funding risk** or "liquidity risk," but do not confuse it with "market liquidity risk." The takedowns are most likely to occur during periods of tight credit. Because the bank is obligated to make the loans, it may have to raise additional funds, including equity, to honor the commitments.

If the bank does not honor the commitment, those customers with legally binding commitments could bring legal actions against the bank. Such actions could give the bank a bad reputation, which could impair its future growth and profitability.

Certain types of commitments are considered irrevocable (i.e., unconditional and binding).[4] These include the following:

1. Asset sale and repurchase agreements. An arrangement whereby a bank sells a loan, security, or fixed asset to a third party with a commitment to repurchase the asset after a certain time, or in the event of a certain contingency.
2. Outright forward purchases. A commitment to purchase a loan, security, or other asset at a specified future date, typically on prearranged terms.
3. An irrevocable revolving line of credit.
4. Note issuance facilities, which will be explained shortly.

Similarly, certain types of commitments are considered revocable. These include credit lines and undrawn overdraft facilities.

Note Issuance Facilities

Euronotes

Note issuance facility (NIF) is one of several terms used to describe medium-term (5–7 years) agreements whereby banks guarantee the sale of a borrower's

---

[3] For additional information on bank loan commitments, see Gerald A. Henweck, "Bank Loan Commitments," in *Below the Bottom Line*, pp. 103–131; Mitchell Berlin, "Loan Commitments, Insurance Contracts in a Risky World," *Business Review*, Federal Reserve Bank of Philadelphia, May/June 1986, pp. 3–12; Thomas F. Brady, "Changes in Loan Pricing and Business Lending at Commercial Banks," *Federal Reserve Bulletin*, January 1985, pp. 1–13; James Chessen, "Off-Balance-Sheet Activities and Bank Capital Ratios: A Further Examination," Federal Deposit Insurance Corporation, November 1985. The amount of loans made under commitments is reported quarterly in the Federal Reserve Board's "Terms of Lending Survey."

[4] Bank for International Settlements, op. cit. The listing presented here is not complete.

short-term, negotiable promissory notes at or below predetermined interest rates. Other terms for similar financial guarantees are revolving underwriting facilities (RUFs), and standby note issuance facilities (SNIFs). For bank borrowers the short-term security is usually certificates of deposit (sometimes called a **Roly-Poly CD Facility**). For nonbank borrowers the short-term debt securities are called **Euronotes.** Euronotes are denominated in U.S. dollars and usually have a face value of $500,000 or more. They are held mainly by governments and institutional investors. As the term *Euronotes* implies, most of the activity in this market involves international banking. The Euronotes are not registered with the Securities and Exchange Commission and cannot be sold in the United States. Several of the major nonbank sovereign borrowers in the Euronote market are the United States, Austria, and Great Britain. The main buyers of Euronotes are European and Japanese banks. However, similar standby arrangements are used for the sale of commercial paper in the United States.[5] Similar types of agreements are called revolving underwriting facilities (RUFs), transferable RUFs (TRUFs), standby note issuance facilities (SNIFs), note purchase facility, multiple component facilities, and Euronote facilities. One contingent risk to banks in these arrangements arises from their roles as underwriters or arrangers.

Arrangers and Tender Panels

The NIF can be organized or underwritten by a single bank (the **arranger**) or by a group of 15 or more banks and financial institutions (the **tender panel**) that have the right to bid for the short-term notes issued under the facility. The advantage of a tender panel is the broader competitive market offered by many institutions bidding for the securities, rather than having one bidder. The tender panel also provides a means to place larger dollar amounts of securities than may be possible for a single arranger.

The arranger or tender panel assures the borrower access to short-term funds (i.e., 90 days) over the 5–7 years covered by the agreement. This process is known as **maturity transformation.** Maturity transformation results in increased credit risk for the arranger or tender panel, which may have to lend the borrower funds if the borrower is unable to sell the short-term securities at the interest rates (or prices) agreed upon. The NIFs also increase the funding risk of the underwriting banks if they are called upon to make the loans.

[5] For additional details see *Recent Innovations in International Banking,* Basle, Switzerland: Bank for International Settlements, 1986; James H. Chessen, "RUFs, NIFs, and SNIFs," in *Recent Legislative and Other Developments Impacting Depository Institutions,* Washington, DC: FDIC, 1985, pp. 1–4; Ian Giddy, "Regulation of Off-Balance Sheet Banking," in *The Search for Financial Stability: The Past Fifty Years,* Federal Reserve Bank of San Francisco, 1985, pp. 165–177.

Securitization

Securitization involves the packaging of illiquid small loans into large securities ($1 million or more) and then selling them to investors. The originating institution may, or may not, **service the loan**—collect the principal and interest for a fee. The loan-backed securities are collateralized by mortgages (residential, multifamily, and commercial), automobile loans, Small Business Administration loans, credit-card receivables, computer leases, mobile home loans, and other receivables.[6] By packaging loans in this fashion, banks can increase their liquidity by their ability to sell small loans that would be difficult to market on a stand-alone basis. Securitization is one of the most important financial innovations in recent years. It is changing the traditional way banks do business. Instead of making loans and keeping them, they are making loans and selling them. Securitization permits the originating banks to act as agents—collecting fees and transferring the risk to the holders of the loans.

Guaranteed

The timely payment of principal and interest on some of the mortgage-backed securities is guaranteed directly or indirectly by agencies of the federal government. As discussed in Chapter 9, the Government National Mortgage Association (GNMA), and the Federal Home Loan Mortgage Corporation (Freddie Mac) stand behind certain mortgage-backed securities that meet their standards. Similarly, the Federal National Mortgage Association (FNMA) developed mortgage-backed securities that are backed by private insurance companies.

With Recourse

Some banks sell loan-backed securities with recourse. In this case the bank guarantees the securities, and if the underlying loans are in default, the bank is responsible for making payments of principal and interest to the security holder. For example, Bank One (Columbus, Ohio) sold a $50 million security backed by credit-card receivables. The "certificates of amortizing revolving debts" (CARDS), are backed by a reserve fund held by the bank. Marine Midland Bank took a different route with a $60 million issue of "certificates of automobile receivables" (CARS) and used a private insurer to guarantee the securities.

When a bank sells loan-backed securities that are guaranteed by agencies of the federal government, the total assets of the bank are reduced by the amount of the sale. But this is not the case for loan-backed securities sold with re-

---

[6] Christine Pavel, "Securitization," *Economic Perspectives,* Federal Reserve Bank of Chicago, July/August 1986, pp. 16–31; Randall J. Pozdena, "Securitization and Banking," FRBSF Weekly Letter, Federal Reserve Bank of San Francisco, July 4, 1984.

course, because the credit risk to the bank does not change. Thus, in the strict sense, securitization with recourse is not an off-balance sheet activity.

INVESTMENTS

Currency and Interest Rate Swaps

A **swap** is an agreement between two counterparties to exchange cash flows that may be expressed in different currencies, and it is based upon some notional principal amount of money, maturity, and interest rates. The counterparties are financial institutions, business concerns, government agencies, and international agencies. In the classic "plain vanilla" interest rate swap, counterparties literally swap their interest payments, which may be at a fixed rate of interest or at a floating rate of interest such as LIBOR (London interbank offered rate). There is *no* transfer of principal between the counterparties. That is why the term *notional* principal amount is used.[7]

Types of Swaps

Currency swaps and **interest rate swaps** are the two principal types of swap arrangements. Do not confuse the term *currency swap* as used here with the currency swap that was explained in Chapter 17 in connection with foreign exchange. The difference between the two is that the currency swap for foreign exchange involves *only* the exchange of principal amounts on two different value dates and no exchange of interest payments between those dates.

As noted earlier, an interest rate swap involves the exchange of a stream of interest payments over time. The three main types of interest rate swaps are:

1. *Coupon swaps,* where interest payments are based on fixed rates (e.g., 11 percent) and floating rates of interest (e.g., 6-month LIBOR).

2. *Basis swaps,* where interest payment are based on two different floating rates of interest (e.g., 6-month LIBOR and U.S. prime commercial paper rate).

3. *Cross-currency interest rate swaps,* which involve three counterparties (A, B, and C) and, for example, the interest payments between A and B are based on fixed rate flows in one currency and interest rate, and the interest payments between A and C are based on floating rate flows in another currency and interest rate.

---

[7] The definitions used here conform with those used in *Recent Innovations in Banking,* 1986. For interest rate calculations involving swaps, see Robert Kopprasch et al., *The Interest Rate Swap Market: Yield Mathematics, Terminology and Conventions,* New York: Salomon Brothers, June 1985. For the use of swaps by banks, see "Equity Bankshares," in *Cases in Bank Management,* Benton E. Gup and Charles Meiburg, eds., New York: Macmillan, 1986, pp. 92–102.

Example of a Swap

Figure 18.2 illustrates a coupon interest rate swap based on a notional amount of $10 million. The swap agreement has a maturity of 7 years, and the payment frequency is semiannually. This is a classic "generic" or "plain vanilla" swap between two banks.

Bank A is the **fixed rate** counterparty—the one that pays the fixed rate of interest; and bank B is the **floating rate** counterparty—the one that pays the floating rate of interest. The figure shows that bank A has fixed rate assets and floating rate liabilities that are mismatched, which is not a good match if market interest rates increase. Bank B has mismatched floating rate assets and fixed rate liabilities, which is not a good match if market interest rates fall. To match their respective balance sheets, both banks exchange streams of interest payments. The fixed rate payer (bank A) pays bank B 12 percent on the notional amount so that bank B will earn a positive spread between its fixed rate liabilities and its assets. Similarly, the floating rate payer (bank B) pays bank A a floating rate based on LIBOR so that the return on A's assets will vary with the cost of its floating rate liabilities.

Let's examine the impact of this transaction on bank A for the first 6 months. The relevant interest rates that we will use in our simplified calculation are:

6-month LIBOR	10.0%
Bank A's fixed rate payment	12.
Bank A's variable rate liabilities	9.0

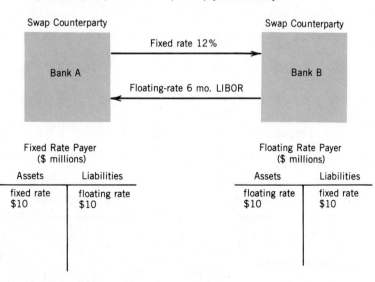

National amount: $10 milion (U.S.)

Maturity: 7 years

Payment frequency: Both counterparties pay semiannually

FIGURE 18.2   Coupon interest rate swap.

Based on these rates, we can determine the net fixed rate cost of funds to bank A in the following manner.

Fixed rate payments made by bank A	12.0%
Minus	
Floating rate payment received	−10.0
Plus	
Interest paid on floating rate liabilities	+ 9.0
Net fixed cost	11.0%

In terms of dollar amounts, Bank A will make the first semiannual fixed rate payment of $600,000 ($10 million × 0.12/2) to Bank B, pay $450,000 ($10 million × 0.09/2) on its floating rate liabilities, and receive a floating rate payment of $502.778 from Bank B. The floating rate payment is based on 181 days and a 360-day year.

First interest period	(1–1 to 6–30)
Number of days	181
6-month LIBOR	10.0%
Principal amount	$10 million

$$\text{Payment} = \frac{\text{Principal} \times \text{LIBOR} \times \text{Number of days}}{\text{Days in year}} \qquad (18.1)$$

$$= \frac{\$10 \text{ million} \times 0.10 \times 181}{360}$$

$$= \$507,777.78$$

Bank A's net fixed cost for the first 6 months expressed in dollar terms is:

Fixed rate payment	$600,000
Plus	
Floating rate liabilities	+ 450,000
Minus	
Floating rate payment received	− 507,778
	$542,222

Because the generic swap is not suitable for all needs, such as call features, deferred payments, and resetting interest rates have evolved. In addition, a secondary market in swaps has developed so that they may be sold or terminated by one of the counterparties.

Risks Associated with Swaps

Counterparties in swap agreements face credit risk and price risk. Credit risk is the risk that the counterparty will default, which will result in an unintended mismatch in the other participants balance sheets. The use of standby letters of credit to guarantee payments is one method of reducing credit risk.

Price risk is the risk that interest rates or exchange rates may change and have an adverse effect on one or more of the participants in the swap agreement. Consider the case of the savings and loan association that wanted to lock in mortgage loan rates of 13 percent and borrowing rates of 11 percent in the early 1980s. They entered into swap agreements as floating rate payers—receiving 11 percent interest and paying a floating rate. By the mid-1980s, homeowners were refining the high cost mortgages at lower rates and the S&Ls and their source of 13 percent income was disappearing. Additionally, they could borrow at about 8 percent, but were stuck with the 11 percent from the swap agreement.[8]

One method of controlling price risk is to enter into an offsetting swap. Another method is to sell the swap in the secondary market, if one can find a buyer.

Over-the-Counter Options, Futures, and Forwards

Over-the Counter Options

In Chapter 17 it was explained that from the option buyer's (seller's) point of view, puts are options to sell (buy) assets and calls are options to buy (sell) them. Put and call options traded on organized stock exchanges are standardized contracts. In other words, the terms of the options contracts (striking price, maturity, etc.) are standardized to facilitate trading. Such standardized contracts, however, did not satisfy the needs of all participants in the market, and an over-the-counter (OTC) market developed for nonstandardized options. OTC options are usually written on treasury securities and currencies that are not traded on exchanges.[9] Although no data are available on the OTC option market, the general consensus is that it is growing rapidly.

Floor-Ceiling Agreements

The concept of options is useful in analyzing some of the off-balance sheet products and services offered by banks. Consider the case of floor-ceiling agreements (sometimes called a collar). A ceiling agreement between a bank and its customer specifies the maximum lending rate on a loan. For example, a corporation obtains a 3-year loan, with interest rates based on treasury bills at 8 percent with quarterly payments. The corporation is willing to pay the bank an upfront fee of 3 percent for 3 years to guarantee that it will not have to pay more than 10 percent over the life of the loan. If the interest rate goes above 10 percent, the bank will compensate the corporation. For example, if the rate

---

[8] "They Swapped—And They're Sorry," *Business Week,* May 26, 1986, p. 111.

[9] Marcelle Arak, Laurie S. Goodman, and Arthur Rones, "Credit Lines for New Instruments: Swaps, Over-the-Counter Options, Forwards, and Floor-Ceiling Agreements," New York: Citicorp Investment Bank, 1986.

goes to 11 percent, the corporation will receive $\frac{1}{4}$ (quarterly settlements) of 1 percent of the loan. On a $50 million loan, the corporation would receive $125,000. In this case, the bank selling the ceiling agreement is analogous to them writing an out-of-the-money put option. The put option is *out-of-the-money* because the striking price of the put option is higher than contract price—the rate at which the loan was made. The corporation is the buyer of the put option, and benefits if interest rates rise.

Floor agreements specify the minimum rate of interest on a loan. If rates go below the floor, of 7.5 percent, for example, the customer may pay the bank the difference between the actual rate and the floor rate. Here the bank is buying an out-of-the-money call option from the corporation. The option is out of the money because the striking price of the call option is less than the contract price—the rate at which the loan was made. Do not be confused by the term *out-of-the-money*. It means simply that the striking price was below (above) the contract price for the call (put) option. Therefore it cannot be exercised for a profit at the present time. An "in-the-money" option is one that can be exercised profitably at the present time. The fee on the floor part of the agreement is less than on the ceiling part because the corporation must pay if the rates goes below the floor. Thus, the total upfront fee of the floor-ceiling agreement to the customer is about 2 percent.

Forward Rate Agreements

A forward rate agreement (FRA) is essentially an over-the-counter interest rate futures contract for bonds or some other financial asset. The buyer and seller agree on some interest rates to be paid on some notional amount at a specified time in the future. The major advantages of FRAs over exchange traded futures contracts is that they can be tailored to meet the needs of the parties involved, and there are no margin requirements.

Buying an FRA (or futures contract) is analogous to buying a call and selling a put, where the forward price is equal to the exercise price of the options. To understand this analogy, keep in mind that the buyer of the FRA is obligated to buy the bond—it is mandatory. Suppose that a bank buys an FRA on a bond at 100 for delivery in 3 months. If the bond is selling at 90 three months from now, the bank must buy the bond (i.e., it is put to the bank) at 100 and then sell it at a loss or keep it in its portfolio at the lower value. On the other hand, if the bond is selling at 110 at that time, the bank will buy the bond (i.e., like a call) and sell it at a profit. Thus, the price of the FRA (or purchased futures) that the bank bought was determined as though it was a purchased call and sold put option. Conversely, the sale of forward contract is analogous to buying a put and selling a call.

Synthetic Loans

Interest rate futures contracts and options can be used to create synthetic loans and securities. To illustrate how this is done, suppose that a construction company, believing that interest rates would decline, wanted to borrow $30 million for 120 days, on a floating rate basis, repricing the loan every 30 days at the CD rate plus 4 percentage points. The current rate of interest on CDs was 10.5 percent, and the initial cost of the loan was 14.5 percent. The bank, however, wanted to make the loan at a fixed rate. To accommodate the customer, the bank resolved the dilemma by using the interest rate futures market to "convert" the floating rate loan into a fixed rate loan, thereby creating a **synthetic loan.** To accomplish this, the bank bought treasury bill futures. If interest rates decrease, the market value of the securities represented by the futures contract will increase and the contracts can be sold at a profit. The profit is used to offset the lower interest from the floating interest rate loan. The details of the transaction are presented in Table 18.1

The top part of the table shows the cost of the loan at floating rates of interest. The interest on the loan from the September 1 to October 1 period was $362,500 ([$30 million × 14.5%]/12 months = $362,500). Using the interest rates shown, the total interest earned by the bank for the term of the loan was $1,310,000.

On September 1, the bank bought three (3) 90-day futures contracts for treasury bills. Each contract is for 10 treasury bills and each treasury bill has a face value of $1 million. The price of each bill is calculated as follows. There are four 90-day treasury bill issues each year. Therefore, the annual interest rate of 11.5 percent is equal to 0.02875 for 90 days, or $28,750 interest per $1 million of treasury bills. The price of a treasury bill is the face amount less the interest, or $1 million − $28,750 = $971,250. Because there are 10 bills in each

TABLE 18.1
DATA FOR SYNTHETIC LOAN

	Dates				
	9/1–10/1	*10/1–10/30*	*10/30–11/30*	*11/30–12/30*	*Totals*
		Loan at Floating Rate			
Loan $30 million floating interest rate	14.5%	13.2%	12.6%	12.1%	
Interest	$362,500	$330,000	$315,000	$302,500	$1,310,000
		Futures Contracts			
	Buy 3 (9/1)	Sell 1 (10/1)	Sell 1 (10/30)	Sell 1 (11/30)	
Yield	11.5%	10.2%	9.6%	9.1%	
Contract value[a]	$9,712,500	$9,745,000	$9,760,000	$9,772,500	
Profit or (Loss)		$ 32,500	$ 47,500	$ 60,000	140,000
					$1,450,000
		Loan at Fixed Rate			
Fixed interest rate	14.5%	14.5%	14.5%	14.5%	
Interest	$362,500	$362,500	$362,500	$362,500	$1,450,000

[a] Contracts are for 10 Treasury bills. Each bill has a face value of $1 million.

contract, a contract would be worth $9,712,500. The bank is required to put up a small margin deposit to buy the contracts. The margin and the commissions are not included in this example. On October 1, the bank sold one (1) of the treasury bill futures contracts at the current market price. Because interest rates declined, the market value of the futures contracts increased and the bank earned $32,500 in the futures market ($9,745,000 − $9,712,500 = $32,500). The gain from the futures market plus the amount of interest paid on the loan total $362,500, the same amount of interest they would have paid on a fixed rate loan.

Similarly, the total gains from the futures market ($140,000) plus the total interest expense on the variable rate loan ($1,131,000) are equivalent to the amount of interest that would have been received on a fixed rate loan ($1,450,000).

The purpose of using the interst rate futures market was to convert the floating rate loan into a fixed rate loan in terms of the interest received by the bank. By using this technique, the bank received the equivalent of a fixed rate loan and the satisfied customer received a floating rate loan.

If interest rates had increased, instead of declined, losses from the futures contracts would have offset higher interest payments from the floating rate loan and the bank would still earn the equivalent of a fixed rate loan.

This example illustrated a synthetic loan. Similarly, banks and others can use futures contracts to convert fixed rate deposits into floating rate deposits, and vice versa.

SERVICES FOR FEES

Cash Management

As mentioned at the beginning of this chapter, banks provide services, which do not involve commitments or contingencies or assets listed on the balance sheet to earn fee income. Cash management systems for business concerns is one example. Cash management systems are used to help business concerns collect remittances and use their bank balances efficiently. Lockboxes are an important part of cash management systems. Lockboxes are post office boxes where customer's remittances are sent and then collected by bankers who deposit them in a business concern's account. Banks receive fees for collecting and processing the funds. With the exception of the computers used to process the funds and an increase in cash (from the collected funds), no other specific items on their balance sheets are directly attributable to cash management systems.

Network

The term **network** refers to a central organization that relies on other companies to provide marketing, distribution, and other functions on a contractual basis. For example, a bank may contract with a discount broker to execute securities transactions for their customers for a fee, part of which goes to the bank. Similarly, some banks have contractual relationships with mutual fund managers (such as Dreyfus) which provide other retail investment services that banks cannot do for themselves because they are prohibited by law (The Banking Act of 1933—*Glass–Stegall Act*) or because it is not efficient to do so.

Banks also use networks to sell insurance, data processing, and other services. Networks permit banks to expand certain specialized services without a major investment on their part.

SUMMARY

A dramatic shift is occurring in the way banks do business. The banking business is changing from making traditional loans and gathering deposits to fee-generating activities that do not appear on their balance sheets, and for which little or no capital is allocated. These activities include a variety of commitments and contingent claims. In addition, banks can use futures and forward contracts to alter the sensitivity of their income to changes in market rates of interest.

In addition, banks are expanding the services they provide to customers (e.g., cash management) which also generate fee income, but do not increase the bank's overall risk.

IMPORTANT CONCEPTS

acceptance participation	loan commitment
arranger	market liquidity risk
basis swap	market risk
cash management	material adverse change clause
commitment fee	maturity transformation
coupon swap	network
credit risk	note issuance facility
cross-currency interest rate swap	off-balance sheet activity
currency swap	out-of-the-money option
Euronote	over-the-counter option
facility fee	revolving loan commitment
floor ceiling agreement	roly-poly CD facility
forward rate agreement	securitization
funding risk	securitization with recourse
guarantee	servicing a loan
interest rate swap	settlement risk
line of credit	standby letter of credit

surety bond   tender panel

swap   trading risk

synthetic loan

REFERENCES

Arak, Marcelle, Laurie S. Goodman, and Arthur Rones. "Credit Lines for New Instruments: Swaps, Over-the-Counter Options, Forwards, and Floor-Ceiling Agreements." New York: Citicorp Investment Bank, 1986.

Bank for International Settlements, Committee on Banking Regulations and Supervisory Practices, "The management of banks' off-balance sheet exposures: a supervisory perspective," Basle, March, 1986.

———. *Recent Innovations in Banking,* Basle, Switzerland, 1986.

Bennett, Barbara. "Off-Balance Sheet Risk in Banking: The Case of Standby Letters of Credit," *Economic Review,* Federal Reserve Bank of San Francisco, Winter 1986.

Berlin, Mitchell. "Loan Commitments. Insurance Contracts in a Risky World," *Business Review,* Federal Reserve Bank of Philadelphia, May/June 1986.

Brady, Thomas F. "Changes in Loan Pricing and Business Lending at Commercial Banks," *Federal Reserve Bulletin,* January 1985.

Cases in Bank Management. Gup, Benton E. and Charles Meiburg (eds.) New York: Macmillan, 1986.

Chessen, James H. "Off-Balance-Sheet Activity: A Growing Concern?" *Regulatory Review,* May 1986.

———. "Standby Letters of Credit," *Economic Outlook,* Federal Deposit Insurance Corporation, November 1985.

———. "Off-Balance-Sheet Activities and Bank Capital Ratios: A Further Examination." Federal Deposit Insurance Corporation, November 1985.

———. "RUFs, NIFs, and SNIFs," in *Recent Legislative and Other Developments Impacting Depository Institutions.* Washington: FDIC, 1985.

Giddy, Ian. "Regulation of Off-Balance Sheet Banking," in *The Search for Financial Stability: The Past Fifty Years,* Federal Reserve Bank of San Francisco, 1985.

Henweck, Gerald A. "Bank Loan Commitments," in *Below the Bottom Line.*

Kopprasch, Robert, *et al. The Interest Rate Swap Market: Yield Mathematics, Terminology and Conventions,* New York: Salomon Brothers, 1985.

Lloyd-Davies, Peter. "Standby Letters of Credits of Commercial Banks," in *Below the Bottom Line,* Staff study of the Board of Governors of the Federal Reserve System, no. 113, January 1982.

Pavel, Christine. "Securitization," *Economic Perspectives,* Federal Reserve Bank of Chicago, July/August 1986.

Pozdena, Randall J. "Securitization and Banking," FRBSF Weekly Letter, Federal Reserve Bank of San Francisco, July 1984.

"The Growth of the Financial Guarantee Market," *Quarterly Review,* Federal Reserve Bank of New York, Spring 1987.

QUESTIONS

18.1. Why did banks substantially increase off balance sheet activities in the 1970s and in the 1980s?

18.2. Briefly describe two broad groups of off balance sheet activities.

18.3. List and define four kinds of risk inherent in banking.

18.4. Distinguish between the issuer, account party, and beneficiary of a letter of credit.

18.5. Define the following terms: (a) acceptance participation, (b) loan guarantee, (c) standby letters of credit, (d) surety bond, and (e) loan commitment.

18.6. What is the difference between a line of credit and a revolving loan commitment? Regarding the latter, what is a MAC clause?

18.7. What is funding risk? What is the potential long-run pitfall of this kind of risk for a bank?

18.8. What are NIFs, RUFs, and SNIFs? Euronotes?

18.9. Who are arrangers and tender panels in NIFs?

18.10. Define the term securitization. What does "with recourse" mean regarding securitized loan portfolios?

18.11. Define a swap. What are two principal types of swaps? What kinds of interest rate swaps are there?

18.12. What risks are involved in swaps? Explain.

18.13. Why has the OTC option market evolved?

18.14. Briefly define the following terms: (a) floor agreements, (b) ceiling agreements, (c) forward rate agreement, (d) synthetic loans, and (e) lockbox.

PROBLEMS

18.1. Corporation XYZ obtains a ceiling agreement from a bank for a five-year loan of $20 million at a rate of 7 percent (tied to LIBOR). An upfront fee of 2 percent is paid by XYZ for the guarantee that rates will not exceed 10 percent.
   (a) If LIBOR goes to 12 percent, calculate the quarterly compensation the bank must pay XYZ.
   (b) What kind of option is this for the bank? XYZ? When is it "in-the-money?"

18.2. Given a forward rate agreement (FRA) on bonds is purchased by a bank at 90 for delivery in three months.
   (a) If the price of the bonds is 100 on the delivery date, what is the profit (loss) of the bank? What type of option is analogous to this example?

    (b) If the price of the bonds falls to 80 three months from now, what is the profit (loss) of the bank? What type of option is analogous to this example?

    (c) From (a) and (b) what can we conclude regarding FRAs and their relationship to options?

18.3. A bank makes a three-month floating-rate loan of $60 million at 15.0 percent. The loan is repriced every 30 days. To hedge against declining interest rates the bank creates a synthetic loan by purchasing and then selling a 90-day T-bill futures contract yielding 12.0 percent every 30 days (i.e., this is done three times). Each contract is for 10 T-bills at $1 million face value for each T-bill. The following interest rate assumptions are made by the bank:

	30 days	60 days	90 days	120 days
Floating rate on loan	15%	14%	13%	12%
T-bill futures yield	12%	11.6%	11.2%	10.8%

Show that the bank has converted the floating-rate loan to a fixed rate loan of 15 percent by calculating the cash inflows on the floating-rate loan and the long position in T-bill futures and comparing their total to the total cash inflows from a 15 percent fixed-rate loan.

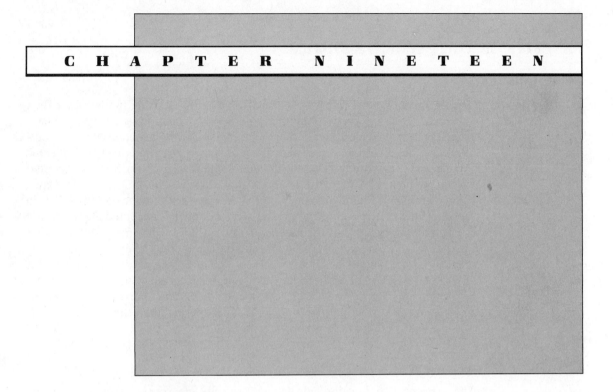

THE PAYMENTS SYSTEM

Payments for transactions are based on paper or electronic systems. The paper-based systems include checks, drafts, and credit card drafts. The electronic system takes advantage of modern technology to exchange payments in the form of electronic debits and credits. This is accomplished through wire transfer of funds, automated clearinghouses, and by other means. This chapter examines the payments system and the role that banks play in it.

BENEFITS OF THE PAYMENTS SYSTEM

Acceptability

The **payments system** refers to various ways of transferring funds, other than currency, from one party to another. A smoothly functioning nationwide payments system provides a wide range of benefits. First, it increases the acceptability of checks drawn on distant banks because the funds can be collected rapidly and at **par value.** This means that a check written for $100 is accepted for the payment of $100 worth of goods and services. Therefore, checks drawn against a bank in Maine are accepted for the payment of goods and services in Hawaii. Earlier in this century, checks were not always accepted at par value.[1]

Checks are the core of the payments system, and will remain so for a long time. Nevertheless, the use of electronic devices for transferring funds is increasing as the payments system evolves. The **electronic funds transfer system** (EFTS) consists of all of the electronic paraphernalia used to exchange funds. For example, transaction cards, automated teller machines, and automated clearinghouses are all part of the EFTS. These terms and others used in connection with EFTS will be explained shortly.

Clearing Arrangements

The presence of a nationwide system permits clearing arrangements to be regulated in the public interest. It is in the public interest that we have a uniform and efficient payments system. This means that terms and conditions for check collection are standardized. **Collection** refers to presenting checks to banks on which they are drawn for payment, and the payment (*remittance*) of those checks. An example of standardization is the imprinted numbers at the bottom of most checks. The numbers are printed in magnetic ink, and are interpreted by receiving banks' check sorters so that the checks can be forwarded to the paying banks for payment. The imprinted numbers include the number of the check (which corresponds with the check number in the upper right-hand corner of most checks), the Federal Reserve Bank District number (ranging from 1 to 12, depending on the bank's location), a routing number used to sort checks to paying banks, and an account number.

About 60 percent of the checks are written for goods or services that are purchased locally, and those that are not deposited in the bank where they are drawn or exchanged by local clearinghouses. A **clearinghouse** is an arrangement whereby banks exchange checks (**clearing**) that are drawn against each other and balances that are due or owed are paid (**settlement**). The net balance is due to or from the clearinghouse agent that represents all of the banks in the arrangement.

---

[1] See James N. Duprey and Clarence W. Nelson, "A Visible Hand: The Fed's Involvement in the Check Payments System," *Quarterly Review,* Federal Reserve Bank of Minneapolis, Spring 1986, pp. 18–29.

BOX 19.1

THE USE OF CHECKING ACCOUNTS

This box reveals some of the results of a survey on the use of cash and transaction accounts by American families. The table shows the usage of checks by family income, age, and education of the head of the household.

SELECTED CHARACTERISTICS OF FAMILY CHECKING ACCOUNTS

	Families Using Checks (%)	Average Number of Checks	Average Size of Checks ($)
Income ($)			
0–10,000	5%	6	$184
10,000–19,999	11	8	167
20,000–29,999	21	9	216
30,000–49,999	25	10	297
50,000 or more	45	10	436
Age of Head (years)			
Less than 35	17	8	288
35–44	22	11	300
45–54	26	10	360
55–64	19	9	276
65 or more	10	6	299
Education of Head (years)			
Less than 12	6	10	200
High school diploma	15	10	380
Some college	20	11	281
College degree	32	8	300
All families	19	9	310

Source: Robert A. Avery, Gregory E. Elliehausen, Arthur B. Kennickell, and Paul A. Spindt, "The Use of Cash and Transaction Accounts by American Families," *Federal Reserve Bulletin*, February 1986, p. 88.

Most checks that are not cleared locally are cleared through the Federal Reserve System. In 1986, the Fed processed 16.2 billion checks. Thus, the payments mechanism consists of a nationwide network of government-controlled facilities and private organizations that exchange funds and information.

Figure 19.1 illustrates the advantage of a clearinghouse arrangment over bilateral collection. **Bilateral collection arrangements** refers each bank sending an agent to other banks to present them with checks for payment. This was the

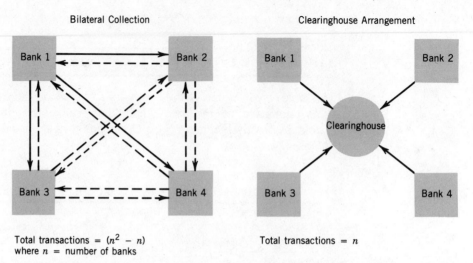

Total transactions $= (n^2 - n)$
where n = number of banks

Total transactions $= n$

FIGURE 19.1   Clearing arrangements. *Source*. Based on James N. Duprey and Clarence W. Nelson, ''The Visible Hands: The Fed's Involvement in the Check Payments System,'' *Quarterly Review*, Federal Reserve Bank of Minneapolis, Spring 1986, p. 19.

arrangement for collecting checks in New York City in the 1850s. It was a workable system while the number of banks involved was small. The total number of transactions involved in a bilateral clearing arrangement is

$$\text{Transactions} = (n^2 - n) \qquad (19.1)$$

For example, the total number of transactions for four banks, each presenting checks to the others, is 12 ($4^2 - 4 = 12$). If there were 100 banks clearing with each other, there would be 9,900 transactions and it would be impossible to operate. In a clearinghouse arrangement, the number of transaction is equal to the number of banks. If there are four banks involved, there would be four transactions.

Role of the Federal Reserve

The passage of the Federal Reserve Act in 1913 marked the beginning of a nationwide, centralized, quasi-government-controlled check-clearing system. The check-clearing process will be explained shortly. The use of the Federal Reserve's extensive communication system for the transfer of funds and information was natural outgrowth of their check-clearing process. Their communications system ties together all of the Federal Reserve offices, the Treasury, other government agencies, and member banks. The communications system is used to: (1) make wire transfers of reserve account balances between member banks, (2) transfer book entries representing U.S. government and federal agency securities, and (3) transfer administrative and monetary policy-related information.

The Federal Reserve also operates automated clearinghouses that will be examined shortly. The ACHs are used to transmit financial entries by electronic means.

Finally, the Federal Reserve is the fiscal agent for the United States. This means that all checks written by the United States for payroll, veterans' payments, social security, or whatever, are drawn against Federal Reserve Banks.

The costs of processing checks are substantial, and the Monetary Control Act of 1980 required the Federal Reserve to make check-clearing and other sevices available to depository institutions subject to reserve requirements for a price. The fees charged cover receiving, sorting, reconciling, delivery of checks, and so on. Institutions send checks to the Fed in the form of **cash letters** containing up to 3,000 items. The amount of each check is itemized, and totaled for the items in the cash letter. Institutions depositing cash letters with the Fed receive credit for their deposits based on the type of items deposited and the time of day when they are deposited. Once the checks are processed and sorted according to the institutions on which they were drawn, the Fed sends a cash letter to those institutions. Accordingly, the fees vary depending on the amount of handling that the Fed does and where the checks are being sent. For example, the cost of a regular cash letter being cleared through a Regional Check Processing Center (RCPCs are centralized processing centers) may be $0.019 per item, whereas nonmachinable cash letters cost $0.13 per item. Nonmachinable items include checks that cannot be processed by the computer because they are mutilated or must be handled manually for some other reason.

Enhances Financial Markets

The existence of a nationwide system for the clearing process enhances the functioning of financial markets by ensuring that funds can be obtained or disbursed quickly. By using the Federal Reserve's communications system to "wire transfer" funds, or by using private wire systems or satellites, banks located in New York, for example, can lend or borrow from banks located anywhere in the country in a matter of minutes. Although this chapter deals with the domestic payments system, it is important to recognize that funds can be wire transferred almost anywhere in the world. Equally important, checks drawn on foreign banks can be cleared, although the process takes longer than it does in the United States.

CHECK CLEARING

An Example of Interregional Clearing

Figure 19.2 depicts the basic elements of the interregional check-clearing system. The process begins when someone writes a check (*payor*) to another party

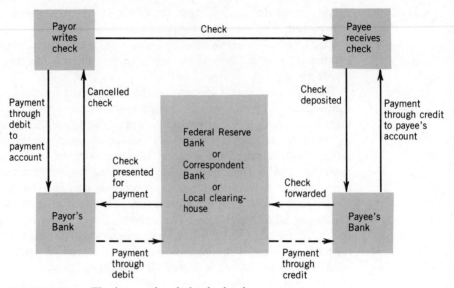

FIGURE 19.2   The interregional check clearing system.

who receives the check (*payee*). By way of illustration, Barbara Bonzano, who lives in Washington, D.C., is vacationing in California and pays for a dress that she bought there with a check drawn on a Washington bank. Surfside Fashions (the payee), where she bought the dress, deposits the check in a California bank. The California bank forwards the check to the Federal Reserve Bank of San Francisco for clearing and settlement.

The Federal Reserve Bank of San Francisco credits the California bank (payee's bank) for the value of the check according to an **availability schedule,** the average length of time it takes to receive payment from the bank on which the check is drawn. Although not shown on the figure, the check may be routed through an automated clearinghouse (which will be discussed shortly), an RCPC, or to the Federal Reserve Bank of Richmond. Credit is usually given on the next business day, and in some cases, two or more business days. The bank in Washington (payor's bank), however, is not debited for the value of the check until it is presented to that bank, which may be several days later.

Float

The difference between the amount credited to the payee's bank and not yet charged to the payor's bank is called *Federal Reserve float*. The Federal Reserve uses airline, charter services, and whatever means of transportation is necessary to move checks from one location to another to minimize the float. But if an ice storm in Washington results in the airports there being closed, and causes the plane carrying the payor's check to be diverted to New York City the float may increase because of the "delayed presentment" (a technical term meaning it's late getting there). Despite natural phenomenon, which increases the float, the check-clearing process is remarkably efficient in getting checks from one part of the country to another, but it is an expensive process for the banks. There are the costs of the sorting and computer equipment, personnel, and related items required to handle checks by the banks as well as the fees paid to the Federal Reserve that were mentioned previously. Estimates for a bank's cost of handling checks range from 6 cents to over $1 per item.

Nonstandard and local holidays also increase the float because checks cannot be presented for payment. Good Friday, for example, is a mandatory nonstandard bank holiday in Connecticut, Maryland, and Hawaii. Nevada Day (October 31) and Pioneer Day (July 24) are mandatory nonstandard holidays in Nevada and Utah, respectively. Mardi Gras is a mandatory holiday in many southern Louisiana parishes and municipalities. In addition, some banks regularly close 1 day in midweek. In the case of midweek closings, the Federal Reserve may charge the bank for checks made available to it, and in the other cases the Fed may delay payments to the payee's bank.

If Surfside Fashions had deposited Barbara's check in a local bank that used a correspondent bank for clearing, instead of clearing directly through the Federal Reserve, the correspondent would probably use the Federal Reserve in the manner described previously. Thus, the Federal Reserve would credit the correspondent bank (now the payee bank) with the amount of the check, and the correspondent would then credit Surfside's local bank.

THE ELUSIVE DREAM OF A CASHLESS SOCIETY

The number of checks written increased from 7.0 billion in 1952 to 56.8 billion in 1984. Because of the increased volume of paper checks that had to be handled, and because of the increased use of computers and credit cards, there were predictions that we would become a cashless society. But that has not happened. Why?

Perhaps the most important reason is the increased efficiency of the processing checks. Faster check-sorting equipment and changes in clearing procedures established by the Federal Reserve make it possible to clear most checks within a day or two—about the same time it takes to do it electronically. The fact that Federal Reserve float declined from $4 billion per day in 1981 to about $500 million per day in 1984 is evidence of the increased efficiency of the check-clearing system. Such improvements in the system were not without costs. The costs were paid, in part, by user fees at the Federal Reserve and capital expenditures by banks for better check-sorting equipment and computers.

It was thought that EFTS would grow more rapidly than it has, and that automated clearinghouses, wire transfers, point of sales terminals, and automated teller machines would be the solution to the problem of handling billions of paper checks. But this did not happen. Nor did the use of plastic credit (or debit) cards solve the problem. In the following sections, we examine these technologies, their strengths and weaknesses.

AUTOMATED CLEARINGHOUSES

An Electronic Alternative to Checks

An automated clearinghouse is similar to the traditional concept of a clearinghouse, except that banks exchange debits, credits, and other information electronically instead of exchanging paper checks. ACHs are designed to use existing computer technology and be high-volume, low-cost substitutes for paper checks. This is especially true for deposits that occur on a routine basis, such as payrolls, Social Security payments, mortgage payments, and insurance premiums. Such payments are for regular, small dollar amounts. The ACHs were not designed to deal with large dollar transfers. They are handled by wire transfers and other systems.

Figure 19.3 shows how ACHs fit into our financial system. Banks, the Federal Reserve, government agencies, savings and loan associations, or other types of financial intermediaries can tie into ACHs through a commercial bank or directly.

The development of ACHs began in 1968 when the Los Angeles and San Francisco Clearinghouse Associations authorized the creation of a committee to study electronic funds transfers. Two years later, a group of California bankers formed the Special Committee on Paperless Entries (SCOPE). The ball

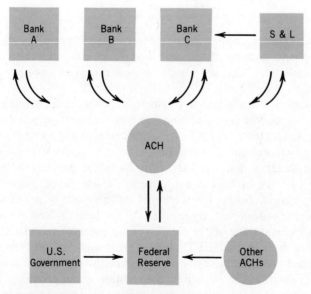

FIGURE 19.3   Automated clearinghouse (ACH).

started rolling and it picked up momentum. In 1970, the American Bankers Association formed the Monetary and Payments System Committee to study the situation. In 1973, 23 similar committees were established to study ACHs. In 1974, the National Automated Clearinghouse Association (NACHA) was formed by regional ACH associations to develop standards and rules to facilitate the interregional transfer of funds.

The first ACH was opened in California in 1972. By the mid-1980s, there were 31 ACHs and 28 Federal Reserve offices in operation serving more than 16,000 financial institutions and 34,000 corporations. Despite the large numbers of financial institutions and corporations participating in the system, only 1.5 percent of the noncurrency payments were handled by ACHs.[2]

Structure of the ACH Payments System

Network

The ACH payments system consists of four components. The first is the network that is used in the clearing/settlement process. This includes the regional ACHs, NACHA, and the Federal Reserve.

Originators and Receivers

The second component includes the 16,000 institutions that use the system. Only a few of these are high-volume, active originators of ACH payments; the majority are low-volume, passive receivers, which leads to a conflict of interest between the two. When making decisions for the ACHs that are governed by the institutions, passive receivers are reluctant to invest in improvements that will enhance the profitability of active users more than theirs. Only those improvements that will benefit both parties at a reasonable cost are acceptable; consequently, not much gets done because they cannot agree on who should bear the cost.

In each institution, there must be sufficient volume and profitability of ACH transactions to justify the cost of originating them, or marketing them to individuals or business concerns. By definition, the acquisition of electronic payment system components implies large capital expenditures for equipment that has a high fixed cost and low variable cost. Therefore, in the long run, there must be a sufficient volume of transactions to cover the costs and make a profit.

Consumers

Individual consumers with checking or transaction accounts are potential users of the ACH system. In order for an individual to originate an ACH payment,

---

[2] The sections of this chapter dealing with EFTS draw heavily on the following special issues of the *Economic Review,* published by the Federal Reserve Bank of Atlanta: "Special Issue: Displacing the Check," August 1983; "The Revolution in Retail Payments," July/August 1984; "The ACH in a New Light," March 1986; "The Automated Clearinghouse Alternative: How Do We Get There from Here?" April 1986.

there must be a payee willing to accept the ACH payment instead of a check. Moreover, the individual consumer may want to make insurance payments through the ACH and mortgage payments by check. Similarly, some individuals may want to receive direct deposit (ACH) Social Security payments and others may prefer checks. Because most institutions are passive receivers, and they make money selling checks and servicing checking accounts, there is little economic incentive for them to market ACH services to individual consumers.

Business Concerns

Some of the same problems arise with selling business concerns on the use of ACHs as occur with individual consumers. But business concerns have additional problems with **corporate trade payments**—payments to vendors and suppliers. The ACH system does not provide adequate message-sending capabilities to accompany payments. For example, an originating corporation may want to explain why the amount sent is different than the amount billed, queries about charges, and other information that is not handled by the ACH system. Such messages frequently consist of 400 words or more. The number of words available for message use is an important consideration for some corporate users.

Another problem concerns check float—the time delay between releasing a check and the time when it is presented for payment. Some observers argue that the financial gain from the float exceeds the savings from the ACH system.

Finally, the ACH system was not designed to handle large-dollar transfers. These are handled by wire transfer.

WIRE TRANSFERS

The major wire transfer systems are the Federal Reserve's Fedwire, CHIPS (Clearinghouse Interbank Payments System operated by the New York Clearinghouse), CHESS (Clearinghouse Electronic Settlement System operated by the Chicago Clearinghouse), and S.W.I.F.T. (Society of Worldwide Interbank Financial Telecommunications). S.W.I.F.T. can be used for international transfers, and in the 1990s plans to include nonbanks, such as brokers, in its network. The predominant feature of the wire transfers is the almost instantaneous transfer of payment data and the security it offers. The cost of using a wire transfer, however, is substantially higher than using the ACH or checks. The cost for sending and receiving a wire transfer may range from $20 to $30 compared to less than $1 for the other means of payment. Clearly wire transfers are not substitutes for most checks.

In addition to the speed of wire transfers, it also offers confirmation of the payment and notification to the receiver that the payment has been made. For example, the offloading of oil from a tanker cannot begin until payment has been made and the seller has been notified. A wire transfer can be used to minimize the time delays made in paying for the oil and notifying the sellers.

Banks that make large-dollar transfers through private wire networks incur some intraday credit risks. Private wire networks usually operate by the transmission of payment messages throughout the day and settle their transactions at the end of the day. This process is called **net settlement.** The time between payment and settlement gives rise to intraday credit exposures. If a participant is unwilling or unable to settle a large debit position, the creditors could be harmed. Because of this, some banks impose dollar limits on transfers and require guarantees.

Wire transfers over the Fedwire do not have credit risk. Transfers are final when the receiver's Federal Reserve bank credits the receiver's account or sends advice of credit. The credit to the receiver is irrevocable. The receiver "guarantees" that the funds will be given promptly to the customer receiving the payments.

AUTOMATED TELLER MACHINES

Cash Dispensers and More

Automated teller machines (ATMs) evolved from single function cash dispensers into complex machines that dispense cash from checking or savings accounts, accept deposits, transfer funds from one account to another, make payments, and provide balances. Some even dispense airline, bus, and ski-lift tickets. Others provide stock market quotations and deposit rates. It is estimated that in 1987, about 75,500 ATMs were installed in the United States. Bank of America is the single largest user with more than 1,350 ATMs.[3]

ATMs can cost $30,000 or more. In addition, the annual maintenance cost may be that much or more. Because of their relatively high costs, two trends are emerging. The first is that many banks are joining networks that permit them to share ATMs. This system permits customers of participating banks to use ATMs throughout the network, which may operate in one or more states or countries. For example, the Plus System, Inc. network offers cash withdrawals at more than 17,000 ATMs in England, Scotland, Wales, Northern Ireland, Canada, Japan, Puerto Rico, and the United States. The Plus System network serves more than 2,300 institutions and 75 million cardholders. Cirrus System Incorporated, another large network, has over 3,000 members, more than 17,000 machines, and 62 million cardholders.

The alternative to networks is for a bank to operate its own (proprietary) system, which is not as convenient for its customers. Beside the obvious cost

[3] Paul Duke, Jr., "Bank Machine Makers Rethink Strategy," *The Wall Street Journal,* June 5, 1986, p. 6; "Crashing the ATM Wall," *ABA Banking Journal,* September 1986, pp. 82–83. For additional information on ATMs, see Steven D. Felgran, "From ATM to POS Networks: Branching, Access, and Pricing," *New England Economic Review,* Federal Reserve Bank of Boston, May/June 1985, pp. 44–61; "Machine Banking," Feaure Section, *American Banker,* December 1, 1987, pp. 1–35.

advantages of sharing ATM equipment and marketing expenses, another advantage is that most of the good ATM locations are already taken by banks, and it is not worthwhile to put one in a bad location.

The second trend is the increased use of cheaper cash-dispensing machines. The logic behind this trend is that about three-fourths of ATM transactions are for withdrawing cash. Deposits account for about 20 percent of the transactions, and the remainder are for other purposes.

Benefits

About 48 percent of bank customers use ATMs, but only a third of those use them on a regular basis. The average ATM handles 5,500 transactions per month (excluding balance inquiries) compared with 4,000 transactions for human tellers. The 5,500 average figure varies widely. Bank of America's ATMs average 9,089 transactions per month. Customers use ATMs twice as much as human tellers to do the same dollar amount of transactions. For example, instead of withdrawing $100 from a human teller, a customer will visit ATMs twice, withdrawing $50 each time.

Thus, ATMs benefit both banks and their customers. From the customer's point of view, ATMs increase the convenience of banking. Transactions can be made 24 hours per day, every day, and at any location where they can use a machine. From the bank's point of view, ATMs replace some human tellers, reduce the error rate in handling transactions, and offer economies of scale if there is sufficient volume. Increasing the volume of ATM transactions is the most difficult task facing banks that are committed to offering ATM services.

POINT OF SALE

Smart Terminals

A point of sale terminal (POS) is an electronic device used for transferring funds and other data in connection with the purchase of goods or services. The terminals are located in business concerns where transactions are made. Some terminals are used to help manage inventory by reading scannable product codes and capturing other sales-related data.

Types of POS Systems

On-line, Real Time

There are three types of POS systems in use. The first is an on-line, real-time system where the retailer is linked directly to the customer's account. The customer's account is debited at the time of the transaction. This type of system is used by Interlink in California. The advantages to the retailer and the bank are reductions in fraud and overdrafts. Fraud is reduced because each customer must use his or her **personal identification number (PIN)** to complete the transaction. Not all POS systems require customer's PINs. This type of system offers consumers the advantage of holding down the costs of the retail goods they buy because of the cost advantages to retailers.

The disadvantages of the on-line POS systems are the high costs of communications and the loss of float by the customers. Where the PIN number is not used, the risk of fraud is increased.

Debit Cards

The second system involves the use of debit cards. **Debit cards** are plastic cards issued by financial institutions to a customer. Information is embossed, impregnated, or magnetically encoded on the card, which may be used to have the cost of goods or services purchased deducted from a customer's account. They look like credit cards, but the difference between the two is that the financial institution's credit is extended to customers with credit card purchases, whereas in the case of debit cards, funds are withdrawn from the customer's account when a purchase is made. By using debit cards, the risk of fraud is shifted from the retailer to the bank. In addition, the average amount customers purchase is higher when they use debit cards than when they use cash.

Several experiments are being conducted between banks and oil companies using POS. Exxon is using its own cards and clearing through Chase Manhattan bank to debit the customer's account. With Chase's access to an ACH, customers' accounts in other banks can be charged. Mobil Oil Corporation and Citibank, N.A., New York, and Barnett banks in Florida are using a similar experiment. One interesting difference between the two experiments is that Mobil requires the use of PIN numbers, whereas Exxon does not. In both experiments the customers get the benefit of paying the "cash price," which is usually 4 cents less than the credit price, when they make a purchase. In still another oil company experiment, Atlantic Richfield Company (ARCO) is charging customers 10 cents per transaction to help defray their costs. The charges will appear on the customer's bank statement. A major advantage to the oil companies is that the average float on their cards is about 45 days. POS will reduce the float to the extent that debit cards are used. Equally important, the average cash purchase at a gas station is about $9. The average credit card purchase is double that amount. Debit cards should have a similar impact on sales. Other experiments include combining debit and credit cards on one card, and letting the customer decide whether to charge the debit or credit card.

Hybrid Systems

The hybrid system is a combination of the debit card and the on-line, real-time systems. The Cactus Switch network in Phoenix, Arizona, is one example of the hybrid system. When a customer makes a purchase, the retailer puts the debit card into a device that records all of the relevant information. Cactus Switch does not require PINs. At designated times during the day, the retailer's information is transmitted to First Interstate Bank, which operates the switch for the ACH. A **switch** is a computer that routes transactions data in an EFT network. Some of the debit cards may be used in ATMs as well as for retail purchases.

Selected Issues

Who Pays the Costs?

Who should pay the costs of the terminals, ATMs, and processing POS transactions? The retailers benefit from increased customer satisfaction, increased sales, and lower costs of operating credit systems. In addition, they reduce fraud, float, and checks written on insufficient or uncollected funds.

The banks benefit from the increased flow of funds, reduced float, lower check collection costs, fewer returned items, and fewer checks written. The banks believe that retailers should pay and the retailers want the banks to pay. To date, most of the research and developmental costs have been borne by large banks and companies that are willing to experiment. As POS systems evolve, other participants will have to share in the costs.

What Does POS Replace?

Do POS/debit cards replace cash, checks, credit cards, or some combination of them? Cash is readily available from ATM networks, check-approval systems reduce a merchant's credit risk, and credit cards are widely accepted. The fact that alternative means of payment are so widely used, and their systems are well established, may be reasons for the relatively slow growth of POS systems.

BANK CREDIT CARDS

Bank credit cards are an outgrowth of travel and entertainment cards issued by companies such as American Express. The first large-scale use of bank credit cards began in the early 1960s, when Bank of America (California) instituted a nationwide credit-card system, which evolved into Visa. By the end of the decade, the use of credit cards was widespread throughout the United States. There are more than 96 million Visa cards and 73 million MasterCards. And both Visa and MasterCard have more than 5 million retail outlets that use their cards. In 1986, Citibank had more than 9 million credit-card accounts (Visa and MasterCard) and Bank of America had more than 7 million. Citicorp, which includes Citibank, accounts for over 16 percent of all credit-card loans outstanding at insured commercial banks. Moreover, the top 100 banks account for 78 percent of all insured bank's credit-card loans.[4]

---

[4] Michael Cacace, "Big Players Win More of Bank Credit Card Market," *American Banker*, September 8, 1986, p. 3; also see "Discover: The New Card in Town, feature section, same issue.

Although bank-related credit cards dominate the scene, Sears Roebuck and Company has introduced their Discover credit card, which is expected to be a significant competitor for the major credit cards and travel and entertainment cards. Discover is part of the growing Sears Financial Network, which includes insurance (Allstate), real estate (Coldwell Banker), and investments (Dean Witter). The Sears Financial Network is part of the firm's strategy to become a major financial service organization as well as the nation's largest retailer.

Common Features

All bank credit cards have the following common features.

1. The credit-card holder has a prearranged line of credit with a bank that issues credit cards. Credit is extended when the credit-card holder buys something at a participating retail outlet. As shown in Figure 19.4, the retail merchant presents the sales draft to the merchant's bank for payment in full, less a service charge discount, which is based on:

  a. the retail merchant's volume of credit-card trade
  b. the average size of each credit-card sale
  c. the amount of compensating balances kept at the bank
  d. some combination of all of these factors

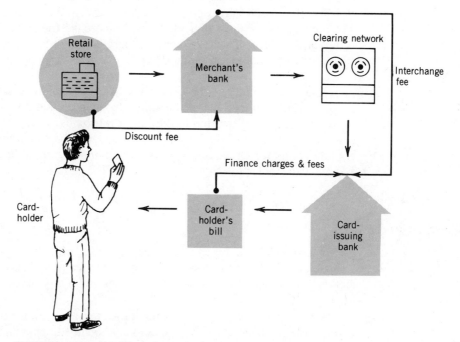

FIGURE 19.4   Credit-card transaction.

The service charge discounts range from nothing to 7 percent or more. The merchant's bank sends the draft through the clearing network to the card-issuing bank, and the merchant's bank receives an interchange fee for its services. Some merchants are transmitting the information to banks electronically (called **data capture**), which is faster than a paper-based system. They benefit from using data capture with reduced service charges. Visa and MasterCard have their own facilities for clearing transactions. The card-issuing bank bills the cardholder, who pays the bank finance charges and fees.

2. The credit-card holder can sometimes pay for the draft in full within a certain period of time (i.e., 30 days), and not be charged any interest on the credit extended, or the holder can pay a portion of the amount due and pay the remainder on an installment basis. The maximum interest rate charged on the unpaid balance is based on each state's law and the prevailing level of interest rates. Banks depend on interest from these credit extensions as a major source of income from credit-card operations. Fees for the privilege of using a credit card are another source of income. Most card issuers charge an annual flat fee, ranging from $12 to $50 or more. Fees are also charged for cash withdrawals, late payments, lost cards, exceeding credit limits, and for other usages. In addition to these fees, banks also profit from the spread between the cost of their funds and the interest earned on the credit extended to cardholders. About 75 percent of the revenue from credit cards comes from interest payments, and most of the remainder comes from annual fees and interchange fees.

Despite potentially high-level profit margins on credit cards, net charge-offs for bad credit-card debt can reduce profits or result in losses. Banks that are aggressive in selling their cards increase their credit risk. In 1985, credit-card charge-offs were about 3 percent of outstanding loans at leading credit-card banks, compared with less than 1 percent for commercial loans.

3. The final feature is the plastic credit card itself, which serves a special purpose. First, it identifies the customer to the merchant. Second, it is used to transfer account information to the sales draft by use of an imprinting machine or some other device. Finally, the credit card may be magnetically encoded, or contain computer chips, allowing the merchant to gain additional information and the cardholder to have access to the EFT facilities.

Credit-Card Plans

There are three basic types of credit-card plans. The first type of plan utilizes a single principal bank to issue the credit card, maintain accounts, bill and collect credit, and assume most of the other functions associated with credit cards.

The second type of plan is for a bank to act as an agent for the principal bank or for Visa or MasterCard. The agent bank's name appears on the credit card. The functions of the agent banks are to obtain new cardholders, establish merchant accounts, and accept merchant sales drafts. The agent banks receive commissions on the business they generate.

The third type of plan is for a bank to affiliate with one or more of the major travel and entertainment card plans, such as American Express. American Express Gold cardholders, for example, may pay their bills to American Express, or borrow directly from the bank against a prearranged line of credit. The bank becomes involved only if the cardholder decides to pay the bill in installments or uses the line of credit.

SUMMARY

The payments system—the various ways of transferring funds from one party to another—is the core of our banking system. Paper-based checks are the most widely used method of transferring payments. Although the paper-based system is costly to operate, it is remarkably efficient and will remain the principal form of payment for years to come.

Automated clearinghouses, which take advantage of computer technology, are becoming increasingly important in the payments system. This is especially true for regular payments, such as payrolls. The system is not widely used for corporate trade payments, however, because of limitations in its message-sending capabilities and other factors. Large payments are commonly sent by wire.

Automated teller machines (ATMs) are an important part of the payments system. They are widely used and accepted by bank customers. Point of sales terminals, however, have not received such widespread acceptance.

Credit cards are a major means of extending consumer credit. The plastic cards are accepted throughout the world as a means of transferring funds.

IMPORTANT CONCEPTS

automated clearinghouse (ACH)	Federal Reserve float
automated teller machine (ATM)	net settlement
availability schedule	par value
bilateral collection arrangement	payee
cash letter	payments system
clearing	payor
clearinghouse	personal identification number (PIN)
collection	point of sale terminal (POS)
credit card	remittance
data capture	settlement
debit card	wire transfer
electronic funds transfer system (EFTS)	

REFERENCES

Cacace, Michael. "Big Players Win More of Bank Credit Card Market," *American Banker,* September 1986.

Duke, Paul, Jr. "Bank Machine Makers Rethink Strategy," *The Wall Street Journal,* June 5, 1986.

Duprey, James N., and Clarence W. Nelson. "A Visible Hand: The Fed's Involvement in the Check Payments System," *Quarterly Review,* Federal Reserve Bank of Minneapolis, Spring 1986.

Federal Reserve Bank of Atlanta. *Economic Review,* August 1983; July/August 1984.

Felgran, Steven D. "From ATM to POS Networks: Branching, Access, and Pricing," *New England Economic Review,* Federal Reserve Bank of Boston, May/June 1985.

"Machine Banking," Feature Section, *American Banker,* December 1, 1987.

QUESTIONS

19.1. What is EFTS? How has it changed the payments system?

19.2. What do the numbers at the bottom of a check indicate?

19.3. What is a clearinghouse? How are checks that are not local cleared? Why are bilateral collection arrangements inferior to a clearinghouse?

19.4. What roles does the Federal Reserve play in the payments system? How did the Monetary Control Act of 1980 affect the Fed's payments operations?

19.5. What is a cash letter? How are they related to RCPCs?

19.6. Describe the clearing process for a check drawn on an out-of-state bank for purchase of goods and deposited with an in-state bank.

19.7. Define the term Federal Reserve float. Does the payee or payor benefit from this float? How do holidays affect float?

19.8. What are ACHs? What payments are especially suited to ACHs?

19.9. What are the four components of the ACH payments system?

19.10. What problems are involved in using ACHs to handle corporate trade payments?

19.11. How do wire transfers differ from using the ACH or checks? Why might the Fedwire be preferred over other wire services?

19.12. How are banks bringing down the costs of ATMs? How do POSs differ from ATMs? What disadvantages may exist with POSs? What advantages?

19.13. How do debit cards differ from credit cards? What is a hybrid system?

19.14. How are service charges on credit cards determined by merchant banks? In what ways do issuing banks earn revenue on credit cards?

19.15. Describe the three basic types of credit card plans.

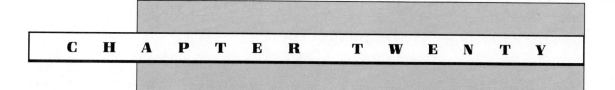

BANK MANAGEMENT ISSUES

The lay of the land looks different from the top of a mountain than from the bottom. From the top one can see how all of the fields, valleys, and rivers fit together in the landscape, and see new horizons in the distance. In the final chapter of this book we are going to take a look from the top. We will consider the landscape that we observed previously, but from a different vantage point. And we will try to see what is beyond the next mountain. To be specific, we know that legal, technical, and economic factors beyond the control of bank managers set the limits within which banks must operate. As these factors change over time, the nature of banking changes. Let's examine some of those changes and see how bank managers responded to them in the past, the present, and strategies that they may use in the future.

THE EVOLUTION OF FUNDS MANAGEMENT

The process of managing funds at commercial banks has changed over the years. This section integrates some of the developments, techniques, and financial instruments that were presented elsewhere in this book. Only those concepts and terms that were not presented previously are defined here.

Asset Management

Following World War II, there was a strong demand for housing, durable goods, and services that were not available during the war. This gave rise to a strong demand for bank loans. It is not surprising, therefore, that from the 1940s until the mid-1960s, bank managers focused most of their attention on the growth and quality of loans and other assets. This was a period when availability of funds and costs of deposits were not major concerns to banks. The costs of deposits was low because market conditions and Regulation Q (both of which are discussed in subsequent sections) held down the cost of funds.

Bank management's emphasis was on making sound lending decisions. Credit analysis to determine a borrower's ability to repay loans, and having sufficient collateral and proper documentation to protect the bank's financial interest were key elements in the lending process. Lending was considered the heart of banking—that's where the action was. Those who were the most successful loan officers—who managed the largest and most profitable loan portfolios—reaped the largest rewards and were promoted to top management positions.

Regulation Q

The Federal Reserve's **Regulation Q,** which limited the maximum interest rate payable on time and savings deposits, was imposed on commercial banks in 1933 and extended to mutual savings banks and savings and loan associations in 1966. The Federal Home Loan Bank Board set the rates for savings banks and savings and loan associations, but followed the rates set by the Federal Reserve.

One reason for estabishing ceiling rates on deposits was to keep bank's costs of funds low so that they would keep the cost of their loans low. Another was to prevent "predatory" competition in interest rates, such as occurred during the 1920s and may have contributed to bank failures at that time. Regulation Q was extended to savings banks and savings and loan associations with the hope that it would help to keep the cost of mortgages low.

Regulation Q acted like a fence. On one side of the fence it protected banks by holding down the cost of acquiring deposits. Accordingly, bank managers did not devote much attention to the cost of funds when interest rates were relatively low from the 1940s through the early 1960s.

Another factor that kept interest rates low was that the Federal Reserve "pegged" interest rates on treasury securities at low levels (not exceeding 2½ percent) to help the government finance its war debts from the 1940s until 1951. This practice ended with **the 1951 accord** between the Federal Reserve and the Treasury that permitted a free market in the interest rates of treasury securities. As shown in Figure 20.1, market rates of interest then began to rise.

On the other hand, Regulation Q hurt banks by prohibiting them from paying competitive rates when interest rates were high after the mid-1960s. Beginning in late 1965, interest rates advanced so dramatically that within a few years their level had doubled. When market rates of interest exceeded the Regulation Q ceilings, individuals shifted their funds from low-yielding savings accounts into higher-yielding marketable securities. This process of withdrawing funds from deposit accounts and investing them in marketable securities is called **disintermediation.** Thus, Regulation Q affected both the availability and cost of deposits.

Banks tried to circumvent the regulatory ceilings imposed by Regulation Q by using deposit premiums and retail repurchase agreements. A retail repurchase agreement is the sale of a retail deposit at a low price with the agreement to repurchase it at some time in the future at a higher price, the difference between the two prices being interest. Another device was to lend depositors part of the amount necessary to buy large CDs at higher interest rates than they could obtain otherwise.

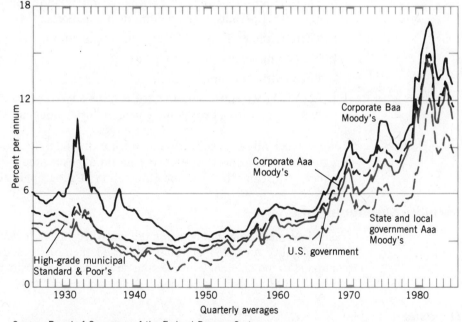

Source: Board of Governors of the Federal Reserve System.

FIGURE 20.1   Long-term bond yields. *Source*. Board of Governors of the Federal Reserve System.

As shown in Figure 20.1, beginning in the mid-1960s, market rates of interes moved irregularly higher until they peaked at record levels in the early 1980s. The interest rate movements reflected economic growth and inflationary expectations. During this period, market rates of interest exceeded Regulation Q ceilings. Because of the failure of Regulation Q to keep lending rates relatively low and because of competitive pressures for savings from money market funds and marketable securities, the Depository Institutions Deregulation and Monetary Control Act of 1980, commonly called the Monetary Control Act, provided for the gradual elimination of Regulation Q.

Deregulation

Deregulation was a cornerstone of President Reagan's political philosophy, and therefore it was not surprising that the 1980 Act had the word *deregulation* in its title, although some would argue that *re-regulation* or *more regulation* would have been more appropriate. Nevertheless, this was a period of deregulation in our history and there are lessons to be learned from other industries, such as the (stock) brokerage and airlines, which were deregulated in 1968 and 1974, respectively. These lessons are:

1. There is always advance warning that deregulation is going to take place. It does not happen instantly.
2. There is an unbundling of existing products and a proliferation of new ones. This permits segmentation of the markets.
3. There is the entry of new, low-cost competitors.
4. New technologies are introduced.
5. Price cutting occurs.
6. Social Darwinism—only the fittest firms survive, frequently by merging with other firms, thereby increasing industry concentration.

We will see all of these factors at work in the banking arena as it becomes deregulated with respect to interest paid on deposits, the variety of products and services it can offer, and the elimination of geographic constraints.

Liability Management

The disintermediation that began in the mid-1960s made it clear to bankers that the availability and cost of funds deserved their increased attention. They responded to the challenge by creating new types of deposits to attract savings and by increasing their use of nondeposit sources of funds.

Deposits

When interest rates were low and competition for deposits was minimal, noninterest-bearing demand deposits, and low-interest paying time and savings deposits were the principal sources of funds for banks. As market rates increased and bank customers became more sophisticated, they disintermediated. Competition for funds intensified in 1972 when the first money market fund was offered to the public. Money market funds located in New England and elsewhere advertised attractive returns and offered toll-free telephone numbers to garner deposits from throughout the United States. This demonstrated to bankers that deposits in their market areas were interest sensitive and fluid.

Competition heated up in 1977 when Merrill Lynch introduced the Cash Management Account (CMA), which combined a money market fund with checking privileges, a margin account, and a debit card.

Bankers began paying higher interest rates on deposits to attract and retain funds. This was made possible by the Monetary Control Act of 1980 that permitted NOW accounts to be offered nationwide and phased out Regulation Q. Beginning in 1983, some of the restrictions on interest rates payable on deposits were removed. By 1986, the only restriction that remained was a $5\frac{1}{2}$-percent ceiling rate on savings deposits.

Several examples of deposits that became increasingly important during this period are money market deposit accounts and money market certificates. Maturities on certificates of deposit ranged from 30 days to 4 years or more, with interest rates payable linked to the size of the deposits and to the maturities. The accounts were an attempt to provide consumers the benefits of interest-bearing checking accounts while others paid the high rates of interest that prevailed in the financial markets.

Nondeposit Sources of Funds

As interest rate ceilings impinged on bank's sources of deposits, they turned increasingly to nondeposit sources of funds. Nondeposit sources of funds include borrowed funds, the sale of certain assets, and equity. These sources are not subject to Regulation Q, and there is no reserve requirements for most of them. The principal nondeposit sources of funds are listed in the following paragraphs.

Federal Funds Purchased. Technically, these are excess reserves of one bank purchased from another. However, the term *Fed Funds* commonly applies to any "overnight" source of funds. They include the sale of securities under agreements to repurchase them from the original seller at a predetermined price. This type of transaction is called a **Repo,** or RP for **repurchase agreement.**

Federal Reserve Discount Window. Banks can borrow on a temporary basis from the Federal Reserve System.

Participations. Banks may sell all or parts of loans to other banks. Banks sell commercial loans, mortgage loans, car loans, and consumer loans. This process of packaging small, otherwise unmarketable loans and selling them to others is called **securitization.** The *ABA Banking Journal* (June 1987, p. 106) published an article entitled "Goodbye, Commercial Loans. Hello, Securitization." The article explained that the future may be securitizing loans instead of the traditional commercial lending.

Eurodollars. For U.S. banks, these are deposits denominated in U.S. dollars in foreign banks. There are reserve requirements on Eurocurrency liabilities of domestic banks.

Commercial Paper. This source of funds is a short-term, unsecured promissory note.

Equity. Equity includes stocks as well as certain debentures and notes.

Asset/Liability Management

New techniques of managing the returns on assets and the costs of funds evolved in response to changing market conditions. Collectively they are referred to as asset/liability management. **Gap management** and **spread management** came into vogue in response to changing market conditions. These terms referred to managing the gap or spread between the return on assets and the cost of funds, the interest rate sensitivity of assets and liabilities, and repricing of loans and deposits. In addition, some banks began to use **duration and immunization** in managing assets and liabilities as well as using it in their security's portfolios.

In general terms, the banks responded to the increased competition by accepting riskier portfolios of assets and liabilities than they had in the protected environment of earlier years. Some observers have argued that the existence of FDIC contributed to the problem by insuring deposits at negligible costs that were unrelated to the riskiness of the insured banks. Bank regulators recognized the increased risks and began to impose higher capital requirements. The additional costs of higher capital, as well as market developments, contributed to the development of financial innovations and off-balance sheet products. For example, one way to increase capital to asset ratios is to sell assets (i.e., securitization).

Financial Innovations

New financial instruments and methods—financial innovations—were created to meet the needs of asset/liability managers. Five broad categories of innovations are:

1. The use of variable rates on mortgage and consumer loans.
2. The development of **financial futures and options contracts** to hedge portfolios.

3. The development of **interest rate swaps** that permitted financial institutions and business concerns to exchange cash flows to meet their needs.

4. Securitization.

5. Electronic transfer of funds, including the widespread use of automatic teller machines (ATM), home banking, "smart" credit cards with electronic chips embedded in them, satellite communications, and so on.

Each of these categories contains a variety of financial innovations. For example, futures contracts are traded on stock market indexes (i.e., index options), financial instruments (i.e., CDs), and on foreign currencies (i.e., yen).

Fee Income

The increased cost of funds and competitive pressures on loan rates forced banks to look for other sources of income. It is not surprising that they recognized the importance of fees for checking accounts, for loan commitments, origination fees, and for other services as a source of income.

Failures

While all of the preceding changes were going on within the banking arena, major external economic forces that had a major impact on banking were occurring. In the first half of the 1980s, the United States went through a period of **deflation**, where the prices of oil, real estate, farm commodities, and so on declined sharply. One effect of the deflation in these commodities was massive loan defaults, which contributed to massive bank failures. In 1987, 201 banks failed, more than at any other time since the Great Depression.

Diversification: The Financial Service Business

The traditional role of commercial banks as depositories for savings and as lenders of short-term, self-liquidating loans has changed. Today, commercial banking organizations are financial service businesses offering a myriad of products and services in order to be competitive. The term **financial services** implies a broad range of products and services, including loans, leases, securities, insurance, investment counseling, and retirement plans.

Competition

Historically, banks competed with banks, retail stores competed with retail stores, and manufacturing firms competed with manufacturing firms, but that has changed. Today, retail stores, manufacturing firms, and other nonfinancial business concerns have entered the financial services business and compete directly with banks. The reason for their entry into the financial service business is that they expect to make a profit. They have a competitive advantage because they are not subject to many of the regulations that limit banking activities, such as rules on geographic expansion or limits on capital or reserve requirements.

The expansion into financial services by nonfinancial business concerns may be a logical extension of their product lines. Such is the case with Sears—the nation's largest retailer—which finances the goods and services it sells. Sears is a major player in consumer installment credit with its Sears and Discover credit cards. In addition to financing the products it sells, Sears Financial Network includes Allstate Insurance, Coldwell Banker, and Dean Witter (securities) to name a few.[1]

General Electric is another example of a nonfinancial business concern that entered the financial service business. GE began by financing the products it sold through General Electric Credit Corporation. But General Electric Credit has gone beyond financing its own products, and today it extends consumer and commercial credit wherever it is legal and profitable to do so.

Other business concerns enter the financial service industry when they believe they can make a profit. K Mart, the second largest retailer in the United States, is leasing space in some of its stores to banks and savings and loans to provide financial services. American Brands, Inc., has two core businesses— packaged consumer foods (i.e., Sunshine Biscuits, Carlton and Lucky Strike cigarettes) and financial services. Their financial service group includes Franklin Life Insurance Company and Southland Life Insurance Company. Even Kinder-Care Learning Centers Inc. (child care) has entered the financial service business by selling insurance to its customers.

Product Diversification

Banking organizations responded to the competitive threats by increasing the number of activities in their holding companies. The Federal Reserve (under Section 4(c)8 of Regulation Y) permitted banks to engage in mortgage banking, leasing, finance companies, and underwriting credit life, accident, and health insurance, and other activities. But the banks wanted more. And in 1981, the Federal Reserve permitted BankAmerica to enter the stockbrokerage business by acquiring Charles Schwab & Company, a discount broker that it later sold. In addition, many banks established relationships with mutual fund distributors, such as Dreyfus Corporation, to market their family of funds. Other banks established relationships with stockbrokers to execute orders for their customers. These contractual relationships permitted banks to get around the Glass–Steagall Act, which had prohibited banks from dealing directly in the marketing and distribution of investment company shares or stocks. A 1987 Supreme Court ruling further eroded the Glass–Steagall Act's prohibitions by

---

[1] For additional information on this topic, see Christine Pavel and Harvey Rosenblum, "Financial Darwinism: Nonbanks—and Banks—Are Surviving," Staff Memoranda SM-85-5, Federal Reserve Bank of Chicago, 1985.

permitting banks to engage in discount brokerage. Some banks even formed **nonbank-banks,** to get around legal corners. Nonbank-banks are those that do not accept deposits or make commercial loans—they engage only in trust activities or consumer lending. The Competitive Equality Banking Act of 1987 attempted to close the nonbank-bank loophole by defining a bank as any institution with FDIC insurance.[2] However, the bill "grandfathered" over 160 existing nonbank-banks existing as of March 5, 1986. This means that Congress closed the barn door after the horses escaped, and is permitting Sears and other firms to operate banks while freezing out new entrants.

Geographic Diversification

Limitations on the geographic expansion of commercial banks have constrained the scope of their activities and shaped the kinds of banking that they do. This point is illustrated by remarks from Henry Wallich, former member of the Board of Governors of the Federal Reserve System who argued that being unable to have a nationwide branch network deprived large money-center banks from a broad base of core deposits and forced them to rely on nondeposit sources of funds. This, in turn, contributed to them being international lenders.

> Lending, unlike branching, while not limited to the state of the bank's residence, nevertheless is affected in some degree by the difficulty of reaching local borrowers. This, together with the limitation on functional expansion beyond activities closely related to commercial banking, such as into securities and other types of financial business, may have helped push American banks in the direction of developing-country lending. Participation in a syndication is a means of increasing assets and earnings when loans to regular customers may be hard to find. This may also help account for the fact that foreign lending by American banks seems to be less oriented toward financing of customer's exports than that of non-U.S. banks.[3]

Relief from geographic restrictions on banking activity came from several sources. First, banking organizations that had finance company, mortgage company, or leasing company affiliates, for example, could operate those affiliates in any state where they could obtain authorization to do so. This loophole permitted Citicorp and BankAmerica, for example, to operate Person-to-Person Finance and Finance America finance company affiliates throughout most of the United States.

---

[2] This definition of a bank is not complete. For more information see 12 U.S.C. 1813.

[3] Henry C. Wallich, "The International Debt Situation in an American View: Borrowing Countries and Lending Banks." Speech before the Verein fuer Socialpolitik, Frankfurt, Germany, February 8, 1985.

Another crack in the geographic roadblock came in 1982 when the Federal Reserve, implementing the emergency powers provision of the Garn-St Germain Act, permitted Citicorp (New York) to acquire Fidelity Federal Savings and Loan, a financially troubled S&L in Oakland, California. The following year, the Federal Reserve approved BankAmerica's (California) to acquire failing Seafirst Corporation (Washington). The most important blow to geographic restrictions came in 1985, when the Supreme Court upheld the laws of Massachusetts and Connecticut permitting interstate banking. Since then, bank mergers across state lines have been approved in various states.

Other important events include:

- Three consumer finance companies (Associates, Household, and Avco), acquiring "nonbank banks"—banks that either accepted deposits or made commercial loans, but did not do both, thereby circumventing banking laws.

- Chase Manhattan Corp. (New York) investing in Equibank of Pittsburgh, and Chemical New York Bank investing in Florida National Banks of Florida.

- The Federal Home Loan Bank Board allowed interstate acquisition of savings and loan associations in California and Florida.

- South Dakota and Delaware opened their doors for out-of-state banks to do credit-card processing and other services in their states. Citibank South Dakota, part of Citicorp, is the biggest bank in the state.[4]

ORGANIZATIONAL STRUCTURE

Forms of Organizations

Changes in banking structure and competition, both de facto and de jure, contribute to changes in the organizational structure of financial institutions. The organizational structure evolves from relatively uncomplicated customer markets located in one place to very complex customer markets located worldwide.[5] For example, consider the *classic pyramid organization* that is shown in Figure 20.2. This type of organization is suitable for uncomplicated customer markets where the bank offers loans and deposits in one geographic location. As banks (and other types of organizations) branch to distant locations, however, they may find a **geographic organization** (such as the one depicted in Figure 20.3) more suitable. In this form or organization, more authority and responsibility is delegated downward to senior officers who are in charge of

[4] Jeffery Kutler, "An Era of Deregulation," *American Banker,* 150th Anniversary Commemorative Edition, December 1986, p. 47.

[5] This section draws on the work of Robert O. Metzger, "Deregulation Calls for Changes in Organizational Structure," *Savings and Loan News,* September 1982, pp. 62–66; also see "And Now, The Post-Industrial Corporation," *BusinessWeek,* March 3, 1986, pp. 64–73.

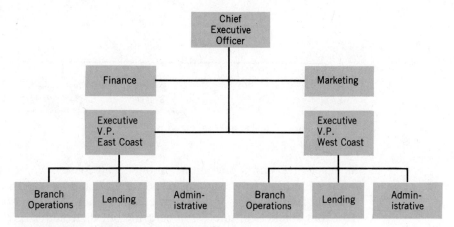

FIGURE 20.2   Classic pyramid organization.

their respective geographic area. For example, as shown in the figure, one Executive Vice President is in charge of East Coast operations and another is in charge of West Coast operations. An alternative to organizing on a geographic basis is to have a **functional organization** that is built around sources and uses of funds. Figure 20.4 illustrates a functional form of organization.

As banks expand in regional and national markets that have different needs, as new business opportunities arise that require particular expertise, and as technology becomes increasingly important in the delivery of financial services, **project-based organizations** become more important. A project-based organization assumes that a business is a stand-alone profit center (see Figure 20.5). Each profit center has its own management team that is responsible for

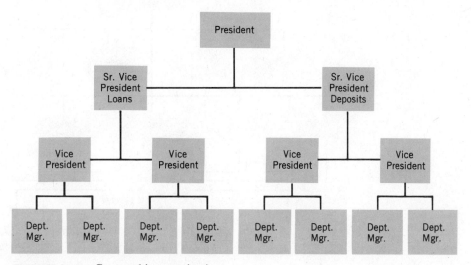

FIGURE 20.3   Geographic organization.

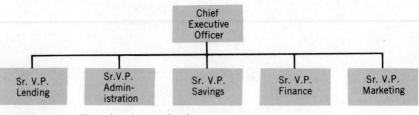

FIGURE 20.4   Functional organization.

its respective unit's operations, profits, and losses. For example, the trust department has its own area of responsibility, and its operations are distinctly different from the rest of the organization for both legal and practical reasons. To avoid conflicts of interest in carrying out their fiduciary responsibilities as trustees, trust departments must separate their activities from those of the bank. Therefore, it is logical to make them a separate profit center.

Sometimes projects are temporary, such as an urban renewal project, and informal lines of communications are established between managers of various areas who must work together on the project. This type of organizational arrangement is called a **matrix.**

In some respects, the **holding company organization** is similar to project-based management because each element of the holding company is a stand-alone profit center. The difference in this case is one of ownership. In the project-based organization, the elements are business units of the corporation.

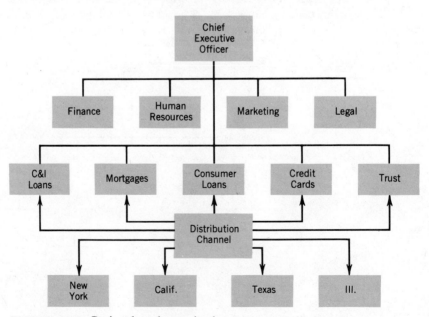

FIGURE 20.5   Project-based organization.

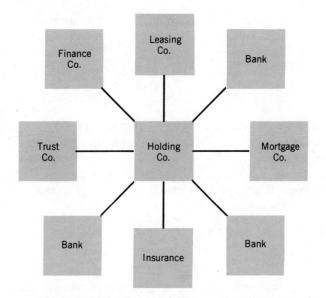

FIGURE 20.6   Holding company organization.

In contrast, a holding company may own only, say, 20 percent of a finance company or leasing company. It could also own 100 percent of the stock, too. But the controls are frequently less in a holding company than in other forms of organization.

The **network** is the final form of organization that is presented here. It is not depicted because it would look like the figure for holding company organizations (Figure 20.6). In a network, a central organization such as a holding company depends on other companies and suppliers to carry out some of its business on a contract basis. For example, some banks have contractual arrangements with mutual funds and stockbrokers to handle some of their retail investment activities. Similarly, they may hire courier services to deliver checks, coins and currency, and other items between branches, banks, clearinghouses, the Federal Reserve, and elsewhere.

Labor Intensive

No matter which organizational structure banking organizations choose, one can make two generalizations about banking.[6] The first is that banks tend to be labor intensive because they believe that personal contact with customers is important. In addition, they are more labor intensive than some of their competitors such as savings and loan associations. One reason for this is that more people are needed to provide the information and credit analysis for the wide

[6] These points are addressed by David B. Zenoff, *International Banking Management and Strategies,* London, England: Euromoney Publications, Inc., 1985, chapter 1.

variety of loans made by banks, compared with the number of people required to make mortgage loans at savings and loans. However, this is changing as savings and loans become more like banks. Nevertheless, the high labor cost is an issue we will address later in this chapter.

Bureaucratic

The second generalization is that banking organizations tend to be bureaucratic. They establish elaborate rules that limit individual decision to protect the organization from fraud or even honest mistakes, and to comply with various rules and regulations. Such processes encourage slow responses by the organizations to change, and inhibit initiative.

PRODUCT AND SERVICE STRATEGIES

Market Strategies

As banking structure changes, organizations change, and the strategies for delivering products and services must change also. Figure 20.7 illustrates a market/product matrix that can be used to aid in the development of strategies.

Market Penetration

The first strategy, shown in cell number 1, concerns present products in the present market. The objective here is to increase market share by cutting prices on products, paying higher interest on deposits, or selling more intensively. For example, a bank may cut the fees on checking accounts to attract new customers, and then induce them to use the other services of the bank. Similarly, a bank can encourage its borrowers to become depositors. In other words, it encourages **cross selling** of products and services.

Product Differentiation

Banks can sell new products in their present market (cell number 2). This strategy works best if the product is differentiated from other products; that is,

Products / Markets	Present products	New products
Present market	1 Market penetration	2 Product differentiation
New market	3 Market development	4 Diversification

FIGURE 20.7   Market strategies matrix.

banks must create a real or imagined difference between their products and services and those of their competitors. For example, a bank may offer consumer loans to teachers, who do not require payments during the summer months when they are not working. Or a bank may offer 95-percent loans (5-percent equity required) on real estate loans when other banks are making 80-percent loans. The fact that the tellers smile or call you by name can be a competitive advantage over institutions that depend primarily on impersonal drive-in windows and automatic teller machines. The point is that banks can attract customers by offering products or services that they believe are more suitable for them (i.e., better value) and different from those offered by competitors.

Market Development

This strategy focuses on present products sold in new markets (cell number 3). The money market funds showed one way of selling products in new markets—the use of toll-free telephone numbers. Similarly, the geographic expansion of Person to Person Finance permitted New York-based Citicorp to have finance company outlets sell existing products (consumer installment credit) in new market areas across the United States.

Diversification

Selling new products in new markets is at the heart of this strategy (cell number 4). The Discover credit card offered by Sears is one example of diversification. BankAmerica buying a discount stockbrokerage firm is another example.

The strategies presented here permit the market to be **segmented** and for firms to establish **niches** within those markets. For example, in order to segment the market, a bank may focus on particular geographic markets or customers. One bank may specialize in lending to small businesses, whereas another deals primarily with large business concerns and international loans. Another bank may offer ''personal attention'' that its competitors cannot or do not offer. These are only a few of the ways that markets can be segmented.

Delivery and Pricing of Retail Services

Part of the evolutionary process that banks face is to establish new methods of delivery and pricing retail banking services. As shown in Figure 20.8, the retail services offered by commercial banks can be divided into three categories—commodity, semipersonal, and personal. Each category has its own characteristics and strategies.

Commodity

Commercial banks offer a variety of retail products and services that are easily understood by customers, and require minimal judgment on their part and can

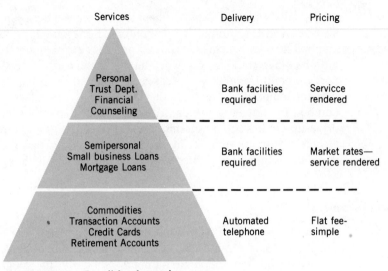

FIGURE 20.8   Retail bank services.

be delivered on a packaged basis. Transaction accounts and credit or debit cards are examples of products that can be considered a "commodity."

Viewed in this context, strategies should focus on how to "package" the commodity and how to "price" it. Because commodity-type transactions require little face-to-face interaction with bank personnel, they should be automated to the extent possible. Automation will help reduce the labor costs that were mentioned earlier. Thus, banks should consider sharing automatic teller machines, the use of direct payroll deposits, preauthorized payments of customers' bills, and the computerized evaluation of credit-card applications (credit scoring) to name a few commodity-type transactions.

The pricing of the commodity should be kept simple. Most customers, for example, may prefer a flat monthly fee for a checking account rather than one based on the number of debit items, the number of credit items, with adjustments for the average daily balance. There is a rule called KISS that some firms use in their decision making, which applies here. KISS stands for Keep It Simple Stupid.

Semipersonal

Semipersonal services are those that require technical knowledge, judgment, and advice. Small business loans and mortgage loans fall into this category. The nature of these services requires considerable customer-bank interaction, particularly on the front-end when the loans are initiated. Therefore, the bank should make it convenient for customers to obtain funds and to get the information they require. Parking, banking hours, and the availability of lending officers are important considerations. By way of illustration, a customer was shopping for a mortgage loan and walked into a financial institution where he asked to see a loan officer. Thirty minutes later the customer was still waiting. He asked when a loan officer would be available and was given a curt reply that someone would be able to see him "shortly." Not wanting to wait any longer, he left and obtained the loan elsewhere. Nevertheless, he decided to call the president of the organization that offended him to let them know how they might improve their service. After 10 rings on the telephone, no one had answered, so he hung up in disgust.

Because business, consumer, and mortgage loans require different amounts of time and knowledge on the part of the bank, the pricing must take into account the time of those involved as well the level of service rendered.

Personal

Personal services require detailed personal knowledge of the customer, technical knowledge, and financial advice. Trust services and financial counseling are examples of services at this level. These services may require substantial customer-bank interaction, and because of this and the knowledge required to give financial advice, the cost of delivery is very high. Therefore, the pricing of these services should also take into account the time and level of service rendered. For example, consider two customers, each with $500,000 under bank management. One customer has all of the funds invested in CDs and money market certificates. The other has all the funds invested in two business concerns that are being supervised by the bank's trust department. Obviously the cost of supervising the business concerns is greater than the cost of rolling over money market certificates, which is why fees must be based on the value of service rendered rather than on the amount of money involved.

RESTRUCTURING THE FINANCIAL SYSTEM

Public Policy Objectives

It is clear that our financial system is in the process of being restructured by design and by default. According to a Congressional study:

> As the barriers between financial sectors, functions and products fell, regulatory strategies that depended on a segregated structure became less effective or even counterproductive. In some areas, regulations have been relaxed, in others, evaded—without a clear understanding of the outcome overall.[7]

---

[7] *Restructuring Financial Markets: The Major Policy Issues,* Committee on Energy and Commerce, U.S. House, 99th Cong., 2d, Sess., July 1986, p. 9. This section draws on this source (including the public policy objectives).

Moreover, the financial markets have become global in nature so that events in China, Africa, and South America affect us. Thus tomorrow's financial system will be different than today's, but how much different is difficult to predict. Nevertheless, there are certain public policy regulatory objectives that will be considered in the restructuring process. These regulatory objectives include:

1. Ensuring access to capital and credit
2. Balancing competition and soundness
3. Enhancing the efficiency of the market system by preventing conflicts of interest and concentration of financial resources
4. Ensuring that the financial system exercises its fiduciary responsibility as a dynamic catalyst in promoting economic growth
5. Protecting consumers

This listing is not complete. Other objectives include separation of banking from commerce, providing for self- and market discipline, and so on.

An Alternative Structure

E. Gerald Corrigan, president of the Federal Reserve Bank of New York, has been a leader in discussing the "specialness" of banks and new financial structures.[8] We are at a turning point in our financial history. We can keep muddling through by not doing much to the existing system except trying to solve problems when they arise. Or we can develop a new financial structure. One structure suggested by Corrigan as a basis for discussion calls for three categories of banking and financial firms. The first is "commercial-financial conglomerates," which may engage in any commercial enterprise and any nonbank financial activity. One of Corrigan's guiding principles is the separation of banking from commerce. Under this scheme, Sears could own or control an insurance company or a stockbroker, but could not own a bank or thrift institution, which includes all institutions that hold "transaction deposits" (deposits that can be withdrawn without prior notice and that are eligible for federal deposit insurance). "Financial holding companies" are the second category. They can own banks and thrifts; for example, an insurance company can own a bank. However, these holding companies cannot be owned or controlled by a commercial firm. Under some circumstances the financial holding companies could have direct access to a payments system and limited access to the Fed's discount window. The banks and thrifts would be subject to reserve requirements.

---

[8] "Are Banks Special?" *Annual Report 1982*, Federal Reserve Bank of Minneapolis; E. Gerald Corrigan, *Financial Market Structure: A Longer View*, Federal Reserve Bank of New York, January 1987, also appears in the *Annual Report 1986*, Federal Reserve Bank of New York; Statement by E. Gerald Corrigan Before the Committee on Budget, U.S. Senate, May 6, 1987. Although others have suggested new or alternative financial structures, Mr. Corrigan's suggestions have been the most widely discussed.

"Bank and thrift holding companies" is the third category. Bank and thrift holding companies may own banks and thrifts, but they cannot be owned or controlled by commercial firms. They may offer a full range of financial services and have normal access to the payment system and the discount window.

An FDIC staff study, *Mandate for Change: Restructuring the Banking Industry* (August 18, 1987) concluded that Glass–Stegall restrictions on affiliations between banks and investment banking firms should be eliminated. In addition, restrictions on Bank Holding Companies concerning affiliations with nonbank affiliates should be phased out, providing that there is "corporate separateness" between the bank and the affiliates.

SUMMARY

Regulation Q, which placed interest rate ceilings on deposits, encouraged bankers to focus on asset management. As Regulation Q ceilings were rendered ineffective by market conditions and competition, management became interested in liability management and then asset/liability management. During the early 1980s, conditions in the financial markets contributed to financial innovations, such as interest rate swaps, that facilitated asset/liability management. The new emphasis in management did not shield banks from deflation and loan failures, which contributed to a large number of bank failures.

As competition to provide financial services expanded to include retailers, manufacturers, and other nonfinancial business concerns, some banks responded to the challenge with product and geographic diversification. In order to compete, banks had to change their organizational structures and develop new market strategies and methods of delivering and pricing their services.

The financial system is evolving rapidly, and the exact form that it will take in the future is not clear. However, we know that because of technology, competition, globalization of financial markets, and other forces, it will be different than the past, or what we have today.

IMPORTANT CONCEPTS

Accord of 1951	disintermediation
asset/liability management	diversification
asset management	duration
classic pyramid organization	equity
commercial paper	Eurodollars
commodity	Federal funds purchased
cross selling	Federal Reserve discount window
deflation	financial futures contracts
deregulation	financial services

functional organization	nondeposit sources of funds
gap management	option contracts
geographic organization	participations (loans)
holding company organization	product diversification strategy
immunization	project-based organization
liability management	Regulation Q
market development strategy	repurchase agreement
market penetration strategy	securitization
matrix organization	segmented markets
network organization	spread management
nonbank-bank	

Some of the terms listed here are not defined in this chapter because they have been defined elsewhere in the book.

REFERENCES

Annual Report 1982, Federal Reserve Bank of Minneapolis.

Corrigan, E. Gerald. *Financial Market Structure: A Longer View,* Federal Reserve Bank of New York, January 1987, also in *Annual Report 1986,* Federal Reserve Bank of New York.

Kutler, Jeffery. "An Era of Deregulation," *American Banker,* 150th Anniversary Commemorative Edition, December 1986.

Metzger, Robert O. "Deregulation Calls for Changes in Organizational Structure," *Savings and Loan News,* September 1982.

Pavel Christine, and Harvey Rosenblum. "Financial Darwinism: Nonbanks—and Banks—Are Surviving," Staff Memoranda SM-85-5. Federal Reserve Bank of Chicago, 1985.

Restructuring Financial Markets: The Major Policy Issues. Committee on Energy and Commerce, U.S. House, 99th Cong., 2d, Sess., July 1986.

Zenoff, David B. *International Banking Management and Strategies.* London, England: Euromoney Publications, Inc., 1985, chapter 1.

QUESTIONS

20.1. What was the major emphasis in bank management in the late 1940s and 1950s? Explain the rationale for this emphasis.

20.2. Did Reg Q originally apply to thrift institutions? Who was responsible for setting deposit rate ceilings for thrifts? What was the reasoning behind Reg Q? How did it affect bank management?

20.3. What was interest rate pegging? When did pegging end?

20.4. In what way was Reg Q harmful to depository institutions? How did banks circumvent Reg Q?

20.5. What legislation called for the gradual elimination of Reg Q?

20.6. If an industry deregulates, what are five consequences that we might expect to occur?

20.7. Disintermediation and higher deposit costs led to what type of bank management? What nonbank financial institution's growth and success was linked to Reg Q? What is a Cash Management Account?

20.8. Name three deposit accounts that resulted from interest rate deregulations. What are nondeposit funds in general? Give five examples of specific nondeposit sources of funds.

20.9. Asset/liability management ushered in what new concepts in managing bank costs and returns? Did these methods increase or decrease bank risk? Explain your answer. If you answered that they decreased risk, why has bank risk tended to increase in the 1980s?

20.10. Asset/liability has led to a number of financial innovations. Give five examples of innovations. Briefly discuss what kind(s) of risk is(are) reduced by each of these innovations.

20.11. Why are nonbank and nonfinancial competitors selling financial services traditionally offered by commercial banks? How have banks responded to market encroachment by these competitors?

20.12. What is the difference between a geographic and a functional organization? What is a project-based organization? Which type of organization does a holding company most resemble? What is unique about a holding company organization? What is a network?

20.13. Briefly discuss the key elements of marketing strategy in banking.

20.14. Distinguish between commodity, semipersonal, and personal retail bank services.

20.15. List five regulatory objectives of financial restructuring.

20.16. What special feature of banks lends support to the idea that banking and commerce should be kept separate to protect the banking system? What is "corporate separateness" in the holding company organization?

INDEX

Accounts receivable as collateral, 145–146
  banker's acceptance, 146
  factoring, 145–146
  pledging, 145
Actuarial method, consumer loans, 253
Add-on interest, calculation of, 29
Add-on-rate, consumer loans, 250–251
Adjustable rate consumer loans, repricing, 252
Adjustable rate mortgages (ARMs), 224–226
  adjustment period, 224
  caps, 225
  convertible mortgages, 225
  discounts, 225
  index, 224
  margin, 225
  negative amortization, 225
  risk in, 225–226
Adjusted balance method, finance charges, 249
Advising bank, 432
Affirmative covenants, 184
Agency, foreign, 398
Annual Percentage Rate (APR), calculation of, 29–30
Annual Statement Studies, 180
Antitrust law, 15
Arbitrage:
  arbitrage tunnel, 427
  covered interest arbitrage, 426–427
  inward arbitrage, 426
  outward arbitrage, 426
  process of, 425
Arrangers, 452
Asset-based lending:
  active participation, 164
  asset values, 163
  characteristics of, 162–163
  finance companies *vs.* banks, 161–162
  leasing, 143
  pricing, 164–165

Asset/liability management, *see also* Dollar-gap management; Duration gap analysis; Interest rate sensitivity
  bank funds, role in, 328–329
  business/interest rate cycle and, 357–358
  defensive/aggressive strategies, 345–346, 347
  dollar-gap management, 347–352
  duration gap analysis, 352–357
  focus of:
    interest rate risk, 341
    net interest income, 329–330, 345
  futures, 366–375
  historical view, 330–332
    liability management, use of, 331–332
  importance of, 327–328
  instruments used in, 346
  interest rate risk:
    determining degree of, 346–347
    and liquidity management, 360–361
  interest rate sensitivity, 334–340
  interest rate swap, 379–383
  interest rate yield, yield curve in management of, 359
  net interest income, 329–330, 345
    determination of, 333
    interest variance analysis, 333–334
  options, 375–379
  simulation models, 360
Asset liquidity, roles of, 91–92
Asset management, 91, 484
Asset sensitivity, 337
Assets/liabilities:
  maturity buckets, 349–350
  nonrate-sensitive assets (NRSA), 335
  nonrate-sensitive liabilities (NRSL), 335
  rate-sensitive assets (RSA), 335, 336
  rate-sensitive liabilities (RSL), 335, 336
Assumable mortgages, 224

Automated clearinghouses (ACHs):
  components:
    consumers, 473–474
    network, 473
    users of system, 473
  development of, 472–473
  issues related to, 474
Automated teller machines (ATMs):
  benefits of, 476
  costs of, 475
  networks of, 475
Automation, banks:
  as marketing tool, 55
  and performance, 53
  types of services, 55
Automobile loans, 242–244
  balloon payments, 243
  lease-a-like loans, 243
Average costs, 290
  average cost *vs.* marginal cost model, 189–190
Average daily balance method, finance
  charges, 249

Back-end loaded approach, investments, 128
Balloon payments:
  automobile loans, 243
  residential mortgages, 220, 227
Bank capital:
  adequacy of, 303
  asset investment aspects, 316
  capital standards, 304, 306–307
    FDIC, 308, 310–312
    risk-adjusted capital requirements, 307–308
    uniform capital requirements, 307
  debt capacity and, 317
  dividend policy and, 316–317
  equity, 300
  financial risk on earnings per share (EPS), 313–314
  internal capital generalization rate (ICR), 318
  long-term debt, 301
  management control aspects, 315
  market conditions and, 315–316
  mergers/acquisitions and, 317–318
  ownership control aspects, 314–315
  primary capital, 305–306
  regulators' view, 303–313
  reserves, 301–302
  roles of, 302

  secondary capital, 306
  shareholders' view, 313–318
  transaction costs and, 317
  trends in, 1970 to 1986, 319–320
    ratio of equity capital to total assets, 319
Bank credit cards, 244–245
  features, 244–245, 479–480
  rise in use, 478–479
  types of plans, 245, 480–481
Bank discount basis yield, calculation of, 27–28
Bank environment, changes in:
  competition, 17–18
  declining market shares, 19
  financial instruments, rise in, 20
  financial reform, 17
  globalization, 19–20
  instability, 18–19
  and risk, 20–21
Banker's acceptance, 97, 146, 275, 434–435
  acceptance participations, 448
  risk factors, 448
  use of, 434–435
Bank Export Services Act (1982), 397
Bank failure:
  and credit risk, 10
  primary causes of, 76, 302–303
  and public confidence, 56
  and regulation, 14, 16–17
Bank funds:
  cost analyses:
    defining cost, 290
    investment decisions and, 293–294
    performance reports and, 291, 293
    weighted average costs, 290–291
  deposits:
    brokered certificates of deposit (CDs), 271–272
    certificates of deposit (CDs), 270–271
    checking deposits, 269–270
    Eurodollar certificates of deposit (CDs), 271
    IRAs/Keogh plans, 272–273
    savings deposits, 270
  nondeposit sources:
    bankers acceptances, 275
    capital notes and debentures, 276
    commercial paper, 275–276
    discount window advances, 274
    federal funds, 273
    repurchase agreements, 274
  sources/uses, and asset/liability
    management, 328–329

Bank holding companies, 275–276
Bank liabilities:
  pricing policy:
    areas covered by, 285
    components of, pricing decision, 284–285
    customer relationship pricing, 288
    deposit pricing matrix, 285–286
    distribution channels and, 290
    loan policy and, 287–288
    pricing committee, 282, 284
    product differentiation and, 289–290
    profitability factors, 286–287
    promotional pricing, 288–289
  structure of, 276–279
    changes in, 1960–1981, 276–277
    insured commercial banks, 277–279
    trends and, 279
Bank Merger Act, 15
Bank of North America, 136
Bank performance:
  CAMEL rating system, 76–77
  external performance:
    market share, 54–55
    public confidence, 55–56
    regulatory compliance, 55
  financial ratios:
    interest sensitivity ratio, 68–69
    profit ratios, 56–62
    risk ratios, 62–67
    tax exposure ratio, 68
  groups interested in, 50
  internal performance:
    bank planning, 52–53
    personnel development, 53–54
    technology, 53
  regulatory monitoring, early warning systems
    (EWS), 74–76
  top performers, study of, 70–74
Bank services:
  commodity services, 497–498
  minimum consumer needs criteria, 281–282
  personal services, 499
  semipersonal services, 498–499
  service charges, 281, 282
Barbell approach, investments, 128
Basis swap, 454
Basle Committee, 399–400
Bilateral collection, clearing process, 467–468
Bill of exchange, and letters of credit, 434
Bill of lading, and letters of credit, 434
Board of Directors, loan policy, 156
Board of Governors, Federal Reserve System,
  400–401

Bonds:
  call provisions, 121
  default risk, 116–118
  pricing equation, 116–117
  rating of:
    junk bonds, 116
    Moody's/Standard & Poors, 114, 115–116
  swapping of:
    as investment strategy, 130–131
    price swap, 130
    spread swap, 131
    tax swap, 130
    yield-pickup swap, 131
  valuation of, 34
Book value, asset-based lending, 163
Branch banks, 16
  foreign, 398
Bridge loan, 247
Brokered certificates of deposit (CDs), 271–
  272
Brokers, 211
Budgets, and planning, 52–53
Business cycle:
  asset/liability management and, 357–358
  phases of, 154–155, 358
    and interest rates, 358
Business plan, and loan request, 172–173
Buydown, residential mortgages, 223

Cactus Switch, 477–478
Call option, 375, 378, 418
Call Report data, 83
Call risk, investments, 121–122
CAMEL rating system, 76–77
  risk measurement, 311
Canadian rollover mortgage, 227
Capacity, and lending consideration, 174, 176
Capital, and lending consideration, 181. See
  also Bank capital
Capitalization, and rate of return on equity
  (ROE), 62
Capital notes and debentures, 276
Caps:
  adjustable rate mortgages (ARMs), 225
  consumer loans, 252
Carry, mortgage banking companies, 236
Cash flow, and value of asset, 31–33
Cash management, 460
Cash plus securities to total assets ratio, 67
Cash to total assets ratio, 66
Certificates of deposit (CDs), 97, 270–272, 346
Character, and lending consideration, 174

Charge-offs:
    loans, 202–204
    recovery of, 202–204
Chattel mortgage, 147
Checking deposits, 269–270
    check overdraft, 244
    clearing process, 466–468, 470–471
    NOW accounts, 269
    Super-NOWs (SNOWs), 269
CHIPS system, 474
Clair, Robert, 70
Classic-pyramid organization, 492, 493
Clean collections, 436
Clearing float, 200
Clearinghouses:
    automated clearinghouses (ACHs), 472–474
    clearing process, 466–468
Clearing process, 466–468, 470–471
    bilateral collection, 467–468
    check processing costs, 469
    clearinghouses, 466–468
    collection, 466
    Federal Reserve, role of, 468–469, 470–471
    Federal Reserve float, 470–471
    interregional system, example of, 469–470
Closed-end, leases, 247
Collateral, 143–149
    accounts receivable, 145–146
    derived demand, effect on, 149
    guarantees, 148
    inventory, 146–148
    and lending consideration, 181
    livestock, 148
    marketable securities, 148
    natural resources, 148
    real property, 148
    residential real estate as, 219
    suitability of items for, 144–145
Collateralized Mortgage Obligations (CMOs),
    233
Collections, 435–436, 466
    foreign:
        clean collections, 436
        documentary collections, 436
Commercial banks:
    constraints on, 10–11
    definition of bank, 4
    deregulation, 17
    first bank in U.S., 136
    functions of:
        financial services, 6–7
        intermediation, 5–6
        payments, 5
    market share, decline in, 19

as profit-earning business, 8
    risk, components of, 9–10
    total assets/market shares, 11–12
Commercial finance companies, asset-based
    lending, 143, 161–165
Commercial and industrial loans, 137, 138–
    143, 150
    dollar size, 150
    and permanent assets, 138
    and temporary assets, 138
Commercial lending, *see also* Loan
        agreements; Problem loans
    borrowing/lending rates, 194–196
    denial for loans, 181–182
    evaluation of loan request:
        capacity in, 174, 176
        capital in, 181
        character in, 174
        collateral in, 181
        conditions in, 181
        financial analysis, 176–180
        industry analysis, 180
    financial guarantees, 205–210
    loan agreements, 182–185
    loan review, 198–199
        function of banks in, 198–199
        purpose of, 198
    loan sales, 210–212
        benefits of, 211–212
        investment banking, 210–211
    pricing of loan:
        effective yield, 186
        frequency of payments, 185–186
        payment accrual basis, 185
    pricing models:
        average cost *vs.* marginal cost model, 189–
            190
        loan expense model, 188
        loan income model, 188
        minimum spread model, 189
        naive model, 186–187
        net bank funds employed model, 188–189
        required rate of return model, 187–188
    prime rate, 190
    problem loans, 199–205
    process in:
        business plan, 172–173
        financial data, 170–172
        initial interview, 173
        loan request, 167–170
Commercial mortgages, construction loans,
    137, 235
Commercial paper 97, 275–276, 488
Commitment fee, 142, 450

Committee on Banking Regulation and
  Supervisory Practices, 399
Commodity Credit Corporation (CCC), 402
  guarantees, 209
Community Reinvestment Act, 15, 230
Compensating balances, 140
Competition:
  financial industry, 489–490
  foreign banks, 19–20
  sources of, 17–18
Competitive Equality Banking Act, 1987, 491
Compound interest, calculation of, 28–29
Concordat, revised, 400–401
Conditions, and lending consideration, 181
Construction and development loans, 137
Consumer Credit Protection Act, 1968, 29
Consumer Leasing Act, 1976, 247
Consumer loans, 138
  add-on-rate, 250–251
  adjustable rate consumer loans, 252
  annual percentage rate (APR), computation
    of, 250
  automobile loans, 242–244
  bank credit cards, 244–245
  bridge loan, 247
  credit decisions, 258–259
    credit-scoring systems, 259
    judgment based, 259
  credit denied, 257
  default risk, 242
  discount rate, 251
  finance charges:
    adjustable balance method, 249
    average daily balance method, 249
    components of, 248
    previous balance method, 249
  historical view, 246
  holder-in-due-course, 257–258
  leases, 247
  mobile home loan, 245, 247
  prepayment, 252–254
    actuarial method, rule of 78s, (sum of
      digits method), 253
  regulation of:
    Equal Credit Opportunity Act, 255
    Truth-in-Lending Act, 248, 254–255
    Uniform Consumer Credit Code, 257
  revolving loans, 244
Consumer protection legislation, 15
Contingent liability, 432, 434
Contracts, foreign exchange transactions, 416
Conventional mortgages, 217
  loan to price ratio, 219
Conversion, options, 421

Core deposits, 266
  interest rates and, 331
Corporate bonds, 114
Corporate trade payments, 474
Correspondent banking, 394–395
Corrigan, E. Gerald, 500
Cost analyses:
  defining cost, 290
  investment decisions and, 293–294
  performance reports and, 291, 293
  weighted average costs, 290–291
Cost/revenue analysis, pricing decisions and,
    286
Country risk:
  foreign exchange transactions, 428
  indicators used, 429
Coupon rate, calculation of, 26
Coupon swap, 454, 455
Covenants, loan agreements, 184–185
Covered interest arbitrage, 426–427
Credit cards, 244–245. *See also* Consumer
    loans
Credit decisions, 258–259
  Code of Ethics, Robert Morris Associates,
    175
  credit bureau in, 257
  credit denied, 257
  credit-scoring systems, 259
  5Cs of:
    capacity, 174, 176
    capital, 181
    character, 174
    collateral, 181
    conditions, 181
  judgment based, 259
Credit exposure, 202
Credit facilities, *see* Loans
Credit risk, 10, 42, 447
  asset/liability management, 341
  and bank failure, 10
  foreign exchange transactions, 417, 427–
    428
  and interest rates, 341
  interest rate swaps, 456–457
  loans, 153–154
Cross-currency swap, 454
Cross-selling, 288
Cumulative gap, 338–339
Currency swaps, 454
  foreign exchange transactions, 423–424
Current deficit-export ratio, 429
Current yield, calculation of, 26–27
Customer relationship pricing, 288
Cyclical industries, loans and, 152–153

Data capture, 480
Daylight overdraft, 141
Dealer paper, 243
Debit cards, 477
Debt capital, 301
Debt-service ratio, 429
Default, loans, 185
Default risk, 37–39
  bonds, 116–118
  consumer loans, 242
  investments, 115–118
Deflation, 489
Deposit insurance, 14
Deposit Insurance National Bank (DINB), 310
Deposit interest cover, 423
Depository Institutions Deregulation
    Committee, 268
Depository Institutions Deregulation and
    Monetary Control Act, 17, 267, 269
Deposits:
  brokered certificate of deposit (CDs), 271–
    272
  certificates of deposit (CDs), 270–271
  checking deposits, 269–270
  core deposits, 266
  deregulation, 267–268
  Eurocurrency liabilities, 95
  Eurodollar certificates of deposit (CDs), 271
  IRAs/Keogh plans, 272–273
  nonpersonal time deposits, 94
  purchased deposits, 266
  regulation, 266–267
  savings deposits, 270
  transactions accounts, 94
  trends in types of, 486–487
Deregulation:
  and bank fees, 281
  deposits, 267–268
  effects of, FDIC, 311
  legislation, 17
  lessons learned from, 486
Discount instrument, 34
Discount interest, calculation of, 29
Discount rate, consumer loans, 251
Discounts, adjustable rate mortgages (ARMs),
    225
Discount window advances, 274
Disintermediation, 485
Distribution, types of, 290
Diversification, 124
  financial services, 489
  loan portfolio, 199–200
  niche in market, 496
  product diversification, 490–491
  as risk management, 41–42
  segmenting market, 497
Dividend policy, development of, 316
Documentary collections, 436
Dollar amount, finance charge, 248
Dollar-gap management, 347–352
  as aggressive strategy, 347–348
  complications of, 349–352
  as defensive strategy, 348–349
  hedging and interest rate futures, 369
  and interest rates, 348
Dollar volume, loans, 150
Due-on-sale clause, residential mortgages, 224
Duration:
  bonds, example of, 35–36
  effects of, 39
  interest rate changes and, 35–36
Duration gap analysis, 352–357
  and aggressive interest rate management,
    355
  and defensive interest rate management, 355
  duration gap measurement, 353–354
    DGAP equation, 354
    interest rates and, 353–355
    market value of equity and, 354
  positive/negative gap, 354
  problems of, 355–356
  zero gap, 349, 354
Duration gap management, hedging and
    interest rate futures, 370–371

Early warning systems (EWS), 74–76
Earnings per share (EPS), and financial risk,
    313–314
Economic instability, effect on banks, 19
Economies of scope, 152
Edge Act, 1919, 396
Edge Act offices, 396
Effective interest rate, 223
Effective yield, pricing of loan, 186
Electronic funds transfer systems (EFTS), 55,
    466
Energy prices, effects of, 90
Equal Credit Opportunity Act, 255
Equity, measurement of, 300
Escrow, 229
Eurodollars, 488
  certificates of deposit (CDs), 271
  deposits, 392
  liabilities, 95
  market:
    development of, 393–394
    forward/forward rate, 440–441
    transaction example, 440–442

Euronotes, 451

European Economic Community (ECC), 401

Evergreen facilities, 140

Exchange rate risk, foreign exchange
transactions, 424

Exchange rates, 412–413
crossrate, 413
currency units per dollar, listing of, 414
direct/indirect rate, 413

Export–Import Bank, 402

Export letters of credit, 431

Export trading companies, 397

Facility fee, 450

Factoring, accounts receivable, as collateral,
145–146

Fair Credit Billing Act, 1974, 15

Fair Credit Reporting Act, 1970, 15

Fair Housing Act, 1968, 229

Fannie Mae, *see* Federal National Mortgage
Association (FNMA)

Farmers Home Administration (FMHA),
guarantees, 209

Federal agency securities, 97, 111–112

Federal Deposit Insurance Corporation
(FDIC), 14, 74, 268, 272, 308, 310–312
bank problems, FDIC response, 310
deregulation, effects of, 311
policy objectives, 310
risk-based deposit insurance proposal, 311–
312

Federal Financial Institutions Examination
Council (FFIEC), 82
minimum consumer needs criteria, 281–282

Federal funds, 97, 273, 346, 487

Federal Home Loan Mortgage Corporation
(FHLMC), 232–233

Federal Housing Administration (FHA),
guarantees, 208

Federal National Mortgage Association
(FNMA), 230–231
commitments, 231
mortgage-backed bonds, 231
mortgage-backed securities, 231

Federal Reserve:
Board of Governors, 400–401
check clearing, role of, 468–469, 470–471
Federal Reserve Board (FRB), 74
Federal Reserve float, 470–471
reserve requirements methods, 92–94

Fedwire, 474

Field warehouse, 147

Finance charges:
adjusted balance method, 249
average daily balance method, 249
components of, 248
previous balance method, 249

Finance companies, foreign, 399

Financial analysis, evaluation of loan request,
176–180

Financial covenants, 184

Financial guarantees:
Commodity Credit Corporation (CCC), 209
Farmers Home Administration (FMHA),
209
Federal Housing Administration (FHA), 208
government loan guarantees, 208
Government National Mortgage Association
(GNMA), 208
parent company guarantees, 207
risk factors, 206–207
Small Business Administration (SBA), 209–
210
standby letters of credit, 205
Student Loan Marketing Association,
(SLMA), 209
surety bonds, 205
Veterans Administration (VA), 208–209
written/oral, 207

Financial Institutions Regulatory and Interest
Rate Control Act (FIRA), 157–158

Financial leases, 143

Financial ratios:
and capitalization, 62
cash plus securities to total assets ratio, 67
cash to total assets ratio, 66
interest sensitivity ratio, 68–69
loan risk ratio, 63
loss rate ratio, provision for loan losses
(PPL), 62–63, 65
net interest margin (NIM), 61
net operating margin (NOM), 60–61
operating expense ratios:
interest expenses, 64
operating expenses, 64
rate of return on assets (ROA), 59–60, 62
rate of return on equity (ROE), 56–59, 60,
62
tax exposure ratio, 68
used by federal bank regulators, 75

Financial service organizations, profitability of,
12–13

Financial services:
fiduciary services, 6
off-balance sheet risk taking, 7
securities related services, 7

Financial system, restructuring of, 499–501

Fisher effect, 37

Fixed income instruments:
  types of, 33
  valuation of, 34–36
Fixed rate mortgages, 220
Float, 200
Floating lien, 146
Floating rate, loans, 154
Floor-ceiling agreements, 457–458
Floor planning, 147
Floors, consumer loans, 252
Forecasts, liquidity, 88
Foreign affiliates, international banking, 395–396
Foreign banks, competition, 19–20. *See also* International banking
Foreign Credit Insurance Association (FCIA), 402
Foreign exchange:
  exchange rates, 412–413
  process of:
    foreign exchange brokers, 412
    interbank market, 412
Foreign exchange transactions:
  arbitrage, 425–427
  contracts:
    credit risk, 417
    delivery of, 417
    maturity of, 417–418
    standardized contracts, 416
  currency swaps, 423–424
  forward market, 415
  forward rates, 417–418
  futures market, 415
  maintenance margin, 417
  mark to market process, 417
  options, 418–423
    conversion in, 422
    example of use, 419–420
    and expiration date, 418
    vs. forwards and futures contracts, 421
    premium in, 419
    put-call parity in, 422–423
    reversal in, 421
    sale of, 420–421
  original margin/security deposit, 416–417
  risks:
    country, 428
    credit, 427–428
    exchange rate, 424
    interest rate, 424–425
    sovereign, 428
    transfer, 428
  spot market, 413, 415
  transaction methods, 415–416

value date, 413
Form for Analyzing Bank Capital (FABC), 304
Forward market, 415
Forward rates, 417–418
  direct/indirect rate, 418
  equation for, 418
  forward/forward rate, 440–441
  forward rate agreement (FRA), 458
  premium/discount, 417
Fraud risk, 9
Freddie Mac, *see* Federal Home Loan Mortgage Corporation (FHLMC)
Front-end loaded approach, investments, 128
Functional organization, 493
Funding risk, loan commitments, 451
Funds, *see* Bank funds
Futures, *see also* Options
  accounting procedures, 374–375
  buyer's position, long/short, 366
  characteristics of, 366–367
  complications in use of, 373–374
  foreign exchange transactions, 415
  forward rate agreement (FRA), 458
  futures contract, 366–367
  hedging, 369–373
    dollar gap position, 369–370
    duration gap, 370–371
    macro hedges, 373
    micro hedges, 373
    steps in, 371–373
  and interest rate swaps, 382–383
  options, 375–379
  trading of, 366
  transaction, example of, 367–369

Gap, *see also* Dollar-gap management; Duration gap analysis
  analysis, 334
  cumulative gap, 338–339
  definition of, 336
  expressions of, 336
  incremental gap, 338–339
  naive gap, 350–351
  net interest income, and interest rates, 337–338
  position at major banks, 339–340
  standardized gap approach, 350
Garn-St. Germain Depository Institutions Act, 1982, 17, 150, 268, 270, 316
General Electric Credit Corporation, 234
General obligation bonds, 112
Geographic factors:
  diversification and, 491–492

geographic organization, 492, 493
loans, 151–152, 158
Ginnie Mae, *see* Government National
Mortgage Association (GNMA)
Glass-Steagall Act, 1933, 7, 111, 266–267, 431,
461
Government National Mortgage Association
(GNMA), 232
guarantees, 208
modified pass-through securities, 232
process in, 232
Graduated payment mortgage (GPM), 226–
227
Growing equity mortgage (GEM), 227
Guarantees, 205. *See also* Financial guarantees
as collateral, 148

Hedging:
futures:
dollar gap position, 369–370
duration gap, 370–371
macro hedges, 373
micro hedges, 373
steps in, 371–373
options, 378–379
macro hedges, 378
micro hedges, 378–379
Holder-in-due-course, 257–258
Holding company organization, 494–495
Holding period yield, calculation of, 27
Home Mortgage Access Corporation, 234
Home Mortgage Disclosure Act (1975), 230
Home mortgages, *see* Residential mortgages

Import letters of credit, 431
Incremental gap, 338–339
Index, adjustable rate mortgages (ARMs), 224
Industry analysis, evaluation of loan request,
180
Industry Surveys, 180
Inflation, and nominal riskless rate of interest,
37
Inspection certificate, and letters of credit, 434
Insurance companies, AAA-rated, 206–207
Interbank market, 412
Interest, simple/compound, calculation of, 28–
29
Interest rate risk, 9, 10, 42
asset/liability management, 341
determining degree of, 346–347
elimination of, 347
foreign exchange transactions, 424–425
and liquidity management, 360–361
loans, 154

non-management approach, 356–357
yield curve in management of, 359
Interest rates:
and credit risk, 341
effective interest rate, 223
and mortgage loans, 221–222, 223
and securities:
liquidity preference, 120–121
price risk, 118–121
yield curve, 119–120
volatility, and bank profit, 18
Interest rate sensitivity:
asset sensitivity, 337
assets/liabilities, classification of, 335
gap:
analysis of, 334
cumulative gap, 338–339
definition of, 336
expressions of, 336
incremental gap, 338–339
net interest income, and interest rates,
337–338
position at major banks, 339–340
liability sensitivity, 337
Interest rate swaps:
basic swap, 454
coupon swap, 454, 455
credit risk, 456–457
cross-currency swap, 454
dollar fixed-rate loan (plain-vanilla) swap,
382
example of, 455–456
and futures, 382–383
mechanics of, 379–381
participants in, 381
price risk, 457
rise of, 379
types of, 382
Interest-reserve ratio, 429
Interest sensitivity ratio, 68–69
Interest variance analysis, 333–334
Interlink, 476
Internal capital generalization rate (ICR), 318
Internal rate of return:
annual percentage rate, 250
calculation of, 27, 29
International banking, 19–20. *See also* Foreign
exchange transactions; International
lending
activities of:
financing of international trade, 394
foreign exchange, 392–393
foreign loans, 392
offshore facilities, 394

International banking (*Continued*)
  debt crisis
    excess oil supply, 404
    illiquid *vs.* insolvent countries, 405–406
    interest rate rise, 404
    oil shocks, 403
    petrodollars, recycled, 403–404
    trade deficit, 406
  foreign banks in U.S.:
    agency, defined, 398
    branch, defined, 398
    finance companies, 399
    investment companies, 398–399
    subsidiaries, 399
  guarantees/insurance:
    Commodity Credit Corporation (CCC),
      402
    Export–Import Bank, 402
    Foreign Credit Insurance Association
      (FCIA), 402
    Overseas Private Investment Corporation
      (OPIC), 402
    Private Export Funding Corporation
      (PERFCO), 402
  participation by U.S. banks:
    correspondent banking, 394–395
    Edge Act offices, 369
    export trading companies, 397
    foreign affiliates, 395–396
    foreign branches, 395
    international banking facilities (IBF), 396–
      397
    representative offices, 395
  regulation:
    Basle Committee, 399–400
    Concordat, revised, 400–401
    regional groups, 401
International Banking Act, 1978, 396
International lending:
  collections, 435–436
    clean collections, 436
    documentary collections, 436
  letters of credit:
    banker's acceptance, 434–435
    banks involved in, 431–432
    and bill of lading, 434
    as contingent liability, 432, 434
    documents required by bank, 434
    export letters of credit, 431
    import letters of credit, 431
    items in, 432
    standby letters of credit, 435
  syndicated loans, 429–431

International Lending Supervision Act, 1983,
  307
International Monetary Fund (IMF), and
  debtor nations, 405–406
International Monetary Market, 377
Inventory as collateral, 146–148
  chattel mortgage, 147
  floating lien, 146
  order bills of lading, 148
  trust receipts, 147
  warehouse receipts, 147
Investment banking, functions of, 210
Investment companies, foreign, 398–399
Investment decisions, and cost analysis, 293–
  294
Investments, *see also* Securities
  policy, development of, 110–111
  risks:
    call, 121–122
    default, 115–118
    marketability, 121
    portfolio, 122–127
    price, 118–121
  strategies:
    bond-swapping, 130–131
    spaced-maturity approach, 127–128
    split-maturity approach, 128
    yield-curve strategies, 128–130
Invoice, and letters of credit, 434
Inward arbitrage, 426
IRA 272–273
Issuing bank, 431

Junk bonds, 116

Keogh plans, 272
Key Business Ratios in 800 Lines, 180

Ladder approach, investments, 127–128
Large Bank Supplement, 77
Leases, 143, 247
  automobile loans, 243
  closed-end, 247
  criteria met by, 247
  open-end, 247
  types of leases, 143
Lender liability lawsuits, 202
Less-developed countries (LDC) debt, 71–72,
  403
Letters of credit:
  banker's acceptance, 434–435
  banks involved in, 431–432

and bill of lading, 434
as contingent liability, 432, 434
documents required by bank, 434
export letters of credit, 431
import letters of credit, 431
items in, 432
risk factors, 447
standby letters of credit, 435, 448–450
Leveraged leases, 143
Liabilities, *see* Bank liabilities
Liability liquidity:
    risks involved, 98–99
    small bands *vs.* large banks, 98
Liability management, 331–332
    and deposits, 486–488
Liability sensitivity, 337
LIBB, 430
LIBOR, 430
Line of credit, 139–140, 450
Liquidity:
    measurement difficulty, 65–66
    regulation:
        loan mix in, 103
        UBRR, 103
    trends affecting, 65
Liquidity management:
    asset liquidity, roles of, 91–92
    estimation of liquidity needs:
        forecasting, 88
        sources and uses of funds statement, 88–90
        structure of deposits method, 90–91
    funds management approach, 99
    liability liquidity:
        risks involved, 98–99
        small banks *vs.* large banks, 98
    liquidity ratio, 99–101
    main areas of, 87–88
    optimum bank liquidity, 101
    primary reserves:
        calculation of reserve requirements, 94–96
        contemporaneous reserve requirements, 92, 93–94
        lagged reserve requirements, 92–93
        legal reserve requirements, 92
        small banks *vs.* large banks, 96
    secondary reserves:
        aggressive liquidity approach, 98
        money market approach, 96–98
Liquidity ratios:
    cash plus securities to total assets ratio, 67
    cash to total assets ratio, 66
    use for liquidity management, 99–101

Liquidity risk, 9
    and interest rate risk, 360–361
Litigation, lender liability lawsuits, 202
Livestock, as collateral, 148
Loan agreements:
    collateral documentation, 183
    covenants, 184–185
    default, 185
    interest rates/fees, 183
    repayment, 183
    representation, 183–184
    type/amount of loan, 182–183
Loan-backed securities, securitization, 453–454
Loan commitments, 142–143
    commitment fee, 142, 450
    funding risk, 541
    line of credit, 450
    material adverse change (MAC), 450
    revolving loan commitments, 450–451
Loan expense model, loan pricing, 188
Loan income model, loan pricing, 188
Loan risk ratio, 63
Loans, *see also* Commercial lending;
    International lending
    approval/supervision of, 156–158
    collateral, 143–149
    commercial and industrial loans, 137, 138–143, 150
    consumer loans, 138, 242–259
    credit policies, 158
    federal limits on size, 150–151
        exceptions to limit, 151
        relative size, 150–151
    leasing, 143
    lending decisions:
        participations in, 152
        scope of services and, 152
        size/location of bank, 151–152, 158
    lending/funding strategies, 154–155
    line of credit, 139–140
    loan commitment, 142–143
    loan review process, 158
    overdrafts, 141–142
    real estate loans, 137–138
    revolving loans, 140
    risks:
        credit, 153–154
        interest rate, 154
    term loans, 140–141
    undesirable loans, 158
    valuation of, 34
    written loan policy, 156
Loan sharks, 246

Loan to price ratio, conventional mortgage, 219
London International Financial Futures Exchange (LIFFE), 415
Long-term debt, 301
Loss rate ratio, provision for loan losses (PLL), 62–63, 65

Macro hedges, 373, 378
Margin, adjustable rate mortgages (ARMs), 225
Marginal costs, 290–291, 294
Marketability risk, 41
  investments, 121
Marketable securities, as collateral, 148
Market liquidity risk, 447, 451
Market penetration, 496
Market risk, 447
Market share:
  automation, as marketing tool, 55
  and earnings, 54–55
Market value:
  asset-based lending, 163
  equity, 300
Mark to market process, 417
Match funding, 190
Material adverse change (MAC) clauses, 142, 450
Matrix organization, 494
Maturity of asset, valuation of, 35
Maturity buckets, 349–350
Maturity transformation, 452
Merchant's discount, 244
Mergers/acquisitions, and bank capital, 317–318
Micro hedges, 373, 378–379
Minimum spread model, loan pricing, 189
Mobile homes, 219
  loans, 245, 247
Modified pass-through securities, 232
Monetary Control Act, 1980, 92, 486, 487
Money market:
  deposit accounts, 270, 285
  money market approach, 96–98
  mutual funds, 269, 271
  principal instruments, 97
Money position, management of, 94–96
Morris, Robert, 136
Mortgage-backed bonds, 231
Mortgage-backed securities, 231
Mortgage banking companies:
  the carry, 236
  origination of loans, 236
  servicing mortgages, 236

Mortgage Guaranty Insurance Corporation, 234
Mortgage insurance, 224
Mortgage Participation Certificates (PCs), 233
Municipal securities:
  general obligation bonds, 112
  taxation and, 112–113

Naive gap, 350–351
Naive model, loan pricing, 186–187
National Automated Clearinghouse Association, 473
Natural resources, as collateral, 148
Negative amortization, adjustable rate mortgages (ARMs), 225
Negative covenants, 184
Net bank funds employed model, loan pricing, 188–189
Net covered position, buying foreign currency, 424
Net interest margin (NIM), 61
Net operating margin (NOM), 60–61
Net settlement, 475
Networks, 460–461
  network organization, 495
1951 accord, 485
Nominal riskless rate of interest, 37
Nonbank-banks, 491, 492
Nonpersonal time deposits, 94
Note issuance facility (NIF):
  arrangers, 452
  Euronotes, 451
  maturity transformation, 452
  tender panel, 452
  types of agreements, 452

Off-balance sheet activities:
  banker's acceptance, 448
  contingent claim, 446–447
  futures, 458
  letters of credit, 447–448
  loan commitments, 450–451
  note issuance facility (NIF), 451–452
  options, 457–458
  risks involved, 447
  securitization, 453–454
  services for fees, 447
    cash management, 460
    networks, 460–461
  standby letters of credit, 448–450
  swaps, interest rate swaps, 454–457
  synthetic loans, 458–460

Off-balance sheet risk taking, 7
Office of the Comptroller of the Currency
(OCC), 74, 304
Offset, 417
Oil crisis:
    excess supply, 404
    rise in prices, 403
Oil-producing nations, petrodolars, recycle,
    403–404
Open-end leases, 247
Open-end credit, 244
Open position, buying foreign currency, 424
Operating expense ratios:
    interest expenses, 64
    operating expenses, 64
Operating leases, 143
Options, 418–423
    call option, 375, 378
    contract specifications, 376
    floor-ceiling agreements, 457–458
    foreign currency futures:
        conversion in, 422
        example of use, 419–420
        and expiration date, 418
        vs. forwards and futures contracts, 421
        premium in, 419
        put-call parity in, 422–423
        reversal in, 421
        sale of, 420–421
    hedging, 378–379
        macro, 378
        micro, 378–379
    International Monetary Market, 377
    over-the-counter, 457
    payoffs for, 377–378
    put option, 375, 378
Order bills of lading, as collateral, 148
Organizational structure:
    bureaucracy and, 496
    classic-pyramid organization, 492, 493
    functional organization, 493
    geographic organization, 492, 493
    holding company organization, 494–495
    labor intensity of banks, 495
    matrix organization, 494
    network organization, 495
    project-based organization, 493
Original margin/security deposit, foreign
    exchange transactions, 416–417
Original maturity, 138
Origination fees, 235
Outward arbitrage, 426
Overdrafts, 141–142, 200
Overnight loans, 273

Overseas Private Investment Corporation
    (OPIC), 402
Over-the-counter, options, 457

Par, selling at/above/below, 34
Participation loan, 152, 211, 430
Par value, 466
Payback period, 223
Payment accrual basis, pricing of loan, 185
Payments system:
    automated clearinghouses (ACHs), 472–474
    automated teller machines (ATMs), 475–476
    bank credit cards, 478–481
    clearing process, 470–471
    point of sale terminal (POS), 476–478
    wire transfers, 474–475
Pay-throughs, 231
Performance reports, and cost analysis, 291,
    293
Permanent financing, 137–138
Personal identification number (PIN), 477
Personnel development:
    job satisfaction, 54
    training, 54
Per unit risk, 288
Petrodollars, recycled, 403–404
Planning:
    bank goals in, 52
    bank objectives in, 52
    budget in, 52–53
    strategic planning, 53
Playing the yield curve, 128–129
Pledging, accounts receivable, as collateral,
    145
Points, residential mortgages, 223
Point of sale terminal (POS):
    issues related to, 478
    types of:
        debit cards, 477
        hybrid systems, 477–478
        on-line, real time system, 476–477
Portfolio risk:
    investments, 122–127
    variability, measurement of, 122–123
Premium:
    options, 419
    premium instrument, 34
Prepayment:
    consumer loans, 252–254
    loans, 183
    penalty, residential mortgages, 223
Previous balance method, finance charges, 249
Price risk:
    interest rate swaps, 457

Price risk (*Continued*)
  investments, 118–121
Price swap, bonds, 130
Pricing policy:
  areas covered by, 285
  components of, pricing decision, 284–285
  customer relationship pricing, 288
  deposit pricing matrix, 285–286
  distribution channels and, 290
  loan policy and, 287–288
  pricing committee, 282, 284
  product differentiation and, 289–290
  profitability factors, 286–287
  promotional pricing, 288–289
Primary reserves, *see* Reserves
Prime rate, 142
  loans, 190
Private Export Funding Corporation
  (PERFCO), 402
Problem loans:
  assessment of, 201
  charge-offs, 202–204
  signs of, 200–201
  workout, 201–202
Product differentiation, 289–290, 496–497
Profit ratios:
  net interest margin (NIM), 61
  net operating margin (NOM), 60–61
  rate of return on assets (ROA), 59–60, 62
  rate of return on equity (ROE), 56–59, 60,
    62
  unraveling profits, 59–60
Profits, and deposit pricing, 286–287
Project-based organization, 493
Promotional pricing, 288–289
Provision for loan losses (PLL), 62–63, 65, 301
Public confidence, value of, 55–56
Purchased deposits, 266
Purchased funds, interest rates and, 331–332
Purchase-money mortgage, 228
Put-call parity, options, 421
Put option, 375, 378, 418
  out of the money, 458

Rate of return on assets (ROA), 59–60, 62
Rate of return on equity (ROE), 56–59, 60, 62
Rates of return:
  add-on interest, 29
  Annual Percentage Rate (APR), 29–30
  bank discount basis yield, 27–28
  coupon rate, 26
  current yield, 26–27
  discount interest, 29

holding period yield, 27
interest, simple/compound, 28–29
yield to maturity, 27
Real estate investment trusts (REITs)
  portfolios, taxation factors, 237
Real estate loans, 137–138. *See also*
  Residential mortgages
  construction and development loans, 137,
    235
  home mortgages, 138
  permanent financing, 137–138
Real Estate Mortgage Investment Conduit
  (REMICS), 233–234
Real Estate Settlement Procedures Act, 1974,
  229
Real property, as collateral, 148
Regulation:
  bank performance:
    CAMEL rating system, 76–77
    early warning systems (EWS), 74–76
    financial ratios used, 75
  compliance, 55
  consequences of:
    on banking structure, 16
    on risk of bank failure, 16–17
  consumer protection, 15
  loans:
    exceptions to limit, 151
    size of loans, 150–151
  reasons for:
    concentration of power, 14–15
    market failure possibility, 14, 16–17
Regulation D, 92, 268
Regulation Q, 16–17, 64, 66, 71, 267, 269,
  280, 330–331, 484–486
  circumvention attempts, 485–486
  purposes of, 484
Regulation Z, 248, 254
Relationship banking, 288
Renegotiable mortgage, 227
Report of Condition, 50, 56, 77, 83
Report of Income, 50, 56, 77, 83
Representation, loan agreements, 183–184
Representative offices, international banking,
  395
Repriceable, 335
Repurchase agreement (repos), 97, 247, 487
Required rate of return:
  determining factors, 37
  elements of, 36–37
  model for loan pricing, 187–188
  nominal riskless rate of interest, 37
Reserves, 301–302
  money position, management of, 94–96

primary reserves:
  calculation of reserve requirements, 94–96
  contemporaneous reserve requirement, 92, 93–94
  lagged reserve requirements, 92–93
  legal reserve requirements, 92
  small banks *vs.* large banks, 96
provision for loan losses (PLL), 301
secondary reserves:
  aggressive liquidity approach, 98
  money market approach, 96–98
Residential Funding Corporation, 234
Residential mortgages, 138
  adjustable rate mortgages (ARMs), 224–226
  balloon payment, 220, 227
  conventional mortgage, 217
    loan to price ratio, 219
  costs related to:
    buydown, 223
    due-on-sale clause, 224
    late charges, 223
    mortgage insurance, 224
    points, 223
    prepayment penalty, 223
  fixed rate mortgages, 220
  graduated payment mortgage (GPM), 226–227
  growing equity mortgage (GEM), 227
  legislation related to:
    Community Reinvestment Act, 1977, 230
    Fair Housing Act, 1968, 229
    Home Mortgage Disclosure Act, 1975, 230
    Real Estate Settlement Procedures Act, 1974, 229
    Title 12, U.S. Code 371, 229
  monthly payments, 220–221
    amount and interest rate, 221–222
    and maturity, 221
    principal and interest, 222
  reverse annuity mortgage (RAM), 227
  secondary mortgage market:
    Federal Home Loan Mortgage Corporation (FHLMC), 232–233
    Federal National Mortgage Association (FNMA), 230–231
    Government National Mortgage Association (GNMA), 232
    private participants, 234
    Real Estate Mortgage Investment Conduit (REMICS), 233–234
  second mortgages, 227–228
    seller take-back, 228
    wraparound mortgage, 228
  shared appreciation mortgage (SAM), 227
  variable rate mortgages (VRM), 226
Residential real estate:
  as collateral, 219
  financing, 219
  housing starts, historical view, 216
  mobile homes, 219
  purchase price, 217–218
Restrictive covenants, 140
Restructuring debt, 428
Retail banking services, 152
  commodity services, 497–498
  personal services, 499
  semipersonal services, 498–499
Retail distribution channels, 290
Retail repurchase agreements, 485
Reversal, options, 421
Reverse annuity mortgage (RAM), 227
Revolving loans, 140, 244
  evergreen facilities, 140
  loan commitments, 450–451
  provisions of agreement, 140
Riding the yield curve, 129–130
Risk:
  credit, 10, 42
  default, 37–39
  diversification and, 41–42
  duration, effects of, 39
  evaluation of:
    CAMEL rating, 311
    in price-maker market, 30
    in price-taker market, 31
    risk index I, 312
  fraud, 9
  interest rate, 10, 42
  liquidity, 9
  marketability, 41
  taxes, effects of, 39–41
Risk-adjusted capital requirements, 307–308
  categories of risk, 309–310
  risk asset ratio, 308
Risk ratios:
  loan risk ratio, 63
  loss rate ratio, 62–63, 65
  operating expense ratios, 64
Risk and return securities, 122–126
Robert Morris Associates:
  Annual Statement Studies, 180
  Code of Ethics, 175
Roly-Poly CD Facility, 452
Rule of 78s (sum of digits method), consumer loans, 253

Savings deposits, 270
Sears Financial Network, 479

Sears Mortgage Securities Corporation, 234
Secondary mortgage market, *see* Residential
     mortgages
Secondary reserves, *see* Reserves
Second mortgages, 227–228
     seller take-back, 228
     wraparound mortgage, 228
Securities:
     corporate bonds, 114
     federal related:
          federal agency securities, 111–112
          Treasury bills (T-bills), 111
     investment bankers, 210–211
     municipal securities:
          general obligation bonds, 112
          taxation and, 112–113
     portfolio composition, 1982–1986, 114–115
     services rendered by banks, 7
     yield on taxable/tax-exempt securities,
          equation for, 41
Securitization, 19, 488
     guarantees, 453
     process of, 453
     sales with recourse, 453–454
Segmented markets, 120
Self-liquidating, 136
Servicing mortgages, mortgage banking
     companies, 236
Settlement risk, 427, 447
Shared appreciation mortgage (SAM), 227
Short position, buying foreign currency, 424
Short-term treasury securities, 346
SIBOR, 430
Simple interest, calculation of, 28–29
Small Business Administration (SBA), 209–
     210
Small businesses, 210
Social constraints, on banks, 10
Sources and uses of funds statement,
     estimation of liquidity needs, 88–90
Sovereign risk, foreign exchange transactions,
     428
Spaced-maturity approach, investments, 127–
     128
Special Committee on Paperless Entries
     (SCOPE), 472–473
Split-maturity approach, investments, 128
Spot market, 413, 415
Spread swap, bonds, 131
Standardized gap approach, 350
Standby letters of credit, 7, 435
     pricing of, 450
     risk factors, 449
     uses of, 448–449

Strategic planning, 53
Striking price, 418
Structure of deposits method, estimation of
     liquidity needs, 90–91
Student Loan Marketing Association (SLMA),
     151
     guarantees, 209
Subsidiaries, foreign, 399
Sum of digits method, 253
Surety bonds, 449
S.W.I.F.T., 474
Switch, 478
Switching strategy, yield curve, 129, 130
Syndicated loans:
     advantages of, 429
     loan pricing:
          fees, 431
          LIBOR, 430
     syndication process, 430
     types of, 430
Synthetic loans, 458–460

Takeovers, 318
Taxes:
     after-tax return, 39
     and municipal securities, 112–113
     yields on taxable/tax-exempt securities,
          equation for, 41
Tax exposure ratio, 68
Tax Reform Act, 1986, 113, 233, 301
Tax swap, bonds, 130
Tender panel, 452
Terminal warehouse, 147
Term loans, 140–141
Time draft, 146
Title 12, U.S. Code 371, 229
Total relationship, in loan evaluation, 157
Trade deficit, 406
Trading risk, 447
Transaction costs, and bank capital, 317
Transactions accounts, 94
Transfer risk, foreign exchange transactions,
     428
Travel and entertainment cards, 245
Treasury bills (T-bills), 97, 111
Trust banks, 6
Trust receipts, 147
Truth-in-Lending Act, 15, 248, 254–255

Uncollected funds, 200
Underwriting, 210–211
Uniform Bank Performance Report (UBPR),
     77, 82–85

liquidity analyses, 103
  sections of, 84–85
Uniform Consumer Credit Code, 257
Uniform Customs and Practices for
  Documentary Credits, 432
Unit banks, 15, 16
U.S. *Industrial Outlook*, 180
U.S. Interest Equalization Tax, 393

Valuation:
  cash flow factors, 31–33
  principles of:
    asset prices and required rates of return,
     34
    for assets of given maturity, 36
    duration measure, 35–36
    life of asset and, 34–35
    par/discount/premium assets, 34
Value date, 413
Variable rate mortgages (VRM), 226
Veterans Administration (VA), guarantees,
  208–209

Warehouse receipts, as collateral, 147
Weighted average costs, 290–291
Wholesale banks, 152
Wholesale distribution channels, 290
Wire transfers:
  major systems, 474
  net settlement, 475
Workout, problem loans, 201–202
Wraparound mortgage, 228

Yield-curve stragegies:
  in interest rate risk management, 359
  investments, 128–130
  playing the yield curve, 128–129
  riding the yield curve, 129–130
  switching strategy, 129, 130
Yield-pickup swap, bonds, 131
Yield to maturity, calculation of, 27

Zero coupon issues, 27